Praise for *The War Between the States, America's Uncivil War*

"The way in which historians describe the War Between the States is by far the worst case of political correctness that I have witnessed in my twenty-six years as a university professor. Thankfully, at long last, we have an antidote to this in the form of the beautifully-written and well researched book, *The War Between the States: America's Uncivil War.* It is comprehensive, learned, and beautifully presented. Every family in America—especially ones with school-aged children—should own it and study it."

—Thomas J. DiLorenzo, professor of economics, Loyola College in Maryland
best-selling author of *The Real Lincoln*

"The best textbook for the high school, preparatory academy, or junior college I've ever read."

—Roger D. McGrath, retired professor of history, UCLA

"Who, you say, needs one more account of The War Between the States and Reconstruction? Well, John Dwyer's *The War Between the States: America's Uncivil War* isn't just "one more" contribution to a garrulous and usually opinionated succession of accounts. Judicious, clearly written, suffused with Christian knowledge and understanding, it stands out a mile."

—William Murchison, senior columnist, *The Dallas Morning News*
best-selling author of *Reclaiming Morality in America*

"Dwyer makes a host of good points and has a well-designed and well-carried out scheme. This will be a greatly useful work."

—Clyde Wilson, professor of history, University of South Carolina

"Partial truths are more dangerous than open falsehoods, as error is more easily concealed and more difficult to uncover. The history of the Civil War taught in secondary schools is typically a partial truth that conceals more than it reveals. Dwyer corrects this error not by adopting a Southern point of view—though that view is rightly included—but with a magisterial account that comprehends both in a tragic story that most Americans have yet to confront."

—Donald Livingston, professor of philosophy, Emory University

"John Dwyer writes engagingly about a topic that has more lives than the toughest alley cat. For many years people on both sides of the issues surrounding the War Between the States have let biases and personal preferences lead their thinking. Instead, we must both know history and think biblically before we can unify our thinking in Christ. Could it be that Mr. Dwyer has taken these steps? Read on!"

—Marlin and Laurie Detweiler, Veritas Press

"Finally, a readable, comprehensive book on the Civil War that does that horrific event justice. Using all the best scholarship, and the skills of a born teacher, historian John J. Dwyer has provided homeschooling parents, and private and Christian schools, with just the book they need. None of the usual pap here: we learn the real reasons for the war, how it was fought, the truth about Lincoln, and what happened afterwards. It was with this monstrous event that America went off the rails. But it is not too late to return to the ideals of the framers. John J. Dwyer shows us that too."

—Lew Rockwell, president of the Ludwig von Mises Institute

"John Dwyer's *War Between the States* continues his tradition of historical works that read like narrative backed by scholarship. He exhibits the courage to challenge long held biases on both sides of the divide with unvarnished facts. I recommend it to my colleagues in classical Christian education as a text for studying America's uncivil war."

—Rodney J. Marshall, President and Headmaster, Coram Deo Academy

Also by John J. Dwyer

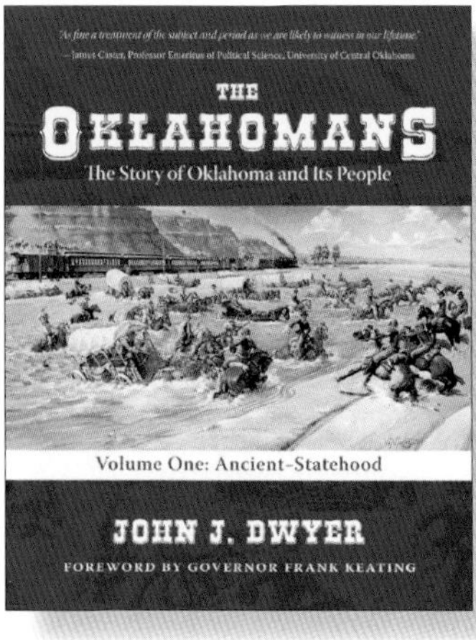

"John J. Dwyer's book *The Oklahomans: Ancient through Statehood* is as fine a treatment of the subject and period as we are likely to witness in our lifetime."

—James Caster, Professor Emeritus of Political Science
University of Central Oklahoma

"A detailed and heroically ambitious history of our state."

—*The Oklahoman*

"An incredible trove of maps and drawings and visuals of all kinds, vivid and colorful . . . John Dwyer has written a wonderful story."

—Frank Keating, former Governor of Oklahoma, from the Foreword

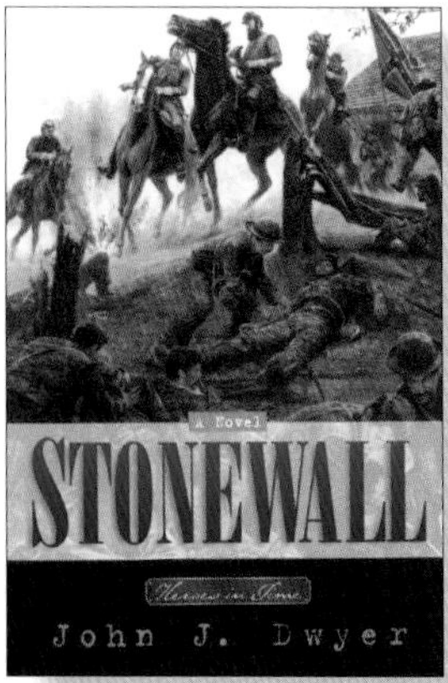

"John J. Dwyer makes one of the great heroes of American history accessible to modern readers."

—*The Oklahoman*

"I still savor with pleasure reading *Lee*. So much good and truth so well told."

—Clyde Wilson,
professor of history,
University
of South Carolina

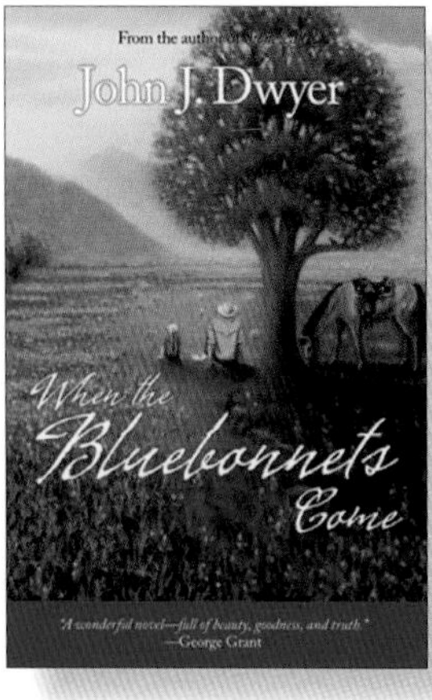

"A must-read for Christian families."

—*Norman Transcript*

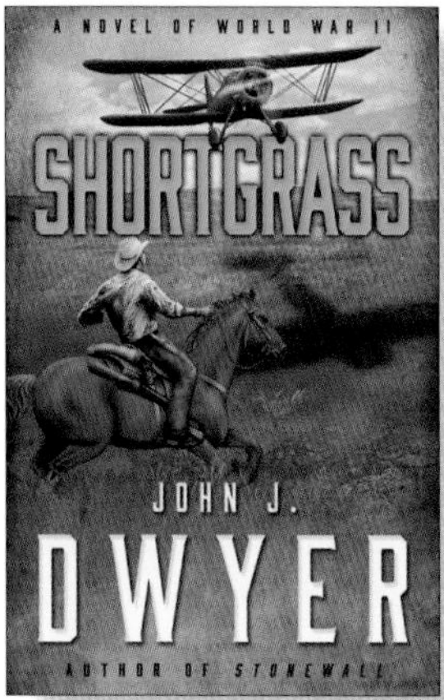

"The difference between John Dwyer and other historical authors is that he doesn't just tell what happened, he shows *why* people did what they did."

—Bob Blackburn,
Executive Director,
Oklahoma Historical
Society

www.johnjdwyer.com

THE WAR BETWEEN THE STATES

America's Uncivil War

THE WAR BETWEEN THE STATES

America's Uncivil War

Author and General Editor
JOHN J. DWYER

Featuring the Artwork of
JOHN PAUL STRAIN

Contributing Editors
GEORGE GRANT · J. STEVEN WILKINS · DOUGLAS WILSON · TOM SPENCER

RED RIVER

Published in the United States of America by Red River Press

For more information about our other books and products or for permission to use material from this text, please contact us:

e-mail: redriverdwyer@gmail.com
Mail: P.O. Box 721664
Norman, Oklahoma 73070

Fourth Printing, 2017
Printed in Korea

Interior design and typesetting: Scott Suckling for MetroVoice Publishing Services
www.metrovoice.org

Cover design: Isaac Botkin
Photographs: Daniel Courter for Soldiers Review
soldiersreview.com

Shenandoah Farewell (page 669): Brenda Robson

ISBN: 978-09768224-0-0

Dedicated to the children of America—

Those of 1861–65, especially they who suffered because of that great and terrible conflict.

Those of today, that they may never so suffer, and that they may never inflict such suffering on the children of other lands.

and to

Helen Miller Dwyer,
Feb. 21, 1925–Jan. 6, 2005,
my beloved mother, who taught me to love history and heroes

Contents

5 Slavery I ... 67

6 Slavery II ... 87

7 Southern Slavery As it Was I ... 105

8 Southern Slavery As it Was II ... 121

The Historical Artistry of John Paul Strain

List of Maps

Introduction

So why another volume on the great and terrible epic of American history, when tens of thousands already exist, and more come off the printing press each year? Because after searching for years, the contributing authors to this work believe that nowhere in that amazing collection exists a single volume that serves as a thorough primer for the causes of the conflict, the war itself, and the aftermath and consequences of it.

Home school parents, Christian school teachers, and adult readers alike have faced two distasteful options when exploring this subject. One, use the same expensive, politically correct textbook their children could get for free at the government school down the street. Or two, employ a virtual library of helpful, informative, fat, and expensive books that together might manage a proper understanding of the war, while filling up a library shelf or book bag.

As a teacher, parent, and reader myself, I wanted one book that covered all the important factors. But I wanted a book which recognized that something as complex as the War Between the States (hereafter referred to as the War) demands more than regional or political partisanship; rose-colored exaltation of a time of chivalry, vision, energy, and valor; and analysis of where battle plans went right and wrong. It demands a full accounting of these and many other factors together.

Why the need to understand the War at all? Many government schools in America now ignore the War and concentrate their American history classes after 1865. As I tell my students, history is not just about the past and it is most certainly not dead and gone. History, the study of one's own people or other peoples, acquaints us with those of the past, that we might better live in the present, and create a better future than we would otherwise.

History is His Story, God Almighty's work of calling out a covenant people for Himself in space and time, throughout human history. Viewed in this context, history can grow very exciting indeed, inspiring, and it might even bring hope, sometimes through events where we would least expect to find it.

So I ask you to come along for the next few hundred pages. I want to demonstrate through the words and actions of those who came before us that some of what we were taught about the War is true and much is not. For instance, it is true that brother sometimes literally fought against brother, that brave men and women, North and South, suffered and sacrificed for what they believed.

It is true that slavery was a divisive and contentious issue in those days, that Americans of African descent have as a race endured a long and hard struggle since their kidnapping and brutal shipment to our shores, and that the War ended American slavery. And it is true that Abraham Lincoln towers over American and even world history for his leadership in the War.

But it is also true that people fought for many different reasons and that slavery drove neither the United States nor the Confederate States to war. It is true that North and South had many real, and, by 1861, even foundational differences. It is true that the Founding Fathers' vision for America and their Constitution were derailed, not preserved, by the War, its outcome, and especially its aftermath. And the story of Abraham Lincoln was more interesting, more tragic, and far more complex than received American history has taught us.

Withal, our story is not that of a "Civil War" of 1861–65, but of a Fifty Years' War in America. By the late 1820s, economic conflict tore at the unity of the country's regions. In particular, controversy over the tariff (the tax the nation charged on imported goods) engendered animosity between the geographic sections, as witnessed by the Nullification Controversy. Fury filled Southerners, who believed the tax, whether or not intentional, to be a colossal transfer of wealth from themselves to those in the North. This contention was connected to the larger issue of what role the Federal government should play in America and its growth. The North, by and large, maintained the necessity for high tariffs, and the need for the strong and energetic national government they would fund—a government more powerful and expansive than most Southerners believed the Founders intended.

These competing visions regarding the role of the Federal government stemmed back to the Federalist versus Anti-Federalist debates of the Constitutional era. But now their import multiplied, fueled by hardening geographic divisions and the other issues. As the Southerners' discontent escalated to a consideration of leaving the Union, the Constitutionality of that act flared on the national stage. Moreover, the debate over the national government's role became a referendum on whether it or the state governments had birthed the Federal Union and whose authority held primacy.

That debate found particular relevance for the Abolitionist minority in the North who wanted slavery (now concentrated in the Southern states) abolished by the Federal government where Northerners held the majority. It did also for the Southern minority who were staunchly pro-slavery, but disproportionately wealthy and influential, and depended on their state governments to protect their right to the practice.

Added to long-held regional, cultural, and even ethnic differences, as well as the size and diversity incumbent in the ever-expanding Union, the debates over the scope and scale of the Federal government meant that increasing numbers of Americans had differences with one another. And all the more as the burgeoning influence of the Scientific Revolution, the European Enlightenment, and rationalism carried the religious persuasions of the North farther from the still largely orthodox Christian South.

When war came, it proved vast beyond the imagining of any of its participants. Slavery was ended suddenly, permanently, perhaps unconstitutionally, and with much harm to both races, but it was ended and American blacks launched on a long uncertain pilgrimage toward equal rights and opportunities. The South was crushed, and the North had to abandon not only the precepts of its own Constitution but those of its Bible to win.

Still, it took a decade of misguided post-war "Reconstruction" to form a nation very different from that birthed by the Founders in 1789. That decade gave rise to the carpetbaggers, scalawags, robber barons, Black Friday Stock Market Crash, the most corrupt Presidential administration in U.S. history, the Gilded Age, the Ku Klux Klan, and lasting enmity between the black and white races in the South.

The War sprang from a half-century (at least) conflict between worldviews and ideologies incapable of cohesion. Ironically, it did not end most of those conflicts, and the victory of the North set in place the evolution of the Federal government, for good and bad, into the unrivaled colossus its early 19th-century mercantile proponents intended.

Still, amidst all the sorrow and destruction, the death and broken dreams, there flowered much courage and heroism, acts of valor and sacrifice now consecrated in the American memory, deeds at once emblematic and formative of what is good and noble in our tradition and character. Legendary, larger-than-life men and women seemed to rise up on every side, many of them devout Christians. Inventions sprang forth, born in the crucible of war and struggle, in many areas, from weaponry to communications—and from transportation to medicine.

And spiritual awakening swept the soldiers of America, its intensity mirroring the worsening of war, and as people and ideals alike died, something else was born—the Bible Belt. If the War was America's time of sorrows, it also opened a window to the selfless bravery of which her sons and daughters are capable.

Now let us learn our past, that we might by the mercy and grace of God be wiser in the present and thus builders of a better future for those who come after us.

— John J. Dwyer

About the Contributors

The Authors

John J. Dwyer is Adjunct Professor of History at Southern Nazarene University and Oklahoma City Community College. He is the former History Chair at Coram Deo Academy, near Dallas, Texas. He is the author of the historical novels *Stonewall* and *Robert E. Lee*, and the former editor and publisher of the *Dallas-Fort Worth Heritage* newspaper. *www.johnjdwyer.com*.

George Grant is Teaching Pastor at Christ Community Church in Franklin, Tennessee, director of King's Meadow Study Center, and coordinator of the Gileskirk Curriculum Project. He is the author of more than three dozen books, including *Forgotten Presidents: The Men Who Served Before George Washington* and the best-selling *Grand Illusions: The Legacy of Planned Parenthood*. *www.kingsmeadow.com*.

J. Steven Wilkins is pastor of Auburn Avenue Presbyterian Church in Monroe, Louisiana. He is the author of several books, including *Call of Duty: The Sterling Nobility of Robert E. Lee* and *All Things for Good: The Steadfast Fidelity of Stonewall Jackson*, and the audio series *America: The First 350 Years*.

Douglas Wilson is pastor of Christ Church in Moscow, Idaho, an instructor at New St. Andrew's College, and editor of *Credenda/Agenda* magazine. He is the author of numerous books on marriage and the family, classical Christian education, and the Reformed faith, including *Recovering the Lost Tools of Learning*, *Reforming Marriage*, and *Standing on the Promises*.

Tom Spencer is secondary principal at Logos School in Moscow, Idaho, where he teaches a course on the War Between the States. He is the author of such books as *The Seven Laws of Teaching: Lessons for Staff Training for the Unabridged Edition*.

The Artist

John Paul Strain is roundly regarded as one of the greatest painters, living or deceased, of American historical art. The publisher is pleased to present over two dozen of his works within this volume. More information about John Paul Strain and his gallery of work can be found at *www.johnpaulstrain.com*.

Acknowledgments

My friend, fellow churchman, and academic colleague Brad Ryden asked me several years ago to teach a series on the War Between the States at the Covenant School in Dallas, Texas. That project led to the development of this narrative.

Respected editor, publisher, and literary agent Steve Laube shared a significant amount of his time to help me better understand the publishing business and how best to proceed with this book. So did Tina and Bob Farewell, Michael McHugh, Rob Shearer, and Doug Phillips. Monica Culberson and Cindy Hauser provided keen and experienced proofreading. Frank Braswell aided the effort in a number of ways, including the securing of some key but elusive illustrations.

Laurie and Marlin Detweiler, founders of Veritas Press and the Veritas School in Lancaster, Pennsylvania, gave us the idea for our online (*www.bluebonnet-press.com*) study guide, which includes study packages for all 38 chapters of this book.

Scott Suckling and his MetroVoice Publishing Services (*www.metrovoice.org*), who for eight years provided outstanding graphics work and typesetting for the *Dallas/Fort Worth Heritage* newspaper my wife and I published, turned in his biggest and best job yet for us with this volume. Ron Hicks, Four Colour Printing, and Everbest Printing, provided attentive, affordable, and quality printing, as evidenced in the pages that follow.

My students at Coram Deo Academy, just north of both Dallas and Fort Worth, Texas, continue to challenge and inspire me, and remind me that indeed the best hope for the Church of Jesus Christ in America and elsewhere lies in them, because they are its future. Coram Deo graduate Brian Frantz provided particularly helpful input, and graduate Lindsey Sobolik's stellar service as my Teaching Aide freed me to complete crucial work on this book I could not otherwise have done.

I want to thank Coram Deo founders Robi and Rodney Marshall, who provided me with the opportunity to teach young people, and who continue to sacrificially commit themselves to educating the younger generation through a curriculum immersed in a comprehensive, robust Christian worldview. Also, Bill "Papa Bear" Rector, our Upper School Principal, a human embodiment of Christ's blending of love and justice. (And whose ancestor, John Rector, rode with Terry's Texas Rangers.)

My longtime friend Tina Jacobson and her terrific B & B Media Group don't know any way but to go the extra mile in publicizing the work of their clients, even for "small potatoes" like John Dwyer and Bluebonnet Press.

I believe that through the years I have seen most of the best artwork devoted to the War Between the States. Never have I seen any that surpasses that of my friend John Paul Strain. Humble, and gifted beyond compare by God, this man made his entire gallery of work available for use in this book, and asked for nothing in return. I hope our readers appreciate this selfless act and visit Jack's website at *www.johnpaulstrain.com*.

My friends George Grant, Steve Wilkins, Doug Wilson, and Tom Spencer—educators, scholars, and Godly men all—amazed me with their selfless donations of their own vast materials related to the many topics this book covers. In addition, George offered indispensable wisdom and insight as our content editor. Kevin Culberson, whose academic brilliance is something to which I can only aspire, made one of the most important contributions of anyone to this project with his seasoned and thorough job of copyediting.

My dear friends and Christian brothers Jim Almond, Gary Campbell, Allen Huffhines, Bill Massie, Paul Perry, and Ken Sibley not only believed in this enormous, half-decade-long project, they stepped into the gap and backed up their convictions with their own hard-earned dollars. If not for these men, dear reader, there would be no *The War Between the States: America's Uncivil War*. May we all be eternally grateful to them for their sacrifice.

My daughter Katie brings me joy and pride in ways only a father with a daughter can truly know. My grandson Luke is my best buddy and possesses a heart as loving and tender as it is bold and daring. Grace, the loving "wife of my youth," helps keep me on the right track, off the wrong ones, and gives me hope that God is not yet through with this oft-doubting, oft-stumbling old native of the Red River country.

—John J. Dwyer
www.johnjdwyer.com

A voice was heard in Ramah,
Lamentation, weeping, and great mourning,
Rachel weeping for her children,
Refusing to be comforted,
Because they are no more.
—Matthew 2:18

PART I Causes of War

Many factors, some not immediately apparent, contributed to the coming of the War of 1861–1865. The first section of this book examines several of the most crucial. We have broken them out into separate chapters (or groups of chapters), each containing its own chronological progression of events from beginning, in some cases before the founding of America, to the brink of war. These include the burgeoning spirit of nationalism, largely imported from European influences, that turned the support of many Americans away from smaller, limited-government states to that of a larger, consolidated nation with a powerful central government.

Meanwhile, as America grew, distinct regional identities and constituencies flowered, in the midst of, and often in conflict with, the spread of nationalism. Chapter 1 chronicles the development—and divisiveness—of both nationalism and regionalism in the United States, as well as some of the factors, including European rationalism, that influenced both.

Later chapters explore other areas of conflict; some are more related to one another than others. They include the differing visions Americans held for what their government—and country—should be, and

The dramatic but—when in view of the events of 1861–1865—eerily prescient sheet music cover for a polka composed by Henry Bellman. An allegorical scene based on the seal of the State of Virginia, it features an armed Minerva-like female warrior standing atop the prostrate figure of a fallen despot. The broken manacles likely represent the state's breaking free from the supposed bondage of a tyrannical central government. The cross likely symbolizes the sacred nature of the struggle.

where the ultimate authority for both should lie. These conflicts evidenced themselves in the disputes over the nature of states' rights, including, but not limited to, secession (Chapter 2) and nullification (Chapter 4).

Contemporary U.S. histories either ignore the subject of economics, including the volatile tariff issue, or relegate it to an obscure role when considering the causes of the War. We demonstrate in Chapter 3 and elsewhere, however, that economics played a crucial role in stimulating the conflict. As suggested, some of the other causes—including nationalism, regionalism, slavery, and the questions over the nature of the American government—exacerbated its effects, and vice versa.

Slavery—what it was and wasn't, and what Americans believed and did not believe regarding it—commands one third of Part I, Chapters 5–8. The prominence we give to slavery is not because of its primacy over other causes of the War, but because of its complexity as an issue, and the large amount of myth and misinformation the modern American has absorbed about it.

Nearly always overlooked in mainstream academic examinations of the War are the disparate religious and worldview perspectives held by large masses of the Northern and Southern sections prior to the War. In many ways, on many levels, these foundational differences contributed to the discord that did not end even with the conclusion of the shooting war. People and nations are always directed by their theological beliefs, whether they realize so or not. In Chapters 9 and 10, we examine what these were in antebellum America and how they guided the people's actions.

Part I concludes with "The Final Hours," which chronicles the fever of events, spinning beyond the control of any man, that unfolded in the months immediately prior to the outbreak of the War. During this dramatic and historic period, the contentions explored in the first ten chapters reach a head, and America plunges into the worst catastrophe in its history.

If Part I seems a bit disjointed, and some of its issues only marginally related to one another, perhaps that bears testament to the fact that many people went to war for many different reasons. Some issues were related to one another, some at most had tenuous connections. So it is that history is comprised of a series of events that, well-studied, are revealed to have had a complex of reasons, none more so than the War Between the States, America's Uncivil War.

1 Nationalism and Regionalism

The face of a new world—the Industrial Revolution in the mid-19th century, which helped propel the commercial, political, and military expansion of western nations.

In that part of the Union where the Negroes are no longer slaves, have they become closer to the whites? Everyone who has lived in the United States will have noticed just the opposite. Race prejudice seems stronger in those states that have abolished slavery than in those where it still exists, and nowhere more intolerant than in those states where slavery was never known.

In the South, where slavery still exists, less trouble is taken to keep the Negro apart: they sometimes share the labors and the pleasures of the white men; people are prepared to mix with them to some extent; legislation is more harsh against them, but customs are more tolerant and gentle.

—Alexis de Tocqueville, *Democracy in America*, 1830

Nationalistic aspirations began stirring in various nations around the world in the late 18th century. The following century they burst into full flower. Before 1750, nation-states such as Italy and Germany did not exist. They arose during the 19th century. As a result, that century was pockmarked

The Spirit of Discovery (The Lewis and Clark Expedition), by John Paul Strain, depicts the energy and expansionist vision of early nineteenth-century America. President Thomas Jefferson appointed his friend and former secretary, Meriwether Lewis, foreground, to lead an expedition of mapping and geographic discovery across the continent. Lewis chose William Clark, far right, as his co-leader. Sixteen-year-old Indian Sacagawea, center with her baby, and Charbonneau, left, her French trapper husband, proved invaluable as guides.

with bloody civil wars. These pitted once-independent states thrown together (often-times forcibly) to create massive nation-states, virtual transcontinental empires in some cases.

Nationalism was a new phenomenon that emerged as a distinct political ideology. Those states that adhered to it sought to be big, strong, progressive, and powerful. They wanted to create a hedge against other large powerful neighbors, absorbing as much territory as possible in order to create as much security as they could. In the process, they wanted to level the circumstances, opportunities, and conditions of as many people as possible within their enlarged boundaries.

Nationalism posited that it was possible to create politically what history, language, culture, and geography had never before created—huge, powerful empires forged solely on the basis of political ideology. This worldwide movement toward nationalism in the 19th century was the context in which American history during the same period unfolded.

America and Europe

A tremendous storehouse of patriotism existed across all sections of America, fostered by the War of Independence from Great Britain and the rest of the nation's history. However, nationalism was a foreign concept. No less than twenty one American colonies existed at the outset of the struggle against the British in 1775. Thirteen of them banded together to fight for their independence. A fourteenth joined them about fifteen years later, a few years after the writing and signing of the Constitution.

These events illuminate a vital characteristic of American history. From the start, Americans tended to think independently and in terms of their regions as opposed to some superpolitical power. By and large, they did not think nationalistically. This is illustrated by the three major political philosophies that emerged from the 1780s debates over the Articles of Confederation—Nationalists, Federalists, and Localists—though these were not necessarily the terms by which they were referred.

The Nationalists wanted a single American superstate with centralized government and a nationwide uniformity on all levels, regardless of regional differences in culture, economic base, or heritage. But the Nationalists were the smallest and least significant group of the three. The Federalists, such as Alexander Hamilton and, initially, James Madison, desired a strong central government, but with significant powers left to the states. The Localists, who comprised the Anti-Federalists movement, believed sovereign power should remain with the states, except for those "enumerated" powers they agreed to consign to the Federal government.

The Localists, or Anti-Federalists, and the Federalists fought one another for preeminence during the first several decades of the nation's history, though various men subscribed to various of the contested positions in varying degrees at various times. Who won the political debate? The Federalists engineered the Constitution and won the first two presidencies with George Washington and John Adams. However, the Anti-Federalists, who formed the bulwark of the new Democratic-Republican Party, elected Virginia adherents to their philosophy as the third (Thomas Jefferson), fourth (James Madison), and fifth (James Monroe) Presidents. (In the 1780s, Madison was considered a Federalist in that he opposed Anti-Federalists in his desire for a strong new Constitution. However, he inclined toward Anti-Federalist positions regarding the issues debated in the 1790s and after.)

Regional Vision

The Federalists rallied to elect the sixth President, John Quincy Adams, though he hailed from the new Democratic Party, which was dominated by Anti-Federalists. But then a series of Westerners with moderate-to-

The Enlightenment

At point after point, the Enlightenment and ancient Christendom clashed. Instead of God and the Bible together providing a standard of absolutes for the authority of a society, the Enlightenment offered relativism, wherein man determined his own standards of authority. Then he typically used the vehicle of government agencies, programs or policies to carry them out.

The Enlightenment produced a very impersonal society, and it profoundly affected the Church, the family, and the state, which were the institutions Christendom previously acknowledged as divinely-ordained. It either mixed them and their roles up or robbed them of their authority and power. Additionally, rather than finding its basis in revealed law as had Reformation-influenced Christianity, the Enlightenment was based on the concept of natural law. This led men to determine through their own observation and judgment what was right and wrong, and to formulate laws sourced in that, rather than Biblical revelation. The last line of the Old Testament book of Judges well describes such a society: "Every man did that which was right in his own eyes."

Rationalism

The theory that the exercise of reason, rather than the acceptance of empiricism, authority, or spiritual revelation, provides the only valid basis for action or belief, and that reason is the prime source of knowledge and of spiritual truth.

Also, rather than the Christian tradition of mediatorial justice, which in effect placed a protective agent between the common citizen and a tyrant or criminal, Enlightenment justice was litigious. That is, it required the individual to fend for his own rights. Mediatorial justice recognized that law is a divine trust merely mediated or administered by governments and institutions. It aimed at peacemaking. Litigious justice attempted to "make law," strong Anti-Federalist philosophies won the Presidency. Indeed, as Europe rushed headlong toward Enlightenment-influenced nationalism, America resisted centralization for the first 35-40 years of its life. The nation chose as most of its Presidents people from regions renowned for their individualism, localism, and adherence to regionalism for their vision of small government, strong local communities, and a weak federal power.

Meanwhile, much of Europe rushed toward large unions. The peninsula of Italy unified. Dozens of small principalities and kingdoms comprising modern Germany came together. America recognized it was a diverse land with diverse people of diverse interests. As a result, in its early days, America was like a United Nations within a single nation. The French scholar and author Alexis de Tocqueville traveled the country for two years in the early 1830s,

Alexis de Tocqueville

through coercion when necessary, utilizing its executors' (evolving) idea of fairness.

Finally, the Enlightenment worldview discarded the old ideas of covenant and tradition in favor of the idea of contract, in particular a social contract between the government and the people or between individuals, forcing them to perform one service in order to receive another. Enlightenment-dominated thinking threw out the idea of covenant.

A covenant and a contract differ profoundly. A covenant is an agreement between God and man or between man and man with God as the divine witness (and far more important than the human witnesses who are also present) to the agreement, as illustrated by the Pilgrims' Mayflower Compact: "We whose names are underwritten . . . do by these presents solemnly and mutually in the presence of God, and of one another, covenant and combine ourselves into a civil body politic . . . ." A contract, meanwhile, is a strictly human instrument established between two or more people, as exemplified by Thomas Paine's "The Liberty Tree." Indeed, the Enlightenment proved no less than the hinge upon which Western Civilization shifted away from its predominate subscription to Christianity.

The Enlightenment

A philosophical movement of the 18th century, concerned with the critical examination of previously accepted doctrines and institutions from the point of view of rationalism.

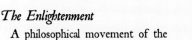

The first great movement to radically change the world according to Enlightenment principles occurred in the 1848 attempt to bring radical revolution to the entire world. It failed, but when Enlightenment thinkers and revolutionaries regrouped, they began to plot a new strategy, one that was patient, multifaceted, and long-term. It led them to success, in only 50–60 years, in transforming civilization. And, as we shall see, it set the stage for a contest of philosophies in the United States that refused settlement other than through a titanic clash of arms.

seeking insights into the phenomenon of its growth and vitality. In his famed book *Democracy in America*, he left many profound insights, as useful in the 21st century as in the 19th. For instance, he declared his belief that the pulpits ablaze from one end of the country to the other with the fire of the Biblical gospel of Christ—rather than the philosophies of the Enlightenment that had swept Europe—were the source of both its greatness and, more importantly, its goodness. And he marveled that so diverse a people as America could cooperate so well with one another.

Northern culture was assiduous—fast-paced, energetic, and driven. Time was its greatest resource, because time was always at a premium.

Such was the basis of the brilliance of the early American experiment in liberty—the allowance for differences within a single confederated goal of preserving unity with diversity. What did this diversity look like? Like three very different worlds, three very different cultures. Three nations really, within a single nation. DeTocqueville spent months touring the country to write *Democracy in America*. According to him and many others, for the first 35-40 years of its history, embracing those differences proved the strength of America. The nation bristled with the industrial might and power of the North, the settled conservatism, traditionalism, and landedness of the South, and the great ambition, sense of destiny, and driving force of the West. The signal problem of early American history was how to reconcile these different personalities.

It was as if the family of America had produced Jacob and Esau, and they were warring from the time they were in the womb until they met on the battlefields of Manassas, Shiloh, and Gettysburg. What made this one nation really three nations bundled together into a single political entity? What held it together and what finally sundered it?

The North

The economy of the North was as diverse as anywhere in the country. Small farms, villages, and family businesses dominated New Hampshire, Vermont, western Massachusetts, central and western Pennsylvania, and everywhere else in the North outside of the Hudson Valley of New York. It was an agrarian, rural economy like most of the world at that time.

The mighty Krupp Iron Works of Germany helped fuel the Industrial Revolution that spread across the Atlantic. In America, the North embraced the European-spawned phenomenon in a way the South and West did not.

America—A Christian Utopia?

Despite the wishful longings of some in the Church, never has a Christian utopia existed in America. The most committed effort toward that end, and one of the strongest in history, occurred in 17th-century Puritan Massachusetts. The early Christian settlements in Virginia, often overlooked in this regard, also strived to form model covenant communities.

By the time of the American War of Independence a century-and-a-half later, however, various philosophical strains—the Aristotelian concept of limited, confederated government from Greek antiquity, (Thomas) Hobbesian statism, and in particular the rationalism of the European Enlightenment—had woven themselves into the fabric of American society, political theory, and even theological thought. They, along with Christian thought and practice, have each contributed to the largely secular 21st century global superpower that is the United States of America.

The ravages, destruction, and sin of war played a key role as well. And not just the War of 1861–65. One of the most brilliant theologians of his generation, New Englander Timothy Dwight, characterized the consequences of the American War of Independence as far more complex and ominous than a heroic triumph of liberty by God-fearing colonists against a tyrannical imperial superpower. Rather, Dwight declared: "Seven years of war had unhinged the principles, the morality, and the religion of the country more than could have been done by a peace of forty years."

Timothy Dwight

From then until the Second Great Awakening a quarter of a century later, skepticism and rationalism spread the length and breadth of the new American nation. And even when the Second Great Awakening occurred, at the turn of the 19th century, it left a spiritual impact less lasting and more man-centered than the original Great Awakening of Edwards and Whitefield.

But there was a difference. A new vision for the future of the region captivated not only urban areas like Boston, Philadelphia, and New York City, as far south as Wilmington, Delaware and as far north as Manchester, New Hampshire, but the small farmers and merchants as well. That vision involved supplying the raw materials, manpower, and capital necessary to drive the engines of commerce.

As a result, the North had a distinctly industrial sense about it, even in those small towns and farms of New England. They envisioned themselves contributing to the greater good of a grand industrialized society, a mechanized colossus that would push the progress of America forward into a new century of grandeur, convenience, comfort, and security unknown to any other people at any time in all of history. The small farms in the North differed from those in the South because they looked to their markets in the cities and how they themselves might contribute to the industrial power of

(One) general cause of the war was the want of intercourse between the people of the North and the South. The great railroads and thoroughfares ran east and west. Emigration flowed from the East to the West. Between the Northand South there was little travel or interchange of opinion. From want of acquaintance the people, without intending it, became estranged, jealous, suspicious. They misjudged each other's motives. They misrepresented each other's beliefs and purposes. They suspected each other of dishonesty and ill-will. Before the outbreak of the war the people of the two sections looked upon each other almost in the light of different nationalities.

—J. C. Ridpath, *History of the United States*, 1888

the society, whereas in the South the small farms looked to the big farms and emulated those as their models.

Thus the North depended economically on every level upon the new and growing industrial power of the urban regions. Soon, small towns out in the hinterlands of the North vied for the privilege to bring new jobs and economic growth to their communities by adding factories, manufacturing plants, and distribution warehouses. So potent did this phenomenon prove that even today every region of America employs the language of the antebellum North—the language of good roads, excellent communication, a growing economy, the expansion of jobs by the bringing in of big industrial combines, more jobs, more dollars, and more development.

Productive Culture

From the 1820s on, this passion for an industrial economy characterized the North. It produced a culture de Tocqueville called assiduous. An assiduous culture is fast-paced, energetic, and driven. Time is its greatest resource, because time is always at a premium. Therefore, an assiduous culture looks askance at time not spent "productively," even as it yearns for such productivity as will allow it to escape to relaxing—and unproductive—venues. (Perhaps no society in history better fits the assiduous mold than Twenty-First Century America with its energy, busyness, and fatigue.)

An assiduous culture is a culture that is progressive, on the move, and in a hurry. As a result, those things that require time, patience, and care are often times bypassed for things more simple, pragmatic, direct, and useful. The fine arts, particularly the architectural arts, disappear. An assiduous culture would have a difficult time, for instance, building a cathedral, because that might take a hundred years. And an assiduous culture often looks careless because it does not care—or it couldn't care less—about those things which take time and patience to develop.

Northern culture had an amalgamated heritage, more mixed than that in any other part of America. It had ethnic neighborhoods in its towns whereas the South scarcely had ethnic regions. For instance, a person could walk for a hundred miles in some parts of South Carolina and never meet anyone who was not of Scots-Irish descent. In New York City, he could walk through three "nations" within two blocks.

Because of its amalgamation, the North had no single cultural consensus. A person might live next door to Poles, around the corner from an Italian bakery, a block away from a Chinese consortium of launderers, porters, and rag pickers, two blocks from the Irish garbage man, and be served along with the rest of the neighborhood by German burghers. The North drew from the energy of each of these national entities. Its heritage was the melting pot.

Because their vision of the world was progressive and they saw themselves as the advance army of the future that would bring prosperity to all, they saw their God and His dogmas in progressive terms as well. They were not a people much interested in the past. Traditions and concepts passed from one generation to the next seemed stale and old. With their new paradigm of progress, innovation, and mechanization, they were going to remake the world themselves. Withal, the dusty old precepts of conservative religion seemed ill-fit for the opportunities that lay before the North.

The South

How different was the South. Firstly, its economy was rooted in agrarianism, or concern for the ownership, cultivation, and tenure of the land, even in the cities like Charleston, Richmond, and Baltimore. Southern cities, too, were steeped in the vision that the land was their greatest resource—that is, the way they used the land and how they passed it on from one generation to the next. Being agrarian meant more than just being agricultural, although

A blazing-hot foundry of the early 19th century Industrial Revolution, where metal was melted and poured into molds.

the South was the breadbasket of the nation. Indeed, by 1860 the South provided 70 percent of the nation's foodstuffs. But being agrarian meant something more. There was a sense that the destiny of families and communities, even the destiny of a family's heritage and legacy, was tied up in its accountability for and responsibility to the land.

Southern culture was aromatic—a more covenantal or community-oriented approach to social interaction, built around the quieter pursuits of conversation and interpersonal relationships, rather than experiences and accomplishments.

Southerners were not ideological in the sense that they vested their hope for the future in ideas such as progress, innovation, mechanization, and capitalization. Rather, they knew good times and bad times would come and go, but as long as the land was there, they felt secure. Their economy revolved around this agrarian notion.

Secondly, Southern culture was what deTocqueville called aromatic. By this phrase he meant antisocial—not in the sense of not liking people, but rather in not liking social excitements. The culture of the South was built around the quieter pursuits of conversation and interpersonal relationships. While an assiduous culture is built around experiences—going and doing things—the Southern culture was not built around going and doing anything. It was built around relationships, constructed quietly and over time, even across generations.

The word aromatic means a more covenantal or community-oriented approach to relationships, rather than an existential or experience-based one. Northern cities were often judged primarily by what sights they had to offer, what things a person might do if they came to the town. In the South, if people were asked the distinctive of their town, they might start telling a family history or recounting historical events that occurred in one place or another which have made that land somehow sacred to their memories.

Southern Heritage

Thirdly, the heritage of the South was contributory. Southerners saw their past as a vital element in the development of their vision for the present and the future. They were not starting from scratch. They often times viewed themselves standing on the shoulders of the giants who had gone before them; therefore, whatever they were doing had to be in continuity with what had gone before. Southerners were not conservative in the sense they merely wanted to preserve the past and keep it the way it was. They wanted to build on the foundations of the past and move forward, but always along a line of continuity proceeding forth from it.

Finally, the religion of the South was collaborative. Again, this does not mean simply conservative or accepting in toto that which their mentors and ancestors from the past bequeathed them. Rather, generally speaking, Southerners required whatever developed in their vision of their relationship with God,

Church, and state, to correlate with all that had gone before. They built upon the foundations once and for all laid for them in the gospel of Christ.

Southerners wanted to see progress, because, to an unusually high degree for an entire culture, they wanted to see the kingdom of God grow, prosper, and ultimately consummate in glory in human history. But they viewed that end not in terms of their own efforts to achieve it by laying new foundations, innovating, and creating, but as a matter of walking in a sense of calling and destiny that had been laid for them long ago, and collaborating with those who had worked in the same fashion in years past.

American mythology has for generations marveled at how two peoples—North and South—so similar, from the same parents, living in the same nation, believing the same Bible, could engage in mutual slaughter and destruction. The truth tells a very different tale. For it would be difficult to find two cultures on the face of the earth more different than these two. They are almost exact opposites. And in a sense, America would have been a Janus-faced monster if not for the fact these two cultural forces were counterbalanced by yet a third, which drew much from both traditions.

The West

The West was a distinctive region. De Tocqueville termed its economy precipitatory. Such a system creates opportunity anew by finding fresh resources, developing new methods, forging ahead with a sense of ambition and progress, and exploiting opportunity as it arises. But it also attempts to fit that sense of progress, industry, and ambition into the context of existing markets, principles, and precepts.

In a sense, the Western economy looked for Northern and Southern opportunities to exploit. So it drew from both North and South in its attempts to make its own way. Firstly, the West was a derivative rather than an independent economy. It depended on the North for manufactured goods and the South for raw materials and natural resources. It would take these and forge them into something new.

Western culture was sanguine—happy-go-lucky and devil-may-care, footloose and free of traditional social constraints that bound both North and South. The people of the West forged their own path in their own way, in a rough and tumble environment.

But, secondly, the West featured a culture de Tocqueville called sanguine. This means happy-go-lucky and devil-may-care, footloose and free of traditional social constraints that bound both North and South. The people of the West forged their own path in their own way, in a rough and tumble environment. This resulted in fiercely independent people with great ambition who "pulled themselves up by their own bootstraps." The West coupled the sense of drive and ambition of the North with the fresh air, wide open spaces, and sense of time of the South.

Thirdly, deTocqueville termed the West's heritage as meretricious or hodgepodge—but not in the sense of the North's amalgamated culture, which resembles stirring and blending multiple cultures together into a near-seamless tapestry. In a mecraous culture, those disparate identities create character traits in communities that are preserved, yet add to the existing character traits of the region. In the West, this phenomenon resulted in numerous "exiled" communities, such as those comprised of Germans, Norwegians, Swedes, and Czechs, as well as many black ex-slaves who made their way into the near West following the Emancipation Proclamation and the War. All this engendered a new vibrancy in the West, distinct from the smothering uniformity of the North and the constraint and narrow social confines of the South.

Revivalism
The belief that the essence of the Christian faith lies in an exciting and dramatic conversion experience that takes place in special meetings outside the ministry and authority of the local church.

Pietism
Desiring a deep devotion to God and believing that a mystical personal experience of Him in one's life—moreso than the comprehension and belief of objective Biblical truth—constitutes true religion.

Western Religion

The West's religion tended to be revivalistic and pietistic. While they were God-fearing as a whole, they were not churchgoing. In the South, many people who maintained the rigors and discipline of regular church attendance did not believe at all points the teachings of their church. In the North, many people abandoned the church altogether because they believed it narrow or unprogressive.

Out West, meanwhile, churches were usually few in number, but the people maintained a simple sort of frontier piety. For instance, when a circuit-riding Methodist or other gospel preacher came through town, they would gather down by the river or out at the fairgrounds to sing psalms and hymns and spiritual songs. They might voice professions of faith and exhibit revivalistic fervor, and the Holy Spirit might seem to fall upon the entire community with fire and passion. And then they might return to their fields, not to attend another church service for six months.

Though Westerners as a whole evidenced earnest piety and sincere belief in God, the doctrines of grace, and the power of the Holy Spirit, these were often disconnected from ordinary life. It was a sort of civic religion, a belief that faith, preaching, and churches were good when they could be found—but they were not expected to be integrated into daily life. The piety of the West was usually without much substance.

In a sense, Westerners expected the Christian religion to be assumed, but not necessarily consumed. One popular tale recounts how the cowboy in the far West, beyond the reach of the organized Church, would tack up a printed poster of the Ten Commandments or the Lord's Prayer on the bedpost or the wall of his bunkhouse. As he went to bed at night, he would look up at the poster—which he could not read—and say a simple prayer, "Lard, them there's my sentiments. Amen."

Nationalism

Thus did three diverse regions—North, South, and West—with their diverse cultures and economies, make up the dynamic of the United States through the end of the 1850s. But the raging fires of ideological passion sweeping across Europe began to invade America. As long as nationalism remained a minor key in American life, no real threat existed that these three very different cultures would come to clashing arms against one another. But once the gospel of nationalism began to be preached, with its insistence upon more centralized governmental control and interregional uniformity, conflict proved inevitable.

In Europe, the passion for nationalism grew violent several times in the years following the Napoleonic Wars which ended in France's defeat at the battle of Waterloo in 1815. By the early 1840s the nation-states of Europe were being racked by calls to unite linguistic or geographical groups into larger, stronger, more progressive and visionary entities. The precepts of nationalism taught that political philosophy could accomplish what religion, heritage, culture, economy, and language never before had. Crusaders began to "rally the troops"— often-times literally—to try and create new entities that would replace the diverse cultures of two thousand years of Christian tradition. Now they wanted unity and uniformity.

Egalitarianism
The doctrine of equal political, economic, and legal rights for all citizens. A distinguishing characteristic is that it seeks to force equality upon everyone in every sphere of life.

The doctrines of the French

"1848 Revolution in Berlin" conveys the enormity of the scale of the nationalistic-socialistic movements that blazed a trail of war across Europe in 1848. Everywhere are seen the revolutionaries' flags, distinct from their enemies' "imperial" German flag scheme of red, white, and black, and identical to the modern German flag.

Revolution, spearheaded by men such as Jean Jacques Rousseau, Maximilien Robespierre, and Voltaire, became the guiding principles of politics. Chief among these was egalitarianism; egalitarianism is different from equality in that it seeks to force equality upon everyone in every sphere of life. Two Germans, Karl Marx and Friedrich Engels—men of radical nationalistic convictions—conceived a plan to bring about this nationalistic unity. Their ultimate objective: to unite the world by imposing a political structure that would level all people and thus consign the old "barriers" of culture, religion, heritage, and economy to irrelevancy.

Nationalism

A modern ideology that emerged in the 19th century. In contrast to national pride or patriotism, nationalism operates on the premise of a centralized state, a politically controlled economy, and a synthesized and amalgamated culture. Where the patriot says, "I love my country," the nationalist says, "My country is better than yours."

Nationalism fostered the idea that bigger was better, that strength and power ought to be invested in a centralized government which would in turn become a sort of benevolent social engineer fixing the woes of society through legislation and education. Two contemporary examples illustrate the philosophy of nationalism in action. If a health problem exists, the central government steps in and proposes a health care reform plan. The government can invade every aspect of a person's life, including what he eats, what he wears, what he can and cannot do on his own property or someone else's, how he can and cannot play his games, what he can and cannot spend.

On the other hand, if the problem is economic, the nationalist will exhort the central government to take action and correct the problems with the economy. If some people do not have jobs, the central government will make certain they either obtain jobs or are paid for not having a job, all in order to provide for the general welfare. Meanwhile, if people make too much money or corner the market on a product in an unfair way, the central government steps in and reduces them to a more reasonable estate.

Communist Manifesto

In 1848, in a fever of creativity, Marx and Engels hammered out a document they called *The Communist Manifesto*. Combined with the nationalistic sentiment of Italy's Garibaldis, Spain's Espanas, Germany's Hohenzollerns, and Poland's Veltas, they created an atmosphere for radical revolution. That very year, the most wrenching series of civil wars and revolutions in all western civilization up to that time occurred simultaneously in battle zones across Europe.

What became the single overarching Revolution of 1848 failed in all eighteen places where it broke out. But the ideas it spawned would survive to define the century that followed.

Around the globe, the 20th century became the century when the ideas of the revolutions of 1848 triumphed. Even before that, the principles of nationalism spearheaded the violent process of unifications of the Italian states by 1870 and the German states the following year.

America's conflict of 1861–65 is rarely considered within this context, at least by Americans. An awareness of it is critical in grasping the key philosophical principles at stake in the struggle between what became the Northern and Southern governments. Just as European theology, fashions, and culture influenced 19th century America, particularly the North, so did European political theory. The tens of thousands of Europeans who participated in the 1848 revolutions and then immigrated to America (again, especially the North) accelerated this influence.

Many of the crucial principles that spurred the uniting of diverse European kingdoms into nationalistic empires likewise inspired the transformation of diverse American regions into a nationalistic empire. The revolutionaries of 1848 faced an America with three different cultures, economies, and religious bases. They determined to remove those differences by a series of political maneuvers.

The *Communist Manifesto* presented a ten-point plan. First was the removal of all pretense to private property ownership. The abolition of private property, Marx and Engels believed, would throw any nation-state into a

Karl Marx

progressive mode where every citizen might be industrious as they contributed toward the state meeting its objectives, and would help push that society forward with great progress into the future.

Second was the development of a graduated income tax. The rich, who could afford it, would pay high taxes. The poor, who could not afford it, might not pay any taxes. The more money a person earned, the greater would be their tax burden. This would accomplish a leveling of the economic factors of the society.

In 1848, the most wrenching series of civil wars and revolutions in all western civilization up to that time occurred simultaneously in eighteen different battle zones across Europe.

The third plank of the Manifesto called for the abolition of the inheri-

The precepts of nationalism taught that political philosophy could accomplish what religion, heritage, culture, economy, and language never before had. Crusaders began to "rally the troops"—often-times literally—to try and create new entities that would replace the diverse cultures of two thousand years of Christian tradition. Now they wanted unity and uniformity.

tance of a person's property by family members, churches, and others when they died through a severe tax penalty called an inheritance tax. This would further remove any semblance of a perpetual elite within a nation, an elite based upon the inheritance of wealth, power, privilege, and name. Such a penalty would force every new generation of a family to start from scratch.

Giuseppe Garibaldi and his Red Shirt volunteers arrive in Sicily in 1860, beginning their military campaign to rid the Italian states of foreign rule and unite them into one nation.

State Control

Fourth would be the confiscation of the rights of certain peoples. Foremost among these were "rebels" and "aliens." This would prevent outsiders from coming in and creating turmoil within a society. Rebels and aliens lost all their rights, as the (nation-) state was now the only mechanism by which rights might be received, and the state would determine who got those rights and who did not; it could abrogate rights at any point or for any cause, but particularly for those whose loyalty to the state seemed suspect, such as aliens and rebels. In this way dissent was squashed. No roiling debates would take place in houses of legislatures. Instead, everything would work harmoniously. Legislative "gridlock" would no longer be a problem, since those who might try to impose an alternative viewpoint would have all their rights stripped from them.

Next, this vision for remaking the world included a series of state-controlled agencies to administer such things as banking; communication and transportation; the mechanisms of the economy such as imports, exports, duties, trading, and the control of the currency of exchange; labor; agriculture—perhaps even making all agriculture communal; and education. The 1848 revolutionaries believed that whole societies could be completely remade through a series of political actions. They did not necessarily place emphasis on what those actions were. For instance, some nationalists accepted certain portions of the *Communist Manifesto* and rejected others. But

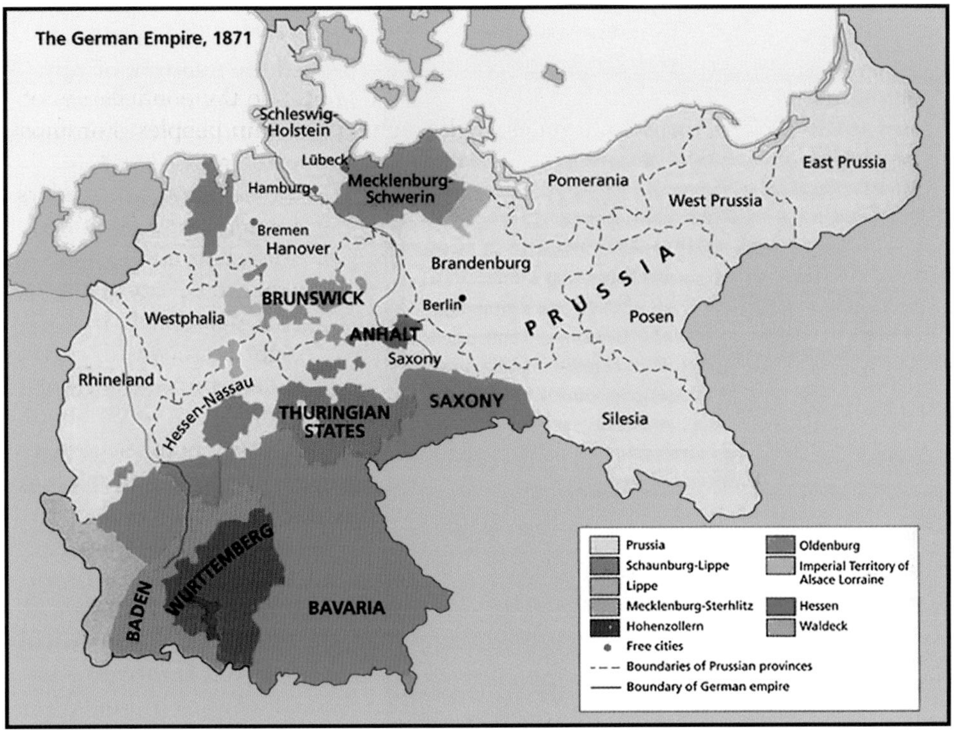

Nationalism and Otto von Bismarck herded all these German states into a powerful central European empire in 1871.

once the principle that a society could be transformed—socially engineered, at the discretion of the "high priests" of politics was established, the basis for nationalism had been laid.

Despite the accomplishments of Marx, Engels, and other European radicals, the communist philosophies so reviled by the majority of twentieth- and twenty-first century Americans had their modern birth not in Germany, Russia or China, but in the verdant democratic fields of early nineteenth-century America.

American Nationalism

America, as a whole, resisted the trend toward nationalism until the 1850s. Then the Whig Party, the old Nationalist Republican Party that such men as Henry Clay and John C. Calhoun had led, dispensed with the vision of those men and began to propound the doctrines of nationalism. A brilliant and eloquent young Congressman from Illinois was the leading champion for nationalism in the House of Representatives during his single term of 1848–1850. His name was Abraham Lincoln. He believed the "house" or the American nation-state had only one way to remain united. It could not, he insisted, remain divided and stand; it must unite itself around nationalistic aims, reduce its differences, smooth over regional distinctions, and become one.

Unification was the clarion cry of the

These soldiers of the 1848 German revolution fought for many of the same nationalistic principles that soldiers of the American Union did, whether or not either realized it.

American nationalists, unity at any cost—even bloodshed, the decimation of centuries of human tradition, the removal of self-determination, majority vote, the will of the people. To the nationalists, the ideals of nationalism superseded even those of freedom and liberty. That vision one day proved the fulcrum, or turning point, upon which the debates of the 1850s and early 1860s hung. Nationalism—and anti-nationalism—ultimately divided the nation and helped bring it to war, and paved the way for a new kind of nation that emerged during the postwar years of Reconstruction and beyond.

Well aware of the revolutions even then spilling blood in all corners of Europe, Lincoln said in an 1848 speech on the floor of the House that would grow more prescient with each year as war neared: "There are two opposing forces in this world. Should we resist these forces, we only delay their conflict. Ultimately these forces will come together. Ultimately we all must choose our sides. And ultimately the destiny of the generations to come will be determined by how we act on this battlefield."

Many of the crucial principles that spurred the uniting of diverse European kingdoms into nationalistic empires, likewise inspired the transformation of diverse American regions into a nationalistic empire.

2 Secession
(States' Rights I)

Washington presiding over the signing of the Constitution.

> *If there be any among us who would wish to dissolve this Union or to change its republican form, let them stand undisturbed as monuments of the safety with which error of opinion may be tolerated where reason is left free to combat it.*
>
> —Thomas Jefferson, First Inaugural Address,1801

With whom did the rule of American law place ultimate political power over the people—the individual states or the national government? From the creation of the Union during the American War of Independence, those conflicting schools of thought contested this question. Only with the defeat of the Southern Confederacy in 1865 was resolution attained, and that by brute force of arms. As with every significant contributing cause to the War, that of States' rights and from it secession, possessed a long, complex, and contentious history, with competing visions for the future of America.

States' Rights

The rights of the states to serve the people by using the powers accorded to them by the social compact theory. The states' rights view held that each state was primarily an independent entity joined in a compact of union, but a union in which they maintained their identity and were not subservient to a centralized national authority.

Patrick Henry

The States' rights issue can best be defined by two opposing early-American political camps. One, the Federalists, championed by Treasury Secretary Alexander Hamilton and more opaquely by President George Washington, argued that the locus of power rested in the national government. The other, the Anti-Federalists, led by such men as Revolutionary War hero Patrick Henry, third President

Confusing Names

If the nomenclature of the Federalist, Nationalist, Anti-Federalist, etc., groups seems confusing, perhaps it is. The group more concerned with strengthening the power of the central government was generally referred to as the Nationalists during the Constitutional Convention that wrote the Constitution. After the Convention, however, they claimed the name Federalists. The group more concerned about protecting the individual states' sovereignty was generally known as the Federalists during the Convention, then the Anti-Federalists later. James Madison himself, who likely would have considered himself a stalwart "federalist," for the most part sided with the "Federalists" neither time. He was aligned with the Nationalists—most of whom were not "nationalists" in the sense of desiring a unified, all-powerful national state, as discussed in Chapter 1—during the Constitutional Convention, but with the Anti-Federalists after that!

The Social Compact Theory

This theory of government states that, regarding human authority, the people are sovereign. They establish state (and other local) governments and delegate limited authority to them. The government is obligated to protect the people's inalienable rights, such as life, liberty, property, and the pursuit of happiness. If the government abuses its power, the people have the right to "alter or abolish" it.

This theory is expressed in the Declaration of Independence, and is evidenced in the ratification ordinances of the United States Constitution by the states of New York, Rhode Island, and Virginia.

Thomas Jefferson, and, eventually, fourth President James Madison, insisted the states retained ultimate power over their own destinies. Upon the answer to that question hinged another question—the constitutionality of a state's right to secede, or leave by its own volition, the Union, without the consent of the federal government.

Secession

A States' right, specifically that of a single state, to leave a union and become its own national entity at any time. Sometimes, as in the case of the War, the departure may cause or extend a conflict that intensifies to the point where the federal government actively coerces the departing state or states, even to the point of sending troops, while the secessionists organize their own separate government and raise their own military force to defend their actions.

Federalism

In this form of government, power and sovereignty are divided between central and regional authorities. Federalism differs from other systems like monarchy, socialism, and feudalism, where the balance of power is weighted heavily toward either central or local government.

Covenant

While covenantalism remained the guiding principle of Southern life to the time of the War, it melted away in place of deist-, Unitarian-, and Transcendentalist-inspired progressivism in numerous key areas of Northern life. The importance of covenantalism—in religion, politics, society, business, and elsewhere—explored in more depth in the "Religion and Worldview" section (Chapters 9 and 10) of this book, can scarcely be overstated. It helps illumine for the modern mind why Southerners were willing to sacrifice and lose what moderns would consider most important—property, health, happiness, even life—for what the average 19th-century Southerner considered even more valuable—the principle, honor, and virtue they felt would be lost should they ignore what they considered the North's long series of covenant-breaking acts. The concept of covenant goes beyond that of social compact in that while it holds man responsible for fulfilling his obligations to his fellow man, God himself judges whether one keeps or breaks the covenant. Thus, man is responsible to his fellow man, as well as to God.

Covenant
A solemn oath and contract of agreement entered into between God and man or between man and man with God as the witness to the oath. Based on the blood covenants of God with His people in the Bible, the Puritans and Pilgrims founded Christian civilization in America based on a covenantal model at every level. Biblically and historically, the man who broke covenant risked losing his covenantal relationship with both the men and the God to whom he was bound.

When considering the constitutionality of Southern secession in the War, two questions loom. First, from the time of America's War of Independence from England, did the states claim the right to nullify laws passed by Congress if the states deemed them unconstitutional? Second, did the states claim the right

Nullification
The rejection or nullifying by a state or states of Congressional acts they deemed unconstitutional. Congress could either change the law or submit it to the states as a Constitutional amendment for ratification or rejection.

to secede from, or depart, the central government if they chose to, if it was necessary for "their happiness"?

When considering the Declaration of Independence and other major events in early American history, the answer to both questions seems clear. Numerous states, from one end of the country to the other, claimed or threatened to exercise such rights up until and even into the War. So perhaps a third question begs asking: Were the states correct in asserting the rights of nullification and secession? That answer lies in the historical documents of American law.

The Declaration of Independence

This watershed document of American history is the actual written divorce decree in 1776 against Britain. It establishes the Founding Fathers' opinion both that government derives its just powers from the people it governs and that those people may adjust or even replace that government if it abuses them. And the Declaration of Independence makes clear that those people are members first not of an independent nation, but of separate individual states. It reads in part:

> We hold these truths to be self-evident, that all men are created equal, that they are endowed by their Creator with certain unalienable Rights, that among these are Life, Liberty, and the Pursuit of Happiness. That to secure these rights, Governments are instituted among Men, deriving their just powers from the consent of the governed. That whenever any Form of Government becomes destructive of these ends, it is the Right of the People to alter or to abolish it, and to institute new Government, laying its foundation on such principles and organizing its pow-

Signing of the Declaration of Independence. (Images of American Political History)

ers in such form as to them shall seem most likely to effect their Safety and Happiness . . .

We, therefore, the Representatives of the United States of America, in General Congress, Assembled, appealing to the Supreme Judge of the world for the rectitude of our intentions, do in the Name, and by Authority of the good People of these Colonies, solemnly publish and declare, That these United Colonies are, and of Right ought to be Free and Independent States, that they are Absolved from all Allegiance to the British Crown, and that all political connection between them and the State of Great Britain, is and ought to be totally dissolved, and that as Free and Independent States, they have full Power to levy War, conclude Peace, contract Alliances, establish Commerce, and to do all other Acts and Things which Independent States may of right do. And for the support of this Declaration, with a firm reliance on the Protection of Divine Providence, we mutually pledge to each other our Lives, our Fortunes and our sacred Honor.

Articles of Confederation

The Articles of Confederation were ratified as the Constitution of the new and United States in 1781 and served as such until the current Constitution took effect in 1789 with the new government headed by President George Washington. The second article staked out the states' view regarding who held ultimate political power over them: "Each state retains its sovereignty, freedom, and independence, and every power, jurisdiction, and right, which is not by this Confederation expressly delegated to the United States, in Congress assembled."

The Articles of Confederation establish the union of states as a "confederacy" and a voluntary "league of friend-

We the People

Article. I

First page of the Constitution

ship." The states declare themselves as sovereign, on the human plane, over their own destinies. They reserve the right to form, remain, or not remain in league with one another, and they convey only specific, limited powers to the association of states they have formed. These powers do not include the right to hold them together in any association against their will.

Treaty with Britain

The supreme achievement under the Articles of Confederation proved to be the treaty of peace with Great Britain in 1783, part of the larger Treaty of Peace among European powers.

Among many planks, the treaty with Britain acknowledged the states as separate and sovereign entities unto themselves: "His Britannic Majesty acknowledges the said United States . . . to be free, sovereign and independent States; that he treats with them as such, and for himself, his heirs and successors, relinquishes all claims to the Government, proprietary and territorial rights of the same, and every part thereof."

Thus Britain too, a foreign power, codifies in writing its recognition of the states as "free, sovereign, and independent"; that is, not as one consolidated whole, but as individual states, and that it will treat them as (separate) individual states.

The Constitution

For the majority of the framers—North, South, and Middle Atlantic—of the 1789 Constitution, the bedrock document of the American people, the states' right of secession was not an issue. It was a given, based both on the previous documents and on the covenantal nature of the Union. Even James Madison, initially one of the more centralist-leaning of the founders, said the Constitution was "a compact between the States in their sovereign capacity." He declared, "The use of force against the (individual) state would probably be considered by the party attacked as a dissolution of all previous compacts by which it might be bound." This would include federal government efforts to hold a state in the Union against its will by force of arms.

The states themselves held similar views. Three of them—New York, Rhode Island, and Virginia—actually included in their written ratifications of the Constitution statements on the subject of a state's right to secede from the new union. New York's ratification ordinance read in part: "That the Powers of Government may be reassumed by the People, whensoever it shall become necessary to their Happiness . . ." Virginia's read in part: ". . . the People of Virginia declare and make known that the powers granted under the Constitution being derived from the People of the United States may be resumed by them (the Virginians) whensoever the same shall be perverted to their injury or oppression and that every power not granted thereby remains with them and at their will . . ."

New York, Virginia, and Rhode Island each declared that if ever the rights they granted to the Union were misused to their harm by the federal government or the other states, it was proper for the offended state to resume its right of self-governance and withdraw from that Union. Perhaps it is worth remembering that during the 18th and 19th centuries in which these events took place, the term "state"—which was usually capitalized as "State"—connoted the idea of a distinct nation or country more than it did a small regional division of a nation as it now does. Written within the "sovereign, free, independent" states context of both the Declaration of Independence and the Articles of Confederation, the Constitution neither forbade American states to secede nor authorized the federal government to prevent their secession.

The use of force against the [individual] state would probably be considered by the party attacked as a dissolution of all previous compacts by which it might be bound.
—James Madison

Kentucky and Virginia Resolutions

Authored by future presidents

The People of Virginia declare and make known that the powers granted under the Constitution being derived from the People of the United States may be resumed by them [the Virginians] whensoever the same shall be perverted to their injury or oppression and that every power not granted thereby remains with them and at their will.

—Virginia's written ratification of the Constitution

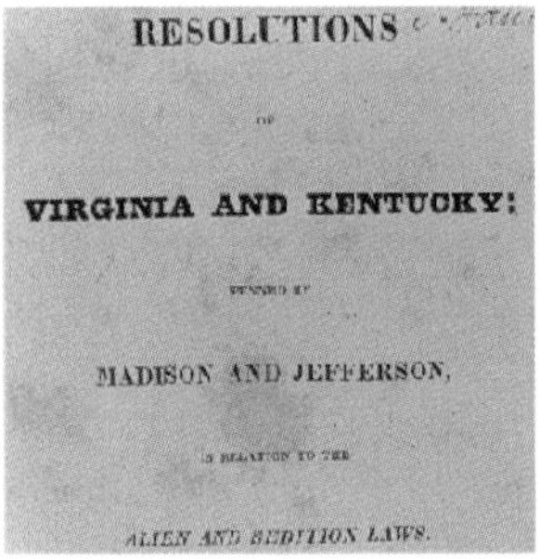
RESOLUTIONS

VIRGINIA AND KENTUCKY;

MADISON AND JEFFERSON,

ALIEN AND SEDITION LAWS.

An original copy of the Kentucky Resolution, penned anonymously by Thomas Jefferson

Thomas Jefferson and James Madison, respectively, these resolutions rejected the controversial Alien and Sedition Acts of 1798, which threatened prison time for Americans who criticized the federal government. The Kentucky and Virginia resolutions reasserted the social compact theory of the Constitution between the states and the national government.

Congress, at that point dominated by the Federalist Party of President John Adams, aimed the Sedition acts primarily at newspapers, specifically newspapers favorable to the opposition Republican party of Jefferson, where Anti-Federalists held great influence. In effect, the Federalists were attempting to muzzle the criticism, sometimes-libelous, visited upon them by these publications. Section 2 of the Sedition Act read: "That if any person shall write, print, utter, or publish . . . any false, scandalous and malicious writing . . . against the government of the United States, . . . then such person, being thereof convicted . . . shall be punished . . .
by imprisonment not exceeding two years."

Alexander Hamilton, Captain, Provincial Company, New York

The Kentucky and Virginia Resolutions charged that the Sedition Act, among other things, ran contrary to the First Amendment of the Constitution, which read: "Congress shall make no law respecting an establishment of religion, prohibiting an establishment of religion, or prohibiting the free exercise thereof; or abridging the freedom of speech, or of the press; or the right of the people peaceable to assemble, and to petition the government for a redress of grievances."

The Virginia document reasserted States' rights on the issue:

> That this Assembly doth explicitly and peremptorily declare that it views the powers of the Federal Government as resulting from the compact to which the states are parties, as limited by the plain sense and intention of the instrument constituting that compact; and that, in case of a deliberate, palpable,

and dangerous exercise of other powers not granted by the said compact, the states, who are parties thereto, have the right and are in duty bound to interpose for arresting the progress of the evil, and for maintaining within their respective limits the authorities, rights, and liberties appertaining to them.

Jefferson's Kentucky Resolution further advocated the states' rights to "nullify" any law they believed not to be in accord with the Constitution:

> Resolved . . . That the principle and construction contended for by sundry of the state legislatures, that the general (national) government is the exclusive judge of the extent of the powers delegated to it, stop not short of despotism—since the discretion of those who administer the government, and not the Constitution, would be the measure of their powers: That the several states who formed that instrument being sovereign and independent, have the unquestionable right to judge of the infraction; and, That a nullification of those sovereignties, of all unauthorized acts done under color of that instrument is the rightful remedy. That this commonwealth does, under the most deliberate reconsideration, declare, that the said Alien and Sedition Laws are, in their opinion, palpable violations of the said Constitution . . .

Thus, two of America's greatest statesmen thundered forth their own declarations that no powers were conveyed by the individual states to the federal government that could be employed to the former's harm, and that if they were, the state could act as necessary to protect itself and its people.

New England Secessionists

For a long time, secessionist fever burned hottest not in the South, but in the North, specifically the far North. Five times combinations of the New England states demonstrated their belief in the constitutionality of secession by threatening to do just that. In 1803, they threatened because of their opposition to Jefferson's Louisiana Purchase. They did not like the slaveowning Southerner's doubling of the land owned by the nation, especially when the increase included a large amount of Southern land likely to host slave-worked cash crops.

Thomas Jefferson

In 1807, New England states again threatened secession, this time over the Embargo Act. That measure, related to the Napoleonic Wars raging between the British and French, prohibited American ships from departing for any other country because of interference with American ships and sailors, mainly by Britain. However, the Embargo Act dealt a withering economic blow to only one nation—America, in particular the New

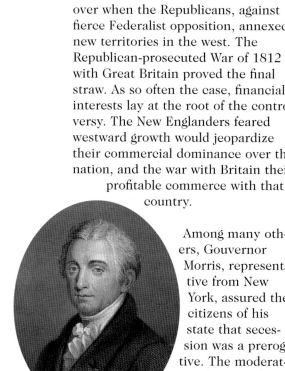

James Madison

England states.

In 1812, New England states threatened to leave the Union over its admission of the state of Louisiana. By 1814, successive Presidential victories by Republican candidates Jefferson and Madison had frustrated the Federalists' national aspirations, and a variety of grievances prompted them to meet at the Hartford Convention in Connecticut to consider secession. Tensions boiled over when the Republicans, against fierce Federalist opposition, annexed new territories in the west. The Republican-prosecuted War of 1812 with Great Britain proved the final straw. As so often the case, financial interests lay at the root of the controversy. The New Englanders feared westward growth would jeopardize their commercial dominance over the nation, and the war with Britain their profitable commerce with that country.

Gouvernor Morris

Among many others, Gouvernor Morris, representative from New York, assured the citizens of his state that secession was a prerogative. The moderating influence of Massachusetts' George Cabot as president of the convention at Hartford steered the assembly more in the direction of demanding constitutional change than secession. However, the ultimate resolution of the issues remained in doubt until the cessation of hostilities between America and Britain caused the New England Commissioners to disperse.

In 1845, New England states yet again threatened to secede, over the annexation of Texas. This time, the speech advocating secession was given by the prominent abolitionist, publisher of *The Liberator* newspaper, and financial sponsor of the murderous John Brown, William Lloyd Garrison. None of these instances, ranging over nearly half a century of time, brought on the New England states charges of treason or accusations that they were unpatriotic. Though not universal, the prevailing political sentiment throughout America was that any state, in New England or elsewhere, who wished to secede could do so.

Defending Secession

Secession was even more ardently defended in both houses of Congress. During an 1848 debate, a tall young first-term congressman from Illinois stood on the floor of the House of Representatives and argued with skill and power in favor of the right of secession. "Any people anywhere, being inclined and having the power," he thundered, "have the right to rise up and shake off the existing government and form a new one that suits them better. This is a most valuable and most sacred right, a right which we hope and believe is to liberate the world." Indeed, his eloquent speech brought some of the first acclaim rookie Illinois Congressman Abraham Lincoln ever received.

Thirteen years later, when the Southern states wanted to exercise the right of secession which the New England states had threatened repeatedly over the past half century, President Abraham Lincoln called it treason. And those New England states who had themselves viewed the federal government as a social compact from which they could depart, now rose up and decried what they viewed as the South's intent to destroy the Union. Garrison railed against the trampling of the very Constitution he had burned publicly and called "a covenant with death and an agreement with hell."

Webster–Hayne Debate

Although the War ultimately settled along North-South geographic lines, a very real East-West sectional tension existed in America virtually as soon as the first organized settlements spread on the leeward side of the Appalachians. This animus continued throughout the 19th century and into the 20th. In the years preceding the War, it manifested itself in many forms. Westerners—comprised largely of citizens residing in what today is considered the American Midwest and Midsouth—suggested that Eastern

Abraham Lincoln, in the late 1840s.

attempts to restrict the sales of western land intended to staunch the westward migration of Eastern industrial workers in search of cheaper land, higher wages, and better working conditions.

One such squabble led to the famous Senatorial debate of 1830 between Daniel Webster of Massachusetts and Robert Hayne of South Carolina. Though rendering little immediate impact, other than national fascination at the oratorical brilliance of the participants, it helped fan the flames of North-South sectional tensions and set the stage for the contentious Nullification Controversy two years later. Webster turned the Senate debate into a referendum on the preeminence of Union, and Hayne rose to defend the banner of state as opposed to national sovereignty.

Webster's dazzling oratory gained lasting fame for his advocacy of the indissolubility of the Union and provided the basis for Abraham Lincoln's eloquent treatises on the necessity of preserving the Union thirty years later. "When my eyes shall be turned to behold for the last time the sun in heaven," Webster declared, "may I not see him shining on the broken and dishonoured fragments of a once glorious Union; on states dissevered, discordant, belligerent; on a land rent with civil feuds, or drenched, it may be, in fraternal blood!"

Hayne exhibited scarcely less brilliance in his simple, cogent defense of States' rights:

Who then . . . are the true friends of the Union? Those who would confine the federal government strictly within the limits prescribed by the Constitution; who would preserve to the States and the people all powers not expressly delegated, who would make this a federal and not a national Union, and who, administering the government in a spirit of equal justice, would make it a blessing and not a curse. And who are its enemies? Those who are in favor of consolidation; who are constantly stealing power from the States, and adding strength to the federal government; who, assuming an

Daniel Webster (1782-1852)

Webster, along with John C. Calhoun and Henry Clay, comprised the great triumvirate of American political leaders during the 19th century. Though they possessed strong, sometimes fierce opinions, if not for their statesmanship and statecraft, the war between the American states would likely have come much sooner than it did. Unlike Calhoun and Clay, Webster was a Northerner, born in Franklin, New Hampshire. Raised in a typical early-New England home of strict Puritanism, he graduated in 1801 from Dartmouth College. After teaching a few years, he was admitted to the legal bar. Almost immediately, attention focused on him because of his incredible rhetorical prowess. He was truly one of the great orators of all time.

The oration Webster delivered at the fiftieth anniversary dedication of the American Revolutionary War monument at the Battle of Bunker Hill was one of the most eloquent in history. It seemed to capture in a few pages all that appealed to Americans and to the preservation of the ideals of the Founding Fathers. It was eloquent, pointed, and thoughtful; and it resisted the tide of political opinion in such a way that it actually moved and changed it.

It concluded:

In a day of peace, let us advance the arts of peace and the works of peace. Let us develop the resources of our land, call forth its powers, build up its institutions, promote all its great interests, and see whether we also, in our day and generation, may not perform something worthy to be remembered. Let us cultivate a true spirit of union and harmony. In pursuing the great objects, which our condition points out to us, let us act under a settled conviction, and an habitual feeling, that these twenty-four States are one country. Let our conceptions be enlarged to the circle of our duties. Let us extend our ideas over the whole of the vast field in which we are called to act. Let our object be, Our Country, Our Whole Country, And Nothing But Our Country. And, by the blessing of God, may that country itself become a vast and splendid monument, not of oppression and terror, but of Wisdom, of Peace, and of Liberty, upon which the world may gaze with admiration for ever.

American students have studied the oration ever since. It remains a model of great oratory, good pacing, substance, humor, the use of history, the appeal to principle, drawing from antiquity, utilizing the authority of Scripture, and making a point relevant to the moment.

Skill and Power

It was inevitable the powers-that-be would soon come to a young New England lawyer of such skill and power and invite him into the political realm. In 1813, he was elected to the House of Representatives as a Federalist from New Hampshire. Almost immediately he became a sort of oratorical sparring partner of Henry Clay, who had come into the House as a War Hawk; Webster opposed the War of 1812.

"When visitors and sightseers come to the capital

Webster's Historic Speech for Union

The following is an excerpt from Daniel Webster's famous speech defending the sanctity of the Federal Union, delivered before the U.S. Senate in 1830 during the Webster-Hayne debate. It greatly influenced the later pro-Union speeches of Abraham Lincoln. Interestingly, Webster's exalted opinion of the Federal Union and his disparagement of the idea of "Liberty first and Union afterwards" found no precedent in the beliefs of most of the early Founders, including Jefferson, Franklin, Henry, and Madison.

It is to that Union, we owe our safety at home, and our consideration and dignity abroad. It is to that Union that we are chiefly indebted for whatever makes us most proud of our country. That Union we reached only by the discipline of our virtues in the severe school of adversity. It had its origin in the necessities of disordered finance, prostrate commerce, and ruined credit. Under its benign influences these great interests immediately awoke, as from the dead, and sprang forth with newness of life. Every year of its duration has teemed with fresh proofs of its utility and its blessings; and although our territory has stretched out wider and wider, and our population spread farther and farther, they have not outrun its protection, or its benefits. It has been to us all a copious foundation of national, social and personal happiness.

I have not allowed myself, Sir, to look beyond the Union, to see what might lie hidden in the dark recess behind. I have not coolly weighed the chances of preserving liberty when the bonds that unite us together shall be broken asunder. I have not accustomed myself to hang over the precipice of disunion to see whether, with my short sight, I can fathom the depth of the abyss below; nor could I regard him as a safe counsellor in the affairs of this Government, whose thoughts should be mainly bent on considering, not how the Union may be best preserved, but how tolerable might be the condition of the people when it should be broken up and destroyed. While the Union lasts we have high, exciting, gratifying prospects spread out before us, for us and our children. Beyond that I seek not to penetrate the veil. God grant that in my day at least that curtain may not rise! God grant that on my vision never may be opened what lies behind! When my eyes shall be turned to behold for the last time the sun in heaven, may I not see him shining on the broken and dishonoured fragments of a once glorious Union; on states dissevered, discordant, belligerent; on a land rent with civil feuds, or drenched, it may be, in fraternal blood! Let their last feeble and lingering glance rather behold the gorgeous ensign of the Republic, now known and honoured throughout the earth, still full high advanced, its arms and trophies streaming in their original lustre, not a stripe erased or polluted, not a single star obscured, bearing for its motto no such miserable interrogatory as '"What is all this worth?" nor those other words of delusion and folly, "Liberty first and Union afterwards," but everywhere, spread all over in characters of living light, blazing on all its ample folds, as they float over the sea and over the land, and in every wind under the whole heavens, that other sentiment, dear to every true American heart—Liberty and Union, now and for ever, one and inseparable!

city," so Washington observers said, "they do not wish to see the monuments, for there are but few. They wish instead to see the great monument of true civilization, the debates of Clay and Webster in the House of Representatives." The influence of their statesmanship was breathtaking.

By 1816, Webster had moved to Boston and begun practicing law. He won a landmark case, *McCulloch v. Maryland*, that dealt with the whole issue of nullification, federalism, the application of tax law, and protectionism. In 1822, he was elected to the House of Representatives from a second state, Massachusetts, where he now lived. This unusual accomplishment demonstrated his political skill and powers of oratory. Five years later, he was elevated to the Senate.

His 1830 Senatorial debate with Robert Hayne of South Carolina helped seed the ground for the great Nullification Controversy two years later. In the Webster–Hayne debate, Webster deftly shifted the issue (whether a state had the right to reject a federal law it considered unconstitutional) to a defense of the Union against ideas emerging in the South that he suggested might jeopardize it. His speech, which lasted two days, became the best known speech ever given in either house of Congress.

In 1841, he became President William Henry Harrison's Secretary of State. Though he never desired to be President, Webster did harbor great aspirations—to maintain the principles of federalism and liberty as the nation expanded. In 1845, he rejoined the Senate, fighting against sectionalism and for the Union during the debates that followed the annexation of Texas.

1850 Speech

In 1850, he was once again appointed Secretary of State, this time by President Millard Fillmore. And during the debate that led to the Compromise of 1850, he added his powerful voice and oratory to that cause. The passage of that key Union-saving bill was due almost entirely to a single speech Daniel Webster gave that lasted only three minutes but which dramatized the whole span of American history and solidified Webster's view of the principles of the Founders in the minds of lawmakers and the public alike.

His life ended on a note whose irony was eclipsed only by the tragedy it held for a nation soon bereft of men able to make peace rather than war. After their long and storied careers, which began at nearly the same time, moved alongside one another, and in many ways resembled each other, Daniel Webster and Henry Clay both died in office in Washington City, as the U.S. capitol was then called, in 1852.

Their oratory, rhetoric, political ideas, laws, and compromises—along with those of Calhoun, who died within two years of them—in many ways outshines those of any other group of statesmen in American history. They thought ahead to, and wrestled with, virtually every issue of Twenty-First Century American political debate, more than a century-and-a-half removed from their lives. "They saved America, they made America," mourned Edward Everett, who spoke just before Abraham Lincoln gave his famous address at Gettysburg. "Oh! That they all died in the span of but two years was a greater calamity than even Gettysburg." The nation was unable to avoid war for even one decade after their passing.

> unwarrantable jurisdiction over the States and the people, undertake to regulate the whole industry and capital of the country . . .

Thus, two great American orators confronted the issue that already, in 1830, faced the American body politic: Some sort of Union needed preserving; was it a federal union with only specific, limited powers vested to the central government by the states, or a national union, where the central government possessed whatever powers it deemed necessary in order to preserve that union?

3 The Tariff

The Northern onslaught upon slavery was no more than a piece of specious humbug designed to conceal its desire for economic control of the Southern states.

—Charles Dickens

Presidential campaign poster for Henry Clay, heading into his Whig party's 1844 nominating convention. *Harper's Weekly, www.harpweek.com*

Economics in general and the tariff (federal taxes charged on products imported into the country) in particular have long been cited as among the causes of the War. But they have traditionally fallen into no better than a second tier of factors, behind such traditional explanations as slavery, States' rights, and secession. Perhaps not until tax historian Charles Adams' landmark 2000 blockbuster, *When in the Course of Human Events: The Case for Southern Secession*, did the desperate nature of the North-South battle over the tariff—in particular, tariffs during Abraham Lincoln's presidency—receive its due as a preeminent cause of the War. Put another way, Lincoln's tariff policy (which we shall shortly discuss)—and his enforcement and the South's defiance of it—fired the already smoldering coals of sectional fratricide and slaughter.

How did such a calamity befall a prosperous and powerful young nation comprised of millions of God-fearing people, and how did it overcome the efforts of some of the greatest statesmen the world has ever known? By the 1820s, how much money Americans gave to their government to be spent, often on others, had become a central issue in the national consciousness.

The North, with its creative genius and abundant, cheap immigrant labor supply pouring across the Atlantic from Europe, caught the full force of the Industrial Revolution that began the previous century in England. Its manufacturing output exploded during and following the War of 1812.

Revenue tariff

A modest tax charged on products imported into the country.

The South, meanwhile, possessed a much smaller population and little industry but abundant natural resources and a large, initially economical labor pool of its own—blacks, mostly slaves but some free. They had been purchased from Arabs or other African tribesmen, then brought to America, first by the English and Europeans, then by Northern mercantilists. Northerner Eli Whitney's invention of the cotton gin in 1793 multiplied the value of slave labor. The gin's colossal ability to churn out cleaned cotton fiber required large numbers of field hands to pick the cotton. This unforeseen combination translated into the potential of enormous cash crop production.

The "fly in the buttermilk" was that as time passed, a tangle of factors drove the North and South, despite their largely shared origins, ever farther apart on many fronts. Not least of these was the divergent effects of tariffs on the sections.

Different Views

To the North, which unlike the South could produce its own finished products and was not as dependent on foreign products, the tariff represented a hedge against market penetration by less expensive import products from Great Britain, France, Spain, and elsewhere. Northern industry had good reason to fear such foreign competition. The Industrial Revolution was still young in America. Many of the nation's manufactories, still in their infancy, could not yet turn out a product of equal quality at equal price to those of some of the European powers. One of many examples was American industry's inability to compete with the wage standards of European-owned plants in the Caribbean and elsewhere.

Thus Northern industry, succored first by the Whig political party, then later by the Republicans in the Congress and Senate, sought to make foreign products so expensive that American consumers would prefer to buy American-made items, as opposed to foreign-made ones. So they favored high, or protective, tariffs on imports. The "tariff" protested by the South (and by some in the North) was more specifically this sort of protective tariff, as opposed to the traditional, much more modest revenue tariff. In contrast, the Southerners with their agriculturally based economy recognized in tariffs of any significant amount an increase in the overhead of planters, whether they purchased from Northerners or Europeans. And when the planters paid more, that expense was passed throughout the rest of the economy.

Plus, Southerners needed no protection for their home products since they viewed foreign nations as trading partners, not competitors, and they wanted no penalties against themselves or these foreign associates. Protective tariffs, especially of the sort envisioned by many in the North, made the South's products more expensive for other nations and consequently reduced the amount of foreign products Southern ships could return home with in trade. So, Southerners often had to purchase inferior Northern goods in place of the foreign merchandise they wanted but whose prices had been artificially increased.

Finally, Southerners complained that most of the revenues taken in by high tariffs against foreign products were then voted toward Northern spending projects by Congress. Indeed, by 1860 the North would hold such a numerical superiority in that body that it needed no Southern votes at all to exercise its will on spending projects. (Though fiscally conservative Northern Democrats sometimes united with Southern Congressmen to block controversial Republican spending bills.)

Tariff of Abominations

In 1816, Congress established an ostensibly temporary tariff on the import of goods manufactured in foreign countries. But rather than terminating the tariff after a few years, Congress increased it in 1824. That same year, John Quincy Adams—newly-elected president due to the solid support of his fellow New Englanders—supported a watershed expansion of federal government action and programs. This expansion necessitated yet more tariff revenue. A new tariff passed the House in 1827 but the Senate deadlocked in the vote necessary to approve it. Vice President John C. Calhoun of South Carolina cast the tie breaking vote—against the tariff.

The next year, yet another new tariff bill arose. This time, in spite of bitter opposition by those who called it the "Tariff of Abominations," the Senate voted it into law. Perhaps more noteworthy than passage of the tariff itself were rumblings of something new down south. The South Carolina legislature sent a blistering protest to the

John Calhoun

Protective tariff

An unusually high tax on imported goods, aimed at protecting a nation's manufacturers from foreign competition by significantly increasing the price of the foreign companies' products and thus hampering their competitiveness.

U.S. Senate calling the new tariff "unconstitutional, oppressive, and unjust." Within weeks, the legislatures of Georgia, Mississippi, and Virginia joined the chorus of protest.

So was birthed a new phenomenon—a unified voice from the South.

Nullification Controversy

Four years later came one of the greatest threats to the Union in its nearly sixty-year existence. In 1832, conflict over whether or not the financial interests of the North could protect themselves by Federal law at the expense of the agricultural states in the South actually pitted the Vice President of the United States, Calhoun, against the President, Andrew Jackson. Ultimately, Calhoun resigned his office, assumed a place in the Senate, and became the great adversary of his former running mate!

> *Nullification*
>
> The right of a state to reject a federal law as unconstitutional and not in the best interest of its citizens, even though all the other states approve the law. The dissenting state stays in the Union, with all the benefits of being a part of American life and liberty, but protects its rights and refuses to accept what the national government decrees on that one law.

In 1832, a new protectionist tariff, passed by the Northern majority over the votes of angry Southerners, created the Nullification Crisis. Once again, important Northern manufactured products were protected by stiff tariffs on competitive imports. But key Southern products such as cotton and tobacco, sold mostly on the world market, were slapped with reciprocal high tariffs at their foreign points of destination.

Calhoun, a South Carolinian, helped that state's governor and legislature draft an Ordinance of Nullification. Nullification is the right of a state to reject a federal law, even though other states say yes. The state stays in the Union, with all the benefits of being a part of American life and liberty, but protects its rights and refuses to accept what the national government decrees on that single issue.

The Calhoun-inspired resolution declared that the state of South Carolina would not participate in the tariff program of the Northern industrial states—including the tariffs of both 1828 and 1832—and would withhold federal revenues so they would not be accomplices in the demise of their own economy. Such was the destiny they envisioned for themselves if they permitted continuation of what had become a massive redistribution of wealth from North to South through the practice of protectionist tariffs in America and the responding foreign countries. South Carolina's act of defiance essentially declared the federal government had no jurisdiction in that state on the issue.

Meanwhile, President Jackson was himself defying the famed Chief Justice John Marshall and the Supreme Court of the United States.

He refused their directive to protect the Cherokee Indians, whose land was being ravaged by gold-greedy whites. Instead, Jackson launched his forcible, ultimately horror-laden removal of the Cherokees out of Georgia and onto their tragic Trail of Tears, which they for generations called "The Place Where We Wept."

Now the hero of the 1815 Battle of New Orleans mobilized federal troops for use against the people of South Carolina too, and beefed up the garrisons in the forts of Charleston Harbor. He was ready to invade the state and fight another war. He pushed the Force Bill through Congress, designed to use the federal military if necessary to force South Carolina to comply with his taxation measures.

States or Union?

The unprecedented Force Bill against a state in the Union evoked shock in many quarters, especially the South. Virginia theologian Robert L. Dabney would later refer to Jackson's bill as "the mere expression of a tyrannical temper and of personal hatreds in that famous renegade to the principles of the (Democratic) party which elected him." The larger issue at stake was one that had simmered on or under the surface of America since before the Colonies declared their independence from Great Britain—was ultimate civil power to rest with the states or the Union of the states?

Jackson thundered forth in support of the Union position during the great debate over nullification: "I consider the power to annul a law of the United States, assumed by one State, incompatible with the existence of the Union, contradicted expressly by the letter of the Constitution, unauthorized by its spirit, inconsistent with every principle on which it was founded, and destructive of the great object for which it was formed."

. . . the mere expression of a tyrannical temper and of personal hatreds in that famous renegade to the principles of the (Democratic) party which elected him.

—Robert L. Dabney regarding President Andrew Jackson's Force Bill

"A deep constitutional question lies at the bottom of this controversy," Calhoun countered. "The real question at issue is this: Has the federal government the right to impose burdens on the capital and industry and freedom and liberty of one portion of the country, not with a view to revenue, but to benefit another portion of the country? Is this right?"

The great statesmen-orators Daniel Webster and Henry Clay spearheaded efforts that crafted a compromise, the Tariff of 1833, which President Jackson signed. It promised to phase out the protectionist tariff over several years and leave primarily a revenue tariff. For its part, South Carolina suspended its Nullification Ordinance. But it also nullified Jackson's Force Bill, which was still in effect. Fortunately, that issue fell by the wayside as the tariff crisis passed. By now, however, speculation ran to all political corners of the nation about when,

The larger issue at stake was one that had simmered on or under the surface of America since before the Colonies declared their independence from Great Britain—was ultimate civil power to rest with the states or the Union of the states?

not if, the Union would break up. People assumed the sectional conflicts had grown too great to overcome.

In the North, many statesmen like Webster worried that the only way the nation could break up was through a great calamitous war. They worried the bloodshed would be enormous, the losses great.

Henry Clay (1777-1852)

Henry Clay was one of three great, dynamic individuals who defined the period of Jacksonian Democracy and whose voices were voices of reason when questions of secession and nullification arose. He was born in "The Slashes" of Virginia's Hanover County, which would later sire famed Confederate General J. E. B. Stuart. His father was killed fighting the British in the American War of Independence, and he was raised in poverty. Like Andrew Jackson, he proved himself incredibly brave during trying times as a young boy.

By 1792, this poor boy with less than three years of formal education secured a court position at the high court of the chancellery. There he caught the eye of the great lawyer George Wythe, who, seeing Clay had a bright mind but little formal education, began guiding him in a reading program through the great literary classics. Young Clay read Thucydides, Plutarch, Augustine, and the English classics of Chaucer, Bunyan, and Milton. He became a Milton scholar and memorized most of Milton's classic work Paradise Lost on heaven and hell.

Experiencing tremendous intellectual growth during this period, Clay was licensed to practice law in 1797 and moved to Lexington, Kentucky. Shortly thereafter, he won the election to the state legislature. He spent the rest of his life in politics. He was elected to the U.S. House of Representatives in 1810 as a leader of the War Hawks. They spurred the country on to another war against Great Britain, the War of 1812. They also helped engineer the concept of "Manifest Destiny," the idea that God ordained the westward expansion of the American republic into a transcontinental empire covering the entire North American continent.

Ironically, this War Hawk was selected in 1815 to negotiate the peace treaty of Ghent with the British. Then, with his eye on politics back home, he negotiated a treaty that saved the Union just before the Hartford Convention could sunder it by the secession of several New England states. He returned home a hero.

Preserving Union

Five years later he again helped save the Union during the conflict over the admission of the state of Missouri when he played a leading role in working out the Missouri Compromise. Five times Clay was elected Speaker of the House of Representatives. By 1824, he was one of America's leading politicians, a noted orator, and twice he had helped save the Union. The Federals' putting him forth as their 1824 Presidential candidate seemed a natural move.

Seeing he did not have the votes to win the election, he threw his support to fellow Federalist John Quincy Adams, son of America's second President, John Adams. Though Adams did not have as many popular votes in the election of 1824 as Andrew Jackson, when Clay threw his support in the House of Representatives to Adams, it swung the election to Adams. Adams immediately made Clay his secretary of state.

In 1828, Clay realized the old political system could no longer meet his political aspirations. He founded a new political party, the National Republicans, not to be confused with either the earlier Republican Party to which Thomas Jefferson and James Madison belonged, nor the later party of Abraham Lincoln. One year later, in fact, the new party changed their name to the Whig Party. The Whigs opposed the Democrats, led by Andrew Jackson and John C. Calhoun.

Clay was elected to the Senate in 1831, then reelected four times. In 1833, he secured a censure of Andrew Jackson, who had defeated Adams in a rematch. The censure was the first against any President. It argued that Jackson had violated the trust of the American people and abused the powers of his office. Many were the complaints that sparked this historic act. They included Jackson's veto of a national bank, his exercise of presidential authority not to enforce several Congressional edicts, and his singular leadership in the murderous ethnic cleansing of the Cherokee Indians, many of whom had converted to Christianity, from the southeast all the way to the Indian Territory (now eastern Oklahoma.)

> ***Mercantilism***
>
> A nationalistic system established on the premise that economic policies benefiting certain groups are good for the nation, and which fosters a structure of imperial state power (at the expense of other nations), as well as special subsidy and monopolistic privileges to individuals and groups favored by the state.

Concerning the latter, Christian missionary Daniel Buttrick suggested that the United States government might more mercifully have executed everyone under one year of age or over sixty. Instead, he said, it had chosen "a most expensive and painful way of exterminating these poor people."

Clay's American System

Henry Clay's early career was marked by great ambition and a desire to be the champion of the people. In his later career he made a series of difficult and unpopular decisions for the sake of the principles in which he believed. Indeed, Clay's censure of Jackson assured the Virginia native's place in history as a great hero to some, but it also fomented such enmity from him in others—many of them powerful men—that it ultimately destroyed his chances of ever winning the Presidency.

At least as controversial as this act was his propagation of what came to be known as his American System. Less charitably likened to 19th-century British mercantilism, this economic philosophy strived for a more powerful and centralized national government than had previously existed in Washington. Clay hoped that government would subsidize both America's industrial foundation and its Westward expansion, and assert the nation's will in economic and thus political matters internationally and even globally.

It does not appear that the power proposed to be exercised in the bill is among the enumerated powers" [of the Constitution].

—President James Madison, upon vetoing an "internal improvements" bill for canal- and road-building subsidies sponsored by Henry Clay

In his book *The Real Lincoln*, economist Thomas DiLorenzo summarizes Clay's American System as advocating "protectionist tariffs, tax subsidies to corporations, and centralized banking." Much of this went toward internal improvements such as railroads, canals, and roads. Abraham Lincoln and both moderate and Radical Republicans melded Clay's American System with Webster's vision for Union as they framed the philosophy and policies of their governments later in the century.

In 1840 Clay ran for president, but William Henry Harrison defeated him for the Whig Party nomination, and then won the presidency. In 1844 he ran again; this time he won the Whig nomination, but lost a heartbreakingly close presidential election to Democrat James K. Polk. In 1848 he ran a third time but lost his own party's nomination by one vote to Zachary Taylor, who became president.

In 1850, Clay helped save the Union for the third time by securing the imperfect, but great, Compromise of 1850. He said, "I do not believe that saving the nation just to save the nation is worth the effort if our compromises ultimately compromise liberty and principle." The statement grew in fame as it rang throughout America, even though many people believed that liberty or principle, or both, were indeed compromised. Still, both North and South would use it when the War sundered the nation into murderous factions in the 1860s.

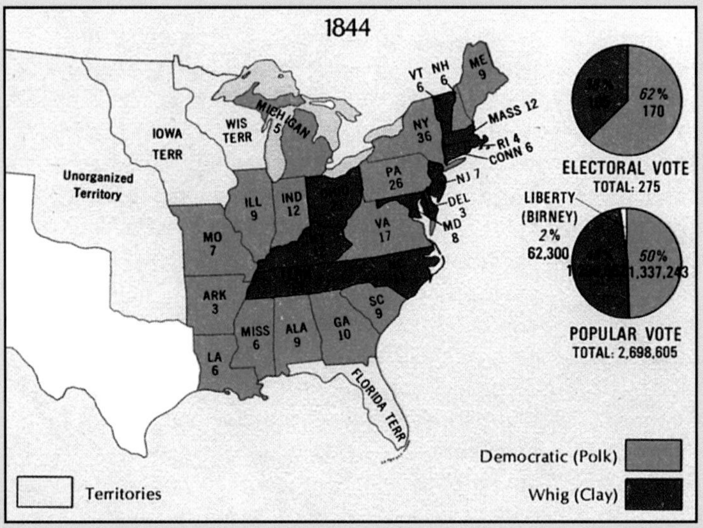

After a life of dedication to the land, in which he played the central role three different times in preserving the Union from disruption, Henry Clay died in Washington at the age of 76. Ironically, many historians believe his "American System" proved instrumental in fracturing that Union—at least the Founding Fathers' vision of it—which he had earlier helped preserve.

1844 Presidential Election (Polk vs. Clay)

Secession Nears

Tension over the tariff and the divergent philosophies of how extensive a role the federal government should play in the national life—and hence how much tariff revenue would be needed to fund that role—grew for the next quarter of a century. By 1860, many Northerners saw the tariff as the permanent and indispensable means for fueling the business growth, national improvements, and westward expansion they favored. Meanwhile, most Southerners believed it broke the uniformity command of the Constitution and wanted it reduced or eliminated. Why? Because Southern taxpayers paid a disproportionate percentage of the national revenue. Though comprising less than one-fifth of the nation's population, they paid approximately 80% of the tariff revenue (see "Why the Tariff Infuriated Southerners" on page 48).

The South reached the breaking point when it witnessed Lincoln and the North's Republican Party congressional forces pressing for more government subsidies of industry, increased Federal land giveaways out West, accelerated internal improvements such as roadways and canals, and a central (national) bank. Every one of these, Southerners knew, would fuel Northern attempts to further increase the tariff, which would arc upward in roughly the same 80–20 proportion.

As the storm clouds of Southern secession gathered, Northern newspapers supportive of Republican Party policies framed the frightening specter in paper and ink. On December 10, 1860, the *Chicago Daily Times* wrote that if the South seceded and established its own low tariff or even tariff-free ports, "In one single blow our [Northern] foreign commerce must be reduced to less than one-half what it now is. Our coastwise trade would pass into other hands. One-half of our shipping would lie idle at our wharves. We should lose our trade with the South, with all of its immense profits. Our manufactories would be in utter ruins. Let the South adopt the free-trade system, or that of a tariff for revenue, and these results would likely follow." Abraham Lincoln thus acceded to the presidency of a nation where an increasing number of people had figured out that Southern secession, like it or not, might well bring economic ruin to the North.

In one single blow our [Northern] foreign commerce must be reduced to less than one-half what it now is. Our coastwise trade would pass into other hands . . . We should lose our trade with the South, with all of its immense profits. Our manufactories would be in utter ruins. Let the South adopt the free-trade system, or that of a tariff for revenue, and these results would likely follow.

—*Chicago Daily Times*, predicting the consequences to the North if the South seceded

A Real Cause

Pennsylvania's most prominent newspaper, the *Philadelphia Press,* wrote eleven days later, the day after South Carolina's secession: "The government cannot well avoid collecting the federal revenues at all Southern ports, even after the passage of secession ordinances; and if this duty is discharged, any State which assumes a rebellious attitude will still be obliged to contribute revenue to support the Federal Government or have her foreign commerce entirely destroyed."

Slavery is not the cause of the rebellion . . . Slavery is the pretext on which the leaders of the rebellion rely, 'to fire the Southern heart,' and through which the greatest degree of unanimity can be produced . . .

—North American Review [published in Boston]

Still, many Southern leaders declared the perceived jeopardy of slavery and white racial hegemony as compelling their secession from the Union. For instance, Mississippi's "Declaration of Immediate Causes" of secession stated: "There was no choice left us but submission to the mandates of abolition, or a dissolution of the union . . . We must either submit to degradation and to the loss of property worth four billions of money, or we must secede from the Union." Alabama Secession Commissioner Stephen F. Hale rued the specter of white Southerners being "degraded to a position of equality with free negroes" under national Republican rule.

The climate of animosity between Southerners and Northern abolitionists and the Southerners' fear of servile insurrection in which these and many other such statements came will be addressed in Chapter 6. For now, suffice to say that even at the time, many other people, North and South, dismissed the claims of slavery being the actual justifier of secession. William Tecumseh Sherman called the issue a "pretext" for secession, the true cause being, he claimed, the dispute over the tariff.

The *North American Review*, published in Boston, announced that "Slavery is not the cause of the rebellion . . . Slavery is the pretext on which the leaders of the rebellion rely, 'to fire the Southern heart,' and through which the greatest degree of unanimity can be produced . . . Mr. Calhoun, after finding that the South could not be brought into sufficient unanimity by a clamor about the tariff, selected slavery as the better subject for agitation." Jefferson Davis himself declared years after the War: "The truth remains intact and incontrovertible, that the existence of African servitude was in no wise the cause of the conflict, but only an incident . . . to whatever extent the question of slavery may have served as an occasion, it was far from being the cause."

Meanwhile, many of the South's own newspapers, including the *Charleston Mercury, The New Orleans Daily Crescent,* and others, pointed straight at the tariff as the primary source of Southern contention with the North. "They (the South) know that it is their import trade that draws from the people's pockets sixty or seventy millions of dollars per annum, in the shape of duties, to be expended mainly in the North, and in the protection and encouragement of Northern interests," editorialized the *Crescent* in January, 1861. "These are the reasons why these people do not wish the South to secede from the Union. They (the North) are enraged at the prospect of being despoiled of the rich feast upon which they have so long fed and fattened, and which they were just getting ready to enjoy with still greater gout and gusto. They are as mad as hornets because the prize slips them just as they are ready to grasp it."

Countless millions of dollars were flowing in a long circuit from the South, through foreign countries, and into Northern coffers, because of protectionist tariffs in America and abroad. The South determined it must stop and the North determined it must not.

"Funeral Obsequies of Free Trade," the pro-mercantilist *Harper's Weekly*'s (www.harpweek.com) contemptuous prediction that President James Polk's low tariff in 1846 would hurt American business and signal the death knell of free trade. Polk and other opponents of heavy central government intervention into economic affairs would have accused high tariffs of causing such a scenario.

Why the Tariff Infuriated Southerners

An examination of some of the nation's compromise tariffs of the 1830s and 1840s by Charles Adams in his book, *When in the Course of Human Events,* reveals approximate total revenues of $107.5 million. These were the amounts charged at Federal ports for the "privilege" of importing products into the United States. According to Adams, the South, with a far smaller population and economy, but much more dependent on imported products than the North, paid $90 million (83%) of this total, the North only $17.5 million (approximately 17%).

Correspondingly, out of a national total of $261 million in exports in 1860, Southern exports counted for $214 million and Northern $47 million. These exports were typically subject to retaliatory foreign tariffs at their point of destination, with the South shouldering an identical 83-17% burden of the load.

In addition, according to Adams, $13 million in fishing bounties were paid to New Englanders, 83% of that, too, originating from Southern coffers. Finally, in a time before Federal Anti-Trust Laws, Northern shipping held a monopoly on business from Southern ports. The South paid these merchants $36 million more.

Growing Northern Congressional dominance drove the tariff higher and higher. Lincoln spearheaded its increase to nearly 40% by the outbreak of war, and nearly 50% by the end of the War.

You are not content with the vast millions of tribute we pay you annually under the operation of our revenue laws, our navigation laws, your fishing bounties, and by making your people our manufacturers, our merchants, our shippers. You are not satisfied with the vast tribute we pay you to build up your great cities, your railroads, your canals. You are not satisfied with the millions of tribute we have been paying you on account of the balance of exchange which you hold against us. You are not satisfied that we of the South are almost reduced to the condition of overseers of northern capitalists. You are not satisfied with all this; but you must wage a relentless crusade against our rights and institutions.

—John H. Reagan
Texas Congressman, January 15, 1861

Lincoln and the Tariff

But what importance did the most powerful individual in all of America assign to the tariff question? Two oft-overlooked conversations President Lincoln had with pro-Union Southerners just prior to the outbreak of the War shed great light on that question.

The first involved Colonel John B. Baldwin, a Virginian respected North and South, who served in the Virginia

Secession Convention. That body was tasked with deciding whether Virginia would follow South Carolina and the other Deep South states or remain in the Union. Baldwin's distinguished reputation helped gain him a private audience with Lincoln at the White House in early April 1861.

The Virginian beseeched the President to pursue a pacific course of reconciliation with the seven seceded states. To do so, he insisted, would keep the eight border states in the Union and assure their aid in bringing the departed states back. Regardless of the free soil and abolitionist policies passed or contemplated by the Republican-dominated Congress—policies repugnant to the seceded states—Baldwin gave Lincoln a personal guarantee. He promised that the peaceful, patient course would ultimately restore the Union—without the massive bloodshed Baldwin likewise promised would result if Lincoln forced a fight. "I ought to have known this sooner!" Lincoln exclaimed, crestfallen. "You are too late, sir, too late! Why did you not come here four days ago, and tell me all this?"

"Only give this assurance to the country, in a proclamation of five lines," Baldwin pled, "and we pledge ourselves that Virginia (and with her the Border States of Delaware, Maryland, North Carolina, Kentucky, Tennessee, Missouri, and Arkansas) will stand by you as though you were our own Washington. So sure am I of this, and of the inevitable ruin which will be precipitated by the opposite policy, that I would this day freely consent, if you would let me write those decisive lines, you might cut off my head, were my life my own, the hour after you signed them."

Lincoln asked how Baldwin would recommend dealing with the new Confederate government. The colonel advised leaving them alone until they could be "peaceably brought back." "And open Charleston, etc., as ports of entry, with ten per cent tariff?" Lincoln asked. "What, then, would become of my tariff?" Upon that question, Baldwin surmised, rested the entire matter. And with it, the interview concluded.

My dear Sir:
[Y]our brother, Dr. William S. Wallace, showed me a letter of yours, in which you kindly mention my name, inquire for my tariff view, and suggest the propriety of my writing a letter upon the subject. I was an old Henry Clay-Tariff Whig. In old times I made more speeches on that subject than any other. I have not since changed my views.

—Abraham Lincoln writing to Dr. Edward Wallace, October, 1859

A few days later, the day after the Confederate firing on Fort Sumter, the Virginia Secession Convention sent a three-man contingent to meet with Lincoln and ascertain his policy toward the seceded states. He indicated peaceful intentions. When one of the Virginians, A. H. H. Stuart, urged forbearance on Lincoln's part and the evacuation of Fort Sumter, the President protested, "If I do that, what will become of my [tariff] revenue? I might as well shut up housekeeping at once."

Still, he signaled to the Virginians a peaceful strategy. Little did they sus-

Robert L. Dabney on Lincoln's Tariff and the War

"What was the decisive weight that turned the scale against peace, and right, and patriotism? It was the interest of a sectional tariff! [Lincoln's] single objection, both to the wise advice of Colonel Baldwin and Mr. Stuart, was: 'Then what would become of my tariffs?'"

"He was shrewd enough to see that the just and liberal free trade policy proposed by the Montgomery (first Confederate) government would speedily build up, by the help of the magnificent Southern staples, a beneficent foreign commerce through Confederate ports; that the Northern people . . . could never be restrained from smuggling across the long open frontier of the Confederacy; that thus the whole country would become habituated to the benefits of free trade, so that when the schism was healed (as he knew it would be healed in a few years by the policy of Virginia), it would be too late to restore the iniquitous system of sectional plunder by tariffs, which his section so much craved.

"Hence, when Virginia offered him a safe way to preserve the Union, he preferred to destroy the Union and preserve his tariffs. The war was conceived in duplicity, and brought forth in iniquity."

pect the very train upon which they returned to Richmond the next day contained Lincoln's dramatic proclamation ordering up seventy-five thousand troops for the violent thwarting of the secession.

It's About — The Money

Indeed, Lincoln and the Northern business and political establishments had good cause for concern. Most of them possessed no great fear over Southern secession itself. They assumed the South would continue as a choice trade partner and some even preferred its departure, along with the sectional rancor that burgeoned. Then, within days of each other in early March, 1861, two events occurred, usually overlooked in chronicles of the War, but destined to exert colossal influence on world history. The United States Congress passed the Morrill Tariff, the highest in the history of the Republic. It featured an average duty of nearly forty percent—forty cents tax for every dollar of value on all foreign goods. The tariff on iron products was well past fifty percent.

Then the new Confederate Congress adopted its Constitution, which included a low tariff at all Southern ports. Overnight, the Northern press, much of it owned by industrial barons whose pocketbooks the tariff directly affected, metamorphosed into ravenous war hawks. Before the month was out, hundreds of leading commercial importers in New York City and Boston, the two largest ports in America, confirmed the worst fears of Northern leaders. They told the collector of customs they would no longer pay the tariff on foreign products unless the same duty was charged at Southern ports.

All those ambitious plans for progress and growth the North had grown accustomed to financing largely with tariff revenue could not continue if that tariff revenue disappeared in the face of free-trading Southern ports. This situation was crystal-clear to Lincoln by the time he ordered up his seventy-five thousand soldiers to retrieve Fort Sumter. It was "now a question of national existence and commercial prosperity," prominent New York banker August Belmont, an associate of the European Rothschild banking establishment, wrote.

It was now a question of war.

"Going to Texas after the Election," more *Harper's Weekly* (www.harpweek.com) ridicule of the advocates of free trade and non-protectionist economics. This cartoon predicts Whig victory in the 1844 presidential election, and manages to lampoon, among others, current president John Tyler, Democratic presidential candidate James K. Polk, former Democratic president Andrew Jackson, and the Republic of Texas.

The central issue in the Civil War, to which all other questions, including slavery and centralization were subordinate, was the movement of American society into modernization. To modernization, the divergent development of the American South presented a formidable obstacle. The South was vast, politically skilled, increasingly unified as the antebellum period wore on, and firmly opposed to economic nationalization in the form of protective tariffs, federal subsidies for the transportation infrastructure, free public lands, and a central banking system. It was opposed to that and opposed to cultural nationalism of its New England variety.

—Professor Clyde Wilson
University of South Carolina

4 Nullification

(States' Rights II)

Any people anywhere, being inclined and having the power, have the right to rise up and shake off the existing government, and form a new one that suits them better. This is a most valuable, a most sacred right—a right which we hope and believe is to liberate the world. Nor is this right confined to cases in which the whole people of an existing government may choose to exercise it. Any portion of such people, that can, may revolutionize and make their own so much of the territory as they inhabit.

—Abraham Lincoln (1848)

In the Nullification Controversy of 1832 over what South Carolina considered the unfair federal tariff, Vice President John C. Calhoun and his native South Carolina squared off against his own running mate, President Andrew Jackson. The South Carolinians vowed to exercise what they considered their clear rights not only to "nullify," or reject, any federal law they believed unjust against their state, but if necessary to secede from the Union. Calhoun resigned his Vice Presidency and sacrificed his Presidential ambitions for this cause, and South Carolina prepared to withstand Jackson's threatened federal military invasion.

In rejecting South Carolina's claimed right of nullification, Jackson maintained that the

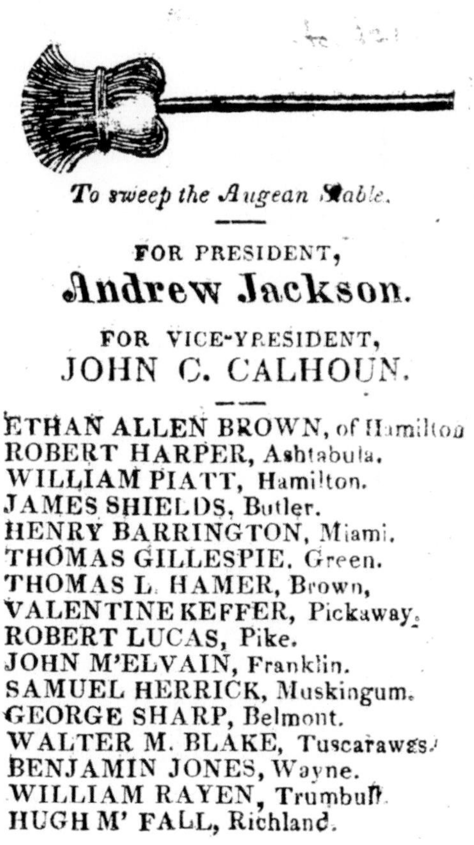

1824 Democratic Presidential campaign poster of Andrew Jackson and John Calhoun. The two giants of 19th-century American history would become bitter enemies.

"more perfect union" elucidated by the Constitution rested upon the preeminence of the confederation of states over the rights of the individual state governments to promulgate their own interests. President Lincoln would maintain the same arguments a generation later, again against South Carolina.

Power Rests With the States

Vice President John C. Calhoun and the South Carolina Legislature

Here are some of the resolutions adopted by the South Carolina legislature in response to President Andrew Jackson's rejection of that state's right to nullify the Federal tariff they considered unfair and unconstitutional:

- That the power vested by the Constitution and laws in the President of the United States, to issue his proclamation, does not authorize him in that mode, to interfere whenever he may think fit, in the affairs of the respective states, or that he should use it as a means of promulgating executive expositions of the Constitution, with the sanction of force thus superseding the action of other departments of the general government.

- That it is not competent to the President of the United States, to order by proclamation the constituted authorities of a state to repeal their legislation and that the late attempt of the President to do so is unconstitutional, and manifests a disposition to arrogate and exercise a power utterly destructive of liberty.

- That the opinions of the President, in regard to the rights of the States, are erroneous and dangerous, leading not only to the establishment of a consolidated government in the stead of our free confederacy, but to the concentration of all powers in the chief executive.

- That each state of the Union has the right, whenever it may deem such a course necessary for the preservation of its liberties or vital interests, to secede peaceably from the Union, and that there is no constitutional power in the general government, much less in the executive department, of that government, to retain by force such state in the Union.

- That the primary and paramount allegiance of the citizens of this state, native or adopted, is of right due to this state.

- That the principles, doctrines, and purposes, contained in the said proclamation are inconsistent with any just idea of a limited government, and subversive of the rights of the states and liberties of the people, and if submitted to in silence would lay a broad foundation for the establishment of monarchy.

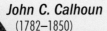

John C. Calhoun
(1782–1850)

Along with Henry Clay and Daniel Webster, John Caldwell Calhoun was one of the three greatest American statesmen in the first half of the 19th century. For nearly 40 years, his leadership skills, ideals, and intellectual power landed him in the center of great national political debate. Calhoun was the only American politician ever to serve as vice president under two different presidents. He also served as secretary of war and secretary of state under two more presidents. He was born in the South Carolina upcountry. The son of a small-holding farmer, Calhoun was educated at a classical log college in Georgia. His advanced studies were pursued at Yale under the tutelage of the strong anti-unionist Timothy Dwight—the renowned grandson of Jonathan Edwards and one of the giants of the Second Great Awakening.

Upon returning to his beloved South, his soaring ambitions enabled his career to advance with astonishing speed. He served in the state legislature and in Congress. Appointed secretary of war in the cabinet of James Monroe in 1817, Calhoun was a War Hawk who supported what was then called the American System—calling for the use of federal power to enforce mercantilist policies and impose high protective tariffs.

Calhoun sought to succeed Monroe as president in 1824. Lacking support, however, he withdrew to run for the vice-presidency with endorsement from both Jacksonians and the followers of the eventual winner, John Quincy Adams. At the time of his election as vice president in 1824, Calhoun was not yet identified with the States' rights position he would later make famous. His views on federal power, however, were undergoing a dramatic transformation—and before long he was converted to both the orthodox Calvinism and the traditional Constitutionalism that dominated his native region.

Timothy Dwight

No longer persuaded that the interests of the South could be served by an active federal government fostering industry, he abandoned what he considered the ideas of political pragmatism for what he viewed as those of principle. As a result Calhoun began repudiating the mercantilist system and broke with the Adams administration. He secretly authored the South Carolina Exposition and Protest, which asserted that a state had the power of nullification over any federal law it deemed unconstitutional.

Supporting Andrew Jackson's presidential candidacy in 1828, Calhoun was reelected to the vice-presidency. His efforts to dominate the Jackson administration were frustrated by Jackson's refusal to endorse a strong states' rights position. In addition, Calhoun was outraged by Jackson's high-handed rule. After the president opposed South Carolina's efforts to nullify the Tariff of 1832, Calhoun resigned from the administration.

His (Calhoun's) rebuttal to Daniel Webster's famed discourse on the indissolubility of the Union possessed a prescience and insight more remarkable with each passing year.

—George Grant

Power Rests With the Union

President Andrew Jackson

The following is a portion of President Andrew Jackson's proclamation to the people of South Carolina rejecting their contention that the Constitution supported their right to nullify, or reject, the Federal tariff, or any other Federal law they deemed unfair and unconstitutional toward their interests.

If the doctrine of a State veto upon the laws of the Union carries with it internal evidence of its impracticable absurdity, our constitutional history will also afford abundant proof that it would have been repudiated with indignation had it been proposed to form a feature in our Government.

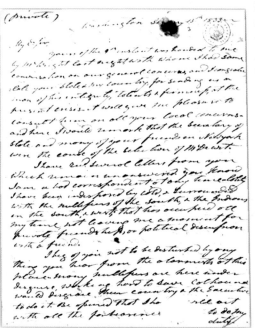

Andrew Jackson's letter to Martin Van Buren attacking nullification.

Our present Constitution was formed in vain if this fatal doctrine prevails. It was formed for important objects that are announced in the preamble, made in the name and by the authority of the people of the United States, whose delegates framed and whose conventions approved it. The most important among these objects—that which is placed first in rank, on which all the others rest—is 'to form a more perfect union.' Now, is it possible that even if there were no express provision giving supremacy to the Constitution and laws of the United States over those of the States, can it be conceived that an instrument made for the purpose of 'forming a more perfect union' than that of the Confederation could be so constructed by the assembled wisdom of our country as to substitute for that Confederation a form of government dependent for its existence on the local interest, the party spirit, of a State, or of a prevailing faction in a State? Every man of plain, unsophisticated understanding who hears the question will give such an answer as will preserve Union. Metaphysical subtlety, in pursuit of an impracticable theory, could alone have devised one that is calculated to destroy it.

I consider, then, the power to annul a law of the United States, assumed by one State, incompatible with the existence of the Union, contradicted expressly by the letter of the Constitution, unauthorized by its spirit, inconsistent with every principle on which it was founded, and destructive of the great object for which it was formed.

Against Jackson

Calhoun now proceeded to confront his erstwhile running mate on the national stage. He authored, behind the scenes, an eloquent defense of the constitutional preeminence of the states in American federal government, with particular regard to nullification (the right of a state to reject or alter a federal law it believes is harmful to its people). His rebuttal to Daniel Webster's famed discourse on the indissolubility of the Union possessed a prescience and insight more remarkable with each passing year. He warned of three immense dangers that could indeed lead to a fracture of the Union. One was the shoving aside of Southern influence in the developing western lands by numerically superior Northern politicians. Another was the unconstitutional usurpation of power from the states by the central government.

Calhoun's third warning concerned the federal revenue tariff and disbursement system (see Chapter 3). He believed raw Northern political power increasingly leaned in favor of that section and against the South: "The North had adopted a system of revenue and disbursements in which an undue proportion of the burden of taxation has been imposed upon the South, and an undue proportion of its proceeds appropriated to the North," he said. ". . . the South, as the great exporting portion of the Union, has in reality paid vastly more than her due proportion of the revenue."

Calhoun remained an influential statesman until his death. Serving briefly as secretary of state in 1844–45 under John Tyler, he engineered the annexation of Texas. He spent the remainder of his career in the Senate, defending Southern rights, advocating strict (conservative) construction of the Constitution, and predicting disunion and civil war if those principles were not respected.

Near the end of his life he delineated his principles in writing. Published just before his death in 1850 as *A Disquisition on Government*, the work is one of the most brilliant speculative works of political thought. It ranks with Thucydides' *History of the Peloponnesian War, Plutarch's Lives*, and Machiavelli's *The Prince*. It wrestles with issues so lofty they are not even a part of normal political course, yet

Henry F. Darby's famous painting of John C. Calhoun, depicted to be around the time of the 1846–48 Mexican–American War.

which lie at the heart of what makes a government work—or not work. *A Disquisition on Government* attempted to forge reasonable legal and political protections for minorities from majority rule. It became the manifesto of the South and remains a classic.

Vermont Threatens

But beyond nullification lurked that previously-mentioned, infinitely more volatile states' right—secession. In 1860, another New England state, Vermont, asserted its treaty rights to secede. Vermont had come into the United States in 1791 as the fourteenth state. Vermont was an independent nation prior to joining with those states that had comprised the thirteen original American colonies. It joined the United States by treaty, not annexation or purchase. This same model brought the Republic of Texas into the Union in 1845.

Most Southerners saw themselves continuing or at least preserving a portion of an old nation, the one begun with the Articles of Confederation, rather than beginning a new one. The states which began that nation, they believed, had the same right to peaceably withdraw.

During the raucous political debates of the 1860 Presidential election season, a plurality of the Vermont state legislature asserted the right to remove themselves from the Union by treaty at any time. Only the outbreak of war in 1861 preempted Vermont's efforts to secede.

Southern Secession

Many traditional American histories have characterized Southern secession as an attempt to preserve slavery and foment insurrection against the United States government. Yet the Confederacy had no interest in harming the Northern states or any state that wanted to remain in the federal Union of states. That the institution of slavery would be prolonged in the South after secession, at least for a period, is true—just as it would be in the North, which had several states and territories of its own where the practice was legal. But a complex of reasons—political, economic, cultural, and religious—in fact drove the South to secede.

Ultimately, most Southerners came to believe they wanted to exist as a separate nation from a North they viewed as growing less and less culturally like them in every way, and less and less accommodating to Southern needs and desires, because of massive immigration and corresponding growth in Northern political power. That burgeoning power, Southerners believed, would elect big-government Northern Presidents, cement Northern control over both houses of Congress (by 1860, the North could already pass a bill in either house without a single Southern vote), and thus, transform the Supreme Court to a Northern-dominated institution. They believed they would be happier and in better control of their own destiny and concerns by leaving the Union.

That Southerners believed the

Union existed as a compact, a covenant, a voluntary confederacy, was reflected in the name they chose: the Confederate States of America. Most Southerners saw themselves continuing or at least preserving a portion of an old nation, the one begun with the Articles of Confederation, rather than beginning a new one. The states which began that nation, they believed, had the same right to peaceably withdraw. In addition to the Declaration of Independence, the Articles of Confederation, and the Constitution, they invoked Jefferson's and Madison's states' rights manifestos in the Kentucky and Virginia Resolutions, respectively, particularly on the right of nullification, as well as the northeastern states' numerous movements toward secession (see Chapter 2).

Lincoln Opposes

Abraham Lincoln publicly fought the notion of secession as a constitutional right, and he fought it with some of the most eloquent language in American history. Some came in his first inaugural, during the period when the Southern states were seceding: "It is safe to assert that no government proper ever had a provision in its organic law for its own termination." And, "We are not enemies, but friends. We must not be enemies. Though passion may have strained, it must not break our bonds of affection. The mystic chords of memory, stretching from every battlefield and patriot grave to every living heart and hearth-stone all over this broad land, will yet swell the chorus of the Union when again touched, as surely they will be, by the better angels of our nature."

But that same grand speech included other language, more ominous to the ears of Southerners. While eschewing the use of aggressive force against the South, including as a preventative to its spreading of slavery to the far west, Lincoln stated that federal property would be kept, if necessary by force of arms.

The real object of those who resorted to secession, as well as those who sustained it, was not to overthrow the Government of the United States; but to perpetuate the principles upon which it was founded. The object in quitting the Union was not to destroy, but to save the principles of the Constitution.

—Alexander Stephens
Vice President
of the Confederacy

Southerners knew that "property" included federal forts in Southern waters, such as Fort Sumter in Charleston Harbor—forts that collected from seagoing vessels the tariff (import tax) which fueled the American government. Such high tariffs the Southerners did not believe should be collected from anyone's ships. But Lincoln would, if necessary, employ the might of the federal government: ". . . to collect the duties and impost; but beyond what may be necessary for these objects, there will be no invasion, no using of force against or among the people anywhere."

In other words, the South would face no military invasion—unless it failed to continue allowing the federal government to collect its high tariffs on

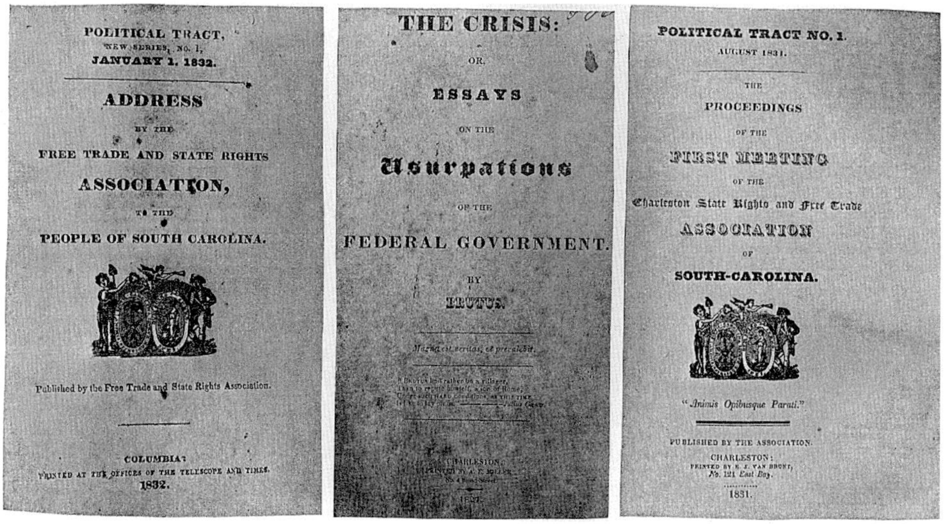
POLITICAL TRACT,
NEW SERIES, No. 1,
JANUARY 1. 1832.

ADDRESS
BY THE
FREE TRADE AND STATE RIGHTS
ASSOCIATION,
TO THE
PEOPLE OF SOUTH CAROLINA.

Published by the Free Trade and State Rights Association.

COLUMBIA:
PRINTED AT THE OFFICES OF THE TELESCOPE AND TIMES.
1832.

THE CRISIS:
OR,
ESSAYS
ON THE
Usurpations
OF THE
FEDERAL GOVERNMENT.
BY
BRUTUS.

POLITICAL TRACT NO. 1.
AUGUST 1831.
THE
PROCEEDINGS
OF THE
FIRST MEETING
OF THE
Charleston State Rights and Free Trade
ASSOCIATION
OF
SOUTH-CAROLINA.

"Animis Opibusque Parati."

PUBLISHED BY THE ASSOCIATION.
CHARLESTON:
PRINTED BY E. J. VAN BRUNT,
No. 121 East Bay.
1831.

An 1832 tract promoting States' rights.

imports entering America through Southern ports. Southern publications caught the drift. One wrote: "It is impossible to doubt that it was Mr. Lincoln's policy, under the name of reinforcing the laws, to retake the forts, to collect the revenue of the United States in our Ports and to reduce the seceded States to obedience to the behests of his party. His purpose therefore was war upon and subjugation of our people."

Contrasting Views

Arrayed against Lincoln's contention that national union preceded state sovereignty and certainly eclipsed it with the formation of the United States were the stated beliefs of Adams, Jefferson, Madison, Monroe, Calhoun, and the original thirteen states themselves and others who joined the Union later. Confederate President—and former U.S. Congressman, Senator, and Secretary of War—Jefferson Davis said, "All we wish is to be let alone. We want to peaceably withdraw as is our right, and have our own nation." Davis countered Northern charges of treason and rebellion with the forceful argument that the Confederacy had no more intention of overthrowing or destroying the United States government than the American colonies had of destroying the British government in the War of the Revolution.

To Southerners, often accused of launching a years-long slaughter of Herculean proportions in order to keep ownership of their slaves, the questions were these: Will the covenantal system of republican government established by the Founding Fathers be preserved or swept away? Will the old nation continue or will a new one take its place? Will true liberty and Constitutional integrity of the states be maintained or will the states lose their integrity and be made slaves of a central government? Invoking the specter of 1776, the South Carolina legislature declared, "No man can, for a moment, believe that our ancestors intended to establish over their posterity, exactly the same sort of Government they had overthrown." They meant by this, government forcing a people to remain under what they viewed as its tyrannical jurisdiction when they no longer wished to do so.

One Southern leader, Alexander H. Stephens, had served Georgia in both the United States House and Senate. He and Abraham Lincoln were close friends. Stephens was a thoroughgoing Unionist who fought against secession, but eventually became the Confederacy's only vice president. He said, "The real object of those who resorted to secession, as well as those who sustained it, was not to overthrow the Government of the United States; but to perpetuate the principles upon which it was founded. The object in quitting the Union was not to destroy, but to save the principles of the Constitution."

Confederate General and ultimate Commander-in-Chief Robert E. Lee of Virginia initially opposed secession. Later, however, he said, "All that the South has ever desired was that the Union established by our forefathers should be preserved and that the government as originally organized should be administered in purity and truth." Lee's father, Washington's famed cavalry chief "Light Horse Harry" Lee, had fought for independence and self-rule against England, as well as to defend his homeland. R. E. Lee believed he was doing no different. The common Southerner considered the contest with the North "The Second War of Independence" or "The War for Southern Independence." In both wars, a land where slavery was legal fought for independence from a land where it was gradually being eradicated.

But not all Southerners opposed Lincoln and the primacy of the national union. One of the most celebrated such men was Sam Houston, the great hero of the Texas revolution against Mexico and a protégé of President Andrew Jackson and Jacksonian nationalism. "When Texas united her destiny with that of the United States, she entered not into the North or South; her connection was not sectional, but national," Houston thundered against a sea of opposition in the Lone Star State.

Men who never endured the privation, the toil, the peril that I have for my country call me a traitor because I am willing to yield obedience to the Constitution and the constituted authorities. Let them suffer what I have for this Union, and they will feel it entwining so closely around their hearts that it will be like snapping the cords of life to give it up.

—Sam Houston

And, ". . . notwithstanding the ravings of deluded zealots, or the impious threats of fanatical disunionists, the love of our common country still burns with the fire of the olden time . . . in the hearts of the conservative people of Texas . . . Texas will maintain the

Constitution and stand by the Union. It is all that can save us as a nation. Destroy it, and anarchy awaits us." Sam Houston had worked for years to usher Texas into the Union and he had no interest in leaving it.

Northerners Too

On the other hand, many Northerners continued to support the constitutionality of secession. Counted in these ranks were some within the camp most fervently opposed to slavery, the abolitionists. Northern abolitionist Lysander Spooner not only supported John Brown and his work, but he also wanted to kidnap Virginia Governor Henry Wise to ransom Brown's release after the attack on Harper's Ferry. But Spooner, too, viewed the premise that war was waged against secession in order to preserve the democratic ideals of liberty and self-determination as a fiction.

"Texas Coming In!" to the Union, an 1845 political cartoon. Democratic presidential candidate James K. Polk, favoring the annexation of Texas, holds an American flag and hails Texans Stephen Austin (waving the Lone Star flag) and Sam Houston aboard a vessel named "Texas." Below the bridge, bedlam sweeps the foes of annexation, including Henry Clay, Daniel Webster, and William Lloyd Garrison.

"Still another of the frauds of these men (who so thought) is, that they are now establishing, and that the war was destined to establish, 'a government of consent,'" he wrote after the war in No Treason: The Constitution of No Authority. "The only idea they have ever manifested as to what is a government of consent, is this—that it is one to which everybody must consent, or be shot. This idea was the dominant one on which the war was carried on; and it is the dominant one, now that we have got what is called 'peace.'"

Still, the majority of Northerners, many of whose fathers and grandfathers had themselves desired to secede from the Union, decried the Confederate secession. The Southerners, they said, were the ones breaking the social compact, breaking the covenant, breaking "the mystical chords of union and shared memory" as Lincoln said.

The British magazine *Quarterly Review*, meanwhile, scoffed at Daniel Webster's famed speech about the indissolubility of the Union by writing that "it does seem the most monstrous of anomalies that a government founded on the 'sacred right of insurrection' should pretend to treat as traitors and rebels six or seven millions of people who withdrew from the Union, and merely asked to be left alone.'"

Secession was assumed by most Americans to be a states' right in their land. And it was the Northern states primarily who asserted that right through the founding era of the nation, the first half of the 19th century, and up to the outbreak of the War. But Lincoln determined to fight, whatever the cost in blood and treasure, for a federalism composed of a sovereign national government. The states, he said, had voluntarily committed sovereign rule over themselves to that central government; such rule precluded their unilateral departure from the union.

The states, [Lincoln] said, had voluntarily committed sovereign rule over themselves to that central government; such rule precluded their unilateral departure from the union.

This view contrasted with the Founding Fathers' vision of a central government both created and restrained by states who were still sovereign in their governance of themselves, and still in social compact with one another. Such states, the Confederates maintained, could leave their union at any time, as freely as they joined it. A sovereign federal government, Lincoln said, could stop them by force of arms. Filmmaker D. H. Griffith perhaps said it best in the title of his controversial silent film masterpiece of 1915, *Birth of a Nation*. The Founders created one nation, with ultimate power rested in the states, according to Griffith, while Lincoln, his armies, the Republicans, and the War created another, with that power resident in the national government at Washington D.C.

Birth of a Nation film poster

States' Right of Secession Asserted

As with every other significant factor that contributed to the War, that of states' rights, including secession, had a long and contentious history in the American body politic. A host of states had demonstrated nearly from the inception of the Union by word and deed their conviction that the states and not the Federal government held the final reigns of power, including the right of secession from the Union if they so chose.

- **1787—New York, Rhode Island, and Virginia Assert Right to Secede**

  Their state conventions adopt the Constitution only after passing legislation that confirms their sovereign right to secede if they deem it necessary for the welfare of their respective states

- **1798-99—Kentucky and Virginia Resolutions**

  They object to the controversial Alien and Sedition Acts. They reassert the social compact theory of the Constitution between the states and the national government. Jefferson's Kentucky Resolution advocates the States' right of nullification.

- **1803—New England States Threaten Secession**

  They object to the Louisiana Purchase.

- **1807—New England States Threaten Secession**

  They object to the Embargo Act.

- **1812—New England States Threaten Secession**

  They object to the admission of Louisiana to the Union as a state.

- **1814—New England States Threaten Secession**

  The Hartford Convention. They object to the War of 1812 with Britain.

- **1832—Nullification Controversy**

  South Carolina objects to the federal tariff and asserts its state's right to nullify it.

- **1845—New England States Threaten Secession**

  They object to the admission of Texas to the Union as a state.

- **1860-61—Southern States Secede**

  Primary among their many objections is the high federal tariff—and newly-elected President Lincoln's support of it—which they believe benefits the North and harms the South. They form the Confederate States of Ameria.

- **1861—Vermont Threatens Secession**

  Halts only when war breaks out.

- **1863—Western Virginia Counties Secede from Virginia**

  During the War itself. Slavery and Federal military pressure are among the issues.

Lincoln's Speech for Union

Abraham Lincoln's First Inaugural Address in 1861 included the following passages, which constitute his ringing declaration and advocacy of a historical case for the federal Union:

> *I hold that in contemplation of universal law and of the Constitution the Union of these states is perpetual. Perpetuity is implied, if not expressed, in the fundamental law of all national governments. It is safe to assert that no government proper ever had a provision in its organic law for its own termination. Continue to execute all the express provisions of our national Constitution, and the Union will endure forever, it being impossible to destroy it except by some action not provided for in the instrument itself.*
>
> *Again: If the United States be not a government proper, but an association of states in the nature of contract merely, can it, as a contract, be peaceably unmade by less than all the parties who made it? One party to a contract may violate it—break it, so to speak—but does it not require all to lawfully rescind it?*
>
> *Descending from these general principles, we find the proposition that in legal contemplation the Union is perpetual confirmed by the history of the Union itself. The Union is much older than the Constitution. It was formed, in fact, by the Articles of Association in 1774. It was matured and continued by the Declaration of Independence in 1776. It was further matured, and the faith of all the then thirteen states expressly plighted and engaged that it should be perpetual, by the Articles of Confederation in 1778. And finally, in 1787, one of the declared objects for ordaining and establishing the Constitution was 'to form a more perfect Union.'*

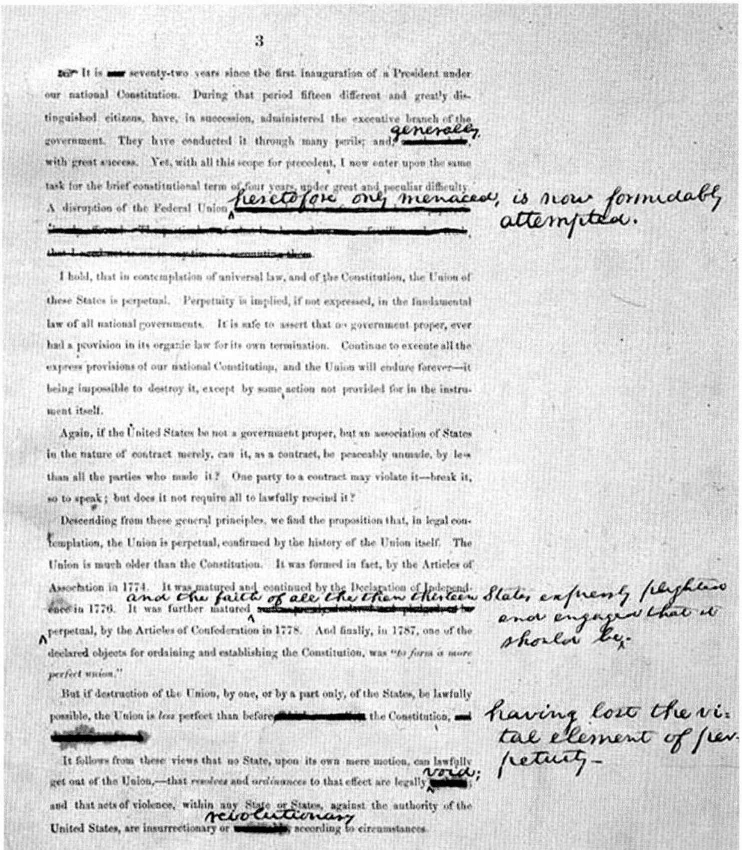

3

[redacted] It is [redacted] seventy-two years since the first inauguration of a President under our national Constitution. During that period fifteen different and greatly distinguished citizens, have, in succession, administered the executive branch of the government. They have conducted it through many perils; and, generally, [redacted], with great success. Yet, with all this scope for precedent, I now enter upon the same task for the brief constitutional term of four years, under great and peculiar difficulty. A disruption of the Federal Union, heretofore only menaced, is now formidably attempted. [redacted]

I hold, that in contemplation of universal law, and of the Constitution, the Union of these States is perpetual. Perpetuity is implied, if not expressed, in the fundamental law of all national governments. It is safe to assert that no government proper, ever had a provision in its organic law for its own termination. Continue to execute all the express provisions of our national Constitution, and the Union will endure forever—it being impossible to destroy it, except by some action not provided for in the instrument itself.

Again, if the United States be not a government proper, but an association of States in the nature of contract merely, can it, as a contract, be peaceably unmade, by less than all the parties who made it? One party to a contract may violate it—break it, so to speak; but does it not require all to lawfully rescind it?

Descending from these general principles, we find the proposition that, in legal contemplation, the Union is perpetual, confirmed by the history of the Union itself. The Union is much older than the Constitution. It was formed in fact, by the Articles of Association in 1774. It was matured and continued by the Declaration of Independence in 1776. It was further matured and the faith of all the then thirteen States expressly plighted and engaged that it should be [redacted] perpetual, by the Articles of Confederation in 1778. And finally, in 1787, one of the declared objects for ordaining and establishing the Constitution, was "*to form a more perfect union.*"

But if destruction of the Union, by one, or by a part only, of the States, be lawfully possible, the Union is *less* perfect than before [redacted] the Constitution, having lost the vital element of perpetuity. [redacted]

It follows from these views that no State, upon its own mere motion, can lawfully get out of the Union,—that *resolves* and *ordinances* to that effect are legally void; [redacted]; and that acts of violence, within any State or States, against the authority of the United States, are insurrectionary or revolutionary [redacted], according to circumstances.

But if destruction of the Union by one or by a part only of the states be lawfully possible, the Union is less perfect than before the Constitution, having lost the vital element of perpetuity.

It follows from these views that no state upon its own mere motion can lawfully get out of the Union; that resolves and ordinances to that effect are legally void; and that acts of violence within any state or states against the authority of the United States are insurrectionary or revolutionary, according to circumstances.

Plainly the central idea of secession is the essence of anarchy. A majority held in restraint by constitutional checks and limitations, and always changing easily with deliberate changes of popular opinions and sentiments, is the only true sovereign of a free people. Whoever rejects it does of necessity fly to anarchy or to despotism. Unanimity is impossible. The rule of a minority, as a permanent arrangement, is wholly inadmissible; so that, rejecting the majority principle, anarchy or despotism in some form is all that is left . . .

Physically speaking, we cannot separate. We cannot remove our respective sections from each other nor build an impassable wall between them. A husband and wife may be divorced and go out of the presence and beyond the reach of each other, but the different parts of our country cannot do this. They cannot but remain face to face, and intercourse, either amicable or hostile, must continue between them. Is it possible, then, to make that intercourse more advantageous or more satisfactory after separation than before? Can aliens make treaties easier than friends can make laws? Can treaties be more faithfully enforced between aliens than laws can among friends? Suppose you go to war, you cannot fight always, and when, after much loss on both sides and no gain on either, you cease fighting, the identical old questions, as to terms of intercourse, are again upon you.

The chief magistrate derives all his authority from the people, and they have conferred none upon him to fix terms for the separation of the states. The people themselves can do this if also they choose, but the executive as such has nothing to do with it. His duty is to administer the present government as it came to his hands and to transmit it unimpaired by him to his successor.

The war therefore was a war between states. In the beginning and throughout the contest the object of the Confederates was to maintain the separate sovereignty of each state and the right of self-government that necessarily carries with it. The object of the Federals on the contrary was to maintain a centralized sovereignty over all the states on both sides. This was the fundamental principle involved in the conflict which must be kept continually in mind.

—Alexander Stephens (in 1884)

5 Slavery I

The Compromise of 1850, Peter Rothermel's classic depiction of some of America's greatest 19th-century statesmen engaged in passionate debate over the bill that would become one of the last great forestallings of war. Henry Clay has the floor, with Daniel Webster to the left, head in hand, Vice President Millard Fillmore presiding in the Senate President Pro Tempore's chair, and former Vice President John C. Calhoun immediately to the right of Fillmore.

One-sixth of the population of the United States are slaves, looked upon as property, as nothing but property. The cash value of these slaves, at a moderate estimate, is two billion dollars. This amount of property value has a vast influence on the minds of its owners, very naturally. The same amount of property would have an equal influence upon us if owned in the North. Human nature is the same—people at the South are the same as those at the North, barring the difference in circumstances.

—Abraham Lincoln (1861)

The first African slaves arrived in the New World just after 1500, bound not for North America but for the Caribbean Islands and Latin America. Later, African slavery was a part of Christian civilization in North America nearly from its beginning in the early 1600s. Slavery was legal in every American colony. At the peak of New England slavery, around 1760, approximately the same percentage of New England families, 25%, owned slaves as did Southern families on the eve of the War a century later.

American slavery rose to the forefront of national controversy during the Constitutional Convention in 1787. The conflict was sourced in two issues at first glance unrelated to it—taxation and political representation. Southern colonies wished to count slaves toward their population totals for purposes of Congressional representation, but not be subject to taxation because of them. The North took the opposite position on both counts. The Three-Fifths Compromise at which they arrived counted each slave as three-fifths of a person for purposes of both taxation and Congressional representation.

Some delegates also wished to stymie the Atlantic slave trade. Some of the states spearheading this effort were Southern. For instance, Virginia was the first colony—and the first land anywhere in Christendom—to outlaw the slave trade within its boundaries. It did so even before the War of Independence from Great Britain, in 1771. Georgia was next, in 1776. Yet the Southern economy grew increasingly dependent on slave labor, especially after the onset of Eli Whitney's cotton gin in 1793. That famed device exponentially increased the rate of cotton that could be processed, and thus revived two flagging enterprises—the cotton industry and slavery. The only catch was that large numbers of cheap-labor field workers were needed to pick the large amounts of cotton the gin could process.

The Constitutional Convention agreed to the Slave Trade Compromise, which prohibited Congress from stopping the transatlantic trade for twenty years, until 1807. However, this compromise permitted a $10-per-head tax levy on each imported slave in the meantime. The prevailing national political attitude at this point, though, was that the individual states had the authority to decide for themselves on questions related to slavery and the slave trade.

Future President James Madison, for instance, considered slavery and its possible abolition a distracting question from the business at hand of forming a new government.

This, despite the tension between the Declaration's "all men are created equal" clause and the practice of slavery. Still, that clause was primarily considered by the Founders to mean all men were created with equal value in the sight of God, and thirty-five of the fifty-five signers of the Declaration owned slaves.

The Slave Trade

The great majority of Americans—North, South, abolitionist, and slaveholder alike—believed the slave trade that brought captive African blacks to the United States, and many other countries, a horrible injustice. "Virginia theologian Robert L. Dabney called it "this iniquitous traffick." Slave trading involved the brutalization of human beings through kidnapping, manstealing, and sometimes murder, mutilation, or torture.

Slave trading involved the brutalization of human beings through kidnapping, manstealing, murder, mutilation, and torture. Its horror was beyond the ability of most modern Americans to imagine.

Surprisingly, most Americans involved directly in the African slave trade were New Englanders, financed by New York City bankers and financial institutions. Many of the wealthiest and most powerful old families of New England gained their fortunes directly or indirectly from the slave trade. According to historian Gail Jarvis, they used "specially constructed ships to transport slaves from Africa. These Yankee clippers were designed to hold a maximum number of slaves using a minimum amount of space . . . These ships would depart New England loaded with trinkets, weapons, and, of course, rum, which would be traded to [African] tribal chieftains in exchange for the Africans they held as slaves. On return trips, the ships would stop in the West Indies and exchange slaves for sugar and molasses, which were taken to New England to be distilled into rum."

African slaves were crammed into these ships like sardines in a tin. From one-fourth to one-third of all slaves shipped from Africa to the Western Hemisphere never made it there alive. Between one and two million blacks died en route. Often, the slaves found themselves jammed into small cubbyholes on the slave ships' lower decks, body on top of body, unable to move. Their journey across the Atlantic lasted anywhere from four days to three weeks. They had little food or water, and sometimes no toilet facilities except where they lay atop one another.

In these unsanitary conditions, disease ran rampant. Weaker slaves often died early in the voyage, only to lay rotting in the cargo holes. Those still alive could not get away from them and often lay atop or beneath them, day after day. The slaves faced dehumanization, brutality, and sometimes the merciless, sadistic beatings of the slave ships' crews.

Opposing Slavetrading

American states began to abolish the slave trade in the 1770s. As mentioned, Southern states, beginning with Virginia and Georgia, led the way in this effort. They believed dealing in human flesh inherently wicked and evil. They recognized in it the sin of manstealing, which Scripture pronounced a capital crime, requiring the penalty of death for the perpetrator. However, the Southern states did not exhibit the same leadership in abolishing slave-owning as they did in fighting the slave trade.

Only 6–8% of the African slave trade to the Western Hemisphere involved the United States. This amount was split almost evenly between Northern and Southern states. Most of the slave traders themselves hailed from Massachusetts, Rhode Island, or Delaware.

Only 6–8% of the African slave trade to the Western Hemisphere—native Africans brought as slaves to the Americas—involved the United States. This amount was split almost evenly between Northern and Southern states. Most of the slave traders themselves hailed from Massachusetts, Rhode Island, or Delaware. While most Southerners considered the slave trade a horrible evil, they felt a responsibility to take these kidnapped, displaced, and disoriented people and "rehabilitate" them into their new society.

Another rationale for white Southerners was that as many as three-fourths of them, too, came to America as some sort of slave, indentured or otherwise—though their status was not permanent or coercive as was that of many African slaves. The best that can be said of this tragic enterprise is, paraphrasing Genesis 50:20, what men meant for evil, God meant for good. Millions of black Americans descended from kidnapped African slaves have found eternal spiritual salvation, as well as earthly opportunity and blessing, by living in America rather than the disease- and war-ridden African nations of their heritage.

Going South

As the second half of the eighteenth century passed, demand for slaves in the North failed to keep pace with that in the South. The latter's terrain and climate rendered Northerner Eli Whitney's cotton gin, when employed in concert with hosts of black field workers, as one of the most successful inventions in American history.

Lacking a financial impetus for slavery, Northeastern states began in the late 1780s to outlaw the importation of slaves and in the late 1790s to phase out slavery altogether. They accomplished this by first decreeing free all children born to slaves. A large number of New England slave traders and slaveowners multiplied their fortunes through this process by selling their slaves to Southerners rather than freeing them. Ironically, many of these sellers' descendants stood in the front ranks of those who condemned Nineteenth-Century Southerners for owning slaves.

A Captured Slave Ship

The May 20, 1860 edition of *Harper's Weekly* reported and illustrated the capture of the slave bark, or ship, *Wildfire*. The United States had outlawed the importation of slaves in 1808, as well as the employment of American ships in the practice, even if they were transporting slaves to other countries. Such was the case when the American steamer *Mohawk*, commanded by a Lieutenant Craven, captured the *Wildfire* off the coast of Cuba on April 30, 1860.

Africans aboard the captured slave ship Barkfire.

According to *Harper's*, the *Wildfire* was owned "in the city of New York." It had left the Congo River in Africa five weeks before with six hundred slaves. One hundred had since died and forty more were ill, mostly from dysentery. The remainder "were generally in a very good condition of health and flesh, as compared with other similar cargoes, owing to the fact that they had not been so much crowded together on board as is common in slave voyages." Some had been slaves in Africa. All—men, women, and children—were totally naked.

President James Buchanan, a Pennsylvanian, recognized the *Wildfire* was not the only vessel still transporting slaves to the Western Hemisphere. He issued the following recommendation: "I would suggest that Congress might authorize the President to enter into a general agreement with the Colonization Society, binding them to receive, on the coast of Africa from our agent there, all the captured Africans which may be delivered to him, and to maintain them for a limited period, upon such terms and conditions as may combine humanity toward these unfortunates with a just economy. This would obviate the necessity of making a new bargain with every new capture, and would prevent delay and avoid expense in the disposition of the captured. The law might then provide that, in all cases where this may be practicable, the captor should carry the negroes directly to Africa, and deliver them to the American agent there, afterward bringing the captured vessel to the United States for adjudication."

This Northern divestiture of slaves created two unplanned and unwelcome consequences. First, Northern slave owners realized a dramatic loss in the market value of their slaves because they could no longer factor in the worth of the slaves' offspring. That is when they began to ship their slaves south to be sold. There, they could bring a larger profit. The second major consequence was that the bulk of nonslaveowning Northern whites viewed the mass emancipation of the black race as a threat to their own security, both economic and physical These Northerners too, for their own reasons, wished the blacks to be forced South. The two developments together resulted in an exodus south of blacks, both slave and free.

19th Century Growth

No organized political anti-slavery effort had yet coalesced, North or South, by the advent of the 19th century. Though individuals and even national leaders such as George Washington and Thomas Jefferson held private concerns about the practice of slavery, only isolated protests had arisen, notably from the Quakers. The prevailing attitude among Southerners, where slavery was more common, was that it was both a moral duty and a regrettable economic necessity they hoped would eventually die a natural death. By 1808, the evils of the slave trade that spawned slavery, on the other hand, were sufficiently manifest that Congress outlawed it without significant objections.

In North America slaveholding was first legally practiced in Massachusetts in 1641.

Land purchases and expansion led by 1819 to an equal number of states allowing and prohibiting slavery. This situation was not planned, but evolved through the addition of states to the Union. For instance, in 1803, Thomas Jefferson's Louisiana Purchase virtually doubled the land area owned by the United States. In 1819, the Missouri Territory, part of the Louisiana Purchase, sought statehood. New York Representative James Talmage introduced an amendment prohibiting the introduction of new slaves into Missouri and freeing slaves over the age of twenty-five upon statehood. The House of Representatives, dominated by the more populous North because of its proportional representation according to state population, voted in favor of the Talmage Amendment. The Senate, with representation distributed equally to each state, and thus equally to the South, voted against it.

The significance of the Talmage Amendment battle was the South's recognition that, since it could not hope to garner control of the House of Representatives, it needed more states in order to maintain power in the Senate. Now the question of whether new states were to be admitted with or without legal slavery first became a serious dispute between North and South. The North tended to hold that slavery in the territories was the purview of Congress. Many Southern leaders grew concerned that denial of the right to slaveowners to take their property into territories would infringe on their Fifth Amendment right of due process; that is, they would be denied the right to their own property.

The Missouri Compromise

The famed Missouri Compromise of 1820, crafted by Henry Clay, sought to assure the continued peaceable admittance of western states into the Union. The overarching objective was continued balance between the number of

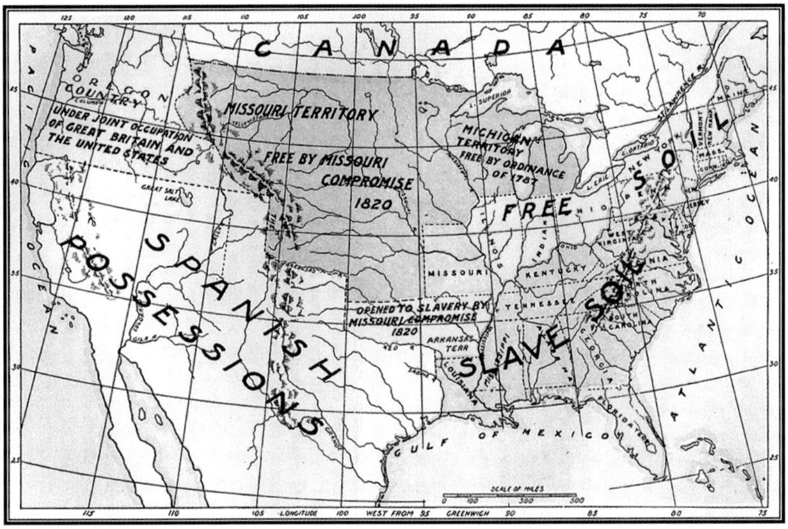

Map of the Missouri Compromise

free and slave states, and hence, political balance in the Senate. This meant that as westward settlement birthed new territories and then new states, some of those states would come into the Union as free states and some would have the opportunity to allow slavery.

The Missouri Compromise allowed Maine into the Union as a free state to balance the admission of Missouri as a slave state. In addition, slavery was forbidden within all territory north of the latitudinal line of 36 degrees, 30 minutes, which runs along the southern border of Missouri. This would include roughly the area containing the modern states of Iowa, Minnesota, Kansas, Nebraska, South Dakota, and North Dakota. South of that line, the area comprising modern-day Arkansas and Oklahoma, slavery was permitted. Lands farther west, still under the control of Spain, were not affected by the Missouri Compromise.

Many Reasons

Though millions of Northerners supported their section's war effort against the South in the 1860s, they did so for many different reasons, and they possessed a variety of views on slavery. At least four sometimes overlapping, but nonetheless distinctive major groups can be identified. Now is perhaps the time to introduce them, because slavery—despite their varying perspectives on it—was the issue around which they eventually coalesced.

One was the the industrialists, whose chief desire was to protect the industrial interests of the Northeast and maintain the South as a place of resources. Another was the radical centralists, who desired revolution along the lines of Marx and Engels' *Communist Manifesto* and remaking the nature of the nation, with the central national government possessing unchallenged authority. A third was the abolitionists, part of a larger category of reformers who wanted to bring salvation by ridding the world—and America in particular—of social sin. The Unionists comprised a final group, whose chief desire was to preserve the Union intact.

All of these groups saw the South as a threat to the attainment of their goals. Slavery gave each group a holy cause by which to accomplish their ends. The industrialists could see the

South removed as an economic threat, which it became due to its cooperation with its European trading partners and especially when it instituted its low tariff ports. The Unionists could preserve the Union from those who would split or destroy the nation. The centralists could use the occasion of war to usher in radical reforms.

None of these people could accomplish their ends easily or on the strength of their own arguments and agenda. They had too little support among the general populace. But with slavery as the leading public issue, the objectives of each group could be attained, and while in pursuit of a righteous cause. It fell to the abolitionists to galvanize public sentiment.

Abolition or Anti-Slavery?

But why was it necessary to heat up public sentiment over an issue like slavery? Did not the vast majority of the nation, North and South, oppose slavery? Yes. But little outrage existed anywhere in America over the practice. America as a whole was antislavery, but not abolitionist. What was the difference?

The abolitionists demanded the immediate freeing of all slaves, with no compensation to those who had purchased them and/or paid for their food, lodging, medicine, and clothing. Those with antislavery sentiment favored some manner of emancipation, preferably gradual and with

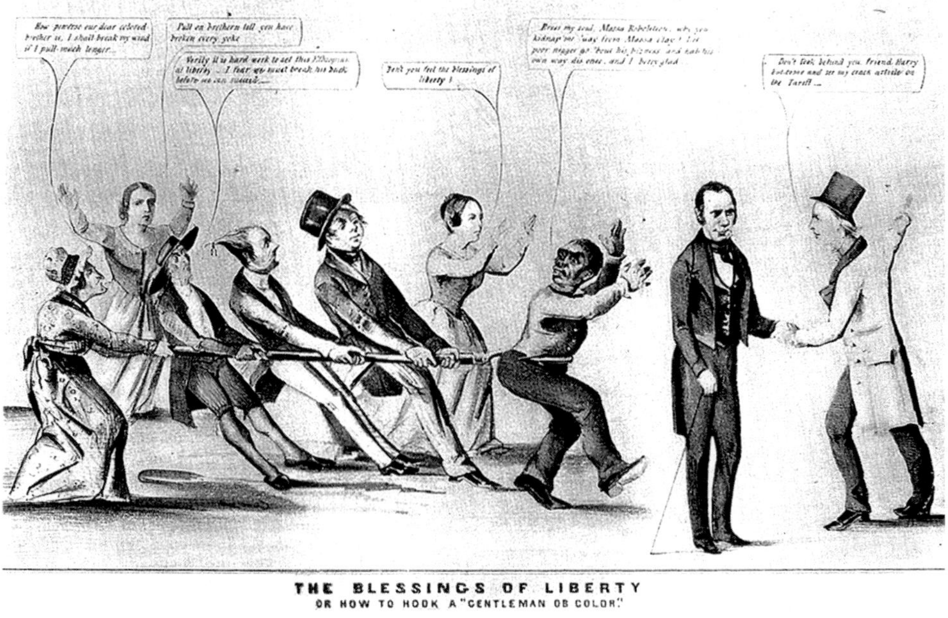

"The Blessings of Liberty," or "how to hook a 'gentleman ob color,'" a caricature of abolitionists and their supposed misguided efforts for slaves. (Images of American Political History)

some form of financial restitution provided the owners. They believed this would minimize the economic—and thus social—disruption, as when the famed Christian social reformer William Wilberforce led the British in just such a successful effort (see Chapter 6).

The desire for financial restitution for slaves was not based on greed, nor was it a ploy to fleece non-slaveowners in a redistribution of wealth. Rather, just as the North had for decades plowed its investment capital into its factories, the agrarian South—rich in natural resources but poor in industrial infrastructure, manufacturing expertise, and cheap immigrant labor—had put its money into the slaves through whom much of its wealth was "manufactured." And after the abolition of the slave trade in 1808, the average cost to purchase a slave rose ever-higher, to the then-substantial price of $1,500 by 1860. By then, so much Southern wealth was tied up in slaves that even without a war, immediate emancipation would have meant economic ruin for thousands of erstwhile slaveowners and likely the entire section.

The South put forth a stream of slave-freeing plans based upon the British model. While a minority of "fire-eaters" argued against any government-induced freeing of the slaves, many Southern leaders urged the eschewing of war and the crafting of a peaceful program of gradual emancipation. Indeed, slavery had never been abolished in any nation by war before 1861.

Abolition—American Style

Still, aside from the fire-eaters and the abolitionists, hardly anyone could figure out exactly what to do about emancipation or slavery in general. The majority of white Americans, North and South, did not want the Negro to become a part of their society, even though they favored the abolition of slavery. But for most whites, abolition meant the abolition of blacks from American life and society.

Thomas Jefferson, third president of the United States, illustrated this ideal. As early as 1790—less than ten years after American freedom from England—he proposed a plan to deport Negroes out of the country. "Deport them to any land which is not likely to become a part of this nation in the future," said Jefferson. It did not really matter where to him, just so they were out of the United States. His concern, like that of most American citizens, was as much the preservation of white superiority in the nation as it was opposition to slavery as an institution. Jefferson believed the black man was inferior to the white man. "It is clear proof because of their color," he said. "That proves it. Black is not attractive."

Jefferson was not unique in his views. Every president from George Washington to Andrew Jackson, with the exception of John Adams and his son John Quincy Adams, were slave owners and believed in the natural inferiority of the Negro. This conviction motivated the formation of the American Colonization Society in 1817. Its purpose was to resettle black

Joseph Jenkins Roberts, first president of the new west African nation of Liberia, which gained its independence in 1847. Roberts emigrated from Petersburg, Virginia to Liberia in 1829 at the age of 20, when the land was still owned by the American Colonization Society.

slaves in Africa. The organization accomplished just that, at least to a degree. It founded the modern west African nation of Liberia. The Presidential administration of slaveholder James Monroe oversaw the effort. The capital of English-speaking Liberia, with its flag that resembles the United States flag, was Monroeville (now Monrovia).

The Colonization Society's plan to export blacks from America had been endorsed by virtually every early American leader—Washington, Jefferson, Madison, Monroe, John Marshall, Andrew Jackson, Henry Clay, Daniel Webster, William Seward, Francis Scott Key, General Winfield Scott—and Abraham Lincoln. Internationally-syndicated journalist Eric Margolis tells the sad, little-known story of what happened when these famed American leaders got their wish in Liberia: "The ex-slaves, in a telling comment on human nature, promptly enslaved local tribes, formed a dynasty and turned the country into a plantation."

With such attitudes toward the Negro pervading the North and the South, the abolitionists faced a big job in stirring up enough people to achieve their goals. So they planned, they wrote, they lobbied, and they preached. They utilized the media to mold public opinion in a way never before done in American history. Sometimes they resorted to wild exaggerations, slander, and outright lies.

The antislavery movement, meanwhile, had at least as much support in the South as in the North. In the early decades of the 19th century, more than two-thirds of the antislavery societies were in the South, not the North. The first antislavery newspaper was published in Jonesboro, Tennessee. State legislation, including in the South, prior to the rise of radical abolitionism was moving toward gradual emancipation.

One such bill was introduced in 1821 in Virginia. Alexander Stephens, later vice president of the Confederacy, declared: "If it had not been for the radical abolitionists, slavery would have been abolished in the states of Virginia and North Carolina. And in Georgia, eight-tenths would have abolished slavery if they could have seen what better they could do with the colored people than they were doing."

The South Hardens

What became of these efforts? The actions of abolitionist William Lloyd Garrison and his cohorts impacted them profoundly and ironically. In 1831, as England systematically disengaged its worldwide empire from slavery, Garrison founded the newspaper *The Liberator.* With it, he threw down the gauntlet to the South in newsprint. Garrison and his associates began to preach a heretofore unheard of brand of radical abolition. Ironically, their revolutionary ideas alarmed more people in the North than they persuaded. But their effect on the South was profound and disturbing. Southerners grew defensive and started to defend slavery with vigor and to oppose even gradual emancipation.

Prior to the advent of Garrison and his network of abolitionist ideologues, most Southerners defended the institution of slavery itself on both Constitutional and Biblical grounds, but not necessarily the manner in which it operated. Southern critics were willing to acknowledge problems with the institution. They believed slavery itself was not evil but was attended in their system with many evils. However, when the fierce, sometimes inaccurate, attacks of the abolitionists began to hit home, the South hardened its position. Southerners began overlooking the shortcomings of slavery and defending it top to bottom, even at points where it was unbiblical and immoral.

Most Northerners did not know the facts about the slave system and had little desire to search for them. Much of what they believed was framed by the abolitionists, who spoke loudest and most passionately on the subject. And the more radical abolitionists of the North were not bashful in declaring their aims. They hoped to start a civil war in the South. But the civil war they had in mind was not between the white citizens of the North and South, but rather the slaves against slaveholders. They wanted to provoke a slave war in the South, blacks against whites. Only when they realized they could force that war did they turn their efforts toward influencing an aggressive Northern political policy toward the South.

Massacred by Slaves

Perhaps Northern abolitionists dismissed the possibility of race war, but Southerners did not. This specter multiplied the effect of the abolitionists' actions on the South. And a series of nightmarish bloodlettings produced a collective chill in Southerners that forever changed their society, all of America, and even the history of the world.

Numerous slave uprisings occurred in the Caribbean, a dozen of them in Cuba alone, during the first half of the Nineteenth Century. The worst involved a barely-believable—and rarely-discussed—sequence of horror unleashed as one of the many consequences of the atheistic French Revolution of Robespierre and Voltaire. In the 1790s, the new French "rulers" freed all black slaves in the French colony of Haiti. This act did not have the intended result. The former slaves raped, tortured, and slaughtered the white French planter class.

The American Colonization Society's purpose: to resettle black slaves in Africa . . . Its work was the foundation of the modern nation of Liberia. The plan carried out by the Colonization Society had been endorsed by virtually every early American leader.

William Lloyd Garrison (1805–1879)

The leading intellectual advocate of abolitionism in the North, William Lloyd Garrison grew convinced as a young man that slavery was an evil so heinous he must oppose it with all the strength he possessed. Garrison was initially committed to pacifism and eschewed violent solutions to slavery. Yet he believed the language of violence and provocation to be quite appropriate in ending slavery. Thus his rhetoric proved inflammatory to the extreme in some areas of the North and nearly everywhere in the South. Most in the former either ignored him or were mildly irritated by his verbosity, but the latter reacted to his words with horror.

He kept the heat turned up on those in the North who were antislavery though not necessarily abolitionist. He challenged them to demonstrate their opposition to slavery by laying their life on the line and by promoting armed rebellion like he was doing. If they did not, he chastised them for compromising. Sometimes employing language even more incendiary than he himself believed, Garrison sought to shift the political center of the issue by shaming moderates and drawing them in his more radical direction.

Among Garrison's many memorable statements was his oft-repeated assertion that the American Constitution was a "compact with the devil" because it allowed for the continuation and perpetuation of slavery. He also called it "a covenant with death and an agreement with hell," and his abolitionist associates in Massachusetts burned it.

Brilliant and articulate, Garrison founded the arch-abolitionist newspaper *The Liberator* in 1831. It never boasted a wide circulation; in fact, Garrison himself was never widely known among the Northern public. When the Georgia state senate indicted him and

The Passion of William Lloyd Garrison

I shall strenuously contend for the immediate enfranchisement of our slave population. In Park Street Church in Boston on the Fourth of July, 1829, in an address on slavery I unreflectingly assented to the popular but pernicious doctrine of gradual abolition. I seize this opportunity to take a full and unequivocal recantation and thus publicly to ask pardon of my God, of my country, and of my brethren the poor slaves for having uttered a sentiment so full of timidity, injustice, and absurdity.

I am aware that many object to the severity of my language, but is there not cause for severity? I will be as harsh as the truth and as uncompromising as injustice.

On this subject I do not wish to think or speak or write with moderation. No! No! Tell a man whose house is on fire to give a moderate alarm, tell him to moderately rescue his wife from the hands of a ravisher, tell the mother to gradually extricate her babe from the fire from which it has fallen. But urge me not to use moderation in a cause like the present.

I am in earnest, I will not equivocate, I will not excuse, I will not retreat a single inch, and I will be heard!

I desire to thank God that He enables me to disregard the fear of man which bringeth a snare and to speak His truth with simplicity and power.

telegraphed the Massachusetts governor for his extradition, the governor did not even know who Garrison was. Yet *The Liberator* exerted great influence. Opinion makers and newsmakers in the North and firebreathing defenders of slavery in the South alike read it.

Garrison became the point man for abolitionism. He founded the American Anti-Slavery Society. Many Northerners considered him a great saint, many Southerners the devil incarnate. So stark and incendiary was Garrison's language that, rather than seeking means to reconcile the increasingly divergent worldviews of North and South, he accentuated and compounded their differences. In fact, he aimed to change the language of debate about slavery, which up until about the time he founded *The Liberator*, was fairly moderate on both sides. He felt if he could move the terms of the debate ever closer to abolitionism, he could actually move even the Southern defenders of slavery toward his viewpoint. He sought not only to win the debate, but to define its terms.

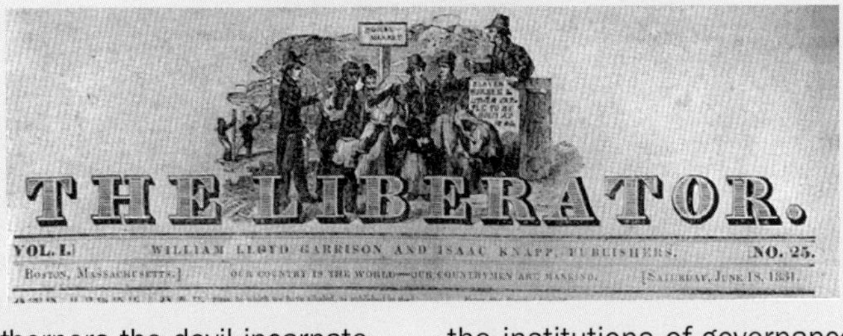

Eventually, Garrison called not only for the impeachment of federal judges, the destruction of the institutions of governance, and the mobilization of every apparatus of society and culture against the great evil of slavery, but for the destruction of the Constitution itself and the rebuilding of the nation upon a new foundation.

When Napoleon Bonaparte acceded to power, he dispatched 45,000 troops to Haiti to wrest control back from the rampaging freedmen. Again, the French could scarcely have imagined what their actions would provoke. Instead of staunching the revolution and restoring their white settlers to power, the French troops themselves were exterminated—by disease and by the freed slaves. Then the blacks proceeded to massacre the entire white population of the island—20,000 men, women, and children—and establish an all-black society on the heels of the century's first true racial genocide. Southerners well knew these stories, and they knew the story of Nat Turner even better.

In August 1831, Turner, a slave and self-styled "preacher," gathered several other slaves and murdered his own master and that man's entire family. Gathering more slaves, more guns, and liquor, Turner stormed across the Virginia countryside massacring every white family he came upon. Fifty-five murders later, he and his gang were captured, tried and hanged. Only thirteen of their shot, sliced, stabbed, or tortured victims were men. Eighteen were women and twenty-four were children.

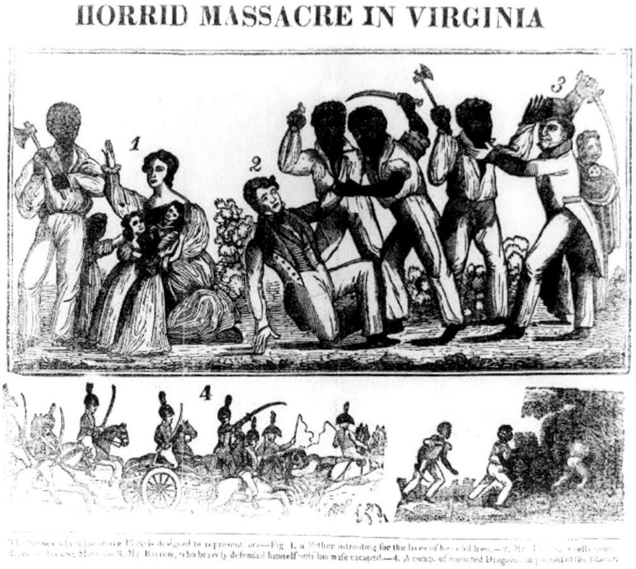
HORRID MASSACRE IN VIRGINIA

"Horrid Massacre in Virginia," a chilling woodcut chronicling the Nat Turner-led 1831 slave rebellion in Virginia. (Library of Congress)

Sad Turnaround

Nat Turner could hardly have done more harm to his own cause. Within months, the pall of his terror hanging like a pregnant cloud of doom over all of Virginia and the South, the Virginia legislature narrowly voted down a plan presented by the grandson of Thomas Jefferson that would have paid slave-owners for the gradual emancipation of their slaves. But for Turner's infamy, the bill might well have passed. Not only that, the legal codes pertaining to slaves in Virginia and other Southern states were tightened, restricting some of the most basic human rights of black bondsmen.

Rev. Dr. William H. White, Stonewall Jackson's pastor in Lexington, Virginia, observed after the War:

> The South was then thrown on the defensive. Stringent laws were enacted which would never have been thought of but for the purpose of a necessary self-defense, and for which we of the South incurred the reprobation of the North.
>
> Previous to the inauguration of this state of things, servants were taught to read, colored men were licensed to preach the gospel (John Jasper of Richmond preeminent among them), the marriage and parental relations were respected, they lived in families, had family worship, and were not only permitted but urged to train their children and govern their households according to the Word of God.

All this occurred as white Southerners, witnessing the horrors of armed slave rebellions at home and abroad—and the apparent support of them by prominent Northern abolitionists—grew stricken with fear at the prospect of masses of armed free blacks loosed in the South. Still, even after the stricter codes passed, the literacy rate of slaves remained between thirty and forty percent. This bore testament to the determination of many slave owners to seek the welfare of their slaves—regardless of whether it meant risking retribution from the law.

In summary, Southern reaction was unfortunate, largely indefensible—and understandable. Most Northern abolitionists had little or no firsthand

Nat Turner (?-1831)

A Virginia slave, Nat Turner was also an articulate underground slave preacher, in a state that ruled the practice illegal. One of the most heinous aspects of slavery was that in many quarters, particularly after abolitionist-spurred Southern paranoia escalated, slaves were proscribed from reading or attending church other than in segregated congregations. Turner grew sickened by such abuses of slavery and no longer content to submit to it. His reading of the Scriptures convinced him it was an unmitigated evil and needed to be opposed with every possible force. So he began to plan a slave rebellion. He launched it in August 1831.

"Nat Turner's Rebellion" slaughtered fifty-five whites, most of them women and children, before Turner and his confederates were caught, tried, and hanged. But this heartbreaking loss of life was hardly comparable either to the shudders of fear in the South or the sense of triumph in some quarters in the North. While Southerners denounced his lawlessness, murderous treachery, and vile acts, many in the North applauded Turner as a hero, liberator, and emancipator.

Turner's short-lived slave rebellion provoked New England abolitionist William Lloyd Garrison toward ever-more radical abolitionist language and provided the impetus behind the founding of his newspaper *The Liberator*. In the end, Nat Turner's violent acts accomplished just what those of John Brown—another self-styled preacher and prophet who fancied he was carrying out the will of God—did. Rather than expediting the end of slavery, they widened the chasm between North and South.

knowledge of slavery in the South. This included Harriet Beecher Stowe, whose classic 1852 *Uncle Tom's Cabin* unleashed a sea change in American opinion over slavery. Mrs. Stowe had never set foot in any state that became Confederate; she gleaned her views from abolitionist writers.

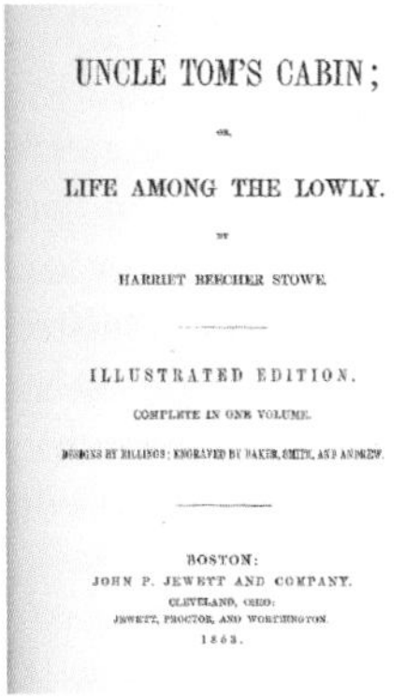

UNCLE TOM'S CABIN;

OR,

LIFE AMONG THE LOWLY.

BY

HARRIET BEECHER STOWE.

ILLUSTRATED EDITION.

COMPLETE IN ONE VOLUME.

DESIGNS BY BILLINGS; ENGRAVED BY BAKER, SMITH, AND ANDREW.

BOSTON:
JOHN P. JEWETT AND COMPANY.
CLEVELAND, OHIO:
JEWETT, PROCTOR, AND WORTHINGTON.
1853.

Time and again, Southerners heard, read, and saw slanderous—and sometimes famous—abolitionist propaganda that had been broadcast in the North and which they knew little resembled the facts of their land. Much such propaganda has passed unchallenged even down into current historiography, secular and Christian. It bears powerful testimony to the power of myth.

The Final Compromise

By 1850, sectional tensions in America were extreme. For the third

Harriet Beecher Stowe (1811-1896)

The seventh child of famous revivalist and theologian Lyman Beecher. Her family was one of the most prominent of the 19th century North, and well-known for its leadership in the Church. Mrs. Stowe strongly believed the domestic arts were the great and glorious calling for women; for her first 30 years, she aspired only to raise a family. She was a committed homemaker and a splendid homeschooler. She read to her seven children for two hours every evening before the fireplace and committed to them a grand treasury of literature and poetry.

But she always loved to write her own stories. When she was thirty one, she published a small collection of short stories. Her husband believed she possessed a great calling in writing and encouraged this gift. Just before her 40th birthday, she published a little book that caused a big rift in the nation. That book was *Uncle Tom's Cabin*. The book did not offer particularly enthralling characters, much of its dialogue strained credulity, many of its stereotypes were overwrought, and even Mrs. Stowe's research was shoddy. She was no eyewitness to slavery herself. She based all her observations about slavery on second- or even third-hand sources.

Yet the little book struck a nerve. Before the end of 1852, its first year in print, it had sold 30,000 copies. Before the War concluded in 1865, it sold more than a million. *Uncle Tom's Cabin* provided an emotional spark, particularly in the North but also in the South, that provoked a wider divide between the two great worldviews that dominated these lands. In 1862, when President Lincoln met the quiet, diminutive New Englander, he said, "So, this is the woman that wrote the book that caused this war."

time, Henry Clay shouldered the lion's share of creating a compromise that preserved the Union. This time, it was the Compromise of 1850. There would be no more successful compromises ever between North and South.

Clay's compromise acknowledged that each region had legitimate arguments. The North, he said, had rightful concerns about the expansion of slavery in the West. Conversely, Clay declared the South had legitimate concerns about the abrogation of property rights the Northern-dominated Congress might impose upon it. Enormous questions abounded over taxation and political representation. The Compromise of 1850 boldly attempted to address all of these. Clay wanted to give everyone as much of what they sought as possible.

For instance, a key component in gaining the South's concurrence on the compromise was that it not only upheld, but broadened, strengthened, and clarified the fugitive slave law.

This law required slaves who escaped from their masters to be returned, if necessary with the cooperation of local or even federal law enforcement officials, no matter what section of the nation they were found in. It applied to all American slaves, whether from Minnesota in the North, border states like Delaware and Virginia, or the Deep South states.

One key component in the new Fugitive Slave Act was that it eliminated the right to trial by jury for a black alleged to be a runaway slave. This included free Northern blacks accused of being such. It also paid a $10 bounty for each fugitive delivered to federal authorities. This provision created the specter of slavecatchers kidnapping free blacks from the North and taking them south for sale. On the other hand, the compromise severely restricted the slave trade itself.

It allowed for the admission of California as a free state. However, the compromise permitted slavery to continue in the New Mexico Territories (the area of present-day New Mexico and Arizona), and further to continue there once that area attained statehood, provided its people approved a constitution that allowed it.

Slavery was the cause of the War, just as property is the cause of robbery.

—George Lunt
19th century Massachusetts lawyer, poet, and author

Indeed, it was the last great attempt to hold the Union together. Only two years later, in 1852, Massachusetts, Illinois, and Rhode Island passed standards of nullification, announcing the Fugitive Slave Act null and void within their state boundaries. They defended these actions by declaring that one of

The famed 1850 political cartoon "The Hurly Burly Pot." It mocked the Compromise of 1850 efforts of a disparate group of political leaders, including David Wilmot, William Lloyd Garrison, John Calhoun, and Horace Greeley, as well as their supposed fellow-traitor from an earlier generation, Benedict Arnold. Savage ridicule in both politics and political commentary is not a recent phenomenon in American society.

the key provisions of the Compromise of 1850 had never been met—abolishing the slave market in the nation's capital itself, Washington D.C. Amazingly, that slave market—the largest in America—was just two blocks from the White House. It remained there for nearly half the War and Abraham Lincoln's presidency. Every time Lincoln walked to a nearby Federal military hospital, for instance, he walked past it.

So those three Northern states said if the great compromise was not to be upheld in the key provision regarding the slave trade—in the nation's capital, no less—they would not uphold it on the key provision regarding the Fugitive Slave Act. In other words, they would not promise to uphold with the force of the courts in their states the slaveowners' rights to arrest and extradition of a runaway slave back to his home.

Harriet Tubman and the Underground Railroad (1820-1913)

For years before legal emancipation freed the great mass of American slaves, the illegal Underground Railroad helped escaped slaves make their way north and find refuge in free states or Canada. It was not a true railroad, though some slaves thought it was. A series of locations called stations helped them move north. Stations could be houses, barns, other structures, even boats. Those who escaped on the Underground Railroad were dubbed passengers. Those who led them garnered the name conductors.

Thousands of people, black and white, participated at some time in aiding runaway slaves. Probably the most famous of them was Harriet Tubman, a black female who herself fled into the woods from the Eastern Shore Maryland plantation where she lived as a slave, then continued north to Philadelphia. One of the many characteristics that set Tubman apart from others who aided the Underground Railroad was that her own newfound freedom did not

satisfy her. Rather, she returned to Maryland to help her parents, her sister, and perhaps as many as 300 other slaves find their way to freedom.

"There was one of two things I had a right to, liberty, or death," said Tubman. "If I could not have one, I would have the other; for no man should take me alive; I should fight for my liberty as long as my strength lasted, and when the time came for me to go, the Lord would let them take me." She developed friendships with numerous leading abolitionists, and John Brown probably confided to her his plans to assault the Federal arsenal at Harpers Ferry.

Slaves on the Underground Railroad, aided by a white family.

The Underground Railroad did not develop according to any preconceived plan or design. Like many other powerful social forces in American history, it formed a bit at a time in response to situations and needs discovered by people contemporaneous to those events. From the late 1830s until the end of the War, between 50,000 and 75,000 slaves successfully escaped their owners. Canada drew many because several Northern states, including Ohio, Indiana, and Abraham Lincoln's home state of Illinois, refused to allow new blacks across their borders.

On some occasions, recapturing slaves who escaped north—even to the northern United States, as opposed to Canada—could prove difficult. Slave owner Edward Gorsuch and Deputy Marshall Henry Kline followed two fugitives to the Pennsylvania town of Christiana. There, local Quakers and free blacks aided the slaves. Gorsuch, a Quaker, and three blacks died in the ensuing gun battle.

Danger and Daring

It could be dangerous for the slaves and those aiding their escape attempts as well. Though only five feet tall, Tubman's courage and aptitude for toughness had to match her compassion for others. More than once, she threatened to shoot with a loaded revolver escaped slaves who straggled behind the group she was leading at the time. She explained why: "If he's weak enough to give out, he'd be weak enough to betray us all, and all who had helped us; and do you think I'd let so many die just for one coward man?"

Tubman soon had a bounty on her own head. But she was never caught. Daring and resourceful, she often disguised herself. She was known to dress up as a man, as well as an old woman.

White abolitionist Martha C. Wright recounted one of Tubman's rescue adventures:

"We have been expending our sympathies, as well as congratulations, on seven newly arrived slaves that Harriet Tubman has just pioneered safely from the southern part of Maryland. One woman carried a baby all the way and bro't two other child'n that Harriet and the men helped along. They bro't a piece of old comfort and a blanket, in a basket with a little kindling, a little bread for the baby with some laudanum (opium) to keep it from crying during the day. They walked all night carrying the little ones, and spread the old comfort on the frozen ground, in some dense thicket where they all hid, while Harriet went out foraging, and sometimes cd not get back till dark, fearing she wd be followed. Then, if they had crept further in, and she couldn't find them, she wd whistle, or sing certain hymns and they wd answer."

There was one of two things I had a right to, liberty, or death. If I could not have one, I would have the other.
—Harriet Tubman

In addition to her work on the Underground Railroad, Tubman worked during the War as a nurse, laundress, and spy in Federal military hospitals on the coasts of Virginia and South Carolina. She distinguished herself in new ways after the War. She moved to New York, married a Federal war veteran, and cared for her parents. She opened a home for elderly blacks. And she worked to open schools for the large number of uneducated former slaves.

Before she died, Harriet Tubman received an invitation from England's Queen Victoria to visit her in London. The tiny old warrior did not have the funds to make the trip. "I always told God," Tubman said, "I'm going to hold steady on you, and you've got to see me through."

6 Slavery II

The Tragic Prelude, the dramatic rendering of John Brown and several of the elements swirling around him and his violent approach to ending slavery. (National Archives and Records Administration)

My paramount object in this struggle is to save the Union and is not either to save or destroy slavery. If I could save the Union without freeing any slaves, I would do it. And if I could save it by freeing all of the slaves, I would do it. And if I could save it by freeing some and leaving others alone, I would also do that.

—Abraham Lincoln (1861)

The conflict between competing financial interests provides the context for much of America's story and growth. The establishment of the Kansas and Nebraska Territories offer a vivid example. They became pawns in the building of the transcontinental railroad. Because of the opportunities for power and wealth that accompanied the transcontinental railroad, it became one of the financial sweepstakes of the century. Nearly ten thousand miles of track had been laid within the American states by 1850. That amount would more than triple in the next decade.

Though differing on the extent of taxpayer involvement, the majority of the people and the government agreed that a transcontinental railroad should be built from the East clear to the Pacific Ocean. That was where consensus ended. Three different routes were advocated by differing factions. One, favored by Northerners, ran westward from the current-day upper midwest to the Oregon Territory in America's northwest corner. Another, favored by Southerners, ran along the nation's Southern rim, from New Orleans through Texas and the Southwest desert to San Diego. A third, in between, was proposed by Illinois Senator Stephen A. Douglas, who happened to be heavily invested financially in the land along which that route would be built.

Stephen Douglas
(Chicago Historical Society)

Kansas and Nebraska

This led Douglas to propose in January 1854 the organization of the Nebraska Territory. It encompassed most of the present-day states of Nebraska, Wyoming, and Montana, as well as the western portions of the Dakotas. Douglas' bill included a provision that the slavery question be decided in Nebraska by popular sovereignty. Popular sovereignty meant agreeing that at a certain point in population growth, a vote would be taken to determine whether the territory would enter the Union as a free or slave state. Northern anti-slavery proponents exploded in fury. To them, Douglas' proposal meant nothing less than the repeal of the old Missouri Compromise—at least that portion of it favorable to them—by allowing for the possibility of slavery north of the old 36-degree, 30-minute dividing line.

Meanwhile, Douglas attempted to secure for the Kansas Territory, just south of Nebraska, the right to decide its own slave policy by popular sovereignty. While doing so, however, he assuaged Northerners with assurances that few Southerners would want to move to Kansas with their slaves, because neither the terrain nor the climate were conducive to growing the crops that made slavery feasible. His more subtle message and aim here were that slavery was a delicate institution needing safeguards, such as special laws, to survive—safeguards which would not be present in Kansas.

John Brown, with and without the beard he sported as a disguise at the time of his 1859 raid on the federal arsenal at Harper's Ferry, Virginia.

In the end, Douglas angered both North and South; Northerners because, being free soilers (requiring all residents to be free), they wanted no possibility of slavery in the territory, and Southerners because they wanted the certain right to move there with their slaves and not be subject to the whims of the popular majority. But the Kansas-Nebraska Act passed in May 1854, opening both territories to the settlement of free soilers and slave-owners, and providing for popular sovereignty to decide slave policy.

Bleeding Kansas

American settlement of Kansas was contentious from the beginning due to the confluence of Northern and Southern cultures. The governor of the territory scheduled a census and election in 1855. Pro-slavery partisans crossed into Kansas from the next-door territory of Missouri, voted for pro-slave territorial legislature candidates, and then returned home to Missouri.

The governor denounced the Missourians, but endorsed the election results, which delivered power to pro-slavery forces. A rump group of free soilers made an unsuccessful attempt in the ensuing months to establish their own territorial government in Topeka. These divergent visions turned deadly. Both free soilers and pro-slavery forces committed violent acts, acts whose severity gradually escalated.

Pro-Southern anger gradually focused on the north central Kansas town of Lawrence. They viewed the schoolhouse and other institutions in that settlement as the epicenter of anti-Southern propaganda and influence. So they sacked the town. Then a grim band of Northerners led by Ohioan John Brown sealed their commitment to instant abolition in blood by dragging five pro-slavery men out of their homes in the middle of the night and butchering them with broadswords in full view of their wives and children. None of the victims owned slaves.

Over two hundred people of all political persuasions died during the reign of terror that came to be known as "Bleeding Kansas." John Brown and his comrades escaped east. To the shock of Southerners, they were not only welcomed into the homes of some of New England's greatest luminaries, but it later came to light that some of those very men had provided the finances that allowed Brown to unleash his terror. But Brown's violence was far from finished, as was that of Kansas.

> *It [is] better that the six millions of white men, women, and children in the South should be slaughtered than that slavery should not be extinguished.*
>
> —Rev. W. J. Sloane
> Third Reformed Presbyterian Church of New York

In 1857, the elected pro-slavery legislature determined to call a convention to write a constitution pursuant to statehood. Anti-slavery forces wrote their own. With anti-slavery forces boycotting, the territory-wide election went in favor of the pro-slavery Lecompton Constitution. Now the governor, aligned with anti-slavery forces and suspecting election fraud, called for a second vote, which pro-slavery forces boycotted. This time, the Lecompton Constitution was overwhelmingly rejected.

The Kansas legislature ignored the second election. They presented the Lecompton Constitution for Congressional approval in hopes of subsequent admittance into the Union as a slave state. President James Buchanan approved of the constitution, but opponents—led by Douglas in the Senate—added an amendment that required a third, carefully-supervised vote in order to attain statehood. With the Kansas population increasingly Northern and anti-slavery, this third vote again rejected Lecompton. Kansas remained a territory, and pro-slavery forces lost hopes of it being admitted as a slave state.

Divisions and Threats

Despite the tumult in Kansas, the issue of slavery did not rivet the attention of the wide sweep of Americans in any section. Still, division mushroomed over it on a number of institu-

Anti-slavery or Anti-slave?

Was "Bleeding Kansas" the result of contention between those who wished to keep blacks in bondage and those who wished them freed? Such a notion would have come as a surprise to many of those "free-soilers" who urged the prohibition of slavery in Kansas. The anti-slavery territorial government proposed a state constitution in the mid 1850s that would have prevented not only slaves, but any other blacks from even entering the state.

The new Republican Party of Abraham Lincoln and others, meanwhile, displayed its sentiments on the issue in its 1856 presidential platform, which read, in part, that "all unoccupied territory of the United States, and such as they may hereafter acquire, shall be reserved for the white Caucasian race—a thing that cannot be except by the exclusion of slavery."

tional fronts around the nation. Anti-slavery Northern Senator Charles Sumner viciously slandered a slave-owning Congressman and kinsman of pro-slavery Southern Senator Preston Brooks in 1856. This resulted in the even more vicious caning of Sumner by Brooks. All of this occurred on the floor of the working senate.

Philosophical divisions not limited to, but certainly spurred by, slavery shook the very foundations of America's greatest Christian denominations. The Baptist church split along a North-South fault line in 1843. The Methodist church did the same in 1844 and the Presbyterian in 1857. Southern fears that the abolitionists intended nothing short of the extermination of their civilization were not eased by the tidal wave of vitriol flowing forth from Northern leaders like the influential Congressman Theodore Stevens of Pennsylvania. He preferred the destruction of the South's land, property, and people to the sundering of the American political union.

Later, when war approached, *Blackwood*'s magazine reported the Rev. W. J. Sloane, pastor of New York City's Third Reformed Presbyterian Church, as declaring "that it was better that the six millions of white men, women, and children in the South should be slaughtered than that slavery should not be extinguished." When a newspaper editor excoriated the pastor for his unchristian stratagem, Sloane riposted, "I affirm that it is better, far better, that every man, woman, and child in every rebel state should perish in one widespread, bloody, and indiscriminate slaughter; better that the land should be a Sahara; be as when God destroyed the Canaanites, or overthrew Sodom and Gomorrah, than that this rebellion should be successful."

Dred Scott

The drama over slavery came to the United States Supreme Court in 1857 with the case of *Dred Scott v. Sandford*. The latter, a Missourian, owned the former, whom he took with him upon moving to the free state of Illinois, then the free territory of Wisconsin. Upon their return to Missouri, Scott, sponsored by abolitionist activists, sued Sandford for his freedom. Citing the Missouri Compromise and its proscription of slavery north of the 36–30 line, Scott maintained he was a free man when in Illinois and Wisconsin and was thus a free man upon his return to Missouri.

Dred Scott

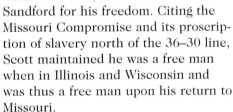

The case roiled all the way to the U.S. Supreme Court. That body ruled 7–2 against the slave. So contentious was the case that every Supreme Court Justice rendered his own opinion. Chief Justice Roger B. Taney's served as a sort of summary of the majority opinions. He ruled that whether or not he agreed with the Founding Fathers, their Constitution did not consider slaves as citizens;

thus Scott had no right to bring suit in a U.S. court. Further, Taney posited that regardless of Scott's sojourn on free soil, he was subject to the laws of the state where he resided, and the laws of Missouri said he was a slave.

Finally, and most controversially, Taney said the Constitution gave no legislative body, including Congress, the right to deprive an American citizen of his property, including slaves. Anti-slavery critics claimed the court not only overthrew the Missouri Compromise, with its ban on slavery north of the 36–30 line, but revoked the right of both the federal and territorial governments to ban slavery, even when popular sovereignty opposed. Future Secretary of State William Seward promised to "reorganize the court and thus reform its political sentiments and practices" when the Republicans won the Presidency. One Cincinnati newspaper roared, "There is such a thing as THE SLAVE POWER. It has marched over and annihilated the boundaries of the States. We are now one great homogeneous slaveholding community."

Weld and the Grimkes

Stereotypes, as powerful as they are distorted, abound about the War, nowhere more so than regarding slavery and race. For generations, the "moonlight and magnolias" portrait of a South replete with happy field slaves wishing no more than to work their whole lives for "massa" held sway in many quarters. In like fashion, abolitionist fiction exerts a powerful influence even today on the American psyche and culture. Evidence aplenty reveals the abolitionists were not above fabricating facts to suit their ends. One famous illustration of this is the work of abolitionist Theodore Weld, who married Angelina Grimke of Charleston, South Carolina. Angelina's older sister Sara moved in to live with Weld and her sister.

Angelina (left) and Sara Grimke

Weld headed the New York Antislavery Society. And he and the Grimke sisters were responsible for one of the most influential abolitionist books of the generation, *American Slavery As It Is*. To research *American Slavery As It Is*, Weld and the Grimkes went to the New York City Commercial Reading Room, which subscribed to a number of Southern newspapers. There they read the daily publications from Richmond, New Orleans, Mobile, Nashville, Chattanooga, and many other Southern cities. Then they subscribed to these newspapers.

They read accounts of men convicted of atrocities against slaves, men on trial for their atrocities against their slaves, and reports of atrocities. The Southern papers conscientiously reported these crimes just as they reported murders, rapes, and thefts. Knowing this, Weld negotiated with the library to buy the newspapers every month as they went out of date. He and the Grimkes took the newspapers home, clipped out the articles reporting atrocities against slaves, and pasted them into a collection of blank-paged notebooks. They developed a sizable file of these atrocities as reported by Southern newspapers. Their thundering conclusion: This is what Southern slavery is like.

Authorized Version

Critics then and now have accused *American Slavery As It Is* of using an unscientific, even misleading method. Were it likewise employed in an investigation of the crime in New York City or the spousal abuse in marriage, they charged, it could paint equally as dark—and unfair—portraits of that great city and Biblical institution as it did of slavery. The book sold 22,000 copies in four months and more than 100,000 copies in the first year, not counting the European edition. It would stand alongside *Uncle Tom's Cabin* as one of the two most influential books anywhere in the world on the American system of

Lincoln's Views on Blacks

Abraham Lincoln rose to national prominence during his 1858 series of debates with his Illinois senatorial opponent Stephen Douglas. Lincoln's eloquent criticism of American slavery helped catapult him into leadership of the young Republican Party. But his own words during the debates demonstrate how different were the views of many anti-slavery Americans around the country from abolitionists who sought not only freedom, but immediate political and social equality for blacks.

> *Make Negroes politically and socially our equals? My own feelings will not admit of this. I will say that I am not nor ever have been in favor of bringing about in any way the social and political equality of the white and black races, that I am not nor have ever been in favor of making voters or jurors of Negroes, nor of qualifying them to hold office, nor to intermarry with white people. And I will say in addition to this that there is a physical difference between the white and black races which I believe will forever forbid the two races living together on terms of social and political equality. And in as much as they cannot so live, while they do remain together, there must be the position of superior and inferior. And I, as much as any other man, am in favor of having the superior position assigned to the white race.*

Ward Hill Lamon, a long time Lincoln colleague and Federal Marshal of Washington during his administration, offered his own thoughts on the subject:

> *None of [Lincoln's] public acts, either before or after he became President, exhibits any special tenderness for the African race. On the contrary, he invariably, in words and deeds, postponed the interests of the blacks to the interests of the whites, and expressly subordinated the one to the other. When he was compelled, by what he deemed an overruling necessity, founded on both military and political considerations, to declare the freedom of the public enemy's slaves, he did so with avowed reluctance, and took pains to have it understood that his resolution was in no wise affected by sentiment.*

What Was Lincoln's Plan for Free Blacks?

A subject as volatile as it is unknown, is Abraham Lincoln's long-declared goal for dealing with free black Americans and those enslaved once they gained freedom. Perhaps no one has described it better than black author Lenore Bennett, Jr. No conservative nor friend of the Confederacy, Bennett wrote in his massive chronicle *Forced Into Glory, Abraham Lincoln's White Dream*:

> *What Lincoln proposed officially and publicly was that the United States government buy the slaves and deport them to Africa or South America. This was not a passing whim. In five major policy declarations, including two State of the Union addresses and the preliminary Emancipation Proclamation, the sixteenth president of the United States publicly and officially called for the deportation of blacks. On countless other occasions, in conferences with cronies, Democratic and Republican leaders, and high government officials, he called for colonization of blacks or aggressively promoted colonization by private and official acts.*

Lincoln's own words, and those of his colleagues, left abundant evidence of his views. Following are a few of the many examples.

> *Let us be brought to believe it is morally right, and, at the same time, favorable to, or, at least, not against, our interest, to transfer the African to his native clime, and we shall find a way to do it, however great the task may be. The children of Israel, to such numbers as to include four hundred thousand fighting men, went out of Egyptian bondage in a body.*
>
> **–Lincoln, 1857**

> *It is still in our power to direct the process of emancipation, and deportation, peaceably, and in such degrees, as the evil will wear off insensibly; and their places be . . . filled up by free white laborers.*
>
> **–Lincoln, February 27, 1860**
> **New York City**

> *But if gradual emancipation and deportation*

slavery, and it became the de facto "authorized" description of it. The book provided the basis for Charles Dickens' chapter on slavery in his book *American Notes*. And Dickens' book inspired Harriet Beecher Stowe to write *Uncle Tom's Cabin*.

Today, despite its distorted, one-sided perspective, *American Slavery As It Is* remains the basis for modern accounts of slavery. One best-selling contemporary Christian author, for instance, quotes Weld's book repeatedly in his own American history book. It is the only book on slavery he footnotes. Such literature as *American Slavery As It Is,* while presenting accurate facts, often utilized those facts to arrive at inaccurate conclusions and might fairly be considered more propaganda than history.

The Secret Six

The abolitionists advanced their cause in other ways as well, including the formation of conspiratorial societies. The decades leading up to the *be adopted, they will have neither to flee from . . . till new homes can be found for them, in congenial climes, and with people of their own blood and race.*

–Lincoln's 1862 State of the Union Address

(It) might well be well to consider, too, whether the free colored people already in the United States could not, so far as individuals may desire, be included in such colonization.

–Lincoln's 1862 State of the Union Address, regarding already-free blacks and the American Colonization Society

He asked Congress to pass a constitutional amendment:

colonizing free colored persons, with their own consent, at any place or places without the United States.

What if Congress refused to grant Lincoln's desire for this sprawling, whites-only enclave, which included states and western territories alike?:

We shall nobly save, or meanly lose, the last best, hope of earth.

Almost from the commencement of this administration, the subject of deporting the colored race has been discussed . . . As early as May 1861, a great pressure was made upon me to enter into a coal contract with this company. The President was in earnest in the matter, wished to send the Negroes out of the country.

–Secretary of the Navy Gideon Welles

(President Lincoln) zealously and persistently devised schemes for the deportation of the Negroes, which the latter deemed cruel and atrocious in the extreme . . .

–Close friend and Federal Marshal Ward Hill Lamon

War saw the rise of political terrorism. While an assassin seeks to change the status quo by murdering prominent people, the political terrorist seeks to change it by provoking a panic in the society after he kills innocent, common people—sometimes en masse—for no apparent reason.

Such were the tactics of John Brown, the Scripture-spewing madman who first gained notoriety for his murderous spree in Bleeding Kansas. His work began to enthrall a group of prominent New England Unitarians, especially as they read reports coming from *Chicago Tribune* reporters traveling with Brown. Inspired by his single-minded savagery in Kansas, six respected New Englanders agreed to finance Brown's efforts to provoke a slave rebellion in the South. Known as "The Secret Six," they were:

- **Dr. Samuel Gridley Howe**, medical director with a worldwide reputation for his work with the deaf and blind. His wife Julia Ward Howe grew even more famous when she wrote a poem named *The Battle Hymn of the Republic*.

- **Reverend Theodore Parker,** a Unitarian minister who rejected biblical authority and biblical doctrine at almost every point. He once stated to Dr. Howe, "What a pity the map of our magnificent country should be destined to be so soon torn in two, on account of the Negro, the poorest of human creatures, satisfied even in slavery with sugar cane and a banjo."

- **Gerrit Smith**, a congressman from New York and Vice President of the American Peace Society.

- **Franklin Benjamin Sanborn**, a graduate of Harvard, who married into a wealthy family and lived comfortably ever after.

- **Reverend Thomas Wentworth Higginson**, another Unitarian minister. He once stated, "I always had money for treason."

- **George Luther Stearns**, enormously wealthy lead pipe manufacturer. He proclaimed his pacifism publicly, but later urged the utter devastation of the South with no remorse.

Harper's Ferry

Bankrolled by these luminaries, Brown and a gang of armed men, including some of his sons, captured the federal arsenal at Harper's Ferry, located at the northern tip of Virginia, on the Potomac River across from Maryland. The first person they shot was a free black man at the town's rail station.

Only a few miles down the Potomac at Arlington, his family plantation, was U.S. Army Colonel Robert E. Lee. His exploits in the Mexican War had prompted American commander-in-chief Winfield Scott to call him the best soldier in the whole country. Now Scott dispatched Lee, who was on leave from his cavalry duties in Texas, to command a detachment of U.S. marines and wrest the Harper's Ferry arsenal from Brown.

Lee sent his young friend and fellow Virginia cavalry officer, Captain J. E. B. "Jeb" Stuart, also on leave from the west, to order Brown out of the arsenal. When Brown refused the command, Stuart sent a detachment of marines storming in. A short fierce gun battle followed in which a number of men fell, including one of Brown's sons. Brown, himself wounded, was captured along with the surviving members of his outlaw band.

A few weeks later Brown was tried and hanged at nearby Charles Town. A contingent of Virginia Military Institute cadets provided a sizable portion of the armed guard assuring the peaceful consummation of the sentence. Commanding the cadets was

"The Storming of the Engine House," from *Frank Leslie's Illustrated News.* Captain Jeb Stuart orders U.S. Marines to attack the Harper's Ferry arsenal captured by John Brown and his men.

one of their professors, Thomas Jonathan Jackson—like Lee and Stuart, a native Virginian.

The Secret Six failed in their original plans and conspiracy. But they succeeded in causing a general panic in the South. This occurred when they were identified for their roles in Brown's raid on Harper's Ferry. Southerners remembered Nat Turner's rampage and a few other slave rebellions, then realized wealthy Northern Unitarians were now financing such ventures. Increasingly, even moderate, pro-Union Southerners feared powerful combinations in the North were out to kill them, and determined their best hope for peace and even survival was to break with the North and its influence.

The words of the leaders of both the New England intellectual elite and the ascendant Northern Republican Party chiseled those impressions yet deeper into the Southern consciousness. Ralph Waldo Emerson, the celebrated poet, transcendentalist, and pacifist, was not against the use of martial force in the case of the South: "If it costs ten years and ten to recover the general prosperity, the destruction of the South is worth so much." Abolitionist leader and Republican Wendell Phillips said, "I hold that the South is to be annihilated. I mean the intellectual, social, aristocratic South—the thing that represented itself by slavery and the bowie knife, by bullying and lynch law, by ignorance and idleness . . . That South is to be annihilated."

Southern Reaction

As the impact of abolitionist propaganda and conspiratorial action grew, Southern states began passing laws forbidding owners to teach their slaves to read. They did not want them reading the propaganda. Indeed, the editorializing of Northern newspapers themselves prompted historian Otto Scott, author of *The Secret Six,* an epic chronicling of John Brown and his exploits, to write, "Until Brown's time, no American, including the heroes of the Revolution, had enjoyed such a steady series of admiring descriptions and slanted reportage as the terrorist received in the North."

I hold that the South is to be annihilated. I mean the intellectual, social, aristocratic South—the thing that represented itself by slavery and the bowie knife, by bullying and lynch law, by ignorance and idleness . . . That South is to be annihilated.

—Abolitionist Leader Wendell Phillips

Such was the context in which various Southerners spoke so as to earn themselves the description in one recent book as *Apostles of Disunion.* Here and elsewhere came accusations that the majority of Southern leaders preferred keeping the whole race of blacks in a subordinate position to whites, even—perhaps especially—if that meant sundering the Union. Some of the accusers further charged them as being dishonest post-war dissemblers attempting to rewrite history to favor themselves; that is, to alter their own pre-war sentiments and statements so that they appeared to have more noble motivations for fighting than racism and slavery.

Were "slavery and race absolutely critical elements in the coming of the war," as that book posits? No doubt for some. For others, they were an instrument to stir emotional support for secession among rank-and-file Southerners by men for whom sectional differences over the tariff, the Constitution, the role of government, and culture had proven unbearable. For many more, the shocking Northern support for the objectives of men like John Brown exacerbated their fears regarding the potential scenarios attendant to racial equality, race war, and racial amalgamation (especially in marriage)—factors cited in the aforementioned text.

But did "slavery and race" in and of themselves cause secession? Another of the many contributions of Charles Adams' *When in the Course of Human Events* is the illumination he sheds on the opinions of foreigners, men committed to neither the Federals or the Confederates, regarding the War. Charles Dickens, whose books confirm he was no supporter of the institution of slavery, thought not: "The South, instead of seceding for the sake of slavery, seceded in spite of the fact that its separate maintenance will expose them . . . to risks and losses against which the Union would afford security." Dickens felt the Southern economy would suffer rather than prosper by continuing as a separate nation, and he posited that Southerners believed this too.

The editorial positions of Dickens' fellow countrymen at the *Times* and *Economist* newspapers in London, meanwhile, evidenced their belief that the high tariff and not slavery primarily precipitated the American war.

Like a range of other issues, slavery and race played a role in the schism between North and South. However, they were neither singularly responsible for the schism nor singularly capable of causing it.

The Arraignment of John Brown and fellow conspirators, as illustrated in the November 12, 1859, edition of *Harper's Weekly* (www.harpweek.com).

Lincoln Elected

Brown's attack on Harper's Ferry—and the subsequent identification of the Secret Six—confirmed for many Southerners the rumors they had not wanted to believe of a massive white Northern conspiracy to start a slave revolt. Now the rumblings for secession began in earnest.

For most Southerners, the election of Lincoln ended all hope for a happy resolution of the controversies. As far as the South was concerned, Lincoln

Abolition of Slavery in Non-Confederate States and Territories

State/Territory	*Year*	*State/Territory*	*Year*	*State/Territory*	*Year*
Vermont	1777	New York	1827	Washington Territory	1848
Massachusetts	1780	Michigan	1837	Oregon Territory	1848
New Hampshire	1783	Rhode Island	1842	Wisconsin	1848
Ohio	1803	Iowa	1846	Pennsylvania	1850
Indiana	1816	New Jersey	1846	California	1850
Illinois	1818	Connecticut	1848	Minnesota	1858

Emancipation Proclamation 1863

Despite the Emancipation Proclamation, slavery continued as a legally-sanctioned practice in the following pro-Union states and territories until the passage of the Thirteenth Amendment in 1865. Even then, it persisted amidst court challenges in pockets of these areas until as late as 1868.

- Kentucky
- Kansas Territory
- New Mexico Territory
- West Virginia
- Delaware
- Montana Territory
- Nebraska Territory
- Missouri
- Maryland

was the candidate of the radical party who promoted radical goals by radical means; he was the candidate of Harriet Beecher Stowe, Theodore Weld, John Brown, and the Secret Six. Southerners believed this even though Lincoln's views on and methods of dealing with slavery both differed markedly from all those people.

For instance, during his presidential campaign, Lincoln repeatedly promised support for the fugitive slave laws, promising one prominent Kentucky Democrat, "The fugitive slave law will be better administrated under my administration than it has ever been under any of those of my predecessors." Still, Southerners saw no way to stay in the Union.

Lincoln won with only forty percent of the popular vote. But he carried every Northern state and with the split in the Democratic Party, North and South, and the running of a Southern third party candidate, he won an overwhelming electoral victory. Abraham Lincoln did not receive one electoral vote from the entire South. Only weeks after Lincoln's election, the first Southern state, South Carolina, seceded. Was slavery the reason for the War, or even a significant factor?

English Emancipation—Peaceful, Successful, and Permanent

Would slavery ever have ended in America without the oceans of blood spilled in the War? In fact, the United States was the only nation where a war was required to end it—even if neither the Union nor the Confederacy went to war over that issue.

Alternatives to war did exist. The abolitionists could have worked within the political system toward a constitutional amendment prohibiting slavery. This approach succeeded in other countries. Or they could have worked, perhaps in league with non-abolitionist opponents of slavery, to pass legislation requiring the gradual emancipation of slaves. Too, the North could have allowed the South to secede, and then worked constitutionally to halt the practice of slavery in the Northern Border States. Or, the North could have done nothing and waited; an increasing armada of modern scholarship (*Emancipating Slaves, Enslaving Free Men*, by Jeffrey Hummel, among others) agrees that slavery was a dying institution financially insupportable in the long term.

William Wilberforce

Finally, as Lincoln suggested, slaveowners could have been remunerated for the freeing of their slaves. This would have helped prevent the financial calamity many who had most of their capital invested in their slaves feared with abolition. The prospects of success varied among these alternatives, but none would have brought the mass slaughter and societal tumult that the War did.

Worldwide Practice

Slavery flourished in France, Spain, Portugal, and many other countries, and on nearly every continent, and had for thousands of years. Nowhere, however, did it prosper more famously than in England. Fortunes of breathtaking magnitude were built on the backs of Caribbean and West Indies plantation slaves. The English engaged in the African slave trade to a far greater degree than ever did the Americans. Many of America's slaves were brought from Africa by Englishmen, as well as other Europeans.

Like America, England excelled in commerce and trade. And like America, its history, though much longer, bristled with violence and bloodshed. Unlike America, England extinguished not only its own slave trade (1807) but the practice of slavery (1833) without secession, the greatest holocaust in its history, or lasting enmity between the sections of its country.

Once a wealthy slave trader, John Newton was now a devout Church of England pastor—and the author of the hymn Amazing Grace. *He exhorted Wilberforce to serve Christ but not to leave public office. "The Lord has raised you up to the good of His Church and for the good of the nation," Newton said.*

How did England and its British Empire peaceably terminate the slave trade upon which an enormous portion of its income depended? First, men like William Wilberforce and Thomas Clarkson worked patiently, for decades, within the God-ordained system of civil government available to them. They did not break laws; they used the law to further the ends of their cause. And they persuaded, rather than forced, people of diverse opinion round to their view.

This grand triumph in British history was not quick and it was not easy. Like other talented and well-placed young men of his generation such as future Prime Minister William Pitt the Younger, Wilberforce reveled in the opulent and decadent society of the world's greatest city, London. After his conversion to Christianity, however, the power, fame, and fortune that had seemed so desirable turned more to dross than gold in his eyes. On the verge of leaving public life in the 1780s, Wilberforce sought the first of two destiny-changing pieces of counsel he would receive from famous Christian converts named John.

Once a wealthy slave trader, John Newton was now a devout Church of England pastor—and the author of the hymn *Amazing Grace*. He exhorted Wilberforce to serve Christ but not to leave public office. "The Lord has raised you up to the good of His Church and for the good of the nation," Newton said. Within two years, in 1787, as Americans were completing their Constitution, Wilberforce would write: "Almighty God has set before me two great objectives. The abolition of the slave trade and the reformation of manners."

Fifty Years' War

For nearly half a century, Wilberforce pursued an urgent, multi-pronged, yet patient strategy in all corners of the country and at all levels of government, first to abolish the British slave trade, then slavery altogether. Time and again, important legislative victories seemed within grasp only to be lost or diluted by compromise for an endless array of reasons. Sometimes the public and their representatives refused to disrupt the vibrant economy. At other times outside events such as the Jacobin excesses of the French Revolution or the slave revolts and massacres in the West Indies sobered the people on abolition. And many times the sheer financial and political power of the slaveowners' lobby in Parliament and elsewhere refused to yield.

But Wilberforce was resolute. "As soon as ever I had arrived thus far in my investigation of the

John Wesley, shortly before his death, writing a letter to William Wilberforce, encouraging him to press forward with his public and legislative opposition to slavery.

slave trade," he wrote, "so enormous, so dreadful, so irremediable did its wickedness appear that my own mind was completely made up for the abolition. A trade founded in iniquity and carried on as this was must be abolished."

Still, the long hard fight and the many bitter defeats often drove him to the brink of despair and giving up. Then would he sometimes pull out the worn yellowed letter from the second famous convert named John. Like the first one, this John too, was by then dead. "Unless God has raised you up for this very thing, you will be worn out by the opposition of men and devils, but if God be for you who can be against you? Are all of them together stronger than God?" wrote John Wesley, in the last letter of his life.

The British succeeded in abolishing slavery not only because they worked within the prevailing system of laws and government; the British government also compensated the slaveowners for the property the latter legally owned and for which many of the slaveowners had paid. Then they provided free land to the now-free men. Finally, they provided free education to the ex-slaves.

American Alternative

Abolitionist zealots in government and out made certain none of these provisions were considered in America. Eventually, their fanaticism discouraged an increasing number of Southerners, even those originally favoring gradual emancipation, from supporting such solutions. At least one New York City newspaper decried the British emancipation, predicting the ruin of both the British colony of Jamaica and the economy of England itself. Unlike the abolitionists, anti-slavery Abraham Lincoln favored such a plan, even after the War began. As Charles Adams reports, many of his fellow Republicans did not. Sen. William Seward, who yearned for the White House himself, excoriated fellow senators from the South:

> *Compensation to slaveowners for their negroes! Preposterous idea! The suggestion is criminal—the demand wicked, unjust, monstrous, damnable! Shall we pat the bloodhound for the sake of doing them a favour? Shall we feed the curs of slavery to make them rich at our expense? Pay these whelps for the privilege of converting them into decent, honest upright men?*

Having said this, Seward (Lincoln's Secretary of State by the time of the Emancipation Proclamation) stood by as Northern states refused to accept the immigration of freed slaves and in some cases (such as in Ohio and Illinois) actually established laws prohibiting blacks from entering their states. Some Northern states forced blacks already living in them to leave. Meanwhile, Southerners were expected to choke down the gargantuan financial calamity of a $3 billion loss of property, while somehow finding resources with which to pay millions of freed slaves who were required to remain in the former slave states.

It is true that the slaves freed by the British lived in colonies far from Britain itself, rather than amongst the free people of the mainland, as in America. However, the distinctives of British emancipation as outlined above would equally have satisfied the challenges of freeing a domestic slave population as a remote colonial one.

Emancipation's Blessings

Britain's ending of slavery opened the way for additional blessings on that nation and mankind. The gospel-preaching churches of 18th- and 19th- century Britain constituted a great bastion of Christian orthodoxy as well as the greatest missionary-sending effort up to that point in the history of the world. Towering names of greatness and legend rose up from the churches of Britain—names like Wilberforce, Newton, Wesley, David Livingstone, Thomas Chalmers, J. C. Ryle, Charles Spurgeon, William Carey, even, late in her life, Florence Nightingale.

The British succeeded in abolishing slavery not only because they worked within the prevailing system of laws and government, but because they compensated the slaveowners for the property they legally owned and for which many of them had paid. Then they provided free land to the now-free men. Finally, they provided free education to the ex-slaves.

As British churches shipped out waves of missionaries, one man told well the reception awaiting them in Africa: "The name of Englishman is already, through the African continent, becoming a simple passport of safety. If a white missionary visits a black tribe, they ask only one question, does he belong to the people who liberated our children from slavery?" The Scotsman Livingstone could take Africans aboard a British warship and introduce the sailors by saying, "Now these are all my countrymen, sent by our Queen for the purpose of putting down the trade of those that buy and sell black men." Indeed, once Wilberforce and the British ended slavery, peaceably and with consideration for all parties concerned, Providence seemed to open the very flood gate of spiritual and material blessing alike to the nation for much of the rest of the century.

To the end of his life, William Wilberforce worked for the freedom of British-owned slaves, and for reform in prisons, among the poor, and in the workplace. Three days after a historic House of Commons vote sounded the death knell of slavery, he died. Among his final words was this testament of joy: "Thank God that I should have lived to witness a day in which England was willing to give twenty millions sterling for the abolition of slavery!" Would that the United States government had offered such to the Southern slaveowners for the emancipation of their slaves, and would that they had accepted it.

Their [the slaves'] emancipation will sooner result from the mild and melting influence of Christianity, than the storms and tempests of fiery Controversy. This influence though slow, is sure. The doctrines and miracles of our Saviour have required nearly two thousand years, to convert but a small part of the human race, and even among Christian nations, what gross errors still exist! While we see the course of the final abolition of human slavery is onward, and we give it the aid of our prayers and all justifiable means in our power, we must leave the progress as well as the result in his hand who sees the end; who chooses to work by slow influences; and with whom two thousand years are but as a single day.

—Robert E. Lee, from an 1856 letter to his wife Mary

7 Southern Slavery As It Was I

Laundry day at "Volusia," a farm off Duke Street near Holmes Run, Alexandria, Virginia, in the early 1860s. Special thanks to Raymond Frederick, Jr. for use of the photograph.

In this enlightened age, there are few I believe, but what will acknowledge, that slavery as an institution, is a moral and political evil in any Country. It is useless to expatiate on its disadvantages. I think it however a greater evil to the white than to the black race, and while my feelings are strongly enlisted in behalf of the latter, my sympathies are more strong for the former. The blacks are immeasurably better off here than in Africa, morally, socially, and physically.

—Robert E. Lee (1856)

I believe the practice of slavery in the South is the mildest and best regulated system of slavery in the world now or heretofore.

—William Tecumseh Sherman (1861)

Robert L. Dabney, a dedicated pastor and theologian who fought for the Confederacy, said the South lost the War because she was under the judgment of God. He cited the example of northern Israel, which led the way in rebellion against God in the 8th and 9th centuries, B.C. Its southern neighbor in the divided kingdom, Judah, remained theologically orthodox and conservative. However, Judah did not avoid final apostasy, but simply traveled that path more slowly than Israel to the north.

God has raised up all nations from one man [Acts 17:26]. All are cousins. And not only are the races connected through God's creation of Adam as recounted in Genesis 1, they are united (this time in harmony) in the redemption purchased by the Son of God.

In a similar way, Dabney believed, the South had not been free from the various currents of unbelief. Although it stood for much that was admirable, he said, the Biblical principle remained—to whom much is given, much is required. And regardless of whether the South was correct about various issues of the War, Dabney cited the hard lesson of Habakkuk, who had to accept that God can use an ungodly nation to judge another nation which is "not as bad" (Habakkuk 1:13).

Some balk at a sympathetic view of the South (to any extent, at any level) because they equate it with racism, which they know is evil. Indeed, all forms of race hatred or racial vainglory are forms of rebellion against God. Such should be vigorously opposed because the Word of God opposes them from start to finish. God has raised up all nations from one man (Acts 17:26). All are cousins. And not only are the races connected through God's creation of Adam as recounted in Genesis 1, they are united (this time in harmony) in the redemption purchased by the Son of God. "You are worthy to take the scroll, and to open its seals; for You were slain, and have redeemed us to God by your blood out of every tribe and tongue and people and nation, and have made us kings and priests to our God; and we shall reign on the earth" (Revelation 5:9–10).

The early church at Antioch contained at least one black man (Acts 13:1). God struck Miriam, the esteemed wife of Aaron and sister-in-law of Moses, with leprosy when she opposed the marriage of Moses to a black woman (Numbers 12). Christians should regard the gift at Pentecost to be a great reversal of Babel and pray that missionary efforts will result in the elimination of racial hatreds in Christ.

Dabney and other Confederate leaders maintained that racism and sympathy for the Southern cause were not necessary companions, but, when Biblically understood, antithetical to one another. Indeed, the economic death of slavery in America might well have been hastened had there been more widespread obedience to Biblical precepts by everyone, whether abolitionists, slaves, slave owners, or otherwise.

In the Bible

In a fallen world, an institution like slavery will be accompanied by many attendant evils. Such evils existed with ancient Hebrew slavery, ancient Roman slavery, and American slavery. How are Christians commanded to respond to

Where the Slaves Came From

The "slave trade" was not initiated by white Europeans. A thriving intracontinental slave trade existed within Africa itself (between African tribes as well as with the Muslims of Arabia) long before the Portuguese arrived in the fifteenth century. The vast majority of Negro slaves were not "kidnapped" out of the jungles by white Europeans or Yankee slave traders, but purchased from African slave traders through tribal mediators.

J. C. Furnas observes in *The Road to Harper's Ferry*, "[I]t is safe to say that ninety-nine in a hundred of the poor devils of Negroes shipped in the trans-Atlantic trade were already slaves, some born so, some become so legally, some forcibly made so—kidnapped if you like—before they were turned over to white men . . . And since slavery was well established along the Guinea Coast when the whites first saw it, kidnapping of free Negroes remained most exceptional even when, as time passed, whites came to buy thousands per year."

Furnas continues, "Even after superior weapons raised the odds for success, raiding remained bad for business. The Guinea trade went best when the Negro trader on the other side of the bargain was confident of his own safety . . . kidnapping [by a European] aroused the keenest resentment, for it defrauded the local chief of his dues and the native traders of their opportunities." The position taken by the Africans was that there was nothing wrong with kidnapping free people into slavery, particularly if they came from other tribes, but this enterprise was the rightful monopoly of the West Africans themselves and not of white Europeans.

"Scenes on a Cotton Plantation," Alfred Waud's rendering of slave life on the Buena Vista Plantation in Clarke County, Alabama. Reprinted from *Harper's Weekly* (www.harpweek.com). In the lower right drawing, a slave preacher holds forth at a church service on the plantation.

such abuses and evils? The New Testament opposes anything like the abolitionism of the United States prior to the War. Instead, it contains many instructions for Christian slaveowners and requires a respectful, submissive demeanor for Christian slaves (Ephesians 6:5–9; Colossians 3:22–4:1, and 1 Timothy 6:1–5). The Bible is not silent on the subject of slavery. But what exactly constitutes slavery or servitude that meets Biblical standards?

One important distinction is often overlooked between Hebrew slavery—slavery in a nation covenanted with God, with laws received from His hand—and the slavery seen in the pages of the New Testament. In the former, God's laws governed and regulated the practice of servitude in a nation called by His name. In the latter, God's laws taught His people how to live within a culture having ungodly laws concerning slavery. In the Roman Empire the system of slavery was, along with the rest of that culture, in rebellion against God. In the Hebrew republic, slavery was akin to indentured servanthood; the only permanent slaves were foreigners (Leviticus 25:44–46) and Hebrews who voluntarily submitted themselves to a more permanent servile status (Exodus 21:5–6).

In the Greco/Roman world, the system of slavery was pagan from top to bottom, with the slaves having virtually no recognized rights. So a vast difference exists between the laws God gave to His covenant people for the regulation of servitude among themselves, and the laws He gave them to regulate their conduct in the midst of a pagan system.

Southern Slavery

Was slavery in the South a Biblical servitude? In some ways, yes, in others, no, as we shall explore in this chapter and Chapter 8. Was the South a nation in covenant with the Lord Jesus Christ? Had it undertaken formally to conform all its laws, including its laws on slavery, to the laws of Scripture? No, in that the South was not a Christian utopia or theocracy, governed wholly by Biblical laws. Yes, in that it contained many conscientious Christians, both slave-owning and enslaved, who endeavored to follow the requirements of Scripture set down in the New Testament for believers in slaveholding societies.

The large number of these believers in the Old South did have the effect of "Christianizing" it. The system of slaveholding in the South was far more humane than that of ancient Rome, although the Christian church had not yet the full influence God intends His kingdom to have in the world. The discipleship of the nations is a process. The South was (along with all other nations) in transition from a state of pagan autonomy to a full submission to the Lordship of Christ. Christian influence in the South was considerable and extensive, but the laws there fell short of the Biblical pattern.

Thus, though the Christian and Reformed influence on antebellum Southern culture was perhaps as extensive as anywhere else in the Nineteenth-Century world, Southern sanctification fell short of the Biblical standard at a number of points, some of them key. That is why someone like Dabney could maintain the justness of the Confederate cause and at the same time acknowledge that the South lost the war because of her sins, declaring famously, "A righteous God, for our sins toward Him, has permitted us to be overthrown by our enemies and His."

The system of slaveholding in the South was far more humane than that of ancient Rome, although the Christian church had not yet the full influence God intends His kingdom to have in the world. The discipleship of the nations is a process.

Slaves preparing cotton for the gin.

Biblical Forms of Servitude

The Bible does not condemn all forms of servitude outright, including some that fell under the designation of American slavery. However, it does condemn many of the practices that accompanied American slavery, as well as the confusion about the administration of that slavery. A major problem was that American slavery/servitude tended to conflate together seven distinctive categories of servitude mentioned in the Scriptures into one or two. Chattel slavery was one of those cited in the Bible, and, when practiced other than in Old Testament Israel, it possessed serious unbiblical components.

How much of Southern (including border states) slavery qualified as unbiblical chattel slavery is debatable. Historians' estimates vary wildly, depending upon the person's underlying presuppositions; they range from 30% to 100% of the practice having possessed unbiblical aspects distinctive to chattel slavery such as permanency and coercion.

How much of Southern slavery qualified as unbiblical chattel slavery is debatable. Historians' estimates vary... from 30% to 100% of it having possessed unbiblical aspects distinctive to chattel slavery such as permanency and coercion.

Nowhere did Southern masters hold the power, however, to take life from a slave beyond what American law allowed for free citizens. Chattel slavery as depicted in the Bible did allow a master this power.

So while a significant percentage of Southern slavery did not comply with Biblical standards at key points, what portion of it technically qualified as chattel slavery in the Biblical sense is less clear.

Following are seven forms of servitude found in the Bible.

Wage slaves—Leviticus 19 gives guidelines and restrictions related to a master's rights over the life, livelihood, and family of this group, who were essentially hirelings. Most had an indigent lifestyle without home or rootedness in the land. Perhaps separated from their family and inheritance, they attached themselves to a wealthy landholder. In exchange for their labor, they often received food, clothing, sustenance, and lodging. They might even be brought into the landholder's family. But these wage slaves were free to depart any time they wished.

Indentures—Unlike a hireling, who often worked on a day-to-day basis, an indentured servant is a contractor who exchanges his labor over a certain period of time with a master in order to achieve some objective. Deuteronomy 15 offers careful regulations for this arrangement.

For instance, the parents of famed American patriot, Patrick Henry, indentured themselves in return for passage on a ship across the Atlantic to Virginia, a secure home in which to settle, pay for their work, and the opportunity to save some of their earnings. In return, they were obligated to labor for seven years for those who had financed their journey and New World beginning, before earning the freedom to do something else.

Servile—Someone who borrows money and is unable to pay it back when due, is required to come and live with the lender while he pays off the debt. The Bible makes it clear the borrower is a slave to the lender, and that condition becomes more acute if the debt is not paid off when owed. Again, comprehensive regulations are offered that protect the slave from abuse. The lender, or master, is subject to prosecution under the law if he does not act responsibly.

Bondsmen—An entire chapter in the book of Exodus chronicles how a thief or destroyer, if prosecuted and convicted according to the statutes of the land, is not to be sent away to prison, but must make restitution for all he has stolen. Exodus 22 lays out this Biblical approach to "victim's rights." It assures restoration to the victim for what has been despoiled. Once again, such Biblical justice carefully regulates the parameters of the bondsman's duties. He is not, for instance, to be treated by the victim as property.

Prisoners of war, aliens and sojourners in the land, peasants, and yeoman—These are people who do not have means and rely on the benevolence of landholders or merchants. They are not put on welfare, but given the opportunity to work. Their freedoms are limited because they are imposing upon the privileges of the landholders. Yet they are not considered property. They have responsibilities and requirements imposed upon them, but when they have fulfilled these, they are free.

Bondslaves—This ancient practice was common in the South after the War. The Biblical Greek word for this group was *doulos*. A *doulos* volunteers to serve a master for life. The Bible offers numerous examples of a person, such as an indentured servant, who is set free from his obligation to a master, but who has come to love that master and identify himself with the master's cause or family. Thus, without compulsion, the servant can tell the master that he, along with his family, desires to serve that man for life.

The Biblical ceremony for this is quite poignant. The *doulos* takes his ear, places it against the door post, and drives a nail through it, then wears a golden ear ring. Wearing an ear ring in the ancient world was the symbol of belonging to someone. As with the preceding categories of slaves, this one is carefully regulated. And according to Deuteronomy 25, all slaves, including the *doulos*, are freed in the periodic "year of jubilee," though the bondslave may choose to repledge himself to his master.

Chattel Slaves—They are the property of their master. Scripture strictly regulated this practice in the theocracy of old Israel. Those strictures and the problematic nature of applying them to nations other than God's Old Testament theocracy of Israel render that portion of American slavery falling into this category Biblically indefensible at key points.

Indeed, one of the great challenges for Southerners was that all these Biblical categories of servitude had precise application only to God's select nation of old Israel. No country since has been governed strictly by Biblical law. A precise application of these categories in the past to any other nation, while desirable where slavery existed, resulted in great confusion about the nature of the Biblical laws governing the institution. That is one reason the various kinds of slavery gradually coalesced into only one or two kinds in the South.

Dabney called this the sin of non-conditionalism. That is, most Americans of all sections forgot the distinctions of the various types of servitude, as well as many of the regulations designed to guide them. Perhaps more accurately, they inherited the collective amnesia of their European forefathers on the subject.

John Jasper (1812-1901)

Here was a man who preached the gospel of Jesus Christ for twenty-five years as a slave and thirty-nine more as a free man. Indeed, God raised him through every manner of economic, social, racial, and fraternal obstacle to national fame as a preacher and man of God—while still a slave. Born a slave in the Williamsburg, Virginia of 1812, Jasper was the last of twenty-four children. His mother Nina held leadership servant positions at large and prestigious farms. She was a Godly woman and her husband, John, was himself a slave preacher.

Tradition relates that one of the saddest consequences of American slavery—the occasional splintering of husband and wife through the sale of one or the other—beset Jasper. Supposedly on the very day of his first marriage, he was sold away to Richmond. He never saw this first of his four wives again and she married another. But before emancipation as well as after, accounts are legion of Jasper's kindness toward white and black alike. While still a slave during the War, he regularly preached to sick and wounded Confederate soldiers in the hospitals of Richmond.

Yet like all great men, conflict and opposition marked his life and career. The ranks of the jealous and covetous escalated alongside his fame and impact for Christ, particularly follow-

John Jasper: The Unmatched Negro Philosopher and Preacher

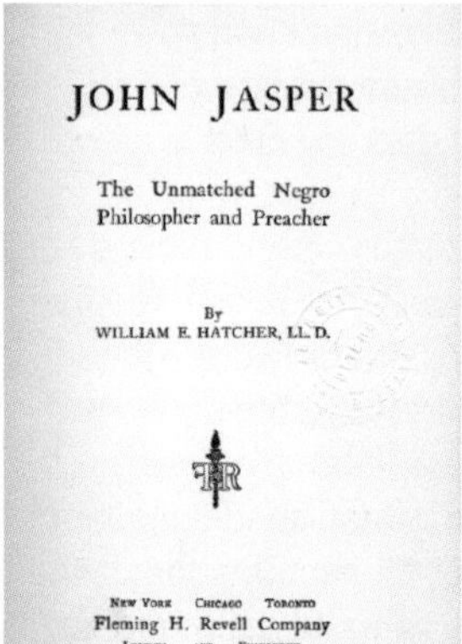

JOHN JASPER

The Unmatched Negro Philosopher and Preacher

By WILLIAM E. HATCHER, LL.D.

New York Chicago Toronto
Fleming H. Revell Company
London and Edinburgh

Hatcher writes how Jasper, responding as he did to any man behind a pulpit who deigned to cast doubt on the tenets of orthodoxy, "felt it a part of his religion to smash, with giant hand, the innovations which the new order was bringing in." Indeed, John Jasper had no use for new innovations, new attitudes or social progress that diluted the old gospel.

One of Jasper's great dreams came to fruition in 1867, when he founded the Sixth Mount Zion Baptist Church in Richmond. The large and stately church lives on today. He was the last, and perhaps the greatest, of the grand antebellum-style preachers, black or white. Jasper believed his call sanctioned by God and man; upon the slave's spiritual conversion, Sam Hargrove, the master he loved, exhorted him to go and preach high and low the gospel that had saved him. Though he never ceased to boom forth in the old slave dialect which stirred so many detractors, some of the most educated theologians of his day marveled at his knowledge of the Scriptures and his grasp of the great doctrines of the faith.

ing the War. White Virginia theologian William O. Hatcher penned his famous biography *John Jasper: the Unmatched Negro Philosopher and Preacher*, in 1909. It remains in print nearly a century later. Hatcher tells how Jasper first gained renown for his electrifying funeral oratories. The author also describes the "double-breasted, Prince Albert-coated, high hat and kid-gloved" black "preachers of the new order." He chronicles how these preachers came to Richmond from fancy schools up north, flush with new power and resentment, and how they sneered at Jasper, whom they considered a reproach to their race.

[John Jasper] felt it a part of his religion to smash, with giant hand, the innovations which the new order was bringing in.

—William O. Hatcher

But the old lion roared back: "He looked this new tribe of his adversaries over and marked them as a calcimined and fictitious type of culture. To him they were shop-made and unworthy of respect. They called forth the storm of his indignant wrath. He opened his batteries upon them, and for quite a while, the thunder of his guns fairly shook the steeples on the other negro churches of Richmond."

Jasper preached his final sermon, on the Biblical doctrine of regeneration, shortly before his death at age eighty-nine. Concluded Hatcher:

> *I would give to the American people a picture of the God-made preacher who was great in his bondage and became immortal in his freedom . . . He was a man of deep convictions, a man with a purpose in life, a man who earnestly desired to save souls for heaven. He followed his divine calling with faithfulness, with a determination, as far as he could, to make the ways of his God known unto men, His saving health among all nations.*

In Families

May a Christian own slaves, even when this makes him a part of a larger pagan system which is not fully Scriptural, or perhaps not Scriptural at all? The abolitionists maintained that slaveowning was inherently immoral under any circumstance. However, the Bible indicates in such passages as 1 Timothy 6:1–4a that Christians may own slaves, provided they own them in conformity to Christ's laws for such situations:

> Let as many bondservants as are under the yoke count their masters worthy of all honor, so that the name of God and His doctrine may not be blasphemed.
>
> And those who have believing masters, let

John Jasper's Greatest Sermon

William Hatcher, author of *John Jasper: the Unmatched Negro Philosopher and Preacher*, concludes that memorable work with a remembrance of what he writes was the greatest sermon Jasper gave in his sixty-four years of preaching. Hatcher witnessed the oration, ostensibly a eulogy for two deceased members of Jasper's Sixth Mount Zion Baptist Church in Richmond. One of the deceased, Mary Barnes, was an elderly saint of rare godliness and splendor of character. Hatcher reported the sermon lasted more than an hour-and-a-half. Following are excerpts as Hatcher recorded them, true to the old slave dialect Jasper never discarded.

> *Grave! Grave! Er Grave! Whar's yer vict'ry? I hur you got a mighty banner down dar, an' you turrurizes ev'rybody wat comes long dis way. Bring out your armies an' furl fo'th your bann'rs of vict'ry. Show you han' an' let 'em see wat you kin do. Ain't got no vict'ry now; had vict'ry, but King Jesus pars'd through dis country an' tord my banners down. He says His peopl' shan't be troubled no mo' forev'r; an' He tell me ter op'n de gates an' let 'um pass on dar way to glory.*
>
> *Oh, my Gord, did yer hur dat? My Master Jesus done jerk'd de sting of death, done broke de scept'r of de king of tur'rs, an' He dun gone inter de grave an' rob it uv its victorous banners, an' fix'd nice an' smooth for His people ter pass through. Mo' en dat, He has writ a song, a shoutin' anthim for us to sing when we go thur, passin' suns an' stars, an' singin' dat song. 'Thanks be onter Gord who give us de vict'ry thru de Lord Jesus Christ.'*
>
> *My bruthrin, I oft'n ax myself how I'd behave merself ef I was ter git to heav'n. I tell you I would tremble fo' de consequinces. Eben now when I gits er glimpse—jist a peep into de palis of de King, it farly runs me ravin' 'stracted. What will I do ef I gits thar? I 'spec I'll make er fool of myself, 'cause I ain't got de pritty ways an' nice manners my ole Mars' Sam Hargrove used to have, but ef I git thar they ain't goin' to put me out. Mars' Sam'll speak fur me an' tell 'em to teach me how to do. I sometimes thinks if I's 'lowed to go free—I 'specs to be free dar, I tell you, b'leve I'll jest do de town—walkin' an' runnin' all roun' to see de home which Jesus dun built for His people.*
>
> *Fust of all, I'd go down an' see de river of life. I lov's to go down to de ole muddy Jemes—mighty red an' muddy, but it goes 'long so gran' an' quiet like 'twas 'tendin' to business—but dat ain't nothin' to the river which flows by de throne. I longs fer its chrystal waves, an' de trees on de banks, an' de all mann'rs of fruits. Dis old head of mine oft'n gits hot with fever, aches all night an' rolls on de piller, an' I has many times desired to cool it in that blessed stream as it kisses de banks of dat upper Canaan. Bl'ssed be*

de Lord! De thought of seein' dat river, drinkin' its water an' restin' un'r dose trees—Oh, what mus' it be to be thar?

Aft'r dat, I'd turn out an' view de beauties of de city—de home of my Father. I'd stroll up dem abneuse whar de children of Gord dwell an' view dar mansions. Father Abraham, I'm sure he got a grate pallis, an' Moses, what 'scorted de children of Israel out of bondige thru' de wilderness an' to de aidge of de promised lan', he must be pow'rful set up being sich er man as he is; an' David, de king dat made pritty songs, I'd like to see 'is home, an' Paul, de mighty scholar who got struck down out in de 'Mascus road, I want to see his mansion, an' all of 'em. Den I would cut round' to de back streets an' look for de little home whar my Saviour set my mother up to housekeepin' when she got thar. I 'spec to know de house by de roses in de yard an' de vine on de poch.' Look dar; see dat on de do; hallelujah, it's John Jasper. Said He was gwine to prepar a place for me; dari it is. Too good for a po' sinner like me, but He built it for me, a turn-key job, an' mine forev'r. Oh, what mus' it be to be thar!

My bruthrin, I dun ferget somethin'. I got ter tek anuth'r trip. I ain't visiti'd de ransum of de Lord. I can't slight dem. I know heap ov'em, an' I'm boun' to see 'em.

Her's Brer Abul, de fust man whar got here; here's Brer Enoch whart took er stroll and straggled inter glory; here's old Ligie, whar had er carriage sent fur 'im an' comed a nigher way to de city.

Here she is; I know'd sh'd git here; why, Mary Barnes, you got home, did yer.

Oh, what mu' it be to be thar!

> them not despise them because they are brethren, but rather serve them because those who are benefited are believers and beloved. Teach and exhort these things. If anyone teaches otherwise and does not consent to wholesome words, even the words of our Lord Jesus Christ, and to the doctrine which accords with godliness, he is proud, knowing nothing . . .

As bewildering as it may be to modern sensibilities, in this passage and elsewhere the apostle Paul, rather than calling for the eradication or even condemnation of the institution of slavery, rather gives instruction to slaves as to how they should honor and serve their masters. He exhorts them to do so in the name of Jesus Christ. And Paul did not deliver such admonitions in the midst of a scripturally sound system of slavery. He spoke in the context of Roman slavery, which was anti-scriptural.

Meanwhile, because of the evil of the slave trade and other shortcomings, the larger system of slavery in the South was certainly unscriptural, in that it fell short of the Scriptural model in various ways. Nevertheless, the Bible prohibits declaring slave*owning* in such contexts as sin. The Bible teaches that a man may be a faithful Christian and a slave-owner in a pagan slave system. If he owns slaves, Scripture places a series of requirements on him, which the Church of Christ may and must insist upon. But beyond those requirements, the Church may not presume to legislate.

In Ephesians 6:5–9, Paul speaks on the subject to both slaves and masters:

> Bondservants, be obedient to those who

> are your masters according to the flesh, with fear and trembling, in sincerity of heart, as to Christ; not with eyeservice, as men-pleasers, but as bondservants of Christ, doing the will of God from the heart, with goodwill doing service, as to the Lord, and not to men, knowing that whatever good anyone does, he will receive the same from the Lord, whether he is a slave or free. And you, masters, do the same things to them, giving up threatening, knowing that your own Master also is in heaven, and there is no partiality with Him.

Paul speaks similarly elsewhere, including Colossians 3:22–4:1. The apostle, speaking with the authority of God's Holy word, gave challenging instruction to Christian master and slave alike regarding their respective roles. But he clearly saw no contradiction between a Christian being a slaveowner and a member in good standing in a Christian church. And he spoke regarding a system of slavery that did not abide many of the Biblical precepts laid out in the Old Testament.

May a Christian own slaves, even when this makes him a part of a larger pagan system which is not fully Scriptural, or perhaps not Scriptural at all?

The Slave Trade

A very plausible argument against slavery comes from the acknowledged wickedness of the slave trade. Advocates of this position often argue that because the Bible prohibits man-stealing (Exodus 21:16; 1 Timothy 1:10), Christians could not consistently participate at any point in a process that resulted from the man-stealing. Exodus 21:16, for instance, states, "He who kidnaps a man and sells him, or if he is found in his hand, shall surely be put to death."

Before discussing whether slave-owning in itself constitutes an indirect support of this capital offense, we should first ask if believers in the South engaged in direct opposition to this evil. Here, the answer is clearly in the affirmative. Dabney, in his *Defense of Virginia and the South*, begins his chapter on the slave trade with these words: "This iniquitous traffick . . ." The duty of Southern Christians was clear—they had to oppose the slave trade. They did so, fervently and zealously. Dabney's vehement attack on the slave trade was representative of many other Christians who were interested in reforming Southern laws regarding slavery.

Were they hypocrites in this opposition because they raised the cry against the slave trade while indirectly supporting that trade by owning slaves? In ancient Rome the acquisition of slaves was not according to the law of God either. A Christian slave-owner in that system, like Philemon, was duty-bound to oppose those features of that society which supported the slave trade, and at the same time was required to treat his slaves in a gracious and thoughtful manner. He was not required to release his individual slaves because of the general societal disobedience. He was not even required to release his slaves if they came into the Christian faith (1 Timothy 6:1–4). At the same time he should have acknowledged that his believing slaves were now Christ's freemen, and they should take any opportunity for freedom provided for them (1 Corinthians 7:20–24):

"Sale of a Slave Family."

> Let each one remain in the same calling in which he was called. Were you called while a slave? Do not be concerned about it; but if you can be made free, rather use it. For he who is called in the Lord while a slave is the Lord's freedman. Likewise he who is called while free is Christ's slave. You were bought at a price; do not become slaves of men. Brethren, let each one remain with God in that state in which he was called.

Could the logic of this have worked its way out over time in a peaceful and Christian form of emancipation, and without nearly 700,000 slain?

Biblical Consequences

But the consequences and ramifications of the African slave trade went far beyond the situation described in Exodus 21. In that situation, when the kidnapper was discovered, he would be tried and executed, and the one kidnapped would be restored to his home. The issues were simple and clear. With the slave trade, the vast majority of the slaves had already been enslaved in Africa by other blacks. They were then taken down to the Guinea coast and sold to the traders, who were usually Arab or European.

The traders transported them, usually under wicked conditions, to those places where a market did exist for their labor. They did this, even though in some of these locations such as the American South the civil leaders had repeatedly and consistently tried to stop the slave traders. Virginia had attempted on no less than twenty-eight occasions to arrest the slave trade, but was stopped by higher (non-Southern) authorities.

If the slaves were not sold in the South, they were taken on to Haiti and

Preparing Slaves for Freedom

Many Southerners who favoured an end of slavery had difficulty imagining how their slaves could get along financially in free society. Some slaves were characteristically immature and undependable. They acted and thought like people in any slave culture. But John McDonogh's plantation was different. This slave-owning Scot had a far-reaching vision to build personal character into the lives of his slaves. He devised a plan to prepare them for productive lives of freedom and personal prosperity based on maturity and entrepreneurial discipline.

A strict sabbatarian, McDonogh would give his Louisiana slaves Saturday afternoons off for their own work if they promised not to work on Sundays. Other planters also gave their slaves Saturday afternoon off. But McDonogh made a contract with his slaves, and he kept it. If they would work for him on Saturday afternoon, and two extra hours each day, he would pay them extra. He paid them 50 cents a day in winter and 62.5 cents in summer. Then, he established a set release price for men of $600 and $450 for women. This was somewhat less than the average market price for healthy field hands. Once they had paid off one-sixth of this agreed-upon price, they would get one free day of their own. Economist Gary North explains, "They could then use their earnings on this free day to speed up repayment. When they "owned" Saturday, the time they spent working for him on Saturday enabled them to buy Friday. When they had bought Friday, they started buying Thursday. When they bought Monday, they were granted their freedom."

As slaves acquired character, they were given responsibilities and privileges of self-governance: rent collection from his white tenants, the agricultural operations, his urban real estate. A jury of six slaves handled all disciplinary matters, which he reviewed. (He would overturn their punishments when they were too harsh. The slaves' jury tended to be overly rigorous in their judgments against fellow slaves.)

McDonogh's vision taught slaves the value of time, work, responsibility, money, contracts and freedom. By selling a slave his freedom, rather than by simply awarding it, this future-orientation would affect the slave's character positively. "Hope," said McDonogh, "would be kept alive in his bosom; he would have a goal in view, continually urging him on to faithfulness, fidelity, trust, industry, economy, and every virtue of good work."

He understood that by allowing a slave to buy his way out of bondage to freedom, the very effort would prepare him for independence. Meanwhile, the efforts of these independence-seeking slaves made him a rich man. At his funeral in 1850,there were many weeping and thankful former slaves.

Brazil, where the condition and treatment of slaves was horrendous. The restoration of these slaves to their former condition was a physical impossibility. In such circumstances, was it a sin for a Christian not to purchase such a slave, knowing that he would take him home and treat him the way the Bible requires? If he did not do so, nothing would be done to improve the slave's condition, and much could happen that would make it worse. The slaves were not stolen cars; they were human beings—and the weight of

Biblical argument suggests the many Christians who treated them lawfully were in no way disobedient.

Virginian Opposition

The requirements for godly treatment of slaves by individual masters is clearly laid out in the Bible, as are the requirements for a godly prohibition of man-stealing on the part of the civil magistrate. Many Southern Christians distinguished themselves in carefully seeking to implement both requirements. Their personal treatment of slaves is discussed later. Regarding their political agitation for a godly abolition of the slave trade, Virginia was the first commonwealth in the world to outlaw the practice, and this after many previous unsuccessful attempts.

"Virginia has the honour of being the first Commonwealth on earth to declare against the African slave trade, and to make it a penal offense," said Dabney. "Her action antedates by thirty years the much bepraised legislation of the British parliament, and by ten years the earliest movement of Massachusetts on the subject . . ."

In 1771, Virginia appealed to the King to stop the trade, saying she had long regarded it as a practice of "great inhumanity." In 1778, Virginia prohibited the introduction of slaves into the state. Georgia was the first state to write a prohibition of the slave trade into its constitution. And the Confederate Constitution (Article 1, Section 9) outlawed the slave trade. In contrast, the slave trade by New Englanders and Northeasterners continued (illegally) until 1861. That year, in fact, the Congress of the United States still appropriated nearly two million dollars in an effort to stamp out the illegal slave trade.

The slave trade was an abomination. The Bible condemns it, and all who believe the Bible are bound to do the same.

"Execution of Gordon, the Slave Trader," reprinted from *Harper's Weekly* (www.harpweek.com). The drawing dramatically depicts the hanging of notorious slave trader Nathaniel Gordon of Maine. The United States Navy steamer *Mohican* caught Gordon in August, 1860, aboard his ship Erie off the west coast of Africa. Lieutenant Henry D. Todd, commander of the Mohican, boarded the Erie and found 900 kidnapped African men, women, and children, filthy and crowded, many of them in poor health. The hanging took place on February 21, 1862.

Where The Slaves Went

Professors Robert William Fogel and Stanley L. Engerman's study *Time on the Cross* examines the origins and destinations of the African slave trade. Fogel later won the Nobel Prize for economics and taught at the University of Chicago and Harvard University. Engerman has headed both the Social Science History Association and the Economic History Association. Their book sent shock waves through academia when published in the early 1970s.

"It is customary to date the beginning of the New World traffic in Africans in the year 1502 when the first references to blacks appear in the documents of Spanish colonial administrators," they wrote. "It lasted over three and a half centuries during which time 9,500,000 Africans were forcibly transported across the Atlantic". That number may be too high an estimate, but it was something else in their writing that surprised many American readers. Fogel and Engerman cited Brazil, not the United States, as by far the largest single Western Hemisphere participant in the slave traffic from Africa. According to them, Brazil accounted for thirty-eight percent of the total, while the British- and French-owned colonies in the Caribbean and the Spanish–American empire totaled together were the destination of fifty percent. Dutch, Danish, and Swedish colonies took another six percent. The remaining six represent the share of the United States.

The slave trade was an abomination. The Bible condemns it, and all who believe the Bible are bound to do the same. Owning slaves, within Scriptural constraints, is not an abomination. The Bible does not condemn it, and those who believe the Bible are bound to refrain in the same way. Reform-minded Christians in the antebellum South reflected the Biblical balance of a hatred of the slave trade and an acceptance of slavery in itself under certain conditions.

The first Baptist church west of the Mississippi River was founded by Joseph Wills, a black preacher.

"It is one of the strange freaks of history," Dabney concluded, "that this [Virginia] commonwealth, which was guiltless in this thing, and which always presented a steady protest against it, should become, in spite of herself, the home of the largest number of African slaves found within any of the States, and thus, should be held up by Abolitionists as the representative of the 'sin of slaveholding;' while Massachusetts, which was, next to England, the pioneer and patroness of the slave trade, and chief criminal, having gained for her share the wages of iniquity instead of the persons of the victims, has arrogated to herself the post of chief accuser of Virginia."

8 Southern Slavery As It Was II

Former slave Sarah Gudgel, 121 years old, as she recounts her life in the 1930s for the *Slave Narratives*.

The Abolitionists in America can be blamed for destroying any chance of Southern support for emancipation and did much to add fuel to the fire of secession. It was impossible to persuade the planters to teach their slaves to read when the Northern Abolitionists were smuggling into the South inflammatory tracts urging slaves to slit the throats of their masters, as well as other criminal acts and violence.

—Charles Adams
When in the Course of Human Events, 2000

If slavery was as bad as the abolitionists maintained it was, why were not multitudes of abolitionists bringing pressure on society to end the evil? Why did not hundreds of slave rebellions occur? The "peculiar institution" of slavery was not perfect or sinless, but the reality was a far cry from the horrific descriptions offered by modern histories, which often mirror 19th-century abolitionist propaganda.

The planter class were for the most part Christians who understood that Scripture did not condemn servitude but it did condemn bad masters. The planter class also provided the U.S. with the most intelligent and most honorable leadership it has ever had.

—Dr. Clyde Wilson
Professor of History
University of South Carolina

Judge George L. Christian observed a far different practice: "In the first place, slavery, as it existed in the South, was patriarchal in its character; the slaves (servants, as we called them) were regarded and treated as members of the families to which they severally belonged; with rare exceptions, they were treated with kindness and consideration, and frequently the relations between the slave and his owner, were those of real affection and confidence."

Prior to the War, the South was often visited by journalists from the North, as well as from Europe. The purpose of their visits was to send back firsthand reports on the nature of the South in general, and of slavery in particular. In the 1840s an Englishman, Sir Charles Lyell, traveled through the nation and published the results of his observations in *Travels in North America in the Years 1841–1842*. Lyell's description of slavery as it operated in the South was widely publicized in the North and pointedly contradicted the abolitionist propaganda. Lyell noted the remarkable affection that existed between master and slave, and the fact that he found the slaves "better fed than a large part of the laboring class of Europe." There were no whips, chains, or accounts of gross mistreatment in Lyell's picture. To Lyell, slavery was a mild, kindly, if inefficient and uneconomical, institution. Others confirmed this view, including Lyell's fellow Britisher, the Earl of Carlisle, James Strictland, and the American Northerner, Frederick Law Olmstead, a staunch opponent of slavery. But their sober testimony was often ignored in favor of abolitionist declarations.

The practice of slavery should be remembered within the context of the Old South as a caste society but not a compartmentalized society. There were specific roles for blacks and whites. One of the drawbacks of such a system, of course, is that it often precluded blacks from pursuing vocations and other callings for which God may have gifted them.

What is often overlooked is the high level of interaction between the races that was a common and everyday experience. Slavery as it existed in the South was not for the most part an adversarial relationship with pervasive racial animosity. Despite the occasional mistreatment of slaves and the aforementioned limitations on opportunities for blacks, because of its dominantly patriarchal character, it was a relationship based upon mutual affection and confidence. The credit for this relative good must go to the predominance of Christianity. The gospel enabled men who were distinct in nearly every way to live and work together, and to be friends.

The Slave Narratives

During the New Deal of the 1930s, American President Franklin D. Roosevelt commissioned a number of journalists to interview former slaves and record their remembrances. The results of the project, collected in the multi-volume *Slave Narratives*, frequently surprises those with certain preconceived notions of the institution of slavery. The reports did not fit with the established and reigning orthodoxy. Thus, despite the verbal testimony of over 2,300 former slaves—not slaveholders—the *Slave Narratives* have been largely explained away (in various ways) ever since and have not had significant effect upon the modern historiography of this period regarding how the institution of slavery functioned.

The narratives portray an amazingly benign picture of Southern plantation life. Affection for former masters and mistresses is expressed with unmistakable devotion. Testimony to the good treatment, kindness, and gentleness of many so-called "heartless slave hold-

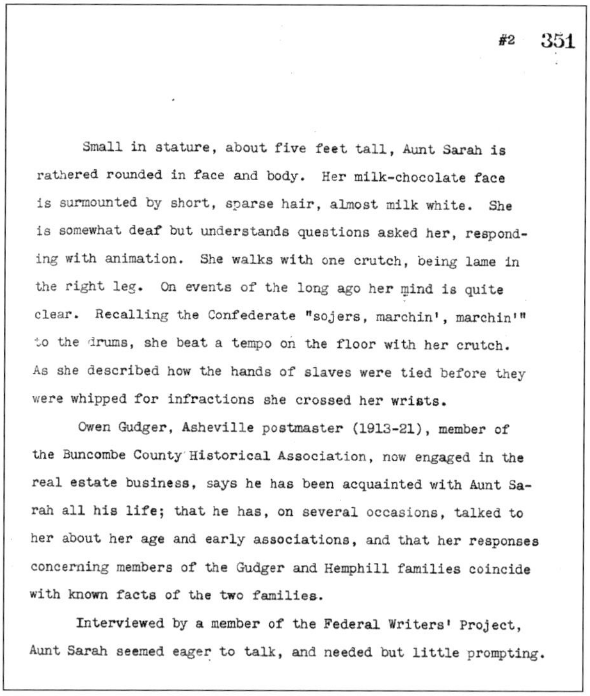

#2 351

Small in stature, about five feet tall, Aunt Sarah is rathered rounded in face and body. Her milk-chocolate face is surmounted by short, sparse hair, almost milk white. She is somewhat deaf but understands questions asked her, responding with animation. She walks with one crutch, being lame in the right leg. On events of the long ago her mind is quite clear. Recalling the Confederate "sojers, marchin', marchin'" to the drums, she beat a tempo on the floor with her crutch. As she described how the hands of slaves were tied before they were whipped for infractions she crossed her wrists.

Owen Gudger, Asheville postmaster (1913-21), member of the Buncombe County Historical Association, now engaged in the real estate business, says he has been acquainted with Aunt Sarah all his life; that he has, on several occasions, talked to her about her age and early associations, and that her responses concerning members of the Gudger and Hemphill families coincide with known facts of the two families.

Interviewed by a member of the Federal Writers' Project, Aunt Sarah seemed eager to talk, and needed but little prompting.

An excerpt from the interview with Sarah Gudgel that appeared in the *Slave Narratives.*

ers" abounds. Many of the old slaves express a wistful desire to be back at the plantation. As recorded in the *Narratives*, slave life was to them a life of plenty, of simple pleasures, of food, clothes, and good medical care. No pervasive cry of rage and anguish appears in the narratives as a whole, nor any general expression of bitterness and outrage. Instead, page after page, expressions of affection appear for a condition which, in the words of one historian, "shames the civilized world."

More often than not, and contrary to a century and a half of bullwhips-on-tortured-backs propaganda, black and white masters worked and ate alongside their charges; be it in house, field or workshop. The few individuals who owned 50 or more slaves were confined to the top one percent, and have been defined as slave magnates.

—Robert M. Grooms

The narratives' overwhelmingly positive view of slavery is striking considering that the period being remembered by these former slaves could arguably be called the most harsh years of the institution—those years when it was under fierce attack, and when slave owners had grown more defensive and in many cases, more restrictive. Modern defenders of the abolitionists dismiss the former slaves' testimony. They claim the slaves were old and their memories were defective, or that as the ex-slaves suffered under the Great Depression, many would think of slavery in a warm , nostalgic way, or that the blacks were talking to white people and weren't about to say things that might get them in trouble.

These explanations are problematic because the testimony is not unanimous. There are those, scattered here and there, who mention atrocities and complain of the meanness and immorality of their owners. There are those whose voices drip with the bitterness brought on by years of unjust treatment and ungodly oppression. They were not too old to remember the outrage they felt; nor had that outrage diminished over the years. They did not look back on their experience with affection and nostalgia. They were not afraid of what "Whitey" might think. In fact, they were happy for the opportunity to make their bitterness known. Their testimony adds the clear note of authenticity to the narratives. There was mistreatment; there were atrocities; there was a great deal of wickedness on the part of some. However, as the narratives make plain, a distinct and very small minority committed these abuses.

Ring of Truth

The *Slave Narratives* have the ring of truth because they present the mixed picture that might be expected in an examination of any human institution. The surprise for moderns is that the mixture contains such an overall positive view of master/slave relations before the War. Dabney, James Henley Thornwell, William S. White, Charles Colcock Jones, and many other defenders of the South

Rev. Charles Colcock Jones

had long acknowledged the existence of mistreatment and wickedness among some slave holders. But they maintained that these instances were relatively rare and infrequent.

Dabney noted: "Now, while we freely admit that there were in the South, instances of criminal barbarity in corporal punishments, they were very infrequent, and were sternly reprobated by publick opinion." Presbyterian pastor White observed: "In all lands there are husbands and fathers who maltreat their wives and children. So there are masters among us who maltreat their slaves. But the prevailing spirit is one of great kindness, showing itself in innumerable ways. Their mutual dependence begets mutual attachment. I could fill volumes with incidents, occurring under my own eyes, illustrating this statement; but I write for my own people, especially my own children, and not for the abolitionists."

The landmark 1970s study, *Time on the Cross,* by professors Robert William Fogel (a Nobel Prize-winner in economics) and Stanley L. Engerman,

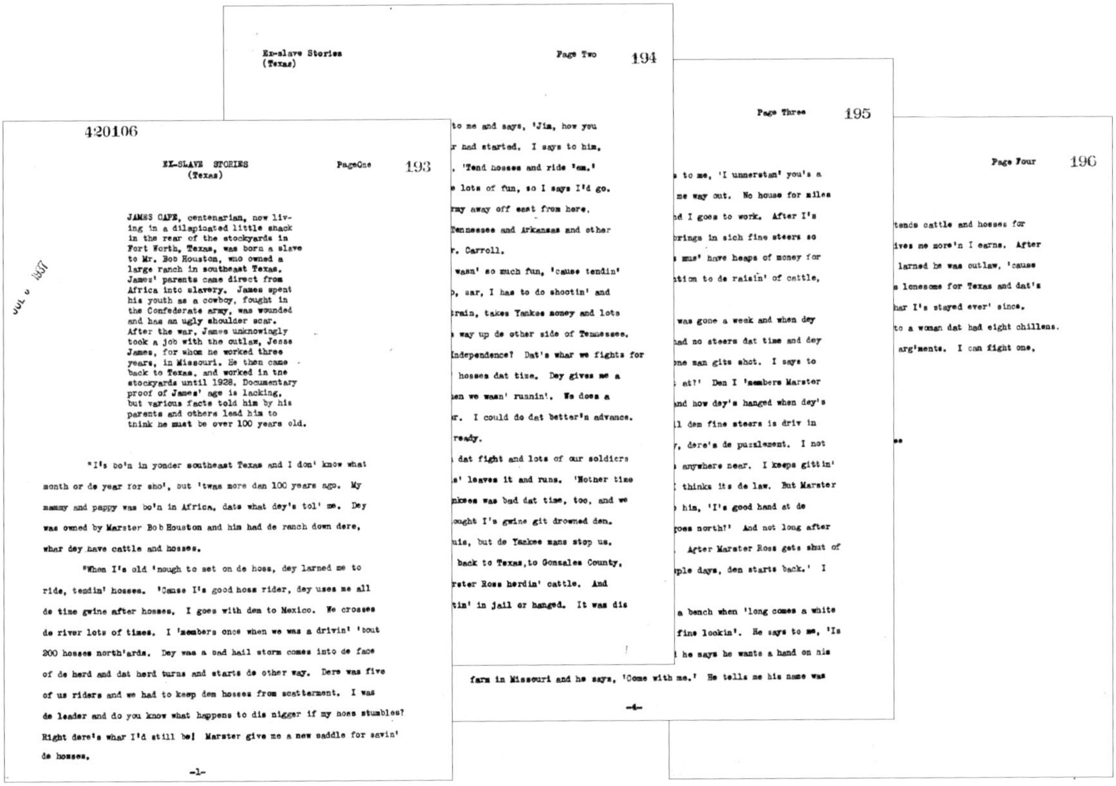
420106

EX-SLAVE STORIES (Texas) PageOne 193

JAMES CAPE, centenarian, now living in a dilapidated little shack in the rear of the stockyards in Fort Worth, Texas, was born a slave to Mr. Bob Houston, who owned a large ranch in southeast Texas. James' parents came direct from Africa into slavery. James spent his youth as a cowboy, fought in the Confederate army, was wounded and has an ugly shoulder scar. After the war, James unknowingly took a job with the outlaw, Jesse James, for whom he worked three years, in Missouri. He then came back to Texas, and worked in the stockyards until 1928. Documentary proof of James' age is lacking, but various facts told him by his parents and others lead him to think he must be over 100 years old.

"I's bo'n in yonder southeast Texas and I don' know what month or de year for sho', but 'twas more dan 100 years ago. My mammy and pappy was bo'n in Africa, dats what dey's tol' me. Dey was owned by Marster Bob Houston and him had de ranch down dere, whar dey have cattle and hosses.

"When I's old 'nough to set on de hoss, dey larned me to ride, tendin' hosses. 'Cause I's good hoss rider, dey uses me all de time gwine after hosses. I goes with dem to Mexico. We crosses de river lots of times. I 'members once when we was a drivin' 'bout 200 hosses north'ards. Dey was a bad hail storm comes into de face of de herd and dat herd turns and starts de other way. Dere was five of us riders and we had to keep dem hosses from scatterment. I was de leader and do you know what happens to dis nigger if my hoss stumbles? Right dere's whar I'd still be! Marster give me a new saddle for savin' de hosses.

-1-

Ex-slave Stories (Texas) Page Two 194

to me and says, 'Jim, how you
r had started. I says to him,
, 'Tend hosses and ride 'em.'
e lots of fun, so I says I'd go.
rmy away off east from here,
Tennessee and Arkansas and other
r. Carroll.
wasn' so much fun, 'cause tendin'
b, sar, I has to do shootin' and
train, takes Yankee money and lots
way up de other side of Tennessee.
Independence? Dat's whar we fights for
hosses dat time. Dey gives me a
hen we wasn' runnin'. We does a
r. I could do dat better'n advance.
ready.
dat fight and lots of our soldiers
s' leaves it and runs. 'Nother time
nkees was bad dat time, too, and we
ought I's gwine git drowned den.
uis, but de Yankee mans stop us.
back to Texas, to Gonzales County,
rster Ross herdin' cattle. And
tin' in jail or hanged. It was dis

Page Three 195

to me, 'I unnerstan' you's a
me way out. No house for miles
nd I goes to work. After I's
brings in sich fine steers so
mus' have heaps of money for
tion to de raisin' of cattle,

was gone a week and when dey
had no steers dat time and dey
one man gits shot. I says to
at?' Den I 'members Marster
and how dey's hanged when dey's
ll dem fine steers is driv in
, dere's de puzzlement. I not
anywhere near. I keeps gittin'
thinks its de law. But Marster
him, 'I's good hand at de
goes north?' And not long after
After Marster Ross gets shut of
ple days, den starts back.' I

a bench when 'long comes a white
fine lookin'. He says to me, 'Is
he says he wants a hand on his
farm in Missouri and he says, 'Come with me.' He tells me his name was

-4-

Page Four 196

tends cattle and hosses for
ives me more'n I earns. After
larned he was outlaw, 'cause
s lonesome for Texas and dat's
har I's stayed ever' since.
to a woman dat had eight chillens.
arg'ments. I can fight one,

ee

The four pages from James Cape's autobiographical account in the *Slave Narratives* offer rich and humorous testimony of his more than 100 years of life as a child of African slave parents, crack Texas horseman and cowboy, Confederate soldier, and unsuspecting ranch hand of the legendary Jesse James. (Library of Congress)

James Cape, over 100 years old, at his Fort Worth home in 1937. (Library of Congress)

cited at the end of Chapter 7, confirms this judgment. They produced perhaps the most thorough examination of plantation records and first-hand accounts ever done; their results contradict the prevailing view of Southern slavery as a perverse and barbarous institution and agree with Dabney, White, and others of the sort.

Pro-Confederate Blacks

Given this testimony, it is not surprising that most Southern blacks (both free and slave) supported the Confederate war effort. Some of course supported it from purely selfish motives. Fully twenty-five percent of the free blacks owned slaves themselves. Most of these free blacks were quite wealthy and knew that a Northern victory would bring economic and social ruin on them, which it did.

But many Southern blacks supported the South because of long established bonds of affection and trust forged over generations with their white masters and friends. They gladly supported the war effort with food, labor, and sometimes fighting. Their loyalty to the principles of the South rivaled and was sometimes even greater than that of some whites. For example, a slave named Robin was captured with his master during Morgan's Raid into Ohio. He was separated from his master in prison and was offered his liberty several times in exchange for taking an Oath of Loyalty to the Union. He refused, saying, "I will never disgrace my family by such an oath." Remember, his "family" was his master's family.

A number of servants captured at Vicksburg were offered their freedom with Federal protection but refused, choosing rather to be sent to Northern prisons to suffer with their fellow (white) soldiers. After their capture, a group of white Virginia slave owners and their slaves were asked if they would take the loyalty oath in exchange for their freedom. A free black among them stated indignantly, "I can't take no such oath. I'm a secesh Negro." A slave in the same group, when he learned that his master had refused to take the oath, proudly replied, "I can't take no oath dat Massa won't take."

That this reflects anything but a servile and cowed attitude is demonstrated by another occasion, when a white planter captured at Point Lookout did agree to take the oath of allegiance. His slave refused. When asked why he refused when his master had not refused, the slave replied with disgust, "Massa has no principles." These facts and many others refuse to conform to modern myths of a harshly oppressed people who constantly seethed with resentment. The fact that very few slave uprisings occurred in the South further confirms the fact that slaves were well-treated and often had a deep loyalty to, and affection for, their masters. The paucity of slave-risings is particularly noteworthy during the course of the War, when so many of the white men were off at war.

Treatment of Slaves

Whenever human society is scrutinized, sin and evil appear. Sometimes in the South slaves were punished, and sometimes by whipping. Engerman and Fogel place this practice in context. Some whippings were severe. Others were as mildly applied as the corporal punishment normally practiced within modern families today. "Although some masters were brutal, even sadistic, most were not," according to *Time on the Cross*.

The *Slave Narratives* contain extended interviews with over 2,300 former slaves. They are overwhelmingly favorable in their judgment of masters as "good men." Out of 331 references in them to masters, eighty-six percent refer to their masters as "good" or "kind." Many planters forbade the practice of whipping except by themselves or in their presence, Engerman and Fogel write, explaining that it was far more in the master's interest to motivate his slaves by positive means. No plantation owner wanted slaves who were sullen, discontent, and hostile, who did just enough to get by, the authors add.

By 1860, thousands of free Southern blacks owned other blacks as slaves, including one hundred twenty-five in Charleston, South Carolina, and over 3,000 in New Orleans.

To achieve the desired response the planters developed a wide-ranging system of rewards, according to *Time on the Cross*. Some were directed toward improving short-run performance, such as "prizes for the individual or the gang with the best picking record on a given day or week." The prizes included items like clothing, tobacco, whiskey, and often cash. "When slaves worked during times normally set aside for rest, they received extra pay—usually in cash and at the rate prevailing in the region for hired labor," explain Engerman and Fogel, who add that planters sometimes developed programs of profit-sharing for their slaves.

All this evidence points to the fact that slaves lived at various levels of income. The pecuniary income received by a prime field hand averaged about fifteen percent more than the income he would have received for his labor as a free agricultural worker, according to Engerman and Fogel. Some slaves saved their money and were quite wealthy after the War. Simon Phillips, a slave from Alabama, said, "People has the wrong idea of slave days. We was treated good. My Massa never laid a hand on me the whole time I was wid him . . . Sometime we loaned the Massa money when he was hard pushed."

In 1860 there were at least a half-dozen free blacks in Louisiana who owned 65 or more slaves. The widow C. Richards and her son, P.C. Richards, who owned a large sugar cane plantation, owned 152 slaves. Black sugar planter Antoine Dubuclet owned over 100.

Conditions Compared

So how were the living conditions of Southern slaves? "Data in the 1850 census suggest that the economic condition of the average free Northern Negro may have been worse than that of the average free Negro in the South," said Engerman and Fogel. "A comparison between New York and New Orleans reveals that New York Negroes lived in more crowded housing, had a lower proportion of craftsmen, and less wealth per capita than free Negroes in New Orleans."

Meanwhile, nearly every slave in the South enjoyed a higher standard of living than poor whites of the South. And the majority had a much easier existence. Most slaves worked under the "task system" which allowed for a great deal of flexibility as work was adapted to the abilities of the individual slave.

Historian Forrest McDonald comments in regard to this "task system": "Normally these [tasks] were light enough so that a worker could complete them in three or four hours. His time was his own when his task was done, and it was not uncommon for slaves, in their free time, to work the acres that were uniformly allotted to them by their masters and thereby to accumulate personal property. It was more common for slaves to double up on their work—to do two or even three tasks in a day—and then to take several days off, during which they might travel many miles by horse or boat to visit friends, family, or lovers on other plantations."

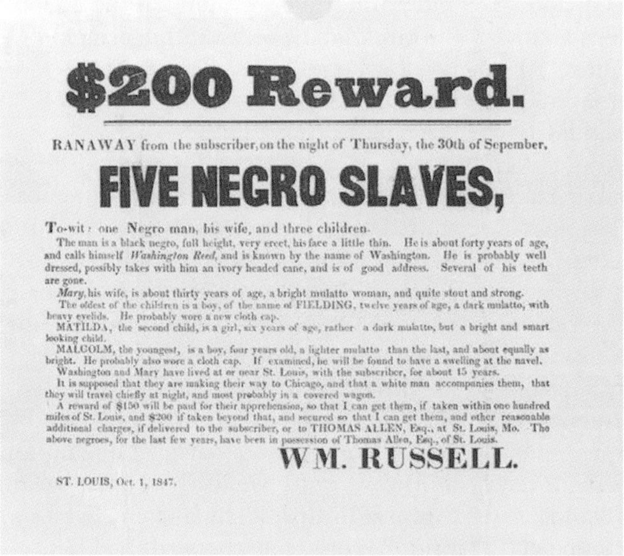
$200 Reward.

RANAWAY from the subscriber, on the night of Thursday, the 30th of Sepember,

FIVE NEGRO SLAVES,

To-wit: one Negro man, his wife, and three children.

The man is a black negro, full height, very erect, his face a little thin. He is about forty years of age, and calls himself *Washington Reed*, and is known by the name of Washington. He is probably well dressed, possibly takes with him an ivory headed cane, and is of good address. Several of his teeth are gone.

Mary, his wife, is about thirty years of age, a bright mulatto woman, and quite stout and strong.

The oldest of the children is a boy, of the name of FIELDING, twelve years of age, a dark mulatto, with heavy eyelids. He probably wore a new cloth cap.

MATILDA, the second child, is a girl, six years of age, rather a dark mulatto, but a bright and smart looking child.

MALCOLM, the youngest, is a boy, four years old, a lighter mulatto than the last, and about equally as bright. He probably also wore a cloth cap. If examined, he will be found to have a swelling at the navel.

Washington and Mary have lived at or near St. Louis, with the subscriber, for about 15 years.

It is supposed that they are making their way to Chicago, and that a white man accompanies them, that they will travel chiefly at night, and most probably in a covered wagon.

A reward of $150 will be paid for their apprehension, so that I can get them, if taken within one hundred miles of St. Louis, and $200 if taken beyond that, and secured so that I can get them, and other reasonable additional charges, if delivered to the subscriber, or to THOMAS ALLEN, Esq., at St. Louis, Mo. The above negroes, for the last few years, have been in possession of Thomas Allen, Esq., of St. Louis.

WM. RUSSELL.

ST. LOUIS, Oct. 1, 1847.

A wanted poster for a slave family who escaped their St. Louis, Missouri owner in 1847.

Family Stability

Only an average of one slave holder out of every twenty-two sold a slave in a year; about one third of those instances occurred during the estate disbursement of deceased persons. In the trading that did occur, some of the families of slaves were broken up, a tragic and abominable occurrence whenever it took place. The Bible gives no support to the legal possibility of separating slave couples or families. So how widespread was this practice?

According to *Time on the Cross,* slave sales records in New Orleans, the largest market in the interregional slave trade, indicate that the destruction of slave marriages was an infrequent consequence of the trade. Chronicling thousands of transactions from 1804–1862, the records reveal that westward migration destroyed about two percent of the marriages of slaves involved in that process. Marriages among whites involved in the westward journey broke up at nearly the same rate. In many cases, among both blacks and whites, a wife refused to accompany her husband on such treks.

Though such extensive slave sale records do not remain from other ante-bellum Southern cities, the age and sex structure of interstate sales at New Orleans do not appear markedly different from those of other south-central cities. Moreover, New Orleans dominated the interregional slave trade. Each year, the city received around one-third of the slaves sold between states.

Myth of Breeding

One of the most volatile topics related to American slavery is the accusation that some slaveowners selected certain black men and women for use as "breeders" of children, similar to how a rancher might utilize his prize bull in hopes of producing offspring of similar mettle. The thesis is often espoused that systematic breeding of slaves for sale in the market accounted for a major share of the net income or profit of slave holders. This thesis, according to Engerman and Fogel, involves two interrelated concepts. First, it is assumed that the slave owners interfered "in the normal sexual habits of slaves to maximize female fertility through... mating women with especially potent men." Second, it is assumed that this raising of slaves occurred with sale as the main motive.

Data contained in the sales records in New Orleans, by far the largest market in the interregional slave trade, sharply contradict the popular view that the destruction of slave marriages was a frequent, if not universal, consequence of the slave trade.

As Engerman and Fogel report, unfortunately for the thesis, "thousands of hours of research by professional historians into plantation records have yet to produce a single authenticated case of the 'stud' plantations alleged in abolitionist literature." Nor was the sale of slaves all that profitable. Slaveowners gleaned more profits from their sweet potato crop than the interregional slave sales.

Furthermore, according to Engerman and Fogel, "proponents of the breeding thesis have been misled by their failure to recognize the difference between human beings and animals." What increases fertility among animals actually reduces fertility among men. Promiscuity increases venereal disease and reduces fertility. Emotional factors, according to *Time on the Cross,* possess "considerable significance in successful human conception." To imply that these factors would not be present in black people is a racist notion.

Had widespread sexual misconduct occurred, the effects on slave morale would have been disastrous. "Distraught and disgruntled slaves did not make good field hands," Engerman and Fogel contend. "Consequently, most planters shunned direct interference in the sexual practices of slaves and attempted to influence fertility patterns through a system of positive economic incentives—incentives that are akin to those practiced by various governments today." Slave owners' written instructions to their overseers frequently contain caveats against "undue familiarity" that could damage slave morale and discipline, according to Engerman and Fogel, who declare that no records have been found containing instructions to overseers that in any way encouraged selective breeding or promiscuity.

Sexual Exploitation?

Did not sexual exploitation undermine and destroy the black family? Critics of the South have consistently answered in the affirmative, among other things accusing slave owners and overseers of turning plantations into personal harems. This argument does not depend on the financial motive for sexual immorality (e.g. the stud farm), but rather on the personal lust of the slave owners or overseers. The musician Neil Young propagated this view in his rock song polemic *Southern Man*—"I seen your black man comin' round."

Again, unfortunately for the thesis, the evidence on which the more expansive assumptions and conclusions are based is scanty at best. Such arguments overlook the real and potentially large costs that confronted masters and overseers "who sought sexual pleasures in the slave quarters," as Engerman and Fogel word it. It would have been much easier, and less risky, for the owner of a large plantation to keep a mistress in town than to risk the possibility of the destruction of his own family by taking up with a slave woman. "For the overseer, the cost of sexual episodes in the slave quarters, once discovered, was often his job," Engerman and Fogel found. "Nor would he find it easy to obtain employment elsewhere as an overseer, since not many masters would be willing to employ as their manager a man who was known to lack self-control on so vital an issue."

Further, to imply that black men would be indifferent to the sexual abuse of their women is to imply that they were somehow less manly than other men who would be indignant over such abuse. This common assumption about slave men is not only unrealistic and unsubstantiated but a racist insult to their humanity. Did slave owners and overseers take sexual advantage of slave women? Undoubtedly, occasional instances of such regrettable behavior occurred, but the evidence is not there for any systematic practice with economic gains in view, according to Engerman and Fogel.

Family Strength

Apart from the motive supplied by Christianity, slave owners had strong economic incentives to promote high standards of morality among their slaves, Engerman and Fogel found. Planters, they write, encouraged strong families not only for the well-being of the slaves, but also for the well-being of the plantation. Strong families promoted happiness and contentment. Happy, contented workers were good workers. Thus, even if a slave owner was not a Christian, there were important reasons to discourage immorality. Marriage was encouraged, as chronicled in *Time on the Cross*; adultery was punished, and divorce was discouraged by the whip.

And slave families were not matriarchal, or dominated by females, as is commonly assumed. *Time on the Cross* examines this subject at length: "For better or worse, the dominant role in slave society was played by men, not women. It was men who occupied virtually all the managerial slots available to slaves . . . Men occupied nearly all the artisan crafts . . ." Also, "It was the male who initiated the period of courtship. And it was the man who secured the permission of the planter to marry." The husband was the head of the slave household, and there was a strong familial bond between family members. Such a bond was not the product of widespread promiscuity.

Living Conditions

Another common myth about American slavery suggests the typical slave was poorly fed. Actually, the typical slave diet was quite good. No deficiency existed in the amount of meat allotted to slaves. "On average, they consumed six ounces of meat per day, just an ounce less than the average quantity of meat consumed by the free population," according to Engerman and Fogel. The high consumption of meat, sweet potatoes, and peas made the slave diet, they write, "not only adequate, it actually exceeded modern recommended daily levels of the chief nutrients."

U.S. slaves had much longer life spans than free white urban industrial workers in both the United States and Europe.

The clothing of slaves, though not lavish, was fairly standard for what the average free white man would have had. Many slaves had far better clothes than poor whites. Regarding shelter, Engerman and Fogel's exhaustive study found that "the most systematic housing information comes from the census of 1860, which included a count of slave houses. These data show that on average there were 5.2 slaves per house on large plantations. The number of persons per free household was 5.3. . . . The single-family household was the rule."

The quality of housing varied. Eyewitness reports from the period, as recounted by Engerman and Fogel, suggest that "the most typical slave houses of the late antebellum period were cabins about eighteen by twenty feet. They usually had one or two rooms. Lofts, where the children slept, were also quite common. Windows were not glazed, but closed by wooden shutters. Chimneys were of brick or stone. Building material was either logs or wood. . . . Floors were usually planked and raised off the ground."

Such housing may sound mean by modern standards, but was actually comparable to the homes of free workers in the antebellum era. According to Engerman and Fogel, "The typical slave cabin . . . probably contained more sleeping space per person than was available to most of New York City's" working-class in 1900. A common tactic of Southern apologists was to point to this discrepancy. "How are you treating your workers?" they would ask the Northerners. "Because they are free, they disappear around the corner at the end of the day, and you continue on with a clean conscience precisely because you do not see the conditions under which they live. We are not as calloused as that."

The most glaring deficiency of Southern slavery when viewed against the righteous standard of Biblical slavery was that portion of it that qualifies as chattel slavery. Unlike Biblically-sanctioned slavery, chattel slavery was permanent and coercive, and it led to other sub-Biblical actions within the institution.

The medical care of slaves was also good. Engerman and Fogel found that the slaves generally received the same medical care, from the same doctor, that the family received. Good medical care is reflected in the statistics for life expectancy. The average life span for an American slave was much longer than that for free white urban industrial workers in both the United States and Europe.

Problems of Slavery

Slavery, though not an evil institution when practiced Biblically, was attended with evils as practiced in the South. It was not in any way perfect or utopian. In fact, as a Southern social institution, generally considered, it was evil.

Christians should be quick to notice the discrepancies between Biblical slavery and that practiced in the South. These differences between the Biblical standard and Southern slavery make impossible an unqualified defense of the institution as it existed and operated in the South.

As mentioned earlier, that institution, as it was established and defended, invited and received the judgment of God. Eugene Genevose, a modern and sympathetic critic of the South, rightly called it "a consuming fire."

As discussed in Chapter 7, the most glaring deficiency of Southern slavery when viewed against the righteous standard of Biblical servitude was that portion of it that qualifies as chattel slavery. Unlike Biblically sanctioned slavery, chattel slavery was permanent and coercive, and it led to other unbiblical actions within the institution. For instance, the cruel mistreatment given to some slaves was wicked (sometimes including immorality and even rape on the part of white owners

The Worst Sins of American Slavery

The three most grievous offenses of slavery as practiced in the American states and allowed by American laws were:

1) The brutal African slave trade that established it and cost the lives of more than a million kidnapped blacks.

2) The lack of a Biblical year of jubilee or other means of ultimate freedom for most slaves. This condemned multitudes of blacks to life-long, even multigenerational, bondage.

3) A raging racism associated with slavery that pervaded America. Particularly unfortunate is the vast number of Christians that fell prey to this attitude.

The Bible states that God has made of one blood all nations of men who dwell on the face of the earth. The Scriptures make plain that on the day of Pentecost (Acts 1), the confusion of Babel was nullified and the glory of every nation, tribe, tongue, and people brought together as one in the kingdom of God.

or overseers), inexcusable, and evil. And though laws protecting slaves from abuse and killing without just cause were on the books, they were not always as specific as they could have been, and were not always enforced as they should have been.

Too, in the decades leading up to the War, the South disallowed the teaching of blacks to read and write, their gathering in public assemblies with whites, and their pursuit of many vocational fields—not to mention the multitude of proscriptions throughout the United States against interracial social discourse such as intermarrying. And underlying the whole institution, North and South, as well as most social discourse in general in the United States, was an endemic societal racism against blacks.

Richard Carruthers, who lived near Houston, Texas, said in the *Slave Narratives:* "My missy, she was good, but the overseer, he was rough. His temper born of the devil, himself. His name was Tom Hill, but us called him 'Devil Hill.' Old Devil Hill, he used to whip me and the other niggers if we don't jump quick enough when he holler and he stake us out like you stake out a hide and whip till we bleed. Many the time I set down and made a eight-plait whip, so he could whip from the heels to the back of the head till he figger he get the proper retribution. Sometimes he take salt and rub on the nigger so he smart and burn proper and suffer misery. They was a calaboose right on the plantation, what look like a icehouse, and it was sure bad to get locked up in it."

Carruthers' recollection and others confirm that for some slaves, cruel mistreatment was not myth but an abiding reality.

Clergy Concerns

As earlier mentioned, James Thornwell of South Carolina and Robert L. Dabney of Virginia—two of the greatest theologians of the 19th century—both possessed grave concerns about the South's peculiar institution, as did Robert E. Lee and many other Southern leaders. Thornwell believed the abolitionists' excesses and infidelity had rendered the North a collection of "Atheists, Socialists, Communists, Red Republicans,

Frederick Douglass (1817-1895)

"My whole future depended upon the decision of this conductor." So went the thrilling account of this runaway slave's escape to freedom aboard a train in his 1881 autobiography *Life and Times of Frederick Douglass*. Young Frederick Washington had borrowed a black sailor's Seaman's Protection Certificate, which attested his free status, and he disguised himself in a sailor's uniform of red shirt, tarpaulin hat, and black scarf tied loosely around his neck. Then he had to change his name from Frederick Washington to Frederick Douglass to conform with the papers as he boarded the Boston to Philadelphia train.

Fortunately, he already knew how to sound like a sailor. "My knowledge of ships and sailor's talk came much to my assistance, for I knew a ship from stem to stern, and from keelson to cross-trees, and could talk sailor like an 'old salt,'" Douglass recalled in his autobiography. But then he found himself face to face with the conductor, who by law was required to return "Douglass" to his owner if he determined he was a slave.

"I suppose you have your free papers?" the conductor asked. "No sir; I never carry my free papers to sea with me," came the reply. "But you have something to show that you are a freeman, haven't you?" "Yes, sir, I have a paper with the American eagle on it, and that will carry me around the world," Douglass said. The conductor's quick glance at the paper—which described the black sailor who actually owned it—satisfied him.

Douglass's Critique of Slavery

Perhaps no one has ever elucidated the worst excesses of slavery with more eloquence and power than the famed black author and orator Frederick Douglass, himself once a slave. However jaundiced Frederick Douglass's eloquent perspective may be accused of being and however infrequent such terrifying episodes may have been in the South, no modern American, certainly no Christian, can look easily past the subject, regardless of what other issues they may believe caused the War.

> *I love the pure, peaceable, and impartial Christianity of Christ: I therefore hate the corrupt, slaveholding, women-whipping, cradle-plundering, partial and hypocritical Christianity of this land. The man who wields the blood-clotted cowskin during the week fills the pulpit on Sunday, and claims to be a minister of the meek and lowly Jesus. The man who robs me of my earnings at the end of each week meets me as class-leader on Sunday*

Jacobins." But he also feared that: "Upon an earth radiant with the smile of heaven, or in the Paradise of God, we can no more picture the figure of a slave than we can picture the figures of the halt, the maimed, the lame, and the blind. That it is inconsistent with a perfect state, that it is not absolutely a good, a blessing, the most strenuous defender of Slavery ought not to permit himself to deny." By the time of the War, Thornwell believed gradual emancipation was the best course of action.

He took the runaway slave's fare and moved to the other passengers.

A remarkable, self-educated man, Douglass learned as a boy to read in the home of his white mistress, then began to teach himself oratory. He became one of the greatest orators of the 19th century. His eloquence was said to rival that of the legendary George Whitefield, the most famous evangelist of America's 18th-century Great Awakening.

Douglass was brilliant and articulate with both word and pen. His autobiography stunned many on both sides of the Atlantic by his perceptions and insights into the institution of slavery and what it did to both slave and master alike. After William Lloyd Garrison heard Douglass speak in Massachusetts, he hired him to be the official orator of the Massachusetts Anti-Slavery Society. Douglass generated great waves in that state and a tremendous amount of support for the cause of abolitionism.

In the 1850s, Douglass and Garrison parted ways philosophically. Douglass grew increasingly convinced that neither slavery nor any other type of social reform could be accomplished without violence. He believed tumult was necessary to promote social change, and he became a strong supporter of the violent overthrow of the institution of slavery. Douglass's conversion to Christianity tempered both his tone and his message in his later years. He became the federal marshal of Washington, D.C., then ambassador to Haiti, the first black to rise to that elevated position in the Federal government.

morning, to show me the way of life, and the path of salvation.

He who sells my sister, for purposes of prostitution, stands forth as the pious advocate of purity. He who proclaims it a religious duty to read the Bible denies me the right of learning to read the name of the God who made me. He who is the religious advocate of marriage robs whole millions of its sacred influence, and leaves them to the ravages of wholesale pollution.

The warm defender of the sacredness of the family relation is the same that scatters whole families—sundering husbands and wives, parents and children, sisters and brothers—leaving the hut vacant, and the hearth desolate . . .

The dealers in the bodies and souls of men gives his blood-stained gold to support the pulpit, and the pulpit, in return, covers his infernal business with the garb of Christianity. Here we have religion and robbery the allies of each other—devils dressed in angels' robes, and hell presenting the semblance of paradise.

Dabney did not think the South should "rest contented" with slavery in its antebellum form. He warned Southerners that it could not be defended unless they were "willing to recognize and grant in slaves those rights which are a part of our essential humanity." Another Presbyterian Pastor, Charles Colcock Jones of Savannah, spent most of his adult life laboring in the education of black slaves. He accused his fellow Southerners of pride regarding the issue of slavery. He believed the withering assaults of the abolitionists had provoked the South to an unwillingness to admit its errors, because that would mean confessing wrong to the North, to other nations, and to the slaves themselves.

One of the great short-comings of Southern slaveowners was their failure to prepare black men and women to shoulder the responsibility of living independently.

Colcock understood the Southern reaction to the abolitionists, but he rejected it. If the South was to defend the Biblical institution of slavery, he maintained, then slavery ought to operate Biblically; covering up wrongs and excesses was inexcusable. Where wrongs are committed, said Jones, they should be corrected.

Still, modern Christians who rightly condemn such infamy are not condemning something defended by the South. This mistreatment was reprobated by the majority of antebellum Southerners as well. Most Southern slaveowners, if learning an overseer had abused a slave, would fire him, and perhaps report him to the law. In some cases, like that chronicled by former slave Henry Lewis of Beaumont, Texas, the slaveowner beat the overseer.

Slave Mentality

An added problem with slavery was its engendering of what can be called a "slave mentality" in the minds of many blacks. That is, that they were incapable of handling responsibilities or accomplishing tasks beyond those of a slave, and that they were innately inferior in some ways to whites and perhaps other races. Not all blacks, as mentioned, were so affected. There are amazing stories regarding the industry and ingenuity of many slaves. One concerned a prominent black artisan, sought all over the South for his work. His master allowed him to travel, and he grew wealthy as he did, paying his master a percentage of his proceeds. Many Southern homes to this day possess work created by this slave.

Many if not most black slaves, however, did imbibe the slave mentality. Indeed, one of the great shortcomings of Southern slaveowners was their failure to prepare black men and women to shoulder the responsibility of living independently. Many complaints appear in the *Slave Narratives* which indicate this. The majority of those interviewed complained that they would rather be slaves again than to be free with all the responsibilities that freedom entailed. Ironically, if the somewhat misguided Christian ethos of many slaveowners had not made slavery so pleasant an experience for the majority of slaves, this mentality would not probably have so strong a hold upon the minds of some of their descendants today.

More Problems

Finally, slavery gave an issue to radical revolutionaries by which they could provoke animosity against the South and, consequently, the "old order" which held sway in America prior to 1861. The War that resulted gave these radicals opportunity to increase the size and power of the Federal Government to undreamed-of proportions. The United States, after 1865, was transformed into a distinctly different entity than it had been before. The nation established by the Founding Fathers—a limited, constitutional republic, and a union of free states—was no more. And a modern, messianic state, seeking to bring salvation by law, was firmly established.

After the death of the old American Republic, the nation created by the new revolutionaries became a nightmare for many newly freed black men and women. The laws ostensibly passed to help them were used more and more to exclude them from the privileges they once enjoyed under the restricted freedom of slavery. For example, licenser requirements and the rise of unionism systematically excluded black artisans and craftsmen from making the living they made before the War. Welfare laws often removed the black man from his position of breadwinner and head over the home, and the black family was gradually destroyed. Blacks were freed from the Southern plantations only to become the slaves of an impersonal state.

Professors Fogel and Engerman observe in *Time on the Cross*:

> What antislavery critics generally objected to was not the fact that slavery constrained the opportunities open to blacks, but the form which these constraints took. While physical force was unacceptable, legal restrictions were not. Thus many one-time crusaders against slavery sat idly by, or even collaborated in passing various laws which served to improve the economic position of whites at the expense of blacks.

In other words, many whites who championed the cause of freeing black slaves failed to support the cause of helping those same men and women after they were free. Henry Banner, a former slave from Arkansas, put it more succinctly: "Before the war you belonged to somebody. After the war you weren't nothin' but a nigger."

Slavery gave an issue to radical revolutionaries by which they could provoke animosity against the South and, consequently, the "old order" which held sway in America prior to 1861. The War that resulted gave these radicals opportunity to increase the size and power of the federal government to undreamed-of proportions.

Unexpected Blessings

In spite of the evils contained in the system, slavery offered benefits for both blacks and whites. First was the influence of Christianity. More than one slave lived to thank God for his servitude—despite all the hardships involved. Martin Jackson of Texas, a descendant of slaves, puts it this way: "I believe that slavery in this country, taking everything into consideration, was a Godsend for the slaves. The twenty million Negroes are descended from four million sent over from Africa. If it had not been for the slave traffic, we would still be living in Africa. I would be a heathen and my children would be heathens."

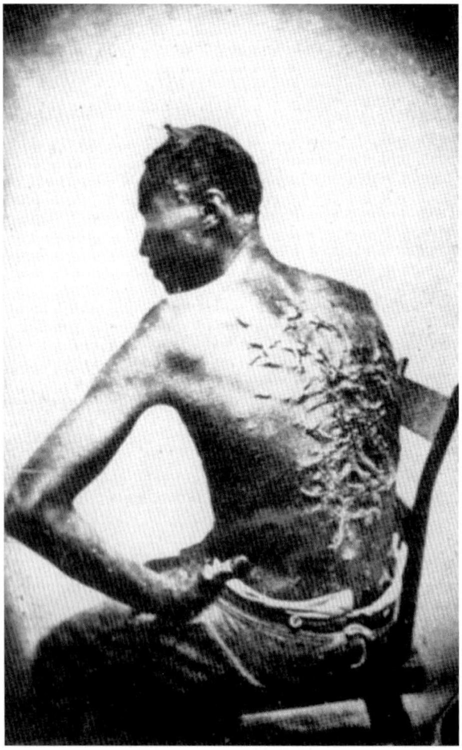

Brutal treatment of slaves was not the norm in 19th-century America. In fact, laws, churches, and community opinion combined with the slaveowner's own self-interest as a bulwark against such abuse. The sad truth, however, is that it did occasionally occur, such as in the case of Peter, pictured here in Baton Rouge, Louisiana, on April 2, 1863. "Overseer Artayou Carrier whipped me. I was two months in bed sore from the whipping," Peter recalled, adding, "My master come after I was whipped; he discharged the overseer." (Library of Congress)

More than one former slave had reason to stand in the place of the Biblical Joseph and say, "Men meant it for evil, but God meant it for good." The slavery they were delivered from in Africa was far worse than what they suffered in this country. Despite its obvious failures, and they were many, slavery produced in the South a genuine mutual affection between the races that had perhaps never existed in any nation before the War or since and which will never be achieved through federally-mandated efforts.

Former slave George Fleming of Laurens, South Carolina said after the War: "I longed to see Marse Sam Fleming. Lawd, chile, dat's de best white man what ever breathed de good air. I still goes to see whar he buried every time I gits a chance to venture t'wards Laurens. As old as I is, I still draps a tear when I sees his grave, fer he sho' was good to me and all his other niggers." Fleming's use of the "n-word" demonstrates the mutable nature of human language. What today constitutes a gross insult did not have the same connotations a century-and-a-half ago.

Former slave Clara Davis of Alabama recalled: "Dem was de good ole days. How I longs to be back dar wid my ole folks an' a playin' wid de chillun down by de creek. 'Taint nothin' lak it today, nawsuh. . . . Dey tells me dat when apusson crosses dat ribber, de Lawd gives him whut he wants. I done tol' de Lawd I don't want nothin' much . . . only my home, white folks. I don't think dats much to ax' for. I suppose he'll send me back dar. I been a-waitin' for him to call."

There is a nobility in these old servants that humbles us. Former slave Nicey Pugh said, "I was born a slave but I ain't neber been one. I'se been a worker for good peoples. You wouldn't calls dat bein' a slave would you, white folks?"

Conclusion

How do we assess these heartfelt reminiscences, and countless similar ones, of former slaves for their masters and their unemancipated lives? Do they reveal the embarrassing servility of former slaves? The unvarnished affection of folks, who happened in the sovereignty of God to be slaves, for their beloved friends whom Providence saw fit to make masters and mistresses? Certainly, such testimonials give us cause to reassess the one-dimensional pronouncements of modern-day politically correct doctrine regarding Southern slavery.

No one needs lament the passing of slavery, and the editors of this volume emphatically do not. But who cannot but lament the damage to both white and black that has occurred as a consequence of the way it was abolished? In many respects, the remedy applied has been far worse than the disease ever was. Christians who doubt this should consider whether it was safer to be a black child in the womb in 1858 or in 2004.

In spite of the evils contained in the system, slavery offered benefits for both blacks and whites. First was the influence of Christianity. More than one slave lived to thank God for his servitude—despite all the hardships involved.

One final entry from the *Slave Narratives* recalls the words of Adeline Johnson of Winnsboro, South Carolina: "I hope and prays to get to heaven. I'll be satisfied to see my Savior that my old marster worshiped and my husband preached about. I want to be in heaven with all my white folks, just to wait on them, and love them, and serve them, serta like I did in slavery time. That will be enough heaven for Adeline."

9 Religion and Worldview I

"The Pilgrims Landing on Plymouth Rock, 1620," by Charles Lucey.

However you boil it, however you slice it, however you cut it down, the American War Between the States was a fight between the largely Unitarian North and the largely Calvinistic and orthodox South.

—Douglas Wilson,
"America's Wars" Conference, 1997, New St. Andrews College

At heart, the War was that oldest and most desperate sort of fight—a religious one. Two waves of European imports had diluted the early Reformed theological bedrock laid in the North by the Puritans and Pilgrims. One wave was human, as millions of non-Reformed European immigrants flooded into the North in the early- and mid-19th century. The other was ideological, as many Northern religious leaders were influenced by non-orthodox theological innovations from liberal German schools of theology and elsewhere.

Reformed
The theology of the Protestant Reformation. It teaches the absolute sovereignty (independence and power) of God in all things. This includes the redemption of His elect people from eternal damnation through the Person and work of Jesus Christ, without contribution from any mortal man or woman. It is also known as Calvinism, or the doctrines of grace.

The South, meanwhile, particularly after 1820, maintained a much more consistent adherence, across all denominations, to the covenantal, Calvinistic doctrines of the Protestant Reformation. This yielded a stricter allegiance than in the North to established norms and creeds, whether politically as to the United States Constitution, or theologically as to the Westminster Confession of Faith, the Heidelberg Catechism, and the London Confession of 1689. Here lay the source of the sections' divergent views on such issues as secession and states' rights.

Calvinism
The branch of Reformed theology influenced by John Calvin's work in Geneva and most commonly defined by five points. They include the total depravity of mankind, the unconditional election of the Christian believer, the limited, definite, or particular atonement of Christ (His successful redemption of His own people, while not dying in vain for non-Christians), the irresistible grace of God over those whom He chooses for His own, and the assured faithful (though not sinless) perseverance of saints till death.

Over a period of centuries, Western civilization had moved away from the old foundational truths of Christendom and toward a revolutionary, Enlightenment-dominated worldview. Now these warring philosophies split America, to no small degree along regional lines. The North as a whole was more progressive, the South more conservative and jealous of preserving the principles of Christendom. This division was cultural as well as political. Though the issue of slavery stirred up the controversy, the real conflict was that the North and South were generally committed to two different worldviews and developing increasingly divergent cultures. These differences evidenced themselves in almost every area of life—music, art, literature, food, entertainment, social relations among the races and sexes, and in how the average person spent the waking hours of their day.

Southern life was rooted in the land and the traditions of family, faith, community, time, and place. In the North, which was becoming a world-class industrial powerhouse, life developed at a faster pace, cut off from ancient homelands and even contemporary family ties. As a result, two different cultures and political environments grew up.

City on a Hill

The Puritans and Pilgrims who migrated from England and Holland to found Christian civilization in North America possessed a Biblical notion of desiring to be a new type of God's chosen Israel, a city set on a hill. They did not believe God spoke and called them out like the original Israel. Rather, they sought to become an example of liberty, dignity, freedom, holiness, and righteousness to the nations, to show them how to live under the Law and Word of God.

Despite this worthy desire, many of the descendants of the New England Puritans turned away from the historic gospel, apparently forgetting its foundation of grace, repentance, humility, and submission to the Lordship of Christ. Yet they retained the goal of being the new Israel and bringing light and salvation to the world, albeit a different light and salvation than before. Conversely, the Southern people believed their society, while imperfect, did not need transforming by other people, least of all the North, with whom they disagreed on many issues and from whom they sensed increasing condescension and derision.

Yet that in many ways is what the War and "Reconstruction" accomplished. Though slavery was an issue for a minority of Northerners, it served as a pretext for many others who had their own reasons to dislike the South, wish it chastened, want it changed, or even desire its destruction. A host of issues provided more direct cause for the war than slavery, issues rooted in theological apostasy. These included economic issues, constitutional issues, and even geographical issues.

John Calvin

The Bible says that as a man thinketh in his heart, so is he. What a person thinks about God determines how he thinks about everything else. Who were the people of the North and the South? Why did they fight? The roots of society are always theological. Thus, to find the answers to these questions, we need to look at what is at the bottom of everything else—their theology.

The Puritans and Pilgrims who migrated from England and Holland to found Christian civilization in North America possessed a Biblical notion of desiring to be a new type of God's chosen Israel, a city set on a hill.

Early Unity

The first two centuries of America's existence, roughly 1600–1800, witnessed a remarkable unity among the

"Embarkation of the Pilgrims," Robert Weir's famed oil painting depicting William Brewster, holding the Bible on his knees, leading the Pilgrims in prayer prior to their departure for America.

people. That unity was based upon a common faith. The vast majority of Americans believed the Bible was the Word of God. For the most part, they followed its teachings. They looked to it as the standard for matters political and personal, as well as for the soul. Most people in all parts of the country also held to the Protestant faith of the 16th-century Reformation. That belief system today is identified by such names as Covenantal, Reformed, and Calvinistic (after the great French Protestant Reformer John Calvin of Geneva).

The first two centuries of America's existence, roughly 1600–1800, witnessed a remarkable unity among the people. That unity was based upon a common faith. The vast majority of Americans believed the Bible was the Word of God. For the most part, they followed its teachings.

Nearly every major early American denomination—Baptist, Presbyterian, Episcopalian, Congregational, Lutheran—would hear a Calvinistic sermon on Sunday. These denominations agreed on theology proper: their view of salvation, their view of God, their view of man, and how salvation is applied. Their differences centered on church government and the definition of the Church. For instance, the Baptists believed the Church consisted of those people who consciously profess having come to trust in Jesus Christ for salvation and then receive baptism. That is why they took the title, Baptists; most other denominations baptized infants prior to any conversion experience. Episcopalians had church government ruled by bishops, Presbyterians by elders, Congregationalists by congregations. Their differences concerned how to go about the work of God, not what to believe about Him and the salvation wrought by Him.

The Great Awakening played a key role in this early theological unity. That historical event of unprecedented American spiritual revival began in 1734 in the Northampton, Massachusetts church of famed pastor-theologian-philosopher Jonathan Edwards. Dominantly Calvinistic, the Great Awakening spread southward through the efforts of evangelical preachers like Englishman George Whitefield and Americans such as the Tennent brothers and Jonathan Dickinson.

Two-Edged Sword

But the Great Awakening wielded a two-edged theological sword. On the one hand, it torpedoed a spiritual malaise that had gripped pulpits and churches throughout the colonies. And it employed theological doctrine no less sound than that originally held by the backslidden or even apostate churches now in spiritual peril. On the other hand, though the revival began in Edwards' church—unplanned and through the effort of God not man as with all true revivals—it grew to full flower outside the auspices of the organized Church. In fact, many established churches and denominations feared and repudiated it.

Indeed, theological soundness had once both anchored the various denominations and held them shoulder-to-shoulder in orthodox solidarity. But though orthodoxy remained strong and theological unity initially recovered with the Great Awakening, that unity soon began to fragment, which in turn rendered vulnerable the orthodox consensus. This occurred because the locus of ecclesiastical power shifted from denominational churches once founded upon a Biblical hierarchy but now grown cool in spiritual ardor, to a more independent, personality driven, and less-biblical ecclesiastical network.

Many of the descendants of the New England Puritans turned away from the historic gospel, apparently forgetting its foundation of grace, repentance, humility, and submission to the Lordship of Christ. Yet they retained the goal of being the new Israel and bringing light and salvation to the world, albeit a different light and salvation than before.

In other words, the denominations had once possessed Biblical systems of multilayered ecclesiastical authority rich with internal checks and balances that both informed their theological distinctives and restrained them from excess and error. Now, though, Church doctrine and practice often hinged on the mutable beliefs

George Henry Boughton's familiar "Pilgrims Going to Church" —Bible in one hand, blunderbuss in the other.

Jonathan Edwards

George Whitefield

and opinions of small groups of men, or even individual men who operated in semi- or complete autonomy from higher authority. Related to these events was the phenomenon of revivalistic evangelists who spoke with oratorical power, while operating outside the established Church. These men could often draw significant financial resources away from denominational churches, as well as exert great influence on the loyalty and theological beliefs of those congregations.

The breaking apart of the earlier theological unity was apparent by the late 1700s. Ironically, as the 19th century unfolded, it was the South which more generally retained the old theology once held by the whole country. New England, the bulwark of Puritan orthodoxy through the 17th and 18th centuries, was rapidly discarding it. For this reason, more than any other, including social, cultural, economic, political, or geographical, the sections began to drift apart.

Differences and Revolution

Differences had always existed between North and South. Even during the Constitutional Convention of the 1780s, Southerners and Northerners alike wrote home, exclaiming the peculiarities of the other in culture, living habits, and other customs. But their theological unity allowed them to work together. By the early 1800s that theological unity was gone, and so their social differences grew all the more stark and intolerable. This proved particularly so for the Northern descendants of the old Puritans. New England's intellectuals and its population in general had begun to chafe under the doctrines of Biblical Calvinism.

Contemporaneous events in Europe exerted enormous influence on all these developments. There, and elsewhere, theological and political revolutions of epic proportions raged, from the 1780s through the early decades of the 19th century. In fact, 1848 was the year of revolution almost worldwide. But in Europe especially and in the German states (no unified "Germany" would exist until Otto von Bismarck used blood and iron to forge it after the War of 1861–1865) in particular, theological radicalism began to flourish.

Many of the men who became the intellectual guiding lights of New England received their training at the German school of Tubingen, where they were immersed in theological radicalism. They would leave America at least semi-orthodox in their Christian beliefs, then return as radical liberals no longer believing the Bible to be the Word of God, Jesus to be the Son of God, the necessity of atonement, the original sin of man, the depravity of man, or the necessity of salvation by grace. They retained the Biblical terminology, but they redefined it. They might continue to preach about such words as resurrection, for instance, but they would replace the spiritual import of the word with a secular meaning. That is why many old speeches and lectures from the New England intellectuals—including clergy—of the early 19th century appear theologically sound at first glance, but less so upon closer inspection and examination of the context.

These intellectuals despised the Biblical doctrines of human depravity and the sovereignty of God, which they believed were enemies of national progress. In their place, they pushed forward such ideas as modernization and advance. As a result, vast numbers of people rejected the old theology because it seemed tied to the past, hindering progress. It seemed negative and discouraging to them. They did not feel uplifted when they heard it.

The ideas of human perfectibility and self-sufficiency proved more palatable to such opponents of the old faith. They would write unabashed thoughts such as, "Yes, I was trained up as a Calvinist, but I never liked it. I hated it. And I was so thankful when I learned differently." Many of these men described their "conversion" to secularism.

Their testimonies sound much like Christian testimonies, except they are talking about being converted to apostasy and turning away from the faith. Strict adherence to the Bible became old fashioned and extreme to them. The evolution of society and its moving forward into a new world, they believed, required a new word, something other than that old-fashioned book. They doubted the relevancy of something written more than two thousand years before—some of it perhaps as much as four thousand years—other than as a resource of helpful living principles, aphorisms, and sayings.

These intellectuals despised the Biblical doctrines of human depravity and the sovereignty of God, which they believed were enemies of national progress. In their place, they pushed forward the humanistic ideas of modernization and advance.

Degrees of Radicalism

This new worldview paradigm can be defined as "rationalism;" that is, a man-centered rather than God-centered view of existence and salvation. Theological radicalism, the departure from orthodox, Biblically-based Christianity, was part and parcel of this worldview. Rationalism took several forms on the American religious landscape, including Deism, Unitarianism, and, farthest from Christian orthodoxy, Transcendentalism.

The adherents of transcendentalism included a galaxy of New England literary and intellectual luminaries, among them the famed poets and traditional American icons Ralph Waldo Emerson and Henry David Thoreau. They believed, in essence, that man was equivalent to God and somehow unit-

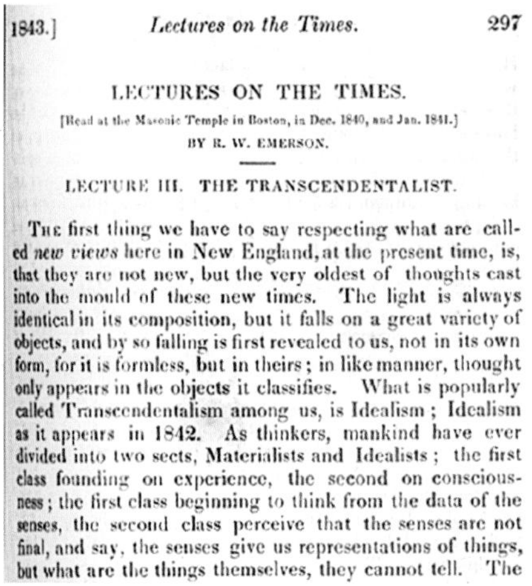

1843.] *Lectures on the Times.* 297

LECTURES ON THE TIMES.

[Read at the Masonic Temple in Boston, in Dec. 1840, and Jan. 1841.]

BY R. W. EMERSON.

LECTURE III. THE TRANSCENDENTALIST.

The first thing we have to say respecting what are called *new views* here in New England, at the present time, is, that they are not new, but the very oldest of thoughts cast into the mould of these new times. The light is always identical in its composition, but it falls on a great variety of objects, and by so falling is first revealed to us, not in its own form, for it is formless, but in theirs; in like manner, thought only appears in the objects it classifies. What is popularly called Transcendentalism among us, is Idealism; Idealism as it appears in 1842. As thinkers, mankind have ever divided into two sects, Materialists and Idealists; the first class founding on experience, the second on consciousness; the first class beginning to think from the data of the senses, the second class perceive that the senses are not final, and say, the senses give us representations of things, but what are the things themselves, they cannot tell. The

Excerpt from "The Transcendentalist," one of Ralph Waldo Emerson's "Lectures on the Times" that appeared in the short-lived transcedentalist publication *The Dial.*

Deism

The belief, claiming foundation solely upon the evidence of reason, in the existence of God as the creator of the universe who after setting it in motioned abandoned it, assumed no control over life, exerted no influence on natural phenomena, and gave no supernatural revelation.

Unitarianism

A monotheist who rejects the doctrine of the Trinity (Father, Son, and Holy Spirit) for a one-person or unitary God, while emphasizing freedom and tolerance in religious belief and the autonomy of each congregation.

Transcendentalism

The belief that knowledge of reality is derived from a person's own intuition or non-demonstrable sources rather than from objective experience or propositional truth such as the Bible. It blossomed into a cultural movement in 19th century New England behind such leaders as Emerson, Thoreau, and Hawthorne.

ed with Him. The Transcendentalists were similar to modern-day humanists, in that they tended toward mankind for the salvation of the world. Their ancestry arguably stretches back to Adam and Eve when those two sinned in the garden by wanting to be like God, to determine good and evil for themselves.

Transcendentalists possessed the desire not to look outside to God and His revelation for their answers, but rather to look inside themselves, where truth can be found if one is sufficiently educated. The Transcendentalists believed man was basically good. So why, they asked, does he do bad things? Not because of himself, they concluded, but because of the society and world around him. The sin and evil in men and women affected and often corrupted otherwise good people. Thus the transcendentalists sought to do away with evil structures and institutions, and reform society, believing man would respond with good character and actions.

The New Vision

Here, the non-orthodox intellectuals' philosophy intersected with the old Puritan vision held by their fathers and grandfathers of seeing God's kingdom reigning on earth. But that earlier vision had Christ as King over all the nations and stated that every rightly-governing nation acknowledged the authority of His Word and Law. Indeed, the new vision intersected with the old but did not merge with it, for God was no longer held to be sovereign over the people, the nation, or in salvation. His sovereignty, in fact, was rejected.

The new vision sought the reformation of institutions and manners, as assessed by their own sin-darkened imaginations. Their fathers, in contrast, had sought the reformation of men's hearts—hearts they believed defiled by the sin nature resident within them, rather than what entered them from outside. Their fathers saw men's hearts as needing replacement, not correction.

How did the Transcendentalists' system of religious doctrine differ with that of orthodox Christianity? It had no need for the Person or atoning work of Christ. It needed no inspired Bible for revelation and illumination. It rejected the need for a Mediator to reveal God to man and provide the bridge of reconciliation and salvation between them. It did so because it rejected the Christian doctrine of man's indwelling sin nature. Rather, ultimate authority and truth, taught the Transcendentalists, was inside of man. He need not look to authority outside of himself.

The Transcendentalists believed man was basically good. So why, they asked, does he do bad things? Not because of himself, they concluded, but because of the society and world around him. . . .Thus they sought to do away with evil structures and institutions, and reform society, believing man would respond with good.

The Transcendentalists, and growing legions of men not of them but influenced by them, saw the answer as better wages and working conditions, safer neighborhoods, nicer friends, fresher food, and more progressive (government) education,

Horace Mann (1796-1859)

Social reform replaced Christian orthodoxy as the central life passion for many key 19th-century Americans, including educator, political leader, and government school advocate Horace Mann. "With government education and a hundred years, all streets will be safe," Mann said. "You will be able to walk anywhere. Men will love one another. It will be like the garden of God again." Mann's gospel of the salvation of humanity was not the Person and work of Jesus Christ, but the work of himself and his colleagues as they developed and spread across America a mandatory, non-Christian, government-controlled school system.

Having rejected the Biblical tenets espoused by Calvinism, Mann no longer believed man was inherently sinful. He believed social problems originated in the community, not people. Therefore he saw transforming American society through government-dictated education as the solution. Mann got his government schools. However, it was not safety, love, and tranquility which accompanied them, but violence, moral debauchery, and family disintegration.

leading to the perfecting of a society that would result in the perfecting of a vast host of its citizens. The Transcendentalists, along with many of their Deistic and Unitarian brethren, possessed dreams of no less breadth and scope than their orthodox Puritan and Pilgrim forefathers. But the new dreams had both a different point of origination and a different source of power. They had a different gospel. The work of enlightened men now effected it, not the Person and work of Jesus Christ. So fierce grew the antipathy toward the old Calvinism in New England that Harriet Beecher Stowe once said, "The only thing in Boston that is worse than an atheist is a Calvinist."

Finney's "Conservative" Radicalism

Not only did a radical rejection of the orthodox Calvinism of the Puritans and Pilgrims occur in America; less known, particularly by contemporary Christians, was the advent of what appeared a more conservative, even evangelical, rejection of it. This developed within the burgeoning ranks of anti-Calvinistic Arminians and Finneyites, or followers of the famous 19th-century revivalist preacher Charles G. Finney.

Not only did a radical rejection of the orthodox Calvinism of the Puritans and Pilgrims occur in America; less known, particularly by contemporary Christians, was the advent of what appeared a more conservative, even evangelical, rejection of it.

Calvinists posited to man no ability to deliver himself from his state of spiritual death and separation of God. God, they said, "regenerated" the dead spirits of certain "elect" men "chosen . . . in Him before the foundation of the world" (Ephesians 1:4). Having done that, He provided them by His grace, or unmerited favor, the repentant faith for their newly-awakened souls to exercise in the Savior Christ. With this, they would be declared innocent of their sin, forgiven for it, and delivered into everlasting spiritual life and fellowship with God, in this life and the next.

While agreeing on man's need for salvation, Arminians generally believed he played some manner of efficacious role in his own deliverance. They also held that God had neither foreordained anyone to salvation or damnation; that, Arminians maintained, rested in the acceptance or rejection by each individual of the saving gospel of Christ. Many Arminians also believed a Christian, having once chosen and received salvation, could lose it by his own action.

Finney's own *Systematic Theology* reveals him as more in conflict with the tenants of Biblical Calvinism than the Arminians. Examined closely, his theology proves the mirror image of transcendentalism, albeit seasoned with more overt Christian terminology. He vehemently rejected the old Calvinism set forth in the 16th-century Reformation that recovered the doctrines upon which Protestant Christianity was founded. He argued that man was not basically sinful. He called the idea of total depravity—that every part of non-Christian man's being is tainted by sin—an anti-scriptural, nonsensical dogma.

"Tent Revival Meeting" reflects the extreme emotional fervor that swept the 19th-century religious camp meetings of Charles G. Finney and other revivalists.

He believed the purpose of Christ's death was to provide men with a stirring example to motivate them to live in obedience. He did not believe that it was necessary as a saving atonement for their sin. "How can another man die for your sin?" Finney asked. God's sacrifice, according to Finney was just to give a person an example. If the person could not be stirred by that example, according to Finney, he was hopeless. He viewed the Reformation doctrine held by Martin Luther and others of justification by faith—central to evangelical, orthodox Christianity—as an absurd heresy: "This error has slain more souls I fear than all the universalism that has ever cursed the world."

Not Miraculous

To Finney, Christianity was not miraculous at all. He writes in his *Systematic Theology:* "There is nothing in religion beyond the ordinary powers of nature. It consists entirely of the right exercise of the powers of nature. It is just that and nothing else. When mankind becomes truly religious, they are not enabled to put forth exertions which they were unable before to put forth; they only exert powers which they had before in a different way and use them for the glory of God." Thus, rather than providing a person with previously-unpossessed strength, Finney believed, Christianity was merely the moral teaching that tutors a person's mind and enables him to exert his own natural abilities in the right direction.

Finney saw no need for renewal in man. The Bible, though, describes all men as being dead in trespasses and sin; God, it says, gives His elect His Spirit to bring them to life and cause them to be born again. He then enables them to obey, love, and serve Him. So Finney viewed spiritual revival as a human-engineered matter wherein the preacher struck the proper emotional chords with his audience, and they did the right things. Again, Finney's own words: "A revival is not a miracle nor dependent on a miracle in any sense. It is purely the philosophical result of the right use of the constituted means."

To Finney, Christianity was not miraculous at all. It was merely the teaching that enabled a man to exert his own natural abilities in the right direction.

Charles G. Finney and Revivalism (1792-1875)

Both the abolitionist movement and later the Northern society that waged war against the South were powered with an engine rarely credited by historians for doing so—atheistic European rationalism. This potent philosophy collided with orthodox Christianity—in particular Calvinism—at nearly every point. For instance, rationalism fueled the Northern philosophical juggernauts of Deism and Unitarianism.

But it also meshed with surprising ease with the conservative reaction to the covenantal Calvinism upon which the first English colonies in America were founded. This was particularly true in "western" areas such as Kentucky. That conservative reaction, revivalistic Arminianism, was in truth an accommodation to rationalism as well, and ultimately a rejection of orthodox Christianity.

One of the foremost American theologian-historians of the later 20th century, the late C. Gregg Singer, said:

> *Even in those denominations which were historically evangelical and held strongly to a trinitarian theology, there were strong influences at work for the creation of a democratic theology, namely a theology which would modify such Calvinistic doctrines as the sovereignty of God and the total depravity of the race, in favor of a theology which would emphasize the love of God at the expense of His justice and holiness; which would insist that man was not totally depraved and could in some degree at least cooperate with God in the achievement of his own salvation and in the bringing about of the kingdom of heaven on earth.*

Singer highlights anew the unbiblical notions of mankind bringing about his own salvation, and through his own ability and effort reforming the society in which he lived. Such ideals had no greater nor more famous champion than Charles Grandison Finney.

Finney was Presbyterian, but in name only. At his ministerial ordination he admitted he had not even read the renowned Westminster Confession of Faith of the Presbyterian Church. Eventually, confronted by one of America's greatest theologians, Charles Hodge of Princeton Theological Seminary, as well as many other Old School (conservative) Presbyterian theologians, Finney departed officially from that church for the Congregationalist denomination.

Finney's theology was an evangelical reaction to Biblical orthodoxy and in fact nearly the mirror image of rationalism. He believed man was sinless at birth, with only a natural inclination to sin. When man by his own will exercises that will in repentance and faith, Finney believed, he becomes sinless. Thus, Finney and a whole generation of revivalistic preachers advocated a religious perfectionism of the same philosophical sort as the rationalism grown so dominant in New England and Europe.

Rejecting Orthodoxy

So rationalism, through both Christian and non-Christian philosophies, brought about the rejection of several pillars of Biblical distinctiveness. These pillars are elucidated in what is traditionally referred to as the theological system of Calvinism. Finney himself held to none of them.

The first pillar was the total and radical depravity of man. The Biblical theology of the rationalists' Puritan forefathers taught that man was incapable of doing anything good apart from the grace of God. But the new view held that man was the master of his own destiny and could shape himself. Not being slaves to sin as the Bible teaches, man was free to make his own choices and determine his spiritual destiny just as he chose his own philosophy of politics and economics.

In this fashion, frontier life influenced frontier theology; in the unsettled or barely-settled west, men depended of necessity on their own strength and ingenuity for nearly everything—food, water, medical treatment, education, and protection from natural elements, outlaws, and Indians. They succeeded or failed depending upon their will power and determination.

Convincing men who daily depended on their own wits for survival that they were totally depraved and could do nothing good proved a hard sell; their entire experience contradicted such a notion. A strong reaction developed against the Biblical notion of man's total depravity.

The second rejected pillar of orthodoxy was the sovereignty of God in man's salvation, as taught in Romans 8 and 9 and elsewhere in the Bible: man cannot save himself, but his salvation is a result of God's grace, sovereignly granted to him according to God's will. But this doctrine smacked of elitism in the minds of a frontier community who despised the notion of a God who Himself determined the destinies of men. They wanted their own destiny in their own hands. They did not cotton to the idea of someone—even Someone—else making this kind of choice for them.

The idea of an elect people chosen by God implied to the frontiersman that some people were better or had more privileges than others. In America, they said, nobody is better than anybody else, and a person becomes what he wants to be. If he pays the price, he can be anything he wants to be; man is the master of his own destiny. These beliefs left no room for a sovereign God, and increasing numbers of Americans rejected the idea.

The idea of an elect people chosen by God implied to the frontiersman that some people were better or had more privileges than others. In America, they said, nobody is better than anybody else. . . . If he pays the price, he can be anything he wants to be; man is the master of his own destiny.

Glory to Man

The next Biblical pillar rejected by Finney and others, and those under their influence, was the substitutionary atonement of Christ, His dying for His people, for those whom God the Father gave Him, as the Bible teaches. This concept proved most offensive of all to the rationalist. All men, they insisted, are equal. How could God make such a discrimination among men? It is not right, not democratic, and against the basic rights of men, they said. The hard truth is that the mentality of nearly the whole country was contrary to this pivotal doctrine, the atonement of Jesus Christ.

The fourth key distinctive rejected by Finney and most frontier people of faith was the irresistible or effectual grace of God. Again, the Bible teaches

"The Burned Over District," the area centered around western New York, that experienced some of the most passionate early-19th-century revivalism—and some of the most bitter aftermath.

that man's inability is counteracted by God's absolute sovereign grace, which comes and makes a man able to repent and believe. No man can believe in Christ apart from God's grace changing his nature, but God does in fact overcome man's enmity by that grace.

This teaching implies a person is helpless to save himself, that salvation is by grace, and that he is utterly dependent on God. Such doctrine offended revivalist preachers like Finney and many of the frontier types alike because it denied man's self-sufficiency and ability to accomplish what needs to be done for himself. They rejected anything that denied man's sovereignty.

Thus at every major point that makes the Biblical gospel distinct, where the Bible gives glory to God, Finney and Arminianism gave glory to man as the indisputable captain of his own soul.

A fifth pillar of the Biblical gospel, the perseverance (in faith and obedience) of the saints, was generally maintained by Finney and the Arminians—but not for the traditionally orthodox reason. They believed the saints persevered not because God did something for them or kept them in the faith, but because they, by the strength of their own will power, upheld themselves in faith.

Thus at every major point that makes the Biblical gospel distinct, where the Bible gives glory to God, Finney and Arminianism gave glory to man as the indisputable captain of his own soul. Calvinism therefore became the enemy of mankind and his best hopes.

Just one hundred years earlier, in the 1720s–1740s, one Arminian preacher had complained that no one would listen to a sermon unless Calvinism was being preached. Now in the 1820s–1840s, a 180-degree change had occurred in the country's theology, and most Americans had no desire to hear anyone preach the old Biblical doctrines of Calvinism.

Discarding Doctrines

This sea change in theology overwhelmed even denominations like the Presbyterians, Congregationalists, and Baptists who were marked by rock-ribbed orthodoxy. They too began to waver. What happened when these denominations arrived west on the frontier with the settlers? The Presbyterians became Cumberland Presbyterians, rejecting old doctrines of the faith. The Baptists, Calvinistic other than the General

Baptists, mostly gave up that Calvinism and became Arminians. The Congregationalists, who carried the legacy of Jonathan Edwards and others, did not even make it much farther than the Appalachian Mountains; when they did they also watered down their doctrine. In summary, every major Christian denomination in America experienced a widespread discarding of these foundational doctrines because they were no longer "popular" among the masses.

New England had been the lighthouse of American Biblical orthodoxy in the 17th and 18th centuries. But that locus had gradually shifted southward.

Lyman Beecher, father of Harriet Beecher Stowe, took the call to be minister of Hanover Street Church in Boston in 1826. In describing the spiritual state of the city at that time, Harriet said Calvinism or orthodoxy was the despised and persecuted form of the faith. It was the dethroned royal family, wandering like a permitted mendicant in the city where it had once held court, and Unitarianism reigned in its stead. Calvinism was despised, she said, and nearly everyone was a Unitarian.

New England had been the lighthouse of American Biblical orthodoxy in the 17th and 18th centuries. But that locus had gradually shifted southward. In the decades leading to the War, the North and West became increasingly radical and man-centered in their theology, while the South for the most part retained, and in some sections grew in its orthodoxy. The Calvinism that once dominated New England now centered in the South. The heirs to the Puritan vision that birthed Christian civilization in America were no longer the children of the Puritans; now they were the people of the South.

By 1830, there was as much difference between the South and the rest of the nation spiritually and theologically as there was economically and socially, and vast differences existed in those latter categories. Among their many accomplishments, Charles Finney and his fellow revivalists succeeded in popularizing the concept of abolitionism among some in both the evangelical and mainstream church circles. This was especially true in areas like western New York and Pennsylvania, and Ohio, who would not otherwise have been influenced by William Lloyd Garrison and his ilk. Indeed, theological differences became one of the great sources of the friction that led to war between North and South.

In the end, Finney and the Transcendentalists, while taking different roads, arrived at the same conclusion, that a person's highest priority in life should be to exert all his powers to bring about social reform. That, both believed, was how salvation came to the world. Even many professing believers within the evangelical tradition, particularly in the North and West, began to view the Church as an engine to bring about social reform, not declare salvation and teach the people how that salvation is to be worked out.

10 Religion and Worldview II

Abraham Lincoln, before the beard and before the Presidency. (Library of Congress)

Evolution is God's way of doing things.
—19th century Northern philosopher and theologian John Fiske

Orthodox Christians, particularly in the South, did not deny the social ramifications of the gospel. They declared that as a person was transformed into a new creature and set into a new spiritual kingdom under a new Lord with a new Word governing his life, he was going to live differently in every area. Thus, they expected from Christians different kinds of businesses, politics, art, and medicine, sanctified with the selfless and God-glorifying attitudes and principles of Jesus Christ. They expected the influence of the gospel to flow everywhere, but they insisted the root cause of that spread is the changed man.

Many in the North believed the Christian men of the South needed more changing yet. They did not consider such resolutions as the Southern Presbyterian Church's in 1864 any Christian blessing to blacks. That resolution said, "We hesitate not to affirm that it is the particular mission of the Southern Church to conserve the institution of slavery and to make it a blessing both to master and slave."

Author and black abolitionist Frederick Douglass, himself not yet a Christian, thundered: "What I have said respecting and against religion, I mean strictly to apply to the slaveholding religion of this land, and with no possible reference to Christianity proper; for, between the Christianity of the land, and the Christianity of Christ, I recognize the widest possible difference—so wide, that to receive the one as good, pure, and holy, is of necessity to reject the other as bad, corrupt, and wicked. To be the friend of the one, is of necessity to be the enemy of the other." A large proportion of the Southern people may have declared their allegiance to Christianity, but in the minds of some in the North, that allegiance failed to substitute for what the critics claimed was a failure to practice the principles of Christianity itself.

A camp meeting during the Second Great Awakening, replete with tents, pulpit box, and a sprawling crowd in the expanses of the American outdoors.

Second Great Awakening

The Charles Finney phenomenon (Chapter 9) occurred in the midst of one of America's greatest religious revivals, the Second Great Awakening. That historic event flowed through two separate currents. One, prominent in its early stages, roughly 1800–1830, particularly in the Northeast, was orthodox. Faithful men of God led that revival. Finney's man-centered revivalism, which dominated the Midwest from around 1830 on, embodied the other. His influence particularly impacted the North.

In the South, the true revival continued. In fact, it continued all the way through the War. A different sort of men led the revival in the South theologically. They included Daniel Baker, James Henley Thornwell, Benjamin Morgan Palmer, Robert Lewis Dabney, John Holt Rice, Thomas Peck, and Moses Drury Hoge. Many of these were men of great theological, intellectual, and moral stature. They were orthodox and Reformed in their theological perspective. And their instruction had a powerful impact on the South.

When these Southerners denounced Finney, some of the Northern theological conservatives joined them. But in the latter part of the Second Great Awakening, most of the Northern conservatives were swept away in the tidal wave of theologically apostate Finneyism. Some of them ended up supporting Finney, including famed New York City pastor Henry Ward Beecher. The harvest of these developments proved profound. For instance, Beecher's daughter joined the radical abolition movement, and Harriet Beecher Stowe's book *Uncle Tom's Cabin* provided an emotional spark that Abraham Lincoln himself credited with helping cause the War. Also, many social reformers, including abolitionists, temperance activists, and women's voting rights proponents, used Finney's revival techniques for their own crusades.

Whereas Finney viewed revival as thoroughly man-centered in its establishment, the South as a whole considered it thoroughly supernatural. As the mass of New England Puritans once had, Southerners considered revival the gift of God, something unable to be scheduled by man and given only by God, to be thankfully received by men who were seeking Him for His mercies.

Different Worldviews

The conflict between these beliefs was no intramural theological squabble among like-minded Christians. It represented two different worldviews. Their contrasting perspectives influenced not only their adherents' view of religious revival, but of everything else as well. The conflict between these worldviews changed the essence and history of the nation and shook the destiny of the entire world.

In the 19th century, the evangelical movement became increasingly identified with political causes from abolition of slavery and child labor legislation to women's rights and the prohibition of alcohol.

Of course, theological radicals also populated the South, just as orthodox Bible-believers lived in the North. And great American theologians lived in the North, such as Charles Hodge and others at Princeton Seminary and George Junkin, father-in-law of future Confederate General Stonewall Jackson.

Contemporary American theologian Michael Horton has offered his own analysis of the significance of the religious phenomenon embodied by Finney:

> Finney's moralistic impulse envisioned a church that was in large measure an agency of personal and social reform rather than an institution in which the means of grace, the Word, and sacraments are made available to believers who then take the gospel to the world. In the nineteenth century, the evangelical movement became increasingly identified with political causes from

Charles Hodge (1797-1878)

One of the greatest theologians in American history, Charles Hodge's theology stood far apart from that of Abraham Lincoln. Yet, his views on politics and the War paralleled Lincoln's rather than the famed Southern Calvinists whose theological views he mirrored. Hodge gained renown as a systematic theologian for over half a century at Princeton, the preeminent seminary of 19th-century America. He towered over the theological landscape as he battled New School progressives in his own and other denominations, theistic evolutionists and other Christian clergy who embraced varying degrees of Darwinian evolution, and all manner of other unorthodox American clergy.

He wrote many books and articles defending the truths of Christianity, including Biblical inerrancy. His *Systematic Theology* stands out even today in the corpus of great doctrinal works studied by orthodox clergy and laymen. Hodge's fame grew during his decades-long battles with Nathaniel Taylor, the Congregationalist leader whose theology reflected much of mainstream Northern clergymen of the day. Taylor, like Finney, argued against the orthodox Christian doctrine of original sin, posited that people could "suspend" their sinful motives—and claimed that spiritual regeneration occurred when they did so—and denied that Christ's death successfully atoned for the sin of others.

Author and theologian David F. Wells describes Hodge's thundering rebuttals:

> *If we are not 'in' Adam, Hodge argued, then we cannot be 'in' Christ, for the way we relate to the one is paralleled in scripture by the way we related to the other. God appointed Adam as the federal head of those whom he represented. The new humanity is not numerically equivalent, however, to the whole of fallen humanity and therefore Christ in his death vicariously suffered in the place only of those whom he represented, which were the elect.*

Hodge also famously confronted Charles Finney and he spearheaded Finney's leaving the Presbyterian church. A member of the Whig Party until 1856, Hodge voted that year for John "The Pathfinder" Fremont, first Republican candidate for President. In 1860 and 1864, he voted for Lincoln, also a Republican.

abolition of slavery and child labor legislation to women's rights and the prohibition of alcohol.

So the Unitarians and Transcendentalists of the North meshed comfortably with the new evangelicals in the North and West. No longer were they enemies with these professing Christians. The faith of the latter drove them to seek reform. Thus was the Puritan vision of applying the gospel to all areas of life—of seeing men's lives as well as the world conformed to the will of God—applied to the man-centered gospel of human perfectibility.

Anti-Slavery

Like Lincoln, Hodge had never declared slaveholding as necessarily a sin, and stood anti-slavery rather than abolitionist at the War's outset. Also like Lincoln, he came to embrace the latter position as a requisite war objective: "This war touches the conscience in too many points to render silence on the part of religious men either allowable or possible." As pointed out by Allen C. Guelzo, however, in *Abraham Lincoln, Redeemer President*, Hodge resisted the popular notion that God necessarily rewarded battlefield victories with his favor and defeats with his wrath and judgment. "Do not the Scriptures and all experience teach us," he wrote, "that God is a sovereign, that the orderings of his providence are not determined by justice, but by mysterious wisdom?"

Like Lincoln, Hodge had never declared slaveholding as necessarily a sin, and stood anti-slavery rather than abolitionist at the War's outset. Also like Lincoln, he came to embrace the latter position as a requisite war objective.

Later in the War, his opinion having crystallized, he wrote that sometimes "political questions rise into the sphere of morals and religion; when the rule for political action is not to be sought in the consideration of state policy, but the law of God." Unlike Lincoln, however, Hodge saw in God's mighty, though sometimes painful, works, not only judgment but redemption: "God not only sees the end from the beginning, but an infinitely wise, good, and powerful God is everywhere present, controlling all events great and small . . . so that everything is ordered by his will and is made to subserve his wise and benevolent designs."

Most orthodox Christians would, however, lament his views on the crucial Biblical doctrine of creation. Rather than espousing the traditional orthodox belief that God created the world in six 24-hour days, each comprised of "morning and evening," Hodge rejected that plain meaning of Genesis. He cited alleged geological facts, which actually constituted the uniformitarian interpretation of data. The American Heritage Dictionary defines "uniformitarian" as "the theory that all geological phenomena may be explained as the result of existing forces having operated uniformly from the origin of the earth to the present time."

Orthodox Christianity can agree that geological evidence, if interpreted by normative (uniformitarian) standards, suggests a millions of years-long life for the earth; however, Christians have long considered "catastrophism" a stronger explanation than uniformitarianism for this phenomenon. Catastrophism posits that a great catastrophic event or series of events interrupted the earth's usual uniformitarian process. That event, occurring in harmony with the Genesis account of the Flood (and flood stories believed by other early civilizations such as the Babylonians), caused a chain of events in a short period of time that would normally take much longer to occur. Thus, catastrophism says, voluminous layers of sediment in the earth, and the various fossils widely separated by them, would indeed normally indicate the passage of perhaps millions of years of time. But under the catastrophic theory, with events expedited, the layers and fossils settled into their places in a much shorter period of time, likely thousands rather than millions of years.

Unlike Lincoln, Hodge saw in God and His mighty, though sometimes painful, works, not only judgment but redemption.

Hodge's position on this issue is all the more surprising because he battled evolutionists, even theistic evolutionists among Christian clergy, with vigor and passion. "What is Darwinism?" he asked. "It is atheism." Plus, he famously defended Biblical inerrancy, or the complete lack of error in the writings of Scripture; the principle of inerrancy seemed to cause even Hodge himself to question his position on the creation issue: "It is of course admitted that, taking this account [Genesis] by itself, it would be most natural to understand the word [day] in its ordinary sense; but if that sense brings the Mosaic account into conflict with facts [millions of years], and another sense avoids such conflict, then it is obligatory on us to adopt that other."

Such was the fruit of the ascendance of Charles Darwin's teachings and evolutionary theory, among even those who disdained him and them. Nonetheless, Charles Hodge, loyal Unionist to the end, endures as one of the great American champions of the Christian faith.

In the year 1826, the Scotch philanthropist Robert Owen founded New Harmony on the Wabash River in southern Indiana. Down the Ohio and up the Wabash came a Boatload of Knowledge—scientists, artists, and educators imported from the East and from overseas to found a New Moral World in the western wilderness. People were invited to come and join a paradise regained by innate human goodness. The noble experiment lasted two years and collapsed in the usual picturesque wreckage of innate human selfishness and inefficiency.

—Ross Lockridge, Jr.
Raintree County, 1948

Finney's Offspring

The upshot of this sea change in American religion can hardly be overstated. Foremost among the many movements it produced were communism and socialism. These were no European or Asian phenomena. They blossomed into fruition in America. Karl Marx was a seven-year-old school child in Germany when the first communist experiment, Robert Owen's New Harmony, Indiana, began in this country. Many other similar—and similarly unsuccessful—experiments in utopian communal living followed Owen's. They included Brook Farm, where Emerson, Thoreau, and Hawthorne all stayed, in West Roxbury, Massachusetts, and Fruitlands, founded by Bronson Alcott, father of Louisa May Alcott, the famed novelist who wrote *Little Women*.

Owen pointed the finger of blame for New Harmony's failure straight at one target:

> The problem is Christian education. We can get people trained in other ways of thinking, then New Harmony will succeed. It will be discovered that the religion of the world, Christianity, is the soul cause of all the disunion, hatred, uncharitableness, and crime which pervaded the population of the earth.

Owen's son, Robert Dale Owen, issued his own credo:

> I believe in a national system of equal, Republican, protected, practical education, the soul regenerator of a profligate age, the only redeemer of our suffering country from the equal curses of chilling poverty and corrupting riches, of gnawing want and destroying debauchery, of blind ignorance and of unprincipled intrigue.

Indeed, it was not German or Russian Marxists who first exported revolution to the world. Americans did. And their actions were rooted in their theological apostasy. The peace movement, the prison movement, the public school movement, and the abolition movement were all rooted and manned by a diversified cadre that included sincere people and sinister revolutionaries alike. This they had in common: it was not the old Puritanism of the early American colonists that drove any of them, but rather the new theology of progress and faith in man.

The upshot of this sea change in American religion can hardly be overstated. Foremost in the many movements it produced were communism and socialism. These were no European or Asian phenomena. They blosomed into fruition in America.

The chief opposition to these unconstitutional movements came from the South. Concurrently, progressives in other parts of the country viewed the South as anti-progress, anti-modern-

"Owen's Proposed Village," Robert Owen's master plan for his New Harmony, IN, utopian community.

ization, and reactionary; as backward, ignorant, and old-fashioned. The term "Bible Belt" was berthed and it was not intended as a compliment.

It will be discovered that the religion of the world, Christianity, is the soul cause of all the disunion, hatred, uncharitableness, and crime which pervaded the population of the earth.

—Robert Owen
Founder of the New Harmony commune

Again, the variant political perspectives of the respective regions were rooted in their prevailing theology. The strict Calvinism and Biblical covenantalism of the South strongly influenced its political view, that government is to be accountable to and strictly limited under the Constitution, itself under the authority of God. Such a philosophy is a covenantal view of government, with covenant defined as a binding compact between two or more human parties and God (see Chapter 2). Meanwhile, the radicalization of its theology had largely driven the North away from such convictions.

Not Infallible

The way a person views the Bible, the Christian's covenant document, affects how he views the Constitution, the nation's civil document. Most Southerners wanted to treat the Constitution the same way they treated the Bible. They followed the practice of "strict construction" as they sought to understand its meaning. That is, they attempted to figure out what the framers' words meant, so as not to depart from that intent.

The political majority in the North, meanwhile, no longer believed the Bible to be infallible. They interpreted it not strictly but loosely, to fit modern circumstances. If the Bible is not infallible, then how authoritative could be the Founding Fathers' Constitution? Thus they also desired the latitude to adapt—their opponents would have said destroy—the received interpretation of the framers' intentions. This new majority did so in accord with a society they believed after nearly a century had changed in ways the framers did not anticipate.

As the North (and West) laid aside covenantally based Calvinism, then, they discarded their covenantal view of government as well. With God no longer sovereign in their mind, the civil magistrates—increasingly those on the Federal level—were depended upon to take His place. Differences over a constellation of issues—and the resulting antagonism—mounted between the sections as their most fundamental beliefs about God and man grew farther apart. The North, and eventually the West, came to view the South as the obstacle to their manifest destiny of sovereign industrial might, social reform, and continental conquest. The South in turn viewed the other sections as forcing upon it a society very different from that envisioned by the Founders and alien to many of its fundamental beliefs.

Overthrowing a Dynasty

Amidst this widening chasm between worldviews, Abraham Lincoln delivered his famous "House Divided" speech to the Illinois Republican Convention in 1858. This brilliantly constructed oration brims over with phrases and slogans still familiar in the 21st century, especially the Biblically inspired "house divided against itself" phrase. Nonetheless, the most important fact about this remarkable speech is the worldview it conveys, a worldview very different from that in the South.

Honorable and unsavory people alike populated every corner of the country before the War, as they do now. No section could claim a monopoly on either. What could be posited to them were prevailing worldviews. For instance, the way Lincoln—and the majority of Northerners—understood the world stood far from the old foundational worldview of Christendom. They were much more attuned to the Enlightenment ideology of nationalism. The "House Divided" speech illustrates this:

> A house divided against itself cannot stand. I believe this government cannot endure permanently half-slave and half-free. I do not expect the Union to be dissolved. I do not expect the house to fall. But I do expect that it will cease to be divided. It will become all one thing or all the other.

Up to this time, the government of the United States was construed to be a series of individually sovereign but confederated states. They did not see themselves as being one thing. But now Lincoln assumed they were one thing and that the issue of slavery was dividing them. He said the states comprised but one house and that its division would toll its fall. Such notions were novel among the American populace when Lincoln spoke them. They sprouted up from the principles of nationalism.

Lincoln continued regarding slavery, but also the constitutionally based political system under which it continued:

> To meet and overthrow the power of dynasty is the work now before all those who would prevent that consummation.

Thus did Lincoln speak of a cultural "dynasty" existing back to the founding of the United States and before, which he said included slavery and which he, crucially, did not therein say included a variety of other cultural, religious, and constitutional issues. He exhorted all those who desired to resist the continuing influence of this dynasty to make war against it and overthrow it. He implicitly exhorted the destruction, not just of American slavery, but of millions of Americans' societal fabric by that of others.

Lincoln complained that his senatorial opponent Stephen Douglas had little quarrel with fellow Democrat and President James Buchanan, whom Lincoln portrayed as the current head of the old dynasty. He faulted Douglas for his embracing it.

"New Harmony on the Wabash," Karl Bodmer's idyllic portrait of the utopian, Christless Indiana community in 1832.

Lincoln Leads

Why, then, were the Southerners so concerned about Lincoln that they gave him no electoral votes at all in the 1860 Presidential election, then pulled their states out of the Union when he won that election? After all, had he not promised, even in his inaugural address, to leave Southern institutions alone and in particular not to do away with slavery, saying it was not expeditious to do so?

Some Southerners feared Lincoln would curb the expansion of slavery to the western territories and states. This they believed would shift the balance of national political power farther away from the South than they believed it already was. The larger issue for most Southerners, however, was their belief that Lincoln wished the overthrow of that old world order, if necessary in the violent manner attempted with the many European revolutions of 1848—revolutions of which Southerners believed Lincoln was a committed heir. Those revolutions sought to usher in a radical change in the nature of society.

Lincoln left no doubt that a cause existed to prosecute, saying, "Our cause, then, must be entrusted to and conducted by its own undoubted friends." Thus the man who declared that a house divided against itself cannot stand now called, in effect, for his fellow partisans to gather round, and said they had a war on their hands, a war they must fight to the end. And not all Americans, but only trusted friends should answer the call.

In 1858, three years before armed hostilities broke out, Lincoln had identified not only friends "Those whose hands are free, whose hearts are in the work, who do care for the results . . ." but enemies:

> Two years ago the Republicans of the nation mustered over thirteen hundred thousand strong. We did this under the single impulse of resistance to a common danger with every external circumstance against us. Of strange, discordant, and even hostile elements we gathered from the four winds and formed and fought the battle though under the constant hot fire of a disciplined, proud, and pampered enemy.

What was the "common danger"? It could only be the Christian worldview. What should be done with the "enemy" who perpetuated that worldview? Overthrow that enemy and change the very nature of the society it animated. Lincoln concluded:

> Did we brave all then to falter now? Now, when the same enemy is wavering, dissevered, and belligerent? The result is not doubtful. We shall not fail. If we stand firm, we shall not fail.

> Wise counsels may accelerate or mistakes delay it, but sooner or later the victory is sure to come.

Old Worldview

The other signal conception of the mid-19th-century American political and cultural arena was articulated three years later, as the Southern states seceded and on the eve of battle, by new Confederate President Jefferson Davis. The modern reader need not endorse Davis' political objectives to recognize how different than Lincoln were the language, tone, and cultural concerns he offered in his inaugural address:

> Fellow citizens, on this the birthday of the man most identified with the establishment of American independence [George Washington], beneath the monument erected to commemorate his heroic virtues and those of his compatriots, we have assembled together to usher into existence the permanent government of the Confederate States. Through this instrumentality, under the favor of Divine Providence, we hope to perpetuate the principles of our revolutionary fathers. The day, the memory, and the purpose seem fitly associated.
>
> It is with mingled feelings of humility and pride that I appear to take in the presence of the people and before High Heaven the oath prescribed as a qualification for the exalted station to which the unanimous voice of the people has called me. Deeply sensible of all that is implied by this manifestation of the people's confidence, I am yet more profoundly impressed by the vast responsibility of the office and humbly feel my own unworthiness.
>
> The purity of an unbridled majority, the most odious and least responsible form of despotism, has denied us both the rights and remedy. Therefore, we are in arms to renew such sacrifices as our fathers made to the holy cause of constitutional liberty. At the darkest hour of our struggle, the provisional gives place to the permanent government.
>
> I deeply feel the weight of the responsibilities that I now, with unaffected diffidence, am about to assume; and fully realizing the inequality of human power to guide and sustain, my hope is reverently fixed on Him whose favor is ever vouchsafed to the cause which is just. With humble gratitude and adoration acknowledging the Providence which has so visibly protected the Confederacy during its brief but eventful career, to Thee our God I trustingly commit myself and prayerfully invoke Thy blessing on my country and its cause.

The larger issue for most Southerners, however, was their belief that Lincoln wished the overthrow of that old world order, if necessary in the violent manner attempted with the many European revolutions of 1848—revolutions to the spirit of which Southerners believed Lincoln was a committed heir.

Thus Davis, rather than seeking their overthrow, celebrated the principles of the Founding Fathers and reaffirmed the old world order out of which these principles grew. The contrast between Lincoln and Davis in these and others of their speeches and writings is stark. Lincoln's thinking was shot through with implicit, and often explicit, images of division, strife, and conflict. Humility and supplication before Divine Providence seasoned Davis' expressions.

A vast chasm existed between these worldviews. The South generally believed in the old traditions of Christendom and self determination, the North to the newer ones of the Enlightenment and nationalism. These differences provided the provocation to war between the sectional rivals. In the North, the Radical Republicans and their associates, including Lincoln, committed themselves to accomplishing what the revolutionaries in 1848 failed to accomplish—the destruction of the old worldview of George Washington and the Founding Fathers.

Radical

Literally, going to the root or origin of the problem. Radical change, then, is change that alters customs, traditions, laws, and constitutions. The [political] Radicals during Reconstruction advocated such changes in the South.

Worldviews and War

Initial events in the War demonstrate this chasm. The early battles occurred in the South, which had no interest in war or invading the North, much less conquering its government. The North, meanwhile, believed the South was in rebellion and, despite Lincoln's expressed desire for self determination and democracy in America, had to be invaded, forced to change many of its societal beliefs and philosophies, and grafted back into the nation.

Even the first shots of the War fired by the South at Fort Sumter were apparently provoked as part of a brilliant strategy by Lincoln and his cabinet both to further their nationalistic aspirations by war and to maneuver the South into starting the conflict, thus rallying the heretofore apathetic Northern people to the colors. By early 1861, the previous Federal Presidential administration of Pennsylvanian James Buchanan had agreed to evacuate all Federal forts in the South. One exception was Fort Pickens at Pensacola, where the U.S. commander and the state forces made a peaceful agreement of mutual non-aggression, pending a political settlement.

Another was Fort Sumter, an island in Charleston Harbor, in South Carolina. There, in early April, 1861, Confederates commanded by General Pierre Beauregard requested the Federal garrison holding the fort to evacuate it. Lincoln still considered Sumter Federal property and believed it his duty to preserve control of it and collect the tariffs generated by it.

The Confederates, meanwhile, recalled that Southern tax money had financed the fort's construction for the purpose of defending the city, in accordance with the obligation of the Federal government under the Constitution. They did not intend to allow the fort to be used as a base to attack them, to illegally blockade their port, and to extort taxes from them.

Now, however, President Lincoln ordered the Federal troops to maintain possession of, rather than evacuate, the fort—while he sent thousands of reinforcements south to them. Was he delivering soldiers surrounded in a hostile territory from starvation? Not only did the Federals have a large stockpile of food and supplies, but Beauregard urged them to leave in peace. And every day during the standoff, he sent supply ships with additional food to feed the garrison.

Toombs's Plea

When Lincoln's initial reinforcement ships arrived, the Confederates did not fire on them, but rather intercepted them and ordered them to return north. Then Beauregard repeated his plea to Fort Sumter commander Robert Anderson that he depart with his garrison. Beauregard promised to let all the Federals go and told Anderson they could keep their weapons. As far as the Louisiana native was concerned, the two sides were at peace.

Anderson refused, whereupon the Confederate government, fearful Beauregard could not ward off the approaching Federal relief squadron that could then continue to bottle up the port of Charleston or attack it, or both, sought to preempt that specter by ordering him to commence a bombardment of the fort. Some Southern leaders, including President Davis's second-in-command, Secretary of State Robert Toombs of Georgia, recognized the folly of firing first, which belied some of the very principles upon which the Confederacy was founded.

Toombs, an arch-secessionist, pled:

> The firing on that fort will inaugurate a civil war greater than any the world has ever seen. Mr. President, it is suicide, it is murder, and will lose us every friend at the North. You will wantonly strike a hornet's nest which extends from mountains to ocean; and legions, now quiet, will swarm out and sting us to death. It is unnecessary, it puts us in the wrong. It is fatal.

How prescient Toombs proved to be. But Davis thought otherwise at the time, and the deed was done.

Beauregard then sent evacuation ships to the fort and again urged Anderson to depart in peace. Once more, Anderson said no. Beauregard realized the Federals would never leave, and the real battle began. The next day, April 13, Lincoln issued a declaration of rebellion that called for immediate conscripts—75,000 of them—from every state in the Union, including the Southern ones. He ordered them to reinforce the Federal army and invade the South.

The North, meanwhile, believed the South was in rebellion and, despite Lincoln's expressed desire for self determination and democracy in America, had to be invaded, forced to change many of its societal beliefs and philosophies, and grafted back into the nation.

Was Lincoln surprised or angered by the shelling of Fort Sumter? His own words written on May 1 to Gustavus Fox, organizer of the Federal relief effort for Fort Sumter, answer that question:

> You and I both anticipated that the cause of the country would be advanced by making the attempt to provision Ft. Sumter, even if it should fail; and it is no small consolation now to feel that our anticipation is justified by the result.

In July, O. H. Browning recorded in his diary that his close friend Lincoln told him that he himself:

> . . . conceived the idea, and proposed sending supplies without an attempt to reinforce, giving notice of the fact to Gov. Pickens of South Carolina. The plan succeeded. They attacked Sumter—it fell, and thus, did more service than it otherwise could.

The firing on that fort will inaugurate a civil war greater than any the world has ever seen. Mr. President, it is suicide, it is murder, and will lose us every friend at the North. You will wantonly strike a hornet's nest which extends from mountains to ocean; and legions, now quiet, will swarm out and sting us to death. It is unnecessary, it puts us in the wrong. It is fatal.

—Robert Toombs to Jefferson Davis, April, 1861

Robert Toombs (1810-1885)

One of the most influential Americans of the Nineteenth Century, Robert Toombs provided nearly half a century of statesmanship to his native Georgia, the Confederacy, and the United States. Born near the town of Washington in Wilkes County, Toombs's energy, fire, and intellect marked him early for leadership. He entered the University of Georgia at age fourteen, but left following a "conduct unbecoming" incident related to a card game. He eventually graduated from Union College in Schenectady, New York, and the University of Virginia Law School.

Toombs earned admission to the bar in 1830, then, between 1838 and 1861, served five years in the Georgia legislature, eight in the U.S. Congress, and eight more in the U.S. Senate. The latter stint ended only with the outbreak of the War. A slaveholder and a champion for his state, he nonetheless worked tirelessly to preserve the Union. He evidenced this on many issues, including his opposition to Southern "fire-eater" secession advocates at the time of the 1850 Fugitive Slave Law; his bill (supported by many free state and slave state advocates alike) calling for a constitutional convention in Kansas to discuss statehood and slavery; and his opposition to annexing Texas and waging the Mexican War, both of which were supported by many Southerners.

By the end of the 1850s, however, Toombs's longheld optimism regarding the preservation of the American Union had vanished. "Show me the nation in the world that hates, despises, villifies, or plunders us like our abolition 'brethren' in the

North," he thundered upon calling for Georgia to secede in March, 1861.

> *". . . here alone am I stigmatized as a felon; here alone am I an outlaw; here alone am I under the ban of the empire; here alone I have neither security nor tranquillity; here alone are organized governments ready to protect the incendiary, the assassin who burns my dwelling or takes my life or those of my wife and children; here alone are hired emissaries paid by brethren to glide through the domestic circle and intrigue insurrection with all of its nameless horrors.*

One of the consequences of Toombs's audacious brilliance was a hot-tempered independence that sometimes caused him difficulty in following authority with which he did not agree. Failing to win the presidency of the fledgling Confederate States in 1861 as he had hoped, he nonetheless gained the high position of Secretary of State when chosen by President Davis. However, he resigned the position within a few months and secured a brigadier-generalship in the field. There, he gained some prestige for his leadership, particularly for a famous stand against Ambrose Burnside's much-larger force on a bridge at the Battle of Sharpsburg, which may have saved Robert E. Lee's Amy of Northern Virginia. Soon, however, he resigned his commission after being passed over for a promotion. He next helped lead the Georgia militia, including in its tenacious, but hopeless 1864 defense of Atlanta.

One of Toombs's many poignant extant letters to his wife Julia reveals that he did not share the tee totaling practices of other Confederate leaders: "We have plenty of jugs & bottles, but they are nearly always empty, We are something like Indians when we have the good luck to get a gallon of whiskey, all hands join & drink it up, & then do without until the next piece of good luck turns up & we get another. I (wish for) you to send me a box of wine by Brewer."

Toombs narrowly escaped capture by the Federals

Robert Toombs's home today.

at war's end. He hid out for awhile, then spent the next two years exiled in Cuba and Europe. In one of his heartfelt letters to Julia near the end of that time, he discusses the upcoming "long journey of five thousand miles from here to Havana & do not know that I shall meet a human being to whom I am known. But if I keep well I shall not mind that especially as I am homeward bound, for altho my hearth Stone is desolate, & clouds & darkness hover over the little remnant that is left of us, and upon all of our poor friends & country men, yet when you get home Washington will contain nearly all that is dear to me in this world."

Toombs returned to Georgia in 1867, and resumed his practice of law, as well as his place of high social and political leadership. Southerners had many reasons to respect him, not least his failure ever to seek a pardon from the Federal government that would have allowed him to regain his United States citizenship. Demonstrating his legendary skills of leadership and political acumen, the old lion dominated the convention that crafted Georgia's new constitution after the end of Reconstruction in 1877.

Tragedy struck in 1883, however, when Julia—his sweetheart since childhood—and former Confederate Vice President Alexander Stephens, his lifelong close friend, died within a few months of one another. Toombs never really recovered from these blows, and he passed away a few days before Christmas in 1885.

Worldviews and Strategy

At this point only the states of South Carolina, Louisiana, Mississippi, Florida, Alabama, Georgia, and Texas had seceded from the United States. As soon as Lincoln proclaimed them in rebellion and mustered an army to attack the departed states, Arkansas, North Carolina, Tennessee, and Virginia all seceded. And the legislatures of Maryland, Delaware, Missouri, and Kentucky met. Those states, too, appeared headed for secession.

The Methodist Church in Maryland . . . voted to send a rebuke to the Federal government for "unconstitutional and unlawful actions denying civil liberties of citizens." So Lincoln sent more troops and confiscated all Methodist Church properties in Maryland where the pastors would not swear an oath of allegiance to the government in Washington . . . he repeated this singular act in Delaware, Missouri, and Kentucky.

In a move with no Constitutional basis or precedent in all of American history, Lincoln sent armies to all these states to arrest their governors and legislators. These elected representatives of their people found themselves arrested and hauled to Federal prisons, or having to escape such action, for the crime of gathering in their state capitols and exercising their sworn duties as representatives of the people to vote on an issue.

Maryland was strongly pro-Southern and oriented to the Southern culture, despite the fact most of its slaves had been set free. At the time Lincoln initiated his campaign of forcible compliance on the state, a bill was in fact on the floor of the Maryland legislature to emancipate the state's remaining slaves. The state's newspapers were pro-South as well. So Lincoln shut them all down and threw their editors into Federal prison, suspending the ancient Western right to the writ of habeas corpus in doing so.

The Methodist Church in Maryland then gathered and voted to send a rebuke to the Federal government for "unconstitutional and unlawful actions denying civil liberties of citizens." So Lincoln sent more troops and confiscated all Methodist Church properties in Maryland where the pastors would not swear an oath of allegiance to the government in Washington. Lincoln repeated these singular campaigns in Delaware, Missouri, and Kentucky.

The variant worldviews evidenced themselves again three months later at the First Battle of Manassas, or Bull Run, the first large-scale slaughter of the War. There, on July 21, 1861, Lincoln sent tens of thousands of Federal troops into Northern Virginia in hopes of fighting one decisive battle that would end what the North considered a treasonous rebellion. The South, defending its own soil against what it considered a violent and aggressive foreign invader, won a thunderous and stunning victory and sent the frantic Federals fleeing in headlong retreat back toward their capital, Washington. Indeed, no Federal armies stood between the victorious Confederates and the White House, with Washington just over twenty miles away.

President Davis, arrived on the field

of battle, decided against the pleas of officers who wished permission to carry the fight across the Potomac River to the capital and secure Southern independence. Tactical and operational considerations figured into his decision, but superseding these was one both strategic and philosophical—the South did not wish to invade or conquer anyone; it wished only to be left alone to go its own way. Never again would the Confederacy have so good a chance to capture the seat of United States power—or secure its own independence.

In the End

Long after the onset of war, Jefferson Davis reiterated the aversion he and most Southerners held for it, and their desire for the principles for which their independence-seeking forefathers fought. But he believed the object of their hopes was gone, swept away in the Enlightenment-fueled march toward nationalism. Now he saw no choice but to protect and defend those foundations for the posterity of his people:

> The confidence of the most hopeful among us must have been destroyed by the disregard they (Lincoln and the Federals) have recently exhibited for all the time-honored bulwarks of civil and religious liberty. Bastilles were filled with prisoners, arrested without civil process or indictment duly-found; the writ of habeas corpus, suspended by executive mandate; a state legislature controlled by the imprisonment of members whose avowed principles suggested to the federal executive that there might be another added to the list of seceded states; elections, held under the threat of military power.
>
> Civil officers, peaceful citizens, and gentlewomen incarcerated for opinion's sake proclaimed the incapacity of our late associates to administer a government as free, liberal, and humane as that established for our common use.

Long after the onset of war, Jefferson Davis reiterated the aversion he and most Southerners held for it, and their desire for the principles for which their independence-seeking forefathers fought. But he believed the object of their hopes was gone, swept away in the Enlightenment-fueled march toward nationalism.

The War which came about pitted the advocates of the old Union against the proponents of a new nation. In many ways the conflict continues today, though in different guises. It is ongoing not because the War officially goes on, but because the issues which provoked it remain. It was a war of two antagonistic faiths between which, in the end, there was no possibility for compromise.

Stonewall Jackson on the Effects of Religion

In his book *Life and Campaigns of Lt. General T. J. "Stonewall" Jackson*, (still in print nearly a century-and-a-half after its publication), theologian Robert L. Dabney argues that the outworking of Christian faith in social interaction is crucial for the believer. Dabney quotes fellow Virginian, Confederate soldier, and Presbyterian Jackson as voicing these words in his final hours of life:

> *The Christian should carry his religion into everything. Christianity makes man better in any lawful calling; it equally makes the general a better commander, and the shoemaker a better mechanic. In the case of the cobbler, or the tailor, for instance, religion will produce more care in promising work, more punctuality, and more fidelity in executing it, from conscientious motives . . .*

> *So, prayer aids any man, in any lawful business, not only by bringing down the divine blessing, which is its direct and prime object, but by harmonizing his own mind and heart. In the commander (Jackson himself) of an army at the critical hour, it calmed his perplexities, moderated his anxieties, steadied the scales of judgment, and thus preserved him from exaggerated and rash conclusions . . .*

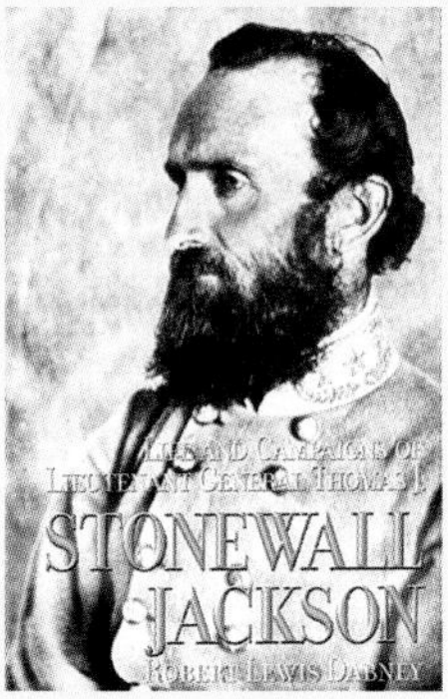

Jackson, recalled Dabney, urged that every act of a man's life should be a religious act. "He recited with much pleasure," Dabney wrote, "the ideas of Doddridge, where he pictured himself as spiritualizing every act of his daily life; as thinking when he washed himself, of the cleansing blood of Calvary; as praying while he put on his garments, that he might be clothed with the righteousness of the saints; as endeavoring, while he was eating, to feed upon the Bread of Heaven.

11 Final Hours

The new national capitol building, still under construction in Washington City (D.C.), 1860.

When a long train of abuses and usurpations, pursuing invariably the same object, evinces a design to reduce (the people) under absolute despotism, it is their right, it is their duty, to throw off such government and to provide new guards for their future security.

—The Declaration of Independence

When Lincoln reinforced Sumter and called for 75,000 men without the consent of Congress, it was the greatest breech ever made in the Constitution, and would hereafter give the President the liberty to declare war whenever he wished, without the consent of Congress.

—Republican Senator Charles Sumner of Massachusetts

When examining the many struggles—political, spiritual, intellectual, ideological, economic, and cultural—explored in the preceding chapters, it is difficult not to conclude that, humanly speaking, the War was avoidable. Only a few extremists on either side actually wanted violent conflict. Nearly everyone seemed to believe war could be avoided. In retrospect, it appears the two sides conducted a series of bluffs calculated to outmaneuver the other—bluffs that in the end failed to attain their desired results.

For most people, the War was neither planned nor carefully strategized ahead of time. This thesis is borne out when examining the political ideas and movements that prevailed in the land leading up to the War.

Northern Philosophies

By 1861, the ideas of nationalism (Chapter 1) dominated the North. Still, a number of positions existed. Out of these came three clear philosophies, each led by capable statesmen. All three intended to carry forth the political policies of the United States while maintaining an appropriate level of Constitutionalism.

One was the conciliators, led by men like Northern Democrat James Buchanan of Pennsylvania, the president from 1857–1861, immediately prior to Abraham Lincoln. The conciliators resembled earlier men such as Henry Clay in their ceaseless search for compromise that would not necessarily solve a looming Constitutional crisis, the crisis between nationalism and regionalism, or the clashing worldviews of Unitarianism in the North and evangelicalism in the South.

Rather, the conciliators sought to find a way to patch things together and live semi-harmoniously with conflicts. This philosophy did not fear diversity or disagreement over fundamental, principial issues. It did not fear division over matters of great import and moment. Even through the first half of the War itself,

JAMES BUCHANAN,
DEMOCRATIC CANDIDATE FOR PRESIDENT OF THE UNITED STATES.

Campaign poster for victorious 1856 Presidential candidate James Buchanan of Pennsylvania, a conservative Northern Democrat who urged conciliation between North and South. Inset is photograph of Buchanan, who preceded Abraham Lincoln as President. (*Harper's Weekly*, www.harpweek.com)

the conciliators hunted for ways to resolve the crisis without solving it.

Hardly any of them, including Buchanan, believed it possible to reconcile entirely the concerns of both North and South. They recognized the vast worldview differences, but they were pragmatists. They cited the common heritage of the sections, that they had together succeeded in becoming the envy of the world, and how the natural resources which lay at their disposal were beyond the wildest dreams of any other nation on earth. They beseeched their countrymen to put peace before ideological purity.

The philosophy of the conciliators was the strongest and most dynamic operating in the North. Perhaps as many as 70–75% of Northerners were in the camp of the conciliators. They did not want war. They wanted to mind their own business, care for their families, and not let politics jeopardize their doing so.

The conciliators held such concerns in common with most Americans of any age, who do not wish for politics to dominate their lives. The American Constitutional system was crafted with this in mind, brilliant in its fostering of a freedom possible because the people's lives were not centered in a politics of constant supervision. Traditionally, Americans have not been statists, whose vision of the world is primarily defined by the doings of the state.

Northern Philosophies

Conciliators—The majority of Northerners. They searched for compromises that would allow the sections to live semi-harmoniously with their differences.

Unionists—Believed that preserving the Union was a non-negotiable issue.

Radicals—Determined to extend the prevailing philosophical visions of the North, such as industrialism and dynamic progressivism, to the South, through bloodshed if necessary.

Northern Unionists

The second significant bloc of nationalistic Northerners, the Unionists, was equally committed to the preservation of the Union, but they believed that union was a principle upon which everyone must agree. Like the conciliators, they were pragmatists in that they were willing to concede almost any principle and offer any sort of compromise in order to achieve consensus. Unlike the conciliators, however, they were intolerant of anyone—North or South—who advocated secession. For instance, the Unionists would have been as adamant in dealing with a conciliator of the previous generation like Daniel Webster as they would have been in dealing with eventual Confederate President Jefferson Davis.

Patriotism amidst division, as the illustrated 1859 sheet music cover for *Our Land; a National Song,* features Columbia or American Liberty, an eagle with the motto *E Pluribus Unum,* and a kneeling female figure—presumably representing Learning or History—holding a laurel wreath and a large book. (*Harper's Weekly,* www.harpweek.com)

Thus, Abraham Lincoln, the primary spokesman for the Unionist philosophy, maintained that no price was too high to pay for preserving the Union, that it—not slavery, tariffs, economics, division of labor, or the political balance between Northern and Southern states—was the only non-negotiable principle. Some of those in the predominant conciliators camp also held strong Unionist sentiments, so these two bodies had some overlap of Northern popular opinion.

Northern Radicals

The third major philosophy held by Northern nationalists was that of the radicals, championed politically by those commonly called the Radical Republicans. They were led by men such as Pennsylvania Congressman Thaddeus Stevens, chairman of that body's Ways and Means Committee, and Ohio Senator Benjamin Wade.

Stevens believed it necessary to extend the prevailing philosophical visions of the North—such as industrialism and dynamic progressivism—to the Southern states. He made it clear in a Congressional speech shortly before the War began that even the bloody wholesale slaughter and destruction of the South was acceptable to attain that objective:

> If their whole country must be laid waste and made a desert in order to save this Union from destruction, then so be it. If the whole countryside must be ploughed under and salted so that nothing will ever grow there again and no one will ever inhabit that territory again, then I would say it is worth the effort. I would rather, sir, reduce them to a condition where their whole country is to be repeopled than to perpetrate the destruction of this people [America] through our agency.

Many, though not all, of the radicals were also abolitionists who desired the immediate and complete termination of American slavery. In short, Stevens and the radicals wished the South made over into the image of the North.

The Radical Republicans, meanwhile, were a tiny but outspoken political minority. Part of the reason they ultimately gained the upper hand was because of other fringe groups, primarily from immigrant communities like those of central and western Europe who fled the defeated revolutions of 1848 and now advocated even more radical visions of the remaking of American society. They wanted to throw out the Constitution altogether and create the perfect proletarian state. They were called prohibitionists and were comprised of radical abolitionists and committed communists.

> *If the whole (South) must be ploughed under and salted so that no one will ever inhabit that territory again... I would rather, sir, reduce them (the South) to a condition where their whole country is to be repeopled than to perpetuate the destruction of this people (America) through our agency.*
>
> —Republican Congressman Thaddeus Stevens

Another man who carried the banner for the Radicals was William Lloyd Garrison, publisher of the abolitionist newspaper *The Liberator*. He believed the Constitution was a "compact with the devil" and needed to be destroyed, and that the United States needed to remake itself more akin to the principles of the French Revolution or the Communist Manifesto of Marx and Engels. This brand of radicalism created a dynamic element on the left, or liberal, end of the political and cultural spectrum,

THE GREAT AMERICAN BUCK HUNT OF 1856.

In this Currier satire of the 1856 Presidential election, Republican abolitionist leaders flounder on the left and American Party candidate Millard Fillmore (right) takes aim at Democratic candidate James Buchanan, the "buck." (*Harper's Weekly*, www.harpweek.com)

and gave great power and suasion to the Radical Republicans, who appeared moderate by contrast.

The upshot of all this was that the more moderate Northerners—the conciliators and Unionists—were opposed by the various Radical factions, who were constantly tugging at them to move more toward the left.

Southern Philosophies

The opposite dynamic was occurring in the South. There, most of the people, including the majority of statesmen, were Constitutionalists. In temperament and character, they closely resembled the conciliators of the North. The main difference was their preference for appealing to the unbending rule of the Constitution rather than compromise.

The Constitutionalists believed secession was a Constitutional corrective to tyranny on the part of the Federal government. Scholars of this bent, North and South, had enunciated the position since the founding of the nation. For instance, a class in Constitutionalism was taught through the first several decades of the nineteenth century at the nation's military academy in West Point, New York. The course examined Supreme Court precedents since the 1790s. The conclusion, as taught to generations of future American military officers, was that secession was a recourse of last resort to preserve Constitutionalism.

Still, the Constitutionalists were moderates. They wanted to remain in the Union. They did not want war, conflict or even secession. Rather, they wanted to preserve the great legacy of Constitutionalism that the South had propounded since the earliest days of the American experiment in liberty. Indeed, Southerners like Peyton Randolph, James Madison, George Washington, Patrick Henry, and Richard Henry Lee had hammered out the vision for Constitutionalism during the country's founding stages.

In the years leading up to the War, Southern Constitutionalists wished to adhere to that standard. They included men like U.S. Congressman Alexander Stephens, who opposed both slavery and secession*ism* but would later serve as Vice President of the Confederacy. Robert E. Lee, too, opposed secessionism and slavery, yet became

Commander-in-Chief of Confederate forces in the field. Even before the War, Lee was one of the most respected men in the South. In the early 1850s he served as superintendent of the military academy at West Point. And he was the son of "Light Horse" Harry Lee, cavalry leader in Washington's Army of the Revolution.

Among the classes Thomas J. (eventually to be known as "Stonewall") Jackson taught as a professor at the Virginia Military Institute was one on Constitutionalism. Like the conciliators in the North, Jackson desired some sort of reconciliation to repair the breach that was growing between the sections.

Alexander Stephens (1812-1883)

A leading contender for the Confederate presidency, Alexander Hamilton Stephens served as its only vice-president. Often called "Little Aleck" due to his frail stature, Stephens was orphaned as a boy and battled illness and depression all his life. But he was brilliant too, graduating first in his class at the future University of Georgia, excelling as a lawyer, and building a large plantation. He proved a kindly master to slaves, and none of them ever attempted to escape. He gained fame during his seventeen years in Congress as one of its keenest intellects and greatest orators.

A close friend of Abraham Lincoln and a staunch Unionist, Stephens supported the Compromise of 1850 that preserved the Union. He also voted a decade later against Georgia's secession, though he did not dispute the constitutionality of the act, only the timing. After it happened, he worked for the Confederacy in every way he knew how. He never ceased, however, exploring possibilities for a cessation of hostilities and reunification with the North, especially on the basis of "a reorganization of its constituent elements and a new assimilation upon the basis of a new constitution." He echoed Thomas Jefferson's philosophy on such matters. Stephens traveled north to meet in person with his old friend Lincoln in February, 1865, in order to attempt a cessation of hostilities acceptable to both warring parties.

As powerful with the pen as he was frail in the body, Stephens later defended the men who

Alexander Stephens on What Caused the War

That the War had its origin in opposing principles, which, in their action upon the conduct of men, produced the ultimate collision of arms, may be assumed as an unquestionable fact. But the opposing principles which produced these results in physical action were of a very different character from those assumed in the postulate (that slavery caused the War). They lay in the organic Structure of the Government of the States. The conflict in principle arose from different and opposing ideas as to the nature of what is known as the General Government. The contest was between those who held it to be strictly Federal in its character, and those who maintained that it was thoroughly National. It was a strife between the principles of Federation, on the one side, and Centralism, or Consolidation, on the other.

Slavery, so called, was but the question on which these antagonistic principles, which had been in conflict, from the beginning, on divers other questions, were finally brought into actual and active collision with each other on the field of battle.

It is the fashion of many writers of the day to class all who opposed the Consolidationists in this, their first step, as well as all who opposed them in all their subsequent steps, on this question, with what they style the Pro-Slavery Party. No greater injustice could be done any public men, and no greater violence be done to the truth of History, than such a classification. Their opposition to that measure, or kindred subsequent ones, sprung from no attachment to Slavery; but, as Jefferson's, Pinkney's and Clay's, from their strong convictions that the Federal Government had no rightful or Constitutional control or jurisdiction over such questions; and that no such action, as that proposed upon them, could be taken by Congress without destroying the elementary and vital principles upon which the Government was founded.

framed the Confederate Constitution:

The whole document utterly negatives the idea which so many have been active in endeavoring to put in the enduring form of history, that the convention at Montgomery was nothing but a set of 'conspirators' whose object was the overthrow of the principles of the Constitution of the United States, and the erection of a great ' slave oligarchy' instead of the free institutions thereby secured and guaranteed. This work of the Montgomery convention, with that of the Constitution for a provisional government, will ever remain not only as a monument of the wisdom, foresight and statesmanship of the men who constituted it, but an everlasting refutation of the charges which have been brought against them.

An arch-defender of States' rights, Stephens clashed with Davis and other members of his administration on numerous issues during the War, including financial policy, conscription or involuntary drafting of soldiers, and suspension of the right of habeas corpus. Still, the two men remained friendly colleagues, and Stephens often defended Davis from his many critics, North and South. When Federals accused Davis of orchestrating a brutal system for prisoners of war, for instance, Stephens called the charges, "the boldest and baldest attempted outrages upon the truths of history which has ever been essayed." Often overlooked are his dedicated wartime efforts to help Confederate soldiers in hospitals and prisons.

One of Stephens's greatest accomplishments came after the War, and following his five-month stay in a Federal prison. His postwar magnum opus *A Constitutional View of the Late War Between the States* remains one of the most profound works on the War and its causes. He returned to the U.S. Congress in 1873 and became governor of Georgia in 1882.

Ready to Secede

The second group of Southerners were those who held the position of ready secessionism. Whereas the Constitutionalists believed secession was a last recourse, the ready secessionists believed it was a recourse available whenever and however it seemed politically expedient. Thus, these Southerners frequently trotted out secession as a threat. They were, however, in the minority, even in the South. Though most Southerners believed in the Constitutional remedy of secession, they did not wish to use it.

Men of strong principle led the ready secessionists. They believed if the majority overran the rights of the minority—as John C. Calhoun predicted long before would happen—the minority must take a stand on principle to whatever degree was necessary. Both Calhoun and his philosophical descendants believed that if mere nullification of federal laws resulted in local regions and the federal government allowed it, then so be it. But if it proved necessary to secede from the Union altogether, then that was a matter of great and profound principle and should be undertaken without fear or hesitation.

Mississippi Senator Jefferson Davis, a former secretary of war and West Point graduate, was an articulate spokesman for this second group. He, too, was a Constitutionalist, but he was not as ready to compromise as men like Alexander Stephens.

Fire-Eaters and Radicals

The fire-eaters comprised a third major bloc of Southerners. Just as many Radical Republicans would have taken umbrage at the adjective "Radical," so most fire-eaters would not have appreciated the name given to them by history. They considered themselves "principled Democrats."

The fiery rhetoric and speeches of the fire-eaters frequently threatened to incite riots in the House of Representatives, Senate, and state legislatures alike. These men were not averse to name-calling, shaking their fingers at opponents, reprimanding the other side of the legislative chamber, or brandishing swords—whether rhetorical or literal.

South Carolina Senator Preston Brooks's brutal caning of Massachusetts Senator Charles Sumner during an 1856 senate session, after Sumner vulgarly slandered another senator—Brooks's cousin—bolstered abolitionist accusations against the "Slave Power" and its leaders. (Images of American Political History)

Southern Philosophies

Constitutionalists—The majority of Southerners. Similar to the Northern conciliators, but they appealed to the unbending rule of the Constitution rather than compromise.

Ready Secessionists—Believed in secession as a recourse whenever politically expedient.

Fire-eaters—More contentious toward the North, more eager to secede.

One such Congressman, Ezekiel Brown, arose in the House of Representatives and thundered:

> I declare on this day that these foolish, godless, perverse, wicked, defiled fools from the North will meet with retribution from God on high. But until then they shall taste the lashings of the Southern patriots who know the truth and walk in it, from this day unto evermore. Amen!

So tensions grew, particularly as the Constitutionalists and conciliators sat with increasing discomfort in the House or Senate and witnessed the fire-eaters and Radical Republicans trade barbs. As if all this were not enough, another group, the radical secessionists, weighed in, tiny but vociferous and more reactionary yet than the fire-eaters. In the same way the reactionary radicals of the North pulled Northern conciliators to the left, the radical secessionists pulled Southern Constitutionalists to the right.

The more radical among this group of Southerners believed the Confederacy itself was too centralized a governing body. Some of them wished for the South to be broken up county by county, each county forming a tiny, independent Greek city-state with its own state department and monetary system, and working in cooperation with its many neighbors.

One final, again tiny, group of Southerners, radical libertarians, held the most extreme position of decentralization. This group should not be confused with the majority of libertarians (or classical, nineteenth-century liberals) antebellum and postbellum who have and do respect legitimate government function and authority. Rather, these radical libertarians believed virtually all government was tyranny, an imposition of forces that stole away their American freedoms. Thus, they advocated the destruction of all forms of government, and the ruination of federalism. South Carolina Senator Preston Brooks was one famous leader who held the philosophy of the radical libertarians.

In summary, most antebellum Americans were quite moderate in their political views. But internal tensions contrived to pull them ever-farther apart, toward more radical or reactionary positions.

Spiraling Toward War

The cauldron in which these many potent philosophies simmered began to boil over in the mid-1850s. The bloody exploits of John Brown and others in Kansas in 1856 presaged both the violence and the division that Americans in a few years would demonstrate en masse. Southerners wondered at the man's murderous villainy while some Northerners, including high political leaders, applauded him and provided him sanctuary from prosecution.

The next year, 1857, Missouri slave Dred Scott brought his suit for freedom against the Federal government and his master before the Supreme Court. The court's decision against Scott electrified the Northern Radicals and proved an emotional rallying cry for them. They framed the ruling as a blessing on slavery, which the justices did not intend.

Lincoln–Douglas Debates

Unionists like Lincoln, too, condemned the Dred Scott ruling. It added fire to the famous series of senatorial debates that took place in 1858 between Lincoln and Stephen Douglas in locations all around Illinois. Lincoln stood strongly against slavery in some debates, particularly those in the more liberal, Radical Republican strongholds in the northern part of the state. He muted his support in the more conservative downstate venues and emphasized his beliefs in the inherent inferiority of blacks to whites and the need to ship them to distant colonies in Africa and Central America.

But he did go on record against slavery, though on a moral rather than a Constitutional basis. He said the moral conscience of the nation must move inexorably toward emancipation.

George B. McClellan would one day gain fame as a top Federal general in the War. At this point a successful railroad executive, he owned a mansion on Lake Michigan in Chicago. He loaned Douglas his private rail car for travel to the debates and escorted him personally to one of them. McClellan's analysis of that debate: "Douglas's speech was compact, logical and powerful—Mr. Lincoln's disjointed, and rather a mass of anecdotes than of arguments. I did not think that there was any approach to equality in the oratorical powers of the two men."

Lincoln lost the election, but he shined in the debates in the eyes of

Paul Ashack's portrayal of Abraham Lincoln speaking during one of his historic 1858 debates with Illinois senatorial race opponent Stephen Douglas. (www.lockport-streetgallery.com)

most and catapulted forward into national prominence, leapfrogging numerous better-known politicos and landing in the forefront of the race for the 1860 Republican Presidential nomination.

Lincoln lost the [Illinois senate] election, but he shined in the debates in the eyes of most and catapulted forward into national prominence, leapfrogging numerous better-known politicos and landing in the forefront of the race for the 1860 Republican presidential nomination.

Meanwhile, in 1859, abolitionist John Brown thundered back into the national spotlight with his capture of the Federal military arsenal at Harper's Ferry, Virginia. After being captured by Federal soldiers and hanged, Brown became the patron saint of the abolitionists, the Radical Republicans, the communists, and even some of the Unionists, who cheered his blood-soaked exploits.

Election of 1860

By now, tensions were white-hot and divisions rife. Men of both Unionist and Constitutional sentiment still dominated the nation's two major political parties, the Republicans and the Democrats, even though the former leaned liberal and the latter conservative. But power struggles abounded in both parties, and both in their own ways painted themselves into political corners.

At the Democratic Presidential Convention, those favoring a states' rights platform that included both state

"The Union Must and Shall be Preserved," 1860 presidential campaign poster for Abraham Lincoln and Hannibal Hamlin (Library of Congress)

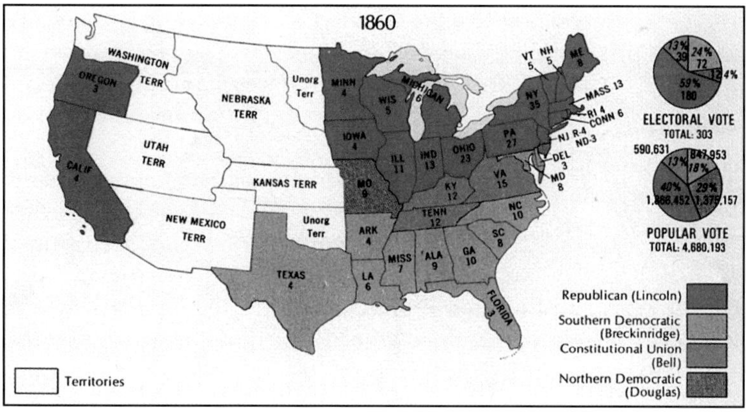

Map of the 1860 Presidential Election: The stark portrait of a nation divided. Abraham Lincoln won the Northern states, John Breckenridge the Southern states, John Bell several of the Border states, and Stephen Douglas the state of Missouri, itself rent in half by Northern and Southern sympathies. (Images of American Political History)

over federal sovereignty and the legality of—though in many cases not the preference for—slavery, stormed out of the convocation. They were furious that supporters of likely presidential nominee Douglas had thwarted Deep South desires that the party platform include a federal code shielding slavery in the Western territories. Though Douglas insisted he would leave the territorial slave issue alone, that did not satisfy the Gulf Coast delegates. Their departure played right into Republican hands, as Democratic support and resources were strewn over three major candidates and other minor ones. As the Republicans united behind Lincoln and the possibility of his election—at first considered unthinkable to Southerners—loomed ever more likely, measured actions grew as scarce as calm tempers in all but the Northern wing of the Democratic Party.

Meanwhile, the more moderate elements among Republicans failed to quell the Radical voices of that party. They voiced the legitimate concern that without its anti-slavery, Federal government-over-states' rights distinctives, the party might struggle to retain its emotional pull over enough people to insure its survival. When the conciliators' views were discarded with Lincoln's nomination, the Republican Party offered little to mollify social, political, and economic concerns now blazing in all corners of the South.

Indeed, the erstwhile Whig Lincoln won not only his new party's nomination, but the election in November 1860. Two striking events towered above the drama that swirled around this historic event. One was division—multiple divisions—of the nation. Though Lincoln won, he received less than 40 percent of the popular vote.

1860 Presidential Election Results

Candidate	Popular Votes	Electoral Votes
Abraham Lincoln (Republican, Illinois)	1,865,593	180
Stephen Douglas (Democrat, Illinois)	1,382,713	12
John Breckenridge (Whig, Kentucky)	848,356	72
John Bell (Constitutional Union, Tennessee)	592,906	39

The conservative political personality of antebellum America evidenced itself in the sweeping majority that voted against Lincoln. But they spread their votes among three major candidates—Douglas, Tennessean John Bell, and Kentuckian John C. Breckenridge, former Vice President of the United States.

Though Lincoln won, he received less than 40 percent of the popular vote.

Lincoln Promises

The other notable happening was the almost immediate secession of South Carolina on December 20. The states of Mississippi, Florida, Alabama, Georgia, Louisiana, and Texas followed over the next two months. But confusion and uncertainty continued. At first glance, Lincoln's Presidential inauguration address (written with the aid of Secretary of State William Seward, as were most of his major speeches) in March 1861, seemed the words of a man with nothing but goodwill and peaceable intentions toward the South:

> Apprehension seems to exist among the people of the Southern States, that by the accession of a Republican Administration, their property (slaves), and their peace, and personal security, are to be endangered. There has never been any reasonable cause for such apprehension. Indeed, the most ample evidence to the contrary has all the while existed, and been open to their inspection. It is found in nearly all the published speeches of him who now addresses you. I do but quote from one of those speeches when I declare that 'I have no purpose, directly or indirectly, to interfere with the institution of slavery in the States where it exists. I believe I have no lawful right to do so, and I have no inclination to do so.

Unionists and others—and many since—criticized the seceding states for

"The Christian's Best Motive for Patriotism"

Virginia theologian Robert L. Dabney's famous sermon following Abraham Lincoln's November 1860 election as U.S. president discusses "The Christian's Best Motive for Patriotism." Dabney based the sermon on the Biblical text of Psalm 122, "Because of the house of our Lord thy God, I will seek thy good."

> *How, then, shall Christians seek the good of this country for the church's sake? First, by everywhere beginning to pray for their country, and along with this, making humble confession of their sins, individual and social; second, by carrying their Christianity into every act of their lives, political or otherwise; by carrying "Christian conscience, enlightened by God's Word," into political duty as had not been done hitherto; obeying the law of God rather than the unrighteous behests of party; choosing out of all the people able men, such as fear God, men of truth, hating covetousness, and placing such to be rulers over them.*

leaving in the wake of the election. According to their accusers, the seceders either overreacted to Lincoln's election or found it a convenient excuse to facilitate what they wanted, which was to leave. Lincoln continued:

> In your hands, my dissatisfied fellow countrymen, and not in mine, is the momentous issue of civil war. The government will not assail you. You can have no conflict without yourselves being the aggressors . . . the mystic chords of memory, stretching from every battlefield, and patriot grave, to every living heart and hearthstone, all over this broad land, will yet swell the chorus of the Union, when again touched, as surely they will be, by the better angels of our nature.

Not Convinced

Was the intent of Lincoln, a consummate politician who exercised exquisite care in the choice of his words in so momentous a speech, limitless forbearance? Voices across the South rose in the negative. One fervent Southern Unionist turned secessionist upon reading Lincoln's speech, and a Mobile, Alabama newspaper recorded his speech that followed: "It is impossible to doubt that it was Mr. Lincoln's policy, under the name of reinforcing the laws, to retake the forts, to collect the revenue of the United States in our Ports and to reduce the seceded States to obedience to the behests of his party. His purpose therefore was war upon and subjugation of our people."

Indeed, a closer reading of the speech finds that Lincoln would:

> . . . hold, occupy, and possess the property and places belonging to the government . . . to collect the duties and impost; but beyond what may be necessary for these objects, there will be no invasion, no using of force against or among the people anywhere.

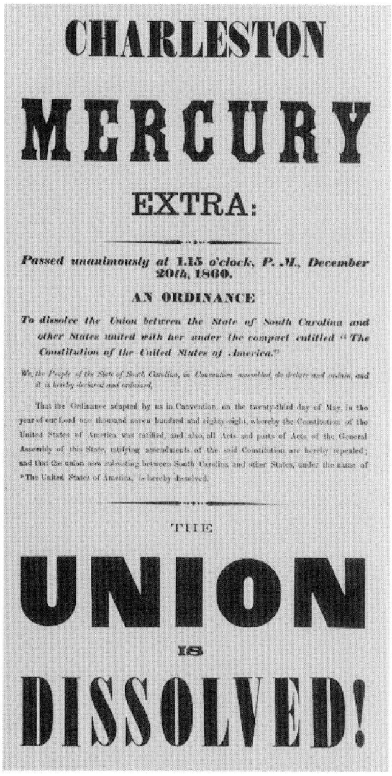

CHARLESTON

MERCURY

EXTRA:

Passed unanimously at 1.15 o'clock, P. M., December 20th, 1860.

AN ORDINANCE

To dissolve the Union between the State of South Carolina and other States united with her under the compact entitled "The Constitution of the United States of America."

We, the People of the State of South Carolina, in Convention assembled, do declare and ordain, and it is hereby declared and ordained,

That the Ordinance adopted by us in Convention, on the twenty-third day of May, in the year of our Lord one thousand seven hundred and eighty-eight, whereby the Constitution of the United States of America was ratified, and also, all Acts and parts of Acts of the General Assembly of this State, ratifying amendments of the said Constitution, are hereby repealed; and that the union now subsisting between South Carolina and other States, under the name of "The United States of America," is hereby dissolved.

THE

UNION

IS

DISSOLVED!

The *Charleston Mercury* newspaper's blazing message to the world of South Carolina's departure from the Federal Union, only weeks after Abraham Lincoln's election.

As explored in Charles Adams's *When in the Course of Human Events*, the first draft of the inaugural address revealed Lincoln's intent that "All the power at my disposal will be used to reclaim the public property and places that have fallen . . ." And Southerners remembered he warned them back in 1856, "We won't let you [secede]. With the purse and sword, the army and navy and treasury in our hands and at our command, you couldn't do it."

So there it was. Southerners needed no soothsayers to interpret for them that "the property and places belonging to the government" meant forts at coastal ports such as Charleston, South Carolina's Fort Sumter, forts that would allow no ships into port without assessing them according to the Federal government's confiscatory tax rate. Lincoln's words did not concern slavery, nor even secession. But he would hold the forts "to collect the duties and impost" and he reserved the (unconstitutional) right of "invasion" or "using of force" to accomplish this.

Various religious observances took place. A national day of prayer for peace in March 1861, featured the involvement of Thomas [soon to be "Stonewall"] Jackson and his pastor, Dr. William White.

The President also supported a little-known proposed constitutional amendment, which the Republican-controlled Congress passed. It would have disallowed the Federal government from stopping or even slowing slavery in states where it remained legal. Thus, both the executive and legislative branches of the government at Washington signaled their unwillingness to take up arms over the issue of slavery.

In February 1861, the provisional government of the Confederate States of America was established in Montgomery, Alabama. The new legislature named Jefferson Davis as president of the nation. A Confederate Constitution followed.

Working for Peace

Attempts were not lacking on many fronts to maintain a peaceful coexistence. In addition to the proposed Constitutional amendment, numerous compromise plans came before both the Senate and the House. Perhaps the one that held the best chance of passage was the Crittenden Compromise, presented by Kentucky Senator John J. Crittenden.

The plan's features included proposed Constitutional amendments that

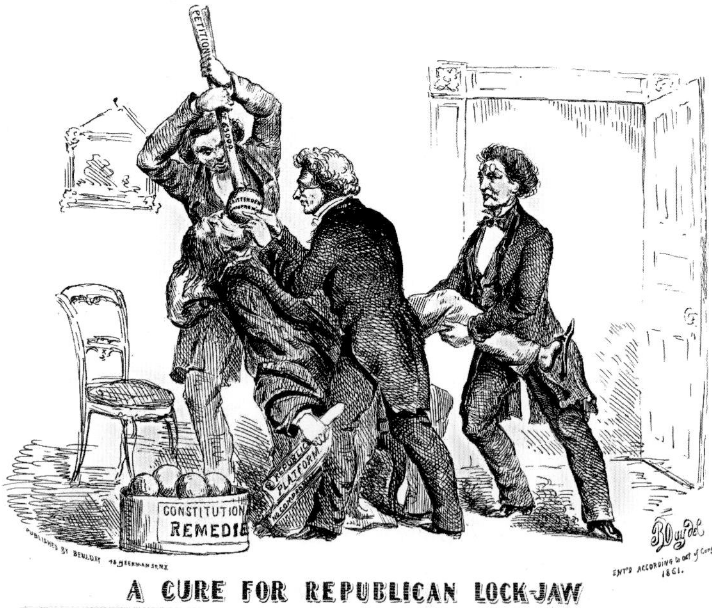

Last ditch congressional efforts strove to maintain harmony between the sections by passing the Crittenden Compromise as an alternative to Northern Radical Republican rigidity on the slavery issue. Three well-dressed men (probably members of Congress) aid a sick man who is grasping a document inscribed "Republican Platform No Compromise." The men drag him from his chair and attempt to push an oversized pill (the "Crittenden Compromise") down his throat, ramming it with a "Petition of 63,000," reflective of popular support for the plan. A box of other "Constitutional Remedies" (containing more giant pills) is ready nearby.

would have protected slavery south of the 36 ∞ 30' line; required Congress to authorize restitution for slave owners who lost slaves in the North due to the violation of the Fugitive Slave Law; and prevented Congress from interfering with the interstate slave trade or slavery in the states in general. The Crittenden Compromise failed a committee vote by one vote.

Various religious observances took place. A national day of prayer for peace in March 1861, featured the involvement of Thomas (soon to be "Stonewall") Jackson and his pastor, Dr. William White.

Federal Major Robert Anderson, who refused to surrender Fort Sumter until fired upon. (TreasureNet)

Fort Sumter

Upon the secession of the Southern states, President James Buchanan, still in office and hoping to ward off war, agreed to remove Federal troops from the forts of Southern ports. Soon, all but one were evacuated. Federal troops retained control of Fort Sumter, set on an island out in Charleston Bay, though South Carolina maintained that state and U. S. Constitutional law alike held the island and the fort were now South Carolina (and eventually Confederate) rather than Federal property.

Within days of taking office, Lincoln was seeking the support of his cabinet to supply—and thus to hold—Fort Sumter. The attorney general and the secretaries of war, navy, interior, and state all opposed the idea. Their fears of such an action included the loss of the fort, secession of the many and large border states, and the "calamity" of civil war.

As discussed in Chapter 10, Davis and the new Confederate government urged the Federals to leave Fort Sumter of their own accord in peace as they had every other coastal fort in the South. But Wall Street and the other New England commercial powers—only now pugilistic toward the South because of the imminent departure of their tariff protection and revenue—leaned on the Lincoln administration with the weight of their commercial might, and by the end of March the President had secret cabinet approval to proceed not only with resupplying Fort Sumter, but to do so with an armed fleet of ships and soldiers.

Indeed, even as the President sought support from his cabinet on Fort Sumter, Seward was hosting a Confederate Commission desirous of working out a peaceful process of secession. And when Lincoln ordered Federal

Pierre Gustave Beauregard (1818-1893)

While one of the most dashing and able commanders in the Confederacy, his sour relations with Jefferson Davis and his own temper and vanity conspired to deprive Pierre Beauregard of even greater success. A Louisianan of French descent, Beauregard demonstrated abundant and varied talents throughout his adult life. He graduated second in his West Point class, served as the chief army engineer in the dredging of the Mississippi River mouth at New Orleans, and ran for mayor of that city.

Beauregard gained the esteemed position of U.S. Military Academy superintendent just three months before the War began. But he lasted only five days in the position before his outspoken secessionist views resulted in his removal. He regained the national spotlight when given command at Charleston, South Carolina, where he the Confederate government ordered him to secure the surrender of the Federal force at Fort Sumter. The Federal commander there, Robert Anderson, had instructed Cadet Beauregard in artillery classes at West Point.

Beauregard's commanding the firing on and subsequent capture of Fort Sumter electrified the world and gave the Confederacy their first military hero.

His commanding the firing on and subsequent capture of Fort Sumter electrified the world and gave the Confederacy their first military hero. Beauregard followed up the achievement just three months later when he masterminded the Confederate strategy at First Manassas, the War's first major battle and a smashing victory for the South. Despite these successes, he crossed swords with President Davis over whether the Confederates should have pursued their beaten foe into the United States capital, twenty-five miles away. Soon, Davis sent him west to serve under Albert Sidney Johnston.

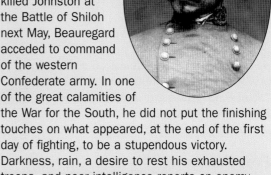

Shiloh Calamity

When a fluke wound killed Johnston at the Battle of Shiloh next May, Beauregard acceded to command of the western Confederate army. In one of the great calamities of the War for the South, he did not put the finishing touches on what appeared, at the end of the first day of fighting, to be a stupendous victory. Darkness, rain, a desire to rest his exhausted troops, and poor intelligence reports on enemy troop movements caused Beauregard to save his climactic attack for the morning.

During the night, however, Don Carlos Buell heroically arrived with tens of thousands more Federal troops. Outnumbered two-to-one, Beauregard had to retreat. Thus, the slaughter at Shiloh shifted the balance of power in the west to the Federals. These events failed to endear him further to Davis, and when the tempestuous Creole went on sick leave, the President replaced him with Braxton Bragg.

Beauregard's record the rest of the War stands high. Returning to Charleston to helm the Confederate defense of the Atlantic Coast, he threw back repeated Federal efforts to capture that city by land and sea for the next year-and-a-half. Sent to Virginia in 1864, he shut down a key

Federal advance on Richmond, pinning Benjamin Butler's larger force inside the Bermuda Hundred peninsula. Then Beauregard performed what may have been his greatest feat as a soldier. With only 2,500 tattered, hungry troops, he stopped cold the assaults of an entire Federal corps of nearly 20,000 men against the key rail junction of Petersburg, some twenty miles south of the capital of Richmond.

A joint resolution of the Confederate Congress thanked him for his defense of Charleston: "a defense which, for the skill, heroism, and tenacity displayed during an attack scarcely paralleled in warfare . . . is justly entitled to be pronounced glorious by impartial history and an admiring country." His fame spread across the Atlantic, and after the War he received offers to command armies in Egypt and Romania, which he declined. He returned to Louisiana and, among other activities, worked as a railroad executive. He also labored for a state lottery, for which Robert E. Lee took him to task.

Major Robert Anderson to hold Fort Sumter, Seward was promising the Southern commissioners the fort would be abandoned within a few days. At Fort Sumter, Anderson and his men faced no danger of starvation, and hence, no need of victualing; the Confederate forces in Charleston, commanded by General Pierre Gustave Beauregard, allowed them to come ashore and purchase whatever they needed.

Back in Washington, the Confederate commissioners, as late as April 7, were still striving to effect an agreement with Seward. Then they heard rumors of a powerful Federal squadron preparing to sail South. "Faith as to Sumter fully kept; wait and see . . ." Seward's intermediary soothed them.

But the next day a pro-Confederate State Department employee passed South Carolina Governor Francis Pickens an anonymous but apparently official government memorandum declaring that rather than being abandoned as Seward had been promising, Fort Sumter would be supplied—by force of arms if Southern resistance was met. Still, Anderson and his men had plenty of victuals—Beauregard had begun sending boats out to the fort each day to provision the Federals himself.

War begins, April 13, 1861, at Fort Sumter, South Carolina. Federal cannon fire out of the fort as Confederate shells streak in from shore batteries and other forts. Miraculously, neither side suffered any casualties.

The Fight Begins

Lincoln's strategy, if Machiavellian, was brilliant. The historic precedent it set would experience revival in later American machinations antecedent to the sinking of the *Lusitania*, the bombing of Pearl Harbor, the Gulf of Tonkin incident, and, possibly, the sinking of the *U.S.S. Maine.* Indeed, the old log-splitter had outmaneuvered the Confederates and left them limited and unappetizing choices. These included allowing the supply of Fort Sumter, thus prolonging the crisis, letting the Federals reinforce Charleston Bay, and casting doubt on the South's legitimacy as a nation. Also, attacking the fort or the relief expedition and giving Lincoln a mandate to declare war.

A fierce debate raged in Davis' own cabinet over the matter (see Chapter 10). Nonetheless, Davis ordered Beauregard to shell Fort Sumter. He did so for half an hour. No one was hurt, and Beauregard sent evacuation boats out to the fort, again urging Anderson to leave with weapons, standards, and honor intact. Obeying Lincoln's orders, Anderson refused, and the battle began in earnest, with the outmanned Federals surrendering when they ran out of ammunition. Even then, the Confederates allowed them safe passage out of the fort and harbor north to home.

Virginia did not take its stand on account of slavery, but on the constitutional principle that each state in the Union was sovereign and none could be forced by the government at Washington to offer up its sons for a war it did not wish to fight.

The Union Divides

The North, until now still averse to a shooting war with the South over any issue, erupted in fury. The next day, Lincoln issued a declaration of rebellion and called for a levy of troops from every state in the Union to form the largest military force in the history of the Republic. He ordered them "to execute the laws of the Union; and suppress insurrections."

The border states of North Carolina, Tennessee, and Arkansas seceded immediately. So did Virginia, cradle of American independence, fifth-most populous state in the Union, and birthplace of four of America's first five presidents. The legislatures of Missouri, Kentucky, Maryland, and Delaware initiated action toward the same end.

Virginia did not take its stand on account of slavery, but on its belief that the Constitution maintained the sovereignty of each state over most of their own domestic affairs. Thus, Virginia believed, none could be forced by the government at Washington to offer up its sons for a war it did not wish to fight. Virginia Governor John Letcher, up to that point an ardent Unionist, summed up the sentiments of the border states: "Our militia will not be furnished to the powers at Washington for any such use or purpose as they have in view."

Two Peoples

Lincoln called the War "essentially a People's contest":

> On the side of the Union, is a struggle for maintaining in the world, that form, and substance of government, whose leading object is, to elevate the condition of men—to lift artificial weights from all shoulders—to clear the paths of laudable pursuit for all—to afford all, an unfettered start, and a fair chance, in the race of life . . . this is the leading object of the government for whose existence we contend.

So was the War preventable? From the comfortable distance of well over a century, it is tempting to say yes and wonder at the misguidedness and violence of that generation of Americans. Surely misguidedness and violence indeed abounded in them—and in every other generation of Americans. More difficult for the modern to grasp is the totality of the American experience leading up to the war. By then, North and South had grown apart on nearly every issue of substance. The North saw its grandiose schemes for internal improvements and services, westward expansion, and continental empire threatened by the South. The South saw its institutions and culture mocked and ridiculed by the North, and its missionary and pastoral candidates rejected by Northern denominational agencies.

The Confederate flag flies over Fort Sumter in Charleston Harbor after its capture from the Federals by Pierre Beauregard's men on April 14, 1861.

The North seethed at the prospect of Southern slavery stretching across the land alongside the transcontinental railroads. The South shook in fury at an increasingly confiscatory tariff system—ratcheted to its highest level in history by new President Lincoln—that redistributed hundreds of millions of dollars per year from Southern to Northern pockets. The North chafed at Southern adherence to the Constitution and state sovereignty. The South bristled at the North's aggressive industrial character, especially when it demanded ever-increasing levels of Southern tax dollars to fuel it.

On the side of the Union, is a struggle for maintaining in the world, that form, and substance of government, whose leading object is, to elevate the condition of men . . . to afford all, an unfettered start, and a fair chance, in the race of life.

—President Abraham Lincoln

In the end, war likely would have come at some point, though perhaps

The Bonnie Blue Flag (Henry Macarthy)

We are a band of brothers, and native to the soil,
Fighting for the property we gained by honest toil;
And when our rights were threatened, the cry rose near and far,
Hurrah for the Bonnie Blue Flag that bears a single star!

Chorus:
Hurrah! Hurrah! for Southern Rights, hurrah!
Hurrah! for the Bonnie Blue Flag that bears a single star!

As long as the Union was faithful to her trust,
Like friends and like brothers we were kind, we were just;
But now when Northern treachery attempts our rights to mar,
We hoist on high the Bonnie Blue Flag that bears a single star.

Then here's to our Confederacy, strong we are and brave,
Like patriots of old we'll fight, our heritage to save.
And rather than submit to shame, to die we would prefer
So cheer for the Bonnie Blue flag that bears a single star.

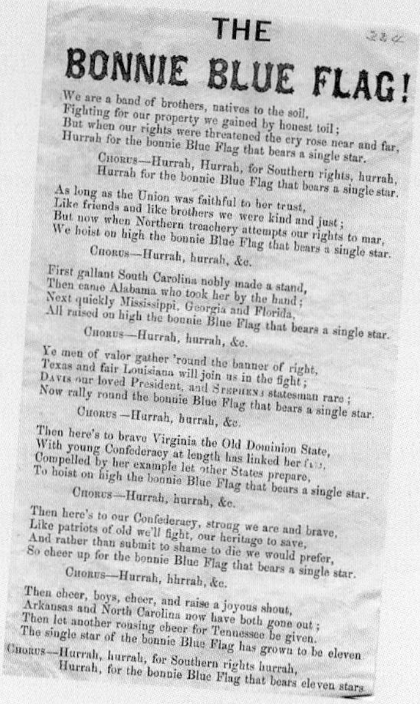
THE
BONNIE BLUE FLAG!

We are a band of brothers, natives to the soil,
Fighting for our property we gained by honest toil;
But when our rights were threatened the cry rose near and far,
Hurrah for the bonnie Blue Flag that bears a single star.
CHORUS—Hurrah, Hurrah, for Southern rights, hurrah,
Hurrah for the bonnie Blue Flag that bears a single star.

As long as the Union was faithful to her trust,
Like friends and like brothers we were kind and just;
But now when Northern treachery attempts our rights to mar,
We hoist on high the bonnie Blue Flag that bears a single star.
CHORUS—Hurrah, hurrah, &c.

First gallant South Carolina nobly made a stand,
Then came Alabama who took her by the hand;
Next quickly Mississippi, Georgia and Florida,
All raised on high the bonnie Blue Flag that bears a single star.
CHORUS—Hurrah, hurrah, &c.

Ye men of valor gather 'round the banner of right,
Texas and fair Louisiana will join us in the fight;
DAVIS our loved President, and STEPHENS statesman rare;
Now rally round the bonnie Blue Flag that bears a single star.
CHORUS—Hurrah, hurrah, &c.

Then here's to brave Virginia the Old Dominion State,
With young Confederacy at length has linked her [illegible],
Compelled by her example let other States prepare,
To hoist on high the bonnie Blue Flag that bears a single star.
CHORUS—Hurrah, hurrah, &c.

Then here's to our Confederacy, strong we are and brave,
Like patriots of old we'll fight, our heritage to save,
And rather than submit to shame to die we would prefer,
So cheer up for the bonnie Blue Flag that bears a single star.
CHORUS—Hurrah, hhrrah, &c.

Then cheer, boys, cheer, and raise a joyous shout,
Arkansas and North Carolina now have both gone out;
Then let another rousing cheer for Tennessee be given.
The single star of the bonnie Blue Flag has grown to be eleven
CHORUS—Hurrah, hurrah, for Southern rights hurrah,
Hurrah, for the bonnie Blue Flag that bears eleven stars

not so total a war. But one man and one man alone held within his grip the power to allow or prevent war in April of 1861. That man was Abraham Lincoln, and for better or worse, the War for Southern Independence was his creation much as is the modern United States of America.

War is never caused by hatred.
Rather, hatred is caused by war.
—Alexander Stephens

PART II The War

The War Between the States began with the firing on Fort Sumter on April 13, 1861, and ended with the surrender of the last Confederate general, Cherokee Indian Chief Stand Watie, on July 23, 1865. In between, upwards of 700,000 Americans, including civilians, died, and countless others fell victim to war-related illness, injury, or wound. To grasp the enormity of those numbers, one should multiply them by approximately ten in order to arrive at a proportionate total should a modern-day war claim a like percentage of Americans.

The Seventh New York marching to war

As the pages which follow evidence, however, the toll taken by this war on America cannot be calculated merely by the statistics of killed and wounded. As with all wars, the uncounted toll is that taken on the souls of people and nations alike. We have attempted not only to chronicle the great people, issues, and events of these tumultuous years, but to go to where the important lessons and morals for all generations, including our own, lie. In a war as desperate and total as that of 1861–1865, that means exploring much that is disturbing, disappointing, and absent from mainstream American histories.

This point opens to another, the editors' belief that true history cannot be divorced from moral history. As orthodox, Bible-believing Christians, we believe that means to study and assess all that occurs in the light of Scriptural standards and principles. Perhaps another way to say this is that we have attempted to approach this work from a Christian worldview. We realize that is a dangerous undertaking, since "Christian worldview" is a term difficult to agree upon. We assume we have fallen short in some places, perhaps many, and we hope that where we have, we might receive correction. But we have at least tried to bring, in our imperfect way, a Christian worldview to bear on all we address, and even to our choices of what we address and what we do not.

The War itself unfolded primarily in two major theaters, East and West. The Eastern Theater roughly entailed the battles and campaigns occurring in Pennsylvania, Maryland, and Virginia; the Western Theater encompassed the action west and south of those states. Though the Eastern Theater encompassed the largest armies and battles, and many of the most famous figures, we believe the Western Theater possessed equal significance, and we have addressed it as such.

To aid the reader in following the flow of this vast conflict, we have divided Part 2 both by the individual years of the War, and into eastern and western chapters for each year. In keeping with the aforementioned Christian worldview approach, the reader will note significant attention paid to acts and undertakings that present clearly moral dimensions, both good and evil. These include atrocities and clearly unbiblical deeds, as well as acts of Christian charity and the movement and expansion of the Church of Jesus Christ in the midst of war.

We present a large number of biographical sketches, particularly in this section of the book, in the belief that history becomes more interesting and understandable to all of us when learned through the experiences, hopes, and fears of human beings. The reader will perhaps note our endeavoring to present not only the stories of soldiers and politicians, but those of people from many different walks of life. Our hope is that this approach will open a clearer window for the reader into the times, and provide a more accurate chronicling of them.

12 War
(1861)

Matthew Brady's famous portrait of President Abraham Lincoln.

Our Union rests upon public opinion, and can never be cemented by the blood of its citizens shed in a civil war. If it cannot live in the affections of the people, it must one day perish. Congress possesses many means of preserving it by conciliation, but the sword was not placed in their hands to preserve it.

—President James Buchanan
Annual message to Congress
December 6, 1860

Why did the worldview differences between North and South ultimately lead to war? Why did the political, social, cultural, economic, and religious conflicts erupt into the bloodiest episode in American history? Why was the nation, founded on such great principles and with such visionary hope, divided, with brother pitted against brother? Historians and pundits have debated the possible answers to these questions ever since the War. Indeed, even at the time, different men and different regions offered different answers. Then and now, the desire has been to boil the issues that divided the country to the simplest definition, to the lowest common denominator. But something as complex as the War is not so easy to

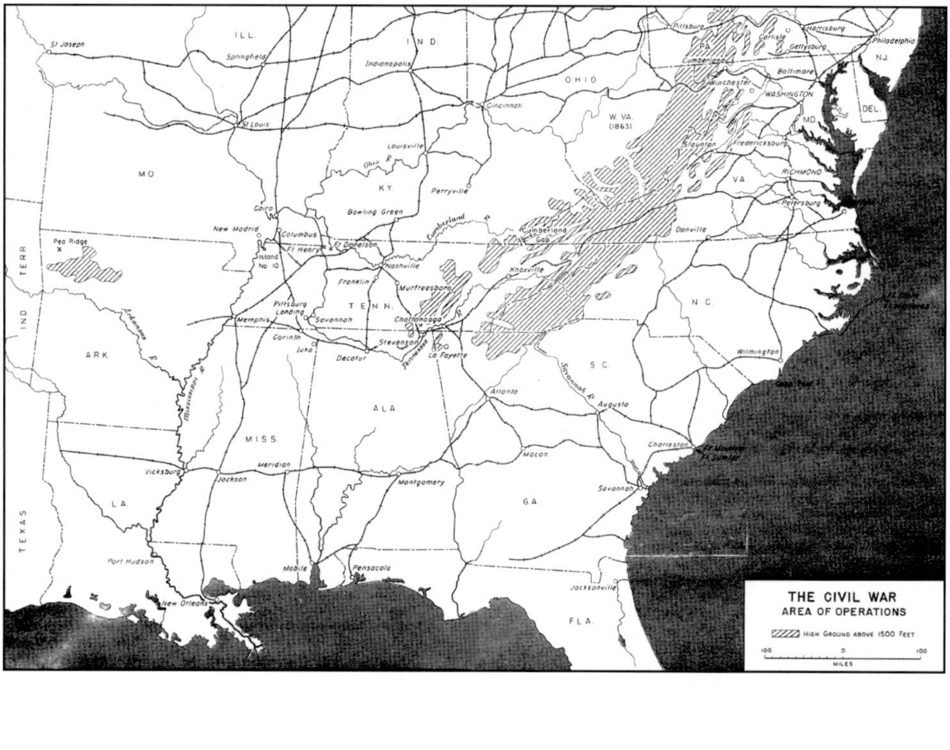

This map reveals much of the vast expanse of operations during the War. Action swept westward beyond these areas, however, through Texas, the Indian Nations (Oklahoma), Kansas, and Arizona Territory (Arizona and New Mexico), as well as to every ocean on the planet. (University of Texas Perry-Castaneda Library Map Collection)

pigeonhole. To argue simplistically that the War was fought over slavery or tariffs or any other single provocation is to vastly underestimate the many and varied interests that ultimately clashed on the battlefields all across the land.

So, viewpoints and philosophies abounded in all sections of America about the aims of the war or if there should even be war. Yet a consensus perspective existed in both the North and the South now that war had come. Confederate aims were simple: independence from the Federal Union, just as their fathers and grandfathers had declared independence from King George III. The North wanted to preserve the Union their fathers and grandfathers had formed by declaring independence from King George, albeit different people had different reasons for wanting to do so. The Crittenden-Johnson Resolution reflected this by stating that the War was not: "waged upon our part in any spirit of oppression, nor for any purpose of conquest or subjugation, nor purpose of overthrowing or interfering with the rights or established institutions of those States, but to defend and maintain the supremacy of the Constitution and to preserve the Union, with all the dignity, quality, and rights of the several states unimpaired; and that as soon as these objects are accomplished the war ought to cease."

Still, minorities on both sides held more ambitious goals for the war. Some Southerners hoped not only to perpetuate their slave-supported influence and holdings, but to extend them west—and perhaps even into Latin America and the Caribbean. The specter of Northern political and military might staggered by the loss of oceans of tariff revenue bothered these folk not in the least. And a small but growing number of Northerners—especially as the Republican Party ascended—wished for more than the mere preservation of the Union. They envisioned an Enlightenment-influenced, communistic societal model featuring man and his efforts, rather than God and especially Christ at the center.

The eventual nature of the War could scarcely be conceived. Consider the words of General George McClellan, first overall commander of Federal forces, at the outset of the conflict: "This rebellion has assumed the character of a war, as such it should be regarded, and it should be conducted upon the highest principles known to Christian civilization. . . . In prosecuting the war, all private property and unarmed persons should be strictly protected . . . all private property taken for military use should be paid or receipted for; pillage and waste should be treated as high crimes; all unnecessary trespass sternly prohibited, and offensive demeanor by the military toward citizens promptly rebuked."

This rebellion has assumed the character of a war, as such it should be regarded, and it should be conducted upon the highest principles known to Christian civilization . . .
—George McClellan

Abraham Lincoln (1806(?)–1865)

Abraham Lincoln, Southern-born, 16th president of the United States, surely stands, even above George Washington, as the American who beyond all others most influenced his nation. Mystery shrouds much of his childhood. His mother, Nancy Hanks, is known, but the identity of his natural father and even his year of birth are debatable. His family's financial trappings were meager, and their frontier surroundings, in both Kentucky and Illinois, were bereft of advantages or influential personal connections. All these factors, as well as his tall and ungainly physical frame, contribute to making the life of Lincoln one of the great temporal American success stories.

He did possess a brilliant mind, surging ambition (and a pragmatism that advanced it), engaging humor, and a simple but at times supremely powerful skill of oratory. His Gettysburg Address and Second Presidential Inaugural speech in particular demonstrate the latter. As Lincoln biographer Joseph Sobran writes, the historical record fails to produce instances of his calling his opponents or even his worst enemies "evil." Rather, he appears to have consistently sought to understand those he disagreed with.

Lincoln excelled as a lawyer; his success, often working for some of Illinois' greatest corporate powers, paved the way first to his election to the Illinois state house, then to the U.S. Congress in 1846.

Lincoln suffered many a bitter personal setback. The great female love of his life was probably Ann Rutledge, whom he engaged for marriage in 1835. But she died before matrimony, probably of typhoid fever. The consensus of accounts from his friends and associates reveals this loss sank him so deep into despair they feared for both his sanity and his life. Indeed, a quarter-century later, long married to Mary Todd, elected President, and heading to Washington from his Springfield, Illinois, home, Lincoln told one friend, "I have loved the name of Rutledge to this day. I did honestly and truly love the girl and think often, often of her now."

He excelled as a lawyer; his success, often working for some of Illinois' greatest corporate powers, paved the way first to his election to the Illinois state house, then to the U.S. Congress in 1846. There he opposed America's initiation of the Mexican War, affirmed the right of individual states to secede from the Union, and established so liberal, even radical, a voting record that his district rejected him in his 1848 reelection bid. Elections he lost and business setbacks he suffered. But he never gave up. He regained his seat in the Illinois House of Representatives and held it four terms. Formerly a Whig, he also gained growing influence with the new Republican Party, founded in 1854.

National Stage

In 1858, Lincoln challenged Stephen A. Douglas, one of the best-known and most powerful men in the country, for Douglas's Illinois senate seat. The Lincoln-Douglas debates that followed established Lincoln's verbal acumen, quickness on his feet, and ability to project a sweeping vision for the entire country—even if that vision changed a bit depending on what part of the state he was debating in at that moment. All this he did, and on the national stage, so that even though Douglas defeated him for the Senate, two years later the two Illinoisans squared off in an epic rematch—for the Presidency of the United States. This time Lincoln won, though Douglas finished a strong second to him in a field of four solid candidates, all of whom established significant followings.

The War likely could have been averted, at least in April, 1861, but for him. And the North likely would have failed to win it, but for him.

Known, and sometimes criticized, for his folksy manner and enjoyment of off-color jokes, Lincoln's presidency was a tempest from its first day. He actually entered Washington City in the dark of night wearing a disguise because death threats already hung over him. Though huge segments of the American public, North and South, opposed him all along the way, he exhibited single-minded tenacity in accomplishing his surpassing objective—the preservation of the full American Union, in a form healthy enough to grow and expand in influence across the continent and beyond. And he won two presidential elections, in 1860 and 1864, whose importance to American, and world, history can scarcely be exaggerated.

The Union several times appeared teetering on the verge of permanent dissolution—following the First Battle of Manassas in 1861, during the unsettling days of Lee's great Northern campaigns of 1862 and 1863, and especially just prior to the victories of Sherman in Atlanta and Sheridan in the Shenandoah during the bitter 1864 presidential race. Lincoln's assassination likely improved his place in history even as it worsened the lot of the entire United States, North and South, during the bitter years of Reconstruction and the Gilded Age of the late 1880s and 1890s.

As with other great men, the legacy of Abraham Lincoln is written according to the views and prejudices of the writer. The War likely could have been averted, at least in April, 1861, but for him. And the North likely would have failed to win it, but for him (See Chapter 11). Left in Lincoln's wake, and supported to varying degrees by him, were emancipation for all American slaves, the preservation of the full Union of American states, the devolving of sovereign governmental power from those states to the national government, and an unprecedented transfer of power from the individual himself and his local community over his own money, property, labor, and persons, to the government at Washington. More than any American in history, today's United States, with all its strengths and weaknesses, is Abraham Lincoln's creation, and the outworking of his vision for it.

President Lincoln reading with his son Tad.

Mary Todd Lincoln (1818–1882)

Abraham Lincoln's wife of 23 years, Mary Todd Lincoln's legacy remains more bitter than sweet, despite her husband's immense triumphs and revered place in United States history. Born into a wealthy, slaveholding Southern family in Kentucky, she was well-educated, cultured, high-strung, and capable of great fits of temper. Her relationship with her husband proved a stormy one from the beginning; at one point, they called off their engagement. How much of their difficulties through the years accrued from her idiosyncrasies and how much from his is difficult to assess. Particularly in the White House, his work consumed him and often separated him from her emotionally as well as physically.

When the War came, four of her five brothers fought not for the North, but for the South—and three died. Three of her four sisters married Confederates—one of whom died. Political enemies of her husband castigated her around Washington for her aristocratic "airs," ridiculed her for the Southern and Western ways she supposedly intended those airs to cover, and accused her(wrongly) of disloyalty to the United States, even treason. For her part, she publicly insulted many of the North's leading ladies, including the wives of Edwin Stanton and U. S. Grant.

The Lincolns' son Willie. His death during the War was perhaps the greatest blow of their lives.

So rent was she with grief when her favorite child, Willie, died in early 1862, she sought the aid of sorcerers and attempted to commune with him through seances. Lincoln himself warned her to control her sorrow or she might land in the lunatic asylum. His violent death perhaps drove her past the brink of insanity, and the cumulative effects of all these and other episodes, including the deaths of two other sons, certainly did. A decade after the War, she was declared insane, though after confinement to a sanatorium, that judgment was reversed. The government established a fund to provide for her financial needs through the remaining years of her life.

Jefferson Davis (1808–1889)

Jefferson Davis's election in February, 1861, to a six-year term as the only president of the Confederate States of America could hardly have been contested. Born not far from Abraham Lincoln's Kentucky birthplace, he came from a respected Mississippi family, graduated from West Point, toiled several years in the Regular army, distinguished himself in Mexican War combat, and then served the United States as congressman, secretary of war under President Franklin Pierce, senator, and chairman of the Senate Military Affairs Committee.

Though a strong proponent of state sovereignty, he had risked his life for the Union on many a bloody Mexican battlefield; he opposed secession, and he grieved when it came. Davis never possessed the eloquence of his counterpart Lincoln, his folksy humor, or his shrewd strategic political brilliance. And many historians have criticized his leadership of the Confederacy. A few examples: his enacting a national conscription law (before the United States's) because it violated local and state control and thus the spirit of the Confederacy; his suspension of the writ of habeas corpus; his long support of the middling western commander Braxton Bragg; his replacement of Joe Johnston with John Bell Hood during the Atlanta Campaign; his failure to appoint Robert E. Lee as commander-in-chief of Southern armies before the Confederate Congress did it shortly before the War's end; and his insistence on spreading troops all across the Confederacy rather than concentrating them at key points.

Born not far from Abraham Lincoln's Kentucky birthplace, Davis came from a respected Mississippi family, graduated from West Point, toiled several years in the Regular Army, distinguished himself in Mexican War combat, then served the United States as congressman, Secretary of War under President Franklin Pierce, senator, and chairman of the Senate Military Affairs Committee.

At least some of those criticisms, and others, ring valid. But many can be refuted. And Davis exercised splendid judgment with many appointments, both in the governmental sphere such as with Postmaster John Reagan and in that of the military when he named a largely-unproven Lee to head the Confederacy's largest and most important army. The very nature of the Southern nation as a confederation made difficult the coordination of troops from many individual states, especially sending them to other sections when their own state was threatened.

Critics also attacked Davis for what they considered a lackluster, defensive strategy of war that offered little chance for victory and independence. Yet Lee was excoriated by many for just the opposite—being too aggressive and sacrificing too many men in his offensive thrusts. In the end, the South would likely have lost a long protracted war no matter who was its President.

Love and Sorrow

Withal, Davis proved himself faithful, brave, and possessed of sterling integrity until the end of his life. Federal soldiers captured him in southern Georgia as he attempted to escape the country at war's end. Their treatment of him as a captured head of state finds little parallel in Christendom; they threw him into prison for two years without a trial or charges, much of the time under brutal conditions.

Jefferson Davis accomplished much in his life and was blessed with a marriage to his second wife Varina that proved one of the great loves of their time. But he bore much sorrow. In addition to the immense travails of the War, prison, and the aftermath; his first wife died of malaria only three months after their wedding day, and all four of his sons died before he, two of them in childhood.

The "White House of the Confederacy," Jefferson Davis's wartime home in downtown Richmond. (TreasureNet)

In his 1500-page magnum opus *Rise and Fall of the Confederate Government*, Davis wrote, "When the cause was lost, what cause was it? Not that of the South only, but the cause of constitutional government, of the supremacy of law, of the natural rights of man." And:

> *In asserting the right of secession, it has not been my wish to incite to its exercise: I recognize the fact that the war showed it to be impracticable, but this did not prove it to be wrong. And now that it may not be again attempted, and that the Union may promote the general welfare, it is needful that the truth, the whole truth, should be known, so that crimination and recrimination may forever cease, and then, on the basis of fraternity and faithful regard for the rights of the States, there may be written on the arch of the Union, Esto perpetua.*

Honored in Jackson, Mississippi in 1884 as "the embodied history of the South," he told the assembled host: "It has been said that I should apply to the United States for a pardon. But repentance must precede the right of pardon, and I have not repented. Remembering, as I must, all which has been suffered, all which has been lost—disappointed hopes and crushed aspirations—yet I deliberately say, if it were all to do over again, I would again do just as I did in 1861."

He died in New Orleans at age 81. Shortly before his passage, a reporter sought insight into all Jefferson Davis had done in the great conflict of 1861–65. He thought about that, then answered simply, "Tell them—tell the world that I only loved America."

Lincoln and the Constitution

The weeks following Fort Sumter witnessed a series of watershed actions by Abraham Lincoln that in themselves forever altered the nature of American government. On April 13, he declared the seceding states in a state of rebellion and called for 75,000 troops to deal with them—a declaration expressly reserved to Congress by the Constitution: "The Congress shall have the power . . . to provide for calling forth the Militia to execute the Laws of the Union, suppress Insurrections and repel Invasions."

On April 15, he called for Congress to return to session—but only on July 15. On April 19, he declared a naval blockade of the South. On April 21, he instructed the U.S. navy to buy five warships—an appropriations act needing the approval of Congress. On April 27, he began the unprecedented, gargantuan, and unconstitutional process of suspending the Constitutional rights of habeas corpus, which protected the civil rights of American citizens. On May 3, he called up thousands more troops—for three year hitches—another act the law authorized only Congress to take. And at about the same time, he ordered the Department of Treasury to pay two million dollars to a New York City company to outfit and arm his army—another appropriations act needing the approval of Congress.

Judah Benjamin, first Confederate Secretary of War and one of a number of prominent Jewish Confederates.

The Confederates' Washington Light Infantry, in camp in 1861.

Each one of these acts—and many more soon to follow—were clear violations of the United States Constitution. The majority of Northerners supported him, however, as the American people have supported other Presidents since when they felt the need to break the Constitution "for the public good." This early series of moves was breathtaking in its

My Old Kentucky Home (Stephen C. Foster)

The sun shines bright in the old Kentucky home;
'Tis summer, the darkeys are gay,

The corn-top's ripe and the meadow's in the bloom,
While the birds make music all the day.

The young folks roll on the little cabin floor,
All merry, all happy and bright;

By-'n-by hard times comes a-knocking at the door—
Then my old Kentucky home, good-night!

Chorus:

Weep no more, my lady,
Oh! weep no more today!
We will sing one song for the old Kentucky home,
For the old Kentucky home, far away.

shrewd efficiency. For instance, by not calling Congress back into session until July, Lincoln presented it with a *fait accompli* upon its return: a war months old from which there was now no turning back—unless Lincoln decided such, which he had no intention of doing. Whether or not Congress would have declared war on the South as had Lincoln, it now had little choice but to fight.

Early Federal Plans

Materially, the War was lopsided from the beginning. The great question is perhaps not why the North

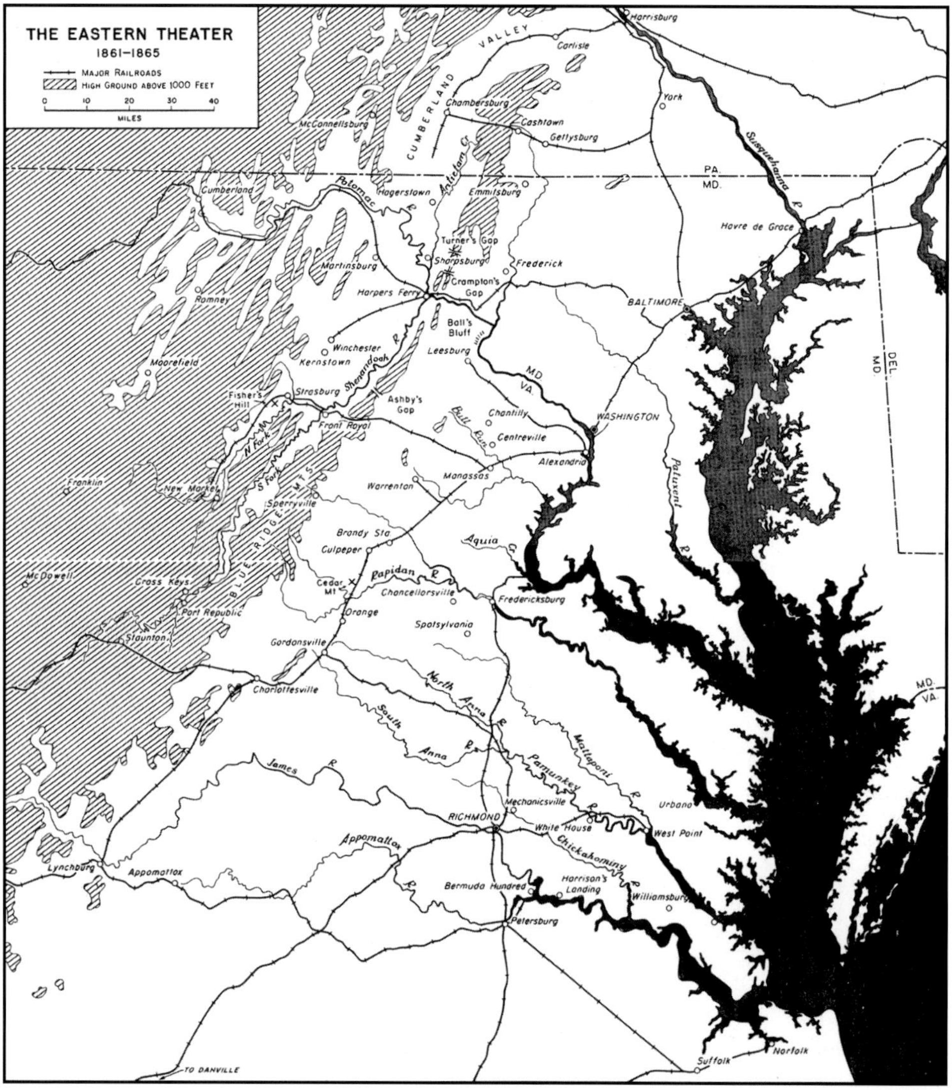

(Courtesy of The General Libraries, The University of Texas at Austin)

won, but rather how the South staved off defeat for so long. The Confederacy's long survival in spite of such disproportionate resources and manpower is at least partly explained by the traditional American character, which is far different from its usual depiction as slow to anger and averse to violence. "All real Americans love a good fight," famed World War II General George Patton, his own grandfather a decorated Confederate officer, declared. The South lasted so long "because Americans are great fighters, great warriors," says author and pastor Douglas Wilson.

Opposing Forces: April 1861

	NORTH	SOUTH
Population	22 million	5.4 million (whites) 3.7 million (blacks)
States	22	11
Soldiers*	2 million	850,000
Manufacturing Output	91%	9%
Railroad Mileage	71%	29%
Ships	50	0
Farms	67%	33%
Factories	80%	20%
Locomotive Production	96%	4%
Firearms Production	97%	3%

* Approximate totals of active soldiers for the entirety of the War

General Winfield Scott led the United States to victory in the Mexican War. A Virginian, he retained his post as commander of the Federal army even after his native state seceded. Sobered by the North's lack of military preparedness and the prowess of Southern military leadership and fighting ability, he proposed the Anaconda Plan. With a name reminiscent of the coiling constriction with which the namesake snake kills its prey, the strategy sought to choke the Confederacy to death with a naval blockade of all Southern ports. This would eliminate the cash the South earned from cotton and other cash crop sales overseas, which it needed to purchase arms and supplies.

The plan also called for taking control of the Mississippi River, which would split the Confederacy in half and further sever its western states from both their sister seceded states and the outside world. Scott believed these strategies, plus pressure from Northern armies, would drain the financial and material life from the

Winfield Scott

South, generate increasing sentiment among its people to return to the Union, and deliver a long-term victory to the United States.

Against the backdrop of the Anaconda Plan, Lincoln made the attack and capture of the Confederate capital at Richmond the primary and

Neighboring Capitals

The Federal capital of Washington City, its formal name during the War, and its Confederate counterpart of Richmond, Virginia, lay only 130 miles apart. Between them fell only two significant geographical obstacles—the Potomac and Rappahannock Rivers. Despite their overarching strategies of war, both North and South poured increasing efforts into protecting their capitals as the fight stretched on.

The United States could scarcely have picked a worse, more vulnerable location for its seat of government. Washington was surrounded by Southern- and secession-sympathetic Maryland and Confederate Virginia. But its very name symbolized the pride of a nation and the new capitol building was still under construction as the War begin.

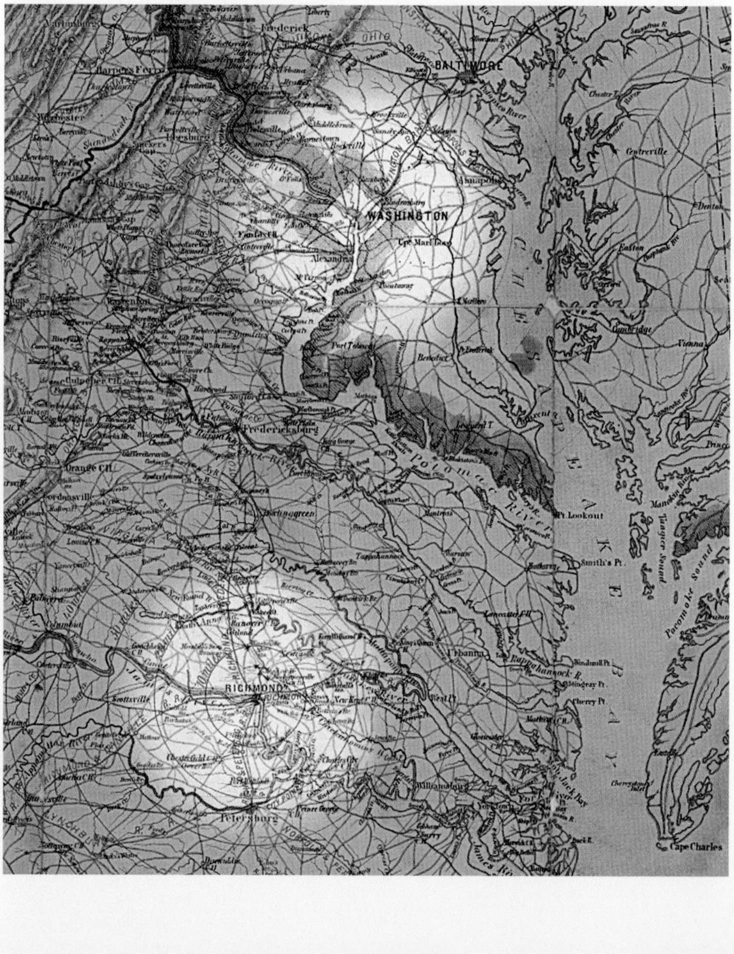

The Confederacy's original capital was Montgomery, Alabama. But the political sway of Virginia and other factors prompted its transfer to Richmond. Historians such as Clarence Carson have suggested that a more central capital location, such as Chattanooga, Tennessee—a major east–west and north–south railhead—may have been preferable. Such a location might have precluded the extreme concentration of Confederate forces in Virginia, which contributed to the loss of important territory and waterways west of the Appalachian Mountains, a primary factor in Southern defeat.

immediate goal of the Federal war effort. And Northerners were by now ready to fight. Their dissatisfaction with Scott's patient plan contributed, along with his advanced age, ill health, and perceived incompetency, to his replacement as Federal military chief with brilliant young General George B. McClellan on November 1.

Southern Strategy

The South, with a smaller population, fewer resources, and more limited military objectives, eschewed plans of invading the North or overthrowing its government. Rather, President Jefferson Davis and his administration pursued a two-pronged strategy. First, they struck a defensive posture intended neither to conquer nor forfeit territory. From the start, controversy beset this approach. The very basis of the Confederacy's existence was state sovereignty; thus, no Southern state wished to be overrun by Federal forces. To maintain the political and military cooperation of all the seceding states, Davis was forced to defend every part of every one of them. This pressured him to extend his military defense lines around the totality of the Confederacy's far-flung frontiers, land and sea. That stretched his outnumbered forces to the breaking point from the very outset of war.

The state sovereignty distinctive further complicated matters for Davis by creating discord and acrimony in his attempts to call forth detachments of troops from one state to defend the ports or borders of another. In the end, a nation founded as a confederation of independent and sovereign states was forced into universal compulsory military conscription at the direction of an increasingly centralized national government, complete with martial penalties for failure to cooperate with that program.

The second prong of Confederate strategy was diplomatic. While hoping that a vigorous and consistent defense would weary the Northern public of war, the South worked diligently to garner diplomatic recognition—and hopefully military assistance—from European titans like England and France. The Confederacy held high hopes such foreign powers, who tended to view it as an important trading partner and the North as a competitor, would come to its aid militarily. However, the Europeans' warehouses were filled to overflowing from the banner Southern crop yields of preceding years. Thus the loss of Confederate products to the Federal naval blockade did not cripple the Europeans as it might otherwise have done. The South's failure to register a devastating blow to the Northern war effort ended its hopes of foreign military intervention against the North.

In the end, a nation founded as a confederation of independent and sovereign states was forced into universal compulsory military conscription at the direction of an increasingly centralized national government, and martial penalties for failure to cooperate with that program.

Robert E. Lee (Part 1) (1807-1870)

Robert Edward Lee learned responsibility early. By the time he was seven years old, bad business dealings had disgraced his father, the famed "Light Horse" Harry Lee, who left home, then died far away. Disaster beset the Lee financial fortunes, the family had to sell their home place, and young Robert was left to tend his devout but very ill mother. Kind, sensitive, and dutiful from the beginning, he began to work to make something of himself and restore the honor of the Lee family name. Later, with the family fortune blasted, pressure weighed upon him to provide even the most basic living for himself and those for whom he would be provider.

Lee received an appointment to the United States Military Academy, where he excelled. He finished second in his class, and to this day is the only cadet ever to complete the school's four-year program without receiving a demerit. His West Point accomplishments gained him a choice assignment in the army's elite engineer corps. For more than fifteen years, he set about construction and preservation tasks great and small, such as saving the city of St. Louis from the encroachments of the Mississippi River.

These deeds landed him a staff position with American Commander-in-Chief Winfield Scott when the Mexican War came. Like Lincoln, U. S. Grant, and many others, Lee lamented that controversial conflict because of its dubious, expansionist objectives. Still, he performed a series of reconnaissance missions on horseback that resulted in a string of American flanking maneuvers and defeats of larger Mexican forces. Lee's legendary solo rides back and forth through the volcanic field of the Pedregal in a howling storm, which other crack soldiers had failed to accomplish, death looming every foot of the way, gained him so exalted a status that Scott called him "the greatest soldier in the American army."

> *What a glorious thought it is that [Charlotte] has joined her little cherubs and our angel Annie in Heaven. Thus is link by link the strong chain broken that binds us to earth, and our passage soothed to another world.*
>
> —Robert E. Lee to his wife Mary upon the death of their daughter-in-law and her babies

After the War, he remained with the army. He gained high marks for his leadership and innovation as West Point Superintendent for three years in the early 1850s. Then he commanded the prestigious 2nd U.S. Cavalry in Texas. In 1859, it was Lee whom President James Buchanan called upon to defeat the looming rebellion led by John Brown. Lee succeeded famously in that endeavor.

Family and Separation

Though he spent many years of his military career prior to the War in lonely isolation from his family Lee and his wife Mary had seven children. For extended periods of time, when he served at remote army posts, they remained at the beautiful Arlington

plantation, inherited from her family, across the Potomac River from Washington City. But Lee visited them as often as he could, and he penned a steady stream of letters to them throughout their separations.

Lee has received criticism, probably with some justification, for continuing in a career that long separated him from his family. However, he viewed his responsibility to provide for them as paramount in importance. All his training and qualifications were for the military; whereas, he believed himself ill-equipped to run a large plantation such as Arlington. Withal, his influence on his own family proved profound. A letter he wrote Mary in 1863 following the death of their daughter-in-law Charlotte and her children, in which he references his deceased daughter Annie, illustrates both his tenderness toward his family and the Christian faith that guided his convictions and his leadership of them:

It has pleased God to take from us one exceedingly dear to us, and we must be resigned to His holy will. She, I trust, will enjoy peace and happiness forever, while we must patiently struggle on under all the ills that may be in store for us. What a glorious thought it is that [Charlotte] has joined her little cherubs and our angel Annie in Heaven. Thus is link by link the strong chain broken that binds us to earth, and our passage soothed to another world. Oh, that we may be at last united in that heaven of rest, where trouble and sorrow never enter, to join in an everlasting chorus of praise and glory to our Lord and Saviour! I grieve for our lost darling as a father only can grieve for a daughter, and my sorrow is heightened by the thought of the anguish her death will cause our dear son and the poignancy it will give to the bars of his prison. May God in His mercy enable him to bear the blow He has so suddenly dealt, and sanctify it to his everlasting happiness!

Wanted: By Both Sides

Northern hopes must have been high when President Lincoln authorized Scott, still commanding U.S. military forces, to offer his fellow Virginian Lee command of all Federal armies in the field against the Confederacy. Lee's loyalty to the United States ran deep. His father, Richard "Light Horse" Harry Lee, had been governor of Virginia and before that, one of Washington's cavalry chiefs in the American War of Independence. Other relatives, such as Henry Lee, also played leading roles in the formation of the United States. His wife Mary's great-grandmother was Martha Custis Washington, wife of George Washington. Too, he supported neither the institution of slavery, which he considered a moral crime against the black race and a greater one against the white, nor, initially, the idea of Southern secession.

Nonetheless, after an evening spent on his knees in prayer and reading his Bible, and pacing the floor of his room, Lee declined the offer. Ending a thirty-two year career and suspecting his beloved Arlington estate must soon be overrun by the Federals, whose capital lay just across the Potomac River from it, Lee wrote his Unionist sister: "With all my devotion to the Union, and the feeling of loyalty and duty of an American citizen, I have not been able to make up my mind to raise my hand against my relatives, my children, my home." Two days later, he accepted a rather less spectacular command—the armed forces of a single state, his native Virginia, against that Federal army of Lincoln's.

Never Against Virginia, by John Paul Strain. President Lincoln's choice of Robert E. Lee to command the main Federal army in quelling the Confederate independence movement was the highest field command an American soldier could obtain. But here Lee spends an agonizing evening in his wife, Mary's, rose garden on their Arlington estate. Later he paced alone in his bedroom, contemplating, praying, and reading his Bible. His midnight decision: he could not lift his sword against his native Virginia.

13 Border States
(1861)

An early stereograph of Soldiers of the 7th New York State Militia, at ease and smoking their pipes in Camp Cameron, Washington City, during the early months of the War in 1861. Note the black servant at right with his head bowed, holding what appears to be an empty boot.(Library of Congress)

The parties to this conflict are not merely abolitionists and slaveholders—they are atheists, socialists, communists, red Republicans, Jacobins, on the one side, and the friends of order and regulated freedom on the other. In one word, the world is a battleground—Christianity and atheism are the combatants and the progress of humanity is at stake.

—James Henley Thornwell
Presbyterian Pastor and Theology Professor

The eight border states laying astride the fault line of secession possessed nearly a quarter of America's total population. Half these states had already gone out with the Confederacy. The importance of the others was scarcely understated by Lincoln's own words: "I should like to have God on my side, but I must have Kentucky." Moreover, to lose Maryland would mean not only a large pool of soldiers and the key city of Baltimore, but the surrounding of the national capital of Washington City by Confederate territory, and the humiliating removal of the Federal government farther north.

I think to lose Kentucky is nearly the same as to lose the whole game. Kentucky gone, we cannot hold Missouri, nor, as I think, Maryland. These all against us, and the job on our hands is too large for us.
—Abraham Lincoln

Without Kentucky, the critical south-flowing waterway of the Ohio River, a prime invasion and supply avenue for Lincoln into the South, would be adjoined by and in the gun sights of Confederate territory. So would other key east-west transportation and communication routes. And the nation's seventh-most populous state and its own enormous cache of fighting men would be lost. "I think to lose Kentucky is nearly the same as to lose the whole game," Lincoln fretted. "Kentucky gone, we cannot hold Missouri, nor, as I think, Maryland. These all against us, and the job on our hands is too large for us."

The Mississippi Valley, locus of the Western Theater of the War, circa 1861.

Missouri had long been caught up in the fratricidal feud of "Bleeding Kansas." With much of its people and government alike sympathetic to the South, Missouri joined the Confederacy late in the year. But Lincoln sent large forces of Federal troops to the state and wrested it back into the Union. However, a "people's war" spearheaded by Confederate irregulars contested Federal regiments in Missouri till the War's end in some of the most desperate and barbarous fighting ever seen on the North American continent. Support for the war was by no means monolithic, even north of the Federal Border States. The Democratic leadership of New York City—opponents of Lincoln and the Republicans—consistently opposed it. So did significant segments of western states such as Indiana and Lincoln's own Illinois.

And as late as March, 1863, the New Jersey legislature proclaimed: ". . . at no time since the commencement of the present war has this State been other than willing to terminate peacefully and honorably to all a war unnecessary in its origin, fraught with horror and suffering in its prosecution, and necessarily dangerous to the liberties of all in its continuance."

Border States

State	Population	Allegiance
Delaware	112,216	Federal
Maryland	687,049	Federal
Virginia	1,596,206	Confederate
West Virginia*	N/A	Federal
North Carolina	991,464	Confederate
Kentucky	1,155,651	Federal
Tennessee	1,109,741	Confederate
Missouri	1,181,992	Federal
Arkansas	435,402	Confederate

* Seceded from Confederate Virginia in 1863

Maryland

One of American history's most bizarre—and overlooked—sequence of events unfolded in Maryland during the year 1861. The state had long been a social and political powderkeg. It nearly surrounded the Federal capital of Washington, while laying between Washington, the industrial powerhouses of New York and New England, and Virginia and the Upper South. It was home to thousands of slaveowners, yet leaned antislavery. It was pro-Unionist in sentiment, but strongly supported what it viewed as a state's Constitutional right of secession. The North needed Maryland, and the South wanted it.

Only one month after Fort Sumter, a large force of Federal troops from Massachusetts troops marched uninvited into Maryland and through Baltimore. There, a furious throng of citizens stoned them. The Federals bloodied the crowd with bayonets and bullets. Then in September, the Lincoln administration ordered a historic action. Without notifying them of charges, or indeed possessing any charges, it hauled dozens of Maryland legislators it suspected of supporting secession out of their homes in front of their families by the darkness of night and threw them into prison. The prison was temporarily located at Fort McHenry, from where Francis Scott Key had written *The Star Spangled Banner*. In fact, Key's own

When thousands of armed Massachusetts troops marched through Maryland without permission, headed for a war the state did not support, furious citizens in Baltimore hurled stones at them. The soldiers responded by unleashing bayonets and bullets alike against the civilians. Four soldiers and a dozen civilians died, and dozens of combatants fell wounded. (Pratt, Fletcher, *Civil War in Pictures*)

grandson was among the host flung into captivity at the fort. He wrote eloquently of how much the nation had changed in less than a half century as he looked upon the United States flag flying at the same location as when his grandfather had written his famous stanzas: "As I stood upon the very scene of that conflict, I could not but contrast my position with his, forty-seven years before. The flag which he had then so proudly hailed, I saw waving at the same place over the victims of as vulgar and brutal a despotism as modern times have witnessed."

Continued Division

In Maryland's November elections, thousands of Federal soldiers from states other than Maryland voted, while residents had to pass through formations of bayonet-brandishing Federals in order to vote. Federal soldiers occupied Maryland throughout the war, even as Confederate sentiment, particularly in the eastern sections, persisted, and slavery continued unabated throughout the state.

> *Federal soldiers occupied Maryland throughout the war, even as Confederate sentiment, particularly in the eastern sections, persisted, and slavery continued unabated throughout the state.*

Though several of the state's largest newspapers sided with Lincoln and his bold actions, at least one did not and published these words: "Maryland implores the President . . . to cease this unholy war, at least until Congress assembles; that Maryland desires and consents to the recognition of the independence of the Confederate States." Nor did the legislature agree, prior to its collective jailing by Lincoln:

> *Whereas the war against the Confederate States is unconstitutional and repugnant to civilization, and will result in bloody and shameful overthrow of our institutions; and while recognizing the obligations of Maryland to the Union, we sympathize with the South in the struggle for their rights—for the sake of humanity we are for peace and reconciliation, and solemnly protest against this war, and will take no part in it;*
>
> *Resolved, that Maryland implores the President, in the name of God, to cease this unholy war, at least until Congress assembles; that Maryland desires and consents to the recognition of the independence of the Confederate States. The military occupation of Maryland is unconstitutional, and she protests against it, though the violent interference with the transit of federal troops is discountenanced, that the vindication of her rights be left to time and reason, and that a Convention, under existing circumstances, is inexpedient.*

The enduring and widespread enmity for the North in the state was evidenced in My Maryland, the state song until 2001. Its opening verses herald the news that "The despot's heel (Lincoln's army) is on thy shore" and call upon the state to "Avenge the patriotic gore that flecked the streets of Baltimore" in the riot with the Massachusetts troops.

Roger B. Taney (1777-1864)

Often castigated by moderns both for spearheading the Supreme Court majority that ruled against slave Dred Scott in that landmark case, and for his epic clashes with Abraham Lincoln over habeas corpus, many legal scholars now consider Roger B. Taney a giant in the history of American jurisprudence. His dramatic career included service as President Andrew Jackson's Secretary of the Treasury. Then, for nearly 30 years—the last of his life—he served as Chief Justice of the Supreme Court of the United States.

During this tenure, in 1857, he led the court's majority in ruling that Scott remained a slave even though he had lived for a period with his master in free soil territory. Legal scholars contend that Taney's leadership stood on firm constitutional footing in its defense of Fifth Amendment property rights. His critics often overlook the chief justice's clear proclamation that he ruled not according to how he himself would have written the Constitution, but rather as he believed America's Founding Fathers had. Indeed, Taney, a Marylander, had already freed his own slaves and wrote often and with power against "the evils of slavery."

Citizens of every stripe—politicians, newspaper publishers, attorneys, business owners, common workers were being hauled from their homes and places of businesses by Federal officers for voicing the slightest criticism of the Federal government or Lincoln, flung into jail, and left there. Taney had no illusions but that that fate likely awaited him if he crossed the President.

Only weeks after the War commenced in 1861, Lincoln suspended the *writ of habeas corpus*, one of the foundational pillars of American—and Western—liberty, and preeminent among all provisions of the Bill of Rights. The *writ of habeas corpus* is sourced in England's ancient Magna Carta. Among other things, it requires a warrant to be issued by a legitimate law enforcement authority before a person can be arrested; prohibits the jailing of a person without his being charged with a specific crime; and does not allow that person to be interred indefinitely without the opportunity of being brought before a legally convened court for the exercise of his rights and the hearing of his case.

The Merryman Case

Despite the central place of *habeas corpus* in American liberty and an armada of opinion ranging from the great British jurist William Blackstone to American Chief Justice John Marshall to President Thomas Jefferson that only Congress—and never the President—could suspend *habeas corpus*, Lincoln did just that in thousands of cases regarding Northerners. One Marylander, John Merryman, was jailed without warrant and kept jailed without opportunity for trial or defense, appealed to Taney. It is difficult for the modern to conceive of the political climate in which Taney received this plea. Citizens of every stripe—politicians, newspaper publishers, attorneys, business owners, common workers—were being hauled from their homes and places of businesses by Federal officers for voicing the slightest criticism of the Federal government or Lincoln, flung into jail, and left there. Taney had no illusions but that that fate likely awaited him if he crossed the President. Yet in *Ex parte Merryman*, he ordered the release of the jailed man. Lincoln ordered his soldiers to refuse. The chief justice then penned an opinion now famous in constitutional law. Delivered directly to Lincoln at his office, it informed the President that he, not Merryman, was breaking the law and the Constitution, and it ordered Merryman's release.

At this point, Lincoln did issue a warrant of arrest—for Taney. Though the federal marshal declined to serve the warrant, Lincoln had established that neither Congress, the Supreme Court, nor the Constitution would stand in the way of his carrying out the actions he deemed best for the country.

Chief Justice Roger Brooke Taney, eighty-five-years-old as Abraham Lincoln issued the warrant for his arrest and dead before the end of the War, recorded his thoughts for history:

> *If the President of the United States may suspend the writ (of habeas corpus), then the Constitution of the United States has conferred upon him more regal and absolute power over the liberty of the citizen than the people of England have thought it safe to entrust to the crown—a power which the Queen of England cannot exercise to this day, and which could not have been lawfully exercised by the sovereign even in the reign of Charles the First.*

James Thornwell, the Confederate Constitution, and Christianity (1812-1862)

Presbyterian clergyman James Henley Thornwell of South Carolina remains one of the greatest of all American theologians. He served as president of the South Carolina College (now University) and professor of theology at Columbia (SC) Theological Seminary. Following are excerpts of a petition he wrote for the General Assembly of the Presbyterian Church in the Confederate States of America to the Confederate Congress. It unsuccessfully urges adjustment of the Confederate Constitution to reflect a distinctively Christian worldview.

> *We are constrained, in candour, to say that, in our humble judgment, the Constitution, admirable as it is in other respects, still labours under one capital defect. It is not distinctively Christian. It is not bigotry, but love to our country, and an earnest, ardent desire to promote its permanent well-being, which prompts us to call the attention of your honourable body to this subject, and, in the way of respectful petition, to pray that the Constitution may be amended so as to express the precise relations which the Government of these States ought to sustain to the religion of Jesus Christ.*

> *The Constitution of the United States was an attempt to realize the notion of popular freedom, without the checks of aristocracy and a throne,*

and without the alliance of a national Church. The conception was a noble one, but the execution was not commensurate with the design. The fundamental error of our fathers was, that they accepted a partial for complete statement of the truth. They saw clearly the human side—that popular governments are the offspring of popular will; and that rulers, as the servants and not the masters of their subjects, are properly responsible to them. They failed to apprehend the Divine side—that all just government is the ordinance of God, and that magistrates are His ministers who must answer to Him for the execution of their trust. The consequence of this failure . . . was to invest the people with a species of supremacy as insulting to God as it was injurious to them. They became a law unto themselves; there was nothing beyond them to check or control their caprices or their pleasure. All were accountable to them; they were accountable to none. This was certainly to make the people a God; and if it was not explicitly expressed that they could do no wrong, it was certainly implied that there was no tribunal to take cognizance of their acts. A foundation was thus laid for the worst of all possible forms of government—a democratic absolutism. . . . The will of majorities must become the supreme law, if the voice of the people is to be regarded as the voice of God; if they are, in fact, the only God whom rulers are bound to obey. . . . We must contemplate people and rulers as alike subject to the authority of God. . . . If, then, the State is an ordinance of God, it should acknowledge the fact. . . . Let us guard, in this new Confederacy, against the fatal delusion that our government is a mere expression of human will.

. . . It is not enough for a State which enjoys the light of Divine revelation to acknowledge in general terms the supremacy of God; it must also acknowledge the supremacy of His Son, whom He hath appointed heir of all things, by whom also He made the worlds.

. . . It is not enough for a State which enjoys the light of Divine revelation to acknowledge in general terms the supremacy of God; it must also acknowledge the supremacy of His Son, whom He hath appointed heir of all things, by whom also He made the worlds. To Jesus Christ all power in heaven and earth is committed. To Him every knee shall bow, and every tongue confess. He is the Ruler of the nations, the King of kings, and Lord of lords.

. . . the separation of Church and State is a very different thing from the separation of religion and the State. Here is where our fathers (America's founders) erred. In their anxiety to guard against the evils of a religious establishment . . . they virtually expelled Jehovah from the government of the country, and left the State an irresponsible corporation, or responsible only to the immediate corporators.

. . . But it may be asked . . . Has the State any right to accept the Scriptures as the Word of God? . . . The State is lord of no man's conscience. . . . He may be Atheist, Deist, infidel, Turk or Pagan: it is no concern of the State, so long as he walks orderly. Its protecting shield must be over him, as over every other citizen.

. . . But if by "accepting the Scriptures" it is

meant that the State may itself believe them to be true, and regulate its own conduct and legislation in conformity with their teachings, the answer must be in the affirmative.

. . . The separation of Church and State is a very different thing from the separation of religion and the State. Here is where our fathers [America's founders] erred. In their anxiety to guard against the evils of a religious establishment, and to preserve the provinces of Church and State separate and distinct, they virtually expelled Jehovah from the government of the country, and left the State an irresponsible corporation, or responsible only to the immediate corporators.

. . . God is the ruler among the nations; and the people who refuse Him their allegiance shall be broken with a rod of iron, or dashed in pieces like a potter's vessel. Our republic will perish like the Pagan republics of Greece and Rome, unless we baptize it into the name of Christ. . . . We long to see, what the world has never yet beheld, a truly Christian Republic, and we humbly hope that God has reserved it for the people of these Confederate States to realize the grand and glorious idea.

The whole substance of what we desire may be expressed in the following or equivalent terms, to be added to the section providing for liberty of conscience:

> *Nevertheless we, the people of these Confederate States, distinctly acknowledge our responsibility to God, and the supremacy of His Son, Jesus Christ, as King of kings and Lord of lords; and hereby ordain that no law shall be passed by the Congress of these Confederate States inconsistent with the will of God, as revealed in the Holy Scriptures.*

Slave Auction in the South

William H. Russell, famed *London Times* reporter, described for the July 13, 1861, *Harper's Weekly* readers a slave auction he witnessed in Montgomery, Alabama shortly after the War commenced :

> *The crowd was small. Three or four idle men in rough, homespun, makeshift uniforms leaned against the iron rails inclosing a small pond of foul, green-looking water, surrounded by brick-work, which decorates the space in front of the Exchange Hotel. The speaker stood on an empty deal packing-case. A man in a cart was listening with a lack luster eye to the address. Some three or four others, in a sort of vehicle which might either be a hearse or a piano-van, had also drawn up for the benefit of the address. Five or six other men, in long black coats and high hats, some whittling sticks and chewing tobacco, and discharging streams of discolored saliva, completed the group. "N-i-n-e h-hun-nerd and fifty dollars! Only nine h-hun-nerd and fifty dollars offered for him!" exclaimed the man, in the tone of injured dignity, remonstrance, and surprise, which can be insinuated by all true auctioneers into the dryest numerical statements. "Will no one make any advance on nine hundred and fifty dollars?" A man near me opened his mouth, spat, and said, "Twenty-five." "Only nine hundred and seventy-five dollars offered for him! Why, at's radaklous — only nine hundred and seventy-five dollars! Will no one," etc. Beside the orator auctioneer stood a stout young man of five-and-twenty years of age, with a bundle in his hand. He was a muscular fellow, broad-shouldered, narrow-flanked, but rather small in stature; he had on a broad, greasy, old*

wide-awake, a blue jacket, a coarse cotton shirt, loose and rather ragged trowsers, and broken shoes. The expression of his face was heavy and sad, but it was by no means disagreeable, in spite of his thick lips, broad nostrils, and high cheek bones. On his head was wool instead of hair. I am neither sentimentalist nor Black Republican, nor negro-worshiper, but I confess the sight caused a strange thrill through my heart. I tried in vain to make myself familiar with the fact that I could, for the sum of $975, become as absolutely the owner of that mass of blood, bones, sinew, flesh, and brains as of the horse which stood by my side. There was no sophistry which could persuade me the man was not a man—he was, indeed, by no means my brother, but assuredly he was a fellow-creature. I have seen slave markets in the East, but somehow or other the Orientalism of the scene cast a coloring over the nature of the sales there which deprived them of the disagreeable harshness and matter-of-fact character of the transaction before me. For Turk, or Smyrniote, or Egyptian to buy and sell slaves seemed rather suited to the eternal fitness of things than to otherwise. The turbaned, shawled, loose-trowsered, pipe-smoking merchants, speaking an unknown tongue, looked as if they were engaged in a legitimate business. One knew that their slaves would not be condemned to any very hard labor, and that they would be in some sort the inmates of the family and members of it. Here it grated on my ear to listen to the familiar tones of the English tongue as the medium by which the transfer was effected, and it was painful to see decent-looking men in European garb engaged in the work before me. Perchance these impressions may wear off, for I meet many English people who are the most strenuous advocates of the slave system, although it is true that their perceptions may be quickened to recognize its beauties by their participation in the profits. The negro was sold to one of the by-standers, and walked off with his bundle God knows where. "Niggers is cheap," was the only remark of the by-standers.

As I was returning to the hotel there was another small crowd at the fountain. Another auctioneer, a fat, flabby, perspiring, puffy man, was trying to sell a negro girl who stood on the deal box beside him. She was dressed pretty much like a London servant girl of the lower order, out of place, except that her shoes were mere shreds of leather patches, and her bonnet would have scarce passed muster in the New Cut. She, too, had a little bundle in her hand, and looked out at the buyers from a pair of large sad eyes. "Niggers were cheap;" still here was this young woman going for an upset price of $610, but no one would bid, and the auctioneer, after vain attempts to raise the price and excite competition, said, "Not sold to-day, Sally; you may get down."

Cowboys and Indians

Over half the present-day Continental American land mass remained beyond the boundaries of established "Christian" civilization when the War began. Texas joined the Confederacy, but a separate war remained to be won on its western frontier with the fierce Comanche Indians. Thus, the state placed a significant portion of its soldiers, including some from the already legendary Texas Rangers, formed in 1854, as a firewall in its west. Other than the Federal naval blockade, little martial conflict reached Texas early in the War. But Texans reached the War in a degree unprecedented in American history. More than 90 percent of all white male residents of the state between the ages of 16 and 60 eventually served in the Confederate military forces.

More than 90 percent of all white male residents of Texas between the ages of 16 and 60 eventually served in the Confederate military forces.

Texan John H. Reagan (1809–1904), Confederate Postmaster General, defied the destruction of war, the Federal naval blockade, and deteriorating Southern financial and living conditions to establish a postal service that not only paid its own way, but earned a profit.

North of the Red River from Texas, site of modern-day Oklahoma, lay the Indian Nations Territory, where several major tribes had been driven from lands farther east, such as during the Cherokees' bloody and heartbreaking Trail of Tears in the late 1830s. The South desired hegemony in Indian Territory as a buffer against Federal invasion into Texas and Arkansas, and the North desired it as a staging ground for the same. The loyalties of the largely Christianized Cherokee, Chickasaw, Choctaw, Creek, and Seminole nations of Indian Territory were split between North and South. However, many had suffered mistreatment at the hands of the United States Government and many were slaveowners, and the majority chose to support the Confederacy, especially early in the War.

The fighting skills of many of the Indians proved far superior to what the warring governments suspected. Notable among a formidable group was the legendary Cherokee Chief and Confederate General Stand Watie. Nearly sixty years old at the War's end, he bedeviled the Federals from beginning to end, gaining renown as a virtual Nathan Bedford Forrest of "The Nations" for his electrifying surprise attacks, audacity in battle, and immunity to capture.

Declaration by the People of the Cherokee Nation of the Causes Which Have Impelled Them to Unite Their Fortunes With Those of the Confederate States of America

Providence rules the destinies of nations, and events, by inexorable necessity, overrule human resolutions . . . In the States which still adhered to the Union a military despotism has displaced the civil power and the laws became silent amid arms. Free speech and almost free thought became a crime. . . . The mandate of the Chief Justice of the Supreme Court was set at naught by the military power, and this outrage on common right approved by a President sworn to support the Constitution . . .

The humanities of war, which even barbarians respect, were no longer thought worthy to be observed. Foreign mercenaries and the scum of the cities and the inmates of prisons were enlisted and organized into brigades and sent into Southern States to aid in subjugating a people struggling for freedom, to burn, to plunder, and to commit the basest of outrages on the women . . . men of the highest character and position were incarcerated upon suspicion without process of law . . . and even women were imprisoned by the arbitrary order of a President and Cabinet Ministers; while the press ceased to be free . . ."

Way Out West

Further north and west, the sprawling, still-sparsely settled territories of Kansas, Nebraska, and the Dakotas, as well as those along the Rocky Mountains and the Continental Divide and west toward the Pacific were Union in culture, geography, and climate. The coastal states of California and Oregon and the territory of Washington were likewise Federal.

Seminole Indian Chief and Confederate military hero John Jumper

The situation in the southwest proved more interesting. Confederate sympathies in New Mexico Territory, site of present-day Arizona and New Mexico, were strong, particularly in the southern half of the territory. In fact, that portion declared itself in alliance with the Confederacy. And the South wanted the territory, which stretched nearly to the Pacific, possessed stockpiles of weapons and supplies at Federal forts, and provided access to a bonanza of minerals and other natural resources. Local militia soon clashed with Federal garrisons in the territory, and Texans, Californians, and Indians joined the melee. By year's end, the Texans spearheaded an effort that forced the surrender of Federal Fort Fillmore and resulted in the naming of Mesilla as capital of the new Confederate territory.

Young New York drummer boys in camp in 1861. What did they experience in the War? Which of them survived it?

The Girl I Left Behind Me (Samuel Lover)

The hour was sad I left the maid, a lingering farewell taking,
Her sighs and tears my steps delay'd, I thought her heart was breaking;
In hurried words her name I bless'd, I breathed the vows that bind me,
And to my heart in anguish press'd the girl I left behind me.
Then to the East we bore away, to win a name in story,
And there where dawns the sun of day, there dawns our sun of glory;
Both blazed in noon on Alma's height, where in the post assign'd me,
I shar'd the glory of that fight, Sweet Girl I Left Behind Me.

14 Stonewall
(1861)

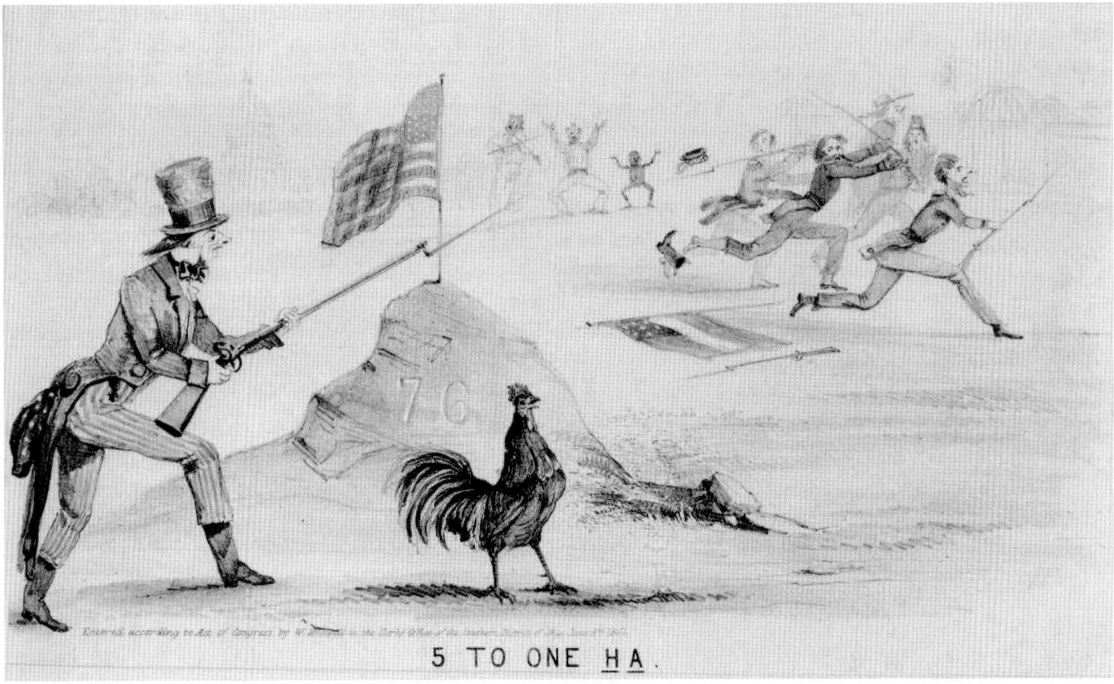

North and South alike expected quick and smashing victory for their cause as the War commenced. Neither imagined what lay ahead. Northern optimism shows in "5 to 1 HA" as Uncle Sam puts five panic-stricken Southern soldiers to flight. A black child and two black men, one fiddling, cheer in the background. (Library of Congress)

See Jackson—his sword in his hand, like the stern rocks around him, immovable stand.

—Margaret Junkin Preston

Neither side contemplated a protracted struggle, much less the marathon slaughter of the flower of two generations. Lincoln's initial levy of troops called for only a three-month enlistment; he saw no need for more. The popular refrain in the South was that the average Southerner was worth ten Yankees in the field. The early skirmishes gave neither side serious pause to reflect otherwise. In Virginia, the Confederates fared well at Big Bethel and Falling Waters, the Federals in the transmountain regions that would soon break off and form the new Union state of West Virginia.

Congressmen, senators, governors, Presidential cabinet members, captains of industry, and the most elegant matrons and maidens of society came forth resplendent in their Sunday best and equipped with picnic baskets of sumptuous virtuosity. They arrayed themselves on the ridge overlooking a plain just north of the key rail junction of Manassas.

Never was the surreal atmosphere more pronounced than at Manassas Junction, northern Virginia, on Sunday morning, July 21. On that day, North and South first collided with all the muscle they could muster. But their armies were not alone on the field. From out of the Federal capital of Washington streamed such a parade of carriages, wagons, and barouches as had rarely if ever been witnessed in America. Congressmen, senators, governors, Presidential cabinet members, captains of industry, and the most elegant matrons and maidens of society came forth resplendent in their Sunday best and equipped with picnic baskets of sumptuous virtuosity. They arrayed themselves on the ridge overlooking a plain just north of the key rail junction of Manassas. Then they watched the most impressively-equipped military force ever to shoulder arms on the North American continent march into battle against an outnumbered contingent of "rebels," which the Washington gliterrati fully expected to be swept into the ash heap of history, along with their newly birthed country, in one afternoon.

In point of fact, the Federals' competent General Irvin McDowell beat his counterparts—Fort Sumter hero Pierre Beauregard and the Confederacy's highest-ranking general, Joseph Johnston—to the punch with a swarming flank attack. The Confederates reeled under the blow and the weight of numbers and were driven back to within a few hundred yards of the rail depot. They knew if that fell, the Federals would control northern Virginia, its key east-west and north-south transportation junction, and a direct road into Richmond itself with no significant force to stop them. Their new nation seemed crumbling about their shoulders as the gray- and butternut-clad hosts scrambled for their lives up one side of Henry House Hill and then down the other.

Irvin McDowell

"There Stands Jackson"

It was the strange man who sat astride his stub-legged little mount at the bottom of that hill that caused the history of the world to be written differently than it might otherwise have been. "There stands Jackson like a stone wall," gasped mortally-wounded General Barnard Bee. The South Carolinian had spotted his old Mexican War comrade, Brigadier General Tom Jackson, mounted amidst the 2,500 men of his Virginia brigade in front of a copse of pine trees. "Rally behind the Virginians, men!"

The Mexican War

The War of 1861–65 is replete with military leaders famous for their exploits in that colossal American struggle. However, many of these men gained fame not only because a great conflict raged and someone had to lead. They also possessed intelligence, courage, toughness, and aptitude at leading other men in battle. This stemmed partly from their participation a decade-and-a-half previous in the Mexican War. That lopsided conflict provided a training ground for an entire generation of men who would lead the far larger and more powerful Federal and Confederate armies against one another in the 1860s.

Many of them, including Braxton Bragg, Ulysses S. Grant, Thomas J. Jackson, Robert E. Lee, George McClellan, John Pemberton, and George Pickett, earned great distinction, honors, and in some cases, fame, for their exploits in Mexico. Among their number was future Confederate President Jefferson Davis. Some of them remained in the service after the Mexican War right up to the War of 1861–65. Many others pursued different vocations, then returned. They all learned much about war and leading men they could have learned no other way than through participation. And they learned, that despite being outnumbered and fighting on the opponents' home ground, good leadership, tenacious fighting, and perseverance could bring victory in battle.

Other Mexican War veterans who played key roles in the later war include Lewis Armistead, David Farragut, Winfield Hancock, John Bell Hood, Albert Sidney Johnston, Joe Johnston, Philip Kearney, James Longstreet, George Meade, John Bankhead Magruder, John Hunt Morgan, John Pope, David Dixon Porter, Raphael Semmes, William Tecumseh Sherman, and George Thomas.

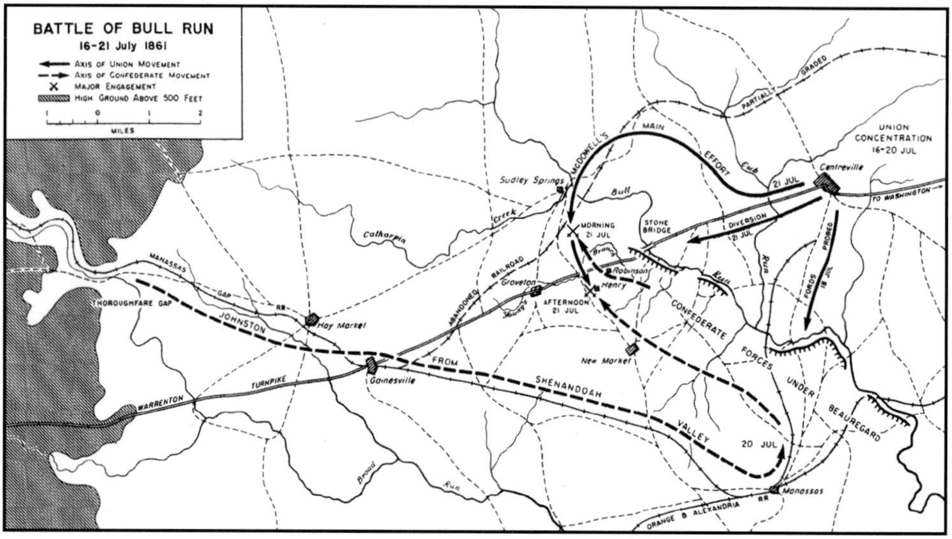

Map of First Manassas, or Bull Run, battlefield. (Courtesy of The General Libraries, The University of Texas at Austin)

As Federal bullets began to fly all about him, Jackson, now forever baptized by Bee as "Stonewall," raised his arms, face, and silent prayers to heaven, beseeching the blessing of God on his men and his cause, which he considered to be the defense of his Virginia homeland. Then one bullet tore off part of Jackson's finger, another struck his horse, and, his face twisted in fury, he shouted, "Reserve your fire till they come within fifty yards, then fire and give them the bayonet; and, when you charge, yell like furies!" And so was born the Rebel Yell.

Jackson's men indeed turned the day for the Confederacy at what Northerners would call the First Battle of Bull Run and Southerners the First Battle of Manassas. The Federal assault was blunted, stopped, and reversed, and the initiative passed to the Confederates. Later in the afternoon, the scales of balance tipped finally to the South. It happened when one last Confederate force arrived on the field. They wore blue uniforms and flew a banner that looked like a United States flag, but they broke the Federal lines and sent them into a headlong retreat all the way back to Washington.

Hurtling from the field, too, were the erstwhile picnickers, champagne glasses and cold chicken legs littering their wake. Among the many prisoners taken by Jeb Stuart and the Confederate cavalry was the governor of Connecticut.

"Stonewall" Jackson pled for permission to pursue his defeated opponent clear into Washington. Neither he nor his superiors who denied his request could conceive that no organized defense now stood between them and President Lincoln himself in the White House twenty-five miles away. Neither could they conceive it would be the best chance they would ever have for victory and independence in the four years of war and the nearly 700,000 deaths which they could not imagine would follow.

We called to them, tried to tell them there was no danger, called them to stop, implored them to stand. We called them cowards, denounced them in the most offensive term, put out our heavy revolvers, and threatened to shoot them, but all in vain; a cruel crazy, mad, hopeless panic possessed them, and communicated to everybody about in front and rear. The heat was awful, although now about six; the men were exhausted their mouths' gaped, their lips cracked and blackened with the powder of the cartridges they had bitten off in the battle, their eyes starting in frenzy; no mortal ever saw such a mass of ghastly wretches.

—Congressman Nathan Riddle describing the Federal soldiers' retreat at First Manassas (Bull Run)

Thomas J. "Stonewall" Jackson (1824-1863)

Thomas Jonathan "Stonewall" Jackson's life was one of the epic, bittersweet sagas of his generation. Hardly any one would have appeared less likely bound for fame and greatness than young Tom Jackson of the western (now West) Virginia mountain country. Tragedy struck his life early, and it struck often. He lost his beloved elder sister when he was three, his father a week later, his mother at age six, and his brother while Tom was still a teenager.

Jackson received an appointment to West Point almost on a fluke; his backwoods education and demeanor rendered him the ill-equipped object of his classmates' scorn when he arrived at the college. Though he finished dead last in his class his first year, that he did not flunk out was a harbinger of the iron will and unshakable determination that would mark him all his life. By the end of his fourth year and graduation, one classmate remarked to another—George McClellan, second man in the class academically—that had they one more year of school, Jackson would have finished top in the class!

He went almost immediately to the 1846–48 Mexican War. It was this war where he first earned fame. In a legendary feat, he, one other man, and one cannon reversed a Mexican assault into the charge up Chapultepec Hill, the capture of the fabled "Halls of Montezuma," and the sealing of Mexican Emperor Santa Anna's fate.

Jackson took an instructor's position at the Virginia Military Institute in 1851. He would teach there for a decade, earning a well-deserved reputation as one of the worst instructors the school ever had because of his rote, wooden lectures. But he also earned a growing respect from those students and professors who got to know him. Probably the greatest love of his life was Pennsylvania-born Elinor Junkin, daughter of Washington College President George Junkin. She and Jackson married in 1853, but barely a year later, she died in childbirth, along with the baby.

Jackson was grief-torn; but these losses, along with

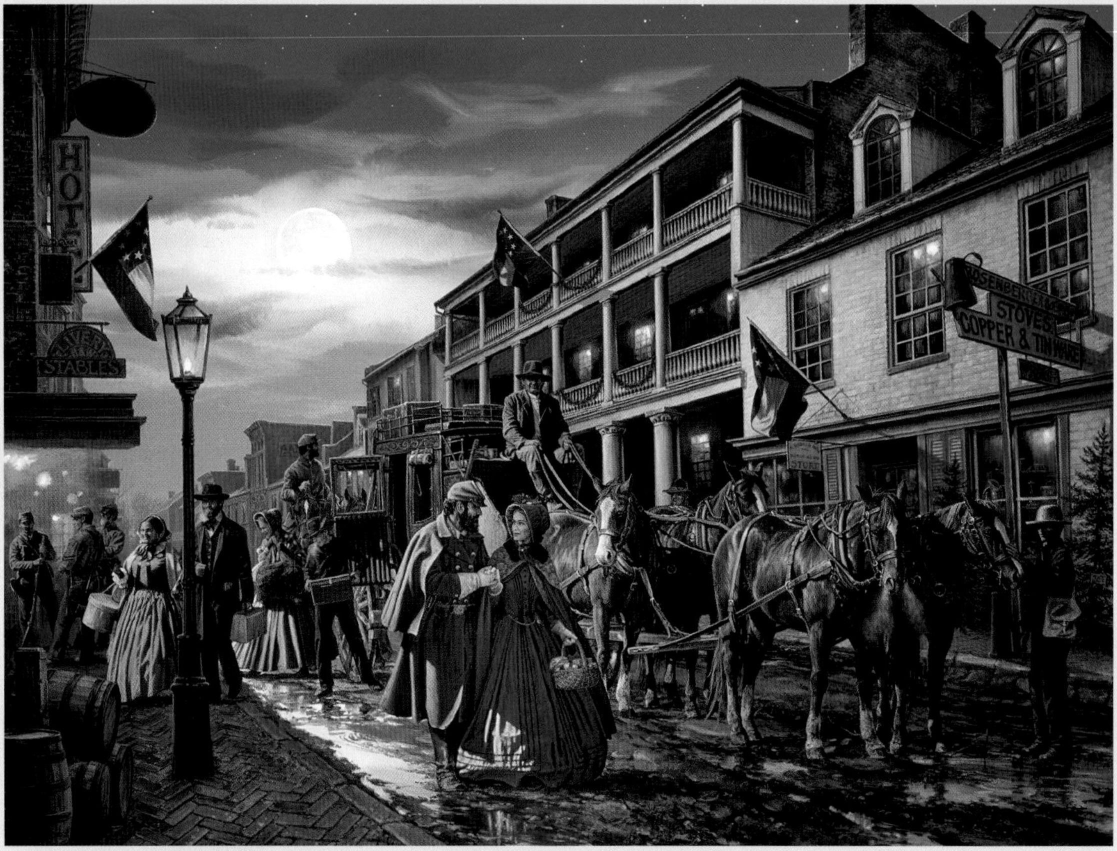

Christmas Moon, by John Paul Strain. Mary Anna Jackson joins her husband Thomas "Stonewall" Jackson at his 1861–62 winter headquarters in Winchester, Virginia. In the days that followed, they would conceive their only child that lived past infancy.

many other contributions to his life by Ellie, aided his growing religious devotion. He and Ellie's sister Maggie became best friends and together started what became one of the most successful black Sunday School classes in the entire South. Despite significant opposition from some whites in the community, and even threats of legal action, Jackson taught the class for years, and Maggie played the piano. Generations of black clergy and other church and educational leaders came forth from the class.

Fame and Tragedy

Jackson and Maggie also apparently fell strongly in love. But a hard trial ensued here as well. The Presbyterian doctrine to which both subscribed prohibited a person marrying their dead spouse's sibling. Though neither Tom nor Maggie agreed with the stricture (which was shortly thereafter expunged from Presbyterian teaching), they chose to honor what they viewed as the God-sanctioned authority over them, as opposed to their own feelings.

In 1857, wedded bliss returned to Jackson as he married Mary Anna Morrison, the daughter of another Presbyterian clergyman and college president. They lost one child in infancy, but had another, Julia, who survived. By the onset of the War in 1861, Jackson was a successful businessman, happy family man, and a devout deacon in the Lexington Presbyterian Church.

His fame on many fields is well known—bestowal of the sobriquet "Stonewall" as he held the gray line and turned the tide of battle at First Manassas; the Spring 1862 Shenandoah Valley campaign in which he defeated three Federal armies, all larger than his own, in half-a-dozen battles, and helped save Richmond from McClellan's powerful host; Sharpsburg, where his outnumbered men wrecked two Federal corps and prevented a rout; and Second Manassas, where his men again held off a vastly larger force and prepared the way for Longstreet's crushing assault.

Despite significant opposition from some whites in the community, and even threats of legal action, Jackson taught the class for years and Maggie played the piano. Generations of black clergy and other church and educational leaders came forth from the class.

He commanded the Confederate right during the devastating victory at Fredericksburg; and at Chancellorsville, he electrified the world with one of the most stunning large-scale ambushes in military history. Again commanding a force only a fraction the size of his foe, "Stonewall" stampeded the Federal Corps of fellow-devout Christian Oliver O. Howard for three miles, and vanquished Fighting Joe Hooker's plans to annihilate the Army of Northern Virginia with his colossal 134,000-man juggernaut.

But the unsearchable hand of Providence again intervened. At the zenith of his success and worldwide fame, and at the very point of cutting off the Federal retreat across the United States Ford of the Rappahannock River and perhaps destroying the entire Army of the Potomac, he was mistakenly shot down by his own men. Jackson alone had perceived the staggering opportunity of sealing off the Federal retreat. Renowned for his secrecy and discretion in military matters, he told only A. P. Hill of his plan. When both men fell from serious wounds, no one was able to communicate Jackson's plan.

Jeb Stuart took over Jackson's command and consummated the smashing Confederate victory the

War chief Stonewall Jackson "crowns" Janie Corbin, one of the many children with whom he developed dear friendships. He perhaps grew closer to this child than any other, but her death to scarlet fever was one of the greatest blows of the War to him. (*The Life of General Thomas J. "Stonewall" Jackson for the Young*)

next day. Smashing, but not fatal. "On such agate points do the balances of the world turn," wrote Winston Churchill of this dramatic sequence of events—and their later consequences. Jackson survived his bullet wounds. However, he died eight days later, probably from pneumonia brought on when stretcher-bearers carrying him from the field at Chancellorsville dropped him and he landed hard on a tree stump, evidently puncturing a lung.

Spiritual Impact

When the long-triumphant Army of Northern Virginia next took the field two months later at Gettysburg, they suffered their first major defeat of the War. The mistakes they made in that campaign, especially during its climactic stages, read like a catalogue of all the miscues that seemed not to occur when Jackson rode with the army. The Confederacy would never again field an army capable of visiting destruction on the Federals of a magnitude that would win Southern independence. And Jackson, along with World War II General George Patton, would be the only American military commander whose tactics and strategy were studied in depth by the Red Army of the twentieth-century Soviet empire. Not everyone, even on his own side, celebrated him. Jackson, often stern and even harsh, failed to work harmoniously with many high-ranking officers who were directly subordinate to him. He court-martialed more subordinates than any other general in the War.

Still, Stonewall Jackson's most lasting impact on the world may prove of a spiritual rather than a martial nature. He spearheaded the great religious revival in the Confederate armies. The Army of Northern Virginia he helped captain was particularly transformed, and upon the South was bestowed a legacy singular in the world and that endures to this day—"the Bible Belt." Theologian Robert L. Dabney—who also served in key campaigns of the War as Jackson's military chief of staff—penned perhaps the most appropriate epitaph for his erstwhile commander. He wrote how the "virtue of the Sacred Scriptures" produced the true greatness of Jackson:

> *May it not be concluded then, that this was God's chief lesson in this life and death! He would teach the beauty and power of true Christianity as an element of national life. Therefore He took an exemplar of Christian sincerity . . . and formed and trained it in an honorable retirement. He set it in the furnace of trial at an hour when great events and dangers had awakened the popular heart to most intense action; He illustrated it with that species of distinction which, above all others, fires the popular enthusiasm, military glory; and held it up to the admiring inspection of a country grateful for the deliverances it had wrought.*
>
> *Thus God teaches how good, how strong a thing, His fear is. He makes all men see and acknowledge, that in this man Christianity was the source of those virtues which they so rapturously applauded; that it was the fear of God which made him so fearless of all else; that it was the love of God which animated his energies . . . that the lofty chivalry of his nature was but the reflex of the spirit of Christ.*
>
> *Even the profane admit, in their hearts, this explanation of [Jackson's] power, and are prompt to declare that it was his religion which made him what he was. His life is God's lesson, teaching that "it is righteousness that exalteth a nation."*

It was the fear of God which made him so fearless of all else.
—Robert L. Dabney

Margaret Junkin Preston (1820–1903)

How unlikely a candidate was Margaret Junkin Preston to attain the enduring mantle of "Poetess of the Confederacy." Pennsylvania-born and Northern-bred, "Maggie" Junkin's father Dr. George Junkin was an acclaimed theologian, educator, and staunch Unionist who believed God had established a sacred compact with the American nation to be His light and defender before the world. Barely five feet tall, auburn-haired, and diminutive, Maggie suffered from a painful and debilitating eye affliction that eventually rendered her blind. An obsessive fear of death also gripped her. And she endured a bewildering shyness, societal mores that hamstrung her writing career because of her gender, and a series of heartbreaking family deaths.

The hardest blow of her life was the loss in childbirth of her younger sister and closest friend Elie, wife of Stonewall Jackson. Their marriage, followed only a year later by Elie's death, turned Maggie bitterly against Jackson. But time, her devout Christian faith, and shared suffering with Jackson over Elie thawed her feelings toward him. Living in Lexington, Virginia, where her father was president of Washington College, she aided Jackson in establishing the Lexington Presbyterian Church's legendary black Sunday School. Its alumni included educators, business leaders, and clergymen. Indeed, if not for a now-extinct Presbyterian Church proscription against

marrying the spouse of a deceased sibling, Maggie might have been Jackson's second Junkin bride. Instead, she married John T. L. Preston, a widower and co-founder of the Virginia Military Institute, and bore him two children.

Disappointed with the response to her one novel, *Silverwood*, a sentimental and thinly-veiled chronicle of herself, Elie, and Jackson, she rose to her greatest work with *Beechenbrook*. An epic poem of the war, its inspiring and heartbreaking prose stretched more than seventy-five pages and carried her renown throughout the South and North and even across the world. When Henry Wadsworth Longfellow compiled his heartfelt *Poems of America,* he asked Maggie's permission to include three of hers.

Fluent in several languages, she wrote hundreds of poems, essays, and book reviews, carried on an extensive correspondence, and articulated her dream for the flourishing of Southern letters. Still legible on her Lexington headstone, worn and ajar, are these words: "Her song cheered the hearts of the Southern people in the hour of their deepest distress. And they sing a new song before the throne."

Beechenbrook

And if never round this altar
We should kneel as heretofore,—
If these arms in benediction
Fold my precious ones no more,—

Thou, who in her direst anguish,
Sooth'dst thy mother's lonely lot,
In thy still unchanged compassion,
Son of Man! forsake them not!

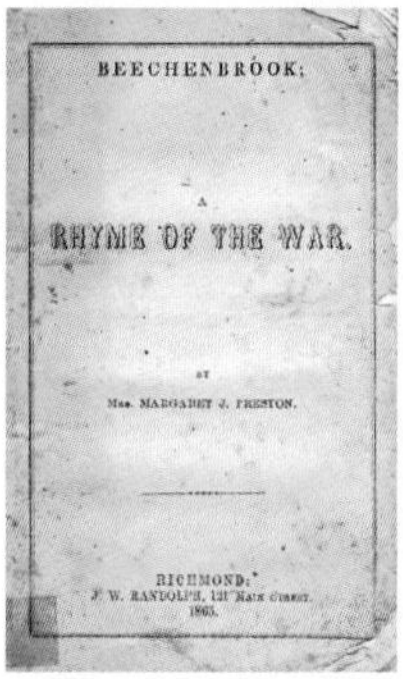

The Federals confiscated this Centreville, Virginia, stone church from its parishioners after the Battle of First Manassas, and converted it to a hospital.

Forming Ranks

The day after the battle of First Manassas, or Bull Run, Lincoln sacked McDowell as commander of the main Federal army in the eastern theater. Whatever the reasons for defeat, and they were numerous, Lincoln wanted a winner, and that is what he saw in McDowell's replacement, George B. McClellan. This brilliant young commander graduated second-highest in the West Point class of Stonewall Jackson in 1846. His early successes in helping the Federals secure the transmountain counties of western Virginia from the Confederacy catapulted him into the North's pivotal position of field command.

Upon His further promotion to General-in-Chief of all Federal armies a few months later with the forced retirement of Winfield Scott, McClellan put into play a sweeping and comprehensive strategy of war. He reorganized the Federal command and organizational structure and called forth an army of nearly 300,000 men to work in concert with the burgeoning United States navy and troop transport fleet. He used the North's roused industrial might—and the then-staggering Congressional war appropriation of one-quarter billion dollars—to arm, equip, and supply his forces to an extent matched only by the rigor of the training he unleashed upon them.

McClellan envisioned a force so overwhelming it would steamroll any opposition the Confederates could muster. He would lead the Federals straight south through the Atlantic states, then west across the Gulf states, defeating secessionist armies and gobbling up every Southern seaport. Then he would turn his forces toward the interior and, buoyed by Northern incursions over waterways like the Mississippi, Ohio, Tennessee, and Cumberland rivers, mop up whatever resistance remained.

Confederate President Davis, meanwhile, stared into the yawning abyss of economic and material overmatching. Against the North's manufacturing muscle—shortly to be the greatest on earth—the South had no arsenals, scarce steel and iron, a skeletal network of factories incapable of producing the necessary equipment and clothing for large-scale war, and a weapons and munitions supply already nearly extinguished. Coupled with the Federal naval blockade and the resultant loss of trade with Europe, all this formed a picture of steadily eroding Confederate war-making capacity and mounting Northern power.

George B. McClellan (1826-1885)

Brilliant and highborn, Philadelphia native George McClellan distinguished himself as a student at the University of Pennsylvania while only 16 years of age. He moved on to West Point and was graduated second in his class, which included Thomas (the future "Stonewall") Jackson and George Pickett. His other prewar friends included future Confederate stalwarts Pierre Beauregard, A. P. Hill, and Joe Johnston, and future Confederate President Jefferson Davis.

McClellan rose to the rank of captain in the Mexican War through distinguished service at a series of battles, including Malan, Camargo, Tampico, Vera Cruz, Cerro Gordo, Churubusco, and Chapultepec. Already proficient in several languages, he later taught himself Russian in order to translate military manuals. He also designed and patented the "McClellan saddle," which boasted special features for cavalry use and remained the standard issue saddle for horse soldiers as long as they remained in U.S. army service. After a series of other assignments, he gained success as a railroad industry engineer and executive. And in 1860, he won the hand of Mary Ellen Marcy, whom he had loved for years. Partly through her influence, McClellan during this time apparently began a lifelong spiritual pilgrimage as a committed disciple of Jesus Christ.

McClellan demonstrated unsurpassed organizational and training brilliance as he built his army into the largest and most powerful fighting force in the history of the Western Hemisphere. In doing so, he also gained a love and trust his soldiers never gave any other commander, including U. S. Grant.

When the War came, McClellan wrote Mary Ellen that he believed God had called him to save the Union and the Christian civil order that accompanied it: "I feel that God has placed a great work in my hands—I have not sought it—I know how weak I am—but I know that I mean to do right & I believe that God will help me & give the wisdom I do not possess." He entered the conflict in command of the Federals' Army of the Ohio. While the South was kicking around other Northern armies at places like Manassas Junction, Virginia, and Wilson's Creek, Missouri, McClellan was leading a successful campaign that shoved the Confederates out of the area which subsequently joined the United States as the new state of West Virginia.

Young Napoleon

Garnering the sobriquet of the "Young Napoleon," he received from President Lincoln command of the Federals' largest and most important fighting force, soon to be named the Army of the Potomac, then leadership of all Federal armies. McClellan demonstrated unsurpassed organizational and training brilliance as he built his army into the largest and most powerful fighting force in the history of the Western Hemisphere. In doing so, he also gained a love and trust his soldiers never gave any other commander, including U.S. Grant.

However, the Democrat McClellan's Radical Republican enemies in Washington, his own preference for a conventional rather than total war—even, if possible, a diplomatic solution—and faulty intelligence reports conspired against him. The latter—the Pinkerton Private Detective Agency's consistent and war-long overestimates of the size of the Confederates' Army of Northern Virginia—contributed to McClellan's cautious approach in his masterfully conceived Seven Days campaign up the Virginia peninsula toward Richmond in the spring of 1862. Though McClellan was decisively defeated in only one of those series of battles, new Confederate commander Robert E. Lee drove him, ultimately, out of the state.

Ceaselessly undermined by duplicitous Secretary of War Edwin Stanton and never regaining Lincoln's full confidence, McClellan watched as the President carved up his command among other, less capable generals. His shining moment, upon restoration to command of the Army of the Potomac, was saving the United States from Lee's September, 1862, Maryland campaign at the battle of Sharpsburg, or Antietam. Even then, he was criticized for only fighting the far-outnumbered Confederates to a draw—despite having captured their battle plans—and for allowing them to return to Virginia.

Lincoln removed McClellan and replaced him again with less capable commanders. The Philadelphia native, his star so ascendant at the War's outset, never received another command. Instead, he ran unsuccessfully against Lincoln in 1864 as the Democratic Presidential nominee. After the War, he served one term as governor of New Jersey, beginning in 1878.

McClellan's Philosophy of War

Major General George McClellan's philosophy of war differed radically from that of later officers in Federal high command. He revealed it in these words to his soldiers in the summer of 1861, when he arrived in western Virginia, at that time still a seceded area:

> *Bear in mind that you are in the country of friends, not of enemies; that you are here to protect, not to destroy. Take nothing, destroy nothing, unless you are ordered to do so by your General officers. Remember that I have pledged my word to the people of Western Virginia, that their rights in person and property shall be respected. I ask every one of you to make good this promise in its broadest sense. We come here to save, not to upturn. I do not appeal to the fear of punishment, but to your appreciation of the sacredness of the cause in which we are engaged. Carry with you into battle the conviction that you are right, and that God is on your side.*
>
> *Your enemies have violated every moral law—neither God nor man can sustain them. They have without cause rebelled against a mild and paternal Government; they have seized upon public and private property; they have outraged the persons of Northern men merely because they loved the Union; they have placed themselves beneath contempt, unless they can retrieve some honor on the field of battle. You will pursue a different course. You will be honest, brave, and merciful; you will respect the right of private opinion; you will punish no man for opinion's sake. Show to the world that you differ from our enemies in the points of honor, honesty and respect for private opinion, and that we inaugurate no reign of terror where we go.*

"Sunday at General McClellan's Headquarters — Divine Service in Camp." McClellan, mustachioed, sits on the camp stool center left, with his head turned. He spearheaded a vigorous campaign of gospel preaching and evangelism in the Northern armies he commanded. (Courtesy of harpersweekly.com)

The Epic of Missouri

Still, bringing nations to full war footing took time. The military clashes of the latter half of 1861 proved inconclusive. Some of the hottest—and most vicious—action exploded, surprisingly, out in the western border state of Missouri. There, Southern sympathizers predominated in the south and west, as well as in the state government. However, those remaining loyal to the North held the majority elsewhere and in the totality of the state, as well as in adjacent Kansas. Further stirring up the seething cauldron in Missouri, in fact, was its contentious relationship with its neighbor to the west, an increasingly Unionist bastion.

Claiborne Fox Jackson, pro-Confederate governor at the outset of the War, pleaded with General Nathaniel Lyon, commander of Federal military forces in Missouri, to allow the state to remain neutral. Lyon answered by commencing a campaign to sweep the state militia and all other secessionists out of Missouri. This included the massacre of twenty-eight pro-Confederate St. Louis civilians, some of them women and children, in early May by one of Lyon's German regiments. Now many state leaders who had been staunch Unionists offered their services to the pro-Southern forces. These included former governor and current president of the state legislative convention Sterling Price.

Separate Federal and pro-Confederate governments sprang up in Missouri, the former bolstered by Lincoln's importation of masses of well-equipped out-of-state troops. Though seizing the initiative, the Federals were successively defeated by Price and former Texas Ranger Ben McCulloch in battles at Carthage, Wilson's Creek, and Hemp Bales. These contests were among the more than 1,100 military clashes in Missouri between 1861 and 1865. This earned the state a regrettable distinction as one of the most ferocious military arenas of the War. At year's end, Missouri was ablaze with competing forces of pro-Confederate and pro-Federal regulars and irregulars.

Separate Federal and pro-Confederate governments sprang up in Missouri, the former bolstered by Lincoln's importation of masses of well-equipped out-of-state troops.

Ironically, the contending philosophies and concerns examined in Part 1 of this text did not inform the attitudes and actions of the average Missourian to nearly the extent they did many people farther north, east or south. Yet this theater of battle, including Kansas, largely overlooked in traditional histories of the War, spawned a parade of colorful, larger-than-life characters—and a desperate fight of the people whose barbarism was perhaps unmatched in the War. That this western conflict could rise up out of a distant, largely unconnected struggle, even absent its undergirding ideologies, is horrifying testament to the unsuspected consequences of violence.

The Battle of Wilson's Creek

Overlooked in the wake of the more famous Battle of First Manassas, this August 9–10 slugfest proved more vicious and, with only a third the participants, claimed nearly half the casualties.

The fall of General Nathaniel Lyon at the Battle of Wilson's Creek. (Courtesy of American Vision)

Nothing less than the fate of a state hung in the balance. Would organized Confederate forces would be cleared from Missouri, or would they gain the opportunity to restore it to Southern control?

The Wilson's Creek National Battlefield southwest of Springfield, Missouri, on State Route 181 recounts the depth of enmity held among Missourians who opposed one another in the War. The site records that pro-Federal antislavery raiders considered themselves "reborn Puritans and their (pro-Confederate) neighbors as nothing but dirt-hauling, whisky-soaked illiterates." Meanwhile, "The Southern sympathizers were the rural Jeffersonian idealists defending their property against the wretches pouring out of Eastern and European slums."

But this fight had far more than just Missourians. It featured one of the most colorful cavalcades ever assembled in a battle. Men from Texas, Arkansas, Louisiana, Kansas, and Iowa fought too, as well as Indians. There were a young Federal scout and spy whom history would call Wild Bill Hickok; teenaged Confederate foot soldiers and brothers Frank and Jesse James; and Cherokee Stand Watie, the highest ranking Indian officer of the War.

Among the commanders, famed Texas Ranger Ben McCulloch had fought with Sam Houston a quarter-century before against Santa Anna at San Jacinto. Franz Sigel was among the many communist revolutionaries in the Federal army from the failed Revolution of 1848 in Germany. The overall Confederate commander, Sterling Price, had been a staunch Unionist and governor of Missouri. Teenaged, part-Cherokee observer Myra Belle Shirley would become the legendary Belle Starr, Confederate spy and Wild West outlaw. Thirty of the Federal officers would become

At Wilson's Creek, there were a young Federal scout and spy whom history would call Wild Bill Hickok; teenaged Confederate foot soldiers and brothers Frank and Jesse James . . . Cherokee Chief and General Stand Watie, the highest ranking Indian officer of the War . . . Teenaged, part-Cherokee observer Myra Belle Shirley would become the legendary Belle Starr, Confederate spy and Wild West outlaw.

generals by war's end.

Frank and Jesse James
Courtesy of Phillip W. Steele

The Confederates had nearly twice as many men, 10,000 to 5,500, but overall Federal commander Nathaniel Lyon, a fiery, red-bearded New Englander, had the edge in weapons, equipment, and organization. After splitting their force, the Federals struck first, attempting to envelope the Confederates between them. Attack and counterattack followed. For two days, doomed soldiers stood mere yards apart and fired into one another's faces until both groups melted away into bloody heaps, and others filled their spots.

Belle Starr
Courtesy of Phillip W. Steele

In the end, the weight of numbers told as so often it did when brave men fought desperately to the death. McCulloch and Price rallied the Confederates, Lyon was killed, and the Federals retreated all the way to St. Louis.

"Wild Bill" Hickok
Courtesy of Phillip W. Steele

Other Early Clashes

Elsewhere in the west, bold thrusts northward by Confederate Generals Albert Sidney Johnston and Leonidas Polk stoppered the Federals, respectively, in mid-Kentucky at Bowling Green and on the Mississippi River at Columbus, Kentucky's western tip. Polk, the former Episcopal Bishop of Louisiana, held his position astride the river by defeating U. S. Grant in November at the Battle of Belmont. In the east, the Federals began to chip away at Confederate coastal fortifications, particularly along the Carolinas. They captured Hatteras Inlet, Ship Island, and Port Royal, among others.

And late in the year the North sealed its absorption of what Lincoln would soon welcome into the Union as the new state of West Virginia. The Federals frustrated a last-ditch salvage mission coordinated by a Confederate general whose lackluster accomplishments in the campaign earned him such epithets as "Granny Lee," "Evacuating Lee," and "The King of Spades." But the Southern critics who imparted such chastening knew not that Robert E. Lee possessed only the authority of an adviser and not a commander in the campaign; nor that his meticulous battle stratagems were repeatedly foiled by the gaggle of incompetent civilians and politicians in actual command. Thus the first calendar year of the War concluded with the Confederacy in apparently solid shape and both U. S. Grant and R. E. Lee smarting from setbacks in the field.

The Trent Affair

America's first War of Independence required significant foreign military intervention from the French to succeed. George Washington and the hearty patriot band of secessionists could scarcely have defeated Great Britain and its German mercenaries alone. The South likewise sought help from abroad when it seceded. Had they received it, this second War of Independence would likely have succeeded as well.

For the first half of the War, an uneasy tension lingered across the Atlantic as Britain, France, and other European powers considered whether to aid the Confederacy militarily or financially or, more likely, whether to recognize the new nation through official channels. The most dramatic evincing of this taut state of affairs was the high seas kidnapping and imprisonment of Confederate diplomats James M. Mason and John Slidell from a seagoing British mail steamer, the Trent, on November 8, by the USS San Jacinto. The Northern public cheered the act—which it considered executed against one new enemy and one old one. The Yankee press blazed its applause, and the House of Representatives passed a resolution of support. But that old enemy was no more amused than the new one over the act. The British demanded an explanation and the freeing of the diplomats. And they sent troops to Canada and formed battle plans to hurl their navy, the greatest the world had ever seen, against the Federals.

Lincoln faced a dilemma. He did not want to cower in the face of a situation that had provided a needed spark to the North. But he also had all the war on his hands he could manage without the world's preeminent empire wading into the fray against him. Secretary of State Seward did not apologize, but he did release Mason and Slidell, and he denied responsibility for the San Jacinto's actions. Then he proclaimed a redeclaration of America's traditional stance against the right to impress, or kidnap, passengers off foreign ships. He did not have to mention that it was British impressment of American sailors which lit the fuse that exploded into the War of 1812 between the two nations.

The Communists and Lincoln

Whether or not Abraham Lincoln believed he was carrying forth the banner for international communist revolution, its founders and many of its adherents did. Karl Marx wrote: "Lincoln is the single-minded son of the working class, who has led his country to the matchless struggle for the rescue of the communist revolution and the reconstruction of the social order." Marx's co-laborer in the worldwide socialistic revolution and in the writing of the *Communist Manifesto*, Friedrich Engels, believed many of the soldiers prosecuting the North's war effort shared such senti-

Friedrich Engels

ments. He wrote: "Had it not been for the experienced soldiers who entered America after the European revolution, especially from the Germanies, the organization of the Union army would have taken longer than it did." "The Germanies" were the array of not-yet-united German kingdoms.

The Federal army had only 15,000 soldiers in 1861, prior to conscription for the War. Of those 15,000, approximately 4,000—over one-fourth—were German veterans, mostly socialists, who had fought in the 1848 European wars as communist revolutionaries to usher in the demands of the *Communist Manifesto*. These German hosts brimmed over with a disproportionately high percentage of men in high command. And those ranks teemed with major generals, brigadier generals, and colonels named Schurz, Schenck, Blenker, Sigel, Osterhaus, and so on. One of these later became governor of Wisconsin, another of Washington, and still another secretary of the interior—all during the Lincoln, Johnson or Grant administrations.

Most of these men believed the War was a continuation in a different venue of the Central European revolutions of 1848 that had sought to usher in a new world order by reconstructing the existing social order. Their vision for the American contest's aims, their prosecution of it, and their perpetuation of it all attested to an Enlightenment-oriented worldview very different from that of old Christendom.

A Federal soldier

15 Virginia
(1862)

Stonewall Jackson leads his army through brutal winter and frozen Allegheny mountain passes into western Virginia in John Paul Strain's *The Romney Expedition.*

I hold that the South is to be annihilated. I . . . mean the intellectual, social, aristocratic South—the thing that represented itself by slavery and the Bowie knife, by bullying and lynch law, by ignorance and idleness . . . I mean a society which holds for its cardinal principle of faith, that one-third of the race is born booted and spurred, and the other two-thirds saddled for the first to ride . . . That South is to be annihilated.

—Abolitionist Leader Wendell Phillips

As the Federals' one-sided naval advantage allowed them to continue snatching one Atlantic coastal port after another from the Confederates, McClellan spent the early months of 1862 building the Army of the Potomac. He faced more opposition than just the Confederates, however. Lincoln waited restlessly for a grand strike against the South to vindicate the enormous Northern efforts—and financial investment. More ominously, Radical Republicans in the administration and Congress intrigued against the young Democratic commander. They knew McClellan to be their political opponent, and they suspected him of having far less ambitious objectives for the war effort than themselves—such as no special interest in emancipating the slaves.

Allen Pinkerton and his secret service organization's assays of Southern troop strength were consistent, convincing—and far overestimated.

Allen Pinkerton and his secret service organization's assays of Southern troop strength were consistent, convincing—and far overestimated. Pinkerton's numbers—200,000 Confederates defending Richmond, for instance—understandably gave McClellan pause. Even Lincoln considered Pinkerton's intelligence trustworthy. Hampered by these and other factors, McClellan found himself relegated by Lincoln in late February to command of only the Federal Army of Virginia.

Meanwhile, Joe Johnston, one of the heroes of First Manassas and the highest-ranking soldier in the Confederacy, continued in command of the South's own Army of Virginia, the chief eastern Confederate force and that which stood against McClellan. Johnston divined the gathering storm. He suspected correctly that McClellan was marshaling his forces for a sledgehammer assault up the peninsula of eastern Virginia which began below Yorktown and was bounded by the James and York rivers and into Richmond. Thus began a series of contentious disputes between Johnston and President Davis that would last the length of the War. Johnston wanted to form a stout defense around Richmond, but Davis insisted that the Virginian confront the Federals farther to the east. Johnston grudgingly consented, but he kept other options open to himself.

McClellan, meanwhile, prepared a combined naval and army assault that would indeed transport his gigantic force of over 100,000 troops out of the

Joseph E. Johnston (1807–1891)

This brilliant Virginian's antebellum military career included combat experience and wounds in both the Seminole and Mexican Wars, cavalry command in mid- and late-1850s "Bleeding Kansas," and quartermaster general of the United States Army. He entered the War as one of only five full generals in the Confederacy. Johnston's parade of accomplishments continued when, with Pierre Beauregard, he commanded Confederate forces as they routed the Federals at First Manassas, or Bull Run, the War's first big battle.

Then Jefferson Davis named him to lead the Army of Virginia, the Confederacy's largest army. But there began a feud with Davis that would last the length of the War and have profound implications for its outcome. Johnston felt the President should stay out of the generaling business; Davis demanded input on strategic, and often tactical, decisions. He also considered Johnston's style too cautious and defensive-oriented.

After launching the opening attack on George McClellan's Federals in the Seven Days Campaign in May, Johnston was shot in the throat and nearly killed. When he returned to action six months later, his successor, Robert E. Lee, had won a series of epic battles; Davis appointed Johnston to a high command in the War's western theater. The two men's enmity escalated when they blamed each other for the fall of Vicksburg.

There began a feud between Johnston and Davis that would last the length of the War and have profound implications for its outcome.

Still, both the Southern people and his own troops esteemed Johnston, and he remained in high command—of the Army of Tennessee—when William Sherman stormed toward Atlanta in the spring of 1864. Johnston had over 50,000 fewer troops than Sherman, but he contested him with a frustratingly-effective defensive plan and thrashed him at Kennesaw Mountain, their only straight-up fight. However, Johnston refused to communicate his plans for defending Atlanta to Davis. The President, fearing (wrongly) he had none, sacked him. It proved one of the greatest mistakes of the War.

Johnston's replacement, John Bell Hood, hurled his army at the Federals, as he believed Davis wished. The outnumbered Confederates were decimated in Tennessee, leaving Sherman free to ravage Georgia and the Carolinas. Finally, in February, 1865, Lee restored Johnston to command. He contested Sherman best as he could, including a courageous stand at Bentonville, North Carolina while outnumbered 3–1.

More than a quarter of a century later, Johnston served as a pallbearer at Sherman's funeral. Despite cold, wind, rain, and a bald head, he respectfully wore no hat, saying Sherman would wear none if the roles were reversed. The eighty-four-year-old warrior fell ill with pneumonia and died within days. Both Grant and Sherman considered Joe Johnston the greatest military commander in the Confederacy.

Chesapeake Bay and land them on the peninsula, thus lessening the overland route to Richmond by thirty miles. But "Little Mac," because of Pinkerton thinking the Confederates far more numerous than Johnston's actual 60,000, had planned on his own force being even larger than the 100,000. In agreeing to McClellan's battle plan, Lincoln had required him to fork over nearly 40,000 men to defend Washington. The President feared a move on the capital by Stonewall Jackson, who loomed out in the Shenandoah Valley with a separate, smaller Southern army. The Shenandoah was the chief overland gateway to Washington from Virginia.

McClellan: Abolitionism vs. Antislavery

George McClellan provides a famous example of a man who opposed both slavery and abolitionism. Many people in all sections of 1860s America held this view. McClellan demonstrated it in his vigorous verbal exchanges with Senator Charles Sumner and other abolitionists.

Soon after my arrival in Washington . . . I had several interviews with prominent abolitionists—of whom Senator (Charles) Sumner was one—on the subject of slavery. I invariably took the ground that I was thoroughly opposed to slavery, regarding it as a great evil . . . but that in my opinion no sweeping measure of emancipation should be carried out unless accompanied by arrangements providing for the new relations between employers and employed, carefully guarding the rights and interests of both. . . . Mr. Sumner replied—others also agreed with him—that such points did not concern us, and that all of that must be left to take care of itself.

My reply was that no real statesman could ever contemplate so sweeping and serious a measure as sudden and general emancipation without looking to the future and providing for its consequences; that four and a half millions of uneducated slaves should not suddenly be manumitted without due precautions taken both to protect them and to guard against them . . . My own view was that emancipation should be accomplished gradually, and that the Negroes should be fitted for it by certain preparatory steps in the way of education, recognition of the rights of family and marriage, prohibition against selling them without their own consent, the freedom of those born after a certain date, etc. . . .

. . . no real statesman could ever contemplate so sweeping and serious a measure as sudden and general emancipation without looking to the future and providing for its consequences.

—George McClellan

I recognized the fact that as the Confederate States had chosen to resort to the arbitrament of arms, they must abide by the logical consequences of the stern laws of war. But, as I always believed that we should fight to bring them back into the Union, and should treat them as members of the Union when so brought back, I held that it was a matter of sound policy to do nothing likely to render ultimate reconciliation and harmony impossible, unless such a course were imperative to secure military success.

Jefferson Davis's Inaugural Address

The Confederate Constitutional Convention, meeting in Montgomery, Alabama, chose Jefferson Davis as the new nation's first president. By the time he gave his inaugural address, on February 22, the country's capital had moved to Richmond. Following are excerpts from that speech:

> *When a long course of class legislation, directed not to the general welfare but to the aggrandizement of the Northern section of the Union, culminated in a warfare on the domestic institutions of the Southern states—when the dogmas of a sectional party, substituted for the provisions of the constitutional compact, threatened to destroy the sovereign rights of the states—six of those states, withdrawing from the Union, confederated together to exercise the right and perform the duty of instituting a government which would better secure the liberties for the preservation of which that Union was established.*

The tyranny of an unbridled majority, the most odious and least responsible form of despotism, has denied us both the rights and the remedy. Therefore we are in arms to renew such sacrifices as our fathers made to the holy cause of constitutional liberty.

—Jefferson Davis

> *Whatever of hope some may have entertained that a returning sense of justice would remove the danger with which our rights were threatened and render it possible to preserve the Union of the Constitution, must have been dispelled by the malignity and barbarity of the Northern states in the prosecution of the existing war. The confidence of the most hopeful among us must have been destroyed by the disregard they have recently exhibited for all the time-honored bulwarks of civil and religious liberty.*

> *The people of the states now confederated became convinced the government of the United States had fallen into the hands of a sectional majority, who would pervert that most sacred of all trusts to the destruction of the rights which it was pledged to protect. They believed that to remain longer in the Union would subject them to a continuance of a disparaging discrimination, submission to which would be inconsistent with their welfare and intolerable to a proud people. They therefore determined to sever its bonds and establish a new confederacy for themselves.*

> *Bastilles filled with prisoners, arrested without civil process or indictment duly found; the writ of habeas corpus suspended by executive mandate; a state legislature controlled by the imprisonment of members whose avowed principles suggested to the federal executive that there might be another added to the list of seceded states; elections held under threats of a military power; civil officers, peaceful citizens, and gentlewomen incarcerated for opinion's sake—proclaimed the incapacity of our late associates to administer a government as free, liberal, and humane as that established for our common use.*

> *The tyranny of an unbridled majority, the most odious and least responsible form of despotism, has denied us both the rights and the remedy. Therefore we are in arms to renew such sacrifices as our fathers made to the holy cause of constitutional liberty.*

The *Monitor* vs. the *Virginia*

The opening battle in the year's eastern campaigns was one of the great combat duels in history. The Federal (Anaconda) blockade of Southern shipping was already taking a toll as 1862 began. Rumors drifted north that the Confederates were refitting the burnt remnants of a former Yankee ship with protective iron plating. On March 8, the *CSS Virginia* entered upon the stage of world history at Hampton Roads, Virginia, where an armada of Federal ships blockaded the estuaries of the James and York Rivers. It incorporated the hull of the old *USS Merrimac*; a new above-water structure slanted at a 45-degree angle and steeled by four-inch-thick iron plates; steam engines; and ten seven-inch guns. Some of the greatest ships in the United States Navy came against it. The Virginia's armored sides took the best they had and unleashed its own blistering fire. It rammed and sank the *Cumberland*, the most powerful frigate in the Federal navy. And it riddled the 50-gun *Congress* with cannon fire, then burned it up. With over 100 Federal guns firing on the *Virginia* from ships all over the harbor and shore batteries up and down the coast, it incapacitated and ran aground the *Minnesota*, the enormous flagship of the fleet, then retired for the evening.

Next morning, the *Virginia* sailed out to finish off the Federal fleet and the blockade. It had already sent one ship down when it spied a fresh foe—the Federals' own new ironclad, the *USS Monitor*. Likened to a "cheese box on a raft" and a "tin can on a shingle" and even stranger in appearance than the *Virginia*, the *Monitor* was so unseaworthy that it had nearly sunk en route to its maiden battle. But it was also smaller, less exposed, faster, and more maneuverable than the *Virginia*, and had a revolving, nine-inch-thick armor-plated turret with two guns—each eleven-inchers.

For four hours the ironclads slugged it out, only 100 yards between them. Each was protected by its armor and suffered little damage. They collided several times, sometimes in ramming attempts, sometimes accidentally. Then the *Virginia* charged alongside, intending to disembark marines and capture its adversary in hand-to-hand combat. But the quicker *Monitor* pulled away. Finally, a *Virginia* shell blast blinded the *Monitor*'s captain and the Federal vessel retreated to safety. With that, the Confederate ironclad withdrew as

The epic duel of ironclads, as the Federals' *USS Monitor* and the Confederates' *CSS Virginia* slug it out. A host of other Federal ships ring the action and fire their own shots at the solitary Southern craft.

well. Though neither ship suffered serious damage, the Federal blockade remained in place. Still, two months later, on May 9, when the *Monitor* and a fleet of other ironclads and heavy wooden ships opened a fusillade on Confederate batteries at nearby Sewell's Point, the *Virginia* reappeared and headed straight for the *Monitor*. The entire fleet, including the *Monitor*, ceased firing and retreated to the cover of Federal forts. The *Virginia* churned back and forth across the area for hours, but its foes remained cloistered within the protective screen of the mammoth shore guns.

For four hours the ironclads slugged it out, only 100 yards between them. Each was protected by its armor and suffered little damage. They collided several times, sometimes in ramming attempts, sometimes accidentally.

Ironically, neither ship survived long after this. The *Virginia* was scuttled just two days later to prevent its capture by the Federals, who had taken Newport News. On the last day of the year, a storm sank the *Monitor* off the coast of Cape Hatteras, North Carolina. But virtually every other ship in the world was now obsolete, and the tactics of naval warfare were forever changed by these ironclad warriors.

The Main Stage

Events transpired far differently during the early months of 1862 in the east than in the west. The War's largest armies locked horns in Virginia. Though McClellan and Joe Johnston (the other key Johnston in Confederate military leadership besides Albert Sidney Johnston, killed at Shiloh) held the theater's, and the War's, main stage, a secondary front developed that turned the equations of Lincoln and McClellan upside down.

As earlier mentioned, Stonewall Jackson commanded a detached division of the Army of Northern Virginia out in the Shenandoah Valley; its presence, then its exploits, so alarmed Lincoln that he siphoned tens of thousands of needed troops away from McClellan. Jackson—outnumbered nearly four to one—confused, defeated, then ran clean out of the Valley three separate Federal armies, each one larger than his own. This not only cost McClellan thousands of troops, it kept him, and Lincoln, looking over their shoulders at the Shenandoah Valley even as they wanted to focus on the Peninsula Campaign they hoped would capture Richmond and end the War.

Then Lincoln, no longer trusting McClellan's ability to deliver victory, reorganized the command structure of the Army of the Potomac; relegated McClellan from general-in-chief and dispersed command of Federal forces in the east among seven men; took an entire corps plus a division from McClellan's attack force; and approved the suspension of Federal military

Thomas Nast (1840–1902)

Uncle Sam, the Democratic Party donkey, the Republican Party elephant, and modern-day Santa Claus are among the many images and icons the brilliant Thomas Nast birthed whose fame have long outlived his own. So, too, did he leave a creative legacy that continues to grow with the work of many in our own time.

The life of Nast, one of the great artists in American history, began in a German military barracks near the Rhine River in 1840. His father played as a musician in the Ninth Regiment Bavarian Band. His mother took him, at age six, to America in 1846. He studied art at the National Academy of Design, and elsewhere, in New York City.

In 1855, upon completing school at age fifteen, Nast began work as a draftsman for *Frank Leslie's Illustrated Newspaper*, one of the most popular publications in America. By 1859, he was drawing for the famed *Harper's Weekly*, which he continued to do for nearly thirty years. The coming of the War provided Nast, still only twenty one, an even larger canvas on which to paint, and he did so in such memorable scenes as the the 7th New York Regiment marching through flag-strewn New York City to war.

The pitiable scenes of battlefield carnage and destruction Nast witnessed affected him profoundly, and his subsequent themes carried him beyond the status of an illustrator. He began to build a gallery as one of the great caricaturists and political cartoonists with his "Peace in 1862," which ridiculed Northerners who did not support President Lincoln's aggressive prosecution of the War. As the conflict progressed, Nast's dramatic battlefield illustrations caused Lincoln to call him the Federals' best recruiting sergeant.

Among his other heralded artistic exploits were works defending American Indians and Chinese immigrants, advocating the immediate abolition of slavery, ridiculing Andrew Johnson and supporting his impeachment, and launching searing broadsides against William "Boss" Tweed and his corrupt Tammany Hall political machine in New York. In fact, historians of the era generally credit Nast with a key role in stirring the public disgust that helping bring down Tweed and sent him to prison.

Born into the cauldron of 1840s German socialism and communistic revolution, Nast's vivid caricatures and editorial cartoons for decades reflected his views from the most liberal, Radical Republican end of the political spectrum. He was an archenemy of the Confederacy, as well as the Democrats and whomever else sought a mild Reconstruction for the South. He grew disgusted with postwar Republican corruption, however, and supported a Democrat, Grover Cleveland, for the presidency in 1884, before returning to the Republican fold in 1892.

Among Nast's other famous images were *Columbia*, his heroic and graceful image of America as a woman, carrying a sword to the downtrodden; the *Tammany Hall Tiger*, his symbol of Boss Tweed's political juggernaut; *John Bull*, his rotund image of the proud and plucky British spirit; and *John Chinaman*, his sympathetic image of Chinese immigrants. Nast also introduced Shakespearean verse to the American popular culture in some of his works. The legendary Dutch painter Van Gogh greatly admired Nast's work, and it likely spurred

It was Thomas Nast' brilliant imagination and artistry that birthed the modern-day concept of Santa Claus into the American consciousness, and framed the Christmas season with him, absent any mention of Jesus Christ. He did so with such famous illustrations as, left to right, "Merry Old Santa," the wartime "Santa Claus in Camp," and "Christmas Supplement," where the pop-up Santa presents a disappointed boy and girl with a bundle of switches.

Van Gogh's long held desire to become a magazine illustrator and cartoonist.

Nast combined understandable imagery, keen political commentary that often worked on multiple levels, and a passion for his subject matter. Thus he was able to propagate his messages to much larger audiences than would otherwise have understood or even heard them. In later years, Nast published *Thomas Nast's Christmas Drawings for the Human Race*, failed in a magazine publishing venture, and received appointment by President Theodore Roosevelt in 1902 as U.S. Consul General to Ecuador. He contracted a fatal case of yellow fever there that same year. Upon his death, *Harper's Weekly* said of Nast, "He has been called, perhaps not with accuracy, but with substantial justice, the Father of American Caricature."

Famous colleagues—John C. Fremont and Kit Carson

Federal General John C. Fremont (1813–1890) clashed with Stonewall Jackson in the latter's Shenandoah Valley Campaign. Fremont was already famous as the legendary "Pathfinder." He led five expeditions to the American West in the 1840s and 50s, during which he traversed more land than any other explorer. The fabled Kit Carson scouted for Fremont on all but one of his Western treks. Fremont's chronicles of these adventures became national best sellers. In 1856, he won the first Republican Party Presidential nomination and nearly beat James Buchanan in the general election.

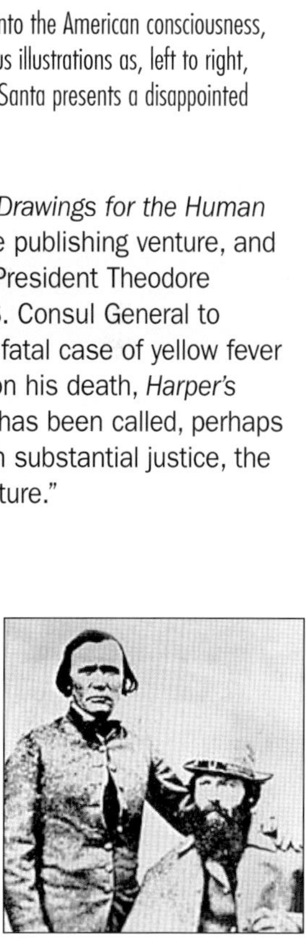

recruiting. McClellan had no say in any of these actions. Within this context, McClellan's caution is understandable. He spent nearly the whole spring slugging his way sixty miles up the peninsula to White House, then laid siege to Richmond.

The Valley Campaign of Stonewall Jackson

As spring unfolded, McClellan stood at the gates of Richmond with his army. And he had tens of thousands more soldiers ready to move up in support. Lee hatched the idea to turn Stonewall Jackson loose in the Shenandoah Valley, now nearly on the western frontier of Virginia. His design: protect the crops of that "Breadbasket of the Confederacy," and so unnerve Lincoln at the prospect of Jackson descending on the Federals' own capital of Washington that he would preempt sending reinforcements to McClellan.

In reality, Lee's plan had less to do with threatening the Federals' seat of government than it did saving the Confederates'. That he would countenance such a plan, much less champion it, provides insight into his audacity, as well as the esteem in which he already held Jackson. For "Old Jack" had less than ten thousand men under his command. Federal Generals Nathaniel Banks, based in Winchester at the north end of the Shenandoah, and John Fremont, out on the western border of Virginia preparing to invade Tennessee, both threw larger forces than that against him, as Irvin McDowell would soon. But they did not have Stonewall Jackson.

Allen Pinkerton (1819–1864)

Scottish native Allan Pinkerton did not emigrate to America until age twenty three. His foiling of a

gang of counterfeiters he came across as he chopped wood on a remote river island, led to his storied career in law enforcement. After rising to become Chicago's first police detective, he responded to the urgings of railroad presidents to launch a private detective service specializing in railroad security.

Pinkerton's many law enforcement innovations helped propel his business to spectacular success. As the War neared, he and his agents labored to protect railroad property in the Border States against secessionists. When death threats loomed against new president Abraham Lincoln, Pinkerton secreted him into Washington City.

The legendary Pinkerton Agency provided the United States its chief source of intelligence and security during the War, and helped frustrate covert Confederate operations in the North. After the War, Pinkerton remained on the national stage as he and his agents doggedly pursued Jesse James and his famed band of former Confederate guerillas. A "Pinkerton" remains a respected security operative to this day.

Beside the Still Waters, by John Paul Strain. Stonewall Jackson suffered his first, and only, battle defeat on March 23, 1862, at Kernstown when a subordinate ordered a retreat without Jackson's approval. Greatly outnumbered, stocked with young, green troops, and pelted with freezing sleet, Jackson retreated to regroup. This memorable scene captures him as he reads his Bible and prays early the morning of March 28, just prior to breaking camp and setting forth on his fabled Shenandoah Valley Campaign.

Following is a brief chronology of his Shenandoah Valley Campaign which shook the world.

March 11—Jackson retreats south up the Valley from his winter headquarters at Winchester.

March 23—Jackson reverses course and, though greatly outnumbered, strikes a portion of Banks' forces just south of Winchester at Kernstown, to prevent him leaving the Valley and reinforcing McClellan. The attack is repulsed, but the thirty-six hundred Confederates fight so ferociously that the Federal government believes his army to be much larger, orders Banks' men to stay in the

Valley, and recalls thousands more already headed for McClellan.

March 24–end of April—Jackson hides his army and rests it in the Valley at Elk Run.

May 8—Jackson marches his men east in a feint toward Richmond, then sends them back west on trains, crosses the Allegheny Mountains on foot, and defeats Fremont.

May 21—Brigadier General Richard Ewell, sent by Lee, reaches Jackson with eight thousand additional troops.

May 23—After churning the length and breadth of the Valley, Jackson fools Banks into thinking he will attack Strasburg but instead defeats another portion of his adversary's forces at Front Royal.

May 25—Jackson defeats Banks at Winchester, collects a colossal store of Federal supplies, and hurls his foe across the Potomac into Maryland.

Late May—President Lincoln, fearing Jackson will cross the Potomac River and attack Washington, orders three separate Federal armies to converge on him at once: Fremont from the west, Banks from Maryland, and McDowell from the east. This torpedoes the latter's intention to reinforce McClellan.

They say that once again Cromwell is walking the earth...

—Francis Lawley
London Times newspaper

Early June—Sustaining his efforts to keep as many Federal troops away from Richmond as possible, Jackson stuns everybody and marches north nearly to Harper's Ferry, on the Potomac, before wheeling south and charging up the Valley, with every Federal in sight in pursuit. Validating their vaunted nickname as Jackson's "Foot Cavalry," his men march 52 miles in 36 hours in a driving rain with no food.

June 8—Dividing his own forces, Jackson sends Ewell to Cross Keys, where he defeats Fremont again.

June 9—Jackson defeats McDowell's forces under James Shields at Port Republic.

June 10—Federal forces retreat north out of the Valley and Virginia.

Stonewall Jackson, with never more than seventeen thousand soldiers under his command, succeeded beyond what anyone could have imagined. While securing Valley farm production, he smashed three separate Federal armies in five battles and six skirmishes and kept nearly sixty thousand troops away from McClellan. Those troops would likely have provided the margin of victory had they been employed in the Seven Days campaign of June and July, which the Federals lost. His "Foot Cavalry" marched 676 miles, an average of fourteen miles a day the whole campaign. Jackson's fame spread across the world.

"They who have seen and heard him uplift his voice in prayer, and then have witnessed his vigor and prompt energy in the strife, say that once again Cromwell is walking the earth and leading his trusting and enraptured hosts to assured victory," wrote Francis Lawley in Europe's greatest newspaper, the *London Times*. "General," said "Old Jack" to Ewell, "he who does not see the hand of God in this is blind, sir. Blind!"

Belle Boyd (1844–1906)

Several pro-Confederate females gained renown during the War as spies for the Southern cause. One of the most famous of these was Belle Boyd, seventeen years young when the conflict began. Inspiring such sobriquets as the "Siren of the Shenandoah" and the "Rebel Joan of Arc," Miss Boyd hailed from Martinsburg in the western mountain section of Virginia that seceded from the Old Dominion and joined the United States. But the rough, sometimes brutal behavior she witnessed the Federals exhibit early in the War turned her implacably against them. Like other such women, her loyalty to the South grew to the point that it took second place not even to the fiercest rag-garbed, diarrhea-laden infantry soldier.

The incident that launched her into prominence occurred at Front Royal during Stonewall Jackson's spring 1862 Valley Campaign. There, staying with her aunt, she raced out of town on foot to the Confederates as they prepared to attack the Federal garrison. Breathless, she informed them the town held only about one regiment of Federals, and Jackson could easily sweep them aside. Accounts vary as to how much of this Jackson already knew; at the least, Miss Boyd confirmed whatever information he had and provided more details. Jackson swept the Federals out and captured the town just as the young spy had predicted.

She proved an intrepid Confederate operative. Twice the Yankees threw her into the Old Capitol Prison in Washington City. Finally, they exiled her to England. The military correspondent for the large and influential *Philadelphia Inquirer* harbored no illusions about her utility:

> *These women are the most accomplished [spies] in Southern circles. They are introduced under assumed names to our officers, so as to avoid detection or recognition from those to whom their names are known, but their persons are unknown. By such means they are enabled to frequently meet combinedly, but at separate times, the officers of every regiment in a whole column, and by simple compilation and comparison of notes, they achieve a full knowledge of the strength of our entire force.*
>
> *The chief of these spies is the celebrated Belle Boyd. Her acknowledged superiority for machination and intrigue has given her the leadership and control of the female spies in the valley of Virginia . . . Last summer, whilst Patterson's army lay at Martinsburg, she wore a revolver in her belt, and was courted and flattered by every Lieutenant and Captain in the service who ever saw her.*
>
> *She has a trained band of coadjutors, who report to her daily—girls aged from 16 upward . . . The reports that she is personally impure are as unjust as they are undeserved. She has a blind devotion to an idea, and passes far the boundary of her sex's modesty to promote its success.*
>
> *During the past campaign in the Valley this woman has been of immense service to the enemy. She will be now if she can.*

Some of the supposed exploits by Belle Boyd and other female spies have gathered a layer of embellishment through the years, including some chronicled by Miss Boyd herself. Still, real and often courageous acts lay behind whatever legends accrued. She and others, North and South, sacrificed their safety, sometimes their freedom, sometimes all their possessions, sometimes even their lives no less than did the bravest soldier.

Jeb Stuart (1833-1864)

"Rugged and a dandy all in one, and his men like it, and his dancing eye too," one of his leather-tough horse soldiers said of James Ewell Brown "Jeb" Stuart. "They say he makes you feel good just being around him. And I guess they're right." With gauntlets of snow-white buckskin half hiding the golden galons on his sleeves, a purple plume festooning his black hat with the brim folded up on one side against the crown, and the great scarlet-lined cape swirling as his spurs jingled, nearly the whole Army of Northern Virginia knew when Jeb Stuart was coming to camp.

The flamboyant Virginian knew his men and his people had few physical amenities to cheer them, but when his sidekick Sweeny lit into his banjo or Jeb himself launched a chorus of *The Girl I Left Behind Me* or *Jine the Cavalry*—or *Rock of Ages* or *I Would Not Live Alway*—despair blossomed into hope. For he was as fearless and capable as Lee and Jackson and as pious. He did not gamble, curse or smoke, and he never took a drink of alcohol after age twelve, when he promised his dying mother he would not. Though he danced and made merry at balls and suppers with the most beautiful belles in the South as they swooned over him, never was a whiff of scandal breathed about him. Indeed, he loved his wife so desperately he named his daughter after her, and he loved the daughter so that her name was among the last words he uttered in his earthly life.

He did not gamble, curse or smoke and he never took a drink of alcohol after age twelve, when he promised his dying mother he would not.

He was shot and nearly killed in 1857 fighting Cheyennes with the U.S. Cavalry on the western plains. But most of this frontier duty proved boring and monotonous. He spent much of it reading two books—U.S. Army Regulations and his Protestant Episcopal Book of Common Prayer. "When I entered West Point I knew many and strong temptations would beset my path, but I relied on 'Him whom to know is life everlasting' to deliver me from temptation . . . and prayed God to guide me in the right way and teach me to walk as a Christian should; I have never for a moment hesitated to persevere; indeed, since coming to this far land I have been more than ever satisfied of the absolute importance of an acquaintance with Jesus our Lord," Stuart wrote during the long lonesome time away from his beloved wife, to whom he wrote impassioned and poor poetry.

In the closing moments of his life, no less than Confederate President Jefferson Davis came to see him. Davis held his hand and asked how he felt. Easy, the pain-racked Stuart replied, but willing to die if God and his country felt that he had fulfilled his destiny and done his duty. He asked those around him to sing Rock of Ages with him.

His Exploits

Stuart first gained fame leading a cavalry charge that swept a New York regiment from the field in the climactic moments of First Manassas. From there, his exploits were legion and his rise meteoric. He "Rode Around McClellan"; his scouting brilliance prepared the way for the thunderous Confederate victory at Chancellorsville, which he himself led after Stonewall Jackson fell; and Robert E. Lee, thrifty with compliments, announced after Jeb's death, "He never brought me a piece of bad information."

For most of the War, Stuart and his horse soldiers outfought the Yankee cavalry no matter how outnumbered and outequipped the Southerners were. And his panache and élan beamed light into some of the South's darkest days. In June, 1863, the improving Federal cavalry ambushed and stung him at Brandy Station, but Stuart and his men still won the 20,000-troop battle, the largest cavalry fight in American history.

The Ride Around McClellan

With the bloody Seven Days Campaign in progress and George McClellan and more than 100,000 Federal soldiers standing at the gates of Richmond, Jeb Stuart, his plumed hat, and 1,200 Southern horse soldiers rode away from the Confederate capital. They seemed headed toward Stonewall Jackson in the Shenandoah Valley. In reality, Lee had sent them to locate McClellan's isolated right flank across the Chickahominy River, in preparation for assaulting it. North of Ashland, Stuart turned his men—who included John Mosby, the future "Gray Ghost"—east, found the Federal right, rode around it . . . and just kept riding.

Calculating the difficulty of returning from whence he came—but moreso applying his credo of "We must substitute esprit for numbers. Therefore I strive to inculcate in my men the spirit of the chase."—Stuart galloped across the communication belt in the Federal rear, clean across the Virginia peninsula, then back home. During the three-day, 100-mile gallop, he snatched nearly 165 Federal prisoners, 260 animals, and as many supplies as he could carry, destroyed abundant Federal property, and shot it out with Yankee cavalry commanded by his own father-in-law, Gen. Philip St. George Cooke, a Virginian Stuart considered a traitor and vowed to kill on sight. "The Ride Around McClellan" cost Jeb Stuart one officer killed, shook Yankee composure, electrified the continent, and engraved the Virginia cavalier permanently in the pages of American history and lore.

The greatest criticism of his career, that he irresponsibly left the Army of Northern Virginia groping in the dark as it moved toward Gettysburg, is wreathed in error. Jeb Stuart acted within both the letter and the spirit of his orders as he moved north. Then he and his cavalry's ferocious rearguard shielding likely saved Lee's army from destruction on its return south after the failed campaign.

He went down fighting, a famous general blazing away with his own revolver, mortally wounded in the May, 1864, Battle of Yellow Tavern while outnumbered 3–1 by Philip Sheridan's mounted juggernaut. One of the histories recorded it thus:

> *And so, with her violets blooming and her linden trees flowering, Virginia grew sadder even than she had been as the famed warrior poet whose feats of daring had brought her renown which could not fade, passed into the upper sanctuary.*

On April 16, a full year after the War began, a bill ending slavery in the District of Columbia became law. Utilizing the appeals process, owners of the world's largest slave market—just two blocks from President Lincoln's bedroom in the White House—would remain open for business for approximately another year.

Seven Days Campaign

The main armies finally crashed into one another June 25 at Seven Pines. The fierce battle blunted McClellan's push on Richmond. But it also resulted in a bullet through the throat and the near killing of Confederate commander Joe Johnston. Davis turned to Robert E. Lee, whose chief service thus far in the War had been the unsuccessful campaign in Unionist western Virginia and as a desk-bound military advisor to the President in Richmond.

Lee arranged for the reinforcement of his army from coastal garrisons Johnston had been unsuccessful in securing. Then he sent several thousand more troops to Jackson in the Valley, to heighten Lincoln's paranoia about that quadrant and the potential for a direct assault on Washington City. Turning his attention to the matters at hand, Lee correctly surmised that McClellan, despite now having an open road into a Richmond protected by a force only one-quarter his own, would hesitate. Then the Virginian engineered an unprecedented series of feints and maneuvers that split his own, smaller, force in half and hurled the Confederates headlong into the Federals in his own offensive thrust.

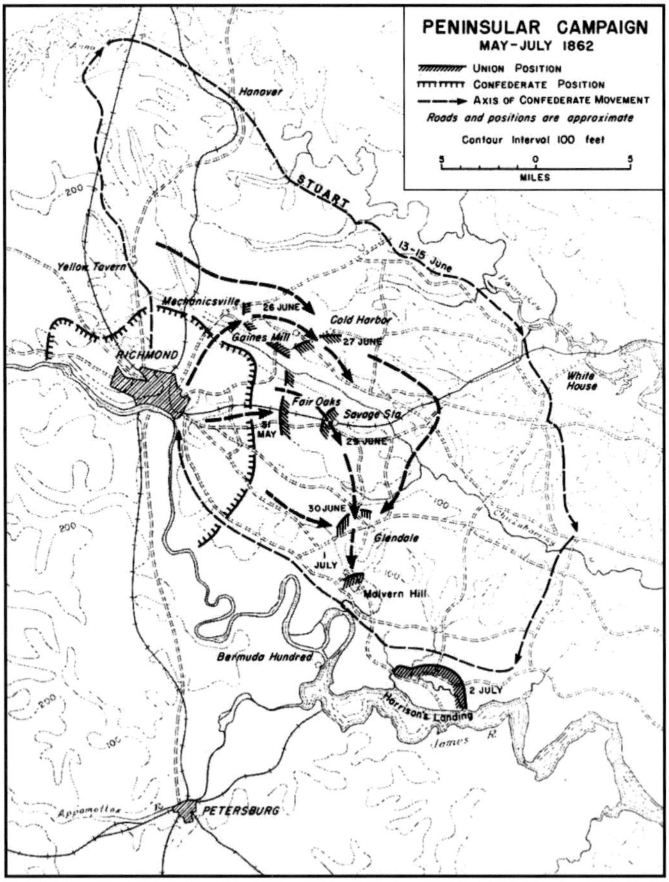

Map of the Seven Days, or Peninsula, Campaign

For the next week, Lee's newly-christened Army of Northern Virginia piled into the Federals at every turn and drove them from the gates of Richmond and out of the state. A whole series of bloody brawls carved their own names into American history—Oak Grove, Gaines's Mill, Savage's Station, White Oak Swamp, Malvern Hill. The Confederates suffered a higher proportion of casualties and won only one battle outright in what came to be known as the Seven Days Campaign. At Malvern Hill for instance, the final battle, Lee attempted to finish McClellan off with a straight-on charge. Massed Federal cannon mounted on high ground, packed with double loads of canister, and favored with an open field of fire, cut down 5,000 Confederates in a failed series of charges whose heroism was matched only by its carnage. However, the psychological effect of Lee's audacity took a higher toll on the Federals than the violence of the attacks themselves. Finally unnerved by the old warrior's ferocity, which cemented for McClellan the veracity of Pinkerton's (false) report that the Southerners had twice as many men as the Federals, the Northern commander ordered a strategic withdrawal down to Harrison's Landing on the James River.

Embarrassed before the court of world opinion by having his splendid army chased away from Richmond, Lincoln would never regain his confidence in McClellan.

The Seven Days Campaign was a bitter setback for the North. Embarrassed before the court of world opinion by having his splendid army chased away from Richmond, Lincoln would never regain his confidence in McClellan. He called that man back to Washington with his troops. He also brought John Pope, flush with success out west in the Kentucky and Mississippi River

Two stereographs of Professor Thaddeus S. Lowe and the Federal military balloon with which he observed and reported Confederate troop positions . . . on the ground . . . and off . . . near Gaines's Mill, Virginia, during the Seven Days Campaign, in May–June 1862.

campaigns, to come and take charge of the newly formed Army of Virginia. In effect, Pope replaced McClellan as chief Federal commander in the east.

Lee was himself disappointed. At several points, the Army of Northern Virginia stood on the brink of annihilating its foe, the main United States army. Each time, mistakes and inexperience hampered the Southrons. Ironically, the failure of Stonewall Jackson to command his men with his usual brilliance and alacrity, cost Lee a couple of his best such opportunities. (Jackson was later found to have been in the throes of physical and mental exhaustion from the demands and lack of sleep of the Valley Campaign). But the Army of Northern Virginia—and its new commander—had written for itself the beginnings of its legend.

Julia Ward Howe and *The Battle Hymn of the Republic* (1819–1911)

Mine eyes have seen the glory
of the coming of the Lord;
He is trampling out the vintage
where the grapes of wrath
are stored;
He hath loosed the fateful lightning
of his terrible swift sword;
His truth is marching on.

Chorus:
Glory! glory, hallelujah!
Glory! glory, hallelujah!
Glory! glory, hallelujah!
Our God is marching on.

In the beauty of the lilies,
Christ was born across the sea,
With a glory in His bosom
that transfigures you and me;
As He died to make men holy,
let us live to make men free,
While God is marching on.

Julia Ward Howe was raised in an aristocratic New York family. She married Samuel Gridley Howe, who gained infamy as one of the wealthy benefactors of John Brown's murderous campaign to unleash a violent servile insurrection against the South. Unitarian, Mrs. Howe preached from those pulpits throughout New England. She believed the idea propelling John Brown's rebellion, freedom for the slaves, would fuel a social change in the United States—the type of change that would bring about the fulfillment of Karl Marx and Friedrich Engels' ten-plank *Communist Manifesto* in America.

During the darkest days of the war for the North, she made a trip to Washington D.C., where she saw the Federal hospitals, depot stations, and supply lines. The horrors of the slaughter gripped her—yet so did the necessity of what she considered a just and holy war. That night, she tossed and turned in her bed until around 3 a.m. Then she rose and penned words, set to the tune of *John Brown's Body Lies A'Moulderin' in the Grave*, which became *The Battle Hymn of the Republic*. Its stirring strains became a paean to Abraham Lincoln, and one of the two or three supreme anthems of the United States's people. And though it reflects her Unitarian faith and is anything but a Christian hymn, the *Battle Hymn* has secured a spot for itself not only in Christian hymnbooks, but as a standard worship service selection, and not only on Lincoln's birthday or the Fourth of July.

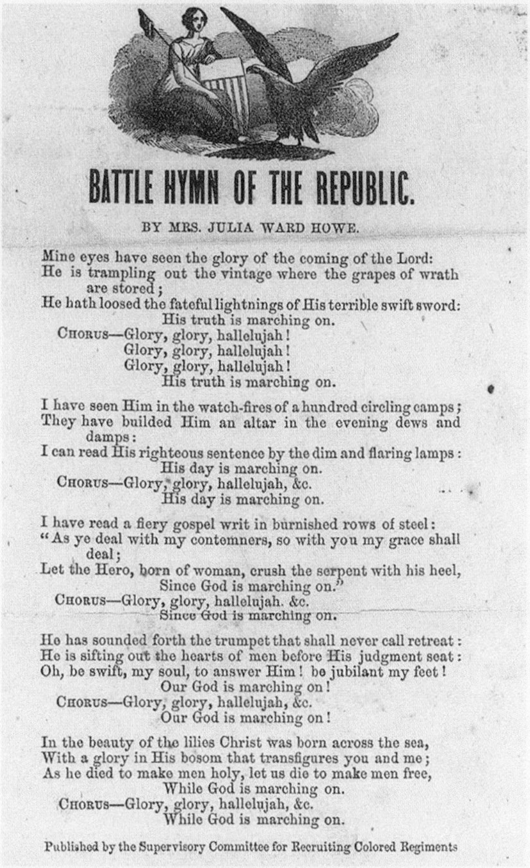

BATTLE HYMN OF THE REPUBLIC.

BY MRS. JULIA WARD HOWE.

Mine eyes have seen the glory of the coming of the Lord:
He is trampling out the vintage where the grapes of wrath are stored;
He hath loosed the fateful lightnings of His terrible swift sword:
His truth is marching on.
CHORUS—Glory, glory, hallelujah!
Glory, glory, hallelujah!
Glory, glory, hallelujah!
His truth is marching on.

I have seen Him in the watch-fires of a hundred circling camps;
They have builded Him an altar in the evening dews and damps:
I can read His righteous sentence by the dim and flaring lamps:
His day is marching on.
CHORUS—Glory, glory, hallelujah, &c.
His day is marching on.

I have read a fiery gospel writ in burnished rows of steel:
"As ye deal with my contemners, so with you my grace shall deal;
Let the Hero, born of woman, crush the serpent with his heel,
Since God is marching on."
CHORUS—Glory, glory, hallelujah. &c.
Since God is marching on.

He has sounded forth the trumpet that shall never call retreat:
He is sifting out the hearts of men before His judgment seat:
Oh, be swift, my soul, to answer Him! be jubilant my feet!
Our God is marching on!
CHORUS—Glory, glory, hallelujah, &c.
Our God is marching on!

In the beauty of the lilies Christ was born across the sea,
With a glory in His bosom that transfigures you and me;
As he died to make men holy, let us die to make men free,
While God is marching on.
CHORUS—Glory, glory, hallelujah, &c.
While God is marching on.

Published by the Supervisory Committee for Recruiting Colored Regiments

Mrs. Howe's Christ, however, is not the Redeemer of the Bible, but a scourging force. The Northern army becomes the incarnation of Christ Himself, a new embodiment of the old gospel ideal of going forth to trample out the great harvest of social transformation. If Mrs. Howe's Christ died to make men holy, it was not by virtue of His atoning sacrifice, loosing them from the bonds of sin and damnation, but by an example of sacrifice that would inspire them to "die to make men free." If her religion did not advocate a final judgment by Christ of all men in the next world, her eyes beheld one now, having "seen the glory of the coming of the Lord" during the War. Indeed, "He hath loosed the fateful lightning of his terrible swift sword" by sending the Federal army rampaging through the farms and homes of the South. Interestingly, she spelled the "his" in this context with a lower-case "h," while spelling it elsewhere with an upper case "h" in reference to President Lincoln.

The gospel of Julia Ward Howe was not one of peace, but of war. As it inspired Northern soldiers into battle and assured them that might makes right, it polarized them further from their brothers and cousins to the south. For those unfortunates, *The Battle Hymn of the Republic* promised only the judgment of God. She whose hymn Christians North and South now sing with emotion did not believe in hell, Christ's Divinity, or His literal final coming. In the end, her anthem sundered two worldviews as it rang forth the great manifesto of human transformation for which Unitarianism calls.

16 Emancipation
(1862)

Francis B. Carpenter's classic depiction of the first reading of the Emancipation Proclamation by Abraham Lincoln and his cabinet.

He would look out of the window a while and then put his pen to paper, but he did not write much at once. . . . when he had made up his mind he would put down a line or two, and then sit quiet for a few minutes.

—Presidential aide Thomas Eckert, describing Abraham Lincoln's first day writing the Emancipation Proclamation

One reason the Confederacy did not win the War was that it never quite marshaled the resources to translate any of its many big victories into a crippling, cataclysmic defeat for the North. Before McClellan even returned to Washington after the Seven Days, for instance, Pope was gathering the Army of Virginia for another march on Richmond. But this time Lee had no intention of waiting on the ever-growing Federal armies to knock at the gates of the capital. He and Stonewall Jackson devised an electrifying plan, the first in a series of bold divisions of the Army of Northern Virginia in the face of much-larger Federal forces.

Jackson and his corps had already swept Nathaniel Banks' Federals from the field at Cedar Mountain. Now they lived up to their sobriquet of "Foot Cavalry" and circled north around Pope's enormous army, marching over fifty miles in two days. Then they destroyed Pope's gargantuan supply depot—which lay between the Federal army and Washington.

Jackson and his corps had already swept Nathaniel Banks' Federals from the field at Cedar Mountain. Now they lived up to their sobriquet of "Foot Cavalry" and circled north around Pope's enormous army, marching over fifty miles in two days. Then they destroyed Pope's gargantuan supply depot—which lay between the Federal army and Washington. Overnight, the Federal shadow was removed from Richmond as an alarmed Pope turned back north to crush Jackson. He crashed into him August 29, the opening day of the Second Battle of Manassas, or Bull Run, close to where the first was fought the year before. Fifty-three thousand Federals charged Jackson's 20,000 Confederates five straight times and could not move them. And Pope seemed to have forgotten that Lee had another corps, the one commanded by James Longstreet. When the battle resumed the second day, Longstreet's men burst undetected upon the outflanked Federals at the climactic point of their attack against Jackson. Lee, with less than 55,000 men, blitzed Pope's 75,000 from the field and sent them hurtling for cover behind the Washington entrenchments.

President Davis had given "Granny Lee," the "King of Spades," command precisely four months before. Then, McClellan was five miles from Richmond. Now Lee's forward outposts were 20 miles from Washington. And another Federal army had been shoved out of Virginia.

John Pope (1822-1892)

A former Illinois farm boy and West Point graduate breveted to captain in the Mexican War for his valorous exploits, John Pope then served as a U.S. Army engineer on the nation's western frontier for fifteen years leading up to the War. Pope first gained acclaim for his Army of the Mississippi's central role in clearing the upper Mississippi River of Southern forces in the spring of 1862, helping capture New Madrid, Corinth, and Island Number Ten, the northernmost Confederate position on the river, just off southeastern Missouri. The gaining of Island Number Ten, in particular, proved a signal triumph for the United States, for it rolled the Confederate presence on the Mississippi south and away from Northern territory.

In a year when Confederate victories in the east were frequent, President Lincoln thought he saw a winner in the brash, courageous, cocksure Midwesterner. He called Pope east to marshal the combined former commands of Generals Banks, McDowell, and Fremont, as well as thousands of new conscripts, into one unstoppable eastern army. These men, already grieved at the removal of McClellan, whom they loved and admired, as theater commander, now heard Pope declare his habit out west of seeing nothing but the backs of his enemies. They recognized the unveiled slight. He supposedly announced that his headquarters would be in the saddle; Confederates joked that Pope put his headquarters where his hindquarters ought to be.

When he encouraged his men to live off the food and supplies of Virginia farms; vowed that all homes in the area of any Confederate resistance would be burned; proclaimed hanging without trial for any Virginia civilian suspected of aiding the Confederacy, and shooting of civilians of any age in areas where Federal troops were killed by what Pope termed "bushwhackers," Lee called him a "miscreant." One of Stonewall Jackson's subordinates reported Pope's measures, heretofore unprecedented in the War, to him and said, "This new general claims your attention, sir." "And, please God, he shall have it," Jackson replied. And have it he did. With Lincoln's simple command "On to Richmond" ringing in his ears, Pope moved his army south into the Virginia Piedmont, intending the capture of Charlottesville and Gordonsville as launch points toward the Confederate capital. But Lee committed the audacious move of splitting his smaller force in two. He sent Jackson, who had 24,000 troops, circling north behind Pope's colossal force of 140,000.

When Jackson defeated Banks' portion of Pope's army at Cedar Mountain, then destroyed Pope's supply base at Manassas Junction, Pope turned in fury on him. But Jackson led him on a chase before choosing ground on the edge of the old Manassas battlefield on which to prepare a fight for Pope. It came August 29, as Pope, convinced Jackson was fleeing before him, threw division after division in uncoordinated assaults against the Confederates. Hugely outnumbered, Jackson held until Longstreet's corps "bushwhacked" Pope's army the next day and routed it. The following day, a disgusted Lincoln returned McClellan to command in Pope's place; the latter was sent northwest to Minnesota.

Lightning at Catlett's Station, by John Paul Strain, depicting the night Jeb Stuart and his men thundered into John Pope's "headquarters in the field" and captured 300 Federal prisoners, $350,000 in U.S. money, a huge stockpile of Federal supplies—and Pope's orders, dispatches, hat, cloak, and frock coat from the Army of the Potomac commander's own tent.

Maryland Campaign

Now Lee embarked on the War's boldest campaign yet. With the Federals still reeling from Second Manassas, he continued north, again splitting his army in two—and crossed the Potomac into Union-held Maryland. The Virginian had several reasons for doing this. He wanted to give Maryland one final opportunity to throw in with the Confederacy, or at least for a large portion of it to do so. He also wanted to cut Federal rail connections between the Northeast and Midwest, perhaps at Harrisonburg, Pennsylvania. Further, he needed the food for his army he could glean from the Maryland countryside. One reason for invading Maryland towered above all others. Lee hoped that carrying the fight into the heart of the United States and making a good showing, maybe winning a decisive battle, might elicit official diplomatic recognition of—and perhaps even military

James G. Longstreet (1821-1904)

His men called him "Old Pete" and Robert E. Lee called him his "Old War Horse." Many people, in fact, called the Dutch-ancestored Longstreet many things. In the end, he was one of the finest corps commanders of the war, probably second only to Stonewall Jackson among Confederates. Reared in the Deep South, the bluff, hulking Longstreet finished low in his West Point graduating class. Like other famed commanders in the War, he first distinguished himself in combat during the Mexican–American War (1846–48). Shared time at West Point and kinship by marriage produced a deep friendship between him and U. S. Grant.

When war came again, Longstreet's cool under fire and immovability while on the defensive spurred him quickly to corps command. His leadership in such Confederate victories as Second Manassas, Fredericksburg, and the Battle of the Wilderness in the East and Chickamauga in the West etched his name into American legend. But Longstreet lost three children in 1862 to scarlet fever and became a brooding man. The rancor between him and his division commander A. P. Hill would have resulted in a duel with pistols had not Lee intervened. He also evidenced jealousy toward Jackson, who, unlike Longstreet, had been entrusted with independent commands. Later, he harbored resentment toward Lee at not providing him the same.

> *Longstreet's cool under fire and immovability while on the defensive spurred him quickly to corps command. His leadership in such Confederate victories as Second Manassas, Fredericksburg, and the Battle of the Wilderness in the east and Chickamauga in the west etched his name into American legend.*

Longstreet failed famously at Gettysburg, then was nearly killed when shot through the neck at the Wilderness in 1864. Ironically, he fell very close to where Stonewall Jackson had, almost precisely one year to the day earlier, and, like Jackson at Chancellorsville, while on the verge of orchestrating a devastating victory that could have rendered doubtful Federal hopes for defeating the South. His corncob pipe and steely nerve accompanied him all the way to Appomattox. When flamboyant Federal General George Custer arrogantly demanded his concession on that field shortly before the surrender, Longstreet faced Custer down and angrily threatened to arrest him if he did not return to his own lines.

Even greater controversy clustered around Longstreet after the War. He angered most ex-Confederates by joining the Northern-dominated Republican Party and garnering lucrative business and government posts partly through his friendship with Grant. When he savaged Lee in his memoirs, anger turned to hatred for many Southerners. Alone among Confederate leaders, no significant monument had been erected to him even by the beginning of the 21st century.

assistance for—the Confederacy from foreign governments such as Great Britain and France.

The campaign began well. The Federals were indeed shaken from the series of beatings Lee and Jackson had dealt them in 1862. News that the Army of Northern Virginia was headed north heightened their concern. Then they lost track of where Lee was. Having deposed Pope from command of the main Federal army, Lincoln reinstated McClellan. Despite the usual vitriol trained on McClellan from his Republican opponents in Washington, the newly-christened Army of the Potomac shook the earth at its soldiers' enthusiastic reunion with the commander who had formed and trained them.

Then, with Jackson gobbling up Union-held Harper's Ferry—and 11,000 Federal prisoners—and Lee marching north through Maryland toward Pennsylvania, Providence intervened on behalf of McClellan and the United States. A Yankee corporal found three unsmoked cigars discarded at an erstwhile Confederate campfire. They were wrapped together with Special Order 191—Lee's official battle plan for the Maryland campaign! Flush with these stunning revelations, McClellan headed straight for Lee with the entire Federal army of nearly 90,000 men. After the Federals stormed through a Confederate force at South Mountain, Lee arrayed his army with its back to the Potomac River at its confluence with slender Antietam Creek. Even when Jackson joined him he had only 40,000 soldiers, less than half the Federal force.

Sharpsburg

What followed, on September 17, 1862, was the bloodiest day in American history. Nearly 23,000 men fell in twelve hours of fighting so brutal that one entire corn field which stood six feet high at sunrise had no blade more than six inches tall by sunset. McClellan first assaulted the Confederate left, held by Jackson. Stonewall's force was savaged, but it wrecked two entire Federal corps and repulsed them. Next came the center, its stacks and piles of corpses rendering it the lasting name of the "Bloody Angle." The outnumbered Confederates were finally pushed back, but not broken.

Blacksmiths proved indispensable to the effective movement of large armies, including these Federals during the 1862 Sharpsburg Campaign in Maryland.

Then the Federals charged into the Confederate right. They drove it back to within a half mile of the Potomac, from which no escape route existed and from which the Federals could turn and roll up the rest of the Southern army. At this point, Jackson's division commander—and adversary—A.P. Hill arrived with his 2,000 men. They saved the day, and the War, for the Confederacy. The battle was a draw, with each side holding the same ground it had at the beginning of the day. But every Federal charge had failed.

"George McClellan at Antietam" (Sharpsburg).

Strategic Victory

Lee expected McClellan to resume the attack the next morning. Even with nearly 50,000 more men than Lee, he did not. But Lee's own generals, including Jackson, declared they must withdraw from Maryland or, squeezed against the Potomac, risk annihilation—or starvation—from the still-growing Federal forces. Under cover of darkness, the Confederates marched back to Virginia. They had dealt several thousand more casualties than they received to an enemy more than twice their number. They had not been beaten, and they had not been driven from the field, and the Federals had not again attacked them. But no threat to the seat of the government in Washington had occurred. The considerable Southern-sympathetic sections of Maryland lay east, beyond the reach of the Confederate invasion and largely unable to rally to Lee's banners. And the Confederacy's last serious hopes for foreign recognition and aid melted away as McClellan pushed the secessionists out of Maryland and deprived them of the opportunity to accomplish a devastating victory that could seal viability before the court of international opinion.

Neither had the United States attained the decisive victory for which Lincoln still clamored. But he considered the Antietam campaign, if not a tactical victory, at least a strategic one. He considered it good enough to afford him a position of strength from which to announce the Emancipation Proclamation. That historic document freed no slaves over which Lincoln had jurisdiction. However, it declared slaves in secessionist areas free. And it confirmed that the War would now be fought to the death, since for the South to capitulate would overnight throw both its economic and social institutions into chaos and possibly destruction.

Burnside's Bridge, by John Paul Strain, the memorable stand by Confederate General Robert Toombs and a few hundred Georgians against the onslaught of Ambrose Burnside's IX Corps.

The Emancipation Proclamation

Lincoln announced the the Emancipation Proclamation on September 22, 1862. He said Confederates could keep their slaves if they quit the War by January 1, 1863. Otherwise, they must free them. Despite the fact that much of the conflict between North and South revolved around the slavery issue, the North never adopted an abolitionist stance during the lifetime of Abraham Lincoln.

> ***Emancipation***
>
> The act of setting free, especially slaves. When an owner sets his slaves free, he emancipates them; when government sets all slaves free, that is the abolition of slavery.

In his first inaugural speech Lincoln said the freeing of slaves was not only inexpedient and impolitic but perhaps even unconstitutional. Several of the states that stayed in the Northern Union—Missouri, Maryland, Delaware, Kentucky, and West Virginia—remained slave states. The District of Columbia, seat of the Federal government, retained slavery too. In fact, for nearly half the War, Lincoln likely walked past the largest slave market on the North American continent every time he went to visit wounded Federal soldiers in the military hospital a few blocks from the White House.

The Proclamation, officially enacted on Jan. 1, 1863, did not actually free any slaves within the jurisdiction of its governmental authority. Rather, it left in bondage the hundreds of thousands of slaves remaining in the Northern (border) slave states, as well as those slaves living in formerly Confederate areas captured by Federal troops. The latter included eastern Tennessee, northern Kentucky, northern Louisiana, the New Orleans parishes of Louisiana, and the parishes of southern Florida. It was

President Lincoln Writing the Proclamation of Freedom.
This print is based on David Gilmour Blythe's fanciful painting of Lincoln writing the Emancipation Proclamation, which was actually issued in 1862 and went into effect in January 1863. Symbolism and messages fill the cartoon, including the bust of Lincoln's strongly nationalist predecessor Andrew Jackson on a mantelpiece near the window, as well as that of his immediate predecessor, President James Buchanan, viewed by Republicans as ineffectual against secessionism, hanging by the neck behind Lincoln. The scales of justice appear in the left corner and a rail splitter's maul on the floor at Lincoln's feet.

essentially symbolic, designed to placate certain sectors within the Republicans' abolitionist constituency and provide certain strategic wartime advantages. Nevertheless, it did lay the groundwork for freedom for the slaves, which would come with the ratification, after the War, of the Thirteenth, Fourteenth, and Fifteenth Amendments to the Constitution.

The Original Proclamation

I, Abraham Lincoln, president of the United States of America, and Commander-in-Chief of the Army and Navy thereof, do hereby proclaim and declare that hereafter, as heretofore, the war will be prosecuted for the object of practically restoring the constitutional relation between the United States and the people thereof, in which State that relation is, or may be, suspended or disturbed; and that, with this object, 'on the 1st day of January, 1863, all persons held as slaves within any State, or any designated part of a State, the people whereof shall then be in rebellion against the United States, shall be then, thenceforward, and for ever, free.

Some in the North, especially those favorable to the Radical wing of the Republican Party, cheered Lincoln's action. More significantly, from the perspective of the great nations of Europe, it cast the North upon the moral high ground in the War and further discouraged England, France, and others from recognizing the Confederacy or offering it succor. Yet the document was met by a firestorm of disapproval even in the North and even among many who supported the ending of slavery. Many abolitionists condemned it for freeing only those slaves over whom Lincoln had no jurisdiction, while leaving in bondage all those over whom he did.

On December 31, 1862, the night before Lincoln's Emancipation Proclamation went into effect, he signed an agreement committing the United States to deport 5,000 American-born blacks. Their destination: Vache Island, off the coast of Haiti. They were to colonize the island, at the cost of $50 a head, to be paid by a group of Northern businessmen.

Conversely, the still-substantial Northern Democratic Party, while willing to fight to the end to preserve the Federal Union, opposed what it perceived as a transforming of the War into a blood-drenched crusade to free slaves. So did much of the Federal army. After the Emancipation Proclamation, the Democratic Presidential candidacy of George McClellan seemed destined to triumph over Lincoln until Sherman captured Atlanta.

"We, Catholics, and a vast majority of our brave troops in the field, have not the slightest idea of carrying on a war that costs so much blood and treasure just to gratify a clique of Abolitionists in the North," Archbishop John Hughes of New York boomed. General Joe Hooker, at the helm of the United States' largest and most important army, opposed the Proclamation and declared that much of his army "would never have embarked in the war had they anticipated this action of the government." U. S. Grant himself owned slaves, through his wife and her family. William Sherman famously urged the same destination for slaves and the Southern cotton they picked—hell.

Many in the North feared Lincoln's decision would harden the War into an implacable duel of annihilation. They attributed this specter to the political humiliation and economic calamity they feared would result to the Confederacy from an immediate release without compensation of the blacks in whom so much Southern capital was invested. Thousands of prominent Southern landowners would go broke without their servants to work or the money to pay them to do so. The former slaves would then starve, and masses of other whites would go bust without the spending influx from the wealthy landowners. Lincoln's home state, Illinois, declared that he had "at once converted the war . . . into the crusade for the sudden, unconditional and violent liberation of 3,000,000 negro slaves; a result which would not only be a total subversion of the Federal Union but a revolution in the social organization of the Southern States."

Lincoln's True Reasons?

Evidence abounds, from Lincoln's own words as well as his actions before and after the emancipation, that something besides the desire to free the slaves fueled the act. Largely unreported by most traditional American histories of the War is the

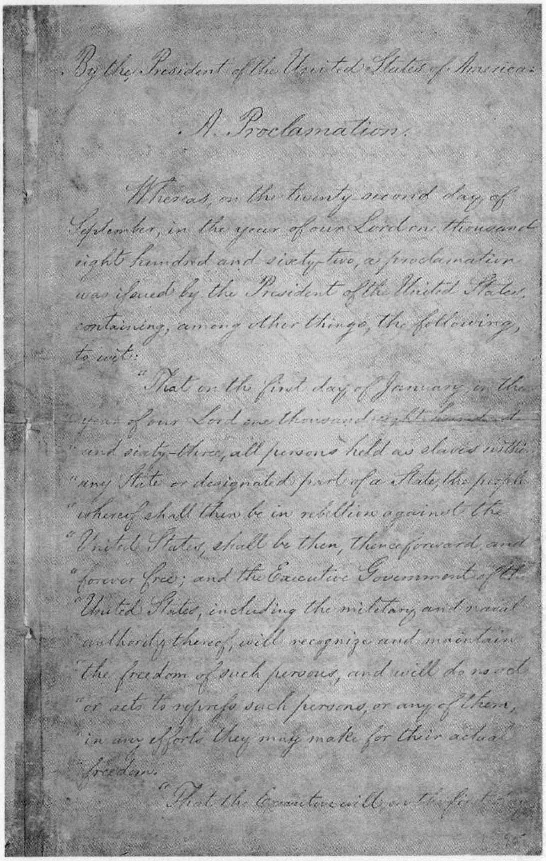
By the President of the United States of America:

A Proclamation.

Whereas, on the twenty-second day of September, in the year of our Lord one thousand eight hundred and sixty-two, a proclamation was issued by the President of the United States, containing, among other things, the following, to wit:

"That on the first day of January, in the year of our Lord one thousand eight hundred "and sixty-three, all persons held as slaves within "any State or designated part of a State, the people "whereof shall then be in rebellion against the "United States, shall be then, thenceforward, and "forever free; and the Executive Government of the "United States, including the military and naval "authority thereof, will recognize and maintain "the freedom of such persons, and will do no act "or acts to repress such persons, or any of them, "in any efforts they may make for their actual "freedom.

"That the Executive will, on the first day

The first page of the Emancipation Proclamation

The Battlecry of Freedom (George Frederick Root)

Yes, we'll rally round the flag, boys,
we'll rally once again,
Shouting the battlecry of freedom,
We will rally from the hillside,
we'll gather from the plain,
Shouting the battlecry of freedom.
Chorus:
The Union forever, hurrah! boys, hurrah!
Down with the traitor, up with the star,
While we rally round the flag, boys,
Rally once again,
Shouting the battle cry of Freedom.

We are springing to the call of our
brothers gone before,
Shouting the battlecry of freedom.
And we'll fill the vacant ranks with a
million freemen more,
Shouting the battlecry of freedom.
Chorus:
The Union forever, hurrah! boys, hurrah!
Down with the traitor, up with the star,
While we rally round the flag, boys,
Rally once again,
Shouting the battle cry of Freedom.

revolt launched against Lincoln by Senate Republicans in mid-December, 1862, just before he signed into law the Emancipation Proclamation. According to Lincoln's old friend Illinois Representative Orville Browning and others, the senators demanded the President conduct a more resolute war effort. They were apparently prepared to bring down his administration if he did not.

This enhanced effort evidently included emancipation as a method of war that would torpedo the South's economy and ability to defend itself. A slave uprising—with the attendant slaughter of white Southern women, children, and old men—lay within the sphere of this projection. At least a howling chorus not limited to the South, but including many of Lincoln's opponents in the North, as well as in Europe, thought so. Horatio Seymour, soon-to-be Democratic Governor of New York, said:

> *The scheme for an immediate emancipation and general arming of the slaves throughout the South is a proposal for the butchery of women and children, for scenes of lust and rapine, arson and murder, unparalleled in the history of the world.*

Fortunately, relations between Southern slaves and their owners proved superior to such an eventuality. But Lincoln himself, when told the Constitution gave individual states and not the national government jurisdiction over slavery, claimed emancipation as a war powers act that he as Commander-in-Chief could employ—for military purposes. Indeed, the President eliminated from an early draft of the decree a call for a violent uprising of slaves.

Slavery to Combat

A portion of the completed Emancipation Proclamation addressed another view Lincoln had in mind for Southern, but not Northern, slaves—impressment into the Federal armies:

> *And I further declare and make known that such persons of suitable condition will be received into the armed service of the United States to garrison forts, positions, stations, and other places, and to man vessels of all sorts in said service . . . [due to] military necessity.*

Not only did he deprive the Confederacy of the labor and other contributions of many Southern slaves, but he employed them instead in the Federal military effort, forcing many blacks into the fighting against their will.

The scheme for an immediate emancipation and general arming of the slaves throughout the South is a proposal for the butchery of women and children, for scenes of lust and rapine, arson and murder, unparalleled in the history of the world.

—Horatio Seymour
Governor of New York

Orville Browning's diary of December 31, 1862, recorded that Judge Benjamin Franklin Thomas of the Massachusetts Supreme Court told Browning that: "the President was fatally bent upon his course, saying that if he should refuse to issue his proclamation there would be a rebellion in the north, and that a dictator would be placed over his head within the week." With the Emancipation Proclamation, Lincoln quelled the Senate revolt. But his lackluster feelings for it resurfaced when he eschewed the urgings of much of his cabinet, including Seward, Chase, Blair, and Bates, and confined his decree to those slaves in Confederate-controlled territory. That is, he freed none of the slaves over which he had control when he had the opportunity.

Frederick Douglass expressed his views on these actions, as well as Lincoln's public declarations regarding the benefits of deporting the bulk of American blacks:

> *Illogical and unfair as Mr. Lincoln's statements are, they are nevertheless quite in keeping with his whole course from the beginning of his administration up to this day, and confirm the painful conviction that though elected as an anti-slavery man by Republican and Abolition voters, Mr. Lincoln is quite a genuine representative of American prejudice and Negro hatred and far more concerned for the preservation of slavery, and the favor of the border Slave States, than for any sentiment of magnanimity or principle of justice and humanity.*

In the end, the Emancipation Proclamation exhibited political sagacity and brilliance, hastened the demise of American slavery, probably triggered the deaths of tens of thousands more men than would otherwise have occurred, and likely contributed to America's future morass in racial relations.

Thanksgiving Day in modern America stems from President Lincoln's setting aside the last Thursday in November as a national day of Thanksgiving. He had earlier designated other days of thanksgiving in order "to subdue the anger which has produced and so long sustained a needless and cruel rebellion."

Clement Vallandigham and the Copperheads (1820–1871)

Most famous—or infamous—of the Copperheads was this Democratic Ohio Congressman. He fit none of the neat politically correct niches constructed by contemporary historians. Though opposing the War, he did not support Southern secession. Though an opponent of Lincoln and the Republicans, he loved the Union first and last and eschewed the opportunity when it came to go over to the South. Just as did his Northern political opponent, Radical Republican Thaddeus Stevens, Clement Vallandigham spoke from conviction, not political expediency or opportunism or a desire for personal popularity. He evidenced this, and an apparent disregard for his political or even physical well-being, in many of his speeches.

"Money you have expended without limit, and blood poured out like water," he thundered to his Republican opponents in Congress. "Defeat, debt, taxation, and sepulchers—these are your only trophies." The Republicans certainly believed he meant what he said. They gerrymandered, or reconfigured to their own advantage, Vallandigham's Congressional district, adding a Republican county to it. He subsequently lost his seat in the

November, 1862, election. If his Northern opponents thought themselves ridded of Vallandigham, they miscalculated. His fury mounted during his final days in office as he excoriated the Republicans about what the War had done to Ohio: “There is mourning in every house and distress and sadness in every heart. Shall she give you any more [soldiers]? Ought this war to continue? I answer, no; not a day, not an hour. What then? Shall we separate? Again I answer, no no, no! What then? . . . Stop fighting, make an armistice.” When Vallandigham told thousands of Democrats assembled at Mount Vernon in May, 1863, that no longer was the Union the reason for continuing the War, but rather the liberation of the blacks—in return for enslaving the whites—they roared their agreement.

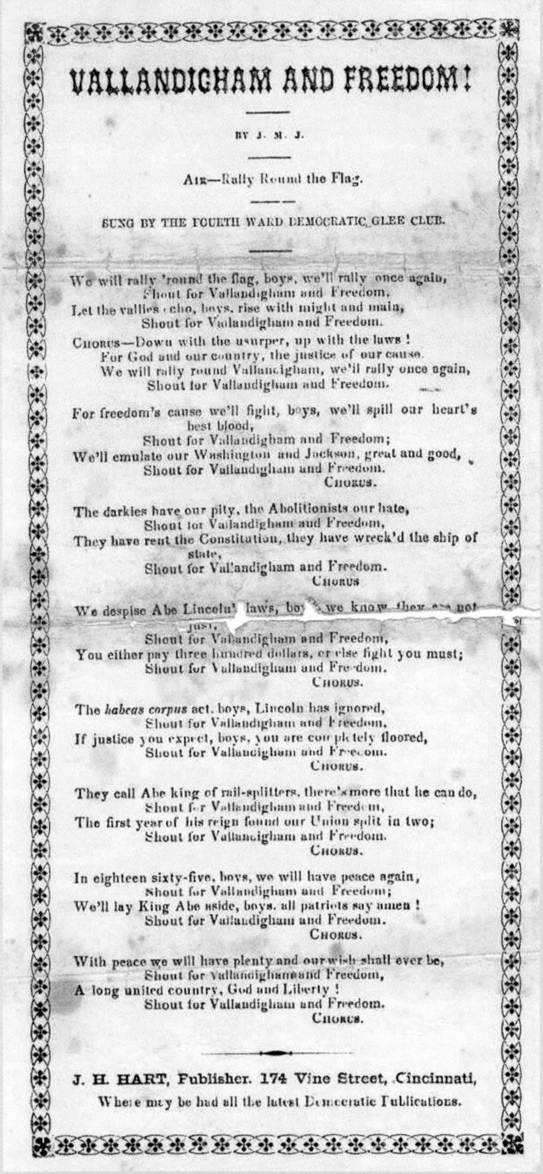

VALLANDIGHAM AND FREEDOM!

BY J. M. J.

AIR—Rally Round the Flag.

SUNG BY THE FOURTH WARD DEMOCRATIC GLEE CLUB.

We will rally 'round the flag, boys, we'll rally once again,
Shout for Vallandigham and Freedom,
Let the vallies echo, boys, rise with might and main,
Shout for Vallandigham and Freedom.

CHORUS—Down with the usurper, up with the laws!
For God and our country, the justice of our cause.
We will rally round Vallandigham, we'll rally once again,
Shout for Vallandigham and Freedom.

For freedom's cause we'll fight, boys, we'll spill our heart's best blood,
Shout for Vallandigham and Freedom;
We'll emulate our Washington and Jackson, great and good,
Shout for Vallandigham and Freedom.
CHORUS.

The darkies have our pity, the Abolitionists our hate,
Shout for Vallandigham and Freedom,
They have rent the Constitution, they have wreck'd the ship of state,
Shout for Vallandigham and Freedom.
CHORUS

We despise Abe Lincoln's laws, boys, we know they are not just,
Shout for Vallandigham and Freedom,
You either pay three hundred dollars, or else fight you must;
Shout for Vallandigham and Freedom.
CHORUS.

The *habeas corpus* act, boys, Lincoln has ignored,
Shout for Vallandigham and Freedom,
If justice you expect, boys, you are completely floored,
Shout for Vallandigham and Freedom.
CHORUS.

They call Abe king of rail-splitters, there's more that he can do,
Shout for Vallandigham and Freedom,
The first year of his reign found our Union split in two;
Shout for Vallandigham and Freedom.
CHORUS.

In eighteen sixty-five, boys, we will have peace again,
Shout for Vallandigham and Freedom;
We'll lay King Abe aside, boys, all patriots say amen!
Shout for Vallandigham and Freedom.
CHORUS.

With peace we will have plenty and our wish shall ever be,
Shout for Vallandigham and Freedom,
A long united country, God and Liberty!
Shout for Vallandigham and Freedom.
CHORUS.

J. H. HART, Publisher. 174 Vine Street, Cincinnati,
Where may be had all the latest Democratic Publications.

Vallandigham and Freedom featured the same tune but a very different viewpoint than the song *Battlecry of Freedom.*

International Embarrassment

Ambrose Burnside took a different view. Transferred after his defeat at Fredericksburg to command of the Department of the Ohio, he dispatched a company of Federal troops to kick in the front door of Vallandigham's house, haul him out of his bed at 2:30 in the morning, and throw him into a Cincinnati prison. “Must I shoot a simple-minded soldier boy who deserts, while I must not touch a hair of a wily agitator who induces him to desert?” Lincoln said in defending his dealings with Vallandigham. “I think that in such a case to silence the agitator and save the boy is not only constitutional but withal a great mercy.” Historian Shelby Foote, in his *The Civil War: A Narrative* trilogy, suggests that Lincoln's analogy was an apples-to-oranges comparison, in that the soldier and the agitator came under different codes of law. Nevertheless, the President posited that a different law prevailed in war than in peace, in the same way that a deathly ill man takes a strong drug he would never ingest when well.

Subsequent to his jailing and especially after a military commission found him guilty of treason and condemned him to prison for the rest of the War, Vallandigham proved more problematic for Lincoln and Northern "hard-war" supporters than ever he could have been while free and even in Congress. A groundswell of support rose up for him across the United States, and their treatment of him became an international embarrassment for the Lincoln administration. "I am here in a military bastille for no other offense than my political opinions," Vallandigham boomed. After several weeks, Lincoln ordered him exiled to the South, from whence he made his way to the West Indies, thence to Canada. During this journey, the Democratic Party of Ohio unanimously nominated him for governor—and he kicked off his campaign across the Niagara River in Canada with an address to the people of his state, lamenting how "usurpers" there had denied him the rights he now enjoyed in another country!

Federal soldiers provided much of the margin of Vallandigham's defeat in the 1863 Ohio gubernatorial battle. But the now world-famed Copperhead was back in business nonetheless, having first returned to Ohio in disguise, then discarding it when he realized Lincoln wanted nothing more to do with making a martyr of him and was leaving him alone. Next year, as the Democratic Presidential Convention prepared to convene, he declared to critics who accused him of pro-Southern sympathies: "Whoever charges that I want to stop this war in order that there may be Southern independence charges that which is false, and lies in his teeth, and lies in his throat!" Never did Vallandigham hold office again, and never did he experience financial plenty. Never did he, either, recant of his desire for "The Constitution as it is, the Union as it was."

What the Copperheads Believed

"Copperheads" were Northern advocates of a peaceful resolution to the conflicts between the sections. Members of the Democratic Party, the major political rival to Lincoln and the Republican Party, comprised the bulk of their thousands-strong ranks.

They supported:

- The Union of Northern and Southern states
- States' rights to govern themselves
- The original, conservative reading of the Constitution
- Peaceful resolution of sectional differences

They opposed:

- High import tariffs
- Secession of states from the Union
- Keeping the Union together by force of arms
- Mandatory military service in the Federal army
- Suspension of habeas corpus, arbitrary arrests, military tribunals for civilians
- Government shutdown of newspapers
- Supporting the Confederacy to the harm of the United States
- Abolition and the Emancipation Proclamation (they feared ex-slaves would flood into their states)

The highest concentration of Copperheads came in the western section of the Northern Union, especially Ohio, Indiana, and Illinois. Though Lincoln came from there, many of his Democratic opponents did as well. The legislature of his home state Illinois was itself controlled by Democrats. These western states had sided with the South and against the

Northeastern industrial interests in many of the contentious prewar issues. So, a degree of tension already existed between them. With the War came a decrease, then a cessation of the Mississippi River trade so important to them. And not only did the bottom fall out of farm prices—even as the cost of transporting these products to the east increased—but the Morrill Tariff, the nation's highest ever, conversely jacked up the prices of manufactured goods for which the westerners looked east.

The Lincoln Administration expressed great concern over Northerners who did not exhibit what it considered sufficient loyalty, or sufficiently enthusiastic loyalty, to the Union and its war effort. After suspending the constitutionally guaranteed writ of habeas corpus early in the War, the President and his lieutenants shut down over 300 Northern newspapers in the course of the struggle, throwing many of their editors and publishers in jail or prison without trials and often without charges. Approximately 14,000 other Northern citizens met the same fate.

Copperheads, at least through the first years of the War, railed famously against what they perceived as a centralized national government run amok and a war waged by it that was destroying the institutions and liberty of the United States. Their ranks were broad and deep, encompassing the New Jersey legislator, Kentucky plantation owner, and Illinois shopkeeper alike. New York Governor Horatio Seymour and Ohio Congressman Clement Vallandigham were among their leaders. But the Federal government came after them with a vengeance, throwing thousands in prison without trials or even charges, shutting down their newspapers, and confiscating their property.

Only one of numberless examples was that of Dennis A. Mahony, editor of the *Dubuque (Iowa) Herald* newspaper. He was taken from his home in the middle of the night and freighted across the country to Washington's Old Capitol Prison. His offense? The Lincoln Administration considered him disloyal because he had challenged the Constitutionality of some of their actions in his newspaper.

I can touch a bell on my right hand, and order the arrest of a citizen of Ohio [Clement Vallandigham]. I can touch the bell again, and order the imprisonment of a citizen in New York; and no power on earth, except that of the President, can release them. Can the Queen of England do so much?

—Secretary of State William Seward

Many Copperheads wore on their lapels the head of liberty, taken from the early American penny. Employing the use of a double entendre, their political enemies thus "coined" their own name for these opponents of the War. The copperhead, opponents pointed out, was not only lethal, but unlike the rattlesnake, it struck without giving fair warning. While many Northerners held Copperhead convictions, many others despised them and truly believed them to be a threat to the United States and its prosecution of the War. Rumors abounded, some of them true, of looming Copperhead plots to undermine the hegemony of the Lincoln administration and the Radical Republican Congress. The public burned, shot, and bayoneted them in effigy.

> *If I tap that little bell, I can send you to a place where you will never hear the dogs bark.*
> —Secretary of War Edwin Stanton

Who was right? Were the Copperheads courageous Constitutional patriots willing to sacrifice their lives for what they believed, or greedy and cynical reactionary traitors of the worst stripe?

> *. . . measures, however unconstitutional, might become lawful by becoming indispensable to the preservation of the Constitution, through the preservation of the nation.*
> —President Abraham Lincoln

They were, at least as they saw themselves, protecting rather than threatening the old Union of the Founding Fathers. But at the same time, they posed a very real threat to some of the military and political objectives of Abraham Lincoln. The answer probably lies somewhere amidst a different question: was Lincoln's idea of a Republic faithful to Washington's?

"The Man of the People!" This cartoon celebrates Copperhead chieftain and LIncoln enemy Horatio Seymour's election as governor of New York. Below him are busts of other New York leaders and scenes reflective of his large Catholic constituency.

Fredericksburg

McClellan was learning from his battles with the Army of Northern Virginia. In October he found out Lee, at Culpeper Court House, had again detached Jackson to the Shenandoah Valley to cast his shadow over Washington. McClellan determined on an all-out attack to demolish Lee before Jackson could come to his aid. Then, virtually on the eve of the attack, November 7, Lincoln dismissed McClellan from command and installed the reluctant Ambrose Burnside in his place. The Radical wing of the Republican Party had won its way. They knew McClellan was not an aboli-

March at Dawn, John Paul Strain's rendering of Lt. Colonel Joshua Chamberlain, right, and Colonel Adelbert Ames leading the 20th Maine regiment through the frigid Virginia winter toward the Battle of Fredericksburg. Both Chamberlain and Ames would win the Congressional Medal of Honor during the War.

The Bivouac in the Snow (Margaret Junkin Preston)

Round the bright blaze gather,
Heed not sleet nor cold;
Ye are Spartan soldiers,
Stout and brave and bold.
Never Xerxian army
Yet subdued a foe
Who but asked a blanket
On a bed of snow.

Shivering, 'midst the darkness,
Christian men are found,
There devoutly kneeling
On the frozen ground—
Pleading for their country,
In its hour of woe—
For its soldiers marching
Shoeless through the snow.

tionist. They suspected him of inordinate sentiment for the South, an unwillingness to carry through to unconditional victory, and a threat to them in the Presidential election in 1864. The Army of the Potomac nearly mutinied upon learning of McClellan's removal. They never loved another commander. Lee was ecstatic; till the end of his life he considered McClellan the best opponent he ever faced.

Burnside followed Lincoln's directive to march on Richmond. He headed straight for the capital, but ran into the Army of Northern Virginia—with Stonewall Jackson—at Fredericksburg, on the Rappahannock River. In order to drive out several hundred Mississippi riflemen—and without warning the civilian populace—Burnside leveled much of the town itself, then crossed the river with pontoons. The Army of Northern Virginia was arrayed across the hills overlooking Fredericksburg from the south. Lee had spent two weeks preparing one of the most formidable defensive positions of the War. Still, he was outnumbered 118,000 soldiers to 75,000.

On December 13, the Federals first attacked the Confederate right, where lay Jackson and his corps. They were stopped. Then Burnside sent his men up Marye's Hill, atop which were Longstreet and his corps, impregnable. Fourteen times the strength and soul of the United States of America charged up that hill, and fourteen times they were cut to ribbons. In some places, the Union corpses were piled so high the men still charging could not climb over them. No Federal got within fifty yards of any Confederate position. At the end of the day, nearly 13,000 United States soldiers had fallen. Once again, however, Lee could not convert the victory into the scale of triumph that could end or change the War. This time because Davis, over Lee's objections, had

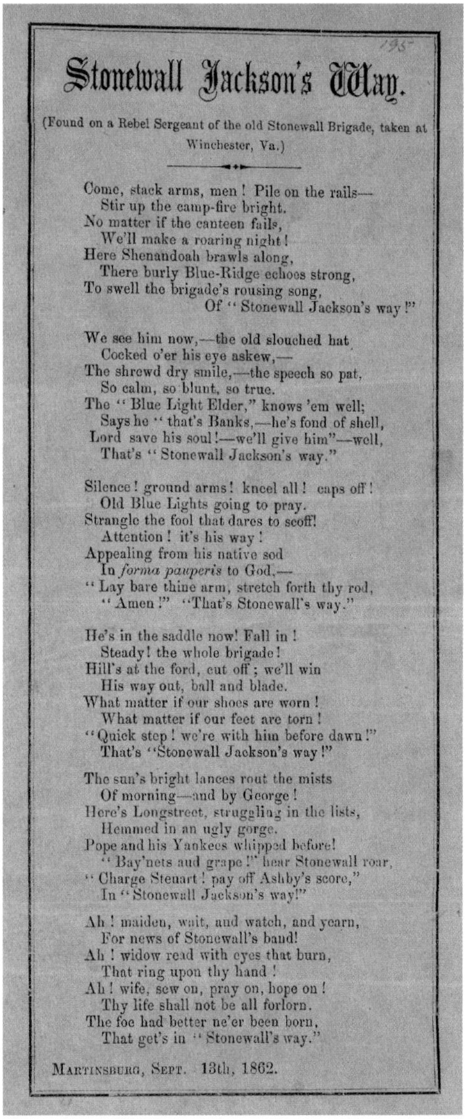

Stonewall Jackson's Way.

(Found on a Rebel Sergeant of the old Stonewall Brigade, taken at Winchester, Va.)

Come, stack arms, men! Pile on the rails—
Stir up the camp-fire bright.
No matter if the canteen fails,
We'll make a roaring night!
Here Shenandoah brawls along,
There burly Blue-Ridge echoes strong,
To swell the brigade's rousing song,
Of "Stonewall Jackson's way!"

We see him now,—the old slouched hat
Cocked o'er his eye askew,—
The shrewd dry smile,—the speech so pat,
So calm, so blunt, so true.
The "Blue Light Elder," knows 'em well;
Says he "that's Banks,—he's fond of shell,
Lord save his soul!—we'll give him"—well,
That's "Stonewall Jackson's way."

Silence! ground arms! kneel all! caps off!
Old Blue Lights going to pray.
Strangle the fool that dares to scoff!
Attention! it's his way!
Appealing from his native sod
In *forma pauperis* to God,—
"Lay bare thine arm, stretch forth thy rod,
"Amen!" "That's Stonewall's way."

He's in the saddle now! Fall in!
Steady! the whole brigade!
Hill's at the ford, cut off; we'll win
His way out, ball and blade.
What matter if our shoes are worn!
What matter if our feet are torn!
"Quick step! we're with him before dawn!"
That's "Stonewall Jackson's way!"

The sun's bright lances rout the mists
Of morning—and by George!
Here's Longstreet, struggling in the lists,
Hemmed in an ugly gorge.
Pope and his Yankees whipped before!
"Bay'nets and grape!" hear Stonewall roar,
"Charge Steuart! pay off Ashby's score,"
In "Stonewall Jackson's way!"

Ah! maiden, wait, and watch, and yearn,
For news of Stonewall's band!
Ah! widow read with eyes that burn,
That ring upon thy hand!
Ah! wife, sew on, pray on, hope on!
Thy life shall not be all forlorn.
The foe had better ne'er been born,
That get's in "Stonewall's way."

Martinsburg, Sept. 13th, 1862.

"Stonewall Jackson's Way" song sheet

restricted him to a defensive formation that precluded a pursuit of the retreating Federals. But as the Union blockade choked the South ever tighter, the North entered the most somber Christmas season it had ever known. "It is well that war is so terrible," Lee said chillingly as he watched the battle of Fredericksburg, "or else we should grow too fond of it."

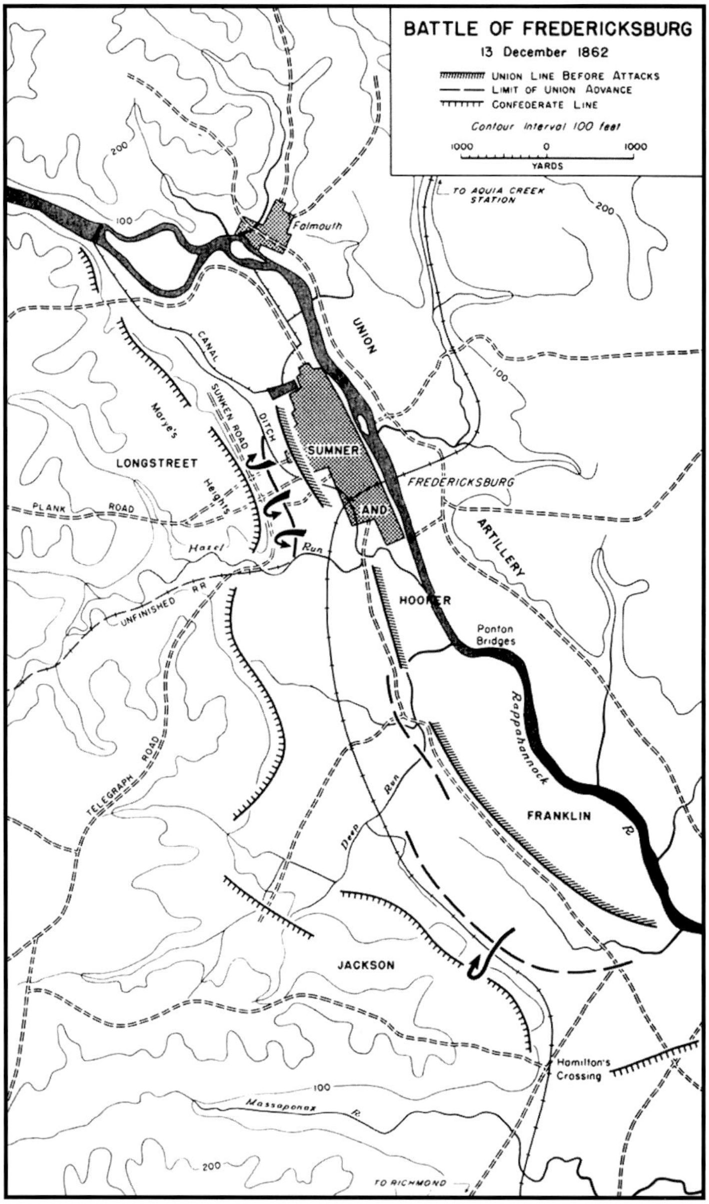

17 Religion
(1862)

(The soldiers, united under) one Lord, one faith, one baptism, . . . were all going down to the one baptism of blood; they were all to take the one cup of suffering; and many were to go into the church invisible . . . before many suns had risen and set.

—American Tract Society missionary regarding Federals entering a bloody campaign

The Great Religious Revival in the Confederate Armies

A frightened, sixteen-year-old Confederate army volunteer entering the camp of his unit in Stonewall Jackson's corps of Robert E. Lee's Army of Northern Virginia would have found a very different scene than he expected. Many of the card decks he saw were tossed aside by repentant soldiers marching the trail to war—and often replaced by prayer books, pocket testaments, or catechisms. Not only was the imbibing of alcoholic spirits frowned upon by many in the army, but when stores of enemy spirits were captured, they were poured out on the ground or burned—and that by order of the boy's own commanding officers.

Unlike most any other army of the day, women of ill repute were not welcome in the van that followed the army, and if it became known a soldier of the South, ranker or officer, was being unfaithful to a wife or causing a wife's unfaithfulness with his own actions, he risked cashiering. The boy would learn, to his surprise, that aside from himself and his fellow greenhorn

"Lee at the Soldiers' Prayer Meeting" (*A Narrative of the Great Revival in the Southern Armies*)

volunteers, gambling and profanity were uncommon in this fearsome army.

Soon, he might be one of those whose captain professed belief in Christ after a soul-searching camp sermon, then called his company together, told them they had followed him into many hard-fought battles, as well as into sin, and that he now wished them to follow him into the service into which he had just enlisted. He might see a log chapel to his left built by a Mississippi regiment for its own services, men streaming in and out of it seven days a week, twenty-four hours a day. He might learn that in this chapel, those Mississippians, half-starved already, had emerged from a time of extended prayer with the decision to give the entire rations allotted to them every tenth day to the hungry civilians of Richmond, a city most of them had never seen. Up ahead, on a hillside to his right, the boy would perhaps hear the chorus of over 2,000 manly voices echoing off the surrounding hills as they sang General Lee's favorite hymn, *How Firm a Foundation*, in an open-air amphitheater built by a Virginia brigade.

Through the months he would witness the sermons and teaching of the greatest preachers in the South: Presbyterians like R. L. Dabney, Beverly Tucker Lacy, James Henley Thornwell, Moses Drury Hoge, and Benjamin Palmer; Baptists such as John Broadus, Robert Ryland, W. F. Broaddus, and J. William Jones; Episcopals like Brigadier General William Nelson Pendleton. Their common message despite denominational distinctives: the proclamation of Christ and Him crucified.

And the once-frightened teenager, callow and acne-faced, would likely join the large proportion of that company professing their own conversion in the next months, and following their captain as he followed Christ, especially after the boy was handed a gospel tract one afternoon while slipping through the muddy camp by none other than Stonewall Jackson himself. If he later doubted the wisdom of his new path, he might be confirmed in it upon overhearing a chaplain tell Robert E. Lee of the many fervent prayers offered on his behalf and Lee responding in a choked voice, "Please thank them for that, sir . . . And I can only say that I am nothing but a poor sinner trusting in Christ alone for my salvation, and need all of the prayers they can offer for me."

> *General Lee used frequently to attend preaching at Jackson's headquarters; and it was a scene which a master hand might have delighted to paint—those two great warriors, surrounded by hundreds of their officers and men, bowed in humble worship before the God and Saviour in whom they trusted.*
>
> —Dr. J. William Jones
> Army of Northern Virginia
> Chaplain

Great Awakening

The sweeping religious revivals in the Confederate armies, particularly Lee's Army of Northern Virginia, comprise one of the great overlooked chapters of the War and one of the preeminent spiritual awakenings in

Confederate Chaplain Lieutenant Bartley Pace Bynum

American history. Perhaps only Oliver Cromwell and his Puritan army of "Roundheads" in the 17th-century English Civil War against King Charles I approached the degree of orthodox devoutness of Lee's army.

A sampling of the abundant contemporaneous accounts of the historic spiritual movement reveal its impact during and after the War. From 1861–65, the Southern armies accomplished a cavalcade of legendary deeds while outmatched in nearly every way. Whilst doing so, they exhibited, from the most senior commanders to the commonest foot soldiers, in a conspicuous and consistent manner, many of the primary attributes of Christian manhood. They exhibited these qualities as well in what they did not do as in what they did. Despite suffering at the hands of the Federals the most brutal prosecution of total war given high government sanction by a Christian nation in at least two centuries, the Confederate States military or governmental high command never approved like behavior. The instances where Southern atrocities occurred were isolated and unsanctioned. Tens of thousands of Confederate soldiers drew strength and consolation from their faith to endure the many horrors of war while Southern fortunes prospered; they did all the more after events turned against the South.

The benefits of the Great Revival in the Southern Armies shone brighter yet after the War as thousands of Southern soldiers emulated the example of Lee, John Gordon, and others, and applied their energies and talents productively to provide for their dependents and rebuild their land. Though some former Confederate soldiers resorted to unlawful and even violent behavior following the War, no doubt many more would have without the profound influence of the Christian faith on them.

How was so much of a spiritual nature accomplished, especially in prolonged surroundings which, though conducive to the occasional "foxhole" conversion, historically prove spawning grounds for every conceivable vice man can imagine? A key component was the piety of Confederate leaders. Lee, Jackson, Jeb Stuart, Gordon, D. H. Hill, Albert Sidney Johnston, Leonidas Polk, and Sterling Price all held exalted rank, yet practiced their faith openly and single-mindedly. A host of other top Southern officers were converted and baptized after the War began. These included Joe Johnston, John Bell Hood, Braxton

Bragg, Richard Ewell, Stephen D. Lee, and President Jefferson Davis himself.

Jackson's Example

These men, and many others, not only approved of efforts to spread the Gospel through the gray ranks, they actively promoted such. Despite having a brigade, then a division, then a corps to lead, Jackson helped spearhead the entire effort. Recognizing the worldliness of Confederate army camps early in the War's months, he fired a letter to his denomination's governing body, the Southern Presbyterian General Assembly:

Christmas Blessing by John Paul Strain. Stonewall Jackson's reputation as a devout Christian spread far and wide. While he and his men were reconnoitering enemy positions in western Virginia during the winter of 1862, a beautiful young woman presented her eighteen-month-old child to him and asked his blessing on the infant. She placed her hand on Jackson's horse Little Sorrel and bowed her head as Jackson prayed God's blessing on the infant.

Each branch of the Christian Church should send into the army some of its most prominent ministers who are distinguished for their piety, talents and zeal; and such ministers should labor to produce concert of action among chaplains and Christians in the army. These ministers should give special attention to preaching to regiments which are without chaplains, and induce them to take steps to get chaplains, to let the regiments name the denominations from which they desire chaplains selected, and then to see that suitable chaplains are secured.

A bad selection of a chaplain may prove a curse instead of a blessing. If the few prominent ministers thus connected with each army would cordially cooperate, I believe that glorious fruits would be the result. Denominational distinctions should be kept out of view, and not touched upon. And, as a general rule, I do not think that a chaplain who would preach denominational sermons should be in the army. His congregation is his regiment, and it is composed of various denominations. I would like to see no question asked in the army of what denomination a chaplain belongs to; but let the question be, Does he preach the Gospel?

Stonewall Jackson Preparing for Battle. The famous scene, the night before the Battle of Second Manassas, where Confederate General Richard Ewell burst into Stonewall Jackson's tent after a long angry ride through a storm and found him on his knees, deep in prayer. "If that is religion," the profane, non-believing Ewell told someone, "I must have it." He soon became a devoted Christian. (*The Life of General Thomas J. "Stonewall" Jackson for the Young*)

When a Catholic priest, with whom "Old Jack" would have had enormous theological differences, heard Jackson had ordered all soldier's tents left behind during a campaign march, the priest requested in person that one tent be allowed taken so that he could receive private confessions from the (few) Catholic soldiers in that corps. Jackson permitted that one tent on the campaign. Indeed, Jackson himself lavished his energies on procuring preachers and chaplains for the army. He, along with Lee and others, restricted Sabbath Day military duties to a minimum. Lee all but required the army's soldiers to attend worship services on that day, and encouraged their participation in worship and prayer services whenever possible through the week. They often did so in facilities Lee encouraged the construction of, in order to house such activities.

During just the four years of the

War, at least 100,000 Confederate soldiers professed saving belief in Jesus Christ for the forgiveness of their sins and eternal salvation. That figure represents approximately fifteen percent of the entire Confederate army and is exclusive of the much higher number who entered the War as professing Christians. History records rare examples of such exhaustive subscription to orthodox Christianity across the width and breath of a nation's entire army, and one engaged in a marathon bloodbath for survival, before or since.

AN EMINENT SOUTHERN CLERGYMAN, During an eloquent discourse, is wonderfully assisted in finding scriptural authority for Secession and Treason, and the divine ordination of Slavery.

Pro-Federal cartoon savagely denouncing the Southern clergy.

The only thing which gives me any apprehension about my country's cause is the sin of the army and people.

—Stonewall Jackson

Robert L. Dabney (1820–1898)

He was an author, pastor, preacher, farmer, mechanic, surveyor, architect, home builder, furniture maker, patent-holding inventor, and political economist. He taught at Union Theological Seminary for 30 years, and turned down both a professorship at Princeton Seminary, at that time the greatest Christian seminary in the world, and the pastorate of the nation's most famous Presbyterian church, Fifth Avenue in New York City. He called his wife Margaret Lavinia Morrison, daughter of another Presbyterian minister, "The first and last love affair of my life." She said she loved him more than life itself.

Soldier, scholar, and theologian, R. L. Dabney left a mark in war and peace that is still felt. Born and reared in Virginia, he was one of eight children of a farmer, local magistrate, militiaman, and Presbyterian elder. Some of the younger

Dabney's most poignant writings are to his brother Charles regarding the deaths of three of his (Robert's) six sons, while little boys, to diphtheria, a horrid disease wherein the throat swells and gradually chokes the victim to death. His three surviving sons were men of character and competence, one of them president of the University of Tennessee.

Like his Southern contemporaries Lee and Jackson, Dabney was a Unionist who loathed the looming specter of war and did all he could to forswear it. He published an editorial entitled "Christians, pray for your Country." He preached and published sermons and articles on peacemaking, even circulating them in the North. On April 20, 1861, he wrote one of the great penetrating American depictions of the awful face of the War he saw fast approaching and its ". . . mountainous aggregate of enormous crime, of a ruined Constitution, of cities sacked, of reeking battlefields, of scattered churches, of widowed wives and orphaned children, of souls plunged into hell . . ."

While he still lived R. L. Dabney was compared to Jonathan Edwards as a thinker and philosopher, Charles Spurgeon as a pulpit preacher, and John Calvin as a theologian.

In War

When the War came, Stonewall Jackson sought out Dabney to serve as his chief of staff. Dabney demurred, but Jackson persisted in his efforts. When Dabney finally accepted, voices across the ranks of Confederate military leadership murmured that one of the most elevated staff positions in the entire army would go to a theologian with no military training or experience. Yet by the time illness and exhaustion forced Dabney from the position, Jackson called him the greatest staff officer he had ever seen. Dabney may have saved Jackson's corps at the Battle of Port Republic. There, he took charge of a battery of Confederate cannon whose commander was down, and, while under heavy fire, commanded their bloody repulse of a Federal charge.

Dabney worked tirelessly all through the War to meet the spiritual needs of Confederate soldiers, preaching, counseling, and distributing gospel literature to them. Withal, Dabney's enormous abilities, and his application of them, rendered him one of the great moral minds in American history. While he still lived he was compared to Jonathan Edwards as a thinker and philosopher, Charles Spurgeon as a pulpit preacher, and John Calvin as a theologian. The all-knowing, all-powerful, all-good God Dabney served for over 60 years was at work in his life even in its darkest hours. As he lay debilitated at home after leaving Jackson's staff, unable even to preach, and having just lost his third son, the idea dawned on him to use his pen for God and country. That is when he began to write a train of classics, including *A Defense of Virginia, The Life and Campaigns of Lt. Gen. T. J. "Stonewall" Jackson, Sacred Rhetoric,* and *Systematic Theology.*

Viztelly's "Prayer in Stonewall Jackson's Camp." Drawn by F. Kramer, engraved by J. C. Buttre.

Later Years

Dabney's voice also resounded as a herald for the hegemony of Christian faith and doctrine over every area of education:

To educate the mind without purifying

the heart is but to place a sharp sword in the hands of a madman. There can be, therefore, no true education without moral culture, and no true moral culture without Christianity. The very power of the teacher in the schoolroom is either moral or it is a degrading brute force. But he can show the child no other moral basis for it but the Bible. Hence my argument is as perfect as clear, the teacher must be Christian. But the American commonwealth has promised to have no religious character. Then it cannot be teacher. If it undertakes to be, it must be consistent, and go on and unite church and state. Are you ready to follow your opinions to this consistent end?

Though renowned in his generation, Dabney did not fall prey to the snare of men-pleasing that besets so many public leaders. In an 1868 letter to his wife he told her that during a recent guest preaching stint, "I let myself loose pretty much, and made the fashionables, who were composing themselves for a genteel doze, wake up, whether they would or not."

After the War, most of his resources donated to the Confederacy and the rest plundered by Federal soldiers, the Virginian moved to Texas. There he helped establish the University of Texas, became the school's first Chairman of Philosophy, and founded a Presbyterian seminary. For nearly the last decade of his life Dabney was blind. Yet he continued to write and teach until, in 1894, the university fired him. It wanted a more "advanced" man.

Shortly before he died, now little heeded and viewed as anachronistic as the Confederacy and its principles he defended, R. L. Dabney lamented, "I no longer have an audience interested in hearing what I have to say." Perhaps it is one of God's providential ironies that, more than a century later, Dabney's influence now reaches more people, in more lands, than even it did whilst he lived.

Our Comfort in Dying

The following excerpt comes from a sermon by Robert L. Dabney.

So must you die, my friend, and I. Though wife and children, and officious comrades be crowding around your bed, and loved ones be stooping to receive your last sigh to their very hearts, and your dying head be pillowed upon the bosom which was the dearest resting place of your sorrows while living, the last approach of death will separate you from them all, and you will meet him alone. The icy shadow of his dart, as it comes near your heart, will obstruct all the avenues of sense by which their sympathy can reach you. Even then, practically, you will die alone; as truly alone as the last wanderer in some vast wilderness, who falls exhausted on the plain, and sees nothing above but the burning sky, or around save the boundless waste; as truly alone as the mariner who, when the ship is rushing before a gale through the midnight sea, drops from the mast-head, and buffets vainly with the innumerable billows amidst the pitchy darkness, while his despairing shriek is drowned by the tumult of the deep.

But then it is that Jesus Christ draws near as an omnipotent Savior. He alone of all the universe has fathomed the deepest abysses of death, has explored all its caverns of despair, and has returned from them a conqueror. He is not only sympathizing man, but omnipresent God, who can go with us into the penetralia of the court of death. When our last labor comes, then let us say, brethren, 'Lord Jesus, receive my spirit.' Where I pass through the valley of the shadow of death, be thou with me; let thy rod and thy staff comfort me.

A catechism of the Southern Protestant Episcopal Church, to be taught to the illiterate, including slaves.

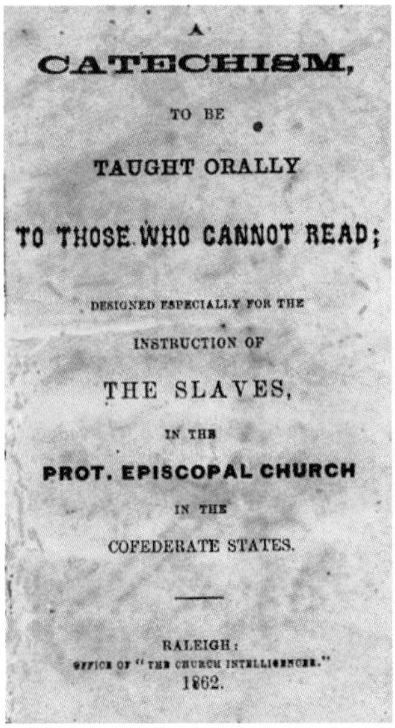

A

CATECHISM,

TO BE

TAUGHT ORALLY

TO THOSE WHO CANNOT READ;

DESIGNED ESPECIALLY FOR THE

INSTRUCTION OF

THE SLAVES,

IN THE

PROT. EPISCOPAL CHURCH

IN THE

COFEDERATE STATES.

RALEIGH:

OFFICE OF "THE CHURCH INTELLIGENCER."

1862.

Handing out gospel tracts in the trenches. (*The Life of General Thomas J. "Stonewall" Jackson for the Young*)

One of the miseries of war is that there is no Sabbath, and the current work and strife has no cessation. How can we be pardoned for all our offenses!

—Robert E. Lee, writing to his daughter Annie

Spreading the Gospel in the Federal Armies

Spiritual devotion increased in both armies as the War progressed. While suffering, deprivation, and the example of devout leaders like Lee, Jackson, and Polk stirred Confederate soldiers, however, contrasting reasons contributed to the burgeoning spiritual fervor of many Northern troops.

Gardiner H. Shattuck, Jr., in his book *A Shield and Hiding Place: The Religious Life of the Civil War Armies*, suggests that Christian commitment amongst the Federal armies lagged during the early years of the War when they sustained so many defeats. Key victories, such as Gettysburg, Vicksburg, and Chattanooga, Shattuck suggests, lifted morale and fostered enthusiasm for spiritual pursuits, which in turn increased the Federals' energy and commitment to their military duties. He writes:

> The revivals, then, were probably the most vivid manifestation of what one historian has termed "the late, war-spawned élan" of the Union troops, and those religious gatherings contributed markedly to stimulating the confidence and enthusiasm that Northern soldiers possessed in the latter stages of the war.

Federal generals like George McClellan and Oliver Howard gave the practice and observance of Christian spiritual disciplines high priority from early in the War. So, too, did William Rosecrans, a central figure through

Members of the 69th regiment New York State Militia gathered with a Roman Catholic chaplain for mass at Fort Corcoran, Washington, D.C.

Chaplains of the Federal Ninth Army Corps, October, 1864. (*Photographic History of the Civil War in Ten Volumes*)

much of the hardest fighting in Tennessee and the western theater. Rosecrans, a Roman Catholic, increased the number of regimental chaplains in the Army of Ohio when he assumed its command in late 1862. He also adhered faithfully to the Fourth Commandment, never fighting on Sundays, even when it appeared to hinder his military efforts. His fortunes and those of his army he placed in the hands of God, who, Rosecrans said, "never fails those who truly trust." McClellan was converted to Christianity in early 1862. He proscribed Sabbath work for his troops, ordering instead regular worship services on that day.

Log chapel built by engineers for Federal soldiers at Poplar Grove, Virginia, during the Petersburg campaign.

Religious Diversity

In the North, devotion and "conversion" did not necessarily represent what they did in the more spiritually homogeneous Southern armies. Unitarian influence was significant, as well as that of many mainline denominationalists who focused more on temporal salvation (earthly happiness and success) than spiritual. For instance, Thomas Wentworth Higginson, colonel of a regiment of freedmen, was a Unitarian and former minister from Massachusetts. He admired the devotion of his "Gospel army" of black soldiers. Another Unitarian minister lauded how the Federal soldier's "duty and patriotism" would transform it to something "clear and generous and pure"—and, according to his own creed, without Christ. Typical of the sentiments of clergy traveling with the Federal armies was one Rhode Island chaplain's comment that his army had "purified" the Shenandoah Valley when they incinerated it.

Just how spiritually "revived" were the military forces of the United States? Across the country, they left a systematic, ever-increasing trail of theft and destruction—against the Southern civilian populace. Famed author Bruce Catton, in his Pulitzer Prize-winning *A Stillness at Appomattox*, writes: "In the winter of 1864, the Army of the Potomac stood at a crossroads. The old army, fired with the spirit of men who had joined out of love of country and who had long since become disillusioned, was gone. The new army, made up of mercenaries, bounty-jumpers, and a hard core of seasoned and embittered veterans, had lost sight of its original goal of radiant victory and had become a ruthless machine of war." A Connecticut soldier called the several hundred late-war recruits his regiment received "the most thorough-paced villains that the stews of New York and Baltimore could furnish—bounty jumpers, thieves, and cutthroats." One veteran called new Massachusetts recruits "some of the most noted, hardened, and desperate villains in this country." Another called New York conscripts "unspeakable" and recalled many of them being shackled with ball and chain, so they would not escape prior to their combat assignments. A New Hampshire veteran said "there were many desperate and dangerous criminals" among Maryland recruits "who would not hesitate to commit any crime that passion, avarice or revenge might incite them to."

In the North, devotion and "conversion" did not necessarily represent what they did in the more spiritually homogeneous Southern armies.

Still another Federal soldier, a newly-enlisted teenager, described the 1,000 men who came in with him late in the War: "If there was a man in all that shameless crew who had enlisted from patriotic motives, I did not see him . . . Almost to a man they were bullies and cowards, and almost to a man they belonged to the criminal classes . . . as arrant a gang of cowards, thieves, murderers, and blacklegs as were ever gathered inside the walls of Newgate or Sing Sing." Yet, religious revivals among Federal soldiers occurred after they joined the army, not before. Though many deserted, some repeatedly in order to claim successive enlistment bonuses, and others would not fight, the power of the saving gospel of Christ fell on many others.

Federals attend worship services on the deck of the U.S. monitor *Passaic* in 1864.

Conversion and Victory

Leonard Moss, too, invoked the synergism between heightened religious enthusiasm and military success in his postwar writings about the United States Christian Commission. He recalled how the drubbing the Army of the Cumberland received at Chickamauga Creek in late 1863 stripped away the resistance many of them had to relying on a power greater than themselves. The arrival of the mighty U. S. Grant to take command reinvigorated them with a confidence imbued with increased spiritual humility. Mere weeks later they accomplished, on successive days, the two most stunning Federal victories of the War, as they overran entrenched Confederate positions on Lookout Mountain and Missionary Ridge. This startled no one more greatly than many of the Federals themselves. One referenced the triumphs as among "the greatest miracles in military history" and "a visible interposition of God." General John W. Geary, who helped lead the attack up Lookout Mountain, had thought it an impossible task. "I have been the instrument of Almighty God," he wrote his wife.

Numerous reports claim the Federal armies arrayed against Lee in Virginia in 1864–65 supported a "pentecostal season" of mass religious conversion and "constant religious interest."

—Gardiner H. Shattuck, Jr.
A Shield and Hiding Place

Numerous reports claim the Federal armies arrayed against Lee in Virginia in 1864–65 supported a "pentecostal season" of mass religious conversion and "constant religious interest." Religious revival broke out during the same period among Sherman's men as they marched through Georgia and the

Rev. Dr. George Junkin (1790–1868) was a renowned theologian and educator—even before his daughter Ellie married Thomas J. Jackson, the future "Stonewall." Junkin was president of Washington College (now Washington & Lee University) in Lexington, Virginia, from 1848-61. But he was a Pennsylvanian, and though no abolitionist, he believed the Union of states to be a divine compact ordained by the Lord Himself, designed to help carry out His purposes among the nations. Tearing it asunder in secession, he warned, would bring forth the wrath of God.

When Virginia seceded, he told Jackson "You will not survive this war" and returned North with widowed daughter Julia. But two of Junkin's own sons fought for the Confederacy; one suffered in a Northern prison camp. His daughter Maggie gained renown as the "Poetess of the Confederacy." Junkin spent much of the War visiting Southern soldiers in Federal prisons, preaching, teaching, and giving them food and other gifts bought from the sale of his own now-meager personal belongings.

Carolinas. Growing numbers of them gathered in nearby churches where they camped on their march, giving thanks to God for the successes of the day. The Christian association of one brigade grew from 50 to 300 members during this time, with hundreds of others attending its nightly meetings.

Black Federal chaplains drew a singular connection between God's hand and the fortunes of war, as witnessed by William H. Hunter, who addressed a crowd of ex-slaves in a Wilmington, North Carolina church after the Yankees conquered that town late in the War. "Thank God the armies of the Lord and of Gideon has [sic] triumphed," Hunter proclaimed, "and the Rebels have been driven back in confusion on and scattered like chaff before the wind." Black soldiers sang "Methodist hymns" when they marched into Charleston at the end of the War. They prayed during gospel-preaching camp meetings that "their cause might prosper and their just freedom be obtained."

Oliver O. Howard (1830-1909)

"The generals (like U. S. Grant and William T. Sherman) who led the North to victory mainly involved themselves with military matters and evinced little interest in cultivating any spiritual sensitivity during the War." So writes Gardiner H. Shattuck, Jr. in his penetrating work *A Shield and Hiding Place: The Religious Life of the Civil War Armies*. The preeminent exception to that maxim among Federal high command was handsome Maine native Oliver Otis Howard, so devout he was known across the North as "The Christian General" and "Old Prayer Book."

Like his contemporary and fellow Maine native Joshua Chamberlain, Howard graduated from Bowdoin College; unlike Chamberlain, Howard then attended the United States Military Academy, graduating in 1855. He served in the army for two years, then returned to West Point to teach mathematics. There he wrote an article entitled "Discipline in the Army," about which he later wrote: "I advocated with as much force as I could a paternal system. I endeavored to show that the general who cared for his men as a father cares for his children, providing for all their wants and doing everything he could for their comfort consistent with their strict performance of duty, would be the most successful; that his men would love him; would follow him readily and be willing even to sacrifice their lives while enabling him to accomplish a great patriotic purpose."

Reading the diary of the famed Christian soldier Hedley Vicars of Great Britain led to Howard's spiritual conversion in 1857. He studied briefly for the ministry, but the War cut short this effort. Howard worked ceaselessly to further the spiritual well-being of his soldiers even as he led them in war. A brigade commander, he insisted on all his regiments holding divine services on the Sabbath. If a regiment had no chaplain, Howard himself conducted that regiment's worship service. One soldier lauded the "eloquent addresses and earnest exhortations" Howard delivered during his sermons. "Though he ranked high among men," the soldier continued, Howard "humbled himself before God."

Howard worked ceaselessly to further the spiritual well-being of his soldiers even as he led them in war. A brigade commander, he insisted on all his regiments holding divine services on the Sabbath. If a regiment had no chaplain, Howard himself conducted that regiment's worship service.

Few men of any rank participated in more of the War's most significant battles than Oliver Howard. He fought at First Manassas, the Seven Days (two Confederate bullets cost him an arm at Fair Oaks), Sharpsburg, Fredericksburg, Chancellorsville, and Gettysburg in just the first two years. His record of battlefield success was not glittering, but it was honorable, and his spiritual impact on the Federal army was exemplary.

With Sherman

Howard's legacy from the final year of the War is militarily more successful but morally more ambiguous. He commanded the right wing of Sherman's army as it burned, pillaged, and in some cases (certainly not sanctioned by Howard) raped and murdered its way through Georgia and the Carolinas. Representative of Howard's central role in this epic rampage was an episode pertaining to Mrs. Louise Cornwell and her property near Hillsboro, Georgia. On November 19, 1864, after Kilpatrick's cavalry stole her livestock, grain, and beehives, torched her cotton gin, its screw, the blacksmith shop, and piles of priceless cotton bales, scarcely any food was left on the property to her and the other females living with her. Then "Old Prayer Book" and his staff arrived, ordering "tea," a light afternoon meal. Mrs. Cornwell and the other females served the Federals, but it took her final scraps of food. She afterwards recalled this extraordinary day, and watching Howard bow his head at her dining room table and pray over the last of her food, which he and his men then proceeded to eat. She remembered the singular sight she observed through a window as he prayed: "The sky was red from flames of burning houses."

The fame of Oliver Howard's name carries forward across the generations through Howard University, the predominantly black Washington, D.C. school he founded, with Congressional help, in 1867 to provide freedmen an opportunity for a college education.

Three months later, Howard held technical command of the occupation of Columbia, South Carolina when three-quarters of the city burned to the ground from fires set by his own drunken troops. No evidence exists, however, that he approved or even knew of the many acts of arson that contributed to the inferno. In fact, he marshaled other troops to fight the blazes. Then he turned over half the (confiscated) Federal cattle herd and half his army's food rations to the city's mayor for distribution to the hungry, homeless citizenry. Still, concerning the fate of the incinerated state capital, Howard said he was reminded of the old politician who, asked if he had attended the burial service of a bitter enemy, replied, "No, I didn't patronize the funeral, but I approve of it."

In Peace

Following the War, President Andrew Johnson named Howard president of the Freedman's Bureau, charged with helming the transition of four million black slaves to freedom. He strived to provide the former bondsmen with food, medicine, education, and other aid. The fame of his name carries forward across the generations through Howard University, the predominantly-black Washington, D.C., school he founded, with Congressional help, in 1867 to provide freedmen an opportunity for a college education. He served as its president from 1869–74.

Howard returned to the army and participated in the Plains Indians Wars. From 1880-82, he led West Point as its superintendent. Still laboring to improve the cause of education for blacks in the South, he founded another institution of higher learning, Lincoln Memorial University, in Harrogate, Tennessee, in 1895. He wrote several books, including *Chief Joseph, Zachary Taylor, Autobiography of Oliver Otis Howard,* and *Famous Indian Chiefs I Have Known*.

Oliver Howard, one arm lost during the Seven Days Campaign, visits the soldiers' cemetery at Gettysburg, where he commanded a Federal Corps.

The headquarters of the United States Christian Commission in the field, at Germantown, Maryland, September, 1863.

He Leadeth Me (Joseph H. Gilmore)

He leadeth me! O blessed tho't!
O words with heav'nly comfort fraught!
What e'er I do, where e'er I be,
Still 'tis God's hand that leadeth me!

Chorus:
He leadeth me,
He leadeth me,
By His own hand
He leadeth me.
His faithful follower
I would be,
For by His hand
He leadeth me.

18 Shiloh
(1862)

The *CSS Alabama* sinks the *USS Hatteras.*

At the outbreak of the war it was found very difficult to raise infantry in Texas, as no Texan walks a yard if he can help it. Many mounted regiments were therefore organized, and afterwards dismounted.

—Sir Arthur James Lyon Fremantle
English Soldier

Many in the more populous east, as well as European observers, tended to overlook the western theater of the War. Events unfolded more quickly there than in the east, and the current turned toward the Federals. When it did, it carried an import only much later acknowledged as decisive in the War's outcome. Two enormous physical realities, both related to water, hampered the Confederacy. Though the territory of the South was large and varied, it had over 3,500 miles of coastline, from which its very life depended upon the import and export of goods. It also had key inland waterways bisecting it—nearly all of them flowing from the North into the South. If the South forfeited control of the Mississippi River from its mouth in the Gulf north to Cairo, Illinois; of its access to the Ohio River which poured into the Mississippi at that point; and of the Cumberland and Tennessee rivers, which flowed northward through Tennessee and Kentucky into the Ohio, three nightmarish scenarios would ensue.

These people are talking about surrendering, and I am goin' out of this place before they do, or bust hell wide open.

—Nathan Bedford Forrest at Fort Donelson

First, the Federals could cut off trans-Mississippi Texas, Arkansas, Indian Territory (Oklahoma), most of Louisiana, and Missouri from the rest of the Confederacy. This would present staggering strategic, tactical, and operational problems for the South regarding supplies, troops, communication lines, etc. Second, they could float masses of troops into the South using the Confederacy's own watercourses. And third, they could starve out the new republic, dependent as it was upon foreign trade. Exacerbating this dilemma, the South had no navy and the North did, and a growing one at that.

The Federals exploded into action all across the west with the advent of 1862. Virginian George Thomas led the bluecoats to victory at the Battle of Mill Springs in January. Then Ulysses S. Grant, through a series of bold thrusts, began to carve his name into the enduring annals of world history. As massed Federal troops pushed Confederate forces down the Mississippi River from Columbus, Kentucky, Grant moved on the outmanned forward Confederates position on the Tennessee River, Fort Henry. He took it, then, without orders, laid siege to Fort Donelson, the forward Confederate position ten miles away on the Cumberland River. He won there, too.

A Way Out, by John Paul Strain. Nathan Bedford Forrest leads his horse soldiers out of Fort Donelson as its Confederate commanders prepare to surrender to U. S. Grant's Federal army.

At Fort Donelson, Grant became a national hero in the United States and gained the lasting sobriquet of "Unconditional Surrender" Grant thanks to the matching initials of that, and his name, and his response to the War's first Confederate request of surrender terms. Within two months, Federal General John B. Pope overran the northernmost Confederate position on the Mississippi, Island Number Ten, off southeastern Missouri. Losing the bulk of Kentucky and Tennessee, as well as most of the Mississippi River, lost the South military stores, manufactories, raw materials, and indispensable food supplies, as historian Ludwell Johnson observed in *North Against South: The American Iliad*. And it shoved the Confederates back into northern Mississippi and Alabama.

The Battle of Shiloh

Two days before Pope's Federal victory at Island Number Ten, Grant's juggernaut ran smack into an assault by Texan Albert Sidney Johnston, whom President Davis considered the greatest soldier in the Confederacy. Grant planned to merge his force with

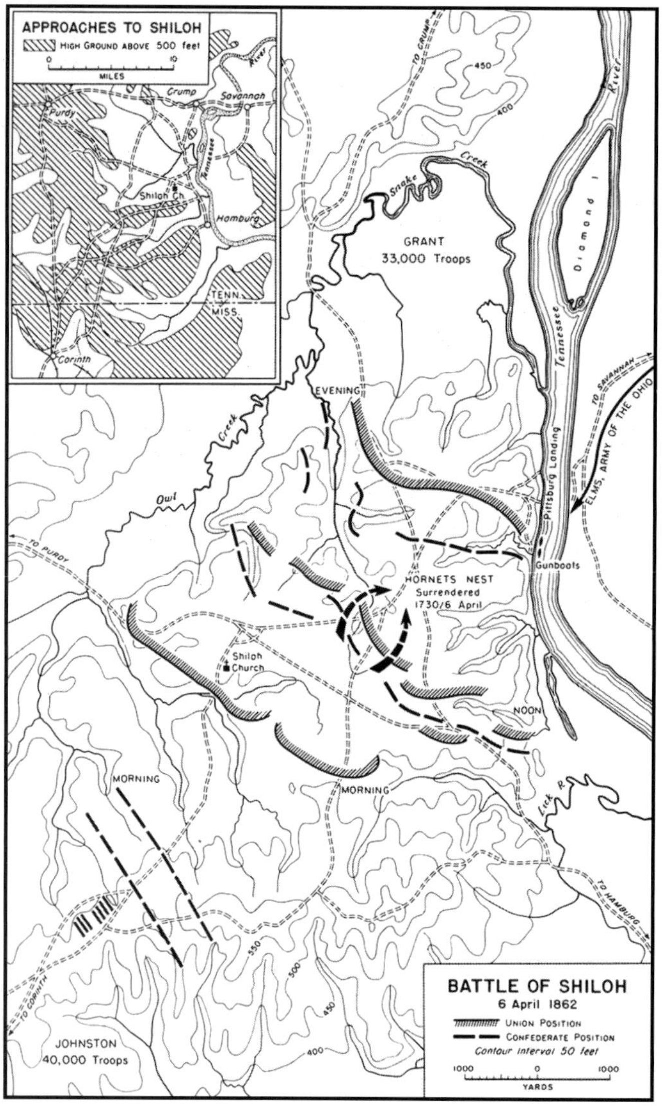

Map of the Shiloh battlefield. (Courtesy of The General Libraries, The University of Texas at Austin)

that of Federal General Don Carlos Buell and move with indefensible might south on Corinth, just inside the Mississippi state line. There lay a key rail junction, the South's only direct connection between the west and the east. But before Grant and Buell could unite, Johnston tore into the former on April 6 in a stunning surprise attack at Pittsburg Landing, near a Methodist church named Shiloh, at the southern edge of Tennessee.

The Confederates wreaked bloody havoc on Grant's force, which was saved by two factors. One was the coming of night. The other was the freak—and mortal—wounding of Johnston. Thinking the battle won against the disarrayed Federals, Johnston's successor—Sumter and Manassas victor, Pierre Beauregard—discontinued the successful attack and pulled his troops back, preparing to mop up the remaining Federals the next morning. By then, Buell had arrived, and the Confederates were outnumbered two to one and had lost the initiative. Beauregard no longer possessed the muscle to complete the job, and he retired from the field. A tactical draw, the Battle of Shiloh was a strategic victory for the Federals. It cost the Confederates their best western general, locked them out of western Tennessee for good, shook the army's confidence, and rendered both the central

Mississippi River and Corinth vulnerable to the Federals.

Less than three weeks later, on April 25, Alabama Unionist and naval admiral David Farragut captured New Orleans, the largest city and most important commercial port in the Confederacy. Its defensive forts reduced by Farragut and his naval squadrons, the city itself fell without further resistance. The loss of New Orleans constituted another bitter blow to the South. And the Mississippi River, the most important in the nation, was now virtually closed to the Confederacy. The only significant outpost remaining to it was Vicksburg, Mississippi. By November, Grant would lay siege to that.

Albert Sidney Johnston (1803-1862)

Just as many historians have pondered how different a course the War might have taken had not Stonewall Jackson fallen in the east—two months before the battles at Gettysburg—so have many considered what the South's destiny may have been had not Albert Sidney Johnston fallen at Shiloh. Confederate President Jefferson Davis certainly did. After the War, he wrote, "The fortunes of a country hung by a single thread of the life that was yielded on the field of Shiloh."

Born in Kentucky, the 1826 West Point graduate served with valor in the Black Hawk Indian War. Tall and handsome, articulate and a devout Christian, he was also rugged and adventurous. But in 1834, he resigned his commission to care for his dying wife. When she died two years later, he moved to Texas and got himself knee-deep into the Texas Revolution against Mexico. The legendary Sam Houston considered Johnston one of the best men he had and named him Brigadier General, then Secretary of War for Texas. A few years later, Johnston spearheaded another Texan war—against the new state's many tribes of indigenous American Indians. In the mid-late 1850s he commanded the 2nd U.S. Cavalry, which famed Texas historian T. R. Fehrenbach has called "the best-mounted regiment that ever rode the American West." Johnston and the 2nd kept the explosive Comanches at bay until they were transferred to Utah.

As the War approached, Johnston returned to the U.S. Army as a brigadier general in California. Like so many other Southerners, however, when his state—which he considered Texas—seceded, he followed. Knowing his abilities, the Federals attempted, unsuccessfully, to keep him from reporting to Richmond for assignment. The high regard the Confederates held for Johnston evidenced itself as well in his immediate appointment as one of only five full generals in the new nation and commander of the Department of the Mississippi. The latter stretched over 1000 miles, from the Appalachian Mountains in the east to the Indian Nations in the West.

Audacious Commander

Johnston soon confirmed the wisdom of those moves. He launched an audacious thrust north to carve a foothold for the South in Kentucky on the Mississippi River and thus provide a shield for

The War Council, by John Paul Strain. Confederate commander Albert Sidney Johnston plots his historic ambush of U. S. Grant and the Federals at Shiloh.

Tennessee from Federal invasion. He held the Federals in check the rest of the year, all the while bereft of every conceivable sort of supplies and commanding a scant 4,000 men. Finally, in January, 1862, U. S. Grant, with 40,000 men, forced him south. But Johnston turned to the offensive after Pierre Beauregard joined him with his own command. He struck Grant like a thunderbolt on the west bank of the Tennessee River at the Battle of Shiloh. There, the Confederates surged forward. But one key position seemed impregnable; in fact, the bloodied Confederate foot soldiers seemed unwilling to charge it again. Johnston rode to the front and center of the entire Southern line and, saber flashing, himself led the charge, which routed the Federal position.

> *When he fell, I realized that our strongest pillar had been broken.*
> —Jefferson Davis, writing long after the War about the fall of Albert Sidney Johnston at Shiloh

A few minutes later, however, even as the battle seemed nearly won, Johnston took a stray bullet in his leg. He shook off the injury and remained in the saddle commanding, not even mentioning the wound to anyone else. But the shot had pierced a femoral artery, and though nearly anyone around him could have staunched the bleeding had they known of it, Johnston insisted that his doctor and staff go attend to wounded enemy soldiers. By the time he paled and swooned in the saddle and men arrived to aid him, he was gone. That the Confederates did not win the Battle of Shiloh that day and instead lost it the next is directly attributable to the events surrounding Albert Sidney Johnston's death. And so, many would say, was Confederate defeat in the west, and hence, the War.

Ulysses S. Grant/Part I (1822-1885)

Like others among the great titans of the War, hardly anyone could have predicted this small, shy man with a father who never really believed in him would be proclaimed by many as the most successful military commander of the War, and possibly in all American history. Even upon his graduation from West Point, Grant stood only 5 feet 1 inch tall and weighed just 120 pounds. His renowned penchant for nondescript, even shabby, dress, stemmed from his mocking by a couple of local toughs when he returned home after graduation in his spiffiest dress uniform and accouterments. U. S. Grant grew into something he was not when he started out, and yet his greatness was animated by attributes he possessed from the beginning. His name provides a metaphor of this paradox. He was born Hiram Ulysses, but West Point administrators erroneously enrolled him as Ulysses Simpson. Henceforward the catchy sobriquets "U. S." and "Uncle Sam" took hold, though most of his friends called him simply "Sam."

The War delivered Grant from a failed career. His mysterious battle with alcoholism, which had likely led to his resignation from the Army in 1854, was another matter. There are as many opinions about the extent of Grant's drinking as there are brands of whiskey. But one of the men closest to him, aide and Colonel John Rawlins, considered Grant's wartime alcoholic intake serious enough to warrant Rawlins's close and constant supervision. Written accounts by Rawlins himself as well as other Federal officers attest to this. Clarence MacCartney quotes just

General U. S. Grant's charge at the Battle of Shiloh. (Courtesy of American Vision)

John A. Rawlins, faithful and able aide to U. S. Grant.

one example in his *Grant and His Generals*, recounting a letter from Rawlins to his fiancee during the late-war semi-siege of Petersburg, where he wrote:

I find the General in my absence digressed from his true path. The God of heaven only knows how long I am to serve my country as guardian of the habits of him whom it has honored. . . . I learn from one of his staff he deviated from the only path he should ever travel by taking a glass of liquor. It is the first time I have failed to accompany him to Petersburg and it was with misgivings I did so. . . . I shall hereafter, under no circumstances, fail to accompany him.

Fighter and Winner

With his victories early in the War at Fort Donelson and Fort Henry, which cleared the Confederates from the Ohio River and helped secure Kentucky for the Federal Union, the North had itself its first big winner. Grant suffered his share of frustrations against the Confederates in the West, but even when he failed, Lincoln saw in him a man who would fight and keep fighting. This led to his receiving command of the Army of the Tennessee, with which he eventually forced the surrender of the key Confederate port of Vicksburg on the Mississippi River.

I never was an abolitionist, not even what could be called antislavery.
—U. S. Grant

Vicksburg proved a pivotal point in the War and Grant's career alike. It won him command of all western Federal forces. A few months later, he led their mighty rally that raised the siege of Chattanooga, won that battle, retired Braxton Bragg to a desk, and left the South reeling. Chattanooga set the stage for Sherman's blazing march through the southeast and Grant's promotion to General in Chief of all Federal armies, then his heading east to supervise the fight against Lee and the Army of Northern Virginia.

Never had Grant faced such a commander nor such an army; after one month of the spring 1864 Wilderness Campaign, the Confederates had felled as many Federals as Lee had in his entire army. The Northern public screamed its outrage and "Grant the Butcher" became a common epithet North and South. He stirred further controversy by issuing his famous General Order #11, which expelled Jews "as a class" from his conquered Southern territories, an act reminiscent of medieval European pogroms. But Lincoln stuck with him and in the end, Grant's ability to combine patience with tenacity, and battlefield composure with strategic brilliance, resulted in the victorious semi-siege of Petersburg just as it had the victorious siege of Vicksburg.

The glittering roll calls of his victories ranks second to none: Fort Henry, Fort Donelson, Shiloh, Vicksburg, Chattanooga, and Petersburg, among others. He became the first full General in the U.S. Army since Washington. He was hailed as the equal or superior of Napoleon and Caesar. The North came to revere him not only for his success; in an army filled with inveterate cursers, his worst epithets were "doggone it" and "by lightning," and even these he used infrequently. One man described him as "the concentration of all that is American. He talks bad grammar, but talks it naturally, as much as to say, 'I was so brought up, and if I try fine phrases I shall only appear silly.'"

Shiloh, a Requiem (Herman Melville)

April, 1862

Skimming lightly, wheeling still,
The swallows fly low
Over the fields in clouded days,
The forest-field of Shiloh—
Over the field where April rain
Solaced the parched one stretched in pain
Through the pause of night
That followed the Sunday fight
Around the church of Shiloh—
The church so lone, the log-built one,
That echoed to many a parting groan
And natural prayer
Of dying foemen mingled there—
Foemen at morn, but friends at eve—
Fame or country least their care:
(What like a bullet can undeceive!)
But now they lie low,
While over them the swallows skim,
And all is hushed at Shiloh.

Private Sampson Altman, Jr., Company C, 29th Regiment, Georgia Volunteers. He fought at Shiloh and died a year later of disease.

David Farragut (1801-1870)

One of several important Federal military leaders who hailed from the South, he also established himself as the most successful naval commander of the War. Born in Tennessee, his true homeland was the sea. The preeminent American naval commander of the early 19th century, Commodore David Porter, took Farragut in as a child. He joined the crew of his first ship at age nine and sailed virtually the rest of his life, other than a few years during which he received a formal education. Farragut (pronounced far-ra-gu) gained combat experience as a child in the War of 1812 against Great Britain. He later sailed throughout the Atlantic, Mediterranean, and Caribbean and fought in the Mexican War.

Like many other Federal commanders, he enjoyed a great advantage in numbers and resources over his Southern foes. Unlike many of them, however, his own abilities shone brilliantly through as well. In April 1862, Farragut, in charge of Federal naval forces in the western Gulf, led a fleet of U.S. warships against New Orleans. Its status as the South's largest city and port, plus its location at the mouth of the Mississippi River over which the United States desperately wished control, placed New Orleans at the

top of the list of Federal objectives in the South. For six days, the Federals shelled Forts Jackson and St. Philip, which guarded access to the city from the sea. But the Southerners held firm.

Then, in a dazzling display of bravado and courage, Farragut simply sailed his fleet past these forts. That put the Federals, with forty ships and 302 guns, in position to attack the city's inner line of seaward defense—a "fleet" of four rams and fire rafts possessing a total of twelve guns. Nonetheless, the defenders went down swinging. One of their fire rafts set Farragut's flagship, the *Hartford*, ablaze and ran it temporarily aground. The fleet suffered widespread damage and nearly 170 Federal sailors perished. For an hour and a half the battle raged. At last, the Federals finished off the tiny Confederate force, opening the way for the Yankee army under Benjamin Butler to enter the city unopposed the next day.

Then, in a dazzling display of bravado and courage, Farragut simply sailed his fleet past New Orleans' sea forts.

Many Glories

Later in the year, Farragut captured the Gulf port of Galveston, Texas, only to have the Confederates take it back three months later. Farragut did yeoman work up and down the Mississippi throughout the Federal campaign for control of that mighty waterway and sundering of the Confederacy. He spearheaded the capture of Louisiana capital Baton Rouge, and Natchez and Port Hudson in Mississippi. However, despite much effort, he failed to capture Vicksburg, the most important Mississippi River stronghold.

Confederate Admiral Franklin Buchanan, who also commanded the ironclad *Virginia* in its memorable first day of battle.

After the victory at New Orleans, Farragut tried for two years to move against Mobile, Alabama. By August, 1864, it was one of only two significant Southern ports still open. Thus was its importance to the Confederate cause multiplied because of the desperate need for supplies from Europe. Once again, as at New Orleans, a massively outnumbered and outgunned Southern defensive force hurtled into Farragut's armada. This time, the Confederate fleet consisted of the ironclad ram Tennessee and three side wheel wooden gunboats, possessing a total of twenty-two guns and 470 sailors. The Federals had eighteen ships, including four ironclad monitors, 159 guns, thirty-three howitzers, and 3,000 men.

It would prove Farragut's greatest day as a commander. Sixty-three years old, he had himself lashed to the rigging high above his ship for a good vantage point as he sailed into battle. The Confederates stunned the Federal fleet by blowing their lead ironclad, the *Tecumseh*, out of the water with an underwater mine; it sank with its crew in thirty seconds. When the Federal line wavered, Farragut sailed his flagship forward, shouting the famous epithet, "D— the torpedoes! Full steam ahead, Dayton!" As at New Orleans, he led a naval charge past the outer forts. And once again, the Confederate fleet went down fighting. Their ironclad, the *Tennessee*, with sixty-four-year-old Admiral Franklin Buchanan and commander and Captain James D. Johnston aboard, took on virtually the entire Federal fleet singlehandedly before Buchanan was nearly killed and the *Tennessee* nearly destroyed.

The Battle of Mobile Bay

Mobile itself did not fall to the Federals until three days after Robert E. Lee's surrender in April, 1865. Farragut's naval victory there, however, terminated its use as a port of entry for Southern goods. Grateful Northern citizens awarded Farragut the then-enormous sum of $50,000 for his exploits, and the U.S. government created the rank of Vice Admiral for him. After the War, he commanded the United States' European squadron and was promoted to full Admiral, the first man to hold that post in the American Navy.

Raphael Semmes and the *Alabama* (1809-1877)

How unlikely that this orphaned Marylander, fighting with a tiny, scratch navy against one of the world's strongest, would emerge as the most famous seaman on earth, and the *CSS Alabama* he commanded, the most famous ship. One of the keys to the United States' winning the War was its naval blockade of the South, which grew more wrenching the longer the fighting went on. As burgeoning Federal industrial might churned out more and better ships, the South cobbled together what little naval forces it could. By War's end, the Federals boasted more than 600 ships and 50,000 sailors, the Confederates less than one tenth of both those numbers.

The South's greatest naval asset was the tenacity and ingenuity possessed by several of its leaders. Naval Secretary Stephen Mallory stretched his scant resources far, and Matthew Fontaine Maury, already known as the "Pathfinder of the Seas," counted mines, then called torpedoes, among his innovations. Bold Confederate commerce raiders, outnumbered and outequipped, using stolen Federal ships, foreign-built ships, and old castoff ships of every stripe, sank over 1,000 Federal vessels. The greatest of these audacious Southern captains was Mexican War veteran Raphael Semmes, 52 years old when the War began. It was Semmes who convinced Mallory to commit significant Confederate resources to attacking Federal shipping. And it was Semmes who wheeled the converted packet ship Sumter out of the Mississippi River in June 1861, took it through a smothering Federal flotilla, and onto the high seas as the South's first cruiser ship.

The CSS *Alabama*

Eighteen Federal ships and one year later, Semmes sailed the English-built CSS *Alabama* out of the Azores Islands west of Africa. It commenced its storied career by devastating the Federal whaling fleet in the Azores, destroying 10 ships in two weeks. Next it captured 11 ships off the east coast of Canada and New England. From there, the *Alabama* hunted the high seas—all seven of them. It tore into Federal shipping anywhere it found it on the globe—off the coast of South America, around the horn of Africa, across the Indian Ocean, at Singapore.

One of the *Alabama*'s greatest exploits was its head-to-head victory over the *Hatteras*, a larger Federal warship, which it sent blazing to the bottom of the sea as it helped blockade the Southern port of Galveston. Finally, in August of 1864, the *Alabama* pulled into Cherbourg, France, for a host of repairs. That is where the powerhouse USS *Kearsarge* caught up with it and challenged it to battle. The *Kearsarge*'s commander, Captain John A. Winslow, was a former messmate of Semmes's during the Mexican War, and like him had more than 40 years experience at sea. He had spent the past year in frustrated pursuit of the *Alabama* all over the waters of Europe. Semmes not only accepted Winslow's offer, he begged the Federal not to leave until he could put the *Alabama* back in order to fight. An international crowd of thousands cheered the famed Confederate warship as it sailed out to do battle four days later.

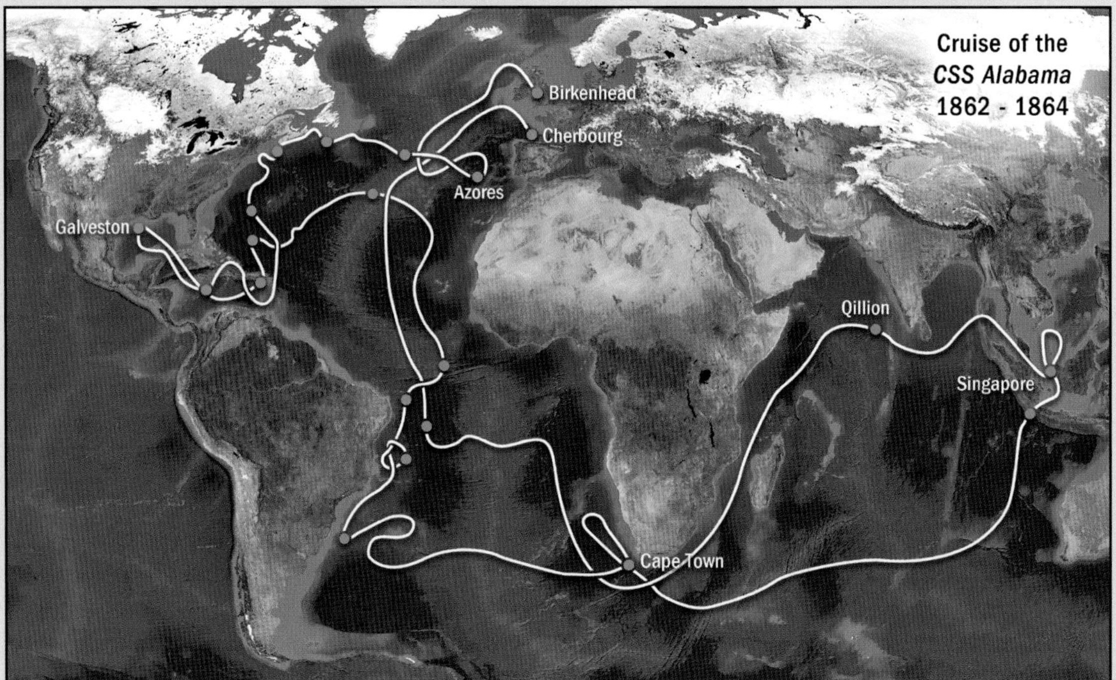

Though apparently evenly-matched, upon closer examination the advantage between the two ships tilted strongly toward the *Kearsarge*. It had the biggest guns—two 11-pound Dahlgrens—significantly more overall firepower, and was freshly refitted. The *Alabama*, meanwhile, had been out to sea for two years, in every conceivable clime, and much of its ammunition was now defective; Semmes compared the ship itself to "the weary foxhound, limping back after a long chase, footsore and longing for quiet and repose." In addition, its seaworthiness, speed, and maneuverability all were diminished. But Semmes stood before his 120-man crew (many of them English) as they prepared for battle and delivered his first and only speech to them:

It was the same thing as if two men were to go out and fight a duel, and one of them, unknown to the other, were to put on a suit of mail under his outer garment.

—Raphael Semmes

> *The name of your ship has become a household word wherever civilization extends. Shall that name be tarnished by defeat? The thing is impossible! Remember that you are in the English Channel, the theater of so much of the naval glory of our race, and that the eyes of all Europe are at this moment upon you. The flag that floats over you is that of a young Republic who bids defiance to her enemies, whenever and wherever found; show the world that you know how to uphold it. Go to your quarters!*

Showdown at Sea

The *Alabama* steamed straight for her foe and launched the first several shots, as well as the first that hit home. It exploded on the *Kearsarge*'s quarterdeck and took out three Federals. Then the *Alabama* fired a shell that tore into the *Kearsarge* stern post and stuck there. Semmes had prayed for just this occurrence, a perfect bull's eye, the night before at church. He eyed it through his telescope, exclaiming "Splendid! Splendid!" and knowing that any second the shell would explode and finish the Federal ship and the dramatic maritime showdown. But Providence overruled him—the shell was a dud and did not explode. Now events veered toward the Federal cause. Round and round the two ships circled each other, like Old West pistolmen in a high noon showdown, except that here, the combatants blazed away with everything they could muster.

Gradually one more Federal advantage—the greatest—evidenced itself. Though the *Alabama*'s

The epic shootout between the CSS *Alabama* and the USS *Kearsarge*.

shells peppered the *Kearsarge*, Semmes noticed that most just bounced off, as did shot when he switched to that. The *Kearsarge*'s jumbo 11-pounders, meanwhile, wreaked havoc with the *Alabama*. Later, Semmes would learn that Winslow had armored his ship with sheet chain. It was, in effect, an iron clad—and Semmes did not even know. "It was the same thing as if two men were to go out and fight a duel, and one of them, unknown to the other, were to put on a suit of mail under his outer garment," he lamented. After nearly 100 minutes of blistering battle, the *Kearsarge* had delivered dozens of direct hits to its wood-constructed foe. Dead men all around him and himself wounded, Semmes managed to leap from the *Alabama* just before she went down. Even then, the Federals could not capture the wily Confederate commander. He escaped on an English yacht.

He returned to lead the maritime defense of Richmond. Then President Davis gave him a brigadier generalship and a high army command in the War's final days. Raphael Semmes's naval record was unparalleled. The Sumter and Alabama between them had sailed more than 75,000 miles, destroyed or captured 66 Federal ships, and cost the United States nearly $7 million. Semmes had nearly destroyed the Federal Merchant Marine force, and he was the only Confederate officer to earn flag rank in both the Army and the Navy.

The Rape of Athens, Alabama

On May 2, 1862, former Russian officer John Turchin (his Americanized name) marched his Federal force into the small north Alabama town of Athens. Confederate soldiers had just retreated through the village, to the cheers of its citizens. Now, however, the people coldly turned their backs on the invaders. Colonel Turchin considered this a slight to his honor and grew furious. According to a *New York Herald* newspaper correspondent, the former Cossack commander told his men he would shut his eyes to whatever they wished to do for the next several hours. The Federals, many of them drunk, set upon the civilian populace of 1,200, looting stores and private homes. They herded resisters away at bayonet point. Women, black and white, suffered sexual assault. One pregnant white woman, her husband suspected of being a Confederate guerilla fighter, miscarried and died after being singled out and gang-raped. Turchin established his headquarters in the home of one of Athens' most prominent citizens, a man named McDonald. The Federal commander refused medical assistance to McDonald's sick daughter; she died from her illness shortly after the Yankees departed.

These depredations disgusted some of Turchin's subordinate officers. They notified his superiors, who convened a court martial against him. The Federals' court-martial records indicate a portion of Turchin's force "quarter[ed] in the Negro huts for weeks, debauching the females." Brigadier General (and future President) James A. Garfield ruled Turchin should be drummed out of the Army for his conduct. President Lincoln disagreed. He not only overturned the verdict of the court martial, but pressed Congress for a quick promotion for Turchin, from Colonel to Brigadier General. Cheering crowds of supporters welcomed the newly-promoted Russian-American home to Chicago as a band played *Lo, the Conquering Hero Comes*.

Benjamin Butler (1818-1893)

Few men factored in more of the important issues and events of his generation, in war and peace. Northerners referred to him as a political general. Southerners called him "Spoons," "Beast," or worse. He was brilliant, charismatic, controversial, and, often behind the scenes, in the thick of many key conflicts of the War and Reconstruction. Butler's political career evidenced one of the most dramatic arcs of his time. A successful Boston attorney, before the War he was an influential Democrat and supported the eventual president for his country's top office. The man he supported, however, was the eventual president of the Confederacy, Jefferson Davis. By War's end, and through the most contentious years of Reconstruction, Butler stood in the vanguard of Radical Republican leadership.

Controversy began to wreath him soon after Fort Sumter. First he occupied Annapolis, capital of Maryland, even as that state's legislature debated whether to secede. Then he put down, in bloody fashion, a riot of Baltimore citizens furious that Massachusetts troops were marching, uninvited, through their state and city. On June 10, 1861, Butler led Federal forces at the War's first official battle, Big Bethel Church in Virginia. Confederates commanded by Stonewall Jackson's brother-in-law, Daniel Harvey Hill, defeated them. However, Butler rallied to lead Federal land forces to victory in the capture of Hatteras Island, North Carolina, two months later.

Hereafter when any female shall, by word, gesture or movement, insult or show contempt for any officer or soldier of the United States, she shall be regarded and held liable to be treated as a woman of the town [prostitute] plying her avocation.

—Benjamin Butler

A year later, after Farragut's naval victory, Butler commanded the Federal occupation forces in New Orleans. The disrespect and venom displayed to them by the citizenry enraged him. When Butler arrived in the city, his troops caught a man who had helped tear down a United States flag raised prematurely over the Mint. To set an example, he convened a drumhead court that convicted the man, then hanged him in full public view from a window of the Mint. This murder had more effect on the men of the city than the women. The latter demonstrated their loathing of the Federal invaders in a myriad of ways. Finally, when one poured a slop jar onto Farragut's head from a window above him, Butler distributed a general order concerning the women of New Orleans that read, in part: "Hereafter when any female shall, by word, gesture or movement, insult or show contempt for any officer or soldier of the United States, she shall be regarded and held liable to be treated as a woman of the town plying her avocation."

Controversy

The reaction proved electrifying—and international. The widower Beauregard, whose gallantry and charm set female hearts aflutter across the South, issued his own order:

Men of the South! shall our mothers, our wives, our daughters and our sisters be thus outraged by the ruffianly soldiers of the North, to whom is given the right to treat, at their pleasure, the ladies of the South as common harlots? Arouse, friends, and drive back from our soil those infamous invaders of our homes and disturbers of our family ties!

After the War, Butler served in Congress and as governor of Massachusetts. And the fame that had eluded him for military glory found him as he championed a hard peace just as he had championed a hard war.

"Any Englishman must blush to think that such an act has been committed by one belonging to the Anglo-Saxon race," said British Prime Minister Lord Palmerston. Should Butler be captured, Davis ordered that "the officer in command of the capturing force do cause him to be immediately executed by hanging." So far did the outrages multiply under Butler's military governorship—including his evident complicity in the systematic theft of citizens' valuables (hence the pejorative "Spoons")—that Lincoln removed him from the position. When Grant prepared to move against Lee and Virginia in 1864, Butler received command of the Army of the James. He was foiled, however, by Beauregard in his efforts to sever Richmond and Petersburg and invade the capital, then bottled up by the Creole's smaller force. Grant sent him away to New York City to subdue rioting. His failed attack on a key Confederate fort at Wilmington, North Carolina at year's end prompted Lincoln to remove him again from command. This time, he was finished as a military commander.

After the War, Butler served in Congress and as governor of Massachusetts. And the fame that had eluded him for military glory found him as he championed a hard peace just as he had championed a hard war. He announced that "if any man stands in the way of the great march of the country . . . he must be taken out of the way." He not only fought for the impeachment of President Andrew Johnson, he conspired to produce false evidence against him. Butler's elevated station as a leader in the Radical Republican House helped enable his participation in a host of sordid postwar freebooting scandals, including the corrupt Carpetbag regime of Bullock in Georgia, the Sanborn contracts, and Credit Mobilier. He fought for the execution of Jefferson Davis, Robert E. Lee, and other erstwhile Confederate leaders; and he fought for the most extreme of Reconstruction policies. In later years, Butler took one final change of course. He switched parties again in 1884 to run on the Greenback ticket—for President.

California troops served the Federal cause on many western fields. Originally formed to guard the U.S. overland mail route, they fought Confederates in Arizona and New Mexico, and Indians in Colorado. They were unable to execute a planned invasion of Texas.

19 The West
(1862)

Raid on the L & N, John Paul Strain's sweeping portrait of one of John Hunt Morgan's famous cavalry rampages through Federal territory. During this raid in early 1862, Morgan's Raiders burned bridges, snatched at least one locomotive, captured countless Yankee railroad cars—and unnerved Northern forces across the Midwest and Northwest. "They are having a stampede in Kentucky," Abraham Lincoln later said.

For all practical purposes, the rebels control the countryside. No loyal man can till a farm or raise a crop . . . or safely travel the highways. . . . The rebels hold the country, while the loyal people are besieged in the towns.

—*Kansas City Journal,* regarding Missouri

The presence of [U.S. Senator James] Lane, and the atrocities he and his troops have committed, have contributed more to make secessionists out of loyal citizens than almost all other causes combined.

—*St. Louis Republican,* regarding Missouri

By early 1862, the Federals had forced ex-Missouri Governor Sterling Price's outnumbered Confederates down into Arkansas. At the beginning of March, young Wild Bill Hickok and other Federal scouts brought word the secessionists were coming back, in strength. Perhaps never did a more diverse contingent take the field for the South. There were the 8,000 Texas and Arkansas frontiersmen of dead-shot ex-Texas Ranger Ben McCulloch, who fought with Sam Houston against Santa Anna a quarter-century before at the Battle of San Jacinto. There were Price's 7,000 battle-hardened Missouri farmers and country boys. And there were Colonel Stand Watie and 2,000 Cherokee, Chickasaw, Choctaw, Creek, and Seminole Indians led out of Indian Territory by their commander, scholarly warrior-poet Albert Pike.

General Earl Van Dorn, given command of the 17,000-man army by President and fellow Mississippian Davis, intended to drive the Federals away from Missouri capital Springfield, then advance on St. Louis, in the process of securing the state for the Confederacy. But by the time he crossed Sugar Creek in far northwest Arkansas, the daunting challenges beyond the standard perturbations of war so often faced by Confederates beset his men. Many were barefoot, most were ill-clothed for the snowy weather, and all were low on ammunition—and hungry. And they had marched over 50 miles in three days, the wintry Northern wind whipping their faces with wet snow every step of the way. Finally they marched all night and straight into the two-day battle of Pea Ridge.

Despite these handicaps, the Confederates, screaming the Rebel Yell, hurtled headlong into the Federals and sent them reeling back. The fight lasted all day and ended with the Southerners seemingly poised for the *coup de grace* the next morning, March 7. Now, however, the Confederates' earlier-mentioned deprivations began to tell. They did not have sufficient ammunition to press home a final attack. They had also lost a series of generals near the end of the first day, most notably the three highest-ranking commanders of the Texans and Arkansans, including McCulloch. Without the latter, uncertainty and confusion seeped over his men, who had promised to storm hell itself if McCulloch ordered them. Perhaps most importantly, the Confederates could no longer escape the toll produced by extended lack of food and sleep.

All this allowed the cool, methodical Federal commander Samuel R. Curtis—West Point graduate, Mexican War commander, and Republican Congressman—to mount an attack of his own. Brilliantly conducted by the red-haired German Franz Sigel, it crushed the Confederate artillery and drove the Southern infantry from the field. With that, though perhaps no one realized it at the time, Missouri was secured for the Union. Van Dorn, undaunted, planned another campaign for the state and was actually returning north within days with 16,000 men. But Davis ordered him to join Joe Johnston and Beauregard in northern Mississippi. "Silent and sad," the victorious Curtis described the place of recent slaughter as he wrote home to Ohio. "The vulture and the wolf have now communion, and the dead, friends and foes, sleep in the same lonely grave."

Franz Sigel

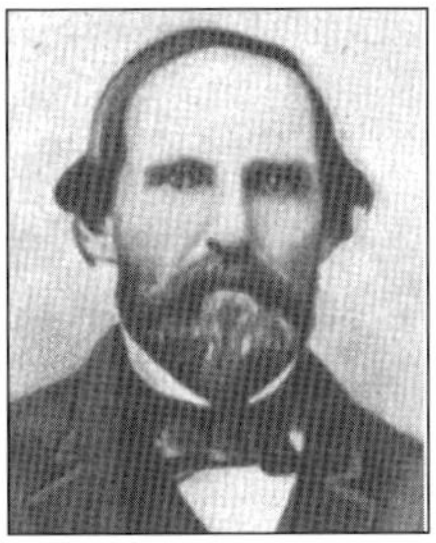
Ben McCulloch

"37th Illinois at Pea Ridge."

Stand Watie (1806-1871)

Refusing to fit any stereotype for standard American history accounts of the War of 1861–65 were the numerous slaveowning American Indians who led Confederate military forces. Such a man was three-quarter-Cherokee Stand Watie, the only Indian to attain the rank of general in either army. Born near Rome, Georgia, and educated at a Christian church mission school in Tennessee, Watie proved himself a leader even as a young man. A frequent correspondent in the 1830s with President Andrew Jackson, he recognized that man's determination to proceed with the ethnic cleansing of the Cherokees from the southeastern United States. When the United States Supreme Court ordered the state of Georgia to leave the mostly-Christian Cherokees alone and let them live in peace on their own land, Jackson defiantly declaimed, "The Chief Justice [John Marshall] has made his ruling. Now let him enforce it."

So Stand Watie, divining the imminent slaughter of his people if they did not leave, helped negotiate the 1835 New Echota Treaty between the United States and the Cherokee Nation to which he belonged. He and a couple thousand other Cherokees left soon after for Indian Territory (present-day Oklahoma). The majority of Cherokees, however, led by Chief John Ross (7/8 Scot and 1/8 Cherokee), opposed the New Echota Treaty and the relocation. They remained in their homeland until the U.S. Army forcibly uprooted them two years later. Broken promises by Jackson—who detested Indians of all stripes—and other Federal officials turned this phase of the Cherokees' westward relocation, in 1838-39, into the tragic Trail of Tears. The Cherokees called it, literally, "The Place Where We Cried." Thousands of them, mostly women and children, died in the open amidst a howling winter and sometimes brutal Federal soldiers en route to their new homeland.

William Penn Adair, colonel of the First Cherokee Mounted Rifles during the War, leader among the post-war Cherokees, and ancestor of modern-day Oklahoma political leader Larry Adair.

Once there, many of Ross's followers harbored bitter resentment against Watie and other leaders of what came to be known as the Treaty Party. Within six months of the larger Cherokee party arriving in Indian Territory, every Treaty Party leader except Watie was murdered. He escaped only by a comrade's warning, his own wits and courage, and the borrowed horse of white Presbyterian missionary friend Samuel Worcester. Years later, Watie and Ross and their two factions made peace, though their variant philosophies would flare again during the War.

A successful planter and journalist, Watie, like many of his educated and devout Cherokee peers, owned black slaves. Though they recognized the economic benefits accruing from slave labor, they also believed their Christian duty was to own slaves, provide a good living environment for them, and make certain they learned the Gospel and the doctrines of Biblical orthodoxy.

Guerilla and General

Watie supported the Confederacy from its start. His influence helped lead the Cherokee Nation into a formal alliance with the South. He and many fellow Cherokees, including John Drew, William Penn Adair, and Clem Rogers (father of famous American humorist Will Rogers), as well as other Indians such as Seminole John Jumper, gained renown for their battle exploits—renown largely ignored in traditional American histories.

After fighting commenced in the Indian Nations, Watie commanded the Cherokee Mounted Rifles, who earned a fearsome reputation, far out of proportion to their numbers, for their accomplishments at such battles as Wilson's Creek in Missouri and Pea Ridge in Arkansas. At the latter, a subordinate recounted Watie's outnumbered Indian horse soldiers charging into the face of blazing Federal cannon, capturing them, then turning them on their fleeing Federal enemy: "I don't know how we did it but Watie gave the order, which he always led, and his men could follow him into the very jaws of death. The Indian Rebel Yell was given and we fought like tigers three to one. It must have been that mysterious power of Stand Watie that led us on to make the capture against such odds."

Sarah Bell Watie, wife of Stand Watie.

Later, Watie's legend grew as a guerilla fighter while commanding Cherokee, Creek, Seminole, and Osage troops. One of his most famous exploits was the capture in a shootout on the Arkansas River of a Federal steamship and its $150,000 cargo. Another was his leading Confederate forces to victory in the Second Battle of Cabin Creek, in Indian Territory. Tragically, the War forced Watie to fight not only Federal troops, who also included Indians, but some of his own people as well. The majority of the Ross faction transferred their allegiance to the North when events turned against the Confederacy.

Saladin Watie, son of Stand Watie

Year after year, Federal armies from all over the west hunted Watie. They never caught him. Brigadier General and Cherokee Chief Stand Watie fought to the bitter end. He was the last Confederate general to surrender, undaunted and unvanquished, on June 23, 1865, nearly three months after Appomattox. He returned to financial ruin and a home burned to the ground by Federals during the War. He spent his final years farming. Tragedy continued to mark his life as his beloved son Saladin, captain, decorated war hero, postwar Southern Cherokee delegate to Congress, and only twenty-one years of age, became the final of his three boys to precede him in death. Like another fabled Confederate general, Robert E. Lee of Virginia, it was said that Chief Stand Watie died at least partly of a broken heart.

The Cherokee Braves flag, the regimental colors of the First Cherokee Mounted Rifles. Similar to the First National Confederate flag, it featured five red stars representing the Five Civilized Tribes - Cherokee, Creek, Choctaw, Chickasaw, and Seminole - that fought for the Confederacy.

E. M. Bounds (1835–1913)

He rose to manhood in the little town of Shelbyville, Missouri, along with his six brothers and sisters. But he lived in a day when true civil war tore apart the society of his state. A fan neither of Southern slavery nor the "human sweat shops" of Northern industry, Bounds did hold an abiding belief in a state's right to secede, as elucidated in *Rawle's View of the Constitution*, taught to West Point cadets since the 1820s. Still, he continued his clergy work in the gospel-preaching Methodist Episcopal Church South at Brunswick Station. He refused to side with either North or South. Then a parade of Northern war crimes unfolded.

On May 10, 1861, came the St. Louis Massacre. A crowd of civilians taunted Federal troops under General Nathaniel Lyon, and the Yankees unleashed a volley that killed twenty-eight people, almost all of them noncombatants, including a baby in its mother's arms. The Federals executed fifty-five civilians in the Brunswick area over the next several months. They included seventeen-year-old John Lenard, accused of bushwhacking, whom Yankee soldiers drowned in the frozen Grand River without trial and whose funeral Bounds performed. In the Palmyra Massacre, Federal Provost Marshal Stracham hanged ten innocent civilians. One young wife begged for her husband's life; Stracham required her to lay with himself. When she could not bring herself to see another innocent person die for her husband, a teenaged boy stepped forward to take his place, asking only that his mother be told he died with honor. The grieving mother

called upon Bounds, her former pastor, to preach the boy's funeral. Bounds, in anguish of soul, preached submission to God-ordained civil authorities, though he wondered if that included authority that defied the higher authority of God. Then he and hundreds of other men and women were seized and ordered to swear an Oath of Allegiance to the United States and pay a $500 bond for release.

> *Without intermission, incessantly, assiduously; that ought to describe the opulence, and energy, and unabated ceaseless strength and fullness of effort in prayer; like the full and exhaustless and spontaneous flow of an artesian stream.*
>
> —E. M. Bounds

Federal Prisoner

The great majority of these prisoners, too, were noncombatants and had done nothing against the Federal government. None had been convicted or even tried for any crime, and the Federals arrested most only because the word "South" appeared in the church name where they ministered or worshipped. Bounds recognized the U.S. government's aim to "convert" clergy to its side in order to control Missouri communities. He would either lose the respect of his people or be arrested. He refused the oath and was sent to a miserable, freezing St. Louis prison. The packed prisoners did not have room to lay down to sleep at night. The women among them were assaulted and raped, often in front of their husbands. Frail, hungry, and shivering with cold, Bounds sang, prayed, and ministered to the men and women around him. He asked the Federal authorities for permission to hold a Christmas worship service to celebrate the birth of Christ and provide the prisoners some joy and hope. His request was denied.

Next, Federal General Samuel Curtis issued Banishment Order 23, exiling Bounds from Missouri until after the War. The Federals shipped him south, locking him in frigid, cramped quarters with little food. He responded by singing hymns. This brought on a salvo of questions from bluecoat soldiers, mostly Irish and English natives. Bounds's joy in his circumstances mystified them. He took the opportunity to speak, teach, and preach the gospel of Christ to these battle-bound soldiers as the source of his joy and hope. Bounds continued to Memphis, then southern Arkansas, and finally northern Mississippi by river barge, train, and foot. At one point, he walked over 200 miles straight in the dead of winter. Eventually, he volunteered for duty as a chaplain in the Missouri Third Infantry, Company B, under the respected General John Bowen.

Again and again, spiritual repentance and reformation swept the men whom Bounds served.

Chaplain in War

Bounds preached and ministered to the Third Missouri and others in the Confederate Army of Tennessee through a succession of the biggest battles in the western theater of the War. The great revivals of the Army of Northern Virginia may be more famous, but Bounds and other preachers saw much spiritual fruit in the western Confederate armies as well. He endured the siege of Vicksburg, where more than a third of his Missouri brigade fell, killed or wounded. The rest, and Bounds, were surrendered when the city fell. He aided his blood-drenched regiment at Kennesaw Mountain and suffered in the trenches with Hood's men as they defended Atlanta. When his men, whom he loved as his own blood brothers, charged through the "Valley of No Return" at Franklin, sixty-eight percent of them did not return, and Bounds himself was sabered in the head trying to rescue his wounded friend and commander, General Alexander Cockrell.

Again and again, spiritual repentance and reformation swept the men whom Bounds served. The darker the events that transpired in the trenches of Atlanta, the greater revival surged. Many times, Federal gunners halted their shelling at night to listen to the Confederates' hymns of praise. The Federals often joined in the singing and shouted forth their own prayer requests. One Iowa soldier recalled: "On duty after dark, the Sixth Iowa heard services carried on late into the night; shouting and singing could be distinctly heard in the Confederate lines. A Missouri chaplain [Bounds] wanted soldiers to be Christians, as they would not fear the consequences after death as others do." After the horror of Franklin, Bounds remained with the 4,000 Confederate wounded and was captured by the Federals yet again. Temporarily released, he ministered to the bleeding town for months before, despite the fact he was a chaplain, being consigned to the Tennessee State Penitentiary until the end of the War.

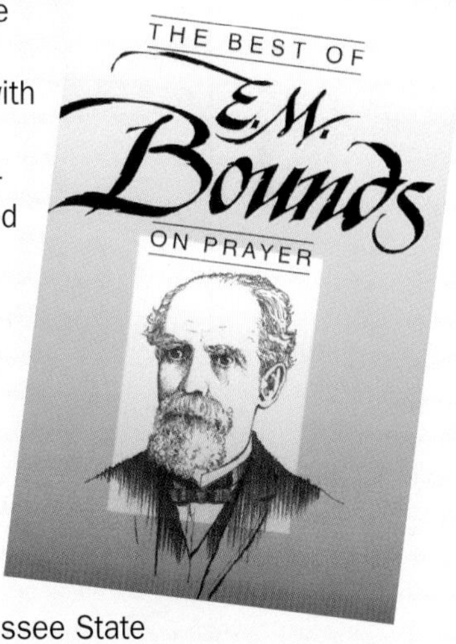

Later Years

After the War, he returned to Franklin, where, in peacetime, he faced one of his greatest challenges. Federal soldiers still occupied the town, and Carpetbag rule proved harsh and unyielding on the poverty-stricken populace. Bitter hatred burgeoned in the hearts of the Tennesseans. For years, Bounds set an example of love and forbearance toward the invaders. And he and others prayed for Christian regeneration in the wounded hearts of the people. Finally it came, with 150 Christian conversions (including a boy named B. F. Haynes who would grow up to be president of the gospel-preaching Asbury Methodist Seminary) and lasting spiritual transformation of the entire area. But Bounds biographer Darrel D. King recounts how Bounds opposed planned or man-generated "revivals," and "was quick to warn that [people] should worship God Himself, not seek after experience or manifestations."

Later he ministered in Alabama—where he performed groundbreaking ministry for blacks—St. Louis, and Georgia. The lasting legacy of Edward McKendree Bounds, however, is his devotion to God, in particular through prayer. His book *Power Through Prayer* has sold innumerable copies and has likely never been out of print since first published. For decades, Bounds' normal daily season of prayer was three full hours, between 4 and 7 a.m. He wrote: "God shapes the world by prayers. Prayers are deathless. The lips that uttered them may have closed in death, the heart that felt them may have ceased to beat, but the prayers outlive the lives of an age, outlive a world. That man is most immortal who has done the most and best praying. They are God's heroes, God's saints, God's servants, God's vice-regents."

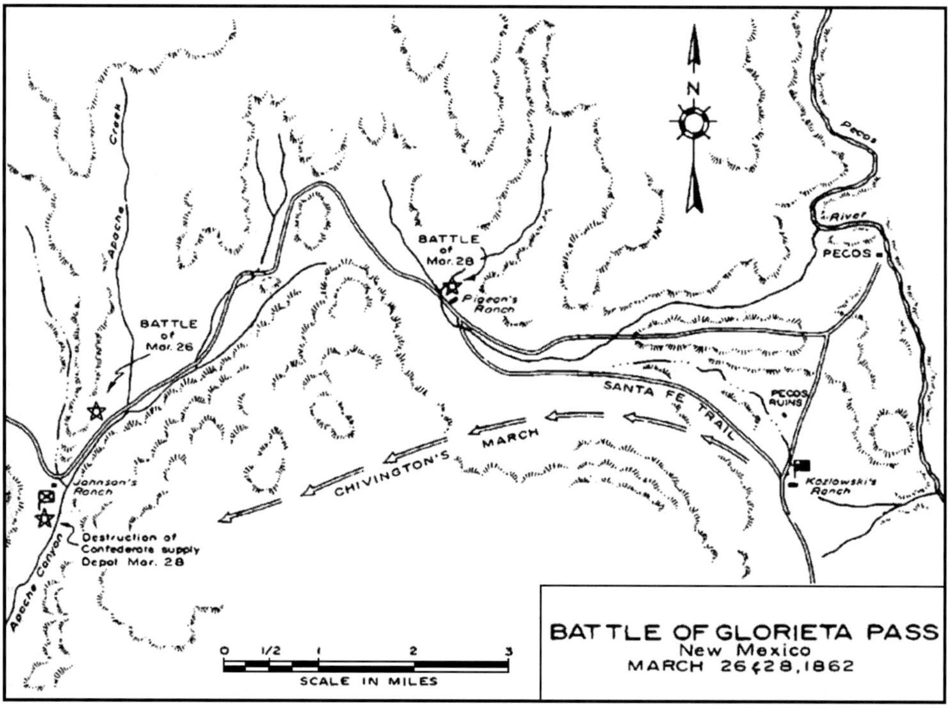

Map of the Battle of Glorieta Pass. (Courtesy National Park Service)

New Mexico Campaign

Buoyed by early success, Confederate General Henry Sibley early in the year campaigned his 3,700 Texans up the state of New Mexico along the banks of the Rio Grande River. They fared well in the southern half of the state, part of the newly declared Confederate Territory of Arizona. Having gobbled up Union Forts Fillmore and Thorn, the Texans crashed into the Federals at Valverde, just south of the 34th parallel line that separated Confederate Arizona and still-Union New Mexico. A brace of heroic but blood-drenched charges straight into the teeth of Federal cannon carried the day for the Texans, and they continued up the Rio Grande.

However, just as Lee and the Confederates in the eastern theater failed to match the martial successes accomplished within their homeland when they crossed into the North, so too did the Texans' fortunes change once they entered Federal territory. They did capture both Albuquerque and the state capital of Santa Fe. But a few weeks later the pivotal event of the entire far west campaign occurred: the two-day Battle of Glorieta. The fight began when the Federals ambushed and bloodied the Texans on March 26 at Apache Canyon. The major part of the battle occurred the next day, when the Texans gained the upper hand against a melange of Coloradans and white and Hispanic New Mexicans. The Federals retreated to their supply base following the battle. The most important action of Glorieta Pass, however, occurred when Colonel John Chivington and 300 hundred Coloradans made a bold charge behind Texas lines and torched the entire

Henry Sibley, Texan commander of Confederates' New Mexico campaign.

Lt. Colonel Manuel Chavez, Second New Mexico Volunteers, guided Federal troops over Glorieta Mesa.

Colonel William Scurry commanded mounted Texas volunteers at the Battle of Glorieta Pass.

The Yellow Rose of Texas (Author unknown)

There's a yellow rose of Texas
That I am going to see,
No other fellow knows her,
No other, only me.
She cried so when I left her,
It like to break my heart,
And if I ever find her
We never more will part.

Oh, now I'm going to find her,
For my heart is full of woe,
And we'll sing the song together,
That we sung long ago;
We'll play the banjo gaily,
and we'll sing the songs of yore,
and the Yellow Rose of Texas
Shall be mine forevermore.

Confederate supply train. New Mexicans, Coloradans, Californians, Utahans, Federal Army regulars, no supplies or supply lines, a hostile citizenry, and barren lands incapable of rendering subsistence to an invading army—they all combined to thwart Sibley and the Texans in their bid to wrest New Mexico from the Union.

They retreated over hundreds of miles of harsh desert to their Fort Bliss base back in Texas. That epic pilgrimage of suffering and survival was in itself one of the great feats of the War. The Federals, happy to allow the Texans to leave without further bloodshed, observed them do so from a distance. Thus, by May ended yet another Confederate threat, that to the Far West. But another, much bloodier war would more than fill its place for the United States—the Indian War.

Braxton Bragg (1817-1876)

The unforgiving court of human history records that Confederate fortunes in the West did not fare as well as those in the East in significant measure because this talented but difficult commander consistently fell just short of winning the sort of victories Robert E. Lee did. The North Carolina native finished fifth in his West Point class, fought in the Seminole Indian War, and received several promotions in the Mexican War for his gallantry as an artillery commander. Courageous and devoted to the Confederate cause, he possessed formidable talents as both a strategist and tactician. But historians have long pondered whether Bragg's frequent migraines, stomach ailments, and other maladies contributed to his surly disposition or vice versa. Surely he was one of the least popular men in high command on either side in the War. A parade of high-ranking subordinates, including Longstreet, Beauregard, Forrest, Polk, and D. H. Hill, detested him; so did many of the men in the ranks. Neither was he ever popular with the public.

He did, however, have one important and loyal friend—Jefferson Davis. Davis, angry with Beauregard for not consummating the Confederate victory at Shiloh, replaced him with Bragg as commander of the Army of the Mississippi. Soon after, Bragg demonstrated the most dramatic, and damaging, feature of his persona—dichotomous penchants for launching bold, successful assaults against the Federals, then failing to carry them through to victory.

He stunned the North by invading Kentucky in late summer before they could move south into Tennessee. His forces won important victories at Richmond and Munfordville. But then he seemed to lose his confidence. Instead of consolidating his gains with further offensive thrusts that might have secured Kentucky—and its enormous manpower base—for the Confederacy, he dispatched a large portion of his army to establish a pro-secessionist state government at Frankfort. Not only did this split his forces, but it gave the Federals pre-

Showdown in Kentucky

President Lincoln had long said that without Kentucky, the Federals could not win the war. Such were the stakes in late August when the Confederates' western commander Braxton Bragg launched a two-pronged attack north into the state from Tennessee. Confederate General Edmund Kirby Smith took one column into Lexington; Bragg moved another toward Louisville. To capture that important Union supply base would accomplish several things. First, it would place Bragg behind (north of) the Federals' Army of the Ohio, commanded by Don Carlos Buell, of Shiloh fame. Second, it would give the South control of the key state, which would draw large numbers of fence-riding Kentuckians into the Confederate army. Finally, it would afford Bragg the opportunity to push further north to

cious time to regain their balance and move against Bragg at Perryville. In this key battle, his men tore into the bluecoats and drove their main line back nearly a mile. Due to his earlier moves, however, Bragg found himself outnumbered better than three-to-one and unable to complete his looming victory. Instead, he retreated gradually out of the state and back into Tennessee, replete with captured supplies and war materiel but without Kentucky.

Unfinished Business

As 1862 became 1863, Bragg inflicted more punishment on the Federals at the central Tennessee battles of Murfreesboro and Stone's River, only to pull away—to the shock of almost everyone, especially the Federals, whose own army had been pummeled. This time, in response to the cascade of complaints from both officers and rankers about what they viewed as Bragg's unnecessary retreat, Davis sent Joe Johnston to investigate. In overall command of the Confederates' western theater of operations since the conclusion of the Kentucky campaign, Johnston advised the President to retain Bragg.

The crowning blow came on the heels of Bragg's, and the western Confederacy's, greatest victory. In the two-day September, 1863 slaughter at Chickamauga Creek, his troops stampeded the Federals back into Chattanooga. It was a decisive and brilliant victory and could have gone forth as one of the epic military triumphs of American history had Bragg followed the urgings of Longstreet and others of his commanders to finish off the fleeing, disorganized Federals. Nathan Bedford Forrest, himself spearheading the pursuit with his cavalry, hastened word back to Bragg that "every hour was worth a thousand men."

Federal Army of the Tennessee Commander William Rosecrans, himself expecting Bragg to chase him right through Chattanooga, rushed his own trains and artillery out of the city. Then, realizing the Confederates were not coming, he stayed there with his army. The regrouped Federals under U. S. Grant used Chattanooga as their base two months later to strike Bragg. They whipped him at Lookout Mountain and Missionary Ridge, drove him out of Tennessee, and set the stage for Sherman's flaming march through Georgia and the Carolinas. Blaming others for the devastating Chattanooga defeats, Bragg resigned and Davis appointed him as his military adviser. In this post, he performed quite well, consistently providing the administration sage counsel on military matters.

the Great Lakes and sever the United States, as the latter was attempting to do to the Confederacy.

On October 8, 16,000 Confederates charged screaming into twice that many Federals at Perryville, drove them back, and captured the ridge upon which they had stood, as well as the advantage. That moonlit night, however, Bragg, knowing Federal repositioning and reinforcements would give Buell a four-to-one advantage the next day, withdrew from the battlefield and then from Kentucky. The final analysis of the battle of Perryville reveals that the Confederates lacked the material resources to wrest Kentucky from the Federals. Still, with 16,000 men they had steamrolled one whole wing of a Federal army that had 55,000 men somewhere on the field at the time; withdrawn with a train of captured field guns, arms, ammunition, mules, supplies, and horses; and restored middle Tennessee and northern Alabama to Confederate dominion. But the South could never mount another serious effort to secure Kentucky. It would, as everyone had suspected, prove a key strategic factor in the outcome of the War.

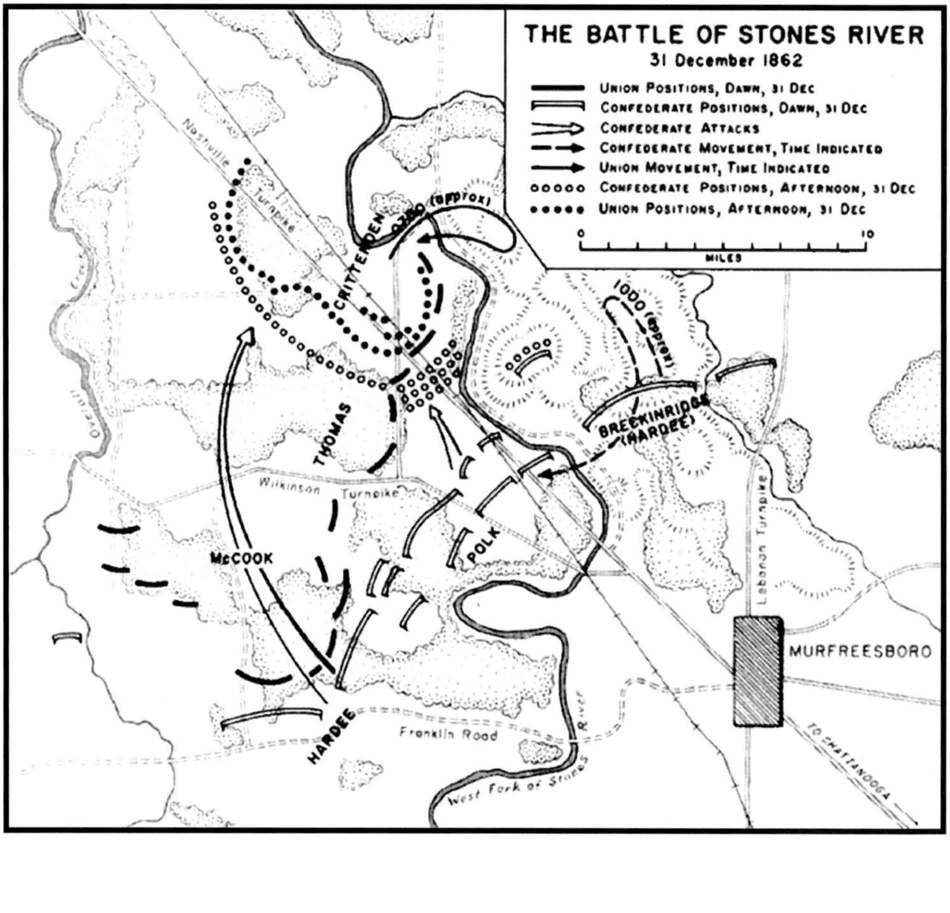

Map of the first day of the Battle of Stone's River. (United States Army Center of Military History)

Vicksburg Campaign Begins

In November, the focus of action in the western theater shifted south. Grant now headed the Federal Army of the Tennessee—one of two major Federal armies in the Western Theater—and thus commanded all Union forces in the strategic northern Mississippi area. But his career was on the ropes. Near-disaster at Shiloh, persistent rumors of his drunkenness on duty, and a spiteful relationship with his superior, Henry Halleck, resulted in his demotion. He began a tenacious campaign against Vicksburg that was critical for both his career and the survival of the full Union. Only Vicksburg prevented the Federals from possessing complete control of the Mississippi River and sundering the Confederacy in half. Grant split his army. He took 40,000 men down the Mississippi Central Railroad from Memphis and Grand Junction, Tennessee, toward Grenada in hopes of diverting the Confederates away from Vicksburg. His chief lieutenant, William Tecumseh Sherman, led another 32,000 men down the Mississippi River from Memphis toward Vicksburg. The Confederates clobbered both Northern forces in late December. Fierce Southern cavalry attacks led by Van Dorn and Forrest captured the Federals' chief Mississippi supply depot at Holly Springs, corralled 2,000 prisoners, and destroyed a mountain of supplies. They also wrecked the Mobile and Ohio Rail line, along which the Federals transported their supplies. Grant retreated back to his base in Tennessee.

Federal commander Williams Rosecrans at the Battle of Stone's River.

Meanwhile, Confederate forces under new departmental commander John C. Pemberton, a native New Yorker, beat Sherman to Vicksburg. They decimated a brave Federal assault at Chickasaw Bayou just north of the town, then counterattacked and swept the field. Sherman suffered nearly 2,000 casualties before he retreated north, Confederate Brigadier Stephen Lee less than 200. The year ended with the Confederates entrenched in Vicksburg and Grant determined to take as long as necessary to remove them and complete the Federal conquest of the Mississippi.

Bloody Middle Tennessee

In middle Tennessee, Rosecrans departed Nashville in late December to drive Bragg's forces out of their winter quarters around Murfreesboro, near Stone's River. The prelude to the contest was a 19th-century battle of the North and South bands, after which the westerners in both armies formed a single massive chorus to sing *Home, Sweet Home*. There was nothing sweet about the battle of Murfreesboro on the last day of the year. Once again Bragg's men hurtled ferociously into the Yankees and drove them back. When darkness finally terminated the fighting, Bragg felt sure the pounding he had dealt the Federals would cause Rosecrans to withdraw. Again boasting superior numbers, however, they dug in and stayed.

Two days later, January 2, 1863, the Confederates charged again, in the Battle of Stone's River. This time, massed Federal artillery stopped them.

A War of Firsts

The North introduced a series of important weapons during the War. These included the first serious use of rifled weapons (and minie balls), as opposed to muskets. This greatly increased firing accuracy and rendered Napoleonic tactics outdated. The United States also inaugurated the use of magazine-loading repeating rifles such as the Spencer and Henry, and machine guns.

Suffering a lopsided, war-long disadvantage in the naval war, the South's innovative naval leaders inaugurated an array of new technologies, including ironclad ships such as the *Virginia*, which overnight rendered wooden warships obsolete; submarines such as the *Hunley*, which blew the Federal warship *Housatonic* out of the water; and electrically-detonated battle torpedoes, first used at Yorktown in May, 1862.

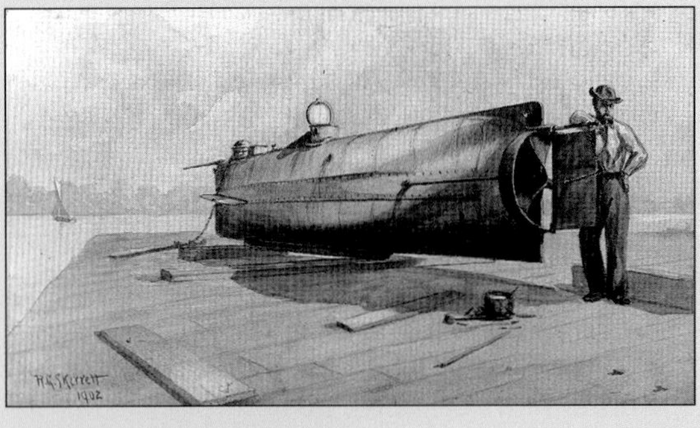
Confederate submarine *H.L. Hunley*

The North, led by scientific professor S. C. Thaddeus Lowe, at the Battle of Fair Oaks, pioneered the use of hot air balloons for observation—and even to direct artillery fire—in war; the South used them to a lesser degree.

For the first time in war, trains were employed for the tactical transport of soldiers when the South's Stonewall Jackson rushed his men to Manassas Junction for the War's first major battle. Their lightning-fast arrival provided the Confederacy with its margin of victory.

Federal and Confederate field telegraphs first connected combat commanders with one another, their forward outposts, and their governmental leaders, greatly increasing the speed and efficiency of their movements.

The elaborately-designed trench systems and earthworks so infamous in later wars such as World War I were inaugurated during the War of 1861–1865 by such commanders as Robert E. Lee, who spent much of his career in the United States Army as an engineer.

The Confederates won the overall battle, but a familiar scenario unfolded. Their lack of resources created doubt, in Bragg's mind at least, that he could force the Federals from the field. Thus, he withdrew south to Tullahoma. More than one third of all the troops involved in the battles of Murfreesboro and Stone's River, nearly 23,000 men, became casualties.

The Confederate Battle Flag

These much-maligned colors have been legislated out of football stadiums, outlawed from public display, expunged from schools brimming with every manner of godless rebellion, and castigated as a dark symbol of ignorance, slavery, racism, and hatred. Ironically, in distant lands, far from America, across the world, this banner is held aloft as a symbol of defiance in the face of tyranny and oppression, the life of the bearer often required as forfeit for the display.

Few who deride it—while flying the U.S. flag that fluttered over every American slave ship and has also been commonly employed by hate groups—know its true identity. The Confederate Battle Flag was originally square in shape; the Confederacy's naval jack was similar, except rectangular. The Battle Flag's design came from the Scottish national flag, which features the same centerpiece pattern. That is the cross of St. Andrew, brother of the apostle Peter and patron saint of the once-Christian land of Scotland. St. Andrew's cross forms the shape of an X, which is the Greek language abbreviation for the word "Christ." It is also the configuration of the cross upon which Christian tradition says Andrew was crucified as a follower of Jesus. The Scots of long ago determined the flag that flew over them would fly for Christ as well as for their people. The people of the South determined the same. The Confederate Battle Flag, to date, is the only Christian flag ever to represent a North American nation.

First National—"Stars and Bars," replaced after First Manassas because of its resemblance to the U.S. flag in the smoke and confusion of the battlefield.

Second National—The "Stainless Banner," replaced because it resembled the traditional white flag of truce or surrender when no wind blew and it hung limp.

Third National—Introduced just one month before Lee's surrender at Appomattox, it added a vertical red panel to the edge of the white field.

Bonnie Blue—The unofficial banner of Southern independence and self-government; previously flown by the Scottish Covenanters and the Republic of West Florida, for both of whom the Confederates felt kinship.

Confederate Naval Jack—The official flag of the Confederate navy, identical to the Battle Flag except for having a rectangular rather than square shape.
(All images courtesy of www.csagalleries.com)

20 Chancellorsville
(1863)

Free blacks enter the Federal lines at Newburn, Virginia, after the Emancipation Proclamation, which declared all slaves in present or former Confederate territory free, took effect on January 1, 1863. (TreasureNet)

Our (Federal) reverses have been misconstrued. They have been the chastisement and expiation imposed by Providence for our crime towards a long-suffering race. Had we succeeded early, we should not have suffered according to our deserts. We must lose other battles, and bury more children; but the results will be attained.

—Massachusetts Senator Charles Sumner

The Confederates repulsed a series of Federal naval attacks along the coast of the Carolinas and Georgia early in the year. Most dramatic of these occurred at the familiar port of Charleston, South Carolina, site of the War's opening salvo. The Federals had long kept Charleston partially blockaded (though many blockade running steamers still made their way in and out), and for a year or more they had launched a variety of efforts to gobble up the key port. Now they commenced to formulating a strategy that would overwhelm the city's defenses. The plan was months in the works and reached its culmination at the beginning of April when a powerful ironclad Northern fleet unleashed a breathtaking attack on Fort Sumter.

Nine vessels, bristling with thirty-

Spies among the Fairer Sex

Some of the most courageous warriors of the War did not wear uniforms. They were not even men. Both North and South benefitted from the exploits of loyal and dedicated women who risked everything—including their lives—for the cause dear to them. They lived among the enemy, clandestinely gathering some of the War's most important information and forwarding it to their own governments.

Rose O'Neal Greenhow (1817-1864)

This rich, beautiful, and charismatic widow lived directly across elite Lafayette Park from the White House and moved in the highest circles of antebellum Washington City society. She remained in the Federal capital when the War came, continuing to socialize with many of the United States' preeminent military, commercial, and political figures. Now, however, she put her contacts to another use—aiding her to apprise the Confederate government of some of the North's most sensitive and classified information. Rose O'Neal Greenhow gained lasting fame by conveying two crucial messages to General Beauregard as he gathered his forces on the plains of Manassas for the War's first great battle. Her initial communiqué con-

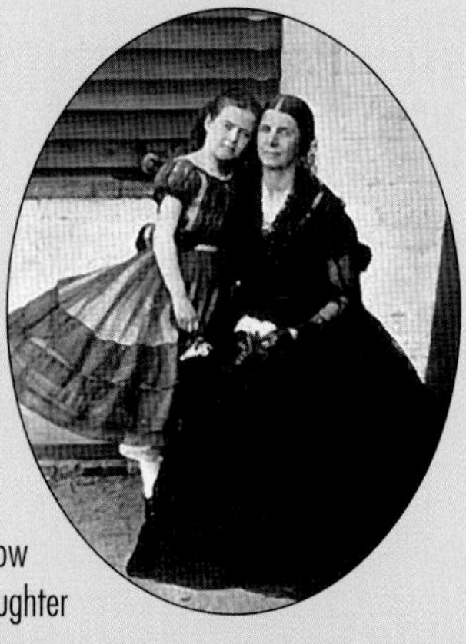

Rose O'Neal Greenhow and her daughter

firmed the timetable for the Federals' mid-July advance into Virginia. When Beauregard requested more information, she responded by alerting him that the Federal divisions of General Irvin McDowell were headed through Fairfax Court House and Centreville on their way to Manassas. This allowed Beauregard to plan and position his forces accordingly. And it contributed to a smashing Confederate victory when, if events had transpired differently, the Southern War for Independence may have ended that day.

The "Rebel Rose," as many called her, persisted in gathering important intelligence and forwarding it to the Confederate government even while in prison.

The Federals long suspected Mrs. Greenhow of espionage, but they had a difficult time figuring out how best to deal with her. Renowned detective Allen Pinkerton, whose agency the Federal government employed during the War, had her arrested within weeks of First Manassas. U.S. agents found a collection of maps and notes in her home containing sensitive Federal military information. They first placed her under house arrest, then consigned her, with her young daughter, to the Old Capitol Prison in Washington. The "Rebel Rose," as many called her, persisted in gathering important intelligence and forwarding it to the Confederate government even while in prison. Finally, the Federals deported her south. She received a hero's welcome in Richmond as large crowds turned out to cheer her. Between fetes and tributes in her honor, she toiled among the horror that was now Richmond's hospitals, helping Confederates wounded and dying from the Seven Days Campaign. "But for you," Davis told her, "there would have been no battle of Manassas."

Foreign Service

Next, the President sent her to Europe as a Confederate agent. From there, she ferried more intelligence to Richmond and represented the Confederate cause before the civil and commercial captains of England, France, and other countries. During her two years in Europe, she also wrote and published her memoirs, *My Imprisonment and the First Year of Abolition Rule at Washington*. In September, 1864, she boarded the Confederate blockade runner *Condor* for the voyage home. On October 1, off the coast of North Carolina, a Federal warship gave chase to the *Condor,* which ran aground on a sandbar. The Rebel Rose feared capture and return to prison—or worse—and requested that she be rowed ashore on a lifeboat. Something else contributed to her request—the $2,000 in gold sovereigns she had raised in Europe, desperately needed by the financially-bereft Confederacy and now stitched into a belt under her clothing. But the stormy sea engulfed the little boat. Several days later her lifeless body, the gold still attached, washed ashore. The weight of the sovereigns had dragged her down and led to her drowning.

The nation for which she was martyred buried her with full military honors at Wilmington, North Carolina. This brave, willful belle's epitaph was perhaps best pronounced by Confederate Naval Secretary Stephen R. Mallory:

> *She started, early in life, into the great world, and found in it many wild beasts; but only one to which she devoted special pursuit, and thereafter she hunted man with . . . resistless zeal and unfailing instinct. . . . She was equally at home with ministers of state or their doorkeepers. . . . [she] had a shaft in her quiver for every defence. . . . If she had displayed the fruits of her bow and her spear. . . . what scalps she might have shown . . ."*

Elizabeth Van Lew (1817–1900)

Small, intelligent, and outspoken, this Richmond resident was born to Northern parents who sent her north to Philadelphia for the schooling they felt was beneath her in Richmond. She remained loyal to the United States her entire life. From her sprawling, 3 1/2-story, six-columned mansion on Church Hill, she watched an early pro-Confederate parade and prayed, "Father, forgive them, for they know what they do." But she did much more than just root and pray for the Federals. At great risk to herself, she labored to aid the large population of Northern soldiers incarcerated in overcrowded, underprovisioned Richmond prisons such as Libby and Belle Isle. She hired lawyers to defend Northern loyalists on trial. She sent couriers through the lines, sometimes even her own servants.

Many such actions did not go unnoticed—nor uncriticized—in the Confederate capital. Even the press focused on her. The *Richmond Examiner* newspaper blared how, unlike a "true woman" would, she and her mother aided not Confederate sick and wounded, but expended "their opulent means in aiding and giving comfort to the miscreants who have invaded our sacred soil, bent on rapine and murder, the desolation of our homes and sacred places, and the ruin and dishonor of our families." More ominously, detectives followed her through the streets and questioned boarders at her house about her loyalty. She repeatedly visited Federal prisoners, often receiving or delivering smuggled letters and even money for them to bribe themselves out. She developed a pose for her prison trips as a demented old woman, shabbily-dressed and talking to herself.

Elizabeth Van Lew and her pro-Federal family's Richmond mansion, within which she hid escaped Federal prisoners.

Secret Agent

By late 1863, officials in the Federal government had learned of Mrs. Van Lew's loyalty and daring. They contacted her, requesting information on many different subjects, including Confederate supplies and transport in the capital, Federal prisoner dispositions, etc. She not only helped orchestrate a major Federal prison break, she began sheltering fugitive Northerners of all stripes inside a secret room high up in her house. After Federal cavalryman Ulric Dahlgren died fleeing his aborted raid on Richmond, Mrs. Van Lew and others learned the Confederates' secret burial place for him, had him removed, and transported his body to the North. By War's end, nearly all the Van Lew fortune, of Elizabeth, her brother, and her mother, was spent in the Federal cause.

Perhaps due to an ironic display of Southern chivalry, even though Confederate authorities grew certain of her pro-Federal activities, never through all her exploits did they arrest her, interrogate her or even search her home. Famed Confederate nurse Phoebe Pember said they were "too delicate minded" to do so. Brigadier General John Winder, inspector general of all Richmond-area Federal prisoner-of-war camps and known as a rough and sometimes even brutal man, actually went to great lengths to aid her pro-Federal brother to evade Confederate Army conscription. Neither Mrs. Van Lew nor her home were bothered by Richmond authorities even when they knew Grant's colossal conquering army was about to enter the capital. "What a moment!" she wrote of that occasion. "Civilization advanced a century . . . Oh! army of my country, how glorious was your welcome!"

Perhaps her greatest tribute came from the most successful general of the conflict. "You have sent me the most valuable information received from Richmond during the war," U. S. Grant wrote her. Upon his taking office as President in 1869, Grant appointed Mrs. Van Lew Federal postmaster in Richmond. She served in that capacity for eight years, then as a post office clerk in Washington for two more. In the end, her bold wartime intrigues left her with little money and few friends. The family and friends of a Federal soldier she had helped during his imprisonment in Richmond supported her during her final years.

The Parting, by John Paul Strain. A. P. Hill was one of the best fighting generals in the Confederate army. He clashed with his superiors Stonewall Jackson and James Longstreet, but his marriage to his wife Kitty was a grand love affair. Here, the Hills part after a respite together during his 1862–1863 winter quarters outside Fredericksburg.

three guns of the heaviest caliber yet seen in the War, including fifteen- and eleven-inch Dahlgrens, comprised the armada. Commanded by Rear Admiral Samuel DuPont, no force had yet been able to touch these ships. Against this, the Confederates brought sixty-four cannons and five mortars from Sumter and elsewhere in the harbor. None had the fire power of the big Federal guns. For two-and-half hours the people of Charleston, in fear, tears, and prayer, watched the blazing spectacle. Then the fleet returned to sea. Half of its turret ships were partially or totally disabled.

Chancellorsville

Eighteen sixty-two had been a year of epic triumphs in the east for the

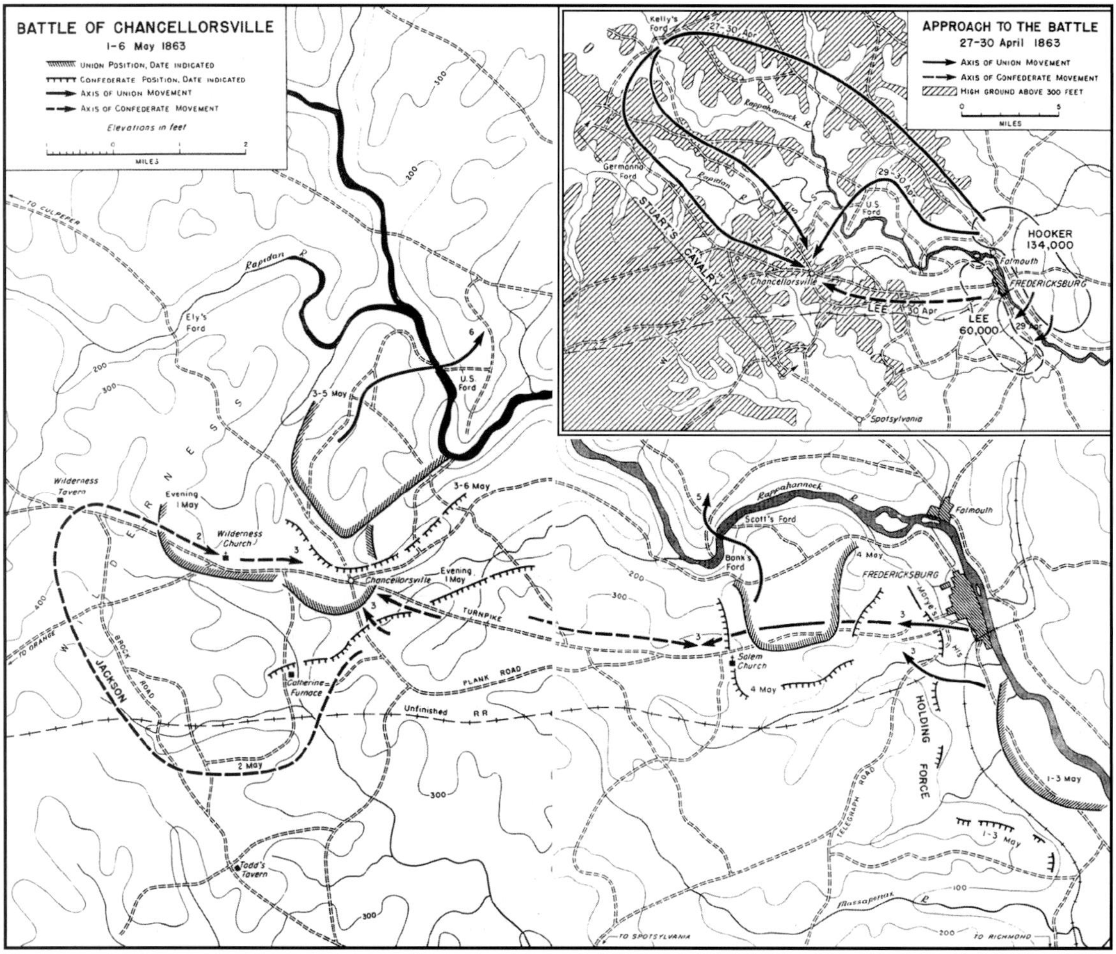

Map of the Battle of Chancellorsville. (Courtesy of The General Libraries, The University of Texas at Austin)

Confederacy. Never before or since have the main field armies of the United States sustained such a pounding from an opponent. But other factors were at play in the outworking of the War. The vast disparity of material resources between North and South not only remained, it expanded, and more rapidly with each passing month. After winning twice at Manassas, in the Shenandoah Valley, in the Seven Days, and at Fredericksburg, the Army of Northern Virginia experienced a keen physical deterioration through the winter months early in the year. Its horses starved, many to death; its men withered to skin and bone for lack of food, then thousands fell prey to dysentery, diarrhea, typhus, scurvy, and pneumonia; its civilians left their war-ravaged homes and farms and fled to cities such as Richmond in search of food, shelter, and medicine.

The awesome industrial might of the North, meanwhile, was only now coming into full swing. So were Northern farms, which differed from those of the South in that the War had touched few of them. Thus, while Lee's men scrounged for the rudiments of life, the Federals came to the field better clothed, better armed, better equipped, and better mounted than ever before. And they were more numerous than ever before as well.

The parade of Northern field commanders continued as Lincoln called upon Fighting Joe Hooker to take command in the east and develop a strategy to defeat Lee and take Richmond. Exhibiting organizational skills, motivational prowess, and tactical acumen, Hooker built the Army of the Potomac into a fighting force whose size and power were unparalleled in American history. By the end of April, when he churned south to confront the Confederates in central Virginia, Fighting' Joe had 134,000 men under his command.

The Army of Northern Virginia's horses starved, many to death; its men withered to skin and bone for lack of food, then thousands fell prey to dysentery, diarrhea, typhus, scurvy, and pneumonia; its civilians left their war-ravaged homes and farms and refugeed to cities such as Richmond in search of food, shelter, and medicine.

Lee, from whom Davis had transferred Longstreet's powerful corps, had less than half that number, barely 60,000. In addition, Southern hopes for foreign intervention had evaporated with Lincoln's signing of the Emancipation Proclamation and the Confederates' continued inability to crush the Federals in the field or threaten their seat of government. The South was alone for good. Loss of the foreign hope, coupled with the vice-grip of the Federal blockade, threatened to choke the very life out of the Confederacy as a viable nation.

Southern hopes for foreign intervention had evaporated with Lincoln's signing of the Emancipation Proclamation and the Confederates' continued inability to crush the Federals in the field or threaten their seat of government.

But Lee was still Lee, and he still had Stonewall Jackson and the fighting men of the Army of Northern Virginia, man for man as deadly an army as perhaps the world has ever known. Hooker not only brought his enormous army south, but he brought an intricate plan that included diversions, feints, stealth, and innovative use of cavalry. Nonetheless, Lee's sagacity, yet another splitting of his army in the face of a much larger force, and an audacious secret march by Jackson, produced a thundering surprise flank attack by "Old Jack" and an electrifying defeat of the Federals that proved the crowning triumph of the Lee-Jackson combination. For even as the battered Federals stumbled back across the Rappahannock in retreat, Jackson lay wounded, his body riddled by mistaken fire from his own men. Ten days later he was dead, and the Confederacy's greatest victory became its greatest loss of the War.

Heat at Catherine's Furnace, by John Paul Strain. Stonewall Jackson and Jeb Stuart's reconnoitering of forward Federal positions near Catherine's Furnace the afternoon of May 1 provided them precious intelligence that led to the spectacular Confederate victory at Chancellorsville. It also nearly got both men killed by a Yankee artillery barrage.

Joseph Hooker (1814–1879)

Dashing, blonde, and cocksure, Joe Hooker advanced up the United States Army ranks in the Far West, the Seminole War, and the Mexican War. But he detested his nickname of "Fighting Joe" and evidenced a difficulty in getting along with his superiors. When the War came, he not only had retired from the army to farm in California, but was at first rebuffed when attempting to secure a commission for action. But he commanded well both while in charge of the Washington City defenses in 1861 and during McClellan's Peninsula/Seven Days campaign the next spring. Then he spearheaded the Federal attack against Stonewall Jackson at Sharpsburg and sustained a bad wound.

Back in action a few months later at Fredericksburg, the married Hooker commanded a corps, then lambasted his superior, Army of the Potomac Commander Ambrose Burnside. "Fighting Joe" wanted the job himself, and he got it by appointment of Abraham Lincoln. By now, his headquarters had earned the well-deserved reputation of "combination barroom and brothel." But he plowed into his new duties with abandon. Discarding, or at least restraining, some of his more unsavory personal habits, he reorganized the Army of the Potomac, improved order and discipline, and rebuilt morale.

I've got the rebellion in my breeches pocket and God Almighty Himself can't take it away from me.

—Joe Hooker

Fighting Joe

"I've got the rebellion in my breeches pocket and God Almighty Himself can't take it away from me," he proclaimed as he moved south across the Rappahannock River toward the Army of Northern Virginia. "May God have mercy on General Lee, for I will have none," he wrote Lincoln. Then Stonewall Jackson's corps slammed into him in the jungle of the Wilderness. At this point, as he later admitted, Hooker lost confidence in Joe Hooker. Over the objections of some of his lieutenants, he slowed his enormous army's advance. Jackson's famous flank attack made mincemeat of the Eleventh Corps of Oliver O. Howard at Chancellorsville. Hooker was nearly killed when a Confederate cannon ball screamed into a post against which he was leaning at his own headquarters building. The ensuing rout represented the apogee of the Lee-Jackson combination and cost the United States 17,000 soldiers in three days. Hooker barely got his army back across the Rappahannock without it being destroyed. Lincoln replaced him with George Meade a few days before the Battle of Gettysburg began.

Like other high-ranking Federal officers who had faced tough sledding in the eastern theater of the War, Hooker gained a chance to redeem himself when transferred west. Only six months after Chancellorsville, his "Fighting Joe" persona seemed to reappear during U. S. Grant's illustrious Chattanooga campaign. He commanded the Federals' bold and decisive charge up Lookout Mountain, and performed well during the successful 1864 campaign against Atlanta. Hooker suffered a stroke in 1868 that ended his U.S. Army career, though he lived another eleven years.

The Death of Stonewall Jackson

Over a week passed between Jackson's wounding and his death. Shot three times, the true cause of his death was probably being dropped from a stretcher by soldiers carrying him from the field. He landed hard on a tree stump. The fall likely punctured his lung, resulting in his death from pneumonia on May 10.

Stonewall Jackson's last days, in which he experienced acute physical suffering, were observed by a host of eyewitnesses, including family, physicians, clergy, and soldiers. They chronicled a number of remarkable comments by the famed general and devout Presbyterian deacon.

He told renowned Presbyterian pastor Tucker Lacy:

> *You see me severely wounded, but not depressed; not unhappy. I believe that it has been done according to God's holy will, and I acquiesce entirely in it. You may think it strange; but you never saw me more perfectly contented than I am today; for I am sure that my Heavenly Father designs this affliction for my good. I am perfectly satisfied, that either in this life, or in that which is to come, I shall discover that what is now regarded as a calamity, is a blessing. And if it appears a great calamity, (as it surely will be a great inconvenience, to be deprived of my arm), it will result in a great blessing. I can wait, until God, in his own time, shall make known to me the object he has in thus afflicting me. But why should I not rather rejoice in it as a blessing, and not look on it as a calamity at all? If it were in my power to replace my arm, I would not dare to do it, unless I could know it was the will of my Heavenly Father.*

"I know you would gladly give your life for me, but I am perfectly resigned," he told his wife Anna. "Do not be sad. I hope I may yet recover. Pray for me, but always remember in your prayers to use the petition, 'Thy will be done.'"

In the presence of Lacy, Jackson's physician and staff officer Hunter McGuire, and others, he discussed his favorite topics of practical religion:

> *The Christian should carry his religion into everything. Christianity makes man better in any lawful calling; it equally makes the general a better commander, and the shoemaker a better mechanic. In the case of the cobbler, or the tailor, for instance, religion will produce more care in promising work, more punctuality, and more fidelity in executing it, from conscientious motives. . . . So, prayer aids any man, in any lawful business, not only by bringing down the divine blessing, which is its direct and prime object, but by har-*

> *In his last letter to me he spoke of our precious Ellie, and of the blessedness of being with her in heaven. And now he has rejoined her, and together they unite in ascribing praises to Him who has redeemed them by His blood.*
>
> —Margaret Junkin Preston

monizing his own mind and heart. In the commander of an army at the critical hour, it calmed his perplexities, moderated his anxieties, steadied the scales of judgment, and thus preserved him from exaggerated and rash conclusions.

Rev. Dr. (and Major) Robert L. Dabney, Jackson's former military chief of staff, recalled:

Again, [Jackson] urged, that every act of man's life should be a religious act. He recited with much pleasure, the ideas of Doddridge, where he pictured himself as spiritualizing every act of his daily life; as thinking when he washed himself, of the cleansing blood of Calvary; as praying while he put on his garments, that he might be clothed with the righteousness of the saints; as endeavoring, while he was eating, to feed upon the Bread of Heaven.

"Before this day closes, you will be with the blessed Saviour in His glory," Anna told him finally, as Robert E. Lee and nearly the entire Army of Northern Virginia prayed for him. Jackson said, "I prefer it." The final words of his life, as he lay comatose, were: "Let us cross over the river and rest under the shade of the trees."

Riding into Battle with Jeb Stuart

In his classic biography *Jeb Stuart*, U.S. Marine Captain John W. Thomason, Jr., chronicles from eyewitness accounts the actions of Stuart in the decisive moments of the Battle of Chancellorsville, after Stonewall Jackson had been shot by his own men:

*Twice the gray infantry, having gained the edge of the woods, rushed up to the breastworks in the clear, and twice the Yankee canister and musketry threw them back. The reports here grow almost lyrical: sober colonels describe Jeb Stuart, on a great bright charger, leading the infantry waves, with a voice that dominated the tumult, and that song (*Old Joe Hooker, won't you come out' the Wilderness*) . . .*

He rode with the first guns into the open where the Turnpike entered the Chancellor clearing. Twice he led the 28th North Carolina regiment in a charge. His fine horse Chancellor is killed early in the day: he mounts another, a big blood-bay, and dashes into a regiment that has broken under the Northern rifles and is running back: snatches their battle flag from the color bearer, turns them about with a ringing, brazen voice, and leads them against the flaming breastworks with their flag in his hands. He rides ahead of the last assault, leaps his big horse through the drifting smoke, over the Yankee fortifications, and the animal stands, with flaring nostrils, above the dead and the debris, between two silent guns. The gray infantry flood up behind him. Jeb Stuart halloos his people forward to the chase, and the fight streamed across the clearing, up from Hazel Grove. . . . Lee's army was united again, and Lee rode upon the field in the midst of his troops.

They say, who saw it, that the moment was such a one as lives in the hearts of men through any after-life of dullness or of glory.

A black family enters the Federal lines with a loaded wagon. (TreasureNet)

The Northern Home Front

Life in the North during the War was different in many respects from that in the South. The greatest affliction, of course, was the sheer scale of human destruction within the Federal armies—360,000 soldiers died in the War, 100,000 more than the Confederacy lost (though the deceased bluecoats represented a lower percentage of their overall population). Hundreds of thousands more were wounded, maimed, or fell seriously ill. Sustaining such fearsome casualties and many defeats in battle exacted a strong mental toll on many Northerners, particularly during the War's first three years.

Several factors prevented the average Northern civilian from suffering to the extent that his counterpart in the South did. For one, only a small fraction of the War was fought on Northern soil. So the North did not suffer the destruction visited by armies marching across the land. Too, Southern armies, particularly the large ones commanded by Lee, the Johnstons, etc., did not practice a policy of total war against Northern civilians as Federal armies often did in the South. Thus, even when Confederate incursions came, homes, businesses, and fields were generally left alone. A number of significant exceptions included the murder and destruction by William Quantrill and other Confederate irregulars in Kansas and Missouri; the rampaging outlawry of Morgan's raiders in Kentucky and Ohio; and the burning of much of Chambersburg, Pennsylvania in 1864.

The North also had no blockade of its ports with which to contend; thus, foreign products continued largely uninterrupted throughout the War. And though the loss of Southern cotton initially hurt Northern industry, the section had already established a thriving industrial and manufacturing society. The War not only helped the North's woolen, flax, and hemp industries as they were substituted for Southern cotton, it spurred the United States to convert many peacetime industries to the very profitable production of war materiel. Even Northern farms maintained strong output, despite enormous numbers of farmers going to war. In general, the North never experienced the dramatic shortage of food, medicine, and other basic life-sustaining products that the South did.

Many Fates

At least 14,000 Northerners suffered imprisonment and many thousands of others endured other bad treatment from the U.S. government due to their varying levels of dissatisfaction with the Federal prosecution of the War, or the fact the North was even fighting the War. But most Northerners put forth whatever effort was asked of them to preserve the full Federal Union. One Boston family lost five soldier sons to the War. Clara Barton and others established unprecedented philanthropic opportunities for the Northern people, and organizations such as the United States Christian Commission and the United States Sanitary Commission gave huge amounts of money, time, and effort to improve the lot of Federal soldiers.

Most Northerners put forth whatever effort was asked of them to preserve the full Federal Union. One Boston family lost five soldier sons to the War.

Matthew Brady set new milestones in photography; medical advances leapt forward due to the exigencies of treating colossal numbers of sick and wounded soldiers; thousands of individuals knitted socks and other items for soldiers and volunteered in the often-times overflowing hospitals. Meanwhile, Northerners patented inventions on all fronts. In some cases, opportunities for blacks in the North increased, and their lot improved. In others, it worsened, as resentful whites discriminated against them, or worse. Some states, such as Ohio, passed laws forbidding blacks even to enter their state. Unlike in the South, no historic revival of Christianity swept the North or its armies. It became wedded to a more powerful and centralized system of government than before the War. This government, working in concert with the Northern industrial and commercial sectors, which both increasingly boomed the longer the War lasted, prepared the way for the great westward expansion across the continent that unfolded following the War. It also prepared the way for the vast post-war expansion of industry by the captains of industry, the so-called "Robber Barons," such as John D. Rockefeller, Cornelius Vanderbilt, and John Pierpont Morgan.

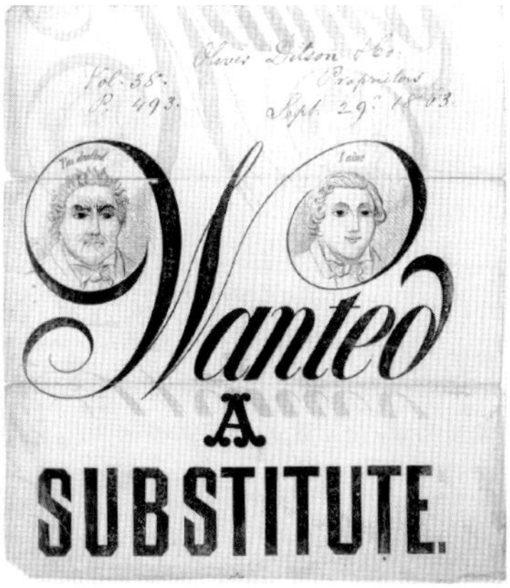

"Wanted—a Substitute," an illustrated sheet music cover that ridiculed the unfairness of the Federals' 1863 Enrollment Act, which allowed men to evade the war draft by paying $300. Poorer men could not do so. Rich men North and South purchased their way out of the sections' conscription drafts, though Federal leaders complained that most wealthy Southern men—from which came many capable battlefield leaders—chose to fight, while a much higher percentage of wealthy Northerners (and potential leaders) paid the $300. (Library of Congress)

New York City Draft Riots

The worst domestic riot in American history did not occur in the 20th century. It exploded at the zenith of America's worst war. Ironically, it broke out only a week after the North's two greatest victories of the War—Gettysburg and Vicksburg—in July, 1863. It raged for four days and involved thousands of people. The New York City conflict proved the worst of a series of other riots, all protesting the perceived unfair application of the Congressional Conscription Act, passed in March. Other incidents, possessing varying degrees of violence, swept Northeastern cities like Boston, Newark, Albany, and Troy; Columbia and Bucks counties in Pennsylvania; and nearly every state farther west, including Kentucky, Wisconsin, Illinois, and Ohio.

The worst domestic riot in American history broke out only a week after the North's two greatest victories of the War—Gettysburg and Vicksburg—in July, 1863.

The New York City causes were many, but centered on two themes: race and politics. A Pennsylvania newspaper's headline of "Willing to Fight for Uncle Sam, but Not Uncle Sambo" summarized the thoughts of thousands of New York City rioters. Largely working-class Irish, they had not liked Lincoln's freeing of the Southern slaves. They certainly did not like the idea of being conscripted, or forced, to fight to keep them free. And the thought that some of those blacks they were forced to go fight for would then compete with them for jobs—helping drive their wages down or even taking their jobs from them—and vote against them, drove many whites to violence. Indeed, blacks had already been employed in New York City to replace striking Irish longshoremen.

Politics played a large role in the onset of the riots as well. As a whole, New York City was at that time a Democratic city. From top to bottom, from governor and mayor to common laborer, a seething resentment roiled against Lincoln and the Republicans. The natural rivalry of politics played a role in this, but so did a host of other issues. These working-class New Yorkers fumed as they witnessed wealthy men, many of them Republicans, purchase their way out of the draft; higher proportions of Democrats than Republicans conscripted; and out-of-state Republican soldiers' votes counted in elections that threatened the Democrats' Tammany Hall New York City political machine.

Days of Horror

On July 13, a vengeful mob wrecked the draft office at 3rd Avenue and 46th Street, then burned it to the ground. They stormed their way to an armory, where they cleaned out over 1,000 rifles. And they commenced upon a frenzy of smashing, looting, and burning. Within a day, the New York City police force was overwhelmed and the draft protesters had control of America's largest city. All the while, portions of the mob chased "isolated Negroes as hounds would chase a fox," hanging many of them once caught. They also torched a black orphanage. White abolitionist Mattie Griffith left a heartbreaking eyewitness account of the slaughter of the city's blacks, a portion of which recalled that "a child of 3 years of age was thrown from a 4th story window and instantly killed. A woman one hour after her confinement was set upon and beaten with her tender babe in her arms. . . . Children were torn from their mother's embrace and their brains blown out in the very face of the afflicted mother. Men were burnt by slow fires."

For three days the rampage—comprised mostly of women and children according to *Harper's Weekly* newspaper—continued. On the fourth day, Lincoln and Stanton had thousands of troops in the city, "fresh" off their victory at Gettysburg. But the rioters did not go down without a fight. They literally shot it out in the streets and from house to house with the Federal soldiers. One eyewitness recounted that

> *there was some terrific fighting between the regulars and the insurgents; streets were swept again and again by grape, houses were stormed at the point of the bayonet, rioters were picked off by sharpshooters as they fired on the troops from housetops; men were hurled, dying or dead, into the streets by the thoroughly enraged soldiery . . .*

The epic tragedy escalated as Federal rifles and cannon mowed down men, women, and children alike. Casualty estimates for the four-day episode ranged from 74 to several hundred. But the draft remained in place, "even if there should be a riot and mob in every ward of every city," said Stanton.

Paddy's Lament (Traditional song of Irish immigrants)

*Well it's by the hush, me boys, and sure that's to hold your noise
And listen to poor Paddy's sad narration
I was by hunger stressed, and in poverty distressed
So I took a thought I'd leave the Irish nation*

*Well I sold me ass and cow, my little pigs and sow
My little plot of land I soon did part with
And me sweetheart Bid McGee, I'm afraid I'll never see
For I left her there that morning broken-hearted*

*Here's you boys, now take my advice
To America I'll have ye's not be going
There is nothing here but war, where the murderin' cannons roar
And I wish I was at home in dear old Dublin*

*Well myself and a hundred more, to America sailed o'er
Our fortunes to be making we were thinkin'
When we got to Yankee land, they put guns into our hands
"Paddy, you must go and fight for Lincoln"*

*Here's you boys, now take my advice
To America I'll have ye's not be going
There is nothing here but war, where the murderin' cannons roar
And I wish I was at home in dear old Dublin*

*General Meagher to us he said, if you get shot or lose your head
Every murdered soul of youse will get a pension
Well in the war lost me leg, they gave me a wooden peg
And by soul it is the truth to you I mention*

*Here's you boys, now take my advice
To America I'll have ye's not be going
There is nothing here but war, where the murderin' cannons roar
And I wish I was at home in dear old Dublin*

*Well I think myself in luck, if I get fed on Indianbuck
And old Ireland is the country I delight in
To the devil, I would say, it's curse Americay
For the truth I've had enough of your hard fightin*

*Here's you boys, now take my advice
To America I'll have ye's not be going
There is nothing here but war, where the murderin' cannons roar
And I wish I was at home in dear old Dublin
I wish I was at home
I wish I was at home
I wish I was at home
I wish I was at home in dear old Dublin*

"The Riots at New York," *Harper's Weekly's* (www.harpweek.com) chilling montage of scenes from the worst domestic riot in American history, July, 1863, in New York City. Thousands of residents, fed up with what they called "Lincoln's War," the draft for it, the perceived inequities of the draft, the deaths and maimings of their loved ones, and the threat to their jobs from some of the very blacks the Emancipation Proclamation determined they were now fighting to free, rose up in armed rebellion against the Federal government. Hundreds of people died.

RUINS OF THE PROVOST-MARSHAL'S OFFICE

FIGHT BETWEEN RIOTERS AND MILITARY

CHARGE OF THE POLICE ON THE RIOTERS AT THE "TRIBUNE" OFFICE

SACKING A DRUG STORE IN SECOND AVENUE

HANGING A NEGRO IN CLARKSON STREET

The Southern Home Front

Stonewall Jackson once said, before the conflict of 1861–65, that "war is the sum of all evils." With evil begetting evil on a colossal scale, the tragic result for the South was that as the horrors of war multiplied on the battlefield, so did they on the home front.

Because of the Federal naval blockade of Southern ports, the Confederacy's dearth of manufacturing and industry, and the ravages of a war fought in the Southland itself, even the most basic of commodities were precious, if not nonexistent, for most of the War. Not only were "luxuries" such as any kind of medicine at all impossible for Southerners to obtain, so were coffee, sugar, baking soda, paper, ink, and spices. By 1865, bacon cost $20 per pound, butter $25 per pound, and flour $1,200 per barrel. To approximate a 2005 equivalent for these prices, one should multiply by a factor of 100 or more. When night came, it was time for bed; not only did nothing remain with which to fuel lamps or candles, no firewood could be found near towns or cities. Thus, those Southern homes which still stood and remained occupied were cold as well as dark through much of the year when night arrived. Of course, thousands of homes in all corners of the South no longer existed at all, fired by a variety of Federal armies.

Shinplaster

Paper money circulated in the South; similar in appearance to little squares of paper soaked in and colored by tobacco juice or vinegar and applied to an ailing leg.

A five dollar Confederate shinplaster.

This shinplaster was Northern-issued as an emergency measure in Minnesota in 1862.

By the end of 1861, the Confederate government had placed over $100 million worth of paper notes in circulation. Historian James I. Robertson well describes the consequences of this flood of unsupported currency: "Soon the entire South was half-buried under a cascade of paper money issued by states, cities, businesses, banks, and anyone else with an engraver and a printing press." Within a year, Confederate scrip was worth only one-third its original value. By 1865, it took 70 Confederate dollars, now called "shinplasters", to purchase one gold dollar, which were by then as rare as a happy Southern face. Just about everybody but the Confederate government printed shinplasters, including railroads, businesses, cities, and states.

Few Southerners of any age did not live at least a portion of the War in fear of imminent attack, pillage, plunder, arson, and perhaps worse on themselves and their homes by the marauding Federal invaders. War and the evils attendant to it brought other tragedies to the besieged South as well. Even early in the conflict, one Richmond newspaper portrayed the erstwhile genial capital city as "full of the vilest licentiousness. Among all loathsome vices imported, gambling [is] so prominent and brazen as to defy public decency as well as law." Thousands of opportunists, adventurers, and swindlers of all shades descended on Richmond and the other major Southern cities from around the continent and even other continents, intent on profiting at the expense of others. Virginia Governor John Letcher announced to the Virginia General Assembly that, "A reckless spirit of money making seems to have taken possession of the public mind. Avarice has become a ruling passion. . . . patriotism is second to love of money."

Many women and children in the South lost their homes and were forced out onto the open road as refugees. Roles changed for even those who kept their homes. Many, particularly in the larger cities like Richmond, had to give up part, most, or all of their dwellings to rent-paying boarders in order to subsist. Many women and some children began to work outside the home in war-related industries, mills, and plants. Thousands of Southern women who owned farms or plantations had few if any men remaining on their land. They had to learn how to run their spreads and often work them side-by-side with slaves, family members, or other workers. Sadly, some poverty-stricken females fell into ill repute, as an abundance of cash-flush customers inhabited the larger cities.

Southern Blacks

Fortunately, the slaves and other blacks who worked on Southern lands committed scarcely a single outrage or crime during the War. Thousands of them left when Federal troops approached; other thousands were "impressed"—forced at gunpoint—by the Federals to join the U.S. Army and thousands left, then later returned to their homes, of their own volition. Famed black educator and wartime slave Booker T. Washington described the feelings of most, however: "To defend and protect the women and children who were left on the plantation when the white males went to war, the slaves would have laid down their lives." Indeed, when a white family was left homeless, hungry, or broke, those blacks dependent on them suffered as well.

Not everyone in the South, however, suffered. A minority of the upper caste, mainly in Richmond and the larger cities, fared quite nicely, some of them even prospering as they exploited financial opportunities presented by the War—sometimes in concert with Northerners of similar ilk.

Withal, how hard Southern pride and defiance was to kill is witnessed by these words of Margaret Junkin Preston, Stonewall Jackson's sister-in-law and the famed, Pennsylvania-born "Poetess of the Confederacy": "The people of Richmond have purposed that if the city cannot be successfully defended, it should only be yielded to the enemy as a barren heap of rubbish, at once the sepulchre and glorious monument of its defenders. . . . Most of us [in Lexington, Virginia] have determined in a like manner not to abandon our hearths and homes even if the Federals burn them down over our heads." Her words proved eerily prophetic.

West Virginia

More than just the Appalachian and Allegheny Mountains had long separated eastern and western Virginia. So had culture, geography, and economics. Slavery was more predominant in the lowland-dominated east, and so was belief in the Constitutionality of secession. As the years passed, relations between the sections worsened. When President Lincoln ordered Virginia to muster thousands of men to help him invade the Deep South, the state's governor and legislator, though mostly loyal Unionists, said no and led the state out of the old Union. However, the 48 Virginia counties west of the mountains, representing nearly 40% of the state's land mass, said yes.

Black Virginian laborers on a James River wharf. (TreasureNet)

Richmond Bread Riot

By Holy Week in April, finding sufficient food to eat was an ongoing problem for many residents across the South. A meeting of women in Richmond protesting the rising cost and decreasing availability of food began at Oregon Hill Baptist Church. Moving toward the governor's mansion, it grew to several hundred people. They petitioned Governor Letcher for food. His promise to comply by afternoon did not satisfy them, and they moved, their ranks still swelling, to the government commissary, where they took bread and other foods. Two women stood most conspicuous in leadership of the protesters. First was Mary Jackson, of fierce countenance and threatening words. As the crowd moved along, six-foot-tall Minerva Meredith, a butcher's assistant brandishing a Navy Colts pistol and a Bowie knife, joined Mrs. Jackson in the lead.

Was the Richmond "Bread Riot" as it came to be known comprised merely of emaciated mothers concerned for the fate of their hungry children, or were more sinister forces at work?

Next they headed for the downtown stores. Somewhere along the way, perhaps from the beginning, "men of the worst character" increased the ranks of the group; by the time it reached the stores and shops, it had become a mob, shattering store windows, smashing down doors, and taking for themselves much more than food, including jewelry, clothing, tools, and household items. Firemen hosed them down, Mayor Joseph Mayo read a warning to them, the Public Guard militia arrived, and the governor gave them five minutes to disperse or be fired upon. Still they stood massed and defiant.

Just as it seemed nothing would stop them and property destruction and theft would breed blood flowing in the streets, President Davis climbed atop a wagon on the street, faced the crowd, and spoke. "You say you are hungry and have no money. Here is all I have. It is not much, but take it." Then he cleaned his pockets of money and tossed it to the crowd. "We do not desire to injure anyone," he continued, "but this lawlessness must stop. I will give you five minutes to disperse. Otherwise you will be fired on." Then he pulled out his pocket watch, but this he did not offer to the crowd. Rather, he stared at it as the seconds passed, glancing at the assembled—and armed—militia as he did. To the President's everlasting relief, the crowd did indeed break up, slowly at first, then with great haste as the five minutes elapsed. They knew that Jefferson Davis, whatever his faults, was a man true to his word once he gave it.

The hungry and the angry during the Richmond Bread Riot.

Rowdy Class

Was the Richmond "Bread Riot" as it came to be known comprised merely of emaciated mothers concerned for the fate of their hungry children, or were more sinister forces at work? Nearly half the forty-seven people arrested were men. Numerous eyewitness accounts recall "young men of the veriest rowdy class" being in the vanguard of the mob as it grew more lawless and vandalous. Mary Jackson herself was roundly portrayed, in print and out, as a veteran "huckster" and "profiteer." According to the *Richmond Examiner* newspaper, the protesters were "a handful of prostitutes, professional thieves, Irish and Yankee hags, gallows birds from all lands but our own . . . with a woman huckster at their head." Too, the mayor testified in court, even the poorest in the city should not have been hungry: "More money [for free food] has been appropriated than has been applied for," he said. Indeed, the mob had robbed some stores of everything except their food, and much of the rice and flour dispensed to the surging Maundy Thursday crowd at the Young Men's Christian Association was flung to the floor and left.

Still, the rampage proved not an isolated phenomenon. Similar, though smaller and less violent episodes occurred in Atlanta and other towns in Georgia, North Carolina, Alabama, and Virginia. Insightful observers recognized in them not just hungry women and children, mischief makers, and plunderers, but something of singular ominousness—the despair and hopelessness berthed by war weariness. If such a spirit took hold, then spread, the Confederacy could not win its independence, no matter how many victories its armies won in the field. Davis did his best to respond, with a speech that was both inspiring and challenging to his people. And he exhorted small and large landowners alike "to devote their fields exclusively to the planting of corn, oats, beans, peas, potatoes, and other food for man and beast," as opposed to cash crops like cotton and tobacco. At the end of the War, the United States government would have to deliver millions of rations to fire-gutted Richmond to prevent the starvation of thousands of its people.

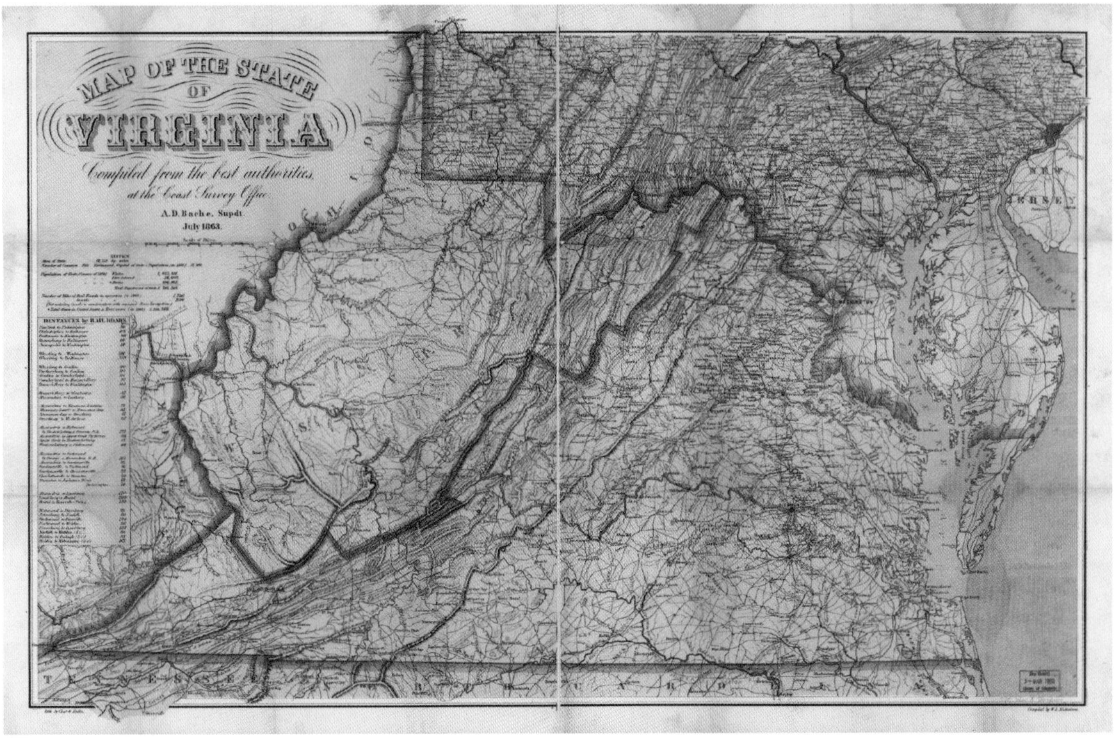

Map of Virginia and West Virginia

Their legislative representatives held their own meeting in Wheeling, at the extreme Northwest tip of the Old Dominion. Claiming the mantle of the loyal legislature of Virginia, they voted themselves permission to separate from their eastern neighbors and form a separate state. To succeed, they had to fight a dreary campaign in the fall of 1861 to rid the area of Confederate military presence. With a larger and better organized force led by George McClellan, they succeeded in defeating Southern forces that included Robert E. Lee in an advisory, though not command, role.

By late 1862, they had drawn up their own constitution, elected their own governor, and applied for admission to the United States as the new state of West Virginia. Lincoln cheered the receipt of more manpower and resources, as well as the securing of a key land mass whose loss would have devastated east-west Federal transportation routes and nearly severed the remaining United States in half. West Virginia entered the Northern Union in June. The new state supplied 32,000 soldiers to the Federal armies. But 8,000 others fought for the Confederacy. Several prominent Confederates hailed from West Virginia, including Stonewall Jackson and Belle Boyd.

21 Gettysburg
(1863)

Williamsport Crossing, by John Paul Strain. General Robert E. Lee leads the Army of Northern Virginia across the Potomac into Maryland and the fateful Gettysburg Campaign.

I cannot hope that Heaven will prosper our cause when we are violating its laws. I shall, therefore, carry on the war in Pennsylvania without offending the sanctions of a high civilization and of Christianity.

—Robert E. Lee, when urged to seek revenge on the Gettysburg campaign for Federal atrocities against Southern civilians.

Lee decided he must carry the fight back North. The Shenandoah Valley, "Breadbasket of the Confederacy," and other rich farming sectors faced imminent and continued threat to their harvests as long as so huge a Federal force remained in Virginia. For the main United States army had sustained another defeat without being destroyed. The Virginian sought to shift the battleground to the fields of the North, both to allow Southern farmers to bring in their crops and so that he could feed his army off the Northern countryside. He also saw this as the best way to prevent Hooker falling upon Richmond with such force that Lee must intervene to stop him. That scenario would preclude the one sequence of events Lee believed could still bring the South independence—a Confederate invasion of the North, decisive battle victory, and threat to Washington.

So disgusted was Lincoln by the Chancellorsville debacle that he pressured Hooker into quitting even as the Confederates marched north into Maryland. He replaced him with George Meade, a solid but unspectacular career officer. The graybacks kept right on marching until they were well into southern Pennsylvania. The two forces crashed together July 1 at the small seminary and college town of Gettysburg. For three days the titanic struggle roiled. The first day, the Confederates swept the Federals out of the town and up into nearby hills, inflicting 5,000 casualties and taking 5,000 prisoners. The next two days, Lee sent his men on a series of epic

Our Southern homes have been pillaged, sacked, and burned; our mothers, wives, and little ones, driven forth amid the brutal insults of your soldiers. Is it any wonder that we fight with desperation? A natural revenge would prompt us to retaliate in kind, but we scorn to war on women and children. We are fighting for the God-given rights of liberty and independence, as handed down to us in the Constitution by our fathers. So fear not: if a torch is applied to a single dwelling, or an insult offered to a female of your town by a soldier of this command, point me out the man, and you shall have his life.

—Confederate General John Gordon
to the panicked citizens of York, Pennsylvania.

uphill charges against the well-entrenched Federals. The Confederates took key ground, but heroic Northern resistance prevented them from capturing the key heights of Culp's Hill, Cemetery Ridge, and Little Round Top from which Lee planned to roll up the entire Federal army. After more than fifty thousand casualties, and following "Pickett's Charge," both armies desisted late in the afternoon July 3. That night, Lee withdrew and marched home, again denied victory in the North. Because of the sheer scale of casualties this time, however, and the continued dwindling of Confederate resources on all fronts, the Army of Northern Virginia—and hence the Confederacy—would never again possess the power to strike a war-winning blow against the Union.

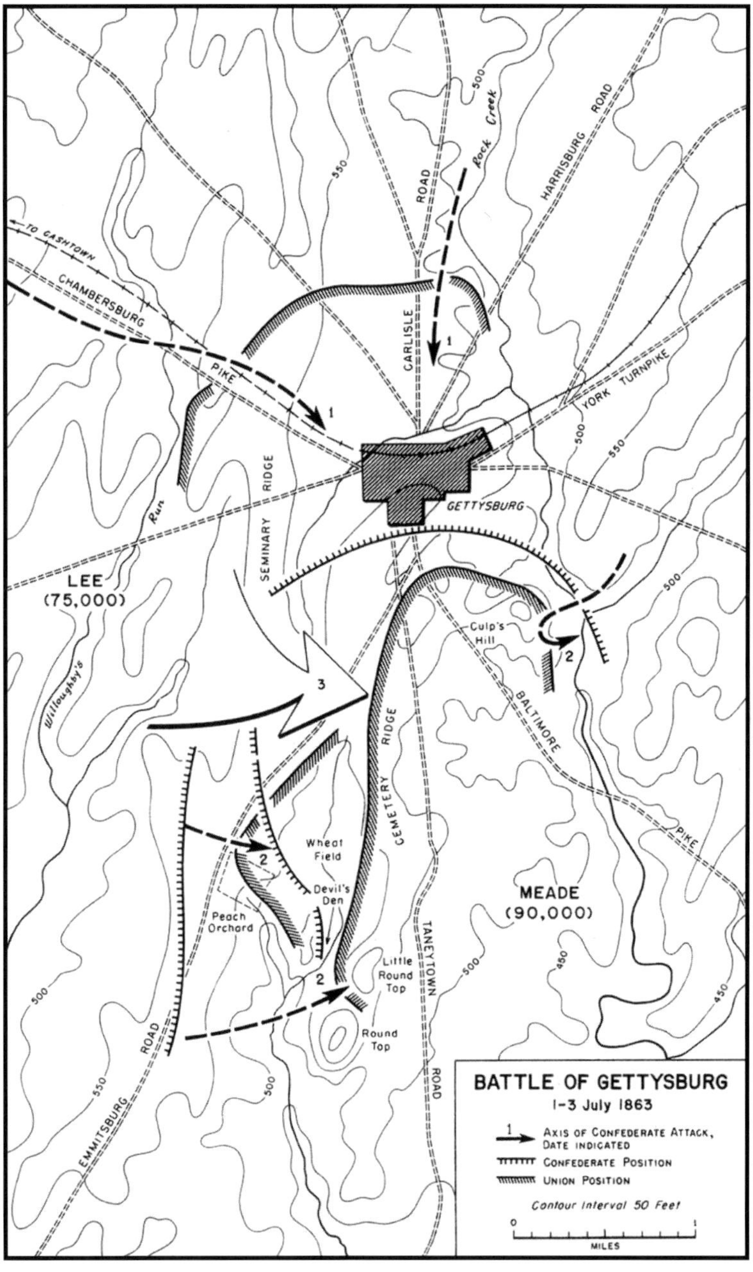

George Meade (1815–1872)

Melancholy, irascible, and honorable, George Meade was born in Spain where his father worked for the U.S. government. He attended schools in Philadelphia and Washington. A year after graduating West Point, Meade began a several-years' stint as a civil engineer. He returned to the army in 1842 as a surveyor in the Corps of Topographical Engineers. He worked there until the War, except for a distinguished tour of duty, including combat, as an officer in the Mexican War. His engineering tasks took him to such places as Delaware Bay, the coast of Florida, and the Great Lakes.

Beginning the War in command of a brigade of Pennsylvania volunteers, Meade rose steadily up the command ladder. Though present at some major Federal defeats in the eastern theater, he handled those portions of the army under his direct command well. After "Fighting Joe" Hooker led the Federals to another defeat at Chancellorsville in May, 1863, then appeared reluctant to continue the fight with Lee, Lincoln looked again for a commander of his main army who would prove aggressive and victorious. He selected Meade. The promotion came at a suspense-racked juncture for the North. On the heels of his smashing victory at Chancellorsville, Lee was moving north into United States territory. Lincoln feared a move on Washington. He ordered Meade to stop the Confederates with an Army of the Potomac that had been beaten time and again by its smaller Southern foe.

Just five days after assuming command, Meade found himself in the bloodiest battle in American history—the three day fight at Gettysburg. Lee and his Army of Northern Virginia possessed unsurpassed confidence in their ability to lick any Federal opponent that came against them. And now they were not only in Maryland, as they had been the year before during the Sharpsburg campaign—they were all the way north, in force, in Pennsylvania.

Gettysburg

But Meade had kept his composure on the pursuit north, and he kept it once the two armies clashed at Gettysburg, even after the Confederates nearly won the battle the first day. He deployed his men along the high ground south of the town hours before the stampeding Confederates could. This—along with Southern command miscues and raw courage on the part of the Federal defenders—provided the balance of victory. In the War's most famous battle, Meade's Federals managed to hold most of the high ground and from that advantage withstand repeated and savage Confederate charges.

In the War's most famous battle, Meade's Federals managed to hold most of the high ground and from that advantage withstand repeated and savage Confederate charges.

Meade won the battle, but he lost more than one quarter of his entire army killed or wounded. And even though he earned a Congressional citation and promotion for his accomplishment, he drew Lincoln's fury for allowing Lee and the Confederates to escape safely back into Virginia. He never really regained the President's confidence, and a few months later Lincoln promoted the aggressive and spectacularly successful U. S. Grant past him to command all Federal armies. Grant would later call Meade "an officer of great merit, with drawbacks to his usefulness that were beyond his control. . . . no one saw this better than himself, and no one regretted it more." Still, he had experience, maturity, and a fine record. Though Grant decided to make his headquarters with the Army of the Potomac and effectively plan its strategy, both he and Lincoln thought enough of Meade to reject his proffered resignation and beseech him to remain in official command of his army. The combination proved good enough to wear down Lee's army and win the War, and to do so without noticeable rancor from Meade.

He held a succession of commands following the War in both the North and the Reconstruction South. Meade resigned one post when Philip Sheridan—with whom he had clashed during the War—gained promotion to lieutenant general and he did not. George Meade was the Army of the Potomac's most successful commander. And his name carries the immortal fame of having beaten Robert E. Lee in the War's greatest battle.

George Pickett and Pickett's Charge (1825–1875)

That the War holds enduring fascination for so many must at least partly stem from flawed, gallant warriors like Virginian George Pickett, concerning whom the lines dividing myth and man, legend and fact, have grown blurry with the years. "Dandified in his dress, he was the most romantic-looking of all Confederates, the physical image of that gallantry implicit in the South's self-concept," wrote respected historian Clifford Dowdey. He finished dead last in the West Point graduating class that included Thomas Jackson and George McClellan. Pickett's uncle had a flourishing law practice. One of his associates had helped secure the boy's appointment. That associate hailed from Illinois, and his name was Abraham Lincoln. He and George Pickett became close friends.

Pickett gained early renown in the Mexican War by being the first man over the wall at the pivotal battle of Chapultepec. There, as his friend James Longstreet watched, Pickett planted the American flag outside "the halls of Montezuma." He served mostly on the western frontier until the War. At Gaines' Mill during the June, 1862, Seven Days Campaign, he took a serious wound—whereupon his brigade went forward in the charge that won the slaughter.

The nearly forty-year-old widower—with flowing mustache and luxuriant auburn hair that fell onto his shoulders in perfumed ringlets—loved Sallie Corbett, a teenager who had loved him since she was a little girl and who called him "My Soldier." When he made major general, it was Sallie who embroidered the two stars in a wreath for his collar. By the time the Gettysburg campaign opened, he had recovered from his wound and commanded a division of five front-line brigades, 9,000 crack troops, in the First Corps of his old friend

Longstreet, who considered him virtually a little brother. But, over Lee's objections, President Davis snatched Pickett's two best and largest brigades before the Confederates headed toward Pennsylvania, to use for defending the Richmond area.

Cemetary Ridge

Pickett neither planned nor ordered the earth-shaking attack that climaxed the Battle of Gettysburg and turned the fortunes of War forever toward the North. His own troops comprised less than half the assault force. But it is his name forever emblazoned across the stupendous brave folly that was and will always be "Pickett's Charge." After nearly three days of sanguinary spectacle, Longstreet placed Pickett in command of the 12,000 soldiers Lee ordered to march up the gentle, mile-long incline to the stand of trees in the center of Cemetery Ridge. They were to cave in the center of the massive Federal line, entrenched atop the sprawling high ground just south of Gettysburg. It was the crescendo of the War's mightiest and bloodiest battle and most of the Army of the Potomac was waiting for Pickett's (and A. P. Hill's) doomed brigades.

The Southerners marched step by step into a roil-

Taking Battery A—Confederate General Lewis Armistead and his men during Pickett's Charge at Gettysburg, by John Paul Strain. How near the balances of fortune swung to the Confederates on that historic day is evidenced by this dramatic scene, where the front rank of Southerners, led by Armistead, actually rolled over the forward Federal skirmishers and their first row of artillery and riflemen, before being overwhelmed by numbers and driven back. Armistead fell mortally wounded beside a temporarily captured Yankee cannon.

ing inferno of shot, shell, bullets, and, at the end, double-packed canister. Thousands fell or disappeared in bloody pink mists. But they did not stop and they did not blink, and they crushed the first Federal line and headed for the next. A couple hundred Confederates actually cleared the final stone wall and reached the assigned tree, then fought hand-to-hand with wave upon wave of Federals until they were annihilated by weight of numbers, perishing amidst heaps and piles of bluecoated bodies. In one hour, nearly half the attacking force was destroyed, a casualty ratio virtually unprecedented in a large-scale action. Lee ordered Pickett to ready his division to parry a Federal counterattack. "I have no division," Pickett famously sobbed. "Come, General Pickett," said Lee gently, "this has been my fight, and upon my shoulders rests the blame. The men and officers of your command have written the name of Virginia as high today as it has ever been written before."

It was the crescendo of the War's mightiest and bloodiest battle and most of the Army of the Potomac was waiting for Pickett's [and A. P. Hill's] doomed brigades.

He was never the same man after Cemetery Ridge, grieving the rest of his life for the thousands who fell that day under his command, and for that George Pickett can be accounted a compassionate—and broken—heart. His later record was tarnished by the embarrassment of being absent while the Federals engulfed his men at Five Forks just prior to the fall of Richmond. When the Federals overran the remnant of his command just before Appomattox, he did not know that Lee had already ordered him relieved of command. Unlike his comrades Longstreet and John Mosby, Pickett, who needed the help more than most of them, rebuffed a substantial postwar position (Federal marshal of Virginia) offered him by President Grant, and even a generalship from the Khedive of Egypt. Years after the War, Pickett and Confederate ranger commander Mosby met with Lee. Relations between Mosby and the two men were fine. Such was not the case with Lee and Pickett. Their fellowship was short and cold. "That old man," Pickett scowled to Mosby after they left Lee, "he had my division massacred at Gettysburg." "Well, it made you immortal," Mosby correctly pointed out.

Lorena (Author unknown)

The years creep slowly by, Lorena;
The snow is on the grass again;
The sun's low down the sky, Lorena;
The frost gleams where the flowers have been.
But the heart throbs on as warmly now
As when the summer days were nigh;
Oh! the sun can never dip so low
Adown affection's cloudless sky.

We loved each other then, Lorena,
More than we ever dared to tell;
And what we might have been, Lorena,
Had but our loving prospered well—
But then 'tis past, the years are gone,
I'll not call up their shadowy forms;
I'll say to them, "Lost years, sleep on!
Sleep on! nor heed life's pelting storms."

It matters little now, Lorena,
The past is in the eternal Past;
Our heads will soon lie low, Lorena,
Life's tide is ebbing out so fast.
There is a future! O thank God!
Life, this is so small a part!
'Tis dust to dust beneath the sod;
But there, up there, 'tis heart to heart.

Joshua Chamberlain and Little Round Top (1828–1914)

Lifelong Maine native Joshua Chamberlain represented the living embodiment of the Northern soldier that, tenacious and enduring as his Southern counterpart, simply would not quit unless he was killed or until he had seen his nation through to victory. A scholar and professor at Bowdoin College before the War, Chamberlain taught rhetoric, oratory, and modern languages. Once the fighting started, his superiors refused to allow him a leave of absence for military service, so in 1862 he feigned departure for a teaching sabbatical and instead enlisted in the Federal army.

He began as a lieutenant colonel in the 20th Maine regiment, eschewing the opportunity to enter at a higher rank. Before the War ended, he would suffer six wounds and a lengthy ordeal of malaria. He was hit by fire at Sharpsburg in September, 1862, Fredericksburg in December, 1862, and

Just as the order went through the Southern ranks to retreat, the erstwhile college professor ordered his men to fix bayonets, then led them roaring over the breastworks and down the hill after the Confederates.

Breastworks at Little Round Top

Chancelorsville in May, 1863. He distinguished himself in the latter battle amidst one of the worst Federal defeats of the War. But it was on the second day of the Battle of Gettysburg that he earned everlasting fame. After the Confederates had captured nearby Big Round Top and knocked three consecutive Federal units off the top of Little Round Top, the hill that shielded the Federal left flank, Chamberlain and the trappers, lumberjacks, and seamen of the 20th Maine dug themselves in atop the rocky, wooded grade. Then five Confederate regiments charged screaming up the hill, straight into the face of everything the eight regiments of Yankees could throw at them. Again and again they came. After five charges, Southern dead carpeted the bloody ascent. Chamberlain and the Federals, though battered and exhausted, remained ensconced on Little Round Top. Just as the order went through the Southern ranks to retreat, the erstwhile college professor ordered his men to fix bayonets, then led them roaring over the breastworks and down the hill after the Confederates. The Federals routed them and preserved the all-important position at the southern terminus of the chain of Federally-held hills stretching south of Gettysburg.

Chamberlain, wounded again at Little Round Top, won the Congressional Medal of Honor for his exploits that day. Then he nearly died from an extended bout with malaria, was shot again at Petersburg in May, 1864—which time the doctors expected he would surely die—and was wounded again at Five Forks at the end of March, 1865. Grant named Joshua Chamberlain, now a major general, to accept the formal surrender of the Army of Northern Virginia at Appomattox. "On our part not a sound of trumpet more, nor roll of drum," he wrote of the deathless event. "Not a cheer, nor word nor whisper . . . nor motion . . . but an awed stillness rather, and breath-holding, as if it were the passing of the dead." As he watched the tattered Confederate remnant pass and remembered the awful scenes, where he and his comrades had faced them, he thought, "How could we help falling on our knees, all of us together, and praying God to pity and forgive us all!"

Chamberlain eschewed the prevailing Federal policy of total war. After Grant required him to torch the homes of Southern women and children during the Petersburg campaign, he wrote his sister: "I am willing to fight men in arms, but not babes in arms." Following the War, the people of Maine elected him governor four times. He also served as president of Bowdoin College.

John Paul Strain's depiction of Joshua Chamberlain and the 20th Maine Regiment defending Little Round Top on the second day of the Battle of Gettysburg. Shortly after, Chamberlain led the counterattack that helped win him the Congressional Medal of Honor.

The Lee–Longstreet Controversy

Lee led the Army of Northern Virginia north in its Gettysburg campaign hard on the heels of Stonewall Jackson's death. The litany of crucial mistakes committed by the Jacksonless Confederates on this epic march are by now nearly proverbial. Miscommunication with cavalry commander Jeb Stuart deprived Lee of important scouting information as he moved north. General Richard Ewell, a new corps commander, failed to grasp Lee's directive to follow up the Confederates' first day victory and overrun the high ground south of Gettysburg, which gave the Federals time to reinforce there. A. P. Hill was also an inexperienced rookie corps commander. He was seriously ill as well and barely able to command his troops. Lee himself was ill, beset and weakened by diarrhea during the worst of the second-day fighting, and possibly the victim of a mild heart attack on the third and final day. He lacked the crisp confidence he possessed two months previous at Chancellorsville—possibly because he lacked Jackson, and he witnessed his current three corps commanders commit a series of un-Jackson-like blunders. Then too, Federal commanders like Winfield Hancock, Governour Warren, Joshua Chamberlain, George

Morning of the Third Day, by John Paul Strain. General Robert E. Lee, accompanied by his most experienced corps commander, James Longstreet, inspects the Confederate lines early on the morning of the climactic third day of the Battle of Gettysburg.

Custer, and Army of the Potomac chief George Meade provided inspired leadership for their men, who put up a tenacious defense against some of the most ferocious assaults of the entire War.

But perhaps the central Southern folly of the campaign was James Longstreet's failure to launch his corps' attack in a timely fashion on the second day of battle, July 2. Longstreet arrived at Gettysburg the previous afternoon. He had already received a field communiqué from Lee that he "intended to fight the next day, if the enemy was there." Yet Longstreet urged Lee to maneuver around the Federals into open country between them and Washington City, seventy-five miles to the south-southeast. This, Longstreet said, would force the Federals to attack to prevent the Confederates falling upon the capital. He envisioned a repeat of the slaughter of Fredericksburg half a year prior. Lee disagreed. He wanted to attack. That night, when Longstreet repeated his case, Lee told his subordinates, "Gentlemen, we will attack the enemy as early in the morning as practicable" and directed them all to make the necessary preparations for prompt action the next day. Longstreet would attack the Federal left.

But perhaps the central Southern folly of the campaign was James Longstreet's failure to launch his corps' attack in a timely fashion on the second day of battle, July 2.

Too Late

Early the next morning, Longstreet pressed his plan yet again, Lee yet again overriding him and finally walking away from his insubordinate lieutenant. All morning, Lee waited for the sound of Longstreet's guns to open the attack. When at 11 o'clock nothing had happened, Lee found Longstreet and gave him a direct order to attack. And the old warhorse did—five hours later. All day he fumed and pouted, as the Federals piled thousands more men onto the high ground south of Gettysburg.

When one of Longstreet's division commanders, John Bell Hood, begged him not to hurl Hood's Texans and Arkansans up steep hills now bristling with Federal soldiers and artillery, Longstreet thrice intoned, "General Lee's orders are to attack up the Emmitsburg Road." He said this knowing full well the Federal force was larger and better entrenched along Cemetery Ridge and the other high ground than it had been when Lee issued his order to attack, and knowing he, Longstreet, had the discretion to countermand the order in such a case. But attack Hood's men did. Withal, they still captured some hard-fought ground and very nearly carried the day on Little Round Top. Had Longstreet responded with alacrity to Lee's designs and launched his attack the morning of July 2 rather than late that afternoon, the doomed valor of Pickett's Charge the next day would perhaps have been unnecessary. As it was, it was very necessary and quite impossible.

After Gettysburg

Lincoln, pleased with the Gettysburg victory over an army that had taken on an aura of near-invincibility, was not pleased with what he considered Meade's lackluster pursuit of the retreating Confederates. Compounding the President's agitation was the rash of mob violence bursting out across the North in opposition to the compulsory military draft. The protesters

"A Harvest of Dead" at Gettysburg.

knew that oceans of Federal blood had been spilled, and still no end to it appeared forthcoming. He wrote to Meade in a letter he never sent:

> Again, my dear general, I do not believe you appreciate the magnitude of the misfortune involved in Lee's escape. He was within your easy grasp, and to have closed upon him would, in connection with our other late successes, have ended the war. As it is, the war will be prolonged indefinitely. . . . Your golden opportunity is gone, and I am distressed immeasurably because of it.

Lincoln did issue an eloquent public "Proclamation of Thanksgiving" to God for the Gettysburg victory.

The two armies returned to Virginia and settled into their familiar positions along the line of the Rappahannock and Rapidan rivers in central Virginia. With autumn, Lee lost yet more thousands of men. Davis called Longstreet with his entire corps, plus two divisions, to Tennessee to support Braxton Bragg in his western campaign. When Lee learned Meade had sent two of his own corps west to counteract Davis' move, the Virginian marched north again in an effort to circle around Meade's flank toward Washington. Lee wanted to draw the Federals away from Culpeper, a launching point for several attractive attack routes toward Richmond. So grievous were Confederate losses in the Gettysburg campaign—28,000 of 75,000 men, or nearly 40%—that Lee had had to reorganize his entire com-

Lincoln's Proclamation of Thanksgiving for the Victory at Gettysburg

In Lincoln's Proclamation of Thanksgiving, he urged the United States public to:

> *. . . render the homage due to the Divine Majesty, for the wonderful things He has done in the nation's behalf, and invoke the influence of His Holy Spirit to subdue the anger which has produced and so long sustained a needless and cruel rebellion, to change the hearts of the insurgents, to guide the counsels of the Government with wisdom adequate to so great a national emergency, and to visit with tender care and consolation throughout the length and breadth of our land all those who, through vicissitudes of marches, voyages, battles, and sieges, have been brought to suffer in mind, body, or estate, and finally to lead the whole nation, through the paths of repentance and submission to the Divine Will, back to the perfect enjoyment of Union and fraternal peace.*

The Gettysburg Address

Though Lincoln was not even the main speaker at the dedication of a cemetery on the site of the bloody Gettysburg battlefield, the tantalizingly short speech he gave on November 19, 1863, is a masterpiece of both penetrating rhetoric and moral politics. His words, though few, have proven immortal. Renowned American author and Lincoln biographer Carl Sandburg in 1946 hailed the address as one of the great American poems. "One may delve deeply into its unfolded meanings," Sandburg wrote,

> *but its poetic significance carries it far beyond the limits of a state paper. It curiously incarnates the claims, assurances, and pretenses of republican institutions, of democratic procedure, of the rule of the people. It is a timeless psalm in the name of those who fight and do in behalf of great human causes rather than talk, in a belief that men can "highly resolve" themselves, and can mutually "dedicate" their lives to a cause.*

Many opposed to Lincoln's prosecution of the War have admired the simple eloquence of this two-minute speech, yet questioned the veracity of its content. Was it "a new nation" America's founders birthed in 1776? (Or did that happen in 1789?) Did the Southern bid for independence constitute a "civil war"? Might secession cause the American federation created in 1789 not to "long endure"? Could "government of the people" "perish from the earth"? Among the more penetrating proponents of such questions was the *London Times*:

> *If Northerners . . . had peaceably allowed the seceders to depart, the result might fairly have been quoted as illustrating the advantages of Democracy, but when Republicans put empire above liberty, and resorted to political oppression and war . . . It was clear that nature at Washington was precisely the same as nature at St. Petersburg. . . . Democracy broke down . . . when it was upheld, like any other Empire, by force of arms.*

And famous American writer H. L. Mencken:

> *The doctrine is simply this: that the Union soldiers who died at Gettysburg sacrificed their*

Abraham Lincoln (center inset) at Gettysburg, prior to giving his famed speech.

lives to the cause of self-determination—that government of the people, by the people, for the people, should not perish from the earth. It is difficult to imagine anything more untrue. The Union soldiers in the battle actually fought against self-determination; it was the Confederates who fought for the right of their people to govern themselves.

The Speech

Following is the matchless text of the Gettysburg Address in its entirety:

Fourscore and seven years ago our fathers brought forth, on this continent, a new nation, conceived in liberty, and dedicated to the proposition that all men are created equal.

Now we are engaged in a a great civil war, testing whether that nation, or any nation so conceived, and so dedicated, can long endure. We are met on a great battlefield of that war. We have come to dedicate a portion of that field, as a final resting-place for those who here gave their lives, that that nation might live. It is altogether fitting and proper that we should do this.

But in a large sense, we can not dedicate—we can not consecrate—we can not hallow—this ground. The brave men, living and dead, who struggled here, have consecrated it far above our poor power to add or detract. The world will little note, nor long remember what we say here, but it can never forget what they did here. It is for us the living, rather, to be dedicated here to the unfinished work which they who fought here have thus far so nobly advanced. It is rather for us to be here dedicated to the great task remaining before us—that from these honored dead we take increased devotion to that cause for which they here gave the last full measure of devotion—that we here highly resolve that these dead shall not have died in vain—that this nation, under God, shall have a new birth of freedom—and that government of the people, by the people, for the people, shall not perish from the earth.

mand structure, down to regimental level. Plus he had neither Jackson nor Longstreet, his best two generals, with him. This told on October 14 when new corps commander A. P. Hill sent two brigades into a Federal ambush at Bristoe's Station. Fifteen hundred Confederates were the forfeit.

Blood and Religion

Meade had pulled prudently back toward Washington, keeping the capital covered but not exposing his own army. Once again, Lee's inability to supply his army forced him to turn away. The Federals forged ahead once more, but Lee laid in wait for them at Mine Run. There, his engineering prowess again evidenced itself as the Confederates constructed some of the best earthworks of the War. These, along with Southern artillery, the rough country, and the cold weather drove Meade back to Culpeper for the winter. Indeed, despite the slaughter at Bristoe's Station, Lee's campaign proved largely successful. The Confederates destroyed tons of Federal supplies, wrecked large sections of their railroad tracks, dealt them nearly 2,300 casualties, and finally forced their retreat.

General George Meade's Army of the Potomac headquarters near Culpeper, Virginia, in late 1863.

Back on the south banks of the Rappahannock and Rapidan, one of the greatest religious revivals in America burst into full bloom amidst the cold, underfed, homesick legions of the Army of Northern Virginia. Lee continued to spearhead the effort, which was birthed the year before amidst the work of Jackson, Dabney, and many others. He issued a proclamation to the entire army that read in part: "God is our only refuge and strength. Let us humble ourselves before him." One Confederate soldier later wrote his account of it: "The most ordinary preachers drew large congregations; scarcely a day passed without a sermon; there was not a night, but the sound of prayer and hymn-singing was heard."

Robert Gould Shaw and the 54th Massachusetts (1837-1863)

Scion of wealthy, aristocratic Boston abolitionists, Robert Gould Shaw's background hardly presaged what he would accomplish during the War and with whom he would accomplish it. He attended the elite Harvard College during the same period as other notables like Henry Adams (son of President John Quincy Adams and grandson of President John Adams) and Rooney Lee (son of Robert E. Lee). Despite his parents' sympathies, Shaw held no strong affinity for the abolitionists or their objectives. Nonetheless, already a captain and combat veteran, in 1863 he accepted Massachusetts Governor John Andrew's assignment to assemble and command his state's new 54th Regiment. Something set the 54th apart from all other Massachusetts regiments before it—only its officers would be white; blacks would fill the ranks of its enlisted men and noncommissioned officers.

Unlike in the brilliant (but brutal and unacceptable for young audiences) motion picture *Glory*, the great majority of Shaw's black troops were freeborn blacks he recruited from the North, rather than abused ex-slaves from the South. Still, the film well chronicles how little confidence nineteenth-century white

"Attack on Fort Wagner" by Robert Gould Shaw and the black 54th Massachusetts regiment. *(Harper's Weekly; www.harpweek.com)*

American society, including Shaw, possessed that blacks could succeed as combat soldiers, as well as how courageous and capable they proved to be. Governor Andrew also called on Frederick Douglass and other prominent black abolitionists to help draw the best possible men to the watershed regiment. Two of Douglass's sons enlisted.

Blacks in the United States army suffered sometimes-brutal mistreatment. The Federal government "freed" thousands of them, then forced them against their will to fight. They were given white officers and paid one-half the rate of whites. They were assigned guard duty, jobs, and risks which whites did not want or refused. Their death rate was astronomical. Of the 186,000 blacks who served in the Federal army, 68,000 died: around 2,000 in battle, over 65,000 from sickness and disease, often from duties served in place of whites.

Shaw took his command with reluctance, but when his mother watched him lead the grand farewell review of the now-trained 54th through the streets of Boston a few months later, she wept for joy and exclaimed, "What have I done, that God has been so good to me!" Her son's character evidenced itself again in his disgust at the total war policy advocated by Lincoln, Grant, Sherman, and other Federals. Ordered to burn down the town of Darien, Georgia, he wrote his wife: "For myself, I have gone through the war so far without dishonor, and I do not like to degenerate into a plunderer and robber—and the same applies to every officer in my regiment."

"Prove Yourselves"

After a couple of minor skirmishes in South Carolina, the 54th received its true baptism of fire on July 18, 1863. Following an unprecedented series of Federal victories that included Gettysburg, Vicksburg, and Honey Springs in Indian Territory, the North had finally seized the momentum. They determined to once and for all assault, capture, and remove from the War Charleston, the very cradle of secession. The Federals had launched various unsuccessful attempts against Charleston. This proved the most formidable yet. Complex and tenacious, it lasted two months and employed both army and navy forces. The climactic infantry attack came against the Confederates' battery at Fort Wagner, a stalwart defensive position bristling with artillery on Morris Island in Charleston Harbor. Wagner's fall would provide the Federals enhanced access to Charleston itself by both land and sea forces.

At dusk, Shaw and the 54th Massachusetts led the 6,000-man Federal rush from a 200-yard wide beach against the fort. It proved one of the most courageous charges of the War and demolished suspicions that black soldiers could not fight as gallantly as white. "I want you to prove yourselves," Shaw told the 54th as they prepared to charge. "The eyes of thousands will look on what you do tonight." But the price for such respect came high. Confederate riflemen and artillerists, outnumbered 6–1 by the attackers, unleashed a desperate fusillade of shot, shell, and bullets that shattered the attack and left the beach a bloody maw beggaring description. One fourth of the entire assault force—over 1,500 men—fell, including nearly half the 54th Massachusetts. Among that number was Robert Gould Shaw, shot through the heart after fighting his way to the parapet. He was buried by the Confederates in a large common grave with some of the men he had led—the privileged "blue-eyed child of fortune" and the descendants of Africa, fighting under the same flag and immortally linked in the history of that flag for their common valor.

Fourth Company, U.S. Colored Infantry at Fort Lincoln,1862. (*Photographic History of the Civil War in Ten Volumes*)

22 Vicksburg
(1863)

"Yankee volunteers marching into Dixie." *Harper's Weekly*'s (www.harpweek.com) fanciful but patriotic depiction of an army of white-hatted, blue-coated, red-vested Uncle Sams marching south to preserve the Union.

The graves of the Texan educated elite lay scattered in a grim procession across six states. . . . Whatever their motivation, and whatever their faults, no group of men ever more bravely sustained a forlorn cause. They gave it a certain haunted holiness few Texans ever completely forgot.

—T. R. Fehrenbach
Lone Star

The War continued unabated in the west with the new year. In middle Tennessee, it brought the climax of the Stone's River battles. In Texas, Confederates, commanded by Virginia General John Magruder, and aided by gunboats padded with cotton bales for protection, recaptured the port of Galveston on New Year's Day. Despite that Texas fight, the Federals increasingly held the advantage in the west as 1863 unfolded. The hopes

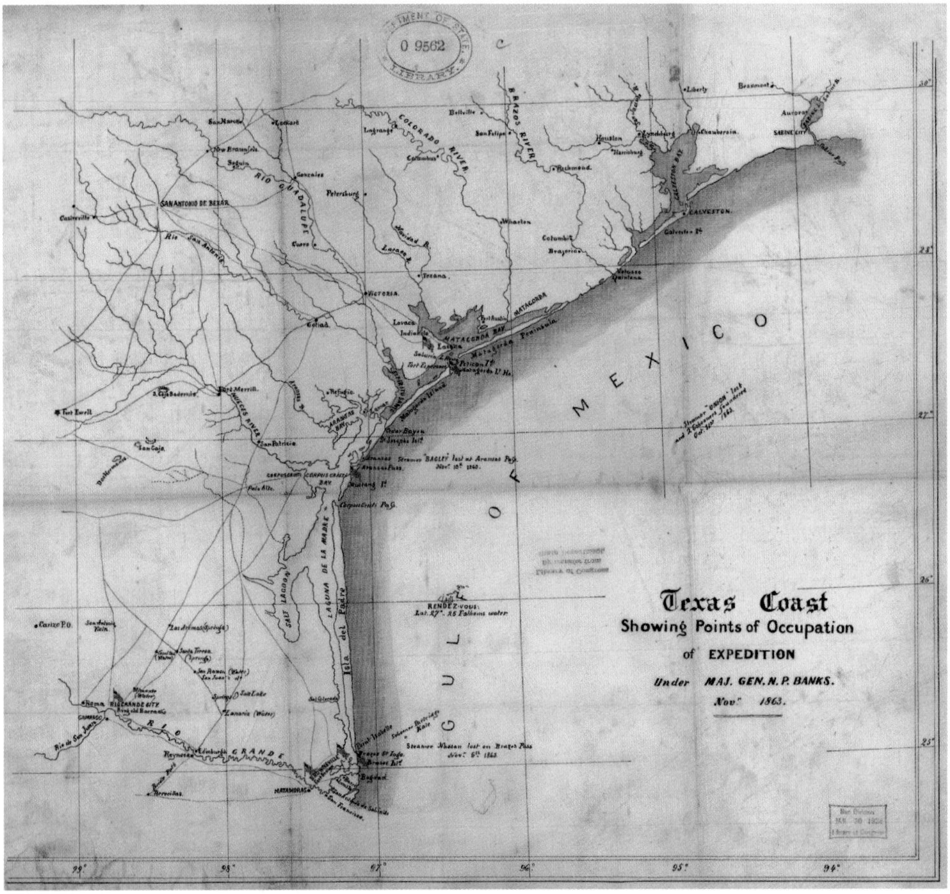

of the Cherokees and other tribes living in the Indian Territory for independence from the United States faded as Federal advantages in numbers and resources mounted. Some Indians who had initially sided with the Confederacy changed sides as they witnessed the South's inability to reinforce and resupply them. Others, such as those led by Cherokee Chief and Confederate General Stand Watie, remained loyal to the South and conducted a fierce guerilla campaign.

In Missouri, Arkansas, and Louisiana, too, Federal organization, resources, and tenacity gradually gained ascendancy. Still, as the old saying goes, "Who overcomes by force hath overcome but half his foe." Everywhere, even in areas under firm Federal control, Southern resentment and rage seethed just beneath the surface—or not beneath the surface at all—against those they viewed as tyrants, despots, and brutal conquerors. This witches' brew of hatred and contempt would shortly explode into infamy in Kansas and Missouri.

Sam Houston and Son (1793–1863)

That the War was oft-times literally a matter of brother against brother is proverbial. In the case of at least one famous family, it was, tragically, father against son. Sam Houston's name stands high in the pantheon of American heroes. He helped his mentor and future president Andrew Jackson win the Creek Indian War, nearly dying in the effort. He served as Congressman and Governor of Tennessee, then lived among and became an official member of the Cherokee Indian Nation. He led Texas to independence from Mexico, commanding at the climactic victory on San Jacinto River. Then he served as the first president of the Republic of Texas and later as governor and senator during Texas's statehood. T. R. Fehrenbach, in his epic saga of Texas, *Lone Star*, addressed Houston's humanitarian views on Indians, especially the more peaceable, Christianized, so-called "civilized" tribes whites had pushed into Eastern Texas:

Houston also was an enigma to his friends, because he loved Indians . . . uniquely among all Western leaders, he proposed a guarantee of Indian rights through the granting of legal title—not mere treaty rights—to Indian lands. Houston recognized a difference between the agrarian and Plains tribes; he believed a place could be made for the former within American civilization.

Houston opposed the secession of Texas from the United States, and he never changed his mind.

By the onset of the War, he was nearly seventy years old, though still governor. Due largely to the influence of his devout wife Margaret, he had become a convert to Christianity late in life, which helped temper his less savory passions and violent ways. But he opposed the secession of Texas from the United States, and he never changed his mind. Neither, however, did he fight to retain the governor's office, from which the state removed him; obstruct Texas' entry into the Confederacy; or accept President Lincoln's offer of Federal troops to keep him in office. Rather, the old warrior promoted a new Texas war with Mexico to divert his state from embarking upon a course he prophesied would bring about its destruction.

His Father's Son

Never before had the beloved "Father of Texas" found the vast majority of his own people opposed to him. The crowning blow came when his own treasured son Sam, believing himself to be fighting for the liberty of his own people no less than had his father a generation before, volunteered to serve in the Confederate forces and received an officer's commission. The elder Houston learned that it was his own extemporaneous patriotic address to a group of young Texans to go forth and do their duty as brave patriots that had convinced young Sam to enlist—for unbeknownst to his father, the eighteen-year-old was part of the group his father addressed!

> *Men who never entered the privation, the toil, the peril that I have for my country call me a traitor because I am willing to yield obedience to the Constitution and the constituted authorities. Let them suffer what I have for this Union and they will feel it entwining so closely around their hearts that it will be like snapping the cords of life to give it up.*
>
> —Sam Houston, 1860

Meanwhile, Margaret gave her son a Bible to take with him to war. It twice saved his life, once when a minie ball shredded it at Shiloh as young Houston carried it into battle with him in his knapsack. The bullet penetrated the Bible as far as where Psalm 70 read, "Oh God: thou art my help and my deliverer." The next day, another bullet nearly killed young Houston, but when a Yankee chaplain found the boy and his Bible, he realized his father had supported the chaplain years before in a ministerial endeavor. The clergyman went to great lengths to see that Houston, lying on a field covered with the wounded and dying, received the medical aid that saved his life. Further suffering awaited Sam Jr. in the Federals' infamous Camp Douglas prison. By the time he returned home on crutches after a prisoner exchange, he stood so emaciated that Margaret, not recognizing him, asked him if he needed help. "Why Ma, I don't believe you know me," the boy said.

Old Sam would not live out the War. He died weeks after the fall of Vicksburg. Only Sam Jr. of all his eight children was mentioned by name in his will. To Sam he left the "sword worn in the Battle of San Jacinto," where the Father of Texas had risked his life and indeed been shot while leading the charge that won Texas its freedom. That sword, Sam Houston wrote his eldest son, was "never to be drawn, only in defense of the Constitution, the Laws, and the Liberties of this Country. If any attempt should ever be made to assail one of these, I wish it to be used in its vindication." Sam Jr. would rejoin the Confederate military ranks. He participated in the victorious Red River Campaign that kept the Federals out of Texas, and then he fought to the end of the War. He carried his father's sword with him all the way.

Benjamin Grierson (1826-1911)

For two years, Southern cavalry wizards like Jeb Stuart, Nathan Bedford Forrest, and John Hunt Morgan had executed breathtaking exploits, frequently behind enemy lines, at the expense of their often-befuddled Federal counterparts. In the spring of 1863, U. S. Grant sought to tun the tables. He needed activity that would draw Confederate defenders away from Grand Gulf, just south of Vicksburg, where he planned to cross the Mississippi River, work his way around the crucial Southern stronghold, and fall upon it from its landward, east, side. Grant set loose a series of diversionary raids. The most dramatic of these aimed to dispense to the Confederates more than a little of their own medicine, of the mounted sort.

The man the Federal high command chose to lead this expedition seemed hardly to fit the part. Pennsylvania-born Benjamin Grierson had until eighteen months before taught music and band at an Illinois school. He evidenced even less outward propensity as a horse soldier than he did as a military man. He carried a lifelong aversion to horses, learned as a boy when one kicked him, crushing a cheekbone, cracking his forehead, and disfiguring him for life. In fact, he objected to the assignment that would enshrine his name in U.S. history books and inspire a fanciful John Wayne motion picture. Nevertheless, on April 17, Grierson led 1,700 Illinois and Iowa horse soldiers south into Mississippi from LaGrange, forty miles east of Memphis. Then he kept leading them south, burning Confederate railroad depots and trains, destroying tracks, capturing 500 Southern soldiers, 1,000 horses and mules, and heaps of arms, ammunition, and supplies.

Grierson's raid traversed the length of Mississippi and landed the Federals at Baton Rouge, the capital of Louisiana.

Grierson's raid traversed the length of Mississippi and landed the Federals at Baton Rouge, the capital of Louisiana, which they held. It accomplished more than drawing needed cavalry away from the Vicksburg defenses in hot pursuit of Grierson and his men; it resulted in the destruction of miles of Mississippi rail line between Jackson and Meridian. This prevented the Confederates from transporting reinforcements, supplies, or arms west to Vicksburg from outside Mississippi. Thus as Grant said, the Grierson raid proved—upon the siege, starvation, and surrender of Vicksburg—"one of the most brilliant" feats of the War. Sherman called it "the most brilliant expedition of the war."

Later in the War, Grierson led some effective cavalry raids in Tennessee and Mississippi, though nothing on the order of his rampage through the latter during the Vicksburg campaign. And he commanded the Northern cavalry when Forrest dealt the Federal army one of its worst thrashings of the War in the west at Brice's Cross Roads. Commissioned colonel in the regular army after the War, he gained additional distinction by leading the 10th Cavalry through more than twenty years of often-arduous duty in the Far West. The 10th was one of the two famous postwar cavalry regiments comprised of white officers and black troopers—"Buffalo Soldiers."

Campaign for Vicksburg

The central strategic drama in the west, however, was Grant's determined campaign against Vicksburg. After the Confederates repulsed him and Sherman, Grant reformed up the Mississippi near Memphis. Through the early months of the year, he tried repeatedly to find a way into Vicksburg. Working in concert with Admiral David Dixon Porter's enormous Federal naval fleet, Grant evidenced both persistence and versatility in his campaign. He launched successive attacks through Williams' Canal, Lake Providence and Bayou Macon, Yazoo Pass, and Steel's Bayou. But the Confederates rebuffed him every time.

Finally, again utilizing Porter's fleet, Grant boldly shipped his army from the west bank of the Mississippi across to the east, south of Vicksburg. Isolating and winning battles against segments of Confederate Departmental Commander John Pemberton's force at Port Gibson and Raymond, Grant circled east to

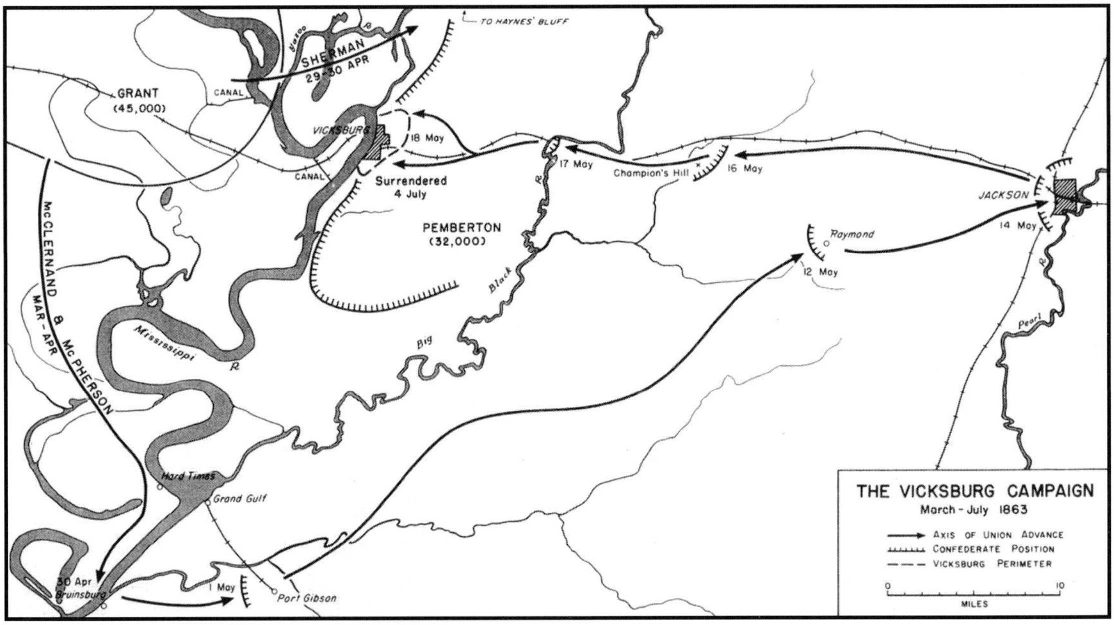

William Sherman's Federals burn much of Jackson, the capital of Mississippi, to the ground.

threaten Vicksburg from its landward side. Forty-five miles farther to the east, Sherman had triple the size force of Joe Johnston's that opposed him. He captured the Mississippi capital of Jackson, burned much of it to the ground, and cut off Vicksburg's supply lifeline.

Meanwhile, one of the costliest Confederate blunders of the War unfolded. Johnston eluded Sherman and ordered Pemberton to merge forces with him to crush Grant. But Pemberton chose instead to follow conflicting orders from President Davis to save Vicksburg at all costs. By the time Pemberton realized the importance of rendezvousing with Johnston, that commander had retreated away and Pemberton found himself trapped between Grant and Sherman.

Grant's execution from the time he departed the west bank of the Mississippi had proven flawless. Now his splendid lieutenants John McClernand and James McPherson led the Federals into the climactic engagement of the campaign at Champion's Hill, just east of Vicksburg. The battle raged vicious and desperate all day. Confederate General John S. Bowen and his division shined, but 6,000 men between the two armies fell, and the Federals shoved Pemberton back. When they beat him worse the next day at the Big Black River, Pemberton retreated into Vicksburg.

"Negro Troops"

This June 20, 1863 *Harper's Weekly* editorial reflects increasing recognition in the North of the ability of blacks to acquit themselves well as soldiers.

> *The magnificent behavior of the Second Louisiana colored regiment at Port Hudson recalls the fact that it is just two years since a warning, uttered in the columns of this journal, that if this war lasted we should arm the negroes, and use them to fight the rebels, was received with shrieks of indignation, not only at the South and in such semi-neutral States as Maryland and Kentucky, but throughout the loyal North and even in the heart of New England. At that time the bulk of the people of the United States entertained a notion that it was unworthy of a civilized or a Christian nation to use in war soldiers whose skin was not white.*

How so singular a notion could have originated, and how men should have clung to it in the face of the example of foreign nations and our own experience in the wars of 1776 and 1812, can only be explained by referring to the extraordinary manner in which for forty years slavery had been warping the heart and mind of the American people. A generation of men had grown up in awe of slavery, and in unchristian contempt of the blacks. And that generation declared that it would not have negro soldiers.

Black Federal troops in combat during "The Battle at Milliken's Bend"

It is very cheering to believers in human progress, and to men who honestly admit that the world moves, to perceive that the short period of two years has sufficed to cure an evil of so long standing, and has educated even the hunkerest Democrat of 1861 into a willingness to arm the blacks. In the abstract, of course, it is a matter of small congratulation that we should at last be doing a thing in itself so obviously sensible and proper that we were clearly fools not to have done it at first. But those who remember how deep the antipathy was, even among antislavery men, to any thing which seemed to involve the remotest risk of negro insurrection; how even the most liberal minds among us shrank from any course of policy which seemed capable of entangling us, under any circumstances, in an admission of negro equality, will feel no common sense of joy at our emancipation from so narrow and mean a prejudice.

We have from time to time recorded the slow progress of negro enlistments, and the constant obstacles which have been encountered by the farseeing men who have desired to raise an army of blacks. When General Hunter raised among fugitive slaves the First South Carolina black regiment at Hilton Head, the officers of his corps—being still uneducated to the times—refused to associate with the few brave men who took command of the negroes; and Secretary Stanton—still barely stammering over the A B C of the work—declined to pay them wages because their skins were too dark. Under the iron rule of Butler at New Orleans a black brigade was organized, and so long as that grim soldier held sway discontent at the measure was prudently silent. But when Banks succeeded a mutiny among the white troops warned the General that his Northern men were not yet sufficiently educated to the times to march side by side with negroes. He wisely solved the problem by sending the blacks into garrison, and keeping the whites in the field. One regiment, it seems, he marched against the enemy, and they, we may be sure, will not, after Port Hudson, be again exposed to sneers or insult. At the Southwest negroes began to pour into our lines when Columbus fell, and the rush has never ceased. Yet, until within a few weeks, no use has been made of them. They came in droves, begging us to employ them as soldiers or laborers—as any thing. But our generals, slow to learn that they were excellent fighting material, and that the lesson of the hour was to arm them, treated them as a nuisance; sometimes fed them in idleness, sometimes sent them back to their masters, in a few cases used them as laborers, but never, until recently, put muskets into their hands. It was not till the month of March last, when Adjutant-

General Thomas (who two years ago was so "sound"—as the phrase was—on the slavery question that he was even suspected of rebel sympathies) went West at the pressing invitation of General Blair and others, that the necessity was discerned of making soldiers of these fugitives. Since then ten full regiments of negroes have been formed, and are being drilled and equipped. It is now stated that ten more regiments will shortly be organized. Indeed there is no limit to the supply of troops which may be drawn from this source. The valley of the Mississippi and its tributaries could furnish, in the course of a year, an army of 100,000 men—enough to hold the country after we have taken it.

At the North, the work of negro enlistments progresses slowly, partly in consequence of the sparse negro population, and partly owing to obstacles created by politicians. In this State no negro regiment has been formed; it is said to be hard work enough to obtain the sanction of the State authorities to the formation of new white regiments. But Massachusetts has already sent off one full regiment, commanded by Colonel Shaw, and another is in process of formation. And the negroes of the District of Columbia will shortly constitute a brigade, and will apply for active service.

Uneasiness is felt in some quarters lest the rebels should execute their brutal threats of hanging the officers of black regiments and selling the privates into slavery. But no apprehension need be entertained on this score. The act of the Rebel Congress on this subject is so ingeniously framed that while appearing to menace our black troops and their officers with dire penalties, it really remits the whole subject of their treatment to Jeff Davis; who, of course, will realize that indignities offered to them would at once be followed by retaliation upon rebel prisoners in our hands. The 8400 prisoners taken by General Grant at Vicksburg are a pretty fair security for our negro troops.

A wide shot of Vicksburg, Mississippi, from across the Mississippi River.

The Siege

Still, the "Confederate Gibraltar" stood defiant. Grant, hoping to capitalize on sagging Southern morale, immediately launched a full-scale assault on the city. The Confederates hammered him back. When the Federals lost over 3,000 men in a series of all-out attacks against Vicksburg on May 22, Grant decided he could not fight his way in. Evidencing his development into one of the great war captains of American history, he remained persistent in his objective, while proving flexible in his methods to attain it. Grant shifted his strategy and began a siege of Vicksburg with his army, which grew to 75,000 men. Pemberton had responsibility not only for his own force that numbered

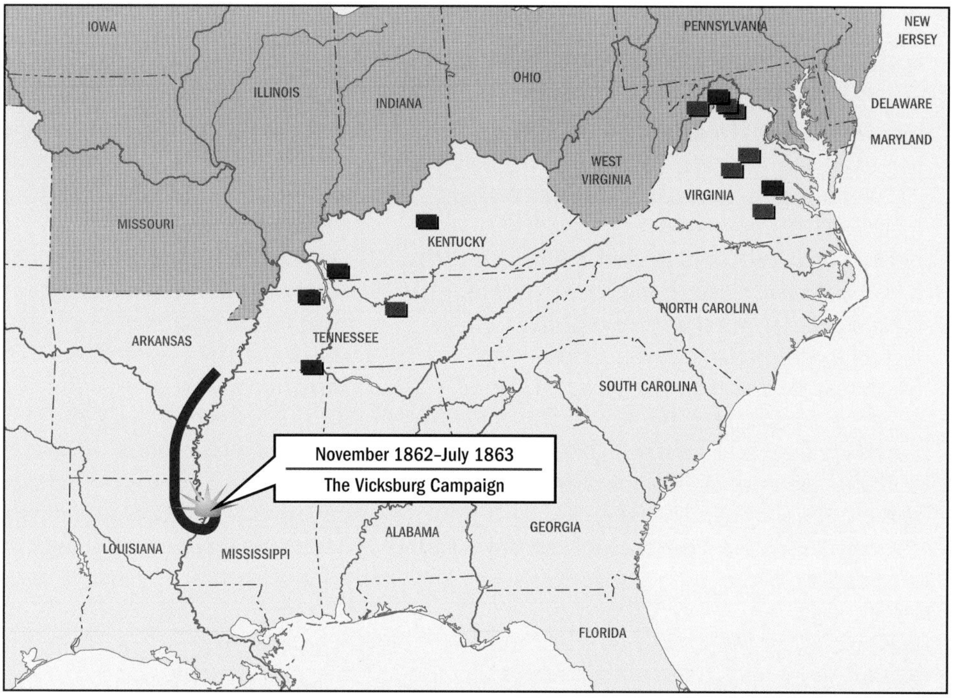

fewer than 30,000, but for the perhaps half of the 5,000 residents remaining in the city.

As further evidence of the evolution of the conflict into one of total war, Grant shelled the town itself, driving the civilian population of aged, women, and children into caves and underground shelters. On July 4—the day of celebration for the War of American Independence—Pemberton surrendered the starving city. He did so over the furious objections of many of his officers and rankers. Not one Confederate position had surrendered nor given way in battle.

One of William Sherman's artillery batteries, trained on the town of Vicksburg.

The 6,000-man Confederate garrison at Port Hudson, 100 miles down the river in Louisiana, remained unvanquished. They had held off a separate Yankee force of 30,000 men for six weeks, and inflicted over 4,000 casualties on them. A few days later, realizing the fall of Vicksburg rendered their own position untenable, these defenders, too, surrendered. The Federals now held the entirety of the Mississippi. "The Father of Waters again goes unvexed to the sea," Lincoln proclaimed. Vicksburg proved a strategic catastrophe for the Confederacy, much worse than Gettysburg.

What it Was Like at Vicksburg

The six-week siege of Vicksburg provided General U. S. Grant and the United States with the biggest victory of the War in the west. The siege proved a horror unparalleled in American history. By its end, nearly half the Confederate defenders were unable to fight because of wounds or illness. Piles of stinking excrement lay mere feet from the soldiers' stations along miles of battlements.

Round-the-clock shelling that destroyed much of the town drove most of Vicksburg's remaining civilian population into an elaborate system of connecting underground caves they themselves dug. Day after day they huddled, mostly in darkness, as shells exploded above and around them. They grew hungry, many of them sick, and so thirsty they drank out of mud holes when they saw one. Some of them died, too, victims of a style of war that proved a harbinger of those to come in the 20th century.

One might have knocked down a full-grown steer with a chunk of it.

—Confederate soldier Ephraim Anderson of Missouri, on how tough was the bread, made from ground-up peas, still available early in the siege.

One shell had exploded in the wall and thrown the entire side of the dining room into the street. Another had alighted in the kitchen, and had blown everything into flinders, "leaving," as the hostess informed me, "scarcely anything recognizable save some bricks and a couple of stove-legs."

—Franc Wilkie, Northern newspaper correspondent, describing the Vicksburg house where he stayed after the siege.

Such a scene of desolation you can hardly imagine. The dressing room was in ruins, the end where the fireplace had been was blown entirely out. The nursery was unthinkable, a hole deep almost as a cistern in the middle of the floor, every room in the house injured and scarcely a window left whole . . .

John Pemberton

—Mrs. W. W. Lord, wife of the rector of Christ Church, describing the rectory.

Rations . . . curtailed to 2 1/2 biscuit and a Slice of Meat per day. . . . the Enemy are close enough to throw clods of dirt and hand grenades at each other. Rations are getting Still Shorter I have an apatite of an oxx.

—Texas soldier (and Pennsylvania native) Alex Frazier, from the "Bull Pen" trenches.

[I] can assure our friends that if it is rendered necessary they need have no scruples in eating the meat. It is sweet, savory and tender . . .

—J. M. Swords, editor of Vicksburg's *Daily Citizen* newspaper, on the tastiness of mule meat.

A few more days will bring us to starvation indeed.

—Dora Miller, pregnant wife and faithful Unionist, upon declining to partake of the food entrees available in the city's market—mule meat and skinned rats.

You must understand that it is not in the usual way we walked down the street, but had to take the middle of the street when we heard a shell, and watch for it. You may imagine our progress

Admiral David Porter's fleet, on the Mississippi River. Porter's flotilla played a key role in the Federals' Vicksburg campaign.

as not very fast. As soon as a shell gets over your head you are safe for, even if it approaches near, the pieces fall forward and do not touch you; but the danger is that sometimes while watching one, another comes and may explode or fall near you 'ere you are aware.

—Confederate Sgt. Will Tunnard

Dogs howled through the streets at night; cats screamed forth their hideous cries; an army of rats, seeking food, would scamper around your very feet, across the streets and over the pavements. Lice and filth covered the bodies of the soldiers. Delicate women and little children, with pale, careworn and hunger-pinched features, peered at the passerby with wistful eyes from the caves in the hillsides.

—Confederate Sgt. Will Tunnard

Then, with the deep boom of cannon taking the place of organ notes and the shells of the besieging fleet bursting around the sacred edifice, he preached the gospel of eternal peace to an assemblage of powder-grimed and often blood-stained soldiery.

—W. W. Lord, Jr., describing the Sabbath Day preaching of his father, a New Yorker, to Confederate soldiers at Christ Episcopal Church.

[The Federals] instantly opened on them with a Parrott gun. As the shells came screaming wickedly through the streets, exploding or entering the building, men, women and children hastily sought shelter to escape the danger. . . . Such an unheard of, ruthless and barbarous method of warfare as training a battery of rifled cannon upon an assembly of unarmed men and worshiping women is unparalleled in the annals of history.

—Sgt. Will Tunnard, describing the shelling of a large number of St. Paul's Catholic Church parishioners gathered in front of the cathedral for Mass.

[We have] set apart all or a portion of the hour between sundown and dark of each day to supplicate Almighty God, that He will pardon our sins, receive us graciously and deliver us from the hands of our cruel enemies. . . . [We ask all Christians] throughout this beleaguered army to unite with us in prayer at that hour.

—Soldiers Christian Association of the 52nd Georgia Regiment

Confederate artillery emplacements sheltered on low ground during the siege of Vicksburg. Their proximity to the Methodist Church (upper right) and the Catholic Church (upper left) witnesses the desperate nature of the battle.

Mary Loughborough and the Caves (1832–1867)

Few people were less likely to have found themselves living in the caves of Vicksburg than Mary Loughborough, a native of New York City who had married a St. Louis attorney. But the War drove her pro-Southern family south. Fortune found her amidst the siege in the summer of 1863 as her father served on the staff of Missouri's General Sterling Price. Loughborough's diary, *My Cave Life in Vicksburg*, is an enduring classic and one of the greatest extant eyewitness accounts of the siege. Many eyewitness accounts attest that the round-the-clock shelling of Vicksburg killed a number of civilians. Among the most poignant chronicles are Mary Loughborough's regarding the deaths of several children, excerpts of which follow. After the War, she raised four children, penned numerous other works, and edited and published the respected *Southern Ladies Journal*.

"A little Negro child, playing in the yard, had found a shell; in rolling and turning it, had innocently pounded the fuse. The terrible explosion followed, showing, as the white cloud of smoke floated away, the mangled remains of a life that to the mother's heart had possessed all of beauty and joy."

"[A homesick little girl tired of being confined in her cave] hastily ran to the house in the interval that elapsed between the slowly falling shells. On returning, an explosion sounded near her—one wild scream and she ran into her mother's presence, sinking like a wounded dove, the life blood flowing over the light summer dress in crimson ripples from a death wound in her side."

"Sitting in the cave, one evening, I heard the most heartrending screams and moans. I was told that a mother had taken a child into a cave about a hundred yards from us; and having laid it on its little bed, as the poor woman believed, in safety, she took her seat near the entrance of the cave. A mortar shell came rushing through the air, and fell with much force, entering the earth above the sleeping child—oh! most horrible sight to the mother—crushing in the upper part of the little sleeping head, and taking away the young innocent life without a look or word of passing love to be treasured in the mother's heart."

> *An explosion sounded near [the cavebound, homesick little girl]—one wild scream and she ran into her mother's presence, sinking like a wounded dove, the life blood flowing over the light summer dress in crimson ripples from a death wound in her side.*
>
> —Mary Loughborough
> *My Cave Life in Vicksburg*

A. J. Hodges and the Common Man of the Land (1833–1910)

Thousands of faded photographs from the War era remain in family attics, boxes, and scrapbooks, the stories of most of the people captured in them lost to history. One exception is Albert James (A. J.) Hodges, a Southern yeoman whose descendants chronicled his life. A Tennessee native, Hodges moved to Texas in 1853. He eventually purchased Denton County land near present-day Pilot Point in North Texas, about fifty miles from the Red River and Indian Territory (modern-day Oklahoma).

In 1858, twenty-four-year-old A. J. married another native Tennessean, fourteen-year-old Mary Margaret Thornton, in Denton County. Never a slaveowner, he worked as a rancher and stockman until the outbreak of war. Along with nearly one thousand other Denton County men, Hodges went forth to defend his homeland. A family history of his life lists the reasons the Texans volunteered for war as "the rights of states to secede from the Union; that the North had violated the Constitution in passing 'personal-liberty laws'; and the North had unfairly imposed taxes on the South for the benefit of Northern interests."

Ex-Texas cavalryman A. J. Hodges in 1880s middle age with his wife Mary Margaret and their eight children.

Hodges joined the First Regiment of the Choctaw and Chickasaw Mounted Rifles at Fort Arbuckle, in the Choctaw Nation (present-day southeastern Oklahoma). The regiment later became known as Company E, 29th Regiment of the Texas Cavalry. Ed F. Bates describes the typical young local soldier leaving for war in his book History of Denton County: "See him as he marches out on dress parade, riding his Choctaw pony, homemade saddle, homemade butcher-knife, old east-barrel shotgun, and an old 'pepper-box' Pistol (old-style seven-shooter)." A. J.'s younger brother Tom and Mary Margaret's brother Jesse also enlisted. Tom lost a leg to a minie ball.

A. J. rode as a Confederate horse soldier for nearly two years, and fought in at least two significant battles in the West. One was Pea Ridge (Elkhorn Tavern) in Northwestern Arkansas, in March, 1862, where he was slashed across the shoulders. Another was the July, 1863, First Battle of Cabin Creek in Cherokee Indian Territory (present-day Northeastern Oklahoma). July 3 proved a day of great activity in the War that year. In the East, the Battle of Gettysburg reached its zenith. On the Mississippi River, the Federal siege of Vicksburg was reaching its climax. Nathan Bedford Forrest and his cavalry were battling Federal cavalry in Tennessee. And in modern-day Oklahoma, the Federals took A. J. Hodges prisoner.

He remained a captive—in four different Federal prisons—for nearly two years, until the end of the war. Broke, without supplies, scarred in the head from another battle wound, and ill from the wretchedness of prison life, he needed more than a year to get home from a Richmond, Virginia, hospital, to which he had gone after the Federals paroled him in March, 1865.

After the war, A. J. sold his land in Texas and moved his family to Arkansas, where he bought land on the border with Indian Territory and near the Pea Ridge battleground. There, he and Mary Margaret became charter members of the Liberty Baptist Church and raised eight children. Some of their descendants remained on that Arkansas land, while others moved west. Ironically, one of A. J.'s great-great-grandsons moved his own family back to Denton County, Texas, in the 1990s. Only later did he learn that he had unwittingly located them just a few miles from the land where A. J. and Mary Margaret began their marriage a century-and-a-half before.

John Hunt Morgan and His Raids (1825-1864)

The epitome of the swashbuckling, daredevil "Rebel Raider" of legend, Kentuckian John Hunt Morgan rose and fell by unharnessed bravado. Unlike other volunteer officers in the War, Morgan had combat experience in the Mexican War, where he rose to the rank of lieutenant. A Lexington, Kentucky, merchant before the War, he organized and trained the Lexington Rifles, a militia of like-minded pro-Southerners. When fighting came, he secured rifles for his militia. This resulted in a Federal warrant for his arrest. He lost his business, too, and his wife died, so John Hunt Morgan rode and led like the fearless man with nothing left to lose that he probably was.

They are having a stampede in Kentucky. Please look to it.
—Abraham Lincoln to his general-in-chief regarding John Morgan's exploits

He gained fame for his four epic raids into Federal territory. Such audacious sallies far into the North with cocksure leadership and thousands of horse soldiers was unprecedented, and it took the Federals a long time to figure out how to deal with it. Included in Morgan's repertoire of innovation was his employment of soldier-tele-grapher George Ellsworth. During raids into the North, Ellsworth would tap into Federal telegraph lines, both to intercept directives to pursue Morgan and to promulgate false information as to his raiders' whereabouts. Often overlooked, especially by Morgan's critics, is how those raids delivered strategic punch as well as tactical. Morgan's first big raid came in the summer of 1862, when he thundered through Kentucky, an exploit that helped throttle a Federal

move on the key city of Chattanooga. With fewer than 1,000 men, Morgan rode more than 1,000 miles through enemy country, destroyed all Federal supplies and arms in 17 different towns, and took 1,200 prisoners—all at the expense of fewer than one hundred men. Three months later, he charged back into Kentucky, captured his home town of Lexington, and wreaked havoc with Federal transportation and communication lines.

He took 4,000 men on his spectacular "Christmas Raid," which frustrated William Rosecrans's campaign to secure Tennessee. In ten days, Morgan and his raiders wrecked two million dollars' worth of Federal property, captured nearly 2,000 bluecoats, and put the Yankees' Louisville and Nashville Railroad out of business for five weeks. Morgan's most famous raid was his electrifying rampage through Kentucky, Indiana, and Ohio in the summer of 1863. By now, the tall Kentuckian claimed attention at the most exalted levels of Federal leadership. Abraham Lincoln told Henry Halleck, his General-in-Chief, "They are having a stampede in Kentucky. Please look to it." With only around 2,000 troopers, Morgan captured 6,000 Federal soldiers, destroyed twenty five bridges, won three battles, and wrecked scores of railroads and other Federal property totaling ten million dollars.

With only around 2,000 troopers, Morgan captured 6,000 Federal soldiers, destroyed twenty five bridges, won three battles, and wrecked scores of railroads and other Federal property totaling ten million dollars.

Noose Tightens

But Morgan had failed to seek permission from his superiors to cross the Ohio River north into the United States proper, and he paid for this unsanctioned exercise of initiative. Despite his accomplishments on the trek, Federal forces led by General Edward H. Hobson, aided by militia and gunboats, defeated Morgan at Buffington Island, Ohio, putting nearly half his force out of commission. Then they captured him at New Lisbon. Despite his high rank of brigadier-general and his regular Confederate army command, the Federals treated Morgan and several of his officers no better than common criminals. They shaved their heads, put them in prison attire, and consigned them to stone cells. Nevertheless, the crafty raider and his lieutenants cut their way through the solid stone with case knives to an underground air shaft and scurried away. Within hours, Morgan had found new clothes and was riding a southbound Yankee train past the very prison in which he had been incarcerated only hours before—while sitting next to an unsuspecting Federal officer!

The aversion of the average Southern soldier to traditional military discipline was proverbial. Morgan inculcated even less a propensity for it in his men, and he would soon bear the consequences. On his final raid into Kentucky in the summer of 1864, certain of his troops—without Morgan's knowledge or sanction—robbed a bank at Mount Sterling, looted stores at Lexington, and burned a portion of Cynthiana. Though he won a battle at the latter and captured the same General Hobson who had earlier captured him, these depredations, along with a subsequent defeat at Cynthiana, further raised the ire both of the Confederate hierarchy and the mounting numbers of Federals pursuing him. With the advent of the autumn of 1864, Morgan led his depleted—and now-tarnished—force to the east Tennessee town of Greeneville to intercept a Northern raiding party. An advanced party of Federals, however, snuck into the town at dawn. Morgan, awakened too late, strapped on his twin Navy Colts and made for his horse. A Yankee trooper shot him in the back and thus was ended the life of John Hunt Morgan, whose fame could scarcely compensate his pregnant second wife for the loss.

William Quantrill and His Raid on Lawrence (1837-1865)

Many names have attached themselves to the event, but whether "Quantrill's Raid," "The Lawrence Massacre," or others, what occurred on the morning of August 21, 1863, in Lawrence, Kansas, was wholesale murder begotten by other murder that birthed yet more murder. Kansas and Missouri had long hosted some of the most vicious and personal fighting of the War. And William Charles Quantrill had participated in more than his fair share of it. His handsome, baby-faced young visage obscured an audacious, autonomous spirit that, unlike most who fought the United States, would not shy from trading outrage for outrage with the North—short of harming women or children.

Quantrill had earned a Confederate captaincy in 1862 for capturing Independence, Missouri, at the head of a partisan band of pro-Southerners. But Jefferson Davis' government would come to lament, and finally disavow, that commission. For never would William Quantrill fight but according to his own rules. He justified his hard brand of war by citing a long train of pro-North atrocities against Southern sympathizers extending back to John Brown's massacre of unarmed men at Pottowattamie Creek in 1856 and even before. He and others watched as Lawrence (eventual site of the University of Kansas), forty miles west of the Missouri line, developed into a pro-Federal bastion with strong nationalist and abolitionist sentiments and a school that vigorously discipled its students in the same philosophies.

For months, Quantrill attempted to persuade the hundreds of men who rode with him to attack Lawrence. However, most of his hard-bitten cohorts considered such a trek a suicide mission, regardless how much revenge—and booty—it might offer. These sentiments changed under the heavy hand of Federal District Commander Thomas Ewing, father-in-law of William Tecumseh Sherman. The tenacity of what Ewing and other Federals termed

"Bushwhackers" drove him to institute extreme measures to suppress them. This Missouri-based guerilla movement who so bedeviled the Federals—sometimes outfighting Regular army cavalry units—fought by stealth and without attachment to any official Confederate military organization. They appeared as ordinary, often-pro-Federal farmers, laborers, and shopkeepers in the day-to-day life.

Total War

That Ewing experienced such difficulty in his quest seems understandable when considering who were some of his prey—Quantrill himself, Jesse James and his brother Frank, Cole and Jim Younger, and William "Bloody Bill" Anderson. From such flesh-and-blood men sprang the myth and legend of the archetypal fearless American outlaw, pistolero, and anti-hero. Many of those who survived the War, such as the James and Younger brothers, continued their outlaw (or resistance, depending on one's point of view) ways for years afterward. For them, the United States government and what they viewed as its tyrannical institutions, rather than the common American citizenry, was their enemy.

Failing to corral these crafty irregulars, Ewing resorted to measures unprecedented even among those such as the Bushwhackers, who abided by a rough code of frontier honor. That code stated that never were women or children to be bothered. But Ewing ordered any females suspected of aiding Confederate irregulars—including their wives, sisters, and mothers—jailed in Kansas City. Having embarked on such internment, and the terror accom-

Quantrill's Raid on Lawrence, Kansas, as illustrated at the time by *Harper's Weekly* (www.harpweek.com).

panying it, Ewing received warnings about the dilapidated old Kansas City building which contained a liquor store and housed some of the female "prisoners." The building, it seemed, was in no wise safe and was in fact susceptible to collapsing.

Ewing ignored the admonitions, and on August 14 the building did collapse, killing four women and seriously injuring numerous others. Unfortunately for nearly everyone on any side of the conflict, one of the dead was the sister of Bloody Bill Anderson. Then, as the Bushwhackers warmed to the Lawrence idea, Ewing ordered all women and children of known pro-Confederate guerillas to leave the state of Missouri and not come back. Now Quantrill's men flocked in from the brush, off the farms, and out of the towns and rallied to his renewed call—this time for utter vengeance on Lawrence, Kansas, home of Kansas Senator James H. Lane, who had long set the tone for the brutal war the Federals waged against Confederate sympathizers in the region.

Lawrence

Quantrill and 300 men rode out of Blackwater Creek, Missouri, headed down a trail of vengeance whose terminus was Lawrence, seventy miles to the west. Along the way, more riders joined them, as well as Confederate Captain Jim Holt and over 100 recruits, whom he joined to the grim column as a training exercise. No one was more surprised than Quantrill when his now-450-man horde thundered into Lawrence just after dawn August 21 and found only twenty Federal soldiers, which they quickly shot dead. The rest of the garrison was out on patrols and scouts. The raiders swarmed through the town, gunning down every male old enough to shoulder a firearm. Some they dragged out of their homes into the street and shot in front of their wives and children. Others, hiding, perished in the flames that brought their homes down over their heads.

Though Holt and others shielded some men, by the time the marauders left, 150 men lay dead and smoke billowed over the town. True to their code, however, the raiders harmed no female in any way, other than to leave them homeless, fatherless or widowed. While the fires of Lawrence yet burned, Federal war parties converged on Quantrill from all points of the map. He and his men responded the guerilla way. They sprang ambushes, set diversions, peeled off, and disappeared into the brush, dodging Yankee cavalry and Kansas Jayhawkers as they went. Quantrill and nearly all his men galloped home safely.

News of the Lawrence massacre electrified America. Most Southerners were barely happier about it than those in the North, knowing Quantrill had no Confederate sanction for such an enterprise and fearing the reprisals the slaughter and pillage would bring. And come reprisals did. Lane, one of the few male survivors of the massacre, ordered murderous counteractions. Each fresh story of government-authorized Federal brutality inspired Quantrill and the 400 men who now rode with him to fight the harder. And both Missouri and Kansas bled the worse.

Still fighting the War his way, Quantrill led a couple dozen men—including Frank and Jesse James and Jim Younger—east as the year 1865 began. This time his mission was nothing short of killing Abraham Lincoln. Traveling through Kentucky, however, he heard John Wilkes Booth had pre-empted him. Then Quantrill fell in an early May shootout. He died a month later.

George Caleb Bingham's dramatic depiction of the results of "Order Number 11," issued by Federal General Thomas Ewing. Order Number 11 demanded that four pro-Confederate Missouri counties be cleared of their entire population. After fifteen days, anyone found still in the area risked being executed on sight by Federal soldiers.

James H. Lane and the Jayhawkers (1814–1866)

"Puzzling," "grim," "eloquent," "violent," "idealistic," "bizarre," "riveting," "paranoid," "heroic," "notorious womanizer," and "highly unbalanced." All these adjectives and many others have been applied to Jim Lane, bold leader of Kansas abolitionists. He traveled a long political pilgrimage. One historian explains that by describing him as "a consummate politician, espousing a different belief for each new crowd of voters, and winning them all with his riveting intensity." He was imbued with inordinate ambition. A decorated colonel in the Mexican War and former lieutenant governor of Indiana, he moved west to Kansas as a pro-slavery Democratic leader, then Congressman. Amidst the free soil-leaning western territory, however, his views shifted as he first became antislavery, then ardently abolitionist. As a Republican in the late 1850s Lane formed the Army of the North, a militia organization designed to protect the rights of free soirees—sometimes at the expense of pro-slavery or pro-Southern citizens. The victims of his often-violent ways bestowed Lane and his marauders with another name—Jayhawkers.

The new state of Kansas elected him to the United States Senate in the same year that Abraham Lincoln won the U.S. Presidency. He won favor with Lincoln by providing members of Lane's "Frontier Guard" to protect the White House and Washington until Regular army units could take over. As the War progressed, Lane further cultivated Lincoln's favor by supporting the President's hard war-soft peace policies. And he garnered the rank of general and raised volunteer troops to fight Confederate forces from Missouri. These included black troops, whom he christened the "Zouaves d'Afrique" for the scarlet pants they wore.

Despite his high political station, no one on any side fought dirtier in the Kansas-Missouri theater than Lane and the Federal cavalry he commanded. They burned, looted, and murdered on a scale with the most desperate Border Ruffians or Bushwhackers. Lane launched a scorched-earth campaign against districts of Missouri that supported or were even friendly to Confederate efforts. When he and his men stormed into Osceola, for instance, they found a Southern ammunition cache. They proceeded to shoot up the town with no mind for who might be in the way, burned most of it down, and stole or destroyed all the townspeople's food of any sort they could lay hands on.

Despite his high political station, no one on any side fought dirtier in the Kansas-Missouri theater than Lane and the Federal cavalry he commanded. They burned, looted, and murdered on a scale with the most desperate Border Ruffians or Bushwhackers.

Battling Quantrill

So mendacious was Lane's trail of fire and death that when William Quantrill rode for Lawrence in August, the fiery Senator's name appeared at the top of the list of men he wanted. But Lane heard the raiders rumbling across the prairie toward town and skedaddled out into a cornfield in his nightshirt. There he hid while one of his arch-foes destroyed his own hometown. He launched a galaxy of reprisals. He ordered Bushwhacker suspects shot on sight. He emptied an entire Confederate-leaning section of Missouri of its civilian population, after which houses, barns, and stores alike were burned to the ground. Two Missouri counties were virtually depopulated, thousands of homeless civilians turned out onto the open road. For years the region was known as the Burnt District.

So mendacious was Lane's trail of fire and death that when William Quantrill rode for Lawrence in August, the fiery Senator's name appeared at the top of the list of men he wanted.

Lane swept to Senate reelection in 1865 and continued to curry White House favor by supporting Lincoln's, then his successor Andrew Johnson's, postwar policies. But years of fratricidal destruction had swung Kansas sympathies toward the vengeful Reconstruction agenda of Thaddeus Stevens and the Radical Republicans. Finally, Lane's ambition found him out. Unwilling to eschew his White House ties, his popularity with his fellow Kansans plummeted. Always susceptible to volatile mood swings, depression, and exhaustion overtook him, and he committed suicide on a farm near Leavenworth in 1866.

Lane's own words perhaps best convey the passion of this much-loved, much-hated man: "I would like to live long enough to see every white man in South Carolina, in hell, and the Negroes inheriting their territory. It would not wound my feelings any day to find the dead bodies of rebel sympathizers pieced with bullet holes in every street and alley of Washington. Yes, I would regret this for I would not like to witness all this waste of powder and lead. I would rather have them hung, and the ropes saved! Let them dangle until their stinking bodies rot and fall to the ground piece by piece."

Federal soldiers, including one black, gather around their log hut company kitchen. The walkway in foreground is constructed of logs.

23 Chattanooga
(1863)

George Thomas at Chickamauga.

You . . . are a coward, and if you were any part of a man I would slap your jaws and force you to resent it. . . . You have threatened to arrest me for not obeying your orders promptly. I dare you to do it, and I say to you that if you ever again try to interfere with me or cross my path it will be at the peril of your life.

—Nathan Bedford Forrest, in person, to Braxton Bragg, over Bragg's insults and dissembling at Chickamauga

With Vicksburg and the Mississippi in hand, Federal attention in the west turned toward Chattanooga. Held by the Confederates under Bragg, the importance of that city could scarcely be understated. It was perhaps the most valuable rail center in all of the Confederacy. It was both a crucial north–south rail junction and the preeminent east–west junction in the South. It lay astride the large and important Tennessee River, which ran virtually the length of the eastern Mississippi Valley before emptying into the Ohio. In addition, it was one of the key strategic points for controlling that vast valley. And it lay less than 100 miles north of Atlanta. It served as the gateway southeast into the South's most populous and prosperous state, heretofore inviolate Georgia, thence clear to the Atlantic. If Rosecrans and his Army of the Cumberland could take Chattanooga and effect such a march, Federal prospects—and the implications for Southern communications, transportation, and supplies, not to mention morale—were breathtaking. The eastern half of the Confederacy severed from the west with the defeat at Vicksburg, they could split the east itself in two.

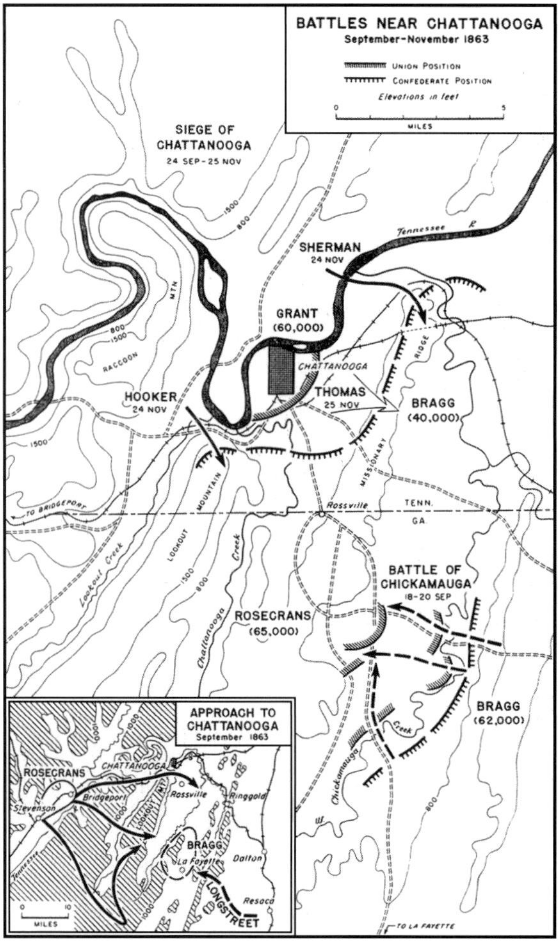

Map of the 1863 Chickamauga-Chattanooga Campaign in Tennessee. (Courtesy of The General Libraries, The University of Texas at Austin)

When Lilacs Last in the Dooryard Bloom'd (Walt Whitman)

When lilacs last in the dooryard bloom'd,
And the great star early droop'd in the western sky in the night,
I mourn'd, and yet shall mourn with ever-returning spring.

Ever-returning spring, trinity sure to me you bring,
Lilac blooming perennial and drooping star in the west,
And thought of him I love.

O powerful western fallen star!
O shades of night—O moody, tearful night!
O great star disappear'd—O the black murk that hides the star!
O cruel hands that hold me powerless—O helpless soul of me!
O harsh surrounding cloud that will not free my soul.

I cease from my song for thee,
From my gaze on thee in the west, fronting the west, communing with thee,
O comrade lustrous with silver face in the night.

Yet each to keep and all, retrievements out of the night,
The song, the wondrous chant of the gray-brown bird,
And the the tallying chant, the echo arous'd in my soul,
With the lustrous and drooping star with the countenance full of woe,
With the holders holding my hand nearing the call of the bird,

Comrades mine and I in the midst, and their memory ever to keep,
for the dead I loved so well,
For the sweetest, wisest soul of all my days and lands—and this for
his dear sake,
Lilac and star and bird twined with the chant of my soul,
There in the fragrant pines and the cedars dusk and dim.

The U.S. cavalry's spanking new Spencer and Henry repeating rifles—which fired as many as 15 bullets in rapid succession before reloading—helped save the Federals' main Western army as it retreated from Chickamauga. Only 535 Yankee horse soldiers unleashed 43,550 rounds in a five-hour shooting spree against the onrushing, single-shot muzzle-loading Confederates. "We thought you had a division there!" one stunned Southern prisoner exclaimed. A division consisted of roughly twenty times as many men.

Lee & Gordon's Mill on the Chickamauga Creek battlefield in 1863.

Rosecrans managed to maneuver the Confederates out of Chattanooga. On September 19 and 20, Bragg, however, consolidating his forces, pounced upon the Federals twelve miles south of Chattanooga at Chickamauga Creek. Lee's "old warhorse," Longstreet, and his Virginia corps, marched from the east, exploited a gap in the Union line and swept thousands of Federals, including Philip Sheridan's entire division, from the field. It was the biggest Confederate victory and the bloodiest battle of the War in the west. The Federals were driven headlong in retreat back to Chattanooga. Only the Federal left, commanded by Virginian George Thomas, held until the Confederates forced their retreat that night. Without Thomas' stand, Rosecrans' entire army may have been bagged. Yet that prospect still loomed the next morning. The chaos and confusion of the Federal retreat were reminiscent of First Manassas. Nathan Bedford Forrest, leading the pursuit, pled for Bragg to complete a task that now seemed eminently possible—nothing short of the destruction of the Army of the Cumberland. But the Confederate commander chose not to, allowing Rosecrans and his army to stagger back into Chattanooga.

Members of the 8th Missouri Federal regiment prior to battle at Chickamauga Creek.

George Thomas (1815-1872)

The immortal "Rock of Chickamauga," Virginian George Thomas was viewed as a traitor to his homeland by Southerners and was one of the greatest Federal commanders of the War. He first gained acclaim as a boy when he rode through the countryside warning his isolated Virginia neighbors about the barbarous murder spree of fugitive slave Nat Turner. But the West Point appointment that ride helped earn him would one day contribute to the downfall of the Confederacy. For after Regular army service in the Mexican War and on America's western frontier, Thomas remained with that army when the War came, outraging friends and family.

He commanded an early Federal victory in the west at Mill Springs, Kentucky, in January, 1862. After performing solidly if not spectacularly later in the year at Perryville, he gained his deathless sobriquet in September, 1863, at the Battle of Chickamauga Creek. Ironically, Chickamauga proved the Confederates' biggest triumph in the west. It would have been even bigger, however—perhaps to the extent of jeopardizing the entire Federal war effort—had not Thomas held his position until nightfall before being forced to retreat. In standing as he did, he gave the rest of the Northern line, swept from the field by Longstreet and the Confederates, a head start in their escape back to Chattanooga. When Grant arrived there to rescue William Rosecrans' besieged Army of the Cumberland, he gave Rosecrans' command to Thomas. The Virginian was not long in repaying the promotion. In November, his troops drove the Confederates off Missionary Ridge in a stunning victory that turned the course of the War in the west and opened the way for Sherman to march down into Georgia.

The immortal "Rock of Chickamauga," Virginian George Thomas was viewed as a traitor to his homeland by Southerners and was one of the greatest Federal commanders of the War.

Historic Victories

When Sherman faced Joe Johnston the following June at Kennesaw Mountain, the biggest battle of the Atlanta campaign, Thomas commanded the uphill attack against the center of the Confederate line. Here, not even the "Rock of Chickamauga" could carry the day. Johnston's men deftly decimated three straight Federal charges. "One or two more such assaults will use up this army," Thomas fretted after the lost battle. The Federals finally pulled away and resumed their attempts to flank Johnston. Thomas's fortunes turned again, however, as Sherman defeated Johnston's replacement John Bell Hood (a far less capable adversary as theater commander), captured Atlanta, and sent the Virginia Unionist north to Tennessee to guard the Federal supply line. Thomas entrenched his well-fed, well-supplied 60,000-man powerhouse in Franklin, awaiting Hood. And come Hood did—with no cavalry and barely half as many men as Thomas, a quarter of those trudging barefoot over the hard winter ground.

After leaving the heart of his army on the bloody fields of Franklin, Hood arrived outside Nashville with a hungry, demoralized, and greatly outnumbered force. Thomas methodically reconnoitered the Confederate positions and planned his attack. Grant, who had previously questioned what he termed Thomas's propensity for "the slows," grew impatient with him as the days passed, and the

Virginian initiated no action. Grant finally boarded a train in Virginia and headed for Nashville to take command of Thomas's army. While he was en route, however, Thomas unleashed both his and John Schofield's men in overwhelming force against Hood. The Confederates held their main position through nearly two days of fighting. Late the afternoon of December 16, however, the Federals broke their line and drove them into a pall mall retreat. Thomas's Nashville victory looms large in the annals of American history because it wrecked the last large Confederate fighting force in the west and cleared the final significant obstacle to Sherman's rampage to the sea.

Chattanooga

Lincoln looked at Rosecrans and saw horrific defeat at Chickamauga—34,000 casualties, half of them Federal. He looked at Grant and, despite the rough-hewn edges, saw a train of major victories stretching back nearly two years. He removed Rosecrans and gave Grant leadership over all the major Western armies—the Ohio, the Cumberland, and the Tennessee. Sherman would take direct charge of the Army of the Tennessee. Within two months, the momentum shifted as Federal armies converged from all points of the map to extricate Rosecrans. Two entire corps marched from the front at Virginia. Sherman came from Mississippi. Grant sacked Rosecrans as Army of the Cumberland commander and replaced him with Thomas. As if that were not enough, Bragg's disagreeable personality finally caught up with him. The latest in a long line of bitter disputes between him and his subordinates resulted in his having Longstreet and 15,000 men—at the worst possible time—sent northeast to contest Burnside's army of 40,000 at Knoxville. Thus, by the time Grant had all his forces in place and attacked Bragg, both the weight of numbers and the initiative had shifted back to the Federals.

Federal engineers constructed this 780-foot-long railroad trestle to ford a valley at Whiteside, Tennessee. Soldiers' tents appear in the foreground.

Bragg had entrenched his army south of Chattanooga on the high ground of Lookout Mountain and Missionary Ridge. On

The Capture of Lookout Mountain.

November 24, the Federals attacked the greatly outnumbered defenders on the former. They could not move them; Sherman's repeated attacks against the Confederate flank were decimated. But, now exposed, the Confederates withdrew after dark. The next day, Sheridan spearheaded a stunning and audacious charge that routed the defenders clean off Missionary Ridge and sent them retreating south into Georgia. Meanwhile, Burnside repulsed Longstreet's attempts to wrest Knoxville from him; the "old warhorse" then led his men back across the mountains to rejoin Lee.

Losing at Chattanooga and failing at Knoxville cost the Confederates all the fruits of their bloody win at Chickamauga. It laid to rest Confederate hopes in Tennessee. And it opened that gateway into Georgia. Long excoriated by Confederates high and low for his middling leadership of the South's chief western army, the Army of Tennessee, Braxton Bragg offered his resignation to his close old friend Davis. The President accepted it, and Joe Johnston acceded to command in his place. And as the year

Yankee ingenuity and initiative at work. Federal engineers build a bridge across the Tennessee River at Chattanooga.

Nathan Bedford Forrest (1821–1877)

During the War, William Sherman called him "that devil Forrest" and said, "I would like to have Forrest hunted down and killed." Long after peace had come, though, he called Bedford Forrest, "the most remarkable man our Civil War produced on either side." The *Chicago Tribune* called him "the Butcher Forrest" after the battle of Fort Pillow, where some of his soldiers shot Federal troops—most of them black—attempting to surrender. Yet he did not sanction their actions, in fact curtailed them, and referring to blacks loyal to the Southern states, declared, "better Confederates did not live." He earned a fortune before the war through cotton, real estate, and slave trading. He took forty-four of his own slaves to war with him and forty-two of them remained with him the entire war. He was shot four times during the War and had twenty-nine horses shot out from under him. But he himself killed thirty Federals. He led the original Ku Klux Klan, then shut it down when he felt its legitimate purposes were fulfilled and that less-honorable men had corrupted its efforts to protect white Southern civilians.

Forrest grew up as a frontiersman on the edge of American civilization and accrued all the violence of that hard land. But he did not drink, smoke, carouse or gamble and a decade after the War he followed his wife's example by professing faith in Christ and living his remaining years as a humble, devout Presbyterian. Despite these enigmatic characteristics, he was essentially a simple man with a simple creed born of duty, loyalty, and honor. He and his cavalry won at Brice's Cross Roads, Holly Springs, Okolona, Cedar Bluff, and a host of other battles and harried Sherman and his communication supply lines till the end of the War.

> *Whenever I met one of them fellers that fit by note, I generally whipped him before he got his tune pitched.*
>
> —Nathan Bedford Forrest recalling his exploits against West Point-trained Federal commanders

Historian Shelby Foote well described what they accomplished during one short period in the fall of 1864:

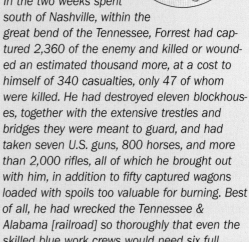

> *In the two weeks spent south of Nashville, within the great bend of the Tennessee, Forrest had captured 2,360 of the enemy and killed or wounded an estimated thousand more, at a cost to himself of 340 casualties, only 47 of whom were killed. He had destroyed eleven blockhouses, together with the extensive trestles and bridges they were meant to guard, and had taken seven U.S. guns, 800 horses, and more than 2,000 rifles, all of which he brought out with him, in addition to fifty captured wagons loaded with spoils too valuable for burning. Best of all, he had wrecked the Tennessee & Alabama [railroad] so thoroughly that even the skilled blue work crews would need six full weeks to put it back in operation.*

To the Death

Forrest and his meager band of 4,500 horse soldiers, which included several dozen black troopers, prompted Sherman to exclaim that it would be: "a physical impossibility to protect the roads, now that Hood, Forrest, Wheeler, and the whole batch of devils are turned loose without home or habitation." Another time, "Uncle Billy" issued orders to "follow Forrest to the death if it costs 10,000 lives and breaks the treasury. There will never be peace in Tennessee until Forrest is dead."

Forrest was defiant and would not countenance capitulation, as evidenced by his leading his men out of Fort Donelson, Kentucky, and refusing to surrender to U. S. Grant with the rest of the Confederate troops there. Perhaps a fitting valedictory to Forrest's wartime exploits occurred at the close of the bloody battle of Shiloh. Covering the Southern retreat with his cavalry, the mounted Forrest was swarmed by a mass of Federal infantry. Shot in the leg, he hauled one bluecoat up off the ground and slung him over the crupper of his horse. Using the doomed soldier as a shield, he muscled his way, shouting and shooting, through the melee and away to safety.

Get there first with the most men.
—Nathan Bedford Forrest

But when the end of the War did come, Forrest made

Thompson's Station, by John Paul Strain. Nathan Bedford Forrest, though outnumbered, leads a charge against Federal forces near Thompson's Station, Tennessee, in March. When the Yankees shot his horse out from under him, Forrest scrambled to his feet and led the charge on foot, driving his foe from the field.

sure his men knew it was time to stop fighting:

> *Civil war, such as you have just passed through, naturally engenders feelings of animosity, hatred and revenge. It is our duty to divest ourselves of all such feelings, and, so far as it is in our power to do so, to cultivate feelings toward those with whom we have so long contested, and heretofore so widely but honestly differed. Whatever your responsibilities may be to government, to society, or to individuals, meet them like men.*

He spent the rest of his life, and most of the fortune he built after the War, financially supporting disabled Confederate veterans and the widows and orphans of dead soldiers. None of these received anything from the U.S. government, while it poured out millions of dollars to Federal veterans.

Spiritual Salvation

In a series of passages in his book *Nathan Bedford Forrest*, Jack Hurst poignantly recounts Forrest's Christian conversion two years before his death and the changed life that followed. One evening, Hurst writes, Forrest accompanied his devout wife Mary Ann to evening worship at the Court Street Cumberland Presbyterian Church she regularly attended in Memphis. Hurst includes the recollection of Rev. George T. Stainback, whose sermon that night centered on Jesus's parable of the builder in the Sermon on the Mount:

> *"He took my arm, and we passed [to] the pavement below," the clergyman, who had known Forrest for a quarter century, would remember two years later. At the sidewalk, Stainback said, Forrest suddenly leaned against a wall and his eyes filled with tears. "Sir, your sermon has removed the last prop from under me," he said. "I am the fool that built on sand; I am a poor miserable sinner." He looked "all shaken," recalled Stainback, who recommended that he study Psalm 51 to find spiritual relief. The next evening the minister visited him for a talk and a prayer, and after the latter, Forrest rose from his knees to say he felt "satisfied. All is right. I put my trust in my Redeemer."*

Later, according to Hurst, Forrest's wartime aide Charles W. Anderson was profoundly struck with his former commander's new "mildness," "softness of expression," and "gentleness" of words:

> *Soon [Anderson] told him . . . that he didn't appear to me to be the same man I used to know so well. He was silent for a moment, then . . . halting suddenly, he took hold of the lapel of my coat and turned me squarely in front of him, and raising his right hand with that long index finger . . . extended, he said, "Major, I am not the man you were with so long and knew so well—I hope I am a better man. I've joined the Church and am trying to live a Christian life."*

He spent the rest of his life . . . financially supporting disabled Confederate veterans and the widows and orphans of dead soldiers.

Finally, Hurst described a scene in the last days of Forrest's life, when his weight had dropped to around 100 pounds. On what would become his deathbed, Forrest told Rev. Stainback how he regretted many words spoken and deeds done in the presence of others even since his conversion. Nonetheless, he said,

> *I want you to understand now that I feel that God has forgiven me for all. . . . I have an indescribable peace. All is peace within. I want you to know that between me and . . . the face of my Heavenly Father, not a cloud intervenes. I have put my trust in my Lord and Saviour.*

ended, William Tecumseh Sherman took charge of the massed Federal forces at Chattanooga and prepared to achieve his destiny.

At home in "Pine Cottage," winter quarters built by these Federal soldiers.

West of the Mississippi

The Trans-Mississippi River situation shaped up even more bleakly for the Confederacy. The Federals had long since snuffed Confederate hopes in New Mexico and Arizona. Now they had swallowed up most of Missouri, as well as Louisiana, particularly its southern regions. The North's growing dominance in the Indian Territory and its victories in Arkansas at Fort Smith and the capital of Little Rock placed most of that state under its heel by the end of the year. Only Texas, now remote and isolated from the main theaters of war, remained solidly under Confederate control.

Forgotten Blacks in Gray

Young Confederates, black and white, armed and ready. *(Black Southerners in Gray)*

Few partisans of the War have been so overlooked as the tens of thousands of Southern blacks who voluntarily committed themselves to the Confederate cause. Across the South, black individuals and groups sponsored fairs and parties, and gave gifts for the War effort. They sponsored balls in Vicksburg and Fort Smith, collected money for soldier relief in Helena, North Carolina, contributed to government loan efforts in Columbus, Georgia, equipped volunteers in North Carolina, gave gold to the treasury in Virginia and food in Alabama, made uniforms in Savannah, and contributed scrap metal for cannon balls in Newburn, North Carolina. In Charleston, the Confederate Ethiopian Serenaders conducted a concert to purchase gunboats and munitions.

Thousands of acts were done freely by blacks across

J. B. White and John Terrill, Sixth Tennessee Cavalry.
(Black Southerners in Gray)

the Confederacy that whites would never have dared ask them to do. The infrastructure of the Southern war effort was heavily dependent upon faithful and loyal black labor. The South depended on its black population and could not do anything, much less go to war, without black involvement and support. On the home front, blacks manned the mines and the munitions factories and kept the crops growing, which in turn kept the army in the field. Many black slaves stepped into the vacated role of white overseers and served there diligently.

The South depended on its black population and could not do anything, much less go to war, without black involvement and support.

Though the Confederate national government did not approve the use of blacks under arms until the final months of fighting, tens of thousands of blacks, free and slave, served in the Southern military some time during the War. The best estimates gauge this count at between 50,000 and 100,000. Moderns who challenge such numbers overlook the fact that the Confederacy never managed to maintain regular enlistment procedures or records; official records do not exist that support the estimated number of white Confederate troops either. Also overlooked is that many, if not most, blacks entered Confederate military service through local or state channels, which was not discouraged, rather than national ones, which was, until March 18, 1865. They worked as body servants, teamsters, and cooks, for quartermasters and engineers, in commissaries, and as construction workers.

In Combat

Even more forgotten—or ignored—are those blacks who served the Confederacy at some time in combat roles. The best estimate of this total number is around 40,000. The *Winston-Salem People's Press* of Salisbury, North Carolina, reported that fifteen free men of color volunteered for the service of the state. Each wore a placard on his hat that read, "We will die for the South." Fifty-three blacks volunteered in Amelia County, Virginia, and two hundred came forward in Petersburg, Virginia, offering to do any work assigned to them "to serve Old Virginia." A group of Savannah, Georgia, blacks sent a letter to the *Savannah Evening News*, requesting the privilege of defending the state. One Charleston, South Carolinian observed "a thousand Negroes who, so far from inclining to insurrections, were grinning ear to ear at the prospects of shooting Yankees." As of February, 1865, 1,150 black seamen served in the Confederate Navy. Black militia-men partially manned the Richmond Howitzers. Two companies of black soldiers marched with the Jackson

Battalion and saw combat at Petersburg.

Nashville had a company of black soldiers. Memphis had several hundred march through the streets under the command of Confederate officers, shouting for Jeff Davis and singing war songs. A black company was established in Augusta, Georgia; blacks were drilled and armed for duty in Montgomery, Alabama; and two companies were raised for duty in Fort Smith, Arkansas. They had no weapons, but they declared themselves ready and determined to fight for their masters and their homes. And fight they did. Beginning at First Manassas, many accounts confirm that black soldiers shot, killed, and captured Federal troops. This sent shock waves through the North. One Yankee newspaper reported after the battle:

> *The war has dispelled one delusion of the abolitionist. The Negroes regard them as enemies instead of friends. No insurrection has occurred in the South. No important stampede of slaves has evinced their desire for freedom. On the contrary, they have jeered at and insulted our troops, have readily enlisted in the rebel army, and on Sunday at Manassas, shot down our men with as much alacrity as if abolitionism had never existed.*

Real Soldiers

The first Federal officer to lose his life in combat, Major T. Winthrop, was probably shot by a black man. A Federal medical officer observed Stonewall Jackson's troops marching through Fredericksburg in 1862 and calculated that about five percent of his force were black men, armed as soldiers, and fully integrated with the ranks. One Federal soldier wrote a letter to the *Indianapolis Star*, which was reprinted by the *New York Tribune*. It said, in part,

> *A body of 700 Negro infantry opened fire on our men, wounding two lieutenants and two privates. . . . We have heard of a regiment of Negroes at Manassas, and another at Memphis, and still another at New Orleans, but did not believe it until it came so near home and attacked our men.*

A Federal medical officer observed Stonewall Jackson's troops marching through Fredericksburg in 1862 and calculated that about five percent of his force were black men, armed as soldiers, and fully integrated with the ranks.

Federal Captain Isaac Haysinger gave the following account of the Army of Northern Virginia as it moved through Frederick, Maryland, in 1862:

> *At 4 o'clock this morning, the Rebel army began to move from our town, Jackson's force taking the advance. The most liberal calculation could not have given them more than 64,000 men. Over 3,000 Negroes must be included in that number. These were clad in all kinds of uniforms. Not only cast-off, or captured, United States uniforms, but in coats with Southern buttons and state buttons, etc.*
>
> *They were shabby, but not shabbier- or seedier-looking than those worn by the white men in the Confederate ranks. Most of the Negroes had arms—muskets, rifles, sabers, Bowie knives, dirks, etc. They were supplied in many instances with knapsacks, haversacks, canteens, and so forth, and were manifestly an integral part and portion of the Southern Confederate Army.*
>
> *They were seen riding on horses and mules and driving wagons, riding in caissons, in ambulances, with the staffs of generals, and promiscuously mixed up with all the Rebel horde.*

The famous black abolitionist Frederick Douglass observed in the fall of 1861:

There are at the present moment many colored men in the Confederate army doing duty not only as cooks, servants, and laborers, but as real soldiers, having muskets on their shoulders and bullets in their pockets, ready to shoot down loyal troops and do all that soldiers may do to destroy the Federal government and build up that of the traitors and rebels.

Some of the best sharpshooters in the Confederate army were black servants. One, his name lost to history, became legendary for the damage he inflicted on the Federal lines. He would perch in the tallest tree he could find in an area and shoot Federal troops. He would often begin with the Federal sharpshooters. He proved so deadly in the area around Yorktown, Virginia, that an entire Federal company was sent to locate and capture him. After many cautious maneuvers, they finally located and surrounded the tree where he perched. "I say big n——, you better come down from there, you are captured," one Yankee shouted up to the sharpshooter. He responded, "Not as this chile knows of!" Those were his final words. He resumed firing and was killed.

These black Confederate soldiers no more fought to preserve slavery than their successors fought in World War I and World War II to preserve Jim Crow and segregation.
—Walter Williams
George Mason University
Professor of Economics

Former slave Jerry May became a Confederate soldier. He died in 1905. When the Sons of Confederate Veterans memorialized him in 1990 and offered a twenty-one gun salute, one of them told an Atlanta newspaper, "We're not honoring this man because he is black, we're honoring him because he was a Confederate soldier." *(Forgotten Confederates: An Anthology about Black Southerners)*

Many Reasons

Why did such widespread support exist among black Southerners for the Confederacy? Some did it not out of patriotism, but to prove their trustworthiness and equality with whites as men and win their freedom after the War. As one black Confederate soldier said, "No matter where I fight, I only wish to spend what I have, and fight as long as I can, if only my boy may stand alone in the street equal to a white boy when the war is over."

Some slaves supported the Confederate cause from a sense of adventure, much more exciting than their usual activities. Perhaps the majority of blacks who chose to actively serve the Confederacy did so, like their white counterparts, to preserve their homes and family, and the way of life they had always known. One Yankee cavalry officer complained in his diary how a shotgun-brandishing black Confederate kept him under guard, training the weapon on his head with unwavering concentration: "Here I had come South and was fighting to free this man. If I had made one false move on my horse, he would have shot my head off." During the march to Gettysburg, one slave stopped to talk with the wife of a Pennsylvania farmer, who sought to enlighten him on the attractions of freedom. She suggested he slip away from the Confederate army and remain in the North as a free man. He replied: "Lady, I live as I wish. And if I did not, I think I couldn't better myself by stoppin' here. This is a beautiful country, but it doesn't come up to home in my eyes."

Story after story from every corner of the South recalls the wartime love of blacks and whites, who had grown up together, for one another. Mobile, Alabama, slave Charlie Adams went voluntarily, as most of the slaves did, with his master's son to the War as his body servant. When asked years after the War during the Franklin Roosevelt administration's *Slave Narratives* project was he not afraid of flying shot and shell, he replied, "No, Madam, I kept way in the back where the camp was, for I didn't like to feel the earth tremble 'neath my feet. But you see, Madam, I loved young Master John, and he loved me, and I just had to watch over that boy."

Monroe Gooch entered the Confederates' 45th Tennessee Infantry as a cook. He was allowed to visit his home when General John Bell Hood raided Federal-occupied Tennessee late in the War, and could have remained. Gooch returned to his unit, however, and remained with them until the end of the War. *(Forgotten Confederates: An Anthology about Black Southerners)*

Other Reasons

Other blacks supported the Confederacy for economic motives. A quarter of a million free black men and women lived in the South—15,000 more than lived in the North. One quarter of the free Southern blacks owned slaves, and most of them had prospered financially. They felt threatened by the Northern invasion and the aims of the abolitionists, whom they saw as a threat to their wealth and social advancement. Large numbers of these blacks enlisted in the Confederate armies. Sometimes they raised their own units, one of which required each man to own at least $25,000 in assets to join. They knew a Northern victory would bring economic and social ruin to them—and it did.

> *Better Confederates did not live.*
> —Nathan Bedford Forrest, praising the black troopers who rode with him in the Seventh Tennessee Cavalry.

Finally, a strong minority of Southern blacks—slave and free—could be classified as Southern patriots. They loved the South and were delighted to be identified with its cause, which they understood to be freedom. They viewed the North as a bully seeking to force its will on others who wished to live as they pleased. Charles Harper said regarding the large number of body servants who accompanied their masters to war and faithfully served them throughout the conflict: "No class of servants had such excellent opportunities to desert or to evidence disloyalty. Yet this class almost never deserted. Black Confederates followed their masters to war, worked as teamsters, foragers, and cooks in the Confederate army, and did yeoman service, shouldering arms and burning gunpowder in combat, and when captured entered Yankee prisons as prisoners of war."

Black soldiers fought for the Confederacy till the bitter end. Groups of them fought in skirmishes at Amelia Courthouse and Farmville the last week of the War for the Army of Northern Virginia, and dozens surrendered with Lee at Appomattox, eschewing freedom and insisting on being paroled with their white comrades. Confederates of African heritage exhibited great courage, resourcefulness, and loyalty. Sixty-five black horse soldiers rode with Nathan Bedford Forrest's cavalry. His opinion of these, the forty-four servants who went to war with him, and other blacks who defended the South: "No better Confederates ever lived." Perhaps historian Ervin Jordan has best summarized the plight of black Confederates:

Numerous Afro-Virginians, free blacks and slaves, were genuine Southern loyalists, not as a consequence of white pressure but due to

their own preferences. They are the Civil War's forgotten people, yet their existence was more widespread than American history has recorded. Their bones rest in unhonored glory in Southern soil, shrouded by falsehoods, indifference, and historians' censorship.

Like many Confederate veteran reunions, this one in Huntsville, Alabama, circa 1928, included both black and white soldiers. *(Forgotten Confederates: An Anthology about Black Southerners)*

Federal soldiers offered freedom to a Confederate master and his slave imprisoned at Point Lookout if they signed a loyalty oath to the U.S. The master agreed and signed. When the slave refused, the Federals reminded him his master had and asked why he would not. Disgusted, the slave replied, "Master has no principles."

Other Black Confederate Soldiers

- James Washington, a sergeant in Company D, 34th Texas cavalry.
- Horace King, who became know as "the bridge builder of the Confederacy" for his engineering skills.
- Sam Ashe, who killed the first Federal officer in the war, Major T. Winthrop.
- Private John W. Buckner, wounded at Fort Wagner helping to repulse the 54th Massachusetts black Federal regiment.
- Louis Napoleon Nelson, who rode as a horse soldier with Nathan Bedford Forrest and his 7th Tennessee Cavalry in such battles as Shiloh, Brice's Cross Roads, and Lookout Mountain.

Steve Eberhardt (right) gained renown during the War for his prowess at securing food for Confederate soldiers. A 1921 Rome, Georgia, newspaper referred to him as "the ancient Senegambian who dresses up in flags and feathers, mostly before Confederate reunion time." (Courtesy Georgia Department of Archives and History.)

Going to the War are these *New York Herald Tribune* reporters and their wagon, in the field.

Christmas Plum Pudding Recipe in the North

A pound of suet, cut in pieces not too fine, a pound of currants, and a pound of raisins stoned, four eggs, half a grated nutmeg, an ounce of citron and lemon peel, shred fine, a teaspoonful of beaten ginger, half a pound of bread crumbs, half a pound of flour, and a pint of milk.

Beat the eggs first, add half the milk, beat them together, and by degrees stir in the flour, then the suet, spice and fruit, and as much milk as will mix it together very thick. Then take a clean cloth, dip in boiling water, and squeeze dry. While the water is boiling fast, put in your pudding, which should boil at least five hours.

24 The Wilderness
(1864)

Mary Tippin, a female sutler with the 114th Pennsylvania regiment Collis Zouaves.

Alas! What sorrow reigns over the land! There is a universal wail of woe. . . . It is like the death of the firstborn in Egypt. Who thinks of or cares for victory now!

—Margaret Junkin Preston

Grant's continued successes in the field across the western theater caused Lincoln on March 9 to promote him to lieutenant general and give him command of all United States military forces. Meade, victor of Gettysburg, retained official command of the Army of the Potomac. Grant, however, rather than working from Washington or splitting his time among the various theaters, tented in Meade's camp and provided direct oversight to the largest Federal army. And Lincoln gave him, unlike previous commanders, not only free rein to conduct operations as he pleased, but whatever he needed with which to do it. All the President asked in return was victory. For once, he felt confident in a commander's ability to provide it.

Sutler
A person who follows an army and sells provisions to the troops.

Grant ordered into play a series of operations. His primary objective, rather than Confederate capital Richmond, was the Army of Northern Virginia and Robert E. Lee in particular. Grant had the insight to recognize that even were Richmond captured and burned to the ground, the Confederacy could survive, and survive to deal much more misery to the United States. But, he saw, if Lee and his army were destroyed, the Confederacy was finished, whether Richmond remained standing or not. Coming east with Grant as cavalry commander of the Army of the Potomac was Philip Sheridan, the volatile little Irishman who had shined at Missionary Ridge and elsewhere.

Grant's Virginia Strategy

1) German revolutionary Franz Sigel and 6,500 men invaded the Shenandoah Valley in the west. Their twin objective was to deny it to the Army of Northern Virginia as an invasion route to Maryland, Pennsylvania, and Washington City; and to destroy its agricultural bounty, which was helping feed Lee's army and keep the Confederacy in the War.

2) Benjamin Butler, reassigned following the ignominy of his New Orleans occupation administration, led 30,000 men up the James River from Fortress Monroe on the Atlantic Coast. His goal: to sunder the rail line between Richmond and Petersburg twenty miles to the south, then threaten one or both of those cities.

3) Grant himself traveled with Meade and the 118,000 men of the Army of the Potomac across the Rapidan River in Central Virginia to crush Lee's Army of Northern Virginia, which could muster barely 60,000 underfed troops.

The Dahlgren Raid

When Brigadier General Judson Kilpatrick and Colonel Ulric Dahlgren rumbled across the Rapidan River the night of February 28 with 4,000 of the most elite horse soldiers in the Army of the Potomac, they intended to make history. They would succeed in that quest, but in a very different manner than they planned. Two factors buoyed Kilpatrick. The first regarded reports that two earlier Federal cavalry raids attempted against Richmond had the potential to succeed because of scant Southern defenses around the Confederate capital. Second was his own personal ambition for no less than the White House itself.

The desire to liberate thousands of suffering Federal prisoners from Richmond's Confederate prisons and to distribute amnesty proposals throughout central Virginia animated President Lincoln.

Thus, Kilpatrick presented a fresh plan directly to the President that would accomplish both of

Return to Clark's Mountain, by John Paul Strain. Robert E. Lee and his army give chase to a diversionary wing of the Dahlgren Raid.

Lincoln's desires, as well as wreak havoc with Confederate supply and communication lines. Kilpatrick next met with Secretary of War Edwin Stanton. The latter had long advocated a harder prosecution of the War than that espoused by Augustine, Aquinas, Calvin, and other Christian proponents of the theory of just war—including Lee, Davis, and other Southern leaders. Plus, Stanton and Kilpatrick were both aware of Lincoln's earlier expression of interest to Fighting Joe Hooker in the kidnapping of Confederate President Jefferson Davis. Dahlgren seems to have caught wind of the project and invited himself aboard. Only twenty-one, he possessed dashing good looks, towering height, a bold appetite for glory, and a decorated war record that included key intelligence service at Gettysburg and a battle wound that had rendered him a wooden leg. He also had a famous father, Rear Admiral John Dahlgren of Dahlgren Gun fame, the U.S. Navy's premier authority on naval ordnance and a close friend of President Lincoln's.

Every Richmond male who could shoulder arms, from fifteen-year-old boys to sixty-five-year-old men, came out against Dahlgren.

The audacious adventure began well. George Armstrong Custer carried off a diversionary attack to the west toward Charlottesville; Kilpatrick's force of 3,000 and Dahlgren's of 460, after splitting up, both destroyed large amounts of Confederate supplies and property; and Dahlgren came within minutes of capturing a train on which rode Robert E. Lee himself.

Lasting Infamy

But by the time Kilpatrick reached the northern extremities of Richmond on March 1, things were souring. He met stiffer resistance than expected, and he retreated from the city. He did so partly because Dahlgren, who should have been thundering into the capital from the south to loose the thousands of Federal prisoners of war, had fallen way behind schedule. Black ex-slave Martin Robinson was supposed to guide Dahlgren to a ford across the James River. However, there was no possibility of crossing it, as it was muddy and swollen beyond its inner banks. Furious, Dahlgren had Robinson hanged from the nearest tree—with Dahlgren's own reins.

Every Richmond male who could shoulder arms again came out against Dahlgren. Fifteen-year-old boys, sixty-five-year-old men, crippled and maimed ex-soldiers, a few soldiers on furlough marched miles on foot to confront the raiders in a nightmarish after-dark rain and sleet storm. Soon, both Kilpatrick's and Dahlgren's forces were hoofing it east through the winter misery in a desperate attempt to reach Federal forces near Williamsburg. Wade Hampton's cavalry ambushed Kilpatrick's much-larger force and sent it reeling. A burgeoning contingent of soldiers, farmers, and other citizenry dogged Dahlgren across the countryside until finally ambushing and killing him on a wooded road northeast of Richmond near King and Queen Courthouse.

But the lasting infamy of what history christened the Dahlgren Raid was yet to come. Thirteen-year-old William Littlepage, rifling Dahlgren's corpse in hopes of finding a watch to replace the one Yankees had stolen from his school teacher, Edward Halbach, found instead a notebook and other papers. He quickly gave them to Halbach,

Thirteen-year-old William Littlepage, rifling Dahlgren's corpse in hopes of finding a watch to replace the one Yankees had stolen from his school teacher, Edward Halbach, found instead a notebook and other papers.

who read in stunned stupefaction: "The released prisoners [are] to destroy and burn the hateful City and do not allow the Rebel leader Davis and his traitorous crew to escape. . . . [Richmond] must be destroyed and Jeff Davis and Cabinet killed. . . . Gut the city. . . . Jeff Davis and Cabinet must be killed on the spot."

> *The released prisoners [are] to destroy and burn the hateful City and do not allow the Rebel leader Davis and his traitorous crew to escape. . . . [Richmond] must be destroyed and Jeff Davis and Cabinet killed. . . . Gut the city. . . . Jeff Davis and Cabinet must be killed on the spot.*
>
> —Excerpts from documents found on the corpse of Ulric Dahlgren

The Federals would officially disavow the papers as Confederate treachery. Dahlgren's father cited an apparent misspelling of his son's name as proof of "bare-faced, atrocious forgery." But adjustments made by a lithographer to a copy of the documents that the elder Dahlgren saw eventually provided an explanation to the supposed misspelling. And the documents themselves were handled by only a handful of men before they reached President Jefferson Davis. All these men corroborated that the publicized version of the Dahlgren papers matched, without alteration, what they themselves read. The first to read them, Halbach, offered lengthy testimony refuting any notion of forgery: "The papers which were thus handed over to the Confederate Government—I state it again—were correctly copied by the Richmond newspapers. . . . Human testimony cannot establish any fact more fully than the fact that Col. Ulric Dahlgren was the author of the 'Dahlgren Papers.'"

"Ugly Business"

"The blood boils with indignation in the veins of every officer and man as they read the account of [Dahlgren's] barbarous and inhuman plot," wrote Lee. The commander of the United States' largest army, Gen. George Meade, victor at Gettysburg, left explicit written record with his wife of his agreement with Lee:

This was a pretty ugly piece of business, for in denying having authorized or approved "the burning of Richmond or killing Mr. Davis and cabinet," I necessarily threw odium on Dahlgren. I, however, enclosed a letter from Kilpatrick, in which the authenticity of the papers was impugned; but I regret to say Kilpatrick's reputation, and collateral evidence in my possession, rather go against this theory.

Despite Lee's anger at the intended slaughter, his counsel alone countered that of high Davis cabinet members and dissuaded the President from ordering the execution of over 100 captured Federals who rode with Dahlgren: "I do not think that reason and reflection would justify such a course. I think it better to do right, even if we suffer in so doing, than to incur the reproach of our consciences and posterity."

Why can the advanced methods of modern science not be

Ulric Dahlgren

used to determine the authenticity of the Dahlgren papers? Because they are not extant to examine. In November, 1865, Stanton requested Francis Lieber (of Lieber Code fame), who had charge of captured Confederate archives, to forward to him all papers and documents found on Dahlgren's corpse. Stanton received the material December 1. Despite exhaustive searching, they have never again been seen. "The suspicion lingers that Stanton consigned them to the fireplace in his office," wrote one prominent historian, voicing the suspicions of many others.

Belief in the veracity of the Dahlgren Papers sparked the Confederate government toward a more aggressive plan to inflame Copperhead antiwar efforts in the North, as well as to kidnap Lincoln. Among other efforts, the Confederate Secret Service recruited the famed actor John Wilkes Booth, a pro-Southern Marylander, to help capture the President. Despite much effort, Confederate kidnapping plans came to naught. This, coupled with the loss of the War, rendered Booth stricken with grief and rage. Primed to deal with Lincoln, realizing that kidnapping him would no longer serve any purpose, and determined that the President should not escape the justice Booth believed he deserved, he murdered him. With no intentions of so doing, the Kilpatrick-Dahlgren raid unveiled before all Christendom to what barbarous depths the War had descended—and not only the War of Quantrill, Lane, and others in the west. Could Abraham Lincoln have been the raid's final victim?

Judson Kilpatrick, standing and holding document, with lady friends and his Third U.S. Cavalry Division staff.

John Singleton Mosby and His Rangers (1833–1916)

So great was the havoc wreaked against Federal forces by the fabled "Gray Ghost," John S. Mosby, and his band of guerilla cavalry that a central region of the War's main theater came to be known as "Mosby's Confederacy." Weighing just 125 pounds, Mosby had the courage and confidence of a giant. He survived seven wounds in the War. Long before secession, he taught himself law while in prison for shooting a University of Virginia classmate.

When war came, the native Virginian and attorney rode in the cavalry at First Manassas, then served Jeb Stuart's cavalry corps as a scout. Mosby hatched the plan that became Stuart's legendary ride around George McClellan's entire main Federal army. Stuart repaid Mosby in late 1862 by approving his request to create a special "Partisan Ranger" force for him to command. This suited Mosby's independent, self-reliant temperament right down to the ground. He chose the northern Virginia counties of Loudoun and Fauquier as his base of operations. Perched astride the main Federal supply line, he could strike north across the Potomac into Maryland, east toward the Federal capital of Washington, or west over the Blue Ridge Mountains into the Shenandoah Valley. Mosby's Rangers came together only when secretly notified of an impending raid. They rode swift horses and carried at least two .44 caliber six-shooting pistols apiece. Mosby eschewed the use of rifles or sabres for the lightning attacks and close-in fighting that marked Ranger operations. His overriding goal was "to weaken the armies invading Virginia by harassing their rear."

Weighing just 125 pounds, Mosby had the courage and confidence of a giant. He survived seven wounds in the War.

For over two years, Mosby's Rangers disrupted the Federal war effort, attacking and burning supply depots, trains, and wagon columns alike, destroying lengthy stretches of rail line, swarming over unsuspecting Federal troop detachments like mad hornets, and drawing the angry attention of enormous numbers of Northern forces. They fought scores of battles and skirmishes, ambushed camp after camp of Federal soldiers, and even kidnapped a Federal general. During one six-month period, Robert E. Lee announced, Mosby's Rangers inflicted 1,200 Federal casualties and collected over 1,600 horses and mules, 230 cattle, and 85 wagons. Two of the best cavalry companies in the United States army—the 2nd Massachusetts and 13th New York—were issued the full-time assignment of chasing Mosby down, but never could. U. S. Grant placed a bounty on Mosby's head and authorized Philip Sheridan's orders to hang on sight men suspected of riding with Mosby—until Mosby began doing the same thing to Federals.

Partisan's Work

Finally, in late 1864, as Sheridan scalded out the Shenandoah Valley, the Federal cavalry chief commissioned Captain Richard Blazer to recruit the 100 best horse soldiers he could find in the Federal army, issue them new repeating rifles, and embark on a search-and-destroy mission against Mosby's Rangers. Blazer got together his elite company and headed out, but on November 18 Mosby ambushed them and wiped out the entire column,

Overturning entire Federal railroad trains was one of the many marks of a raid by Mosby's Marauders.

except for two men, and took all their weapons.

Some historians calculate the War lasted as much as a year longer than it otherwise would have due to the exploits of Mosby and his men, who totaled fewer than 2,000 for the entire war and never numbered as many as 1,000 at one time. Mosby proclaimed his philosophy in his own words:

> *A small force, moving with celerity and threatening many points on a line can neutralize a hundred times its own number. The line must be stronger at every point than the attacking force, else it is broken. The military value of a partisan's work is not measured by the amount of property destroyed or the number of men killed or captured, but by the number he keeps watching.*

Some historians calculate the War lasted as much as a year longer than it otherwise would have due to the exploits of Mosby and his men, who totaled fewer than 2,000 for the entire war and never numbered as many as 1,000 at one time.

Like another stalwart Confederate commander, James Longstreet, Mosby sustained the wrath of his own Southern people after the War when he supported Grant (the man who had once placed a bounty on his head but who later became a close friend) for president, and joined the Northern-dominated Republican Party. In his later years, Mosby's friendship with powerful U.S. government officials—including presidents like Grant—led to a series of high level posts for him in both government and industry. He proved himself worthy of such appointments. As consul to Hong Kong, he exposed an elaborate ring of corruption in the United States' Far East foreign service offices. His actions led to an investigation that resulted in sweeping reform. And so well did he acquit his duties enforcing Federal fencing laws in Nebraska for the Department of the Interior, that local politicians forced his transfer elsewhere. Living in California at the dawn of the 20th century, the small old man, now blind in one eye, befriended a little boy named George S. Patton. The old warrior and the future warrior—himself the grandson of a Confederate officer—rode horses while the Gray Ghost regaled Patton with the long-ago saga of Mosby's Confederacy and what it took to lead men to victory in fierce combat against an implacable foe.

In an inconspicuous little grave behind an old church in the village of Flint Hill, Virginia lie the remains of Albert Gallatin Willis, a young seminary student who died on October 14. Willis rode with Mosby's Rangers during the War. Because of those hard-riding guerillas' harassment of Federal troops, supply trains, wagons, and stores, General Philip Sheridan, with U. S. Grant's concurrence, ordered Mosby and any of his men hung upon capture. In October, the 2nd U.S. Cavalry captured Willis and a now-unknown comrade and sentenced them to die by hanging. As a ministerial student, however, Willis was offered a chaplain's exemption. Refusing to doom his companion, the single, twenty-year-old soldier offered himself as a substitute for his married comrade and died in his place, so the other might go free. In his final moments, Willis professed aloud his "Christian readiness to die," prayed for his executioners, and was hanged.

Fire in the Valley, by John Paul Strain. John Mosby and his Rangers ambushed Phil Sheridan's 525-wagon train at Bush Marsh Creek, near Berryville, Virginia. Mosby's Rangers burned many wagons and captured 200 prisoners , 500 mules, 50 horses, and 200 cattle.

The Wilderness Campaign

Grant moved straightway to get to grips with Lee. But never before had he encountered the leader whom the Federal's new eastern subordinates warned him was on a level beyond any Confederate commander in the west. Grant was insulted at the insinuation he perceived of Lee being too much for him to handle. Then he found himself lured by the Virginian into a savage fight among the tangled density of the Wilderness, which, when smoke and then fire were added to the mixture, negated both the Federals' numerical and artillery superiority. Plus, Lee struck the first blow, which counted heavily in the confusion and mayhem. For two days, May 5–6, the great armies slashed and blazed at one another, sometimes in isolated pockets of one or two men each. On the second day, the Federals appeared ready to sweep the field when Longstreet's corps, mostly Texans, came to the rescue. So thrilled was Lee that he attempted to lead the counterattack himself. The Texans screamed, "Lee to the rear! Lee to the rear!" and refused to charge until Lee relented. When they did charge, it turned the tide of the battle. If not for a spooky reprise of history, the Confederates again might have crushed the main Federal army.

What saved them? For one, Lee's best corps commander was shot and nearly killed by his own men while supervising a thunderous victory in the Wilderness. So had it happened, on every count, to Stonewall Jackson—and almost a year before to the day. The loss of Longstreet (for nearly six months) blunted Confederate hopes for a victory of monumental proportions. But in a way it still was. Ulysses S. Grant, in his first all-out fight with Robert E. Lee and the Army of Northern Virginia, took a thrashing and lost nearly 20,000 men.

Federal General Winfield Hancock, whose alert and steadfast leadership helped save the Army of the Potomac from destruction at the Battle of the Wilderness.

Spotsylvania

Unlike previous Federal commanders, Grant did not retreat to the ramparts of Washington to lick his wounds. "Whatever happens, there will be no turning back," he told Lincoln. He moved southeast around Lee's right flank and a race began to reach Spotsylvania Courthouse, where Grant hoped to cut Lee off from Richmond—and his supply base. The Confederates won the desperate race, but barely. It gave Lee the opportunity to construct some of the strongest earthworks of the War. For nearly two weeks the armies slugged it out. The combat grew ferocious, crazed, beyond anything even many of the battle-hardened veterans themselves had yet seen. On May 12, 7,000 men fell on each side at the "Bloody Angle." But Grant never could turn Lee's right flank, as he attempted over and over to do. When the Federal commander disengaged and again looped to the southeast, he had lost another 18,000 men.

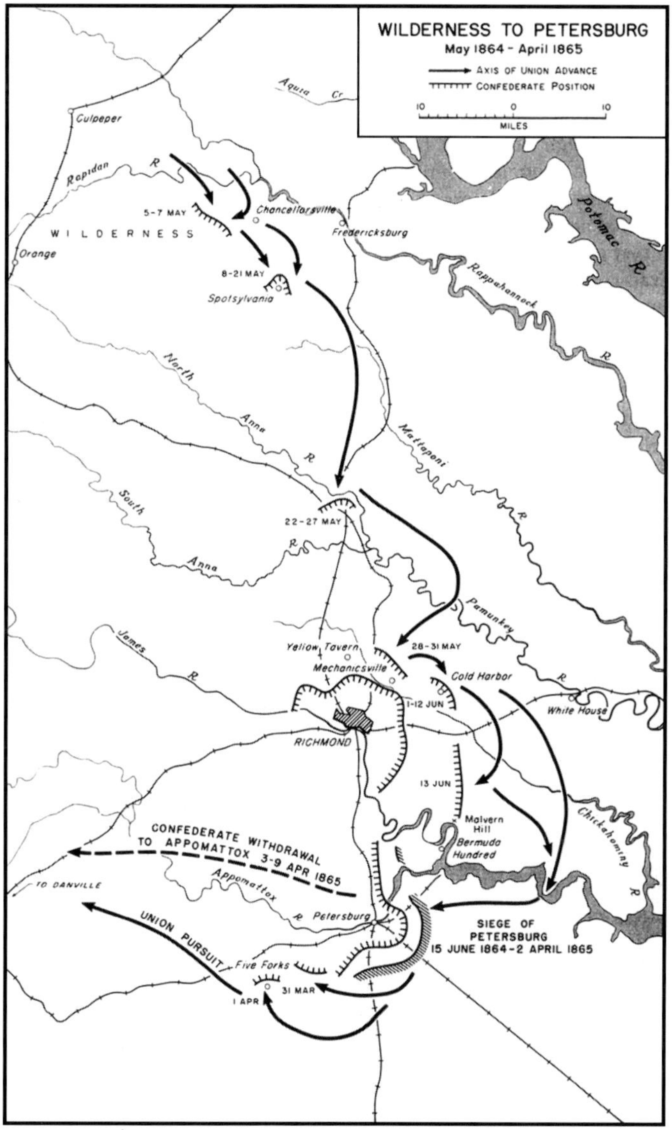

Map of the Wilderness to Petersburg campaign. (Courtesy of The General Libraries, The University of Texas at Austin)

Lee, outnumbered at least two to one the whole Wilderness Campaign, was inflicting double the number of casualties he was receiving. But he had lost Longstreet, and his other two corps commanders—Richard Ewell and A. P. Hill—were ill, and so was Lee. Plus, he knew he must finally lose the War if this battle of attrition continued. Meanwhile, the past two weeks had been the bloodiest two of the War for the North—and the two most shattering defeats of U. S. Grant's career. Plus, his other advances in Virginia—in the Shenandoah and toward Richmond from the James—had been stuffed.

Yellow Tavern

One bright note for the North was Sheridan's rampage down the heart of Virginia from Spotsylvania toward Richmond with a gargantuan force of Federal cavalry. They accomplished more in a few days than any previous Federal cavalry had done in the east through three years of war. Among other feats, they torched a three-week supply of food for the Army of Northern Virginia, destroyed over a hundred Virginia Central railway cars and two locomotives, freed nearly 400 Federal prisoners, and took 300 Confederate prisoners.

I should have been the hero of the hour. I could have gone in and burned and killed right and left.

—Philip Sheridan, on not riding into Richmond

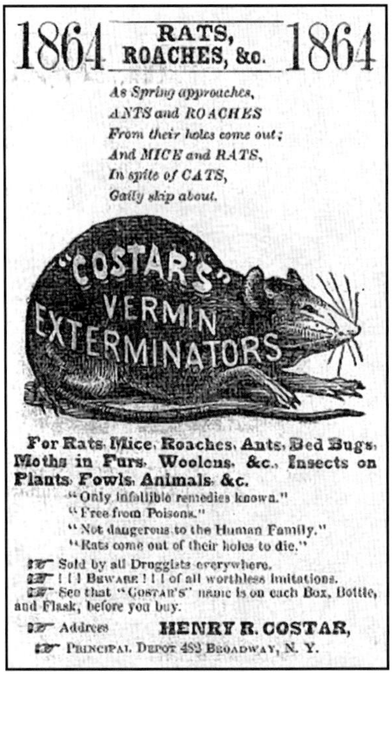

Prisoners of war North and South may have slept with vermin, and the people of Vicksburg may have eaten them, but some places in America still had the wherewithal to purchase Costar's Vermin Exterminators to rid themselves of such creatures.

Grant wanted Lee's communication with Richmond disrupted. And he knew Jeb Stuart, outnumbered, outgunned, and outhorsed, had no choice but to peel off with his Confederate horse soldiers from Lee's vanguard and challenge Sheridan. Otherwise, the Yankees would thunder right on into Richmond, defended by a skeleton force of old men, boys, and invalids. Indeed, Stuart did come out against Sheridan, six miles north of Richmond at Yellow Tavern—4,500 Confederates against nearly 13,000 Federals. But despite realizing it likely meant his doom—and possible loss of personal prestige and plaudits—in a straight-up fight with Sheridan, Stuart had left fully half his men with the Army of Northern Virginia, so as not to leave Lee without "eyes"—as Sheridan had Grant. Stuart's skillful placement of his troops at Yellow Tavern slowed Sheridan down and forced him into an all-day contest. This in turn deterred the Federal cavalry chieftain from advancing beyond the capital's outer defensive perimeter as he hoped, because of approaching darkness, a now-raging thunderstorm, and most of all because he feared significant Confederate reinforcements were now converging, which they were. "I should have been the hero of the hour," Sheridan lamented later on not riding on into Richmond. "I could have gone in and burned and killed right and left."

Jeb Stuart may have helped save Richmond once again, but he could not save himself. A retreating, unhorsed Michigan trooper gutshot him. "Go back and do your duty as I have done mine and the country will be saved!" the Virginian shouted as he was carried from the field. "I had rather die than be whipped!" In barely more than twenty-four hours, the incarnation of Confederate knighthood and chivalry requested of a clergyman the singing of *Rock of Ages*, then said, "I am going fast now, I am resigned; God's will be done." Less than thirty minutes later, the man whom Federal General John Sedgwick called "the greatest cavalry officer ever foaled in America" was dead.

Matthew Brady's famous portrait of U. S. Grant during the spring Cold Harbor battle.

Cold Harbor

Shortly after he learned that Beauregard had bottled up Butler's much-larger Federal force between Richmond and Petersburg, Grant again looped around Lee's right flank. After a desultory action at the North Anna River, he did so yet again, then again. Now the two forces faced one another at the key junction of Cold Harbor, just northeast of Richmond. Frustrated and impatient, Grant unleashed an all-out frontal assault against the Confederates on June 2. Over 7,000 Federals fell in little more than an hour. If Grant did not discern the possibilities at Cold Harbor, many of his battle-seasoned veterans did. Scores of their corpses were afterward found by the Confederates with self-written notes pinned to their uniforms that featured their name and words such as, "June 3. Cold Harbor. I was killed." The Battle of Cold Harbor only ended when the Federal soldiers threatened to mutiny rather than attempt another attack. A chorus of rage rose up across the North. For all its physical deprivations and disadvantages, in less than one month, the Army of Northern Virginia had hung 60,000 casualties on Grant. This number was equal to the number of soldiers in Lee's entire army.

"The Very Darkest Hours"

Horace Greeley (1811–1872) long published the pro-Republican *New York Tribune*, one of America's most influential newspapers, and spoke the famed words, "Go west, young man." In his book *American Conflict*, he recalled how desperate the War grew for the North:

> *The very darkest hours of our contest—those in which our loyal [Federal] people most profoundly despaired of a successful issue—were those of July and August, 1864. . . . Cold Harbor was an exceedingly expensive and damaging failure—damaging not merely in the magnitude of our loss, but in its effect on the morale and efficiency of our chief army. It had extinguished the last hope of crushing Lee north of the James and of interposing that army between him and the Confederate capital.*
>
> *The failure to seize Petersburg when it would easily have fallen, and the repeated and costly failures to carry its defenses by assault, or even to flank them on the south; the luckless conclusion of Wilson's and Kautz's raid to Staunton River; Sheridan's failure to unite with Hunter in Lee's rear; Sturgis's disastrous defeat by Forrest near Buntown; Hunter's failure to carry Lynchburg and eccentric line of retreat; Sherman's bloody repulse at Kennesaw, and the compelled slowness of his advance on Atlanta; Early's unresisted swoop down the Valley into Maryland, his defeat of Wallace at the Monocacy, and his unpunished demonstration against the defenses of Washington itself; the raids of his troopers up to the suburbs of Baltimore, on the Philadelphia railroad, and even up into Pennsylvania, burning Chambersburg and alarming even Pittsburg; and finally the bloody, wretched fiasco of the Mine explosion before Petersburg; these and other reverses relieved by a few and unimpressive triumphs, rendered the midsummer of 1864 one of the gloomiest seasons of our great struggle for the upholders of the national cause.*

I received to-day a kind letter from Reverend Mr. Cole, of Culpeper Court House. He is a most excellent man in all the relations of life. He says there is not a church standing in all that country, within the lines formerly occupied by the enemy. All are razed to the ground, and the materials used often for the vilest purposes. Two of the churches at the Court House barely escaped destruction. The pews were all taken out to make seats for the theater. The fact was reported to the [Federal] commanding officer by their own men of the Christian Commission, but he took no steps to rebuke or arrest it. We must suffer patiently to the end, when all things will made right.

—Robert E. Lee to his wife Mary

Mary Boykin Chesnut (1823-1886)

Perhaps the most famous diary of the War was not published until nearly twenty years after the death of its author. Mary Chesnut was a highborn Charlestonian. Both her father and her husband James represented the state in the U.S. Senate. The former was also governor of South Carolina. She and her husband owned one of the vastest chain of plantations on the continent; it included over 1,000 slaves. He became a well-regarded adviser to President Davis and a Confederate brigadier general. Chesnut lived to see—and her readers with her—the bombardment of Fort Sumter from a rooftop; a kitchen utensil with a prewar price of less than one dollar in gold costing $1,000 in paper money; Southern planters mortgaging their possessions to provide for their servants, who had no work to do, while they themselves fought and died on the battlefront; the wives of Davis's cabinet officers and military commanders gathering in homes to knit socks for barefoot soldiers; people going to market with their money in their basket, then returning home with their purchases in their pocket.

The people who moved in and out of Mary Chesnut's life represent a virtual roll call of the greatest names in the Confederacy.

How incisive a portrait was Chesnut's journal, not only of the contemporary wartime South, but of the plumbline connecting it back to the birth of America, is found in the following paragraph (and many others) from Chesnut's record:

> *Saw at the Laurens's not only Lizzie Hamilton, a perfect little beauty, but the very table the first Declaration of Independence was written upon. These Laurenses are grandchildren of Henry Laurens, of the first Revolution. Alas! we have yet to make good our second declaration of independence—Southern independence—from Yankee meddling and Yankee rule.*

> *[General John Bell] Hood has written to ask them to send General Chesnut out to command one of his brigades. In whose place?*

High Society

The people who moved in and out of Chesnut's life represent a virtual roll call of the greatest names in the Confederacy: President Davis, Vice President Stephens, Generals Lee, Jackson, Longstreet, Stuart, Joe Johnston, Hampton, Hood, and many others, and virtually every high office holder in the wartime government. Thus they appear:

> *General Lee had tears in his eyes when he spoke of his daughter-in-law just dead—that lovely little Charlotte Wickham, Mrs. Rooney Lee. . . . Detached from General Lee, what a horrible failure is Longstreet! oh, for a day of Albert Sidney Johnston out West! . . . Mrs. (Jefferson) Davis is utterly depressed. She said the fall of Richmond must come; she would send her children to me and Mrs. Preston . . . One more year of Stonewall would have saved us.*

For all her endowments and the rich contribution she left history of the momentous times during which she lived, Chesnut lived in circles very easy for modern Americans to condemn. While much of the South teetered near starvation or died of maladies related to malnourishment, her table remained replete with bounty. She describes one such Christmas feast, nearly three years into the War: "We had for dinner oyster soup, besides roast mutton, ham, boned turkey, wild duck, partridge, plum pudding, sauterne, burgundy, sherry, and Madeira. There is life in the old land yet!"

She rued the sickening scenes that abounded in hospitals filled with soldiers from social stations far lower than hers, and she condemned the practice of women serving amongst them as nurses. And Christians might wince at what her early twentieth-century editor describes "her steadfast loyalty to the waning fortunes of a political faith, which, in South Carolina, had become a religion." That "religion" evidences itself in such diary entries as the following: "Somebody counted fourteen generals in church today. She suggested that less piety and more drilling of commands would suit the times better. There were Lee, Longstreet, Morgan, Hoke, Clingman, Whiting, Pegram, Elzey, Gordon, Bragg, and—oh, I forget the others." Still, she wrote with honesty and without guile, even when it presented her and hers in a less than favorable light. *A Diary from Dixie* remains among the greatest and most illuminating chronicles of the War's home front.

Federal pontoon bridge across the James River toward Petersburg in June.

Besieging Petersburg

Grant, as was his hallmark, kept grimly about his business. Like McClellan and all the others, unable to conquer Richmond, he shifted strategy and effected a brilliant movement of his entire army across the Virginia Peninsula, thence across the James River on pontoon bridges to front Petersburg. Losing that city, twenty-two miles south of Richmond, would slit the capital's supply jugular to the south and leave it isolated and, soon, surrounded. From there, its fall could only be a matter of time. Grant launched an entire corps against

> ***Pontoon***
> A flat-bottomed boat or other structure used to support a floating bridge.

The Battle of the Crater

U. S. Grant possessed no great enthusiasm for a long siege of Petersburg. He approved a plan proffered by members of a rugged regiment of Pennsylvania coal miners to tunnel their way more than 500 feet to a position directly under the center of the Confederate defenses. There they rammed four tons of gunpowder, which on July 30 blew nine companies of Lee's men to smithereens. More than 15,000 Federals stormed forward, including a large force of the first black soldiers to come against the Army of Northern Virginia. But thousands of them marched down into a massive deathtrap of their own—the crater left by the explosion.

The Crater as it appeared in 1865.

The Confederates were blind with fury at the staggering blow, and this inauguration of black troops against them confirmed their suspicions that the United States intended a colossal "servile insurrection & massacre" against the South. The graybacks counterattacked with resistless power. They—and the crater—stopped the Federal rampage dead in its tracks and sent the Northerners into a pell mell retreat. That day, the Army of Northern Virginia inflicted over 4,000 casualties on its enemy, while losing barely more than one third that number. Renowned Confederate Artillery Commander Porter Alexander acknowledged that "some of the Negro prisoners, who were originally allowed to surrender by some soldiers, were afterward shot by others, & there was, without doubt, a great deal of unnecessary killing of them." "A stupendous failure," Grant fretted, "the saddest affair I have witnessed in the war."

Famed Jewish Confederate nurse and widow Phoebe Pember offered chilling lamentation following the Battle of the Crater. After all previous battles, expressions of hatred for the enemy were

Robertson Hospital

absent from the words spoken by the Southern soldiers she tended, including those maimed and dying. Never had they so much as uttered off-color language around her. No more. Now they cursed, she said, and "their eyes gleamed, and teeth clenched as they showed me the locks of their muskets to which the blood and hair still clung, when after firing, without waiting to re-load, they had clenched the barrels and fought hand to hand."

As Confederate casualties mounted and resources declined, many Richmond residents donated their homes to serve as hospitals. Judge John Robertson's home became Robertson Hospital. Under the leadership of Sally Louisa Tompkins, it served over 1,300 soldiers, only 76 of whom died. Tompkins, a devout Episcopalian renowned for her love of the Bible, ran the hospital for nearly four years. President Davis appointed her as a captain of cavalry, unassigned, making her the only woman ever to hold an officers' commission in the Confederate army.

Sally Louisa Tompkins

The Nurses

Until the watershed exploits of the famed English noblewoman Florence Nightingale in the Crimean War (1853–56) and after, nursing was considered beneath the dignity of respectable people. Most people could not abide the idea of respectable women, in particular, engaging in the intimate contact with strangers that nursing sometimes necessitated. Female nurses were thought a disreputable bunch of drunks, slatterns, thieves, and prostitutes. Society viewed hospitals themselves as dirty, even dangerous death camps for the poor and deranged.

But Nightingale's book *Notes on Nursing* gained a wide reading in America and influenced the country toward accepting women, even women of high social station, as nurses for common people, including soldiers in war. Confederate nurse Kate Cummings wrote in her diary, "I knew that if one woman [Florence Nightingale] had done it [nursing] another could. . . . And as to the plea of its [a hospital] being no place for a refined lady, I wonder what Miss Nightingale and the hundreds of refined ladies of Great Britain who went to Crimea, would say to that!"

Still, nurses North and South experienced resentment from both men and women throughout the War as they tended soldiers amidst often very unladylike surroundings. Well-known Confederate nurse Phoebe Pember recalled her first meeting with one surgeon, when "there was no mistaking the stage whisper as the little contract surgeon informed a friend in a tone of ill-conceived disgust, that 'one of them had come.'" Indeed, female nurses faced innumerable clashes—with doctors, other hospital employees, patients, and the families of patients, often amidst terrifying and heartwrenching surroundings. They often

Beauregard's 2,500 well-entrenched Petersburg irregulars. Surpassing even his feats at Fort Sumter and First Manassas, the Louisiana native repulsed three straight days of attacks and held the city. On June 18, Lee's whole army marched into Petersburg and positioned themselves behind the elaborate defensive works. While Lee could not replenish his shrinking army, Grant's kept

Interior view of Confederate Works—Petersburg, VA

worked through the night, six or seven days a week, all the while worrying over the safety of their own loved ones. And Southern hospitals, especially, faced constant shortages of doctors, nurses, medicines, medical equipment, and food.

Despite all this, humorous incidents often preempted even such horrifying scenes. In the so-called "pea riot," patients angry with the lack of variety in their menus hurled their peas, plates, and spoons at one another, to the floor, and against the walls of their mess hall. When one nursing matron approached and tasted the pea stew in question, to the delight of the convalescents she agreed the peas definitely constituted fighting food! During one hospital "bread rebellion," soldiers stormed the bakery, slung the half-cooked bread about the yard, beat the baker, and threatened to hang the steward before a plucky nursing matron shamed them with a reminder that she was the only one willing to stew their rats for them.

Female nurses faced innumerable clashes—with doctors, other hospital employees, patients, and the families of patients.

One wartime investigation determined that female nurses not only aided the wounded, sick, and dying, they did so more effectively than their male counterparts. The investigating committee found the mortality rate among hospitalized soldiers to be ten percent when male nurses attended the patients, but only five percent when female nurses did. Just as Florence Nightingale and her intrepid Crimean band pioneered nursing as a respectable, even noble, endeavor in Britain and Europe, so did the many devoted nurses, Federal and Confederate, in the War help elevate the practice to the esteemed status it holds today.

Phoebe Pember (1823–1913)

Alabama widow Phoebe Pember was one of the many Jews who played key roles in the Confederate war effort. She also became one of the most famous nurses in American history. Pember served as matron-in-chief for one division of Richmond's Chimborazo, the largest hospital in the Confederacy—and likely the world—from November, 1862 until after the capital fell in 1865. Chimborazo served over 76,000 patients during the War.

Never was Pember's job easy, but in the beginning the Confederacy had no organized system of care for the wounded and ill soldiers, or even specific locations designated to provide care. One hospital inspector lamented "The confused and disorganized state of the medical department. . . the lack of order or system in the hospitals behind the lines, and the almost utter hopelessness of adequate hospital arrangements." Then the country passed the Hospital Act of 1862, which permitted women's employment in military hospitals. Thereafter, Pember and many other female nurses sparked a dramatic improvement in both conditions and organization within the hospitals through their dogged devotion and their many innovative ideas.

Pember and many other female nurses sparked a dramatic improvement in both conditions and organization within the hospitals through their dogged devotion and their many innovative ideas.

The work was long, stressful, and, especially after big battles and as the Federal blockade choked the South off from medical supplies and nearly everything else, at times overwhelming. On occasion, though, Pember found time to engage in the lively, if spartan, social life that permeated upper class Richmond throughout the War. During one game of charades, she dressed in Confederate gray, then pulled some hardtack out of one pocket and a chunk of bacon out of the other and proceeded to chew on both of them. She executed the sequence three times, waiting in vain for anyone to guess the word she was acting out: "ingratiate" (in-gray-she-ate).

Many of Pember's challenges were as unusual to hospital work as they were frustrating to handle. For instance, whole families, many of them left homeless by the War or otherwise refugeeing, would descend on Chimborazo and other Southern hospitals, often staying weeks or even months. The visiting relatives of patients created innumerable disturbances, including lounging on beds that were needed for soldiers, embarrassing the men, and laughing without realizing someone nearby was dying. Among the greatest irritants to Pember were the "women visitors who persisted in using pipes and filling the wards with smoke."

The wife of one soldier stayed at her bedridden husband's side for months, despite repeated polite attempts to exit her. One day Pember found the man gone but his bed filled by his wife and their newborn baby. The patient matron finally managed to send the wife away, only to discover the woman, evidently bereft of food or medicine at home, had left her daughter behind for the hospital to tend. Pember sent the husband home with the child and a quart of milk. The baby's name: Phoebe. Following the War, Pember wrote her famous memoir *A Southern Woman's Story*, which chronicled her experiences at Chimborazo.

Dorothea Lynde Dix (1802–1887)

When the War started, American social reformer Dorothea Lynde Dix already possessed international renown as a pioneer in the movement for humane treatment of the insane. A native of Hampden, Maine, she for many years ran a school in Boston. In 1841 she visited a jail in East Cambridge, Massachusetts. Its appalling conditions left a lifelong impression on her. The random mixing of criminals with the insane particularly disturbed her. She set out to investigate similar institutions around Massachusetts. What she found led to her writing her famous 1842 memorandum to the state legislature. Dix's efforts led to the founding of state hospitals for the insane across the country. The influences of her crusade reached as far away as Canada and Europe. She also accomplished significant work in the study of penology.

Dix's efforts led to the founding of state hospitals for the insane across the country.

She volunteered for nursing duty as soon as the War began. The United States surgeon general appointed her to the exalted position of superintendent of all female nurses. By the end of the War, over 3,000 women would serve under Dorothea Dix, ministering to the needs of Federal, and sometimes Confederate, soldiers. Some of the better-known included Clara Barton, Mary Ann "Mother" Bickerdyke, and Mary Walker. The latter was the lone female surgeon in the Federal army. The Confederates captured her during the War.

Over 3,000 women served under Dorothea Dix, ministering to the needs of Federal, and sometimes Confederate, soldiers.

growing, in spite of his colossal losses. He now had 140,000 men; soon Lee would be outnumbered nearly five to one.

Grant had won at Vicksburg with a siege. Now, retaining Lincoln's support despite continued clamor and outcry in the North, he proposed to lay siege to Petersburg in order to get at Richmond. Lee's options were dwindling. Behind earthen trenches—and fronted by Grant's own now-entrenched forces—he no longer possessed even the ability to maneuver, as he had during the Wilderness Campaign. The Virginian wanted to leave the cage that was being constructed around him and head for open country, where his strategic and tactical prowess would be less harnessed. But President Davis insisted he defend the Confederate capital to the end. Now it was only a matter of time.

Clara Barton (1821–1912)

Famous American humanitarian Clara Barton is best remembered for founding the American Red Cross. Long before she did that, however, she proved herself one of the most important women in the entire Federal war effort. A native of North

She never forgot what she saw at that horrible battle.

Oxford (now Oxford), Massachusetts, she taught school from 1839–54, then clerked in the U.S. Patent Office before the War. While still working at the Patent Office, she traveled to the Battle of Sharpsburg. Her singular accomplishment in this action was that she brought with her desperately-needed medical supplies and food early in the battle, before the Regular army supplies arrived. She never forgot what she saw at that horrible battle. It spurred her to arrange service with the chief U.S. quartermaster for the regular provision of wagons and supplies in many later battles. She herself nursed in both army camps and on the battlefields. And the government appointed her superintendent of nurses for the Army of the James in 1864. In 1865, President Lincoln appointed her to search for missing Federal prisoners. Her exhaustive investigation identified thousands of previously-unidentified dead at Andersonville Prison.

Barton persuaded President Grover Cleveland to sign the treaty in 1882 and support Red Cross work in catastrophes other than war.

She worked behind the German lines for the International Red Cross during the Franco-Prussian War in 1870. Seven years later, after returning to the United States, she organized the American Red Cross, then led it for 27 years. Much to the chagrin of countries around the world, Lincoln and other United States presidents had long refused to sign the Geneva treaty for the care of war wounded. Barton persuaded President Grover Cleveland to sign the treaty in 1882 and support Red Cross work in catastrophes other than war.

Bestowed with the reverent nickname "The Angel of the Battlefield," she also wrote several books about the Red Cross.

25 Shenandoah
(1864)

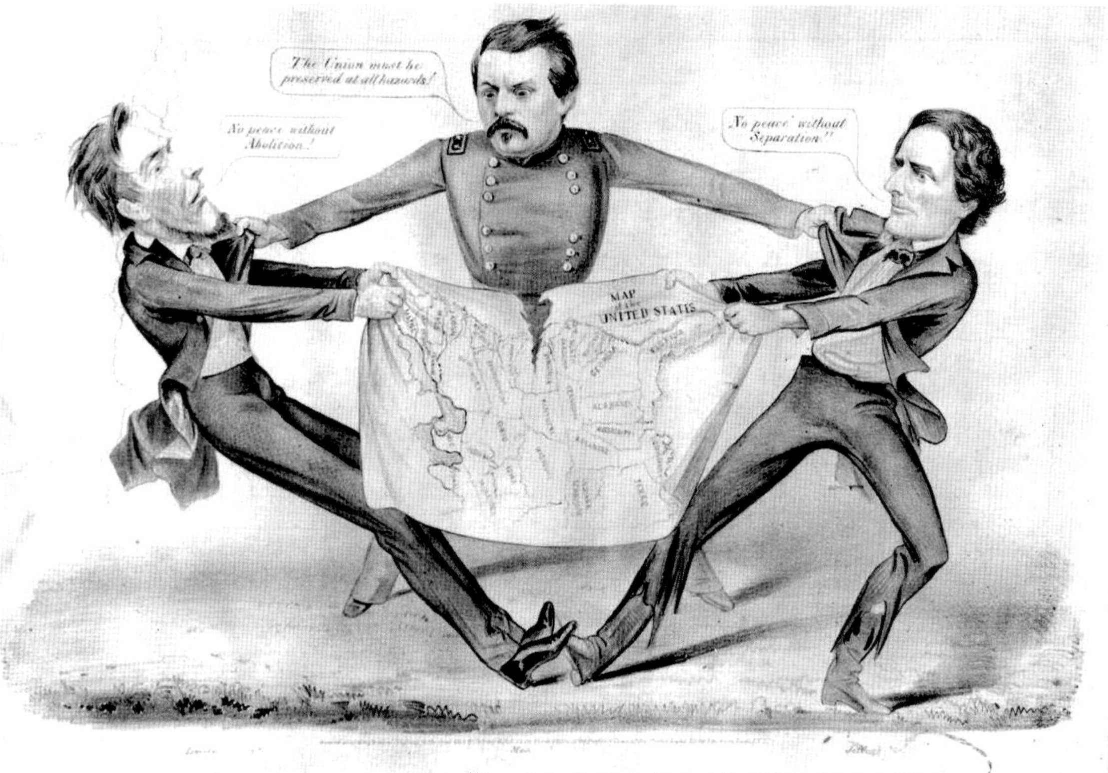

THE TRUE ISSUE OR "THATS WHATS THE MATTER".

This cartoon promotes Democrat George McClellan in the 1864 U.S. Presidential election against Abraham Lincoln. It depicts him as able to lead America to a peaceful solution of the dispute between North and South.

(The Confederates) are fighting from different motives from us. We are fighting for the Union . . . a high and noble sentiment, but after all a sentiment. They are fighting for independence and are animated by passion and hatred against invaders.

—Federal officer from Illinois

The Federal expedition ordered into the Shenandoah Valley by Grant had been throttled at New Market on May 15. Anchoring the center of the outnumbered Confederate line were 247 Virginia Military Institute college boys. A few days later, Grant sent another, larger, force of 22,000 men, commanded by General David Hunter, into the sumptuous valley. Though a Virginian, Hunter detested slavery and the Confederacy, perhaps partly due to having received a blazing scar from a grayback at First Manassas. He wrecked, burned, and looted his way through the Upper (southern) Valley. When he reached Lexington—home to the Virginia Military Institute and to the now-deceased Stonewall Jackson—

The Wade-Davis Bill

Passed in 1864 by both the U.S. House and Senate, the Wade-Davis resolution illuminated the developing chasm between the war—and peace—aims of Abraham Lincoln and other moderate-leaning Republicans, and the dominant Radical Republican Congressional forces. A strong and growing Union, fueled by audacious tariff rates, proved Lincoln's preeminent motivation as President. "[Charles] Sumner and Zachariah Chandler in the Senate, Thaddeus Stevens and George W. Julian in the House—Jacobins all and accomplished haters, out for vengeance at any price," according to historian Shelby Foote, sought a uniform, centrally controlled nation organized and administered according to the dictates of the *Communist Manifesto* of Karl Marx and Friedrich Engels.

Lincoln's 1863 "Proclamation of Amnesty and Reconstruction" sought reentry to the United States of both the Confederate states and their people. The people, except for high-ranking Confederates, had only to swear allegiance to the U.S. and support for its government. A state had only for ten percent of the number of its citizens who voted in the 1860 Presidential election to take the oath of loyalty, then form state constitutional conventions to establish new state governments and Congressional delegations.

Ben Wade

If Lincoln's proclamation sought to promote reunion, the Wade-Davis Bill, authored by Congressman Ben Wade and Senator Henry Winter Davis, seemed to discourage it. Among its contentious planks: 1) Fifty, rather than ten, percent of qualified voters in the Confederate states he shelled the town (which had no soldiers remaining) with cannon fire, then burned the V.M.I., its faculty homes, part of Washington College (founded on a grant by George Washington), and the homes of prominent citizens, including Governor John Letcher. Then Hunter turned east toward the key rail junction of Lynchburg (across the Blue Ridge Mountains) and a rendezvous with Sheridan's high-flying cavalry, sent by Grant to tear up more of the Virginia Central Railroad.

Now the Federal rampage came to a screeching halt. Riding hard to avenge Jeb Stuart, and well aware of the brutality of Sheridan, Hunter, and other Federal generals against Southern civilians, was Stuart's successor as Army of Northern Virginia cavalry commander, forty-six-year-old Wade Hampton. Sent by Lee, who correctly assessed Sheridan's destination, Hampton and his 5,000 Confederate horse soldiers crashed into Sheridan's cavalry at Trevilian Station. The June 11–12 contest was one of the most vicious, sanguinary cavalry duels of the War. The climactic sequence occurred when Hampton's men, outnumbered nearly two-to-one, shredded repeated charges by Custer's dismounted horse soldiers.

---

must sign the loyalty oath. In addition, the Wade-David Bill required an "iron-clad" oath that one had never been disloyal to the Union, not just that one now supported the United States and its government. 2) Not only high-ranking Confederate leaders, but anyone who had voluntarily borne arms for the Confederacy was disqualified to vote or participate in the new state government processes. Thus, Southern Unionists and Unionists immigrating from the North would seize power in the South. 3) The actual program of Reconstruction would not occur until after the War, when Congress regained most of its Constitutional authority to conduct it from the President, who held such powers in time of war. 4) Harsher specific strictures against the South would ensue once Congress gained control of the program. 5) An erstwhile Confederate state must abolish slavery before readmittance to the United States—even though slavery was still permitted in several pro-Union states. 6) The former Confederate states must all exclude from political rights all high-ranking civil and military officers of the Confederacy, and repudiate all debts incurred "under the sanction of the usurping power."

In addition to all this, Federal-occupied Tennessee, Arkansas, and Louisiana organized loyal governments under Lincoln's plan but Congress, led by the Radicals, refused to recognize them—they refused to allow their representatives and senators seats in Congress and they refused to count their electoral votes in the presidential election of 1864. This provided one of many examples of Republican Party chicanery in that election, which is explored in greater detail later in this chapter.

If Lincoln's proclamation sought to promote reunion, the Wade-Davis Bill, authored by Congressman Ben Wade and Senator Henry Winter Davis, seemed to discourage it.

The moonscape left by Federal naval artillery of Hampton Roads, Virginia homes. All that remains of most are chimneys surrounded by charred rubble.

Amazing Manifesto

Plus, the "Ironclad Oath" of 1862 remained in force. This prohibited anyone who had held office in or voluntarily supported the Confederacy from holding Federal office. Lincoln allowed the bill to languish, neither signing nor vetoing it. Why? He opposed its transfer of control over Reconstruction from him to the Radical-controlled Congress. He feared the adverse effect on his November reelection chances when the public—North and South—learned the bill required immediate and total abolition. And he challenged the Constitutional authority of Congress to abolish slavery—the same authority he had claimed for himself upon issuing the Emancipation Proclamation. No doubt, too, he shared Secretary of Navy Gideon Welles's view that the bill "was as much an object of Mr. Henry Winter Davis and some others to pull down [Lincoln's] Administration as to reconstruct the Union. I think they had the former more directly in view than the latter."

Lincoln's refusal to sanction the Wade-Davis Bill generated the Wade-Davis Manifesto, an amazing article in Horace Greeley's *New York Tribune*, one of the nation's most powerful newspapers. Published in the heat of

Lincoln's uphill reelection battle with Democratic General George McClellan, the Congressional leaders of the President's own party denounced his "political ambition," termed his opposition to their bill a "stupid outrage," and unleashed numerous personal insults. "To be wounded in the house of one's friends is perhaps the most grievous affliction that can befall a man," Lincoln responded. "While everybody was shocked at [Lincoln's] murder," Radical Republican Indiana Representative Julian later wrote, prophetically, "the feeling was nearly universal that the accession of Johnson would prove a Godsend to our cause."

Federal soldiers playing dominoes in camp.

Jacobin

The term "Jacobin" finds its source in the violent, radical egalitarian revolutionaries of the late-18th-Century French Revolution. It references the place where the original conspirators met prior to and during the terrifying, slaughter-filled uprising. They gathered in an abandoned monastery of the French Jacobine Order.

A Jacobin typically opposes government in a secret and unlawful manner or by violent means. Distinguishing trademarks of Jacobin philosophy include: 1) Espousal of democratic, majority rule—in preference to a Constitutional Republic based on written standards and principles immutable by changing popular opinion, despite 2) extreme concentration of civil authority in a central government structure, and requiring 3) replacement of existing religious worldview and precepts at all levels of society with atheistic ones promulgating the central state as supreme authority and the locus of the people's affections and loyalty. The Jacobin—American, French, or otherwise—proposes that just claim on men's obedience to authority is founded not on covenantal, constitutional or even contractual authority, but on the consent of the individual himself.

A Jacobin typically opposes government in a secret and unlawful manner or by violent means.

Jacobins should not be confused with Jacobites, the partisans and adherents of King James II of England after he abdicated the throne, and his descendants, the Stuart claimants to the throne after 1688. Jacobites opposed the "Glorious Revolution" of 1688, which enthroned King William and Queen Mary, and led to the 1689 English Bill of Rights. Jacobitism has no particular ideology associated with it, other than opposition to the recognized Stuart or Hanoverian monarchs.

Marching on Washington

Bitterly disappointed, Sheridan retreated back to Grant. This left Hunter on his own to face Confederate Corps Commander Jubal Early, the latest successor to Stonewall Jackson, at Lynchburg. Seething with rage, "Old Jube's" troops confronted Hunter's from the east, while Confederate guerillas blocked their retreat back into the Shenandoah. Hunter's retreat turned into a humiliating race for survival that carried him all the way into the mountains of West Virginia and out of the War. Then Early headed down the Shenandoah with his own army—13,000 men with rags for clothes and bare feet for shoes. They did not stop until they had left Virginia, entered Maryland, defeated a smaller Federal force commanded by Lew Wallace at Monocacy, and arrayed themselves at the gates of Washington for two full days. At one point, President Lincoln visited the city's defensive ramparts and observed the Confederates through field glasses. The stunned Federal capital, convinced Grant was about to reduce Richmond, now trembled at the prospect of the Confederates marauding into Washington with their own army.

McCausland, acting outside Early's orders and without Lee's knowledge or approval, evacuated the Chambersburg population of 3,000 and set fire to the business district.

All this was a spectacular boost to Confederate morale and a bracing jolt to Lincoln and the Federals—who had thought the War well in hand on all fronts—even when Early sidled back to Winchester in the Shenandoah without

Confederate Quaker artillery guns. (TreasureNet)

Lew Wallace (1827-1905)

Lew Wallace commanded Federal troops in some of the War's most important battles; helped send John Wilkes Booth's co-conspirators to their deaths; was governor of New Mexico; negotiated face to face with the Billy the Kid (then sent Pat Garrett to kill him); served as the American ambassador to Turkey; and wrote the best-selling novel of the entire 19th century. The Indiana native's father David was governor of that state. The younger Wallace graduated West Point and saw action in the Mexican War. Later, he crafted a career as an attorney and got elected to the Indiana State Senate as a Democrat in 1856.

Rising quickly from colonel to general in the War, Wallace saw action in both the east and the west. He served well at Romney, Fort Donelson, and while in charge of the defense of Cincinnati in 1862–63. He also commanded a division at the pivotal battle of Shiloh. In 1864, he pulled together the only Federal force to stand between the Potomac River and the outskirts of Washington against Jubal Early's victorious troops. Outnumbered nearly two to one, Wallace put up a good fight before Early swept him aside. But it was after the War that fame gathered itself to Wallace. First, he sat on the commission that tried Booth's cohorts in the Lincoln assassination and related attacks, such as on Secretary of State William Seward. Then he chaired the controversial commission that tried, convicted, and condemned to hanging Confederate Major Henry Wirz, commandant of Andersonville Prison. From 1865–67, he helped gather arms and men for the Mexican rebels fighting the occupation forces of France. He won election to Congress as a Republican in 1870.

He also traveled to the Middle East as part of his research for *Ben-Hur*, the famed novel of first-century Israel and early Christianity. In the course of his work on that book, which he subtitled A Tale of the Christ, Wallace, not theretofore a believer, embraced in faith the Christ of whom he wrote. Ben-Hur was not only great writing; it was a historic achievement. It sold more copies than any other novel of the 19th century, and it established for the first time the novel as a widely-accepted art form among those in the American Church. Later it was adapted twice into motion pictures, the 1959 Charlton Heston version winning the Best Picture Oscar and still tied for the most Academy Awards won by any movie. Released in 1880, the book was one of five Wallace wrote.

Ben-Hur was not only great writing; it was a historic achievement. It sold more copies than any other novel of the 19th century and it established for the first time the novel as a widely accepted art form among those in the American Church.

Wild West

Wallace wrote much of *Ben-Hur* while resident in the Santa Fe governor's mansion of New Mexico. President Rutherford Hayes appointed him to that position in 1878, hoping he might quell the legendary Lincoln County range war. That murderous feud between warring gangs featured a holsterful of names now fabled in American lore, including William "Billy the Kid" Bonney, Pat Garrett, John Chisum—and Wallace himself. For it was Wallace who looked Bonney in the eye and offered him a pardon, then revoked it after the gunman was convicted of murder. And then it was Wallace who sent Garrett and the posse after Bonney on the hunt that climaxed in the outlaw's July, 1881, death in Fort Sumner.

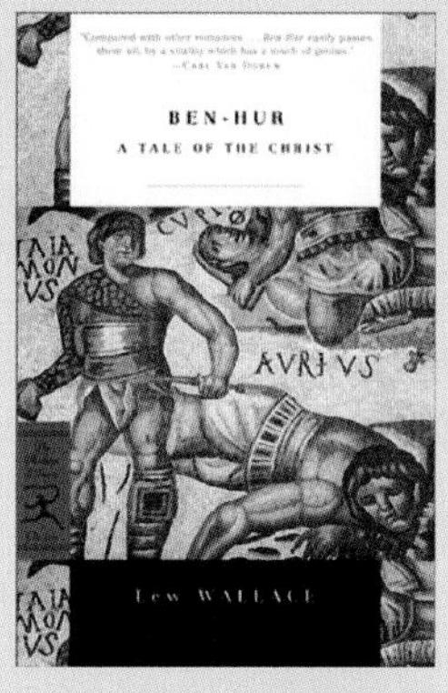

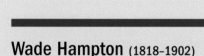

Indeed, New Mexico was the better for Wallace, but his own words evidence the frustration of ceaseless battle with murderers, robbers, and rapists; wronged, unhappy Indians; and crooked politicians. "All calculations based on our experiences elsewhere fail in new Mexico," he lamented. His successor, he promised, "will do just as I did, have the same ideas, make the same attempts, and with the same heartiness of effort, soon cool in zeal, then finally say, 'All right, let her drift.'" Even if Wallace grew disillusioned, others recognized his accomplishments in the roiling territory. "We believe Governor Wallace to be about the only reputable and worthy gentleman who was ever appointed to a federal office in New Mexico," one New Mexico newspaper announced.

Ben-Hur found its way into the hands and heart of another ex-Federal general and Christian, James Garfield, now President of the United States. Garfield delivered Wallace from New Mexico by naming him minister to Turkey, where he served from 1881–1885 and established an excellent relationship with the Sultan. So moved was Garfield by the novel that he appointed Wallace in hopes he "may draw inspiration from the modern east for future literary work."

Wade Hampton (1818-1902)

The name Wade Hampton looms large in the historical landscape of South Carolina, the South, and America. Hampton was a leader of his people long before the War, all through it, and for long after. Born in Charleston and raised near Columbia, he proved himself a peerless athlete and horseman. He graduated from South Carolina College and studied law before taking over the management of the family's sprawling complex of plantations. He was caring and considerate of his many slaves, who reciprocated his kindness.

Hampton's dealings with the black bears of the Mississippi swamps were a different matter during the years he ran family plantations in that state. Though a crack shot, once Hampton cornered a bear, he relished going up against it with nothing but his hunting knife and his own tall, powerful physique, courage, and wits. He killed as many as eighty bears in such fashion, and had both the witnesses and scars to prove it.

Elected to the South Carolina State Senate, though he evinced political ambition neither before nor after the War, he issued a memorable speech against the reimportation of slaves to America. *New York Tribune* publisher Horace Greeley called it "a masterpiece of logic, directed by the noblest sentiments of the

Christian and patriot." When war came, Hampton was one of the richest planters on the North American continent. But his plantation experience convinced him the institution of slavery was an increasingly unprofitable one and probably on its way to oblivion, at least in the South. And like Lee, Jackson, and many other Southern war leaders, he was a staunch Unionist who did not advocate secession. Still, he raised his own "Hampton's Legion" of infantry, cavalry, and artillery at the War's outset. They fought with desperate valor at First Manassas, and Hampton sustained the first of several battle wounds. He moved steadily up the ranks of Confederate cavalry command, finally succeeding the deceased Jeb Stuart as leader of all Robert E. Lee's horse.

Dramatic, Defiant

Many of Hampton's most dramatic exploits rarely grace the pages of War histories. For instance, it was Hampton—with only 300 troopers—who chased down Judson Kilpatrick's Yankee cavalry force of better than ten times that number after their aborted March raid on Richmond, ambushed their sleeping camp in a cold dark howling storm, and chased them clean out of the area. A year later, with the Confederacy on the brink of collapse, he ambushed Kilpatrick again near Fayetteville during Sherman's march through North Carolina. This time, Hampton's again-outnumbered horse soldiers stormed through the main Army of the West cavalry camp, wreaking havoc and nearly capturing Kilpatrick (who fled into the woods on foot in his nightshirt) himself, before the Federals drove them off.

After assuming Stuart's command, Hampton led a daredevil raid of Federal cattle that delivered enough beeves to feed Lee's entire army at Petersburg for forty days. And his June victory over Philip Sheridan at Trevilian Station was one of the most decisive defeats of the War for the Federal cavalry chieftain. It thwarted Sheridan's initial attempt to rendezvous with Federal infantry rampaging through the Shenandoah Valley. Fiercely defiant to the end, Hampton refused to surrender his cavalry to Sherman when Joe Johnston laid down his arms. He told one Federal officer during the treating, "If I were in command, no surrender would ever be written. You'll never see me give up. I'll go to Mexico and fight with Maximilien." Undefeated and unchastened, he and his horse soldiers eluded the Federals, rode away, and considered heading west for a last stand before finally giving up the hopeless fight.

Though a crack shot, once Hampton cornered a bear, he relished going up against it with nothing but his hunting knife and his own tall, powerful physique, courage, and wits.

Few men sacrificed more in the War than Hampton and lived to tell about it. The Federals wounded him at least five times, burned down his mansion, left him in financial ruins, and killed his sons in battle. With carpetbaggers and scalawags ravaging the postwar ruins of South Carolina, he labored to convince the Federal government that his state was committed to a peaceable Union and again deserving of home rule. No less a visiting Northern speaker than John Quincy Adams II endorsed Hampton's efforts, proclaiming of him, "If he is a rebel, he is just such a rebel as I am and no more."

Years later, in 1877, it was Hampton who led the people of South Carolina finally out of the misery and bondage of Reconstruction and back into political control of their own state. He did it by winning an epic race for governor against the incumbent carpetbagger, his Federal troops, and the might of U. S. Grant's corrupt government in Washington. One chronicler penned perhaps the truest epitaph for Hampton, who also served as a U.S. senator. The author wrote how his native state had "turned to General Wade Hampton, who was to his people what Washington was to the colonies, and for much the same reason."

attacking Washington. For two more months, he kept the Federals at bay and commanded the Valley. He even won another battle, on July 24, at Kernstown against future Indian-fighter George Crook. And Early detached two brigades of cavalry under John McCausland north to Chambersburg, Pennsylvania. There, under Early's orders, McCausland ordered the town's merchants to pay him $100,000 in gold or $500,000 in Yankee greenbacks. He warned that if they refused, he would fire the town. Early intended the plan to recoup some of the property values lost in the smoke and ashes of Shenandoah homes torched by Hunter.

The Pennsylvanians rejected the Confederate demand. Now McCausland, acting outside Early's orders and without Lee's knowledge or approval, evacuated the Chambersburg population of 3,000 and set fire to the business district. The flames spread and wiped out over half the town's buildings and homes. In both North and South, the sporting atmosphere of the "picnic affair" at the First Manassas battlefield must by now have seemed like something out of a different lifetime.

Winning the Shenandoah

Grant had had enough. He sent his best eastern theater commander, Sheridan, into the Shenandoah—with 40,000 troops. He wanted Early's 13,000-man army destroyed. But that

Sheridan's final charge at Winchester. (Courtesy of American Vision)

Philip H. Sheridan (1831-1888)

Five feet five inches tall and barely one hundred fifteen pounds, "Little Phil" Sheridan emerged as one of the most colorful characters and greatest fighters of the war. Born to Irish immigrants, he grew up in Ohio. His pugnacity evidenced itself early, when his bayonet attack of an older cadet officer landed him a one-year suspension and near-expulsion from West Point.

Sheridan's uncertain, and undistinguished, early military career continued with the coming of the War. Serving as quartermaster and commissary in Missouri with Samuel Curtis's Army of the Southwest, he evidenced sloppy bookkeeping and careless observance of the rules, and barely escaped a court-martial. However, once he secured a commission as Colonel of the 2nd Michigan Cavalry in May, 1862, Sheridan began to thrive. Within two months, he advanced to command of a brigade. His military training, superb horsemanship, and fighting spirit, especially during the tumult of battle, spurred his advance up the ranks while a key lieutenant in U. S. Grant's successful western campaigns.

In the United States, Sheridan's record was one of fierce loyalty and unfettered triumph on hallowed fields like Missionary Ridge, Yellow Tavern (where his men mortally wounded Jeb Stuart), Cedar Creek, and Five Forks.

Sheridan distinguished himself in several key battles. He commanded a division in the key October, 1862, Federal victory at Perryville, Kentucky. His tenacious refusal to give ground at Stone's River, Tennessee, a couple of months later garnered him promotion to Major General. In November, 1863, he led the reckless and brilliant charge up Missionary Ridge that clinched the Chattanooga campaign and opened the way for Sherman's March to the Sea.

When President Lincoln brought Grant east in early 1864 as General-in-Chief of all Federal armies, Grant brought Sheridan with him, first as Cavalry Chief for the Army of the Potomac, then as commander of the new Army of the Shenandoah. Sheridan cleared that Valley, the "breadbasket" of the eastern Confederacy, of Southern forces, then commenced to destroy it—home, crop, and livestock—from one end to the other.

Southern hatred of him for this unprecedented feat mounted after the war for his harsh policies as a Reconstruction-era occupation commander in Texas and Louisiana. So controversial was Sheridan's rule that Grant himself removed him from one post. American Indians tasted his hard ways as he directed the post-war campaign against them on such fields of civilian massacre as the "Battle" of the Washita River.

The German military leadership consulted Sheridan while he toured the Franco-Prussian War in the early 1870s. His chronicle of the successful Northern prosecution of the recent American contest left the tough Prussians astounded and offended at what they considered the unchivalrous nature of the Federal policy of total war. His record in the United States, however, was one of fierce loyalty and unfettered triumph on hallowed fields like Missionary Ridge, Yellow Tavern (where his men mortally wounded Jeb Stuart), Cedar Creek, and Five Forks.

One of Sheridan's singular contributions to the Federal triumph was his innovative—and insistent—notion that Northern cavalry be used strategically in their own right and in overwhelming force, not just as escorts for the infantry, artillery, and supply trains. According to journalist Sylvanus Cadwallader, who knew Grant well, the latter esteemed Sheridan above all his other generals, including William Sherman. Sheridan succeeded Sherman as General-in-Chief of the United States Army in 1883. His personal memoirs were published in 1888, only a few days before he died in Nonquitt, Massachusetts, honored and revered by his wife and children, and the United States he had served for nearly forty years.

was not all. Though Federal generals had been wreaking havoc on Southern property and land for two years or more, never had such high official sanction been given to the practice, and that on so massive a scale. "Do all the damage to railroads and crops you can," Grant ordered Sheridan. "If the war is to last another year, we want the Shenandoah Valley to remain a barren waste."

Sheridan's troopers watering their horses on a Shenandoah Valley farm they have just torched.

Burning the Shenandoah Valley

The Shenandoah Valley, or "Great Valley of Virginia," enveloped its namesake river and reached from the upper tip of the Old Dominion at Harper's Ferry south through most of the length of the state. It served as the "Breadbasket of the Confederacy." Its lush rolling fields fed Southern civilians and Lee's Army of Northern Virginia alike. Stonewall Jackson conducted his famed "Valley Campaign" through the Shenandoah in the spring of 1862. Still a raging battlefield, his successor Jubal Early drove through it to the gates of the Federal capital at Washington City two years later. Grant determined to eliminate both this threat and the Valley's productive capacity. He notified Washington City that a Federal host should be assembled: "to eat out Virginia clear and clean . . . so that crows flying over it for the balance of the season will have to carry their provender with them. . . . Hunter should make all of the Valley south of the Baltimore and Ohio road a desert as high as possible . . . and the people should be notified to move out."

But it was Sheridan, not Hunter, who crushed organized Confederate resistance from the Valley a few months later and promised, "the Valley, from Winchester up to Staunton, ninety-two miles, will have little in it for man or beast." He proved true to his word. The Federals destroyed more than 2,000 Shenandoah barns, 70 mills, nearly 4,000 horses, nearly 11,000 cattle, 12,000 sheep, and tons of crops of all stripes. They also burned down dozens of homes and plundered hundreds of others. Scores of eyewitness accounts, Northern soldiers and Southern civilians alike, recount such scenes as pump handles being destroyed so families could not draw water from their wells, the salting of other wells, and tent pegs driven through the heads of pigs and other stock the Federals did not take or want, so the owners could not eat them.

The gallant intervention of Federal Lieutenant Colonel Thomas F. Wildes with Sheridan saved the town of Dayton from being burned to the ground. Wildes could not save the rest of a nearly fifty-square-mile-area surrounding Dayton. Sheridan ordered that area torched—homes and all—because he believed a false report concerning the death of a subordinate officer. For years, this benighted region carried the unwelcome title of the Burnt District. Overshadowed by William Sherman's epic march to the sea, the burning of the Shenandoah itself evidenced total war on a grand scale. It delivered terror to the very homes of the people. It brilliantly accomplished its military objectives. The armies and people of the South would grow hungrier and more needy even than they were.

I rode down the Valley after Sheridan's retreating cavalry beneath great columns of smoke . . . I saw mothers and maidens tearing their hair and shrieking to Heaven in their fright and despair, and little children, voiceless and tearless in their pitiable terror.

—Confederate staff officer of Jubal Early's

George Armstrong Custer (1839–1876)

Of all the larger-than-life characters who emerged from the War, only a few have eclipsed George Armstrong Custer as an enduring icon. The changing perceptions of him have in many ways reflected the shifting views of successive American generations. Famous even during the War as the "Boy General"—youngest in either army—with the gaudy uniforms and the flaxen ringlets falling about his shoulders, the Michigan native gained near-godlike status with his 1876 death on the hills above the Little Big Horn River in Montana. Yet his apogee, perhaps, came with the turn-of-the-nineteenth century release of the painting Custer's Last Stand, a heroic rendering of the warrior that became as familiar to Americans of that and ensuing generations as portraits of Washington or Lincoln. Custer's Last Stand also helped crystallize into the collective consciousness the concept—and duty, if necessary—of facing long, even hopeless, odds with unflinching courage.

Custer was endowed with formidable talents, including a battlefield persona that, if not fearless, appeared to be so. He also possessed a remarkable capacity to lead men well in the midst of chaos and danger.

Indeed, Custer was to the end of his life a fearsome and manly warrior. One of the worst overall cadets at West Point—he finished last in his class—he was one of its best horsemen. And less than a week after leaving "The Point," he was proving it on the bloody field of First Manassas. On an otherwise dismal day for the Federals, Custer and his Michigan "Wolverines" cavalry showed well in his first command of troops in combat. He was endowed with formidable talents, including a battlefield persona that, if not fearless, appeared to be so. He also possessed a remarkable capacity to lead men well in the midst of chaos and danger. Custer fought in all but one significant Army of the Potomac and Army of the Shenandoah cavalry action; he finished second only to Philip Sheridan in rank within the latter, victorious, organization.

Heroic and Savage

Among his many exploits were stopping Jeb Stuart's cavalry advance on the second day of battle at Gettysburg, then leading his brigade against Stuart at Yellow Tavern a year later, when one of Custer's troopers killed the graycoat cavalry chieftain. After Sheridan arrived from the west, Custer's troopers played a key role in clearing Jubal Early's Confederates out of the Shenandoah Valley. He then commanded one wing of the Federals' destruction of that Valley. He also shined at the Federals' Five Forks victory that helped break the Petersburg stalemate (his brother Tom, a captain, personally captured some Confederate battle flags), and he rode with Sheridan all the way to Lee's surrender at Appomattox Courthouse—where Custer stole a parlor table for a souvenir.

His status as a national hero grew as he became the point man in the United States government's postwar campaign of extermination against the Plains Indians. Too, the Indian wars coupled him with the same military command team that had won the War—President Grant, General-in-Chief Sherman, and Lieutenant General Sheridan. They

General George Custer observes his division burning wide swaths of the Shenandoah Valley. (Courtesy of Battles and Leaders of the Civil War)

also revealed more clearly the characteristics that have not worn as well in American history annals—his ambition, glory-seeking, and brutality. Custer often dispensed savage discipline against his own troops; he was court-martialed and sent home for nearly a year after one such incident.

At the 1868 Battle of the Washita he led a dawn attack against a sleeping Cheyenne village and slaughtered over one hundred Indians, mostly women and children. A series of errors in judgment on Custer's part led to the disastrous June 25, 1876 encounter between the 265 troopers he led and thousands of vengeful Indians led by Crazy Horse and Sitting Bull. "I regard Custer's massacre," President Grant said, "as a sacrifice of troops brought on by Custer himself, that was wholly unnecessary—wholly unnecessary."

Rear Admiral David D. Porter and staff aboard his flagship, the *USS Malvern,* at Hampton Roads, Virginia, near the end of the year.

First, the outmanned Confederates defending the Valley had to be dealt with. Sheridan began that process by defeating them in September in the Third Battle of Winchester. Three days later, he did so again, at Fisher's Hill. Now Sheridan burned and looted his way up the Shenandoah. A month later, Early made his last stand, at Cedar Creek, north of Strasburg. There, he launched a dawn ambush that sent thousands of Federals hurtling into headlong retreat. But the starving Confederates, outnumbered even here at least two-to-one, stopped to gorge themselves with food from the abandoned Federal camps. Seeing his men streaming to the rear in disorder, Sheridan grabbed a regimental pennant and galloped over the field, rallying them to a ferocious counterattack that overwhelmed the exhausted Confederates and drove those who were not captured from the field.

The Battle of Cedar Creek finished both the Confederate threat to Washington, and the Shenandoah Valley as a source of food for the South. Even more importantly, it—and Sheridan's Valley Campaign—helped boost Lincoln to victory in his tough presidential reelection race against the Democratic standard-bearer, his former commanding general George McClellan. Lincoln's triumph assured the North would press the War on to a decisive conclusion and the surrender of the South.

Shenandoah (Author unknown)

Oh, Shenandoah, I long to see you,
Away, you rolling river.

Oh, Shenandoah, I long to see you,
Away, I'm bound away, 'cross the wide Missouri.

Oh, Shenandoah, I love your daughter,
Away, you rolling river.

Oh, Shenandoah, I love your daughter,
Away, I'm bound away, 'cross the wide Missouri.

Farewell, goodbye, I shall not grieve you,
Away, you rolling river.

Oh, Shenandoah, I'll not deceive you,
Away, we're bound away, 'cross the wide Missouri.

1864 Presidential Election: Lincoln vs. McClellan

One of the most dramatic Presidential elections in United States history occurred in the next-to-last year of the War. The November showdown pitted Republican incumbent Abraham Lincoln against Democratic challenger and Lincoln's former Army of the Potomac commander, General George McClellan. The backdrop to the contest possessed immense drama of its own. Not only did Lincoln and McClellan represent opposing political parties and philosophies; the President blamed McClellan for many Federal military failures in the east, while McClellan blamed Lincoln and his political allies for dooming his efforts. But the election issue of the day turned on whether or not the United States would prosecute what had become a brutal war effort to the extent of crushing the South and winning total victory. Lincoln would do that, unless the South acceded to his demands on all the major issues. McClellan would likely attempt a negotiated peace, provided the Confederate states returned to the Federal Union. Never in history were the stakes higher, for everyone, in an American Presidential election.

1864 Presidential campaign poster for the Democratic ticket of General George B. McClellan and George A. Pendleton.

So gloomy did Lincoln's reelection prospects grow by late August that his ally Henry J. Raymond, editor of the *New York Times* and chairman of the Republican National Executive Committee, wrote him:

I feel compelled to drop you a line, concerning the political condition of the country as it strikes me. I am in active correspondence with your staunchest friends in every state, and from them all I hear but one report. The tide is setting strongly against us.

Lincoln himself wrote the following note, sealed it, and had his entire cabinet sign their names in concurrence, not knowing what it said. No one else saw it until after the election. It read:

This morning, as for some days past, it seems exceedingly probable that this Administration will not be reelected. Then it will be my duty to so cooperate with the President-elect as to save the Union between the election and the inauguration; as he will have secured his election on such ground that he cannot possibly save it afterwards.

Turnaround

Then Sherman captured—and burned—Atlanta. Sheridan shoved the Confederates from the Shenandoah and scalded it out. And Farragut sealed off one of the South's final ports at Mobile Bay. Plus, McClellan and the Democrats possessed problems of their own. Most wanted reunion with the South, but some did not care; some wanted peace, others to fight on. More difficulties yet faced the Democrats as the Republican Party power structure, in charge of both houses of Congress and the Presidency for the past several years, intensified a multifaceted campaign that had for years bedeviled the out-of-power Democrats. Democrat-leaning newspapers such as the *Chicago Tribune* had been shut down temporarily or even permanently by the hundreds, and individual opponents of the Republicans had been thrown into jail without trials or even charges; anti-Republican candidates and voters had been arrested across the North in all levels of elections; and Democratic voters had been threatened and driven from polling places, their meetings prohibited, and their names removed from ballots.

1864 Presidential campaign poster for Abraham Lincoln and his new vice presidential running mate, Southern Democrat Andrew Johnson.

Plus, many Federal soldiers of Republican persuasion were not limiting their fighting to the battlefield. They were often the means by which the aforementioned sanctions were carried out against Republican opponents. Lincoln sent them home on furlough to vote, and on at least one occasion they threw Democratic commissioners delivering ballots to soldiers in the field into prison, again without charges. Sometimes they enforced the discarding of Democratic soldiers' votes, which were either not counted or were replaced by Republican ballots. This gargantuan mischief paid dividends for the Republicans. In both the midterm Congressional elections of 1862 and the Presidential election of 1864, Federal military control of the Border States provided inexplicably favorable Republican results in those areas. In 1862, it saved the Republican majority in the House of Representatives; in 1864, it perhaps saved Lincoln's presidency.

Silly and Wise

Indeed, though Lincoln won the popular vote 2.2 million to 1.8 million and swamped McClellan in the electoral college 212 to 21, a closer examination of the results is illuminating. Lincoln fared little if any better in the non-border Northern states during the 1864 Presidential election than he did in 1860. He improved astronomically in the Border States—and the Border States alone. He won Connecticut by just 2,000 votes and New York by less than 7,000. The soldier vote made the difference in both, as well as in Pennsylvania, Maryland, Indiana, and even Lincoln's home state of Illinois. Had McClellan won those six states, he would have won the electoral college and the election. Withal, the shift of 38,000 votes—less than 1 percent of the total vote—in the right places would have given McClellan the victory. The enduring, but unanswerable, question remains: how many votes were the product of mischief?

Still, such an enormous and competitive contest for so high an office, conducted in the midst of a raging continental-wide war, spoke highly of the foundational institutions of the United States. Lincoln agreed, stating that for all

> *its incidental and undesirable strife . . . a people's government can sustain a national election in the midst of a great civil war. . . . In any future great national trial, compared with the men of this, we shall have as weak and as strong, as silly and as wise, as bad and as good. Let us therefore study the incidents of this, as philosophy to learn wisdom from, and none of them as wrongs to be revenged.*

Meanwhile, the Army of Northern Virginia stood at its posts behind the earthworks of Petersburg, immersed in filth, stench, vermin, disease, hunger, exhaustion, and homesickness. Perhaps worst of all, they knew that scores of their homes in all corners of the South were being looted and even burned, their livestock slaughtered, their wells salted, and their families left destitute or even turned out onto the open road. A growing number of these Southern soldiers left the lines to go home and try to bring in a crop or protect their families. Others, starving and freezing, simply crossed over to the Federal lines for food and clothing. Most, however, remained in the lines while the prospects for independence and self-governance dropped with the temperature as another bitterly cold winter beset Virginia.

26 Sherman
(1864)

"Marching through Georgia."

Their families back home, like the nation at large, conceived of them as moral, honorable young Americans, ideal products of the world's most enlightened system of government. In fact, they were potentially cruel and heartless pillagers, many of whom awaited only the opportunity to plunder, burn, and rape.

—Burke Davis, speaking of William Sherman's soldiers
Sherman's March

Following the Federal victories around Chattanooga in November, 1863, Grant appointed Sherman commander of all Federal forces in the west—though the "west" might now be more accurately called the Deep South. As Grant and Meade would hunt Lee, Sherman was to hunt Joe Johnston. But Grant gave Sherman the added admonition of "inflicting all the damage you can against their war resources." How open-ended was that official order Sherman was shortly to demonstrate.

The opening military chapter of the year was the Federal invasion of Confederate Florida. Admiral John Dahlgren's fleet accompanied a 7,000-man force which captured Jacksonville without a fight on February 7, then proceeded inland. Two weeks later, the Federals ran into Georgians and Floridians commanded by General A. H. Colquitt, two miles east of Olustee. The Confederates defeated them and short-circuited Federal plans for the conquest of the state.

Columbia guns of the Confederate water battery defending the entrance to Pensacola, Florida.

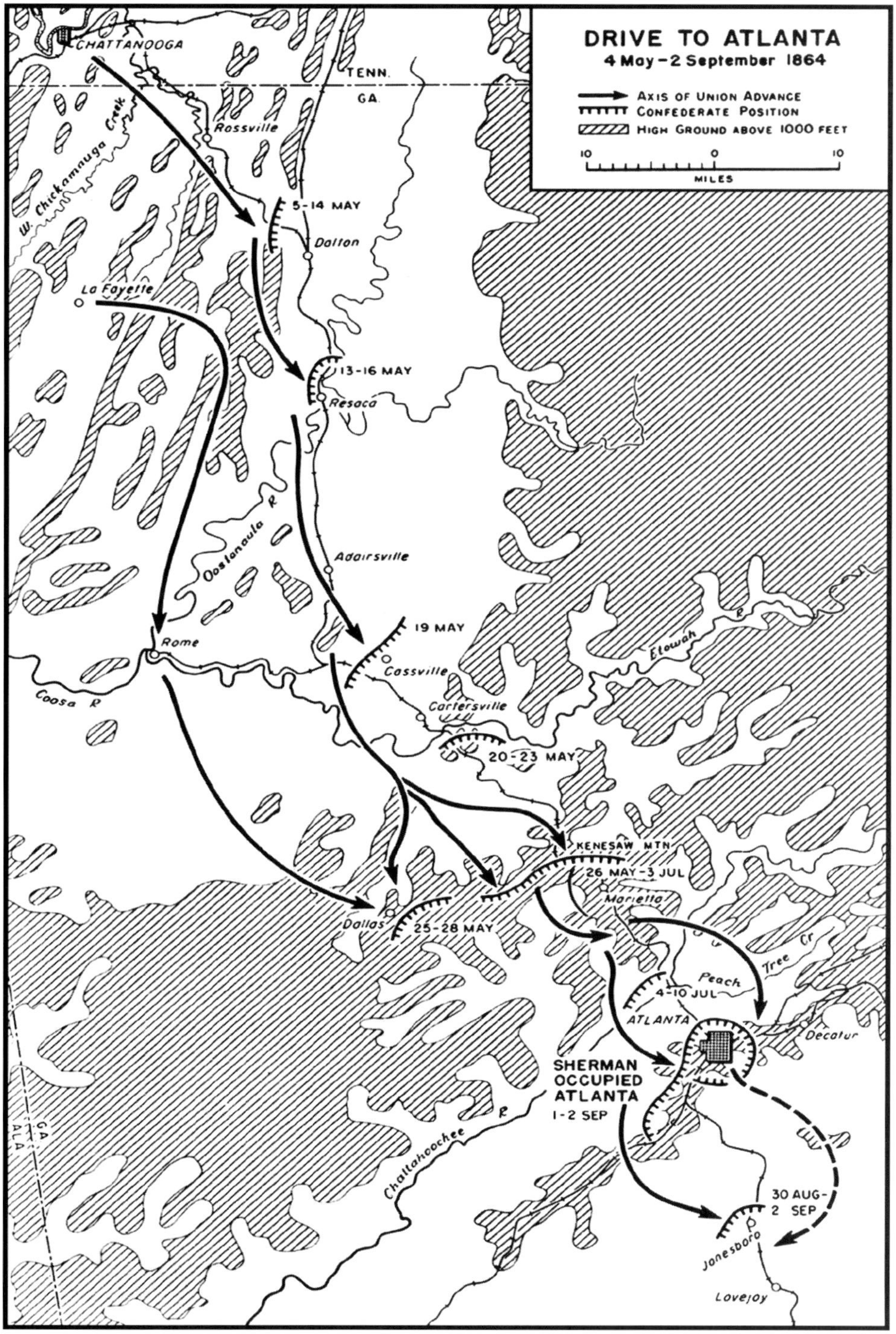

Map of the Atlanta Campaign. (Courtesy of The General Libraries, The University of Texas at Austin)

Leonidas Polk (1806–1864)

The famous “Fighting Bishop” of the Confederacy, Polk held the highest military rank in the War of any clergyman. His old West Point classmate Jefferson Davis personally lobbied him to take a commission at the exalted rank of Major General. He did this not only because he believed Polk would prove a splendid leader, but because of the prestige and credibility he believed this one man would bring to the entire Southern cause of independence. The North Carolina-born clergyman counted President James K. Polk among his kinfolk. The Protestant Episcopal Church ordained him as a deacon in 1830 and bishop over all Louisiana in 1841. A young man when appointed to that high position, he held it for twenty years.

Polk, also a wealthy plantation owner with 400 slaves, accepted Davis's offer and stepped down from his bishopric. He shouldered key commands in every significant engagement of the main western Confederate army, including the big victory at Chickamauga, until his death in 1864. Early on, Polk beat U. S. Grant in a race to the key Mississippi River station of Columbus, Kentucky, in September, 1861.

Two months later, he shellacked Grant's assault on the Confederate stronghold. The following spring, Polk helped persuade Albert Sidney Johnston to launch his pulverizing first-day attack on Grant at Shiloh. Polk himself commanded a corps and helped lead the Confederates to near-victories at the battles of Perryville, Kentucky, and Murfreesboro, Tennessee. Then he commanded an entire wing of the thunderous victory at Chickamauga.

The famous “Fighting Bishop” of the Confederacy, Polk held the highest military rank in the War of any clergyman.

But he faced conflict from more than just his Northern opponents. He received it, surprisingly, from many of his fellow clergy—not only in the North, but in the South too. Many of the latter, even if prone to support the service of chaplains in the Confederate armies, could not brook Christian ministers participating in the killing of other men. And he, like nearly every other officer in the Confederate command hierarchy of the west, developed a fatal lack of confidence in Braxton Bragg's ability to lead the Army of Tennessee, the main Southern army in the west.

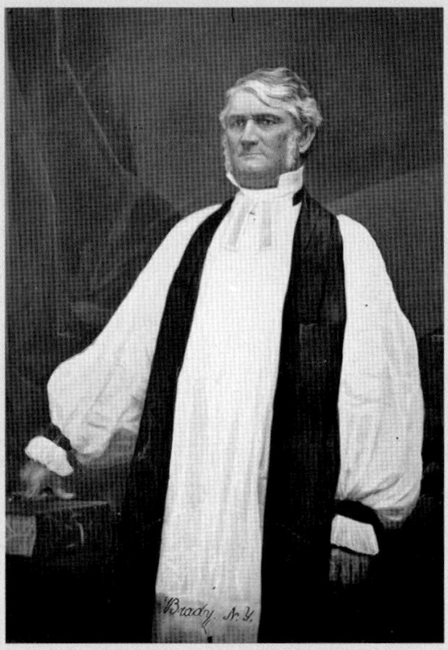

Polk urged Bragg's sacking after Murfreesboro, where Bragg's hesitation precipitated yet another second-day reversal of fortunes for the South. After he did so again following Bragg's failure to capitalize on the Chickamauga victory, President Davis transferred Polk to Mississippi to help defuse the contentious situation. This move spared the Fighting Bishop a share in Bragg's command-ending calamities at Lookout Mountain and Missionary Ridge, which ensued almost immediately.

Vanishing Breed

The end for Polk came June 14 when a Federal shell sheared directly through his body as he reconnoitered a Federal position at Pine Mountain, Georgia, during Sherman's campaign against Atlanta. Joe Johnston, by then commander of the Army of Tennessee, wept over Polk's body as it lay bleeding on the battlefield. Johnston placed his hand upon the old bishop's head and said, "We have lost much. I would rather anything but this." For it was Leonidas Polk who baptized Johnston during the War upon his profession of Christian faith; he baptized John Bell Hood, Johnston's successor at the helm of the Army of Tennessee, too.

Though Polk never proved a great military commander, he was solid, and his sterling example as a soldier and a Christian man helped lift the spirits of a devastated South following the War. Books and articles alike, such as Gabriel Manigault's 1867 "The Decay of Religion in the South," cited Polk as primary among those men who had demonstrated not only their patriotism, but, part of a now-vanishing breed, the author feared, had defended the "religious truth" of orthodox Christianity for which the Confederacy tried to stand.

Concerning Polk's death, historian Shelby Foote wrote of "the contribution he made to the army's moral tone, which was one of the factors that enabled it to survive hardships, defeats, retreats, and Bragg. Northerners might express outrage that a man of the cloth, West Point graduate or not, should take up the sword of rebellion; Southerners took his action as strong evidence that the Lord was on their side, and they on His."

Andersonville

The very mention of the name Andersonville invokes visions of pestilence, plague, and sadistic villainy. Forgotten by history is that the Confederates built Camp Sumter near the Andersonville Depot in southern Georgia to solve the very problems that eventually bedeviled it. They intended Andersonville to alleviate the frigid, overcrowded, disease-ravaged prisons in Richmond and elsewhere. Choice land wedged between verdant fields and crosshatched with clear streams was intended to address food and water shortages and provide fresh healthy air and surroundings. What unfolded soon after the prison's opening in February, 1864, could scarcely have been more different than what was planned.

The pitiable scenes of Andersonville Prison beggar description. Overflowing, disease-laden latrines; fetid swamps from which to drink; swarms of malaria-carrying mosquitoes; too little food and that often times worse than no food at all. Plus, Confederate doctors and surgeons had little or no medicines for the prisoners because they had no medicines for their own men due to the Federal blockade that had been tightening since the War began.

Federal prisoners gathering in August to receive rations at the infamous Andersonville Prison.

Food and supplies were scarce too—for Federal and Confederate alike—largely because the scorched-earth policies of generals like Sherman and Sheridan were destroying Southern food crop production, and Sherman and his invading army had cut the food and supply line to Andersonville. Of the 41,000 Federals imprisoned on the 17 acres there—as many as 32,000 at one time during the worst months—only about 26,000 returned home alive. The others died of smallpox, dysentery, gangrene, scurvy, typhus, pneumonia, and a galaxy of other hideous ailments.

Of the 41,000 Federals imprisoned at Andersonville, only about 26,000 returned home alive. The others died of smallpox, dysentery, gangrene, scurvy, typhus, pneumonia, and a galaxy of other hideous ailments.

Unfinished Story

To finish the story of Andersonville here, however, as do books like MacKinlay Kantor's Pulitzer Prize-winning novel *Andersonville* and movies like *Andersonville* and *The Andersonville Trial*, is to tell an incomplete, and inaccurate, story. Two key factors are little known: the efforts of Prison Commandant Henry Wirz and the Confederate government itself to relieve the horrific situation. The Confederates designed Andersonville in expectation that the policy of the North and South continuing their exchange of prisoners would continue.

Upon his ascension to general in chief of Federal armies at the beginning of 1864, however, Grant discontinued the policy. The Federals placed the blame on the South, faulting them for not including black prisoners as well as white in exchanges.

Prisoners of War

	Total	Deaths	Percent
Federals	270,000	22,576	8
Confederates	220,000	26,246	12

The Confederates agreed to count black Federals who were not escaped slaves. And Andersonville, with over 30,000 prisoners some months in 1864, counted less than 100 blacks among that number.

No less a Northern patriot than the legendary poet Walt Whitman wrote that Secretary of War Stanton and General Benjamin Butler (Grant's representative). . .

> *had taken [their] stand on the exchange of all black soldiers, has persisted in it without regard to consequences, and has made the whole of the large and complicated question of general exchange turn upon that one item alone, while it is but a drop in the bucket. . . . In my opinion, the anguish and death of these ten to fifteen thousand American young men, with all the added and incalculable sorrow, long drawn out, amid families at home, rests mainly upon the heads of members of our own Government.*

Through Judge Robert Ould, Confederate Commissioner of Prisoner Exchange, the Confederate government tendered a series of offers to the United States government, including: to purchase medicines from the U.S. for the exclusive relief of Federal prisoners; to allow Federal surgeons within Confederate lines to dispense the medicines themselves; to resume exchange of Federal prisoners for Confederate prisoners, on a man-for-man basis; and to return all sick and wounded Federal prisoners without requiring a like number of Confederate prisoners in return.

The Federals made no reply to any of these offers for months. Grant gave his own answer on August 18:

It is hard on our men held in Southern prisons not to exchange them, but it is humanity to those left in the ranks to fight our battles. At this particular time to release all rebel prisoners North, would insure Sherman's defeat and would compromise our safety here.

The Confederates' Libby Prison, alongside the James River, after the Federals captured Richmond in April, 1865.

Petitioning Lincoln

Finally, Wirz approved the desperate request of Andersonville prisoners that a team of them be allowed to travel north and petition President Lincoln directly to relieve the suffering thousands. Wirz himself coordinated the trip, and outfitted, equipped, and transported the Federals. New York infantryman Edward Wellington Boate helped lead the contingent.

For three days they waited in Washington for an audience with the President. Lincoln refused to see them. Boate recorded his bitter reaction:

You [Federal] rulers who make charge that the rebels intentionally killed off our men, when I can honestly swear they were doing everything in their power to sustain us, do not lay this faltering unction to your souls. You abandoned your brave men in the hour of their cruelest need. They fought for the Union, and you reached no hand out to save the old faithful, loyal, and devoted servants of the country. You may try to shift the blame from your own shoulders, but posterity will saddle the responsibility where it justly belongs.

Thousands more Federal prisoners died after this failed, late-August mission, before a Federal ship finally arrived near the end of the year to pick up sick and wounded prisoners. By then, the Confederates had already moved many of the surviving prisoners to healthier locations. Thousands were transported North, however—with no Confederate prisoners exchanged in return. The parents of Vermont cavalryman Joseph P. Brainerd honored him with a small monument at their St. Albans home, near the border with Canada. They had no doubt where the blame lay for their son's death. The marble slab read in part: "on the 11th day of Sept. 1864, entirely and wholly neglected by President Lincoln . . . "

Federals playing baseball at the Salisbury, North Carolina, Confederate prison. (TreasureNet)

Henry Wirz (1822-1865)

Assistant Adjutant General, Confederate States Army, Henry Wirz was the infamous commander of Camp Sumter—better known as Andersonville Prison, due to its close proximity to that town and railroad station. Captain Wirz was a Swiss native and veteran of that Republic's army. He established a commendable record as a Confederate soldier before his assignment to Andersonville. While fighting as a sergeant in the Army of Northern Virginia at the battle of Seven Pines or Fair Oaks during the Seven Days Campaign, he caught a rifle ball in his right arm. The date: May 31, 1862, the same day Joe Johnston, at that time the Army's commander, was nearly killed.

Wirz almost lost his arm and suffered pain and the debilitation of it for the rest of his life. Just twelve days after falling, however, he was assigned to duty related to martial law under Provost Marshal John Winder in Richmond. Winder sent him on an inspection tour of Confederate prisons, then to command the prison at Tuscaloosa, Alabama. President Davis dispatched him on secret assignment at the end of 1862 to the Confederate representatives in England and France. Wirz served the Confederacy in Europe all through 1863.

He returned to the South in February, 1864. Two months later, he received command of Andersonville, where conditions were already horrific after only weeks in operation. His wife and three young daughters lived with him in three borrowed rooms at a nearby Andersonville home. Written accounts abound by Andersonville prisoners accusing Wirz personally of cruel, even sadistic, violence against them, and of commanding the prison in a manner that fomented such acts by his guards. Many of these accounts were spawned by the testimony offered during Wirz's trial before a Yankee military tribunal.

Wirz's Trial

The conducting of those proceedings surely furnishes one of the most shameful and unjust episodes in American history. Secretary of War Edwin Stanton placed General Lew Wallace in charge of the investigating commission. From the beginning, Wallace made no pretenses about his opinion of Wirz. Of 160 witnesses, fifteen of them offered testimony suggesting Wirz himself murdered prisoners. The testimony of all 15 has since been refuted.

Of 160 witnesses, fifteen of them offered testimony suggesting Wirz himself murdered prisoners. The testimony of all fifteen has since been refuted.

One witness testified he saw Wirz shoot a prisoner in cold blood—on a day Wirz lay deathly ill in an Augusta hospital. Other men accused him of shooting other prisoners, men whose names appeared on no death records. Still others recounted his brutal beatings of victims—though Wirz's left shoulder was withered and his right arm useless. One man testified Wirz kicked the man's stepfather, also a prisoner, into a role call formation, threatening to deprive him of food for a week—even though the stepfather was in the hospital at the time and Wirz himself miserably sick at home. One former prisoner whose Andersonville diary gained renown recited a litany of Wirz's supposed crimes—though he admitted he had not witnessed any of them.

The *piz de resistance* was "Felix de la Baume, grandnephew of the Marquis Lafayette." The final and star witness for the prosecution, he not only chronicled Wirz's violence with passion and eloquence, he presented his own sketched illustrations of the evil deeds. This witness received the compliments of Wallace and his commission, as well as a choice position with the Department of the Interior.

Then, after Wirz was hanged, some Germans in Washington recognized "de la Baume" as Felix Oeser of Saxony, a deserter from a New York regiment, and a liar. Meanwhile, Wallace outdid himself discounting the abundant testimony to Wirz's good character and lack of violent ways. Finally, after hearing medical experts swear that Wirz was physically incapable of so much as slapping anyone, much less killing them, Wallace and the tribunal pro-

The execution of Henry Wirz's. Some of the Federal soldiers surrounding the scaffold chanted and cheered.

nounced him guilty and sentenced him to hang.

Last Minute Offer

Never again was Wirz allowed to set eyes on his wife, waiting in Washington for weeks to see him; nor was she even allowed to take his body afterwards. The one certifiably criminal Confederate at Andersonville, quartermaster and cookhouse manager James Duncan, received a 15-year prison sentence, but escaped after less than a year and was not recaptured. In the end, the death rate among the Confederate guards at Andersonville was nearly that of the prisoners. Most of the 149 Federals who died of gunshot wounds arrived at the camp already shot. Andersonville guards killed only 11 prisoners, with several of those accidental or deliberately provoked by prisoners.

Wirz himself had no idea he had committed war crimes on any level. He remained at his post in Andersonville with his wife and three daughters until the Federals arrived, assuming he would receive the amnesty agreed to by Sherman and Johnston. The famed testaments of prisoners like Robert Kellogg, John Ransom, and John McElroy have since been proven full of errors and falsehoods.

According to Wirz's attorney, Louis Schade, the night before his execution, representatives approached Schade and Wirz's Catholic priest, Rev. Father Boyle. They informed the two that "a high Cabinet officer wanted to assure Wirz that if he would implicate Jefferson Davis with the atrocities committed at Andersonville his sentence would be commuted." Two hours before his hanging, Captain Henry Wirz, lonely, ill, brokenhearted, his arm in a sling, and his life in the balance, rebuffed the overture, adding, "If I knew anything about him, I would not become a traitor against him, or anybody else, even to save my life."

The question lingers: did Henry Wirz's trial concern him or Jefferson Davis? United States Army Judge Advocate Major Glen W. LaForce authored a 1988 article for *The Army Lawyer*. He condemned Wirz's trial not only as a miscarriage of justice, but a national disgrace: "Wirz was a scapegoat, tried in order to incriminate the Confederate leaders and to deflect criticism from Secretary of War Edwin M. Stanton."

The Raiders

Added to all the other problems Federal prisoners faced at Andersonville were "The Raiders." This vicious and criminal organization formed out of the prison population itself. Led primarily by brutal men from the big cities of the northeast, the ranks of the Raiders grew until they were hundreds strong. They used strength of numbers and brutal force to intimidate, bully, rob, beat, and even kill other prisoners. Many Raiders lived quite well at Andersonville, at the expense of thousands of their fellow soldiers.

Finally, after months of rampant, murderous criminal behavior, a heroic cadre of mostly-western prisoners led by men like Leroy "Limber Jim" Key and Alfred Hill formed organized opposition to the Raiders. They intended to fight fire with fire, and they did when the two groups crashed together one night in a climactic mass brawl that left scores of casualties. But Key, Hill, and their men, seething with rage, thrashed the Raiders, then established their own camp "Police," with Wirz's approval, to prohibit a revival of the gang. Wirz also allowed the prisoners to hold trials within the prison grounds, complete with prosecutors, defense attorneys, and jury—all drawn from the ranks of the Federals. Six Raiders were hanged for their misdeeds; others were found guilty and allowed to live, receiving various punishments.

Northern Prisons

The Federal government, while stymieing the succor of its own men at Southern prisons such as Andersonville in 1863, then preventing their release through exchange in 1864, publicly cast the blame for these acts on the South. Northern public opinion responded in outraged protest and demanded retribution. Their prison commandants and field commanders provided it in several ways, including:

1) Reduction of available food to Confederates in Northern prisons, and placing them on diets of cornmeal and pickles.
2) When Federal military operations, including the destruction of rail lines, prevented delivery of blankets and other winter clothing to Federal prisons in the South, similar items—most of them sent by their families—were confiscated from Confederate prisoners in the frigid Northern prisons.
3) The Federals turned back a British ship loaded with enough free winter supplies for 8,000 Confederates in Northern prisons without allowing delivery of its cargo.

Then the U.S. Congress codified these practices with the infamous Lane Resolution, whose preamble well conveys its antipathy to Biblical precepts, the rules of just war, international law, and the United States' own Lieber Code: "Rebel prisoners in our hands are to be subjected to a treatment finding its parallels only in the conduct of savage tribes and resulting in the death of multitudes by the slow but designed process of starvation and by mortal diseases occasioned by insufficient and unhealthy food and wanton exposure to their persons to the inclemency of the weather." Indiana Senator Henry Smith Lane, along with fellow Radical Republicans Benjamin Wade of Ohio and Morton Wilkinson of Minnesota, spearheaded the bill. They proclaimed its practice would force the Confederacy into providing better food, shelter, and clothing for Federal prisoners.

Senator Henry Smith Lane, sponsor of the Lane Resolution

Many Northerners disagreed. "The enemy are reported to be without the means to supply clothing, medicines, and other medical supplies even to their own troops," General Dan Sickles, who lost a leg but (later) won the Medal of Honor at Gettysburg, wrote Lincoln. Other prominent Senators who opposed the Lane Resolution included Republican Charles Sumner of Massachusetts and Democrat Thomas A. Hendricks of Indiana. But they were outvoted 24–16. Though the Lane Resolution remained in force only a short time, the practices it espoused continued.

These actions saved no Northern lives and took more Southern ones at death camps such as Johnson's Island, Ohio; Point Lookout, Maryland;

Confederate prisoners at the notorious Camp Douglas in Chicago.

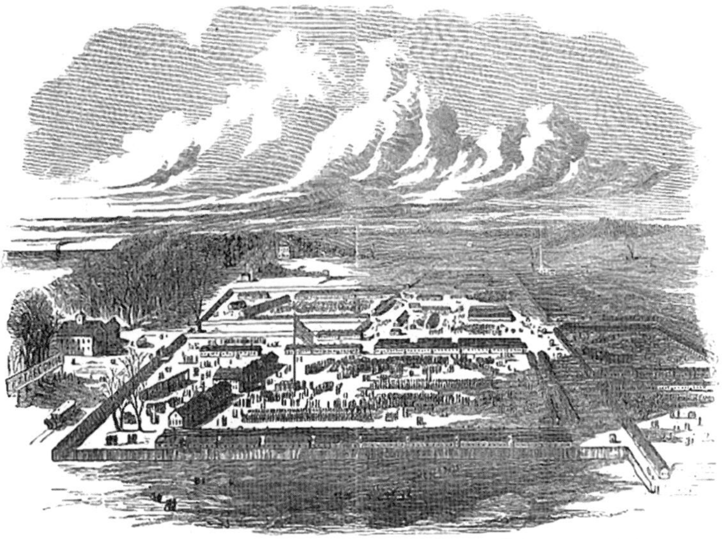

CAMP DOUGLAS, NEAR CHICAGO, ILLINOIS, WHERE SEVEN THOUSAND REBEL PRISONERS ARE QUARTERED

REBEL PRISONERS AT CAMP DOUGLAS, CHICAGO, ILLINOIS

Rock Island, Illinois; Camp Douglas, Illinois (the largest); and Elmira, New York (the worst). The mortality rate at Camp Douglas for the four winter months of 1864–65 was its highest of the War. It equaled the death total for the first four months of operation at the much-larger Andersonville Prison in Georgia. In fact, Camp Douglas's overall war toll of 4,000 was comparable to Andersonville's, though no motion pictures or television programs have ever been produced about it.

A Terrible Thing

Oceans of misery and thousands of deaths occurred in both Federal and Confederate prison camps. Individual cases of wrongdoing, brutality, and even sadism occurred in both. But a couple of episodes demonstrate a distinction between the situations North and South. Federal General in Chief Halleck complained that soldiers in his enormous Northern armies were "overclothed, overfed, and overstocked." Yet, one Southern officer imprisoned at Johnson's Island, wrote:

> *Sir, it is a terrible thing to be hungry from day to day, from week to week, from month to month—to be always hungry! . . . Should it be a matter of surprise that men dwindled from 200 to 140 and 100 pounds . . . that they grew pale, cadaverous . . . that they pounded up old bones, and boiled them over and over, until they were as white as the driven snow; that they fished in the swill-barrel at the prison hospital; that they greedily devoured rats and cats.*

Meanwhile, the Army of Northern Virginia's entire 30,000-barrel reserve supply of flour in Richmond was transferred to Federal prisoners in 1864.

Lean Confederate captives headed for prison.

In short, the North possessed abundant resources with which to supply the needs of its Southern prisoners, while the Confederacy could barely feed itself. Nonetheless, the Confederate Congress passed a bill requiring that Federal prisoners receive the same rations as Southern soldiers. Abundant evidence demonstrates that the Confederacy wished throughout the War to clear all the prison camps through exchange, and on the whole did its best to feed and supply Federal prisoners with the limited resources it possessed.

And the hard truth presents itself that the United States, in accord with its strategic objective to diminish the Confederate armies through attrition, preferred leaving the captured soldiers of both sides in prison. And even though the Federal government could have fed, clothed, doctored, and otherwise supplied its Confederate prisoners, those prisoners suffered deprivation and died in even larger proportions than their Federal counterparts down south.

The Federals' Old Capitol Prison in Washington, D.C.

to defend Atlanta, sacked him. In his place he advanced Major General John Bell Hood, a brave Texan who understood Davis expected the Confederates to fight to save Atlanta, and whose own nature fit with such a philosophy. Unfortunately for the Confederates, Hood had sparse resources and in Sherman he was facing what was proving to be one of the greatest generals of the War.

Still, the Texan threw his Army of the West into the Federals with savage ferocity in a series of battles before Atlanta. The Confederates fared well in some, such as the July 22 Battle of Atlanta, where they stopped another Sherman flanking move dead in its tracks. Hood, however, lost over 10,000 men at Decatur, to the Federals' 3,000, and more than 5,000 at East Point. Davis, whose decision to replace Johnston would prove one of his worst of the War, ordered Hood back to Atlanta. Confederates held off the Federals for several weeks as they barraged the city with shot and shell, but on September 2 Hood evacuated his troops and the invaders took the city.

An even bigger mistake—some historians think the biggest strategic error of the War by either side—was

Davis' refusal to allow Forrest to ride north from Mississippi into Tennessee and Kentucky and attack Sherman's communication lifeline. It stretched behind him from Georgia all the way north to the Ohio River at Louisville. Robert E. Lee, Joe Johnston, and Georgia Governor Joe Brown all urged this action, knowing no Federal cavalry could contend with Forrest. Sherman himself feared the specter as he clawed his way slowly toward Atlanta, even with an unimpeded supply pipeline. Instead, Forrest remained in Mississippi, and Sherman remained supplied.

Some historians think the biggest strategic error of the War by either side was President Davis's refusal to allow Forrest to ride north from Mississippi into Tennessee and Kentucky and attack Sherman's communication lifeline.

Great Catastrophe

"Women and children," Hood wrote after the War of the siege of Atlanta, "fled into cellars and were forced to seek shelter a greater length of time than at any period of the bombardment. . . . It was painful, yet strange to mark how expert grew the old men, women and children in building their little underground forts, into which to fly for safety during the storm of shell and shot." Never had American civilians conceived of a "Christian" army bombing them in their homes, schools, and churches, much less an army comprised of other Americans. But the fate of the people of Atlanta would grow much bleaker.

All the pictures and verbal descriptions of hell I have ever seen never gave me half so vivid an idea of it as did this flame-wrapped city tonight.

—A Federal staff major as Atlanta burned

The fall of Atlanta, "the workhouse and warehouse of the South," was one of the greatest catastrophes of the War for the South. It dismantled most of the key lines of supply, communication, and transportation remaining to the Confederates in the Deep South; it deprived them of one of their largest cities and greatest commercial centers; and it sounded a note chill as death to the nation's morale and future.

Most important of all, it was the singular event (in concert with Sheridan's burning of the Shenandoah and Admiral Farragut's capture of Mobile, Alabama) that swung the momentum in the United States Presidential election campaign toward Lincoln, who had looked headed toward a crushing defeat. A Lincoln defeat likely meant a negotiated truce, the end of the War, and Confederate independence; a Lincoln victory meant war—savage and total—until the South surrendered and the Confederacy fell. All this, plus Sherman burned down more than one-third of Atlanta as he left. Then he ordered the remaining thousands of civilian population and homeless refugees out of the city and onto the open road as winter approached.

Shipped North by Sherman

When Federal cavalry sent by Sherman arrived at the textile mill towns north of Atlanta, he ordered their commander, General Kenner Garrard, to burn the mills, since they produced rope, clothing, and other goods for the Southern war effort. Sherman's directives concerned the mill workers as well:

> *I had no idea that the factories at Roswell remained in operation, but supposed the machinery had all been removed. Their utter destruction is right and meets my entire approval, and to make the matter complete you will arrest the owners and employees and send them, under guard, charged with treason, to Marietta.*

Lest any confusion exist regarding Sherman's orders, he reiterated:

> *I repeat my orders that you arrest all people, male and female, connected with those factories, no matter what the clamor, and let them foot it, under guard, to Marietta, whence I will send them by cars to the North. Destroy and make the same disposition of all mills save small flouring mills manifestly for local use. . . . Useful laborers . . . are as much prisoners as if armed. The poor women will make a howl. Let them take along their children and clothing, providing they have the means of hauling or you can spare them.*

The Federals held hundreds of Roswell women, children, and a few old men for five days in the open town square under the broiling summer sun. The invaders had already "confiscated" most of their property, including wedding rings, and burned many of their homes. Finally, Sherman exclaimed, "Send them to Indiana and turn them loose!" The town of New Manchester lost so many of its people and so much of its property and buildings that it simply vanished from existence. According to historian David Evans in *Sherman's Horsemen*, most of the "traitors" were women and young girls. Meanwhile, the significant segment of Roswell residents who worshiped at the Presbyterian church no longer had that edifice for comfort and succor. Garrard ordered it turned into a Federal field hospital.

Moving Out

On the evening of July 8, the Federals began moving out nearly 2,000 terrified, heartbroken noncombatants. Within a few days, Federal soldiers would pack them onto railroad cars like cattle and

Boxcars full of Southern civilian refugees soon to be sent away from the Atlanta rail depot before Sherman burned it and much of the town.

William Tecumseh Sherman (1820-1891)

Legendary Federal General William Tecumseh Sherman helped lead the United States to victory in two of its most momentous conflicts. In doing so, he changed, perhaps forever, the way the nation fought its wars. Born in Ohio, Sherman was orphaned when young. Thomas Ewing, a United States Senator and Presidential cabinet member, raised him and helped him receive an appointment to West Point. After graduation, Sherman served several years in the South; his familiarity with its geography would help him in his campaigns during the War. He served in various staff officer positions during the Mexican War, then worked as a banker, lawyer, and realtor until the late 1850s. Then, he served as superintendent of the Louisiana school that would become Louisiana State University.

send them away. James and Walter Kennedy movingly describe the scene in their book *The South Was Right*:

> *With little or no concern for homes, more than two thousand women and children were torn from their families and shipped north. The vast majority of these people were never to see their loved ones again. In all, more than two thousand women, children, and a few old men were collected. Families were divided. Children were separated from their mothers. Tearful mothers were forced to watch as children, who had worked in the the factories, were dragged away from home—almost none of them would ever be heard from again.*

A reporter for the *Cincinnati Daily Commercial* newspaper wrote:

> *Think of it! Four hundred weeping and terrified Ellens, Susans, and Maggies transported, in springless and seatless army wagons, away from their lovers and brothers of the sunny South, and all for the offense of weaving tent-cloth and spinning stocking yarn!*

Some female factory workers who for various reasons remained in Roswell found that no advantage a few days later when Garrard issued whiskey to his men. "Upon this occasion," recalled one Federal Sergeant Magee of his rip-roaring drunk fellow soldiers, "their delirium took the form of making love to the women."

A Louisville, Kentucky newspaper report offers a portrait of the captured mill workers as they arrived North: "These people are mostly in a destitute condition, having no means to provide for themselves a support." As chronicled in books like *Turn Homeward*, *Hannalee*, and *North Across the River*, perhaps the saddest chapter of this very sad story is the final one. Soon after reaching the North, nearly all record of these mostly-poor, illiterate mill workers ends. What happened to them? Were they prevented by force from going home? Did they marry Northerners? Melt into Northern families? Succumb to prostitution to provide for themselves? Perish from disease? Probably all of these. No evidence exists that most of them ever returned South to their families and homes. They disappear from history.

Sherman liked the South, was offered an officer's commission in the Confederate Army, and reentered private business in the North rather than the military when War came, so disgusted was he that Congress had not worked it out peaceably. Nonetheless, by mid-May, 1861, he was in the U.S. Army as a colonel. He moved up the ranks, but his rise proved turbulent. Early in the War, he was transferred from one command when he claimed he needed at least 200,000 men to invade Eastern Tennessee. George McClellan said "Sherman is gone in the head." Suspicions about his emotional stability, and his sanity, dogged him even amidst his great victories.

And the Confederates proved a tenacious foe. Sherman fought in the Federal defeat at First Manassas (Bull Run), was wounded and nearly killed at Shiloh, drubbed at Chickasaw Bluffs in the Vicksburg Campaign, and repelled at Kennesaw Mountain during the Atlanta campaign. He was unsuccessful in other engagements as well, but he succeeded in many more, climaxed by his rock-ribbed stand at Missionary Ridge during the pivotal Chattanooga battle. Thereafter began the smashing chain of triumphs—Atlanta, the March through Georgia, and the Carolinas campaign—that bestowed upon him immortal fame.

Why He Succeeded

Numerous factors contributed to Sherman's colossal success. He was a brilliant strategic commander, adept at implementing the resources available to him. Also, he had a tremendous advantage over his foe with those resources, especially during the final year of the War, when his most important missions took place and the South's manpower and supplies were depleted. He also had excellent Army commanders serving directly under him: George Thomas, the "Rock of Chickamauga"; James B. McPherson; and John M. Schofield. Even his cavalry commander during the Georgia and Carolinas campaigns, the immoral, sometimes irresponsible Judson Kilpatrick, accomplished Sherman's designs for his role: "I know Kilpatrick's a h— of a d— fool, but that's just the sort of man I want on this expedition."

And there was his enduring friendship with Grant. "Grant stood by me when I was crazy and I stood by him when he was drunk," Sherman later said. "And now we stand by each other always." In Sherman, Grant had a selfless commander, one he could trust to give everything he had to the task at hand, as well as to the ultimate objective of restoring the full American Union.

Grant, meanwhile, was a commander who believed in Sherman. He provided him opportunities to prove himself in situations great and small, stood by him through difficult times, and took him along as Grant himself ascended the ladder to exalted command. For instance, when Grant acceded to overall command in the western theater, he placed Sherman in charge of the Army of the Tennessee, the largest Federal army in the West. When

William Sherman during the 1864 Atlanta Campaign.

Lincoln named Grant Commander-in-Chief of all Federal military forces, Sherman took over in the West—and Grant himself went east, so great was his trust in Sherman.

Finally, Sherman succeeded because he possessed a passion for the Federal Union and a corresponding loathing of the Confederacy, which historian Burke Davis describes him as considering "a kind of idiotic and criminal conspiracy." Sherman summarized his wartime thoughts regarding the people of the South:

> *Satan and the rebellious saints of Heaven were allowed a continuous existence in hell merely to swell their just punishment. To such as would rebel against a Government so mild and just as our was in peace, a punishment equal would not be unjust.*

Grant stood by me when I was crazy and I stood by him when he was drunk. And now we stand by each other always.
—William T. Sherman

Another War

After the War, when Grant became president, Sherman replaced him as Chief of the Army. They, Phil Sheridan, and George Custer waged another war together, this time against the Plains Indians. This conflict proved even more brutal than the War, with mass slaughters of defenseless civilians on both sides. Sherman made plain his opinion on the matter when he wrote Grant:

> *We must act with vindictive earnestness against the Sioux, even to their extermination, men, women, and children. Nothing else will reach the root of this case.*

But he was a hero to the United States—at least to those sections of it outside of the South. His fame and popularity escalated with his newfound brilliance as an after-dinner speaker. For most of the quarter-century he lived after the War, his name ranked at the head of the list of both Democratic and Republican Presidential possibilities. His memorable riposte on the subject: "I will not accept if nominated and will not serve if elected."

William Tecumseh Sherman's success in Georgia and the Carolinas legitimized the theretofore-scorned practice of "Total War"—unleashing the might of military forces against not just an army, but against a whole people, young and old, male and female, armed and unarmed—as a sanctioned practice of United States political policy. The nation has employed it ever since, in such venues as the Plains Indians Wars, the Philippines, World War II, Vietnam, Serbia, and Iraq. As one contemporary American children's history book on the War, popular in Christian schools, approvingly writes:

> *[Sherman's] army did a lot of destroying. It was cruel, because many innocent people were hurt. But Sherman may have been right. He probably shortened the war.*

Though it brought him success, adoration, fame, and fortune, Sherman himself declared, "War is hell." He expounded on that sentiment at war's end with revealing words worthy of contemplation by latter-day generations of Americans:

> *I confess, without shame, I am sick and tired of fighting—its glory is all moonshine; even success the most brilliant is over dead and mangled bodies, with the anguish and lamentations of distant families, appealing to me for sons, husbands, and fathers. . . . It is only those who have never heard a shot, never heard the shrieks and groans of the wounded and lacerated (friend or foe), that cry aloud for more blood, more vengeance, more desolation.*

John Bell Hood (1831-1879)

Possessed of apparently limitless courage, this tall, sad-faced Kentucky native who adopted Texas and whom Texas adopted, mirrored as well as any single man the changing fortunes of the Confederacy. His famed Texas Brigade in Longstreet's Corps established itself as one of the greatest fighting units in American history. Charging straight into a sheet of fire and steel, it spearheaded the attack that won the key victory at Gaines's Mill for the Confederates during the Seven Days Campaign.

Hood and his Texans again led the way in Longstreet's crushing attack that won Second Manassas. One Yankee soldier described their stunning entrance as "like demons emerging from the earth . . . mad with excitement, rage, and the fearful desire for blood." The Texas Brigade, now part of Hood's Division, broke the Federal attack that had threatened to overwhelm the Confederate left during the early hours at Sharpsburg.

The second day of Gettysburg, it was Hood's men who swarmed over the Peach Orchard, the Wheatfield, Round Top, and Devil's Den, and who came so close to taking Little Round Top, against such gargantuan odds. "I do not hesitate to pronounce this the best three hours' fighting ever done by any troops on any battlefield," Longstreet proclaimed even after Hood and his men fell just short of their objective.

The second day of Gettysburg, it was Hood's men who swarmed over the Peach Orchard, the Wheatfield, Round Top, and Devil's Den, and who came so close to taking Little Round Top, against such gargantuan odds.

Hood himself was wounded so badly at Gettysburg that he lost the use of his left arm. His corps was one of the two Longstreet used to mow back the Federals in the famous victory at Chickamauga.

Hood lost a leg on that field. Yet with a useless arm and a cork leg, he still could ride nearly as well as most men with two legs and two arms, according to General Gustavus Smith.

Texas Boys

Hood and his men once more etched their name onto the tablets of American history during the May 5–6 Battle of the Wilderness. There, as U. S. Grant and Robert E. Lee fought head-to-head for the first time, the Federals were driving the Confederates from the field. Lee himself, watching in vain for reinforcements, was in danger of capture. But then a small cadre of lean men in hole-filled hats and colorless rags for uniforms appeared through the smoke and fury.

"Who are you, my boys?" Lee cried. "Texas boys!" came the answer. "Hurrah for Texas!" Lee, normally calm and quiet even on the battlefield, shouted. "Hurrah for Texas! Texans always move them!" Then the Virginian himself rode toward the onrushing Federals, leading Hood's Texans in counterattack. "Lee to the rear! Lee to the rear!" screamed the Confederates. They barely managed to catch him and stop him, refusing to charge until he rode to safety. Hood and his men not only saved the day, they turned the tide of battle. Grant lost over 18,000 men in his first encounter with Lee.

Yet for all the magnificence Hood demonstrated in battle after battle while commanding brigades and divisions, he proved just as spectacular a failure when Davis made the fatal decision to replace Joe Johnston with him as Commander of the Army of Tennessee during the Atlanta campaign. Pressured by Davis to go on the offensive, and inclined that way by nature, Hood initiated a series of bloody skirmishes with Sherman that failed to keep the Federals from taking Atlanta. Unlike Pemberton at Vicksburg, Hood eluded Sherman, then effected a series of artful and distracting maneuvers in his rear. But the ruin of the Army of the Tennessee and the end of the War awaited when Hood moved north into Tennessee. A crippling tactical victory at Franklin that saw much of the heart of his army fall was followed by his ill-advised and disastrous move on George Thomas at Nashville. Hood's army was decimated and only fragments of it played any further role in the now-hopeless attempt to stop Sherman's rampage.

Hood and his men not only saved the day, they turned the tide of battle. Grant lost over 18,000 men in his first encounter with Lee.

Yet John Bell Hood had proven an indispensable component in many of the triumphs that kept the South in the War as long as it was. And like tens of thousands of other Confederate soldiers, his extreme sufferings during the War likely had a redemptive outworking—his own spiritual salvation. After professing his belief and trust in Jesus Christ, he was baptized by Lieutenant General Leonidas Polk, the "Fighting Bishop." Hood, his wife, and one of their eleven children died of yellow fever in New Orleans in 1879.

Dueling Generals

When Sherman decided to force the remaining thousands of civilians out of Atlanta, he asked Hood for a truce to get them through the lines. For two days, the two foes shot verbal volleys back and forth.

> *Permit me to say that the unprecedented measure you propose transcends, in studied and ingenious cruelty, all acts ever brought to my attention in the dark history of war. In the name of God and humanity, I protest.*
>
> —John Bell Hood

> *In the name of common sense, I ask you not to appeal to a just God in such a sacrilegious manner. You who, in the midst of peace and prosperity, have plunged a nation into war—dark and cruel war—who dared and badgered us to battle, insulted our flag, seized our arsenals and forts . . . God will judge us in due time, and he will pronounce whether it be more humane to fight with a town full of women and the families of a brave people at our backs, or to remove them to places of safety among their own friends.*
>
> —William Tecumseh Sherman

27 Franklin
(1864)

That Devil Forrest, by John Paul Strain. Nathan Bedford Forrest's stunning nighttime charge against a much-larger Federal force clears the road to Nashville for John Bell Hood ill-fated invasion of Tennessee.

"Gentlemen, n-----s and cotton started this war, and I wish them both in hell."

—William Tecumseh Sherman

The War in Missouri had grown more vicious with each passing year. The St. Louis civilian massacre, the deaths of Bill Anderson's sister and the other women in Kansas City, Quantrill's raid on Lawrence, the Cass County expulsions—these and countless other bloody exploits had stained the honor of both sides. Even the Indian practice of scalping was now plied by white Federal and Confederate alike against the other.

Sterling Price made another attempt to wrest the state back from the United States when he led his army into the two-stage October 21–23 Battle of Westport. The fight ranged across most of Jackson County in the Kansas City area. The Confederates broke the Federals' front lines, then cleared them out of the town of Independence. But Price got squeezed between two enemy forces—which included Kansas militia—along the Big Blue Creek, now part of Kansas City, Missouri. Here the tide of battle turned in favor of the Federals.

Price and his men escaped into Kansas, where the Federals attacked them at the Battle of Mine Creek two days later. In the only major battle

Nathan Bedford Forrest's Navy

Forrest's non-West Point-tutored military mind shone again in mid-October, against the huge Federal supply depot at Johnsonville, on the Tennessee River in northern Tennessee. Working to wreak havoc on Sherman's supply line chain, the "Wizard of the Saddle" launched a diversion to obscure his assault on Johnsonville. He began with the disruption of Federal river traffic on the Tennessee north of Johnsonville. However, after capturing then destroying one Yankee transport ship, Forrest hauled in two more, the *Undine* and the *Venus*. Then he put former riverboat skipper Captain Frank Gracey of the 3rd Kentucky in charge of training soldiers to man both boats. Having done that, Forrest's "horse marines" set about creating chaos on the river with their new two-boat "navy," then battling a whole fleet of Federal gunboats.

Meanwhile, with all Federal attention in the area turned toward that rumble, Forrest's main force descended upon totally-unsuspecting Johnsonville. His artillery turned the Federals' three gunboats, 11 transports, 18 barges, stockade fortress, row of warehouses, acres of open-air materiel, and two freight train-loads of supplies into one gargantuan inferno. The scene "beggared description," said one Federal. Forrest estimated the loss at $6,700,000 (in 1864 dollars). The Federals abandoned Johnsonville, but Forrest lost his navy. The *Venus* was recaptured, and Gracey, running out of fuel and single-handedly fighting nine Northern gunboats mounting 100 guns, burned the (Federals') *Undine*.

fought in Kansas, the Confederates repulsed the Federal assaults, then made their way back through Indian Territory to their base in Arkansas. Missouri remained, permanently, in Federal hands.

Gettysburg of the West

Hood could have remained near Sherman and dogged him from behind once he marched east from Atlanta, while placing cavalry in his front to slow him and reduce his opportunities for destruction. Instead, the Confederate commander headed for Tennessee. He wanted to cut off the Federals from their supply and communication bases. Doing that, perhaps he would even be able to push on through Tennessee to the Ohio River. That feat would create a number of intriguing possibilities, including liberating Tennessee, forcing the retreat of Sherman from Georgia, and rendezvousing with Lee in Virginia against Grant.

But Sherman had sent George Thomas, the "Rock of Chickamauga," to deal with just such a situation, and two corps under John Schofield to back him up. Filled with rage at the devastation they observed visited on their homeland by the invaders, Hood's army caught up with Schofield's 30,000 men on the last day of November at Franklin, fifteen miles south of Nashville.

Goober Peas (Armand E. Blackmar)

Sitting by the roadside on a summer day,
Chatting with my messmates, passing time away,
Lying in the shadow underneath the trees,
Goodness, how delicious, eating goober peas!

Chorus:

Peas! Peas! Peas! Peas! Eating goober peas!
Goodness, how delicious, eating goober peas!

Just before the battle the gen'ral hears a row;
He says, "The Yanks are coming, I hear their rifles now."
He turns around in wonder, and what d'you think he sees?
The Georgia militia, eating goober peas!

I think my song has lasted almost long enough,
The subject's interesting but the rhymes are mighty rough;
I wish this war was over, when free from rags and fleas,
We'd kiss our wives and sweethearts, and gobble goober peas!

John Chivington and The Sand Creek Massacre (1821–1894)

This famed chapter of the U.S.–Plains Indian struggle happened on November 28, while the War still raged. Bloody battles, as well as pitiless murder parties, had already been unleashed in the area between westward-migrating white Christian civilization and the aboriginal pagan tribes of Cheyenne, Arapahoe, and others. But as the well-known Cheyenne chief Black Kettle and hundreds of his people lay nestled in their blankets along Sandy Creek before dawn, they slept with the promise of peace and safety issued by the Federal garrison at nearby Fort Lyon. President Lincoln himself had awarded Black Kettle a medal for his peacemaking efforts, along with an American flag that now flew from his lodgepole.

Black Kettle's antagonist was Colonel John Chivington, a bluff, six-foot-four-inch former circuit-riding Methodist preacher and hero of the Battle of Glorieta Pass two years before. There, he had led the audacious rear assault that destroyed the Confederate supply train and doomed their entire Far West campaign to defeat. "I have come to kill Indians," he announced upon his arrival at Fort Lyon. When asked by Regular Army troops if that included women and children, he boomed, "Nits make lice."

"I have come to kill Indians," Chivington announced upon his arrival at Fort Lyon. When asked by Regular army troops if that included women and children, he boomed, "Nits make lice."

Chivington set out from Fort Lyon with 700 men. Heavily-armed, they toted 150,000 cartridges, 20 bags of powder, a ton of lead, and four howitzers. Most of his main force of 600 men were raw recruits, mostly miners, signed on for 100 days. They intended to rid eastern Colorado once and for all of Indian menace. Captain Silas Soule, also a veteran of Glorieta Pass and other Western action, commanded another 100 men, Regular Army troopers from Fort Lyon.

After an all-night ride through the winter air, "Chiv" and his men thundered into the Cheyenne camp at dawn. As his terrified people swarmed to him, Black Kettle ran a white flag up his pole to accompany the American. It mattered not. The Federals not only killed their quarry, they took Bowie knives and other weapons and carved off their scalps and every other conceivable body part. They also tossed "papooses" in the air, then ran them through. Chivington claimed the deaths of 400–500 Cheyenne warriors. The actual body counts was 28 men, 105 women and children. Nine soldiers fell dead and 38 wounded, most of these shot down in the crossfire of one another's bullets.

Much More Murder

The unspeakable scenes horrified the First Colorado regiment, commanded by Soule. They refused to participate and watched the bloodletting from a distance. "Murder pure and simple," Soule called it. A furious Chivington threatened afterward to kill Soule too. Many other Coloradans shared the sentiment, though by no means all. Indeed, Soule was murdered on the streets of Denver a few months later, after being named Provost Marshal of Denver. He was walking with his wife of one week at the time of his shooting. The accused man was captured by Soule's replacement, Lieutenant Cannon, then escaped—after Cannon was poisoned to death.

A Congressional investigation of the Sand Creek Massacre condemned it as an attack on law-abiding civilians. Chivington was cashiered from the Colorado militia and his burgeoning political career destroyed. Black Kettle himself escaped the Sand Creek apocalypse, only to be massacred along with another Cheyenne settlement at the "Battle" of the Washita less than four years later by General George Custer and his pony soldiers. In an 1868 interview in the *Denver Inquirer* newspaper, Chivington defended his actions at Sand Creek: "How reviving to a soul . . . to know that God has given invincible might to quell the wicked of the earth and give dominion to the good, the wise, the just—the true believers! This world is delivered to our hand, sir, delivered for dominion! Our Savior bids us make His excellence supreme! . . . Oh the Indian . . . he's dumb, sir, dumb as a dog, he's ignorant of what can lift him! What will save him? Offer him salvation! Offer life! As he is, he'll never read a word you're writing. I will! I am what conversion means!"

Federal soldiers attack the Cheyenne village at Sandy Creek, Colorado.

All Chivington ridded Colorado of was peaceable Indians. No chief of any tribe dared take the white man's side after what happened at Sandy Creek. The slaughter, and atrocities, on all sides escalated, and hatred—lasting hatred—with it. The *Denver Inquirer* pronounced its own epitaph four years later after witnessing Colorado reap its whirlwind:

We say this: the uniform of these United States should ever be the emblem of humanity and justice. The colonel [Chivington] broke the honor of that trust. He planned and put in hand a massacre so foul it would have set to shame the veriest "savage" of all who were the victims of his cruelty. The toll of the Indian Wars is not the count of bodies only. It is invisible. It attacks the mind and heart. It puts the soul to trial by asking, "This nation under God? How shall it grow from roots so deeply set in wrong? And when it does, its fruit—how can it prove a savor to our spirit?"

The toll of the Indian Wars is not the count of bodies only. It is invisible. It attacks the mind and heart. It puts the soul to trial by asking, "This nation under God? How shall it grow from roots so deeply set in wrong? And when it does, its fruit—how can it prove a savor to our spirit?"

—The Denver Inquirer

View of Nashville, 1864, from the capitol.

Now Hood, superlative as a division commander, began to evidence his shortcomings in higher command. The Federals were dug in about as deep as an army could dig itself. Artillery shielded them on every side. Hood did not even wait to bring his own heavy guns up. No less bold a commander than Nathan Bedford Forrest beseeched him not to attack, since the Federals had no intention but to keep moving north anyway.

The doomed valorous epic of Gettysburg appeared now to replay itself in the west. No battle in the War proved more desperate or murderous than Franklin.

Hood would not be dissuaded. He sent nearly 20,000 men forward over wide open ground on a front stretching nearly two miles across. The doomed valorous epic of Gettysburg appeared now to replay itself in the west. No battle in the War proved more desperate or murderous than Franklin. Time after time the Confederates charged screaming into the well-entrenched enemy, who blazed away with new multi-shot repeating rifles while the Southerners used single-shot muzzle loaders and bayonets.

Over 6,000 Southerners, including twelve generals (among them Pat Cleburne, the "Stonewall of the West," and Texan Hiram Granbury), fell. But they would not quit. "It is impossible to exaggerate the fierce energy with which the Confederate soldiers that short November afternoon threw themselves against the works, fighting with what seemed the madness of despair," wrote one Federal officer. The fighting raged into the night. Finally, Schofield, his own forward lines crushed, left his dead and wounded and fell back to Nashville.

Western Troop Strength Fall 1864
Middle Tennessee/Northern Alabama/Northern Georgia

Federal	135,500
Confederate	42,500

(Prior to the battles of Franklin and Nashville)

Destruction at Nashville

Indeed, it can be fairly stated that the remaining flower of the Confederate Army of the West sacrificed itself on the altar of its country at Franklin. It was not the same army that stood against the combined attacks of Thomas and Schofield December 15 at Nashville.

With many more of his men debilitated by sickness brought on by the unusually frigid winter, and outnumbered 55,000 to 39,000, Hood managed to hold the Federals off for most of two days. But then they broke his line and surged forward. The Federals carted off fifty-four cannons and thousands of Confederate prisoners in the Battle of Nashville, which crushed the last threat to Sherman's juggernaut across Georgia to the Atlantic.

That epic procession began in mid-November. Even without Thomas's and Schofield's 60,000 men in Tennessee, Sherman had a force of 63,000 infantry and cavalry. Facing him were 13,000 scattered Georgia militia—mostly old men and young boys—and a couple thousand horse soldiers under Joe Wheeler. They did their best, but Sherman entered Savannah, on the Atlantic, on December 22. "I beg to present to you as a Christmas gift the city of Savannah with one hundred and fifty heavy guns and plenty of ammunition, and also about 25,000 bales of cotton," he wrote President Lincoln. Now Sherman would turn north through the Carolinas. If he kept marching, which he planned to do, he would join Grant and destroy the Army of Northern Virginia.

It can be fairly stated that the remaining flower of the Confederate Army of the West sacrificed itself on the altar of its country at Franklin.

The Indian Nations

The Federals, with their immense advantage in resources and numbers, had gradually gained the upper hand in the land occupied by the "civilized" Indian nations, roughly the eastern half of present-day Oklahoma. Southern control was rolled back far south of the Arkansas River, aid from the Confederate government choked off, and the families of pro-Confederate Indians driven south into Texas for their safety.

Illustrative of the brutal nature of Indian Territory warfare was Federal Colonel William A. Phillips' 1864 campaign south through the territory toward Texas. Phillips sent a circular to

Joe Wheeler (1837-1906)

Long overshadowed by fellow Southern horse soldiers like Nathan Bedford Forrest, Jeb Stuart, and even Wade Hampton, Joe Wheeler was one of the greatest cavalry commanders of the War. Robert E. Lee called only a few men "outstanding," and Wheeler was one of those. A native Georgian born to New England parents, he fought Indians in New Mexico for two years between graduating from West Point and the War's beginning. He moved quickly up the Confederate military ladder.

Soon after leading a regiment of Alabama cavalry at Shiloh, he found himself assigned command of all horse in the Army of Mississippi, one of the Confederacy's western armies. As such, he coordinated a superb effort of scouting and reporting Federal troop movements during the Murfreesboro and Chickamauga campaigns. But some of his greatest work came during the most difficult time of the War for the South. After the fall of Atlanta and destruction of the main western Confederate forces up at Franklin and Nashville, "Wheeler's Raiders" provided the only sustained resistance to Sherman as he burned and looted his way to the Atlantic.

Controversy came with Wheeler's actions, some of it from his own side. Complaints arose that Sherman and his bummers were not the only ones hard on Georgia's crops and livestock. The state's Governor Joe Brown (who gained infamy after the War for throwing in with the carpetbaggers) called Wheeler and his men horse thieves and bellowed, "General Wheeler . . . [has] demonstrated . . . that he is not capable of commanding 10,000 cavalrymen."

"Wheeler's Raiders" provided the only sustained resistance to Sherman as he burned and looted his way to the Atlantic.

Wheeler, risking his neck and those of his men night and day month after month against a colossal, unstoppable foe, fired back: "During the last five months my command has been without wagons or cooking utensils. With orders to subsist on the country, its food has been limited to bread baked upon boards and stones and meat broiled upon sticks." That, and his men had been paid nothing for a year and had never been issued uniforms. Meanwhile, they averaged sixteen miles a day on horseback. He drew inordinate ire from the Federals as well when on two occasions some of his men tracked down, slit the throats of, and placed warning notes on the corpses of bluecoats who had raped and killed Southern women.

Primal Combat

Wheeler and his cavalry fought Sherman's army with all they had, several times engaging in combat that descended to the most desperate and primal levels. On three separate occasions, they nearly captured Judson Kilpatrick, commander of all Sherman's cavalry. The first occurred in late November, when the Confederates mounted a last-ditch—and successful—stand that saved Augusta from Kilpatrick and his men. "Kilcalvary" escaped capture only by leaping to safety from a house the Confederates did not notice, where he was "socializing" with some black women.

Early the next year, Wheeler and his men ambushed Kilpatrick in Aiken, South Carolina, again nearly nabbing him. They did get his hat. Then in March, 1865, near Fayetteville, North Carolina, they stampeded into Kilpatrick's camp at dawn. This time he dove out a window from a bed he shared with an Irishwoman and fled on foot, wearing only his night shirt. The Federal infantry dubbed the incident "Kilpatrick's shirt-tail skedaddle." Kilpatrick himself called it "the most formidable cavalry charge I ever saw." The next month, at Bentonville, North Carolina, the last substantial clash between Sherman and the Confederates, Wheeler and his horse soldiers broke the most dangerous Federal attack of the battle. Historian Burke Davis described them as "reckless riders who held reins in their teeth and fired big navy pistols with both hands."

But Joe Wheeler's work and life had only just begun when the War ended. Not yet 30 years old, he not only served two terms in the U.S. Congress, he ascended to leadership as the ranking Democrat on the House Ways and Means Committee. When the Spanish-American War exploded with the *USS Maine*, the government appointed Wheeler major general in command of all volunteers. Though ill, he was present at the famous Battle of San Juan Hill; he fought at Las Guasimas; and he commanded a cavalry division at Santiago. All this he did while more than 60 years of age.

Later still, he commanded a brigade of cavalry in the Philippines and gained the rank of Brigadier General, in the United States army he had once fought, before finally retiring from active service in late 1900 at the age of 64. Wheeler wrote books and articles and worked until the end of his life to improve the lot of his adopted state Alabama and all of the South, and aid their return to equal status in the Union.

Joe Wheeler, still a vigorous horseman and leader of man, decades after the War, around the time of the Spanish-American War.

Santos Benavides and His Brothers (1823–1891)

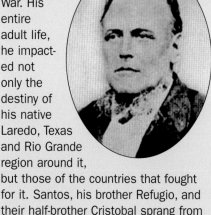

Santos Benavides was the highest-ranking Hispanic officer on either side in the War. His entire adult life, he impacted not only the destiny of his native Laredo, Texas and Rio Grande region around it,

but those of the countries that fought for it. Santos, his brother Refugio, and their half-brother Cristobal sprang from a long line of Mexican community, business, and political leaders. His great-great-grandfather was the founder of Laredo. Santos himself won election as mayor of Laredo in 1856, when he was only 33, then chief justice of Webb County in 1859. He further established his leadership by commanding several campaigns against the Lipan Apaches and other Indians.

Santos' times were tumultuous ones, and he led his people through many historic events. Sometimes his relations with political parties and governments shifted. But he retained an abiding vision for his people. He wanted Laredo and the Rio Grande region around it to be well-represented in whatever body politic to which they were accountable, while remaining as self-reliant and self-governing as possible. For instance, he and other leaders in the far north Mexican provinces (which still contained Laredo) supported the Federalist cause of local autonomy as they politicked and sometimes warred against Santa Anna and the Centralists who wanted power centralized in Mexico City, far to the south. Santos fought in combat for the Federalists in the Mexican civil war as a young man. Frustrated with the Federalists, however, he sided with Texas and the Americans in the Mexican War. Then, concerned that it jeopardized the independent character of northern Mexico, he opposed the American-drawn Treaty of Guadalupe Hidalgo which ended that war and annexed Laredo and the surrounding area to the United States.

Santos Benavides was the highest-ranking Hispanic officer on either side in the War.

With the South

The Benavideses sided with the Confederacy from the start. The South's adherence to the principles of States' rights squared with their own strong regionalism. The family's influence in the Rio Grande region, their resources, and their personal skills marked them as valuable assets for the secessionists.

Refugio Benavides, Atanacio Vidauri, Cristobal Benavides, and John Leyendecker, officers of the Benavides Texas Cavalry, 33rd Regiment.

The Confederates commissioned Santos as a captain. Within a month of the firing on Fort Sumter, he confirmed the wisdom of that rank. Mexican rebel Juan Cortinez, long a nemesis of border-dwelling Americans—though his own mother dwelt north of the Rio Grande and opposed his actions—launched a series of raids on Zapata County, on the north bank of the river. When Cortinez and a large force surrounded Benavides and a few dozen Hispanic and white Confederates at Redmond Ranch in Zapata County, Benavides refused to flee and stood his ground. Then, fearing Cortinez and another force was ransacking the county seat at Carrazo, Benavides and his men broke through and ambushed them, defeating them and chasing the survivors all the way back to Mexico. He also squelched other local challenges to Confederate rule.

He rose to the rank of Colonel of the Benavides Texas Cavalry, 33rd Regiment, in late 1863, with authority to form his own regiment of partisan rangers. His younger half-brother Cristobal was promoted to captain at the same time and placed in command of a company in Santos' regiment. Santos' greatest military triumph was his April defense of Laredo against the Federals. With Cristobal, Refugio, and forty other men, most of them kinsmen, he held off 200 Yankee soldiers. Santos used everything he could muster to protect the town—including cotton bales he and his men used for cover.

With his ammunition running out and knowing that Colonel Rip Ford and his Cavalry of the West were riding south sweeping the Federals out of the Rio Grande Valley, Santos sent word to Ford; he would keep fighting if Old Rip would just bring him some more ammunition. The Benavideses and their cohorts held until Ford's April 15 arrival. The Yankee General, Edmund Davis, whom Santos held off, had once offered him a brigadier generalship in the Federal army because of his influence with Mexicans along the river.

With Laredo secured, the Benavideses and their colleagues mounted up and rode down the Rio Grande with Ford, driving the Federals out of Texas. On June 23, Cristobal helped lead the Confederate assault on Federal forces at Las Rucias. Refugio charged too. Riding in the front rank of the charge, Cristobal's horse was shot out from under him; dodging bullets he charged forward on foot. After the victory, his superiors singled him out for gallantry. Santos, Refugio, and Cristobal were among the last soldiers in the entire Confederacy to lay down their arms.

After the War, Santos served in the Texas state legislature from 1879–1884. He continued to struggle for the cause of regional independence from centralized national authority. His guiding influence shifted Hispanic support in Webb County toward the conservative Democratic Party, while ending the control of the Republicans and their platform of more activist and centralized government. Refugio married the daughter of a Confederate general, raised ten children, and won election several times as mayor of Laredo. Cristobal focused his efforts on his sheep, cattle, and mercantile enterprises and became one of the wealthiest men in Webb County.

Federal troops invade Brownsville, Texas, in November, 1863.

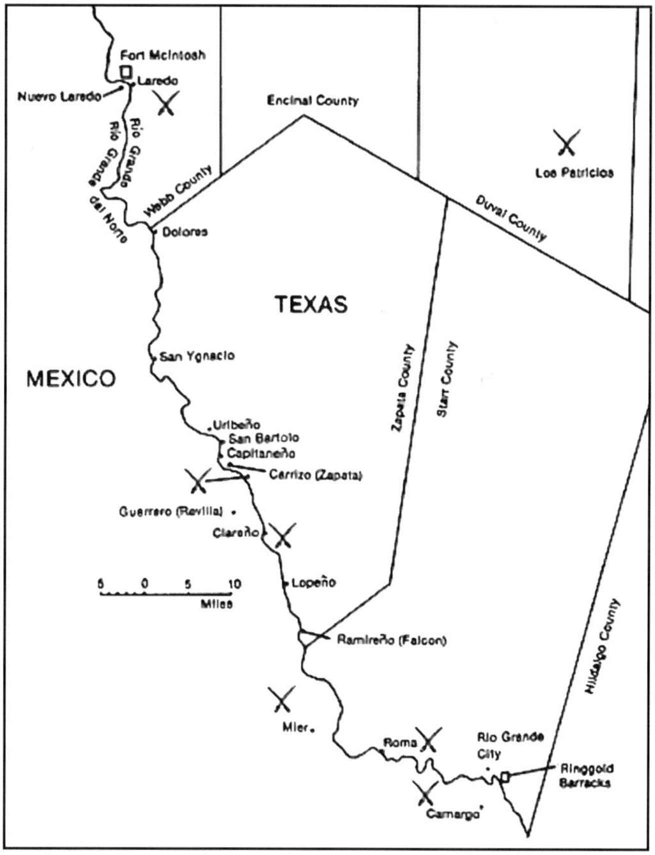

Battles of the Upper Rio Grande region in Texas.

his troops, which read: "Do not kill a prisoner after he has surrendered. But I do not ask that you take prisoners. I do ask that you make your footsteps severe and terrible." Then Phillips stormed south down the Texas Road, burning homes and crops as he went.

Cherokee Chief and Confederate General Stand Watie unfolded a tenacious guerilla campaign of hit-and-run assaults that kept the Federals off-balance and looking over their shoulders.

On February 13, 1864, several hundred of his Kansas cavalry troopers ambushed and massacred less than one hundred Confederates—many of them American Indians—on or near the Middle Boggy River west of modern-day Atoka, in far southeastern Oklahoma. The Federals took no prisoners, and Confederates who recovered their dead comrades' bodies said many had only superficial wounds, but their throats had been slit and some were scalped.

The Second Battle at Cabin Creek, which reversed a Federal victory there the year before, gained Watie and Gano special commendations from Jefferson Davis himself.

After the Battle of Middle Boggy, Phillips continued his rampage, stealing all available food and capturing women, children, slaves, and livestock. According to Oklahoma Historical Commission official Whit Edwards, the Federals killed another 110 Confederates, mostly Indians, in their homes, because of Phillips's no-prisoners policy. "He hoped this would be the final blow to the Confederate resistance," Edwards says. "Instead, the brutal treatment of the wounded only served to strengthen the resolve of the resistors."

Indeed, Cherokee Chief and Confederate General Stand Watie deftly adjusted his strategy to meet these changing and vicious circumstances. He unfolded a tenacious guerilla campaign of hit-and-run assaults that kept the Federals off-balance and looking over their shoulders. So effective were Watie and his multi-tribe melange of warriors, that despite occupying most of Indian Territory, no Federal troop column, no Federal wagon train, no Federal fort was beyond the Indians' striking reach.

After a series of successful raids, the electrifying climax to the Southern Indians' resistance movement came on September 19. That is when the Confederates ambushed a mammoth, 300-wagon Northern supply train in an audacious night raid deep behind Federal lines. Watie conceived of and crafted the entire attack. Devout Baptist minister, physician, and Brigadier General Richard Gano of Texas led it. Gano's 1,200 rough-riding Texas cavalrymen and 800 Oklahoma Indian soldiers, led by such men as Seminole Chief John Jumper and Creek Chief C. W. Grayson, routed the Yankee defenders, seized half the wagon train and burned the other half, then fought off Federal pursuers and drove their bounty all the way down the Texas Road, across the Red River, and safely into the Lone Star State.

The haul came to $1.5 million (approximately $75 million in 2003

Tenting on the Old Camp Ground (Walter Kittridge)

We're tenting tonight on the old camp ground,
Give us a song to cheer
Our weary hearts, a song of home,
And friends we love so dear.

Chorus:
Many are the hearts that are weary tonight,
Wishing for the war to cease;
Many are the hearts that are looking for the right,
To see the dawn of peace.
Tenting tonight, tenting tonight,
Tenting on the old camp ground.

We are tired of war on the old camp ground,
Many are dead and gone,
Of the brave and true who've left their homes;
Others been wounded long.

We've been fighting today on the old camp ground,
Many are lying near;
Some are dead and some are dying,
Many are in tears.

dollars). It clothed Watie's whole army—mostly in blue—and fed them and their dependents for more than a month. The Second Battle at Cabin Creek, which reversed a Federal victory there the year before, gained Watie and Gano special commendations from Jefferson Davis himself. It was the final significant clash of the War in "The Nations."

28 Appomattox
(1865)

Galusha Pennypacker leads the Federals ashore in *Landing at Fort Fisher,* by John Paul Strain. The capture of Wilmington, North Carolina, and the fort closed the Confederates' last open port on the Atlantic.

A mighty army, a navy absorbing nearly the whole mercantile marine, vast military stores, a martial law, a national debt, a heavy taxation, enormous dues—all things which it was long the object of all constitutional statesmen to prevent—have now been established without resistance, and have transformed the government.

—Horace Greeley

As the fifth calendar year of war began, the Confederacy clung to its lone remaining open port in the East—Wilmington, North Carolina. By the end of January, however, after months of Federal assaults and episodes of furious combat, Wilmington's Fort Fisher and the city itself had fallen. Confederate Vice President Alexander Stephens called the event "one of the greatest disasters which has befallen our Cause." But month after month, the future of two nations hung on the events transpiring along a thirty-five mile-long chain of trenches and earthworks circling Petersburg and Richmond.

Every move Grant made, every plan he devised, was based on the long-term strategy of wearing down Lee's army by siege.

As had all of his predecessors, U. S. Grant had failed to reach Richmond the year before. So, beginning in June, 1864, after Grant moved his Army of the Potomac south across the James River, the soldiers and the action centered on Petersburg. Historian James I. Robertson has well described Grant's three-pronged strategy for reducing Petersburg. First, he had tenacity and patience in equal measure, as well as Lincoln's support, especially after the President's reelection for another four-year term in the White House. Grant recognized that time was his ally; his well-fed, well-supplied army grew stronger, while Lee's starving, freezing one was withering away. Indeed, Federal General Butler said, "The fact is incontestable that a soldier in our army would have quite easily starved on the rations . . . served out to the Confederates soldiers before Petersburg."

Not only were Southern soldiers growing weak with hunger; the few horses they still possessed were too weak for the critical duty of pulling wagons. And these words penned by a Confederate staff officer help illumine why desertions further sapped the defenders:

> Hundreds of letters addressed to soldiers . . . in which mothers, wives, and sisters told their inability to respond to the appeals of hungry children for bread, or to provide proper care and remedies for the sick; and, in the name of all that was dear, appealed to the men to come home and rescue them from the ills which they suffered and the starvations which threatened them.

Every move Grant made, every plan he devised, was based on the long-term strategy of wearing down Lee's army by siege. Sam Grant possessed complete confidence this course would provide eventual victory, which he believed would end the War and restore the full Federal Union.

Wilmington, North Carolina, a few weeks after it fell to the Federals. Released Federal prisoners make their way to waiting transports.

Secondly, Grant knew both Richmond and Petersburg, and the army defending them, depended on the railroads that brought food and supplies from the South and West. So he attacked these, hoping to starve the cities and the soldiers into surrender, as he had done Pemberton's men and Vicksburg. Well before the beginning of the year,

Lincoln's Second Inaugural Address

Abraham Lincoln's second presidential inaugural address, delivered on March 4, 1865, is considered by many people as one of the greatest speeches in American history. Lincoln sought to convey resolution and explanation for the conflagration; unlike previous speeches, he invoked the practice of slavery—and the fight against it—as the signal cause for the conflagration.

Both parties deprecated war; but one of them would make war rather than let the nation survive; and the other would accept war rather than let it perish. And the war came.

One eighth of the whole population were colored slaves, not distributed generally over the Union, but localized in the Southern part of it. These slaves constituted a peculiar and powerful interest. All knew that this interest was, somehow, the cause of the war. To strengthen, perpetuate, and extend this interest was the object for which insurgents would rend the Union, even by war; while the government claimed no right to do more than to restrict the territorial enlargement of it.

Neither party expected for the war, the magnitude, or the duration, which it has already attained. Neither anticipated that the cause of the conflict might cease with, or even before, the conflict itself should cease. Each looked for an easier triumph, and a result less fundamental and astounding. Both read the same Bible, and pray to the same God; and each invokes His aid against the other. It may seem strange that any men should dare to ask a just God's assistance in wringing their bread from the sweat of other men's faces; but let us judge not that we be not judged. The prayers of both could not be answered; that of neither has been answered fully. The Almighty has His own purposes. "Woe unto the world because of offenses! For it must needs be that offenses come; but woe to that man by whom the offense cometh!"

> *Both [North and South] read the same Bible, and pray to the same God; and each invokes His aid against the other.*
>
> —Abraham Lincoln

If we shall suppose that American Slavery is one of those offenses which, in the providence of God, must needs come, but which, having continued through His appointed time, He now wills to remove, and that He gives to both North and South this terrible war, as the woe due to those by whom the offence came, shall we discern therein any departure from those divine attributes which the believers in a Living God always ascribe to Him? Fondly do we hope—fervently do we pray—that this mighty scourge of war may speedily pass away. Yet if God wills that it continue, until all the wealth piled by the bond-man's two hundred and fifty years of unrequited toil shall be sunk, and until every drop of blood drawn with the lash, shall be paid with another drawn with the sword, as was said three thousand years ago, so still it must be said "the judgments of the Lord are true and righteous altogether."

With malice toward none; with charity for all; with firmness in the right, as God gives us to see the right, let us strive on to finish the work we are in; to bind up the nation's wounds; to care for him who shall have borne the battle, and for his widow, and his orphan—to do all which may achieve and cherish a just, and a lasting peace, among ourselves, and with all nations.

> *With malice toward none; with charity for all; with firmness in the right, as God gives us to see the right, let us strive on to finish the work we are in . . . to do all which may achieve and cherish a just, and a lasting peace, among ourselves, and with all nations.*
>
> —Abraham Lincoln

Larger Issues

These simple profound lines provoked admiration from beyond the United States, even from such Southern-leaning publications as the London *Times*. Lincoln reached past the normal bounds of an inaugural address or even a political manifesto. He courted larger issues, eternal issues. Neither is Lincoln's fabled political brilliance absent. Though casting the slavery question—and the bitter harvest he saw accruing from it—in bold relief, he carried it past the realm of a simple Radical Republican solution. Rather, he invokes the name, purposes, and inscrutability of Almighty God. Yet, though Lincoln's God was Judge, in this case of the sin of slavery, he conveyed no sense of Him as Redeemer, working His judgment for redemptive purposes.

Other questions arise as well. If slavery indeed precipitated the "woe" of the War, why did the God whose name Lincoln invokes never in His own Word, either through the prophets, the apostles or Christ the Lord Himself, condemn the institution of slavery? And whose fight was it—God's or Lincoln's? Critics would charge that even as the President rued the "terrible war," that the South "would make war rather than let the nation survive," he himself had refused a peaceable parting and now refused a peaceable reunion; he caused the suffering and deaths of tens of thousands of prisoners, North and South, by long refusing to reinstate the exchange program or allow adequate medicines, food, and clothing to either army's prisoners; he approved the concerted—and unprecedented—policy of total war pursued by nearly all of his top generals and their armies.

In the end, to some, Abraham Lincoln's second inaugural address evidences cruel hypocrisy and worse theology. To those pleased with the War's outcome, it rings through the years not only with eloquence but with penetrating wisdom.

only one rail line—the Southside—linked the area to Confederate supply sources. Finally, Robertson concludes, the Federal commander expertly employed his advantage in numbers. He kept ceaseless pressure on Lee's troops with artillery fire (including 2,000-pound Dictator guns, which lobbed 200-pound shells at the Confederates from two miles away), sharpshooting riflemen, and attacks first at one end of the Confederate line, then the other, with pressure all the time on the middle. Not a day passed without Confederate casualties. Lee's men barely had enough ammunition; Federal soldiers complained because they were required to fire at least 100 shots every day at something.

Davis Restrains Lee

In February, President Davis finally appointed Lee Commander-in-Chief of all Confederate armies. What likely would have been a splendid idea two or three years before now mattered little. Lee was fighting for the survival of his own Army of Northern Virginia and could offer scarce benefit of his wisdom and cunning to dwindling Southern forces elsewhere.

But the old "Gray Fox" as many, North and South, now called him, had fight left in him yet. He again urged

Band members of the 114th Pennsylvania Regiment infantry.

The Federals' powerful thirteen-inch mortar "Dictator," mounted atop a railroad flatcar during the Petersburg siege.

Davis to allow him to remove his men to open country. He envisioned a junction with Joe Johnston to the south, their defeat of Sherman, and then a renewed confrontation with Grant, this time in concert with Johnston. Davis would not have it, refusing to allow the abandonment of Richmond, even if it required the destruction of his greatest army to hold it. In this, his perspective seemed to differ from Grant, who had long considered Lee and the Army of Northern Virginia, and not the Confederacy's capital or any other city, the primary threat to Federal victory and the continuance of the Union.

What could Lee have accomplished if allowed several months earlier to move into country with room to innovate and maneuver? The Army of Northern Virginia had drubbed Grant's forces all spring, and others sent against it for four years—could it have reached that junction with Johnston and merged forces? What would have been the result of a pitched battle with Sherman? With Grant? Such delicious hypotheses will forever be debated. Even should Lee and Johnston, however, have fared well in straight-up fights against Grant and Sherman, which they had previously done, the watershed issue remained one of attrition—the attrition of the Confederate army, while the well-fed Federals grew ever more numerous.

Last Hurrahs

Up to the very end of his defense of Petersburg, Lee watched and probed for an opening against the Yankees. He felt he had it on March 25, when he approved a daring plan authored by Georgia General John Gordon. It involved a surprise attack on the Federals' Fort Stedman, its capture, then use of it as a launching stage to roll back Northern forces in adjacent forts and engulf Grant's entire left wing. The thirty-two-year-old Gordon, who developed into one of Lee's best and most innovative generals in the War's later stages, participated in the attack himself. The Confederates succeeded in capturing Fort Stedman and 1,000 prisoners and turning its guns onto adjacent forts. Then, however, the Federals' enormous advantage in numbers and firepower overwhelmed the attackers and drove them back to their own lines, with the loss of over 5,000 men; the Federals lost only 3,000.

John Gordon

Lee was unable to muster another offensive until March 31, when George Pickett, of Gettysburg fame, unleashed an attack on the right terminus of the Confederate line that drove the Federals back six miles to Five Forks, a key confluence of five major roads. Lee ordered Pickett to "hold Five Forks at all hazards." He did, against staggering odds, all day, that night, and into the next day. Pickett had only 10,000 troops; the Federals, now commanded by Sheridan in that quadrant, had 50,000. Then, however, with Pickett away at Colonel Thomas Rosser's infamous shad bake with Lee's nephew and cavalry chief Fitz Lee, the Federals finally crashed through. They caved in the Confederate right, wrested away their final rail line, and rendered the entire Southern line vulnerable.

Climactic Battle

All that night, the Confederates felt the fury of the mightiest artillery barrage of the whole war. Grant followed it early the next morning, April 2, with a coordinated attack at numerous points. By now, the Federal advantage in soldiers was better than 4 to 1, 150,000 to 35,000. Bluecoats poured over the Southern lines; the Confederates fought desperately—and savagely—to hold them off. At Fort Gregg, little more than a dug out hole in the ground, 214

By now, the Federal advantage in soldiers was better than 4–1, 150,000 to 35,000.

Matthew Brady (1823-1896)

This New York-born son of Irish immigrants provides one of the great success tales of the 19th century. His story is a mosaic containing the brightest and darkest shadings of the mythical American dream. When only sixteen years of age, Brady met the famous Samuel F. B. Morse, who had already invented the telegraph. Through Morse, Brady gained exposure to the new daguerreotype imaging process, the forerunner to modern photography.

Several factors contributed to Brady's meteoric rise in the 1840s both as a pioneer in the artistic techniques of portraiture and in New York City society. He had talent, energy, a flair for experimenting with the flood of technological advances in the daguerreotype process, and a showman's ability to market and promote his product and himself. The last was not harmed by his first gallery's location on Broadway—across the street from a museum run by P. T. Barnum of circus fame.

Brady's thirty-five crews produced a photographic chronicle that featured a treasury of other sorts of shots, such as soldiers drilling and in camp, and the carnage of post-combat battlefields. And Brady himself took still-familiar photos of the War's greatest personalities, including Grant and Lee.

By 1845, "Brady of Broadway's" flair for showmanship rivaled that of Barnum himself, and his portrait subjects included the most famous Americans of his generation—former Presidents like Andrew Jackson, statesmen like Henry Clay and Daniel Webster, and an array of other notables, including Dolley Madison, James Fenimore Cooper, John J. Audubon, and naval hero Matthew Perry. Brady's success multiplied in the 1850s. He opened an even more lavish gallery and his employment of the new "wet plate process" propelled him into the (supremely profitable) forefront of producing unlimited numbers of both positive prints and enlargements. All the while, Brady maintained an unprecedented standard of innovation and creativity in such areas as the high-quality equipment he used, his large proficient staffs, and his groundbreak-

Matthew Brady, center, wearing hat, under fire with a Federal battery in the Petersburg, Virginia lines.

ing processes of print enhancement and retouching.

Lincoln and War

Brady's star reached its zenith with the approach of the War. In 1860, both Edward, the Prince of Wales, and Republican Presidential candidate Abraham Lincoln requested his services. Soon the prince became King Edward, and upon his election, Lincoln proclaimed, "Brady and the Cooper Union speech made me president!"

A Brady photographic unit during the War near Petersburg, Virginia. (TreasureNet)

It was the War, however, that seemed to offer Brady professional and financial opportunities yet undreamed of even by him. He marshaled his own brigade of field photography units and dispersed them from one end of the War to the other. The technical limitations of the day prevented certain types of photography Brady desired. For instance, since the exposure time for an individual shot remained several seconds, pictures with movement—such as during battles—proved unfeasible. Brady's thirty-five crews, however, produced a photographic chronicle that featured a treasury of other sorts of shots, such as soldiers drilling and in camp, and the carnage of post-combat battlefields. And Brady himself took still-familiar photos of the War's greatest personalities, including Grant and Lee.

Brady sunk his whole fortune . . . into his watershed wartime enterprise. He failed to recoup anywhere near his investment either from the public or the government.

But even as the self-promotion aspect of his entrepreneurial genius grew, he found less tolerance for it within the grim context of the nation's most horrific war. Many of his best workers left him in disgust when he claimed credit for photos they themselves had taken, sometimes half a continent removed from him. And Brady sunk his whole fortune of $100,000 (millions of dollars in today's money) into his watershed wartime enterprise. He failed to recoup anywhere near his investment either from the public or the government.

Incredibly, his later years found him living in cheap boarding houses and working for other photographers. After the death of his beloved wife of 37 years, Juliet, in 1887, his life grew sad and lonely. Still, Matthew Brady was the preeminent photographer in the world during an age that stretched from the first daguerreotypes to the dawn of motion picture film. His efforts, more than anyone else's, preserved for history what the War looked like.

My poor friends, you are free—free as air. . . . Liberty is your birthright. God gave it to you as he gave it to others, and it is a sin that you have been deprived of it for so many years. But you must try to deserve this priceless boon. . . . Don't let your joy carry you into excesses. Learn the laws and obey them; obey God's commandments and thank him for giving you liberty, for to him you owe all things.

—Abraham Lincoln to former slaves
upon his April 4 entrance into Richmond

Confederates stood against 6,000 Federals. When the "fort" finally fell, over 500 Federals had as well. Thirty Confederates remained.

Under Gordon's adroit leadership, Confederates along the east, or left, ranges of their line actually counterattacked and drove the Federals back. But another corps commander, A. P. Hill, was shot through the heart by a twenty-nine-year-old Pennsylvania carpenter named John Mauck. And Lee telegrammed President Davis: "I advise that all preparations be made for leaving Richmond tonight. I will advise you later, according to circumstances."

Federal and Confederate dead side by side at Fort Mahone after the Yankees stormed the Petersburg lines.

The Confederates retreated to their inner line of defenses, held off the massive attack, and kept the Federals out of Petersburg. But at 3 a.m. the next morning, Lee began moving his army out of their fortifications toward the one narrow corridor left open to him: west. It was what he had urged be done many months ago, and he allowed to his stalwart adjutant Walter Taylor: "Well, Colonel, it has happened as I told them at Richmond it would. The line has been stretched until it has broken."

Meanwhile, a procession of trains carried Davis, other key administration officials, government employees, and Confederate archives southwest out of Richmond toward the rail junction at Danville, North Carolina, where the temporary new capital would be. They had barely departed the capital before the wind caught fires set by the Confederates to destroy ammunition and supply warehouses and swept them out of control. Nearly 1,000 structures perished, including most of the city's central commercial and governmental districts. This, as deserters blue and gray, an assortment of other malcontents, and scores of starving civilians descended upon everything from vacant stores to the rivers of whiskey running in the streets from broken kegs.

Final Retreat

Lee hoped to make Amelia Courthouse, thirty-six miles from Petersburg, and collect meal rations for his men there, then loop south toward Danville, perhaps put his army in railroad cars, thence move toward a junction with Johnston. But though April 3 passed without sign of the Federals, most of Grant's army was in hot pursuit of the Confederates. Sheridan's cavalry thundered forward, intending to get in front of Lee and block his further progress.

On the 4th, Lee reached Amelia Courthouse. The Confederate Commissary Department, long an ineffectual—and likely corrupt—organization had indeed sent a mountain of stores. But they were comprised of ammunition and other supplies and no food. The head start Lee had gained on the Federals with his canny nighttime escape from Petersburg vanished as he halted his hungry army for a whole day while Confederate wagons scoured the countryside for food.

On the 6th, Sheridan's cavalry, followed by tens of thousands of Federal infantry, swooped down on the

Richmond in ruins, April, 1865.

Confederates' rear at Sayler's Creek. They destroyed the remnants of Lee's supply wagons, along with the corps of Richard Ewell, who was himself captured, as was Lee's son Custis. Eight thousand Confederates were lost. Meanwhile, Lee found the way to Danville blocked by the Federals, so he continued west. He hoped to reach Appomattox Courthouse, where he had ordered trains to bring his army food from Lynchburg, farther west. But by the time he reached Appomattox on April 8, he was surrounded by Grant, Meade, Sheridan, Ord, Custer, and 80,000 other Federals. The Confederates shouldered 8,700 muskets.

On the 4th, Lee reached Amelia Courthouse. The Confederate Commissary Department, long an ineffectual—and likely corrupt—organization had indeed sent a mountain of stores. But they were comprised of ammunition and other supplies and no food.

Even as correspondence regarding the possible terms of a cessation of hostilities began between Grant and

Messages Sent Between Grant and Lee

Ulysses S. Grant and Robert E. Lee exchanged a series of historic battlefield communiqués during the final days of their struggle. The texts of these messages, minus salutations, follow. The final two were penned at the Appomattox Courthouse ceremony and represent the terms of the Confederate surrender.

1) **Grant to Lee, 5 p.m., April 7:**
General: The results of the last week must convince you of the hopelessness of further resistance on the part of the Army of Northern Virginia in this struggle. I feel that it is so, and regard it as my duty to shift from myself the responsibility of any further effusion of blood, by asking of you the surrender of the C.S. Army known as the Army of Northern Virginia.

2) **Lee to Grant, April 7:**
I have received your note of this date. Though not entertaining the opinion you express of the hopelessness of further resistance on the part of the Army of N. Va.—I reciprocate your desire to avoid useless effusion of blood, and therefore before considering your proposition, ask the terms you will offer on condition of this surrender.

3) **Grant to Lee, April 8:**
Your note of last evening in reply to mine of same date, asking the condition on which I will accept the surrender of the Army of Northern Virginia is just received. In reply I would say that, peace being my great desire, there is but one condition I would insist upon, namely: that the men and officers surrendered shall be disqualified for taking up arms again against the Government of the United States until properly exchanged. I will meet you, or will designate officers to meet any officers you may name for the same purpose, at any point agreeable to you, for the purpose of arranging definitely the terms upon which the surrender of the Army of Northern Virginia will be received.

4) **Lee to Grant, April 8:**
I read at a late hour your note of today. In mine of yesterday I did not intend to propose the surrender of the Army of N. Va.—but to ask the terms of your proposition. To be frank, I do not think the emergency has arisen to call for the surrender of this army, but as the restoration of peace should be the sole object of all, I desired to know whether your proposals would lead to that and I cannot therefore meet you with a view to surrender the Army of N. Va—but as far as your proposal may affect the C.S. forces under my command & tend to the restoration of peace, I shall be pleased to meet you at 10 A.M. tomorrow on the old state road to Richmond between the picket lines of the two armies.

5) **Grant to Lee, April 9:**
General: Your note of yesterday is received. As I have no authority to treat on the subject of peace the meeting proposed for 10 A.M. today could lead to no good. I will state, however, General, that I am equally desirous for peace with yourself, and the whole North entertain the same feeling. The terms upon which peace can be had are well understood. By the South laying down their arms they will hasten that most desirable event, save thousands of human lives, and hundreds of millions of property not yet destroyed. Sincerely hoping that all our difficulties may be settled without the loss of another life, I subscribe myself . . .

6) **Lee to Grant, April 9:**
I received your note this morning on the picket line, whither I had come to meet you and ascertain definitely what terms were embraced in

your proposition of yesterday with reference to the surrender of this army.

I now request an interview in accordance with the offer contained in your letter of yesterday for that purpose.

7) **Grant to Lee, April 9:**
Your note of this date is but this moment (11:50 A.M.) received. In consequence of my having passed from the Richmond and Lynchburg road to the Farmville and Lynchburg road I am writing this about four miles west of Walker's church and will forward to the front for the purpose of meeting you. Notice sent on this road where you wish the interview to take place will meet me.

8) **Grant to Lee, April 9:**
General . . . I propose to receive the surrender of the Army of Northern Virginia on the following terms . . . The officers to give their individual paroles not to take up arms against the Government of the United States until properly exchanged, and each company or regimental commander to sign a like parole for the men of their commands. The arms, artillery, and public property to be parked, and stacked, and turned over to the officers appointed by me to receive them. This will not embrace the side arms of the officers, nor their private horses or baggage. This done, each officer and man will be allowed to return to his home, not to be disturbed by the United States authorities so long as they observe their paroles, and the laws in force where they may reside.

9) **Lee to Grant, April 9:**
General: I have received your letter of this date containing the terms of the surrender of the Army of Northern Virginia as proposed by you. As they are substantially the same as those expressed in your letter of the 8th inst., they are accepted. I will proceed to designate proper officers to carry the stipulations into effect.

Lee, the Virginian kept fighting, ceaselessly searching a way of deliverance for his army and his country. He sent Gordon's infantry and nephew Fitz Lee's cavalry on one final attack to break out the morning of April 8. It stunned and savaged the Federals' front lines and rolled them back more than a mile. Then, as the Confederates crashed into the van of the Federal infantry, Custer scuppered Lee's desperately needed supply trains at nearby Appomattox Station. The Federals sealed off the way to Lynchburg, and, on Palm Sunday, April 9, it was over.

Lee's Surrender

How impossible for any history book, novel, play, or film to capture the overwhelming drama of Palm Sunday, April 9, 1865. Surrounded with no route of escape, outnumbered in arms better than 10 to 1, the attack that would complete the annihilation of his legendary band of brothers, the Army of Northern Virginia, about to commence, Lee sighed deeply and lamented, "Then there is nothing left for me to do but go to General Grant, and I would rather die a thousand deaths."

A New Day at Appomattox, by John Paul Strain. Robert E. Lee and Ulysses S. Grant, mounted peacefully alongside one another, after the surrender of Lee's Army of Northern Virginia.

Sheridan urged Grant to loose the Federals for the annihilation, but his petitions were rebuffed.

The surrender scene at Wilbur McLean's home in Appomattox Courthouse was indeed the stuff of which legends, and legacies, are comprised. The tall, courtly Southern aristocrat in his finest uniform, towering over the short Midwesterner whose mud-spattered garb offered no indication of his exalted rank. They exchanged pleasantries, Grant recalling their Mexican War experiences, warming as he talked, Lee more reserved. But the Virginian expressed his appreciation upon reading Grant's magnanimous surrender terms, which included permanent and irrefutable pardon for Lee. When they finished, Lee walked out, mounted Traveler, and rode through the assembled Federal hosts. If his soldiers were licked, they did not yet know it. When they heard what was happening, they converged on him, reaching up to touch him, pat him, make some sort of contact, even with his boot or with Traveler, or with the horse's bridle. They begged him not to give up. "General, we'll fight 'em yet!" "General, say the word and we'll go in and fight 'em yet!" "Blow, Gabriel, blow! My God, let him blow, I am ready to die!" Some cried, some cursed, some sat staring in stupor. When Lee rode away, they made an enormous lane for him, removed their hats in respect, and by the hundreds and hundreds, these hard fierce men who had only quit fighting even now because "Marse Robert" said to, began en masse to weep, without shame.

John Suckling—immigrant, blacksmith, and one-time Burgess of Hollidaysburg, PA—entered the Federals' Pennsylvania 6th Cavalry as a private at the age of 37. The 6th was involved in the Appomattox Campaign until Lee's surrender on April 9, on which day they fought at Clover Hill near Appomattox Court House.

Back at Wilbur McLean's, the proceedings had taken a less dignified turn since Lee's departure. Led by Phil Sheridan and his brother Michael, the Federal officers who remained conducted an auction of the McLean family's possessions. General Ord paid $40 for Lee's signing table, Phil Sheridan $20 for Grant's, Michael Sheridan another amount for a stone inkstand. McLean, who had not invited anyone to plunder the contents of his home, slung the proffered money on the floor. Soon, he witnessed a veritable flock of blue-clad human vultures, albeit of high rank, consuming everything of value that belonged to him and his family, down to the chopping up and passing out of cane-bottomed chairs and the cutting into strips of the upholstery from his chairs and sofas.

Grant knew nothing of these outrages. Rather, he later recorded his sentiments on the occasion: "As [Lee] was a man of much dignity, with an impassable face, it was impossible to say whether he felt inwardly glad that the end had finally come, or felt sad over the result and was too manly to show it. Whatever his feelings they were entirely concealed from observation; but my own feelings, which had been quite jubilant on the

The Wilbur McLean house in Appomattox Courthouse, Virginia, around the time of Robert E. Lee's surrender there of the Army of Northern Virginia to U. S. Grant and the Army of the Potomac.

Lee's Last Address to His Troops

Headquarters, Army of Northern Virginia

April 10th, 1865

After four years of arduous service, marked by unsurpassed courage and fortitude, the Army of Northern Virginia has been compelled to yield to overwhelming numbers and resources. I need not tell the survivors of so many hard-fought battles, who have remained steadfast to the last, that I have consented to this result from no distrust of them, but, feeling that valor and devotion could accomplish nothing that could compensate for the loss that would have attended the continuation of the contest, I have determined to avoid the useless sacrifice of those whose past services have endeared them to their countrymen.

By the terms of the agreement, officers and men can return to their homes, and remain there until exchanged. You will take with you the satisfaction that proceeds from the consciousness of duty faithfully performed; and I earnestly pray that a merciful God will extend to you his blessing and protection.

With an increasing admiration of your constancy and devotion to your country, and a grateful remembrance of your kind and generous consideration of myself, I bid you an affectionate farewell.

R. E. Lee, General

receipt of his letter, were sad and depressed. I felt like anything rather than rejoicing at the downfall of a foe who had fought so long and valiantly, and had suffered so much for a cause, though that cause was, I believe, one of the worst for which a people ever fought."

Before us in proud humiliation stood . . . men whom neither toils and sufferings, nor the fact of death, nor disaster could bend from their resolve; standing before us now, thin, worn and famished, but erect, and with eyes looking level into ours, waking memories that bound us together as no other bond.

—Major General Joshua Chamberlain
Federal officer who formally accepted the surrender
of the Army of Northern Virginia

29 Assassination
(1865)

"The Assassination of President Lincoln," by Currier & Ives.

Lincoln represented a perfect fulfillment of everything the North had hoped to gain; he had destroyed slavery, preserved the Union, and provided an image of sacrifice and rebirth.

—Gardiner H. Shattuck, Jr.,
A Shield and Hiding Place

Jefferson Davis succeeded in eluding Grant's mammoth forces. The Confederate President hastened south with a coterie of his most trusted government officials. Cheering crowds greeted them in North Carolina, South Carolina, and Georgia. Meanwhile, Abraham Lincoln in Washington correctly perceived that though Confederate armies remained in the field, the surrender of the Army of Northern Virginia meant nothing less than the fall of the Confederate States of America. He traveled to Richmond to see Grant. He found a starving, war-ravaged city, its heart incinerated, many of its former slaves thrilled to see, touch, even to bow before him. He had always wanted all the states, including those in the South, in the Union, accountable and providing tariff revenues, and at peace within the Union. He wished all those things still, despite shrill and ominous Radical Republican cries for the blood of Confederate leaders and the further chastening of the South.

"Satan Tempting Booth to the Murder of the President." *(Harper's Weekly,* www.harpweek.com)

Lincoln had much reason for optimism upon his return to Washington, as he headed to popular Ford's Theatre with his wife Mary the evening of Good Friday, April 14. There, one of the most famous actors of 19th-century America, John Wilkes Booth, shot him through the head and killed him as he watched the play *Our American Cousin*. Secretary of State Seward was seriously wounded at his residence in a coordinated attack by one of Booth's conspirators. Though Booth had the cooperation and knowledge of only a tiny band of cohorts, unspeakable rage spread through the North—and the Northern armies. Overnight, those who liked Lincoln developed a lifelong love for him as the savior and martyr of the

United States. Those who cared not one way or the other for him were stirred to vengeance on his behalf and that of the Union, from which the "rebellion" had cut down 360,000 men and maimed hundreds of thousands more.

Booth's killing by Federal pursuers twelve days later in a Virginia barn did not keep ex-Confederate soldiers from being assaulted and beaten by Federal troops in every corner of America. Much worse,the most extreme wing of Congress—the Radical Republicans led by Thaddeus Stevens in the House and Charles Sumner in the Senate—now had the opportunity they wanted to unleash a peace on the South in some ways worse than the War that was slowly concluding. For Southern armies remained in the field in North Carolina, Texas, Alabama, Indian Territory, and elsewhere. And many of the officers and rankers comprising them had no intention of turning their swords into ploughshares as they witnessed the long train of Federal outrages against their land and people multiply, especially after the murder of Lincoln.

The most extreme wing of Congress—the Radical Republicans led by Thaddeus Stevens in the House and Charles Sumner in the Senate—now had the opportunity they wanted to unleash a peace on the South in some ways worse than the War that was slowly concluding.

John Wilkes Booth (1839–1865)

John Wilkes Booth provided the *coup de grace* to the disastrous bloodletting that was the War. Booth's assassination of Lincoln helped no one but the Radical Republicans, who leveraged Northern outrage over it into the hard Reconstruction policy Lincoln himself discouraged. Least of all did it help the devastated South Booth loved.

A Maryland native, he was born into the most famous theatrical family in America. His internationally-renowned father Junius Brutus, his brothers, and Booth claimed positions all over the political spectrum. Early on, young Wilkes evidenced a powerhouse talent for the stage. But never did he apply himself to the disciplined practices necessary for true and sustained theatrical greatness. Though he became one of the most revered actors in America, earlier in his career, while still raw and sometimes unprepared, audiences in Northern cities booed him. Worst of all, at one performance in the "City of Brotherly Love," the crowd screeched in laughter at him. Booth remembered these nightmarish experiences till the end of his life. He also remembered how somewhat less-sophisticated Southern audiences in Richmond and elsewhere forgave his gaffes and embraced his rough but transparent charms—embraced them, loved him, and catapulted him to the most popular actor of his generation in the South.

Though never in the official employe of any Confederate organization—military, governmental, or otherwise—by the time the War started, Booth's detestation for the North and what he considered its brutish culture had escalated right alongside his burgeoning affection for the South. Vain and high strung by nature, his emotions grew more taut when he learned that a persistent raspiness of voice—noticed only by a handful of critics and attributed to cold or flu—in fact indicated permanent damage to his vocal chords. His physicians attributed it to years of wear and tear without proper rest, voice lessons, or preparation prior to practices and performances. Booth's undisciplined work habits had found him out.

Early on, young Wilkes Booth evidenced a powerhouse talent for the stage. But never did he apply himself to the disciplined practices necessary for true and sustained theatrical greatness.

Smuggler

As the War progressed, the celebrity Booth possessed in both the United States and the Confederacy aided his becoming an accomplished smuggler of medicines and other precious, immensely expensive items in the South. He also watched with mounting fury as Abraham Lincoln—whom Booth had met and who considered Booth his favorite actor—shifted the U.S. to a strategy of total war. Booth saw this manifest itself in numerous ways, including the suffering of the Southern people brought about by the Federal blockade-induced deprivation of food, medicine, and nearly every other type of supply. All the while, he recognized he had no prospects for a future on the stage. An alternative means to lasting fame developed in his mind, and one by which he could serve the South, his adopted country. He would present a plan to the Confederate government proposing that he and a group of associates kidnap Lincoln. After all, the revelation of the infamous Dahlgren papers had laid bare supposed Federal plans not only to capture Jefferson Davis, but to murder him and his entire cabinet.

Lewis Payne, who attacked and nearly killed Secretary of State William Seward. (TreasureNet)

Though never endorsed by the Confederacy, Booth did indeed spearhead an attempt to kidnap Lincoln. It failed. Only as the blockade and fighting ground the South down and the end neared for the Confederacy did Booth turn to his own, non-government-sanctioned final solution—murdering Lincoln. By the time Booth learned that Lincoln was to attend *Our American Cousin* at John Ford's Washington theater, the War was lost and Booth was inconsolable—and in a unique position to strike at Lincoln.

Ford's Theater

First, he remained one of America's most famous actors, and well-liked as well. He actually received his mail at Ford's Theater. He could come and go anywhere and anytime he pleased around its environs. And Booth knew firsthand how notoriously lax Lincoln's personal security was. Not long before, at another performance, the President had requested Booth to join him in the Presidential Box. How the actor relished spurning the invitation. But on Good Friday evening, April 14, Booth would visit Lincoln's box without an invitation. Sure enough, he had no problem finding himself standing behind the President and placing a pistol to his head, with no security personnel in sight.

When he shot Lincoln, a Federal officer sitting in the box lunged at Booth, who whipped out a hunting knife and slashed his arm. Then he leapt from the box to the stage, catching his spur on a United States flag hanging from the box and breaking his ankle. He shouted "Sic semper tyrannis!" (Death to tyrants!), then wheeled, ran from the building, jumped on a waiting saddled horse, and rode over the one unguarded bridge leading out of the city, across the Potomac, and into Virginia. It took twelve days to corner Booth in a Virginia tobacco barn that Federal agents set afire before one of them shot him in the back as he fought it out with them.

Booth had coordinated other attacks to coincide with his on Lincoln. One conspirator nearly killed Secretary of War Seward. Six people died on the gallows for their roles in the attacks. All but one were apparently involved. The other, Mary Surratt, was a widowed mother whose only crime seemed to be that Booth and some of his associates sometimes lodged at her boarding house, as did many other people. No evidence has ever been produced that she even knew about the conspiracy to kill the President, much less participated in it in any way. Yet she was hanged with the rest.

Booth remained one of America's most famous actors. Not long before, at another performance, the President had requested Booth to join him in the Presidential Box. How the actor relished spurning the invitation.

The private box in Ford's Theater where Abraham Lincoln was shot. (TreasureNet)

Worse Evil Yet

Now the Federals placed a bounty of $100,000 in gold on Davis' head, plus whatever gold—estimated to be several million dollars—was found in his procession. Before dawn May 10, he was caught near the south Georgia town of Irwinville, put in chains, and transported to a solitary prison cell in Fortress Monroe on the Virginia peninsula. Most of the key Federal military leaders, including Grant and Sherman, still desired to let the South turn to the task of rebuilding itself, provided its people kept the peace. Confederate leaders, too, like Lee, Longstreet, and Johnston, urged their men to follow this path, for the sake of their own wives and children. And the more discerning of them trembled that, though they believed Lincoln had reduced the U.S. Constitution to an irrelevant rag and had waged

Sergeant Boston Corbett, who claimed he shot John Wilkes Booth. (TreasureNet)

a barbarous war against not only Southern armies but the Southern people, the Radicals who would now wield power were far worse.

Clement Vallandigham, most prominent among the antiwar Northern "Copperheads," and whom Lincoln lieutenants had thrown in jail then exiled to the South, agreed. Even he lamented the President's assassination as "the beginning of evils." Those who had opposed Lincoln's total war policies had begun "to turn to him for deliverance," Vallandigham said, because, "His course in the last three months has been most liberal and conciliatory."

But John Wilkes Booth's bullet had kindled a wrath—or perhaps stoked what was already there—in the bosom of those who had preferred the destruction of the South to its well-being even before Lincoln's death. And among their ranks were now the most powerful men in the United States. Their words were many and fierce. Perhaps most chilling of all, however, was one line spoken by Radical Republican Senator Ben Wade, co-author of the Wade-Davis Manifesto, and an arch-enemy of Lincoln. Wade's words were not spoken in anger. Nor were they offered in sadness. Rather, they resounded happy and hopeful. With Lincoln's death, he promised with polytheistic fervor, now, "By the gods, there will be no trouble running the government." More than anything else said during these black days, Ben Wade's words proved a harbinger of things to come.

The hanging of Booth's accused conspirators. Mary Surratt, wearing a dress, appears on the left. (TreasureNet)

O Captain! My Captain! Walt Whitman (1819-1892)

Following is a portion of the classic ode written to honor President Lincoln by one of America's most celebrated poets.

O Captain! my Captain! our fearful trip is done,
The ship has weather'd every rack, the prize we sought is won.
The port is near, the bells I hear, the people all exulting,
While follow eyes the steady keel, the vessel grim and daring.

But O heart! heart! heart!
O the bleeding drops of red,
Where on the deck my Captain lies,
Fallen cold and dead.

O Captain! my Captain! rise up and hear the bells;
Rise up—for you the flag is flung—for you the bugle trills,
For you bouquets and ribbon'd wreaths—for you the shores a-crowding,
For you they call, the swaying mass, their eager faces turning.

Exult, O shores! and ring, O bells!
But I with mournful tread,
Walk the deck my Captain lies,
Fallen cold and dead.

The Religion of Abraham Lincoln

Most serious scholarship posits that Abraham Lincoln was a skeptic and a deist, if not an infidel, in his years as an Illinois lawyer, which lasted through the 1850s. The chronicle of Lincoln's possible later conversion to Christianity while he was president, however, has gained wide coinage in recent years, particular in Christian circles. Adding credence to the conversion theory are Lincoln's numerous eloquent sayings (many of them penned by Treasury Secretary William Seward) that invoke the names of God and the Bible. He called the latter "the best gift God has given to man. But for it, we could not know right from wrong." He encouraged his countrymen toward "firmness in the right, as God gives us to see the right." He warned that "intoxicated with unbroken success, we have become too self-sufficient to feel the necessity of redeeming and preserving grace, too proud to pray to the God that made us."

Less well known are Lincoln's various flirtations, including while president, with such non-Christian practices as spiritism. Almost from the time of his inauguration, Lincoln was approached by spiritists. Eventually, his wife invited mediums to the White House. There and elsewhere the President attended seances. He obtained several books on spiritism. Grief over the death of their young son Willie—and in Mrs. Lincoln's case at least, the possibility of communicating with him—apparently prompted this interest in spiritism.

Other preachers came forth with never before told reports of Lincoln's faith.

What moral philosophy did guide Lincoln? Many Lincoln scholars—and the man himself—posit that it was the "Doctrine of Necessity." Orville Hickman Browning referred to his intimate friend as a "thorough fatalist." He summarized the doctrine of necessity as held by Lincoln as a belief

> *that what was to be would be, and no prayers of ours could arrest or reverse the decree . . . men were but simple tools of fate, of conditions, and of laws. Thus, no one was responsible for what he was, thought, or did, because he was a child of conditions.*

Christianizing Lincoln?

Following Lincoln's death, a chorus of voices, many from Northern clergy, rose in witness to his Christian conversion and beliefs. In the spring of 1865, just weeks after his death, J. G. Holland of Massachusetts interviewed longtime Lincoln law partner and confidant William Herndon for a book Holland was writing, *The Life of Abraham Lincoln*. "What about Mr. Lincoln's religion?" Holland asked. Herndon, who loved Lincoln and admired him as a great man, replied, "The less said the better." "Oh, never mind," Holland said with a wink, "I'll fix that." Holland's main source in the book was Illinois Superintendent of Education Newton Bateman, who once shared an office with Lincoln in the Illinois state capitol. Lincoln, said Bateman, offered him detailed testimony about his precise belief in Christian doctrine. When confronted by Herndon, however, Bateman admitted he had fabricated the story.

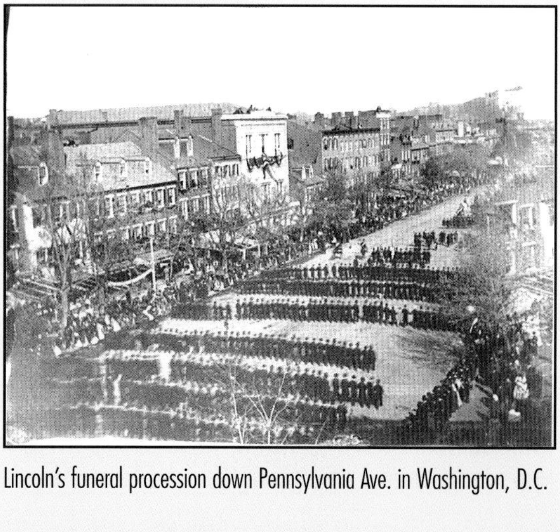

Lincoln's funeral procession down Pennsylvania Ave. in Washington, D.C.

Other preachers came forth with never before told reports of Lincoln's faith. Many shared a common thread—years earlier Lincoln had evidenced being a believing Christian. Dr. James Smith of the First Presbyterian Church in Springfield, Illinois, a fiery abolitionist Republican, said Lincoln was converted and that he joined his church. Later research, however, revealed that Lincoln never joined the church, casting doubt on Smith's conversion claim. A state evangelist for the Disciples of Christ Movement declared that Lincoln had professed faith to him out in the woods and that they had gone to a little pond where Lincoln was baptized. No other evidence or testimony, including by Lincoln, exists for this account.

One Baptist preacher recounted Lincoln's intense prayer life. He told about his great interest in the Bible. And he told the now-famous story of Lincoln's final moments of life the night of his assassination at Ford's Theatre. There, the preacher said, Lincoln's attention was focused not on the play, but on a conversation with his wife Mary. "I want to know more about Jesus. I want to go to Bethlehem, I want to see the place where He was born,'" the preacher declared Lincoln as saying. Then, the account continued, Lincoln leaned over to Mary and said, "Perhaps we could go to Jeru—." At that point, the preacher claimed, as Lincoln began to say "Jerusalem," John Wilkes Booth fired his infamous shot. The last words of Lincoln, the preacher said, indicated his desire to know more about Jesus.

A Different Picture

Many of Lincoln's closer associates presented a different picture. Mrs. Lincoln never said her husband was a Christian. "He didn't have faith in the usual sense," said she. "His faith was more of a divine portrait. But he was a man who believed in dreams." Neither she nor any of Lincoln's closest friends ever referred to his Christian conversion, nor his belief in the deity or resurrection of Christ.

Hans Morgenthau, a great admirer of Lincoln, questioned whether Lincoln's frequent public references to biblical persons and events possessed any religious significance. "Skepticism and fatalism, then," said Morgenthau, "are the dominant moves of Lincoln's religiosity. References to God, Almighty God, the Lord, the Savior, Providence, appear routinely and add nothing to the substance of Lincoln's religiosity." Close friend Ward Lamon wrote that Lincoln was never a member of any church, nor did he believe in the divinity of Christ or the inspiration of Scriptures. Herndon declared after Lincoln's death, "I never heard him use the name Jesus but to confute the idea that He was the Christ. . . . He had no faith in the Christian sense of the term."

Mrs. Lincoln never said her husband was a Christian. "He didn't have faith in the usual sense," said she.

And Herndon recorded the words of others who spoke to him about Lincoln's religious views. Another close friend of Lincoln, Leonard Swett, told Herndon in 1866, "You asked me whether he changed his religious opinion toward the close of his life. I think not." Mrs. Lincoln told Herndon her husband was never a "technical Christian."

The final year or two of his life, Lincoln did exhibit

NATIONAL PICTURE
WASHINGTON MADE
AND
LINCOLN SAVED
OUR COUNTRY
YOUR SONS THE GREATEST AMONG MEN.

"National Picture. Behold Oh! America Your Sons. The greatest among men," a pro-Federal drawing from *Harper's Weekly* (www.harpweek.com), suggesting a patriotic link between George Washington and Abraham Lincoln.

a mournful, even haunted visage. He spoke in milder terms of his adversaries the Confederates, even as he orchestrated a campaign of total war against them. He proclaimed his desire for the departed states to be forgiven and reconciled within the Federal Union. Herndon commented on the "purifying process" of war, tragedy, and suffering that he said elicited in his friend "charity, liberality, kindness, tenderness, toleration, a sublime faith, if you please, in the purposes and ends of his Maker."

In the End

Cosmopolitan magazine said in its March 1891 edition that John G. Nicolay, the President's wartime private secretary, was closer to the martyred Lincoln than any other man, that he knew him as a President and a man more intimately than any other man. Six weeks after the assassination Nicolay told Herndon, "Mr. Lincoln did not to my knowledge in any way change his religious ideas, opinions or beliefs from the time he left Springfield [in 1861] to the day of his death." Lincoln's life, even in its closing chapters, offers substantial evidence that he was a deist, a humanist, and a fatalist. Maybe the closing words of Allen Guelzo's largely-laudatory portrait *Abraham Lincoln—Redeemer President* best sum up the enigmatic issue of the American icon's spirituality:

Perhaps, in the end, he hoped to find some beginning of an answer after the presidency was laid down, in Jerusalem or some other place of pilgrimage. But it is more likely, as Lincoln confessed to Aminda Rankin in 1846, that "probably it is to be my lot to go on in a twilight, feeling and reasoning my way through life, as questioning, doubting Thomas did." Those words make him something very different from the scoffer or deist or infidel in New Salem in 1831. But neither were they the confession of a convert or a prophet. They were, instead, the lonely murmur of abandonment, deathlike in the leafless trees.

Lincoln—Hero or Villain?

Abraham Lincoln saw the United States in its largest dimension—as a noble experiment in self-determination that had to be preserved, even if that meant violating the principles of self-determination. In the long history of tyranny and oppression, he believed that the American democracy—sustained by a muscular national government—was man's great hope and that it must be saved even if it was necessary to resort to non-democratic coercion. To him the great ideal of democracy overshadowed the practical realities of democracy. Lincoln's profound conviction of the enduring value of this experiment in a unified government sustained him throughout the long bitter years of the War.

> *Of all the men I ever met, he seemed to possess more elements of greatness, combined with goodness, than any other.*
>
> —General William T. Sherman

> *Of more importance, perhaps, was his assault upon the Constitution, and especially upon the Bill of Rights. . . . Lincoln was scarcely in office before he began to subordinate it to military measures, and by the end of the Civil War it was in such a state of decay that it has never recovered. Every guaranty of the Bill of Rights was heaved overboard. The American people, North and South, went into the war as citizens of their respective states, they came out subjects of the United States. And what they thus lost they have never got back.*
>
> —H. L. Mencken

> *What a noble soul was his—noble in all the noble attributes of God. . . . No common mortal had died. The Moses of my people had fallen in his hour of triumph. . . . Ah! never was a man so widely mourned before. The whole world bowed their heads in grief when Abraham Lincoln died.*
>
> —Elizabeth Keckley
>
> Washington seamstress and former slave

Mary Custis Lee (1808–1873)

Their love began in storybook fashion. She was heiress to one of the greatest family dynasties in America. He was a handsome noble soldier from similar background, but one fallen on hard times in finances and name alike. They would finish in storybook fashion as well, but almost nothing fit that mold for the nearly forty years in between. It is true that Lee himself suffered much, but all the South loved him and much of the North respected him, and at least part of his honor grew out of his sufferings.

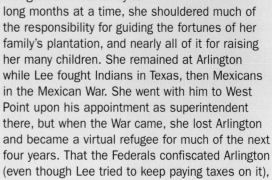

Mary Custis Lee, great-granddaughter of Mrs. George (Martha Custis) Washington and heiress to one of Virginia's preeminent families, suffered physical and emotional pain impossible to now grasp. A degenerative arthritic condition afflicted her from early adulthood and finally put her in a wheelchair, garnishing her life for decades with unremitting pain. She bore more suffering than just physical. From nearly the beginning of her marriage, her husband was assigned to distant posts hundreds, sometimes thousands of miles away. She accompanied him when she could, but this proved increasingly difficult as her health deteriorated and the number of Lee children increased—eventually to seven.

With Lee absent from Arlington and his family for long months at a time, she shouldered much of the responsibility for guiding the fortunes of her family's plantation, and nearly all of it for raising her many children. She remained at Arlington while Lee fought Indians in Texas, then Mexicans in the Mexican War. She went with him to West Point upon his appointment as superintendent there, but when the War came, she lost Arlington and became a virtual refugee for much of the next four years. That the Federals confiscated Arlington (even though Lee tried to keep paying taxes on it),

"Of the proud army . . . "

A memorable tribute to Robert E. Lee and the Army of Northern Virginia came from one of the South's most implacable enemies, Horace Greeley, Republican publisher of the *New York Tribune*, among America's most influential newspapers. He spoke of them in his book *American Conflict*:

> *Of the proud army which, dating its victories from Bull Run, had driven McClellan from before Richmond, and withstood his best effort at Antietam, and shattered Burnside's host at Fredericksburg, and worsted Hooker at Chancellorsville, and fought Meade so stoutly though unsuccessfully before Gettysburg, and baffled Grant's bounteous resources and desperate efforts in the Wilderness, at Spotsylvania, on the North Anna, at Cold Harbor, and before Petersburg and Richmond, a mere wreck remained.*
>
> *It is said that 27,000 were included in Lee's capitulation, but of these not more than 10,000 had been able to carry their arms thus far on their hopeless and almost foodless flight. The rebellion had failed and gone down; but the rebel army of Virginia and its commander had not failed.*

chopped down much of its forest, stole nearly all her finery—much of which came from Martha and George Washington—then turned the grounds into a Federal cemetery (burying men right up to the walls of the main house to preclude crops ever again being grown there) left her fighting bitterness the rest of her life.

> *While much of upper-crust Richmond persisted in gay social pursuits, Mary Lee established a veritable assembly line of female knitters that provided socks, mittens, and scarves for Confederate soldiers all over the continent.*

During the War, while separated from the family by hundreds of miles because of fighting, her eldest daughter died. So did a beloved daughter-in-law and a grandchild.

Her Legacy

Mary Boykin Chesnut's classic memoir of the War *A Diary from Dixie* chronicled how, while much of upper-crust Richmond persisted in gay social pursuits, Mary Lee established a veritable assembly line of female knitters that provided socks, mittens, and scarves for Confederate soldiers all over the continent:

Then we paid our respects to Mrs. Lee. Her room was like an industrial school: everybody so busy. Her daughters were all there plying their needles, with several other ladies. . . . When we came out someone said, "Did you see how the Lees spend their time? What a rebuke to the taffy parties!"

But Mary Lee's greatest legacy was her patient, selfless, often unseen embodiment of Christian

Mrs. Lee's Cake Recipe from Old Arlington

Twelve eggs, their full weight in sugar, a half weight in flour. Bake it in pans the thickness of jelly cakes Take two pounds of nice "A" sugar, squeeze into it the juice of 5 oranges and three lemons together with the pulp. Stir in the sugar until perfectly smooth, then spread it over the cakes as you would jelly—putting one above another till the whole of the sugar is used up.

—Mrs. Robert E. Lee

Half quantity:

Cake:

6 eggs, separated,
1 1/2 c. sugar,
1 1/2 c. flour.

Non-Icing:

1 1-lb. box confectioner's sugar, sifted, or 2 c. superfine,
4 T. orange juice plus 1 T. rind,
4 t. lemon juice plus 1 T. rind.

Preheat oven to 350 degrees. Grease and flour bottoms only of layer pans. To mix by hand, beat yolks light, add sugar gradually, beating until very light; fold in flour, then beaten whites. To mix with a stand mixer, beat whole eggs 15 minutes in all, starting on low and increasing to high; when soft peaks form, fold in flour. Bake about 20 minutes for 3 layers, less time for more, thinner layers. To ice, follow directions in the original, reserving slightly more of the juice-and-sugar mixture for the top.

womanhood toward those around her. She worked tirelessly to save Grace Episcopal Church of Lexington, where the Lees worshiped, during the years following the War, and to aid its ministry to the bleeding community and beyond. Upon hearing of daughter Agnes' conversion, she wrote to her:

> *It is very late my precious little daughter, but I cannot let another day pass without telling you the real happiness your letter afforded me, you for whom I have felt so anxious to heart that God had sent his spirit into your heart & drawn you to himself. Remember what He says, 'Those who seek me early shall find me.' The promises of God are sure and cannot fail. Therefore seek Him with all your heart. . . . You must pray for your sister & for your brothers who are out of the fold of Christ. Think what a happiness to your Mother to be able to present all her children at the throne of God & to be able to say, 'Here I am Lord & the children Thou hast given me.' Pray for your Mother that she may be more faithful in her prayers & example. . . . I accept, my dear child, your penitence for all your faults towards me & freely bestow my forgiveness.*

Among the ocean of published tributes and eulogies to Mary Custis Lee was this:

> *It is enough to say that in intelligence and refinement of taste, in kindness of heart and attractiveness of manner, in cheerfulness under the heaviest reverses of fortune and the agonies of bodily pain, in sympathy and in benefactions towards the impoverished and suffering people of her country, in her manifold and ceaseless self-denials and labors on behalf of religion and the church of her fathers and of her choice, in all this she was an ornament to her sex, was worthy of her illustrious husband.*

The front of Mary and Robert E. Lee's Arlington, facing east toward Washington across the Potomac River, after its capture by the Federals.

When Johnny Comes Marching Home (Patrick Sarsfield Gilmore)

When Johnny comes marching home again,
Hurrah! Hurrah!
We'll give him a hearty welcome then,
Hurrah! Hurrah!
The men will cheer, the boys will shout,
The ladies they will all turn out.

Chorus:
And we'll all feel gay,
When Johnny comes marching home.

The old church-bell will peal with joy,
Hurrah! Hurrah!
To welcome home our darling boy,
Hurrah! Hurrah!
The village lads and lasses say
With roses they will strew the way.

Chorus:
And we'll all feel gay,
When Johnny comes marching home.

Black Federals collecting the bones of dead soldiers at the Cold Harbor (Virginia) battlefield.

30 Gotterdammerung (1865)

A new kind of war. The ruins of Columbia, South Carolina, after fires destroyed three-fourths of the capital city the night the Federal occupation began. (TreasureNet)

Now the truth is, we fought the holiest fight ever fought on God's earth.
—William Tecumseh Sherman

Sherman moved north out of Savannah in February. His men advanced in two separate columns. One, cavalry commanded by Judson Kilpatrick of "Dahlgren Raid" infamy, moved along the coast, heading for Augusta in north Georgia. The other, larger, one marched inland, its destination South Carolina, specifically the capital of Columbia. Confederate cavalry under Joe Wheeler saved Augusta from the fate of so many other towns on Sherman's marauding path when they ambushed and defeated the Federals at Aiken and nearly captured Kilpatrick himself. Columbia was not so fortunate. Sherman's strategic feints and thrusts had found the city with only 5,000 defenders, which had to retreat before a force more than ten times their number. Columbia surrendered peaceably, but flames engulfed the city by the time the Federals left.

Sherman's strategic feints and thrusts had found [Columbia] with only 5,000 defenders, which had to retreat before a force more than ten times their number. Columbia surrendered peaceably, but flames engulfed the city by the time the Federals left.

Wade Hampton, whose own home perished in the blaze, blamed Sherman's drunken bummers, as did scores of other townspeople. Sherman denied it, citing orders he had issued against such destruction. He accused Hampton's men for accidentally starting the fire with huge bales of cotton. One of Sherman's own generals, Henry Slocum, perhaps revealed the truth: "I believe the immediate cause of the disaster was a free use of whiskey," said Slocum. "A drunken soldier, with a musket in one hand and a match in the other, is not a pleasant visitor to have about the house on a dark windy night." And in his own memoirs, Sherman wrote, "The [Federal] army having totally ruined Columbia, moved on toward Winnsboro." When Sherman's army finally crossed into North Carolina, they left its southern neighbor one great heap of ashes and rubble.

Adalbert John Volck's sketch of black slaves concealing their white master from a Federal search party. (Library of Congress)

Sherman's March

This rampage of fire and sword was one of the greatest military feats in American history and the most brutal large-scale attack ever orchestrated against American civilians. Sherman marched out of vanquished Atlanta on November 15, 1864, headed for the sea at Savannah, 300 miles away. He intended to destroy everything in between that could conceivably contribute to the Confederate war effort, whether crops or livestock for food, manufacturing plants for supplies, railroads for transportation, or telegraph offices and lines for communication. Georgians had good reason to fear Tecumseh Sherman; he had burned or demolished all or much of several towns already, including Randolph, Tennessee, and Meridian and Jackson, Mississippi. "I intend to make Georgia howl!" he crowed.

William Sherman and his key generals during his decisive campaign through Georgia and the Carolinas. From left: Oliver O. Howard, John A. Logan, W. B. Hazen, Sherman, Jeff C. Davis, H. W. Slocum, Joseph A. Mower, and Frank Blair. Sherman's greatest lieutenant in the campaign, James Birdseye McPherson, was killed in battle near Decatur, Georgia, shortly before he was to be married.

First, he wanted assurance that Atlanta's gigantic role in the Confederate war effort could never resume. He burned most of it to the ground. Only a few hundred homes and a handful of buildings survived. Then, overriding the plaintive petitions of the city's mayor, he issued an order singular in American history—forcing nearly all of the thousands of residents remaining in the city out onto the open road and into the gathering winter as homeless refugees.

Across the state—for 300 miles, on a 60-mile-wide front—his army marched, pillaging, plundering, burning, and killing in a manner never before contemplated by Americans North or South. In at least one memorable instance, he marched Confederate prisoners of war across ground to test it for mines. But he also wiped out the vast autumn harvest desperately needed by hungry Confederate armies. Upon marching into beautiful Savannah, which surrendered without a fight on December 22, Sherman found crack Admiral David Porter waiting offshore as ordered, with a fleet of ships. Sherman himself estimated the financial toll on Georgia at over $100 million, in 1865 dollars.

South Carolina

When he turned north into South Carolina, the "Cradle of Secession," a month later, his execution grew even more brilliant—and terrifying. While the scant Confederate forces conducted a traditional

Charleston, viewed from the Circular Congregational Church. (TreasureNet)

The "Sister Churches" in Charleston at the end of the War. (LOC)

defensive effort, Sherman eschewed major battles and towns (such as Augusta) for their own sake, remaining focused on the larger strategic concerns. Nearly one hundred years would pass before military scholars recognized—and emulated—the landmark brilliance of Sherman's comprehensive strategic maneuvers and multifaceted "total war" philosophy.

The country itself—flooded, swampy, and tangled, appeared impassable for a massed army. But Sherman sent out scouts in canoes, as well as pioneer (engineering) corps, which included many blacks, to clear paths, construct corduroy roads with the wood of felled trees and saplings, and string pontoon bridges across waterways. His rate of advance was breathtaking—425 miles in fifty days, in the face of a desperate enemy. "I wouldn't have believed it if I hadn't seen it happen," Confederate General William Hardee exclaimed.

A fever of vengeance mounted in the Federal army as they marched nearer with each passing day to the state capital of Columbia. Whole sections of country were so thoroughly plundered, then scalded out, that nothing man-made stood in them but blackened chimneys and heaps of rubble and ashes. A Northern newspaper reporter described a typical scene, wherein Sherman's bummers:

> *came up to a retired plantation house, just set on fire. The soldiers were rushing off on every side with their pillage. An old lady and her two grandchildren were in the yard alarmed and helpless. The flames and smoke were shooting through the windows. The old lady rushed from one to another beseeching them at least to save her furniture. They only enjoyed the whole thing, including her distress.*

The Federals demolished whole towns that lay in their path: Robertsville, Hardeeville, Sheldon, Purysburg, Grahamville, Lawtonville, McPhersonville, and Beaufort Bridge. Many were never rebuilt and passed into history.

Columbia

When the Federals arrived in Columbia on February 17, the drunkenness, looting, and vandalism reached epic proportions. Then fire, earlier put out, broke out anew and got caught by the wind. The scenes which followed seemed as though conjured out of the fiery cataclysm of Wagner's *Gotterdammerung*. Within 24 hours, three-quarters of the entire city lay in ashes, and thousands of old people, women, children, the sick and the maimed, sat and lay in stunned hungry stupor along the streets of the city.

An embarrassed Sherman blamed the fire on Wade Hampton and his recently-departed Confederate cavalry. But the citizens of Columbia had no doubt who was to blame—drunken, marauding hordes of Federals, some of whom had taken axes to the hoses of fire trucks attempting to extinguish the flames. "As far as the eye can reach," wrote seventeen-year-old Emma LaConte, "nothing is to be seen but heaps of rubbish, tall dreary chimneys and shattered brick walls."

By the time the Army of the Ohio entered North Carolina, its neighbor to the south lay in ruins. Fully one-half the property of all South Carolina was destroyed. Asked why he had not exercised more alacrity to keep order among his men when they entered Columbia, especially considering the many ominous portents of looming disaster, Sherman dismissed the question. "I would not have done such a harshness to save the whole town," he snapped. "They were men, and I was not going to treat them like slaves."

Though the propensity for vandalism and larceny of Southern property grew to near-universal proportions in Sherman's army, certain elements of it merited special infamy, such as the New York regiments whom one Sherman biographer said were "filled with big city criminals and foreigners fresh from the jails of the Old World."

Though the propensity for vandalism and larceny of Southern property grew to near-universal proportions in Sherman's army, certain elements of it merited special infamy, such as the New York regiments whom one Sherman biographer said were "filled with big city criminals and foreigners fresh from the jails of the Old World." Many of the slaves to whom Sherman supposedly brought liberty did not escape the wrath of his roving bands of supposed "foragers." Neither Sherman nor much of his army had any particular interest in the rights, or even the freedom, of blacks.

The bummers ransacked plantation homes and slave cabins alike. One frequent bummer exercise was to hang a slave by his neck until he confessed to the bluecoats where were hidden the valuables of the plantation owner. By the time Sherman reached Raleigh, North Carolina, in mid-April, Lee had surrendered and the War in the east was ending.

Rape

Many accounts of Sherman's epic campaign acknowledge its vast destruction of property, but not its outrages against the Southern people—in particular, the rapes committed by Federal soldiers. Any accurate accounting is obscured from history because of the utter shame felt by victims of that generation when admitting such assaults. But many episodes are known.

Mrs. Kate Nichols Latimer of Milledgeville, Georgia, wife of a Confederate officer, was raped by Federal soldiers, then descended into mental illness and finally death in a mental institution. Near Aiken, South Carolina, bluecoats raped the daughter of a Baptist minister. An Illinois soldier raped a Georgia woman, then was court-martialed and turned loose in the Georgia countryside. Famed diarist Mary Chesnut's husband James, a Confederate General, reported the gang-rape and murder of a beautiful young

The ruins of St. Finbar's Church in Charleston. (Library of Congress)

The ruins of Secession Hall in Charleston. (Library of Congress)

"Mrs. M." north of Columbia. "A brute named Bryant" in the 12th New York cavalry raped a sixty-five-year-old Goldsboro, North Carolina woman, as well as a young girl from nearby Kinston.

But the mass of outrages were perpetrated against black females. Renowned novelist William Gilmore Simms reported their plight at the hands of Sherman's conquering troops during the destruction of Columbia: "The poor Negroes were victimized by their assailants, many of them . . . being left in a condition little short of death. Regiments, in successive relays, subjected scores of these poor women to the torture of their embraces." How many Southern women suffered like atrocities will never be known, but such acts contributed to the despising of William Sherman's name in the South that lasts even to this day.

Militarily, Sherman's March was a towering success. At its outset, Southerners had no idea he could accomplish such a mission. In the North, even Grant and Lincoln worried and gave only grudging consent. But in the end, Sherman's chief adversary Joe Johnston said the world had seen no army the likes of the Yankee commander's "since the days of Julius Caesar." And the campaign sealed the fate of the Confederacy in both the east and the west.

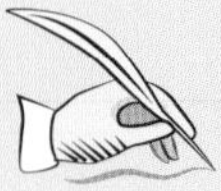

Sherman's "Bummers"

"Foragers" according to the average Northern soldier, "criminal looters" according to the average Southern civilian victimized by them.

First the pulpit and seats were torn out, then the siding and the blinds were ripped off. Many axes were at work. . . . The building tottered, the beautiful spire, up among the green trees, leaned . . . vibrating to and fro. . . . By the use of long poles the men increased the vibratory motion of the building, and soon, with a screeching groan the spire sunk down . . . and as the structure became a pile of rubbish, some of the most wicked of the raiders yelled out: "There goes your d----- old gospel shop."

—Federal Sergeant Fleharty describing the Yankees' destruction of the village church at Hardeeville, South Carolina.

Sherman and the Nun

As Sherman's army neared Columbia, Sister Baptista Lynch sent a request to him for protection of the Ursuline convent where she served as mother superior, and for its nuns and sixty young students. She had been a girlhood schoolmate of Sherman's sister and had taught his daughter Minnie in Ohio. Sherman responded that neither the convent, nor any other private property in the capital city would suffer harm. He promised the same to an aged priest sent by Sister Baptista.

An early stereograph of Broad Street in Charleston and the remains of the Roman Catholic Church. (Library of Congress)

Then young Federal cavalry officer Thomas Fitzgibbon arrived at the convent, offering his personal protection. "This is a doomed city," Fitzgibbon insisted. "The whole army knows it. I doubt that a house will be left standing." But Sister Baptista's further message reminding Sherman of his promise was answered with yet another assurance of safety from him, and another still when she petitioned him once the city began to burn.

As the flames neared the convent, Father O'Connell led a last benediction. The dozens of children, as young as five years old, several of them under ten, knelt praying when the chapel door was smashed in by "the most unearthly battering . . . like the crash of doom. Drunken soldiers piled over each other, rushing for the sacred gold vessels of the altar, not knowing they were safe in the keeping of one blessed of God."

Father O'Connell led the girls past the cursing bluecoats toward a nearby church. The Ursuline building stood long after the surrounding structures fell, but it too succumbed to the blaze. Finally, the cross towering above it crashed down in flames at 3 a.m. "Oh, holy! Yes, holy!" hooted the laughing Federals at the sight, as they puffed cigar smoke into the nuns' faces. "We're just as holy as you are! . . . Now, what do you think of God? Ain't Sherman greater?"

Inside the church, the nuns calmed the children, some of whom shook and sobbed. Then more soldiers crashed through the church's doors and shouted, "All out! We're blowing up the church!" Now the girls rushed, terrified, out into the hedges of the church cemetery, where they quailed and huddled around Sister Baptista, refusing to reenter the church.

Sherman arrived in person after sunrise. He took Sister Baptista's hand and announced, "Oh, there are times when one must practice patience and Christian endurance." "You have prepared for us one of these moments, General," she replied. When Sherman blamed the raging inferno on the people of Columbia for leaving liquor for his men, Sister Baptista motioned to the heap of smoking ashes that had been the convent, and the city beyond, and said, "General, this is how you kept your promise to me, a cloistered nun."

Marching Through Georgia (Henry Clay Work)

Bring the good old bugle, boys!
We'll sing another song;
Sing it with a spirit
That will start the world along;
Sing it as we used to sing it,
Fifty thousand strong,
While we were marching through Georgia.

Chorus:
"Hurrah, hurrah! We bring the Jubilee!
Hurrah, hurrah! The flag that makes you free!"
So we sang the chorus
From Atlanta to the sea,
While we were marching through Georgia.

So we made a thoroughfare
For Freedom and her train,
Sixty miles in latitude,
Three hundred to the main;
Treason fled before us,
For resistance was in vain,
While we were marching through Georgia!

Chorus:
"Hurrah, hurrah! We bring the Jubilee!
Hurrah, hurrah! The flag that makes you free!"
So we sang the chorus
From Atlanta to the sea,
While we were marching through Georgia.

The Theory of Just War

The idea of "civilized" warfare is distinctively Christian. It aims to preserve the moral distinctives of Christianity even during and after war, as well as to restrain the state from establishing itself as an all-powerful god unto itself. It reflects the desire to avoid war as a fundamental idea in the Christian view of politics, as opposed to the romanticization of war as a pagan one that reflects a disregard for the sanctity of life.

The first Geneva Convention on War in 1863 minced no words: attacking defenseless cities and towns, as well as plundering and wantonly destroying civilian property, were war crimes, performed by war criminals.

Gradually coming to be known as the "Theory of Just War," a set of moral standards judging the rightness of military engagements was observed and respected (with many lapses, such as during the Thirty Years War) for nearly 1,500 years in the Christian West. The concept arose from a chain of sources: Ambrose, revered 4th-century Bishop of Milan; his protégé, renowned theologian St. Augustine of Hippo; the Christianization of Europe during the Middle Ages under the leadership of Alfred of Wessex, Charlemagne, and others; the famed clergyman and scholar Thomas Aquinas; the impact of Catholic and other jurisprudence on international law; the Protestant Reformation giant John Calvin; and 17th-century Dutch lawyer and Reformer Hugo Grotius's landmark book *The Law of War and Peace*.

Generations of West Point graduates, including most of those who led the armies of the North

Sherman versus Johnston

The Confederate Congress named Lee military commander-in-chief in February; now he appointed Johnston head of all forces in the Carolinas and ordered him to concentrate them and drive Sherman back. Johnston could only marshal 20,000 men, but in one final desperate attempt to halt Sherman's juggernaut on March 19, he threw them against Slocum's wing, which he discerned to be isolated, at Bentonville. Johnston hoped to destroy this force, then deal with Sherman's main wing on a different field.

Many of the bloodied Federals considered Bentonville the most horrific fight they had ever seen. The Rebel-yelling Confederates drove them back and almost swept them from the field. The Federals finally held, and did so until Sherman arrived with the rest of his army. Now Johnston was outnumbered better than 3–1. Nonetheless, he smashed one attack, held his ground for two days—further delaying Sherman's junction with Grant—then, surrounded on three sides and seeing no evidence of eagerness on Sherman's part to attack, moved north under cover of night.

Sherman rendezvoused with General John Schofield's corps in Goldsboro

---

and South, had learned the code of just war. For many years leading up to the War, they learned it from none other than Henry Halleck—Lincoln's general in chief the first three years of the War. Halleck himself wrote General Order No. 12, and taught it to the cadets. In the following excerpt, the order addresses wanton plunder of private property during war:

> *The inevitable consequences . . . are universal pillage and a total relaxation of discipline; the loss of private property, and the violation of individual rights . . . and the ordinary peaceful and noncombatants are converted into bitter and implacable enemies. The system is, therefore, regarded as both impolitic and unjust, and is coming into general disuse among the most civilized nations.*

Even Sherman acknowledged his understanding of the consequences in Christendom—in particular, in America—of waging unjust war when he wrote a friend after the War: "I know that in the beginning I, too, had the old West Point notion that pillage was a capital crime, and punished it by shooting." The first Geneva Convention on War in 1863 minced no words: attacking defenseless cities and towns, as well as plundering and wantonly destroying civilian property, were war crimes, performed by war criminals. Only necessities, it declared, could be taken from a civilian population, and those must be paid for. But Lincoln never signed on to the Geneva accords.

Henry Halleck

The Principles of Just War

A consensus summary of criteria necessary before the use of force is justified:

1) It must have a just cause.
2) It must be pursued only as a last resort, protective and defensive in nature, after all other options are exhausted.
3) It must be declared by proper, God-ordained civil authority, in keeping with the tenets of such biblical passages as Romans 13:1–7; or by a lower order oppressed and forced into repeated unbiblical actions by a leviathan central power.
4) The evil caused by the war must be less than the evil to be righted. This includes the practice of proportionality, a reasonable and proper level of response.
5) The war must have a reasonable probability of success.
6) No military action can be undertaken that seriously threatens civilians or their property, much less deliberately targets them.

Admiral John Dahlgren and his famed Dahlgren gun in Charleston (SC) harbor. Dahlgren maintained the innocence of his son Ulric from the worst charges of the Kilpatrick-Dahlgren raid on Richmond until the end of his life.

No One Blameless

Whether the contestants in the War passed muster on several of the established criteria for just war is debatable. Incontestable is their failure in multiple instances on at least two points. One concerned whether the evil caused by the War was less than the evil intended to be righted. Another was whether the armies eschewed military action that seriously threatened civilians or their property, and especially that which targeted them.

Neither North or South was blameless. However, a key distinction marked them. Confederate outrages such as Quantrill's murderous raid on Lawrence, Kansas, McCausland's burning of Chambersburg, Pennsylvania, the destruction and plunder of some of Morgan's raids in Kentucky, and the murder of surrendered Federal soldiers at such places as Fort Pillow and the Battle of the Crater were unsanctioned—even condemned—by the South's high command.

Even after Federal generals such as Pope and Butler had savaged the Southern homeland, when Robert E. Lee took the Army of Northern Virginia north on the Gettysburg campaign, he issued his famous General Order No. 73 to all his soldiers:

> *It must be remembered that we make war only upon armed men, and that we cannot take vengeance for the wrongs our people have suffered without lowering ourselves in the eyes of all whose abhorrence has been excited by the atrocities of our enemies, and offending against*

Him to whom vengeance belongeth, without whose favor and support our efforts must all prove in vain.

The commanding general therefore earnestly exhorts the troops to abstain with most scrupulous care from unnecessary or wanton injury to private property, and he enjoins upon all officers to arrest and bring to summary punishment all who shall in any way offend against the orders on this subject.

Six Confederate soldiers were executed by firing squads during the campaign for vandalism, one of them for taking fence railing to kindle a fire. Federal atrocities were not only vastly more numerous, they were championed by the most powerful men in the United States military and political power structures, including Lincoln, Stanton, Grant, Sherman, Sheridan, Halleck, and the Republican leaders of both the Senate and House. Some Federal generals, such as George McClellan, Joshua Chamberlain, and Robert Gould Shaw, opposed such actions and at least one, Don Carlos Buell, resigned his commission because of them. But the North triumphed, and hardly a war since, anywhere in the world, has been won according to the standards of just war.

Black Federal teamsters. (Library of Congress)

A Confederate Soldier's Prayer (Author unknown)

I asked God for strength, that I might achieve.
I was made weak, that I might learn humbly to obey.

I asked for health, that I might do greater things.
I was given infirmity, that I might do better things.

I asked for riches, that I might be happy.
I was given poverty, that I might be wise.

I asked for power that I might have the praise of men.
I was given weakness, that I might feel the need of God.

I asked for all things, that I might enjoy life.
I was given life, that I might enjoy all things.

I got nothing that I asked for but got everything I had hoped for.
Almost despite myself, my unspoken prayers were answered.

I am, among all people, most richly blessed.

March 23, bringing "Uncle Billy's" strength to nearly 90,000 men. Combined with Grant, the Federals would have 220,000 soldiers to hurl against Lee's 35,000 and whatever remained of Johnston's force, now less than 20,000. But within thirty days, Lee had surrendered, and President Davis had given Johnston, yet unvanquished in the field with his army, permission to treat with Sherman about surrender. This he did, arriving on April 26 at terms similar to those between Lee and Grant.

Confederate bugler Bentley Weston, Company A, 7th South Carolina cavalry. (LOC)

Final Acts

The Federals' Southern-born Admiral Farragut had led the long-sought capture of the Confederate port city of Mobile, Alabama, on April 12. But some Confederates had not yet surrendered, and a few subordinate acts remained to be played out. On May 12–13 came the final battle of the War. Texas' Calvary of the West, led by Mexican War and Texas

John S. "Rip" Ford and the Last Battle of the War (1815–1897)

How long a shadow does John Salmon Ford cast over Texas history, as well as significant segments of United States, Confederate, and Mexican history? Acclaimed Texas historian T. R. Fehrenbach wrote that beginning with his migration to the state in 1836, "over the next five decades, he was to be the only man in Texas history who was involved in a major way in every action or controversy of his time."

The native South Carolinian raised volunteer troops in Tennessee for the Texas fight for independence, then became a lawyer, medical doctor, publisher of several newspapers, state representative, twice state senator, one of the first captains in the Texas Rangers, mayor of both Austin and Brownsville, decorated leader of a Ranger spy company in the Mexican War, legendary commander of the Cavalry of the West in the War, and finally, Superintendent of the State Deaf and Dumb Institution.

A voracious reader and a Presbyterian, destiny seemed to draw Ford along the parallel tracks of learned professional leadership and warrior-defender of his people. Arriving in Texas too late for action in the war for independence against Mexico, he gained distinction for his military service during the Mexican War, then helped lead Texans in their frontier and border fights with Indians and Mexican bandits during the late 1840s and early 1850s. Ford ranged west to El Paso, north to the Canadian River in present-day Oklahoma, and south into Mexico.

Texas governor Hardin Runnels placed Ford in charge of all state forces for the 1857–1858 Canadian River Campaign against rampaging Indians. Ford led his troops to victories in two major battles that quashed the uprisings. When the Mexican-American rebel Juan "Cheno" Cortinas terrorized Brownsville and the lower Rio Grande, Runnels again called on "Old Rip Ford." Ford thrashed the Mexicans twice in battles where he himself led six-shooter-firing charges into the teeth of Cortinas' numerically superior forces.

First he drove them across the river out of Texas, then into the mountains of interior Mexico. Texans assigned Ford a key role in the secession convention that opposed Sam Houston, removed him from office, and took the state from the United States into the Confederacy. Ford then spearheaded the successful capture of $3 million worth of Federal military installations and property in Texas and the removal of their armed forces.

Fighting Yankees

Many historians consider the defense of the Texas land and Gulf Coast borders one of the great military accomplishments of the Confederacy. And one man's name towers above all others in that feat—Rip Ford. With his "Cavalry of the West," a small scratch band of irregulars, including boys in their early teens and men in their sixties; little food or supplies; atrocious land and weather conditions; and a case of malaria that nearly killed him, Ford, in the saddle, personally led one of the most amazing campaigns of the War.

Over 6,000 Federal troops had invaded the lower Rio Grande Valley and cut off Texas' critical supply line through Mexico. With only a fraction that many men, Ford rode south out of San Antonio, defeated the Federals at Las Rucias and Ebonal, and drove them hundreds of miles back, out of Brownsville, and out of Texas onto tiny Brazos Island, just below South Padre Island. This, along with Confederate victories in the Red River campaign, at Sabine Pass, and at Galveston, cleared the Federals out of Texas, except for a few remote and isolated coastal positions.

Rip Ford's crowning military achievement was winning the last battle of the War. Recognizing its approaching denouement, he and Confederate General James Slaughter signed a truce covering the Rio Grande with Federal General Lew Wallace. More than a month after Lee's surrender at Appomattox, however, an ambitious young Yankee "political general" named Theodore H. Barrett, desiring at least one combat engagement to spur his future political career, disobeyed orders and brashly reinvaded the Texas mainland. Employing a melange of Indiana and New York troops, a black regiment, and some Unionist Texas cavalry, Barrett took Palmito Hill, between Brownsville and the mouth of the Rio Grande.

Rip Ford's crowning military achievement was winning the last battle of the War.

Furious at the truce-breaking, Ford thundered in from Brownsville on May 13. Once again he personally led the Cavalry of the West as they crushed the Federal force and shot, slashed, and trampled them every step of the hellish seven-mile retreat back to Brazos Island. Several hundred Federals were killed, wounded or captured; less than a dozen Texans were wounded and none killed.

Rip Ford remained a leader of Texas the rest of his life. However, a weakness for gambling contributed to his dying nearly broke—nearly broke, but much honored. One of his final acts was co-founding the Texas State Historical Association.

Ranger veteran John S. "Rip" Ford, thrashed a foolish Federal attack at the Battle of Palmito Ranch, near Brownsville on Texas' Rio Grande border with Mexico. Thus the final battle of the struggle was a Confederate victory, as was the first. Ford disbanded his men rather than surrender, but the remnants of Edmund Kirby-Smith's Trans-Mississippi Confederate Department—now chiefly Texas—gave up the fight on May 26.

"A Man Knows a Man," a memorable illustration from the April 22, 1865 edition of *Harper's Weekly*, conveys the common sacrifice and cause that war brought together black and white Federal soldiers.

It was left, however, to the legendary Cherokee Chief and Confederate Brigadier General Stand Watie to tender the final Southern surrender. On June 23, 2–1/2 months after Lee's capitulation at Appomattox, he and his Indian horse soldiers ceased their fight and returned to their burned and pillaged homes. The war for Southern independence was over, and the Confederate States of America were no more.

PBS's Civil War Series

Dr. James I. "Bud" Robertson, respected historian, best-selling author, and Alumni Distinguished Professor of History at Virginia Polytechnic Institute and State University, succinctly analyzed the PBS *Civil War* series: "The less you know about the Civil War, the more you'll enjoy the program." Robertson said that as an historian his main problem with the series was not its imbalance, but the number of factual errors it contained. Factual errors are those whereby data is presented that is materially different from actual facts. They do not include inconsequential items such as showing the body of the same man after several different battles. Robertson counted 17 factual errors in one half-hour segment. On a pro rata basis that adds up to hundreds of errors.

A Soldier Speaks about War

General Oliver Howard commanded a Federal corps in the battle of Gettysburg. In his autobiography he left a poignant treasury of his sentiments regarding the horrors of war and the need for forgiveness.

It is sometimes said to me that writing and speaking upon the events of war may have a deleterious influence upon youth. I can conceive of two reasons of such a warning—one, that a soldier by his enthusiasm may, even unconsciously, infuse into his writing and speech the war spirit, and thus incite strong desires in younger minds for similar excitements and deeds; and secondly, a soldier deeply affected as he must have been in our great struggle for national existence, may not take sufficient pains in his accounts of historic incidents to allay any spirit of animosity or dissension that may still exist.

But with regard to the first, I think there is need of a faithful portraiture of what we may call the after-battle, a panorama which shows with fidelity the fields covered with dead men and horses; and the wounded, numerous and helpless, stretched on the ground in masses, each waiting his turn; the rough hospitals with hay and straw for bedding, saturated with blood and wet with the rain; horses torn into fragments; every species of property ruthlessly demolished or destroyed—these, which we cannot well exaggerate, and such as these, cry out against the horrors, the hateful ravages, and the countless sufferings because of war. They show plainly to our children that war, with its embodied woes and furies, must be avoided, except as the last appeal for existence, or for the rights which are more valuable than life itself.

. . . these, cry out against the horrors, the hateful ravages, and the countless sufferings because of war. They show plainly to our children that war, with its embodied woes and furies, must be avoided, except as the last appeal for existence, or for the rights which are more valuable than life itself.

—Oliver O. Howard

When I dwell on the scenes on July 4th and 5th at Gettysburg, the pictures exhibiting Meade's men and Lee's, though now shadowy from time, are still full of terrible groupings and revolting lineaments.

There is a lively energy, an emulous activity, an exhilarating buoyancy of spirit in all the preparations for an expected battle, and these feelings are intensified into an increased ardor during the conflict; but it is another thing to see our comrades there upon the ground with their darkened faces and swollen forms; another thing to watch the countenances of friends and companions but lately in the bloom of health, now disfigured, torn, and writhing in death; and not less affecting to a sensitive heart to behold the multitude of strangers prone and weak, pierced with wounds, or showing broken limbs and every sign of suppressed suffering, waiting for hours and hours for a relief which is long coming—the relief of the surgeon's knife or of death.

As to the second reason, any feeling of personal resentment towards the late Confederates I would not counsel or cherish. Our countrymen—large numbers of them—combined and fought us hard for a cause. They failed and we succeeded; so that, in an honest desire for reconcilement, I would be the more careful, even in the use of terms, to convey no hatred or reproach for the past. Such are my real convictions, and certainly the intention in all my efforts is not to anger and separate, but to pacify and unite.

Red Fox (Wilfrid Knight)

No monuments nor marble shafts
Keep silent record of the time
When grey clad ranks of warriors rode
The Indian Nation line.

But mists of time have not eclipsed
The Ancient stories of his day,
And still the whsipered words are heard,
"Stand Watie passed this way."

The noon of darkness casts its spell:
Dutch Billy's bugle sounds once more
And Watie heads his column out
To ride through legend's door.

Now once again the muskets fire
While "Eagle" Buzzard's spirit soars,
And smoothbores spew their deadly hail
As Watie leads to war.

But now—the Red Fox rides nor more,
No bands of men, with muffled sound
Slip through the night to strike at dawn;
The fight is thru, the moon is down.

Now who will sing old Watie's song,
And who will tell his tale,
And who will keep the rendezvous
Along the Texas Trail?

PART III Post-war and Reconstruction

The years following the War did not witness a gentlemanly shaking of the hands, reuniting, and proceeding forth as a bloodied but strengthened Union. If the oceans of blood spilled and the numberless atrocities and cruelties committed during the War left bitterness and hatred, the vengefulness and corruption that abounded following the War only multiplied that hurtful legacy.

Nameless refugees, lost to history like most of the other thousands of American families who lost their homes, and often their loved ones, to the War.

These years break into two periods. The immediate post-war period, from 1865 until early 1867 (Chapters 31 and 32), witnessed a variety of competing approaches on the part of the triumphant Federals to repairing the nation's economy and property, preserving the political goals for which the United States fought, and returning the warring sections to a peaceful union. President Andrew Johnson, the Democrats in Congress, and some moderate Republicans favored generally mild and charitable policies toward the South and a return to a more strict construction (literal interpretation) of the Constitution than had been practiced by the Federal government during the War. They held varying degrees of commitment to the rights of former slaves and other blacks.

Thaddeus Stevens and the burgeoning Radical wing of the Republican Party in government generally advocated much more authoritarian treatment of the former Confederate states and a looser construction (less literal interpretation) of the Constitution. As a whole, they also placed a higher priority on effecting legislation to improve the civil rights of black Americans.

The coming of the Military Reconstruction Acts in early 1867 signaled the post-war political triumph of the Radical Republicans and most of their agenda, and the onset of the long harsh period Northerners termed Reconstruction, but many Southerners called Deconstruction (Chapters 33–37). Some Reconstruction-era actions, notably the Freedman's Bureau and the Thirteenth, Fourteenth, and Fifteenth Amendments, aimed at and sometimes achieved noble ends, though unconstitutional methods and divisive consequences beset even the best of them.

American blacks at long last had their freedom and the official Union was preserved, but the manner in which both these objectives were accomplished created additional problems that did not end with Reconstruction in 1877. While many supporters of the Radicals' Reconstruction considered it a good idea that did not go far enough, or even failed, opponents considered it a bad idea that succeeded all too well.

31 Peace

The ruins of a Charleston, South Carolina, home, destroyed by Federal shelling.

Our fields everywhere lie untilled. Naked chimneys and charred ruins all over the land mark the spots where happy homes, the seats of refinement and elegance, once stood. Their former inhabitants wander in poverty and exile, wherever chance or charity affords them shelter or food. Childless old age, widows, and helpless orphans beggared and hopeless, are everywhere.

—A Mississippi farmer writing to his brother

Even as the Congressional leaders of Lincoln's own party rushed to seize the reins of governmental power following his death, the fallen president was transformed overnight into a hero and martyr; some eyes, not unaware of his falling on Good Friday, viewed him a a saint. A train of Christian ministers sought to burnish his heroic epitaph with a crown of Christianity for which his own utterances had offered scant support. Lincoln also emerged as a towering figure of forgiveness—even as some in the government he left behind crafted plans of breathtaking scope that, if carried out, would leave forgiveness aside and visit apocalyptic wrath on the fallen South.

And fallen, and crushed, it was. Formerly the region had held many of the most important posts in government. It maintained control over the

Approximate Percentage of Southern Losses Between 1860 and 1870

Total property value, excluding slaves	41%[a]
Total property value, including slaves	63%[a]
Land Under Cultivation in Louisiana	30%
Land Under Cultivation in Virginia	30%
Land Under Cultivation in South Carolina	33%
Value of Farms	33%[b]
Value of Farm Implements in South Carolina	67%
Corn production	33%
Cotton production	45%
Wheat production	50%
Sugar production	63%
Rice production	66%

[a] in 1865; [b] in 1880

Richmond, Va. Ruins of paper mill with water-wheel

Federal judiciary up until the War. Four of the first five presidents were Southerners. Despite its numerical inferiority, the South was a cultural and intellectual center, and counterweight to New England. It had more colleges and more schools for all age levels than the North, both in proportion to population and in absolute number. It had both the financial and intellectual resources to lead America, and had since the time of Patrick Henry and George Washington. But no more. Historian Ludwell Johnson, in his book *North Against South: The American Iliad 1848–1877*, quantified the devastation, as seen in the adjacent table.

Shattered South

By 1870, total property value in the eleven former states of the Confederacy remained one-third less in 1860. Meanwhile, Northern wealth increased to two-and-a-half times its value in 1860. What little industry, communication lines, and transportation network the South had lay in rubble. Many of its towns and cities, and millions of square miles of its land were literally burned to ashes. The worst toll was the human. Everywhere was hunger, disease, and exposure. One Federal official wrote:

> It is a common, an every-day sight . . . women and children, most of whom were formerly in good circumstances, begging for bread from door to door. . . . They must have immediate help or perish. . . . Some are without homes of any description.

Two hundred sixty thousand Confederate soldiers, or one-fourth of the entire white male population of the Southern states between the ages of 16 and 60, died in the War. Another one-fourth suffered serious wounds, illness, maiming, or a combination of the three. Proportionate casualties in early 21st-century America would total nearly thirty million. In addition, historian Jeffrey Hummel in *Emancipating*

Not everyone was suffering at war's end, as evidenced by this humorous November 4, 1872 *Harper's Weekly* (www.harpweek.com) advertisement for Taylor & Young Pioneer Yeast Powder.

MISTRESS: "Why, Bridget, what are you doing—nailing those biscuits down to the tray?"
COOK: "Yes, faith, Mum, or they'd be afther liftin' the tops off your oven, Mum—this Yaste Powdher's so moity powerful."
(Messrs. Taylor & Young, and the Trade generally, are successfully proving the Pioneer yeast Powder a good thing with which to "raise the wind.")

Slaves, Enslaving Free Men, has documented that around 50,000 Southern civilians, many of them black, perished during the conflict by causes directly related to the Northern war effort against the populace. Thousands of frightened or embittered Southerners emigrated out of the region to which their forefathers had, in many cases only a generation or two or less before, come. They moved to Canada, Europe, the Caribbean, Central America, South America (particularly Brazil), and west to Texas, the Plains states and territories, the Far West, and California and Oregon.

Two Phases

Such was the context within which the lamentations of the so-called "Reconstruction Era" must be placed. Actually, at least two separate phases comprised the overall postwar and Reconstruction period. Immediately following the War, President Johnson's more moderate agenda of reconciliation with and rebuilding the South held sway. This featured plans for the erstwhile Confederate states to reform their own state governments, comprised of men elected by their own citizens. It also incorporated the resumption of duly-elected Congressional representatives from the Southern states.

Even though Radical Republican influence chipped away at Johnson's Reconstruction agenda, not until early 1867, with the first of a series of Congressionally-passed Reconstruction Acts, did the process move full force into a second, much more hostile and divisive phase. From the ruins of Southern civilization, and as the triumphant United States sought to "reconstruct" the South into its own image, came the Carpetbaggers, the Scalawags, the Ascendants, and the Ku Klux Klan.

And came the centralization of the American government and banking system, Black Friday and the Gilded Age, transcontinental American expansion, the spoils system of the U.S. political process, the genocidal extermination of the Plains Indian tribes, a theretofore-unseen worldwide American imperialistic presence, and a vicious enmity

Birth of the Klan

The little south Tennessee town of Pulaski had suffered more than its share. As the ruined South suffered under the heel of Federal military occupation, a recent cyclone had swept through the town, destroying more homes, buildings, and human life alike. Indeed, the six young erstwhile Confederate soldiers who gathered Christmas Eve Night 1865 in Judge Thomas M. Jones' law office had lost all their property and possessed business prospects. "Boys, let's start something to break this monotony, and to cheer up our mothers and the girls," said one of them, Captain John C. Lester. "Let's start a club of some kind."

It was a time of mysterious societies and clubs, secret initiation rites and ceremonies, and passwords nationwide. Soon, another of the young veterans, Captain John B. Kennedy, suggested a name for the new club: "Kukloi," from the Greek word "Kuklos," meaning band or circle. A third soldier, James R. Crowe, said, "Call it Ku Klux," and no one will know what it means. Lester added: "Add Klan as we are all Scotch-Irish descent." When he said the words "Ku Klux Klan," it was the first time they ever fell from human tongue. Crowe suggested they don a distinctive costume, and they raided their host's linen closet, robing themselves in stiff linen sheets and pillow cases. Masquerading, too, was a popular endeavor of the day.

John C. Lester, originator of the original, post-War Ku Klux Klan, which was designed as a men's social club.

Riding horses, the men thought, would increase the drama and strengthen the impression, so they mounted and rode—the horses cloaked in white linen too. They visited the homes of their mothers and sweethearts, saying not a word, but leaving baskets of food and whatsoever other necessaries they could scrounge for the needy women. They cheered the whole unhappy town by these endeavors, and by waving and making various comic gestures.

In her book *Authentic History of the Ku Klux Klan*, Susan Lawrence Davis writes: "Aside from the amusement they had created, it was reported on the streets, that many of the idle negroes thought they had seen ghosts from the nearby battlefields, and had with haste gone back to their former masters, only too willing to work." The tiny fraternal organization began to seem like a very good idea indeed.

between the black and white races that has yet to melt away fully.

Northern Factions

Though factions and opinions abounded, the majority Northern Republican Party contained two dominant wings. The more moderate of the two featured men such as the now-deceased Lincoln, Carl Schurz, Lyman Trumbull, and, surprisingly, William Sherman. Also, though a Democrat, the new president, Andrew Johnson, vice president under Lincoln, who ran on their 1864 National Union ticket.

Andrew Johnson (1808–1875)

Few Americans of his generation or any other lived a life as replete with adventure, drama, and danger, on the national stage, as the 17th President. Like the two other leading Federal politicians of the 1860s, Abraham Lincoln and Thaddeus Stevens, Johnson entered the world in poverty, in a log shack in Raleigh, North Carolina. By age four, he was a penniless orphan, bound as an apprentice—one of the Biblically-, and Constitutionally-, sanctioned forms of slavery—for food, clothing, and shelter until reaching manhood.

Remarkably, this future President never attended any school. He did manage to learn to read and write. He migrated west to Greeneville, Tennessee, where he married a woman from a respectable family and became the proprietor of a small tailor shop. With thrift, labor, and enterprise, he built the store into a prosperous concern. And her teaching expanded his scant educational experience. Johnson's hardscrabble background created in him a distaste that never left him for large plantation owners and others he considered part of the aristocratic class. Granted opportunity to pursue political interests due to his business success, he proved a splendid debater—and enjoyed it too.

Johnson opposed the centralization of the national government as ardently as did Thomas Jefferson and he hated policies supportive of privilege and monopoly as much as Andrew Jackson.

He opposed the centralization of the national government as ardently as did Thomas Jefferson:

> *Your States . . . are sinking into mere petty corporations . . . mere satellites of an inferior character, revolving around the great central power here in Washington. There is where your danger is. It is not in centrifugal power being too great, but in the centripetal influence all drawing here . . . I believe that governments are made for men and not men for governments . . . I am opposed to consolidation or to the concentration of power in the hands of the few.*

And he hated policies supportive of privilege and monopoly as much as Andrew Jackson:

> *The tendency of the legislation of this country is to build up monopolies . . . to build up the money power . . . to concentrate power in the hands of the few. The tendency is for classes and against the great mass of the people.*

To Washington

Johnson graduated from local politics to the United States Congress in 1843, at age 35. He served there for a decade, until winning election to the U.S. Senate, where he remained even after the War began. Though a Southerner, a Democrat, and no abolitionist, his loyalty to the Union coupled with his animus toward both secession and plantation slaveowners caused him to side with the North.

His views on slavery mirrored Lincoln's: "My

position is that Congress has no power to interfere with . . . slavery; that it is an institution local in its character and peculiar to the states where it exists, and no other power has the right to control it." Like Lincoln, Johnson preferred shipping the blacks to distant colonies.

Even when Tennessee joined the Confederacy, Johnson remained in the Senate. In 1862, he accepted President Lincoln's appointment as military governor of Tennessee, which meant whatever that part of it the Federals military controlled. Hoping Johnson's influence might help draw Southerners back into the Union, which might help end the War, Lincoln named him his vice presidential running mate for the 1864 Presidential election.

When Lincoln died, Johnson became only the third man to inherit the office upon the death of the President. At first, with Johnson's tough talk toward the South, it looked as though he and Radical leaders like Thaddeus Stevens in the House and Ben Wade in the Senate would mesh nicely. But when the emotion of the assassination tempered, Johnson pursued a post-war program akin to Lincoln's and much more conciliatory with the South than the Radicals'. With this, the Radicals unleashed a furious campaign not only to defeat Johnson in the legislative arena, but to destroy his reputation and, ultimately, to remove him from office. Some of them even wanted him dead, which would have been the likely outcome had they gotten their way and Johnson been arrested, tried, and convicted for complicity in Lincoln's death.

Impeachment

Behind Stevens' determined and innovative leadership, the House did manage to impeach Johnson in 1868, but the Senate failed by one vote to remove him from office. Still, the Radicals' comprehensive assaults on him crippled his effectiveness his final year in the White House. Though Johnson would have liked a second term, he did not even win his own party's nomination, due to fears he would be unelectable in the 1868 race.

Never did Johnson's stalwart character shine through with more brilliance than when he won election again to the Senate in 1874. There he capitalized in full on the opportunity to stand against President Grant and other Radicals who had bedeviled him when he resided in the White House. Noteworthy, too, is the fact that by 1874, the white Southern Democratic majority—most of them ex-Confederates—held sway again in Tennessee. Yet they respected the former Yankee vice president enough to send him to Washington as one of their two most important representatives. Johnson's benedictory triumph was short-lived. He died later in 1875.

Perhaps Andrew Johnson offered up his own most profound epitaph when, late in his life, he surveyed the social and political morass around him and declared:

> *I feel prouder in my retirement than imperial Caesar with such a corrupt Congress at his heels, for . . . when degeneracy and corruption seem to control Departments of Government; when "vice prevails and impious men bear sway, the post of honor is a private station." When I accepted the Presidency . . . I accepted it as a high trust. . . . I did not accept it as a donation, or as a grand gift establishment; I did not take it as a horn of plenty, with sugar plums to be handed out here and there. Thank God, I can stand before the people of my State and lift up both hands and say in the language of Samuel, "Whose ox have I taken, or whose ass have I taken? At whose hands have I received bribes and had my eyes blinded? If there by any, let him answer."*

March of the victors. James Taylor's memorable depiction of the Federals' Grand Army of the Republic as they marched down Pennsylvania Avenue in Washington, D.C. The grand review lasted three days, May 23–25, 1865. The U.S. capitol looms in the background. (TreasureNet)

In general, this more moderate wing was best marked by its determination to preserve a single Federal union of states—though the reasons or priorities for doing so varied according to the individual. This group leaned antislavery or even pro-slavery rather than abolitionist, and they possessed no great love for the African race and no bold plans for their social and economic transformation. Most in this group would have been just as happy, or happier, to have all blacks leave the country, or at least stay out of the North.

Its adherents did not possess the ideological zeal for a makeover of the United States along the lines of the *Communist Manifesto* and the European revolutions of 1848. When the Confederacy fell, the moderates (most of whom had never harbored great hatred for the Southerners, though some did for their secession) desired to welcome back the beaten states, sans slavery, and help rebuild their economy, which the moderates believed would be profitable, socially and financially, for everyone.

The other wing, the Radicals, included men like Congressional leader Thaddeus Stevens, Senate leaders Ben Wade and Charles Sumner, and military leaders like Benjamin Butler. They saw abolition as one of many components of the Marxist revolution they desired. They had much to build—a pro-Republican black voting base in the South, new schools across the South espousing Northern philosophical doctrines and historical views, one-party domination of the whole country, and a nationalized, Washington-based transcontinental empire fueled by railroads, manufacturing, and tariff revenue.

And they had much to destroy—the domination of Christian orthodoxy everywhere in the United States, the leadership of plantation owners and other landed and propertied men in the South (as well as their Northern Democratic philosophical allies), the strict adherence to Constitutional law, and the notion of individual state social, political, economic, and religious sovereignty. To succeed in all this, they knew the South must not only be rebuilt, but transformed, from top to bottom.

Sherman versus Stanton

The process would not be easy, and it would not be quick. The South was physically crushed but ideologically defiant. The contention between the Northern Radicals and their more moderate associates, meanwhile, burst into public view with the feud between Stanton and Sherman. Lincoln, fearful of a protracted guerilla war with thousands of bitter Confederates, had persuaded Sherman that a quick reestablishment of the existing Southern state governments was the best course in restoring the Union. So when he treated with Joe Johnston in April 1865 after Lee's surrender, Sherman agreed to that process, as well as amnesty for all Johnston's soldiers.

Stanton, who feared the Democrats drafting Sherman, by now a national hero, as their next presidential candidate, erupted in fury. He orchestrated a reversal of the Sherman-Johnston treaty regarding Southern political leadership. Then the Secretary of State unleashed a salvo of public charges, among other things accusing Sherman of helping the Confederacy's leaders stay in power, its soldiers to remain armed, its slaveowners to keep their slaves, and its president to escape. Northern newspapers, taking the cue, claimed everything from Sherman's involvement in the murder of Lincoln to his "stark insanity." Attorney General James Speed, a Stanton political ally, warned President Johnson's cabinet of Sherman's supposed plans to take over the government as dictator.

Sherman penned thoughts to his wife Ellen that illumine many of the differences in the Republican Party's major factions:

> Stanton wants to kill me because I do not favor the scheme of declaring the Negroes of the south, now free, to be loyal voters, whereby politicians may manufacture just so much more pliable

Edwin J. Stanton (1814-1869)

An Ohio native like so many Federal leaders of the War era, he graduated from Kenyon College and pursued a career in law, then politics. One of the many distinctives of his career was his high level service in the administrations of three consecutive Presidents. A Democrat before the War, he served Democrat James Buchanan as Attorney General during the latter part of that man's term, which ended in early 1861. Then Abraham Lincoln hired him as his Secretary of War, though he knew Stanton was not only a Democrat, but opposed Lincoln and the Republican Party platform. He came in time to realize Stanton detested him personally as well.

Stanton, embracing the Radicals' agenda, supported total war as necessary to defeat the Confederacy—war against the South, against Democrats, against Northern citizens, against whomever he thought unhelpful in the Federal effort. Grant described Stanton's "natural disposition to assume all power and control in all matters that he had anything to do with" and how "he cared nothing for the feelings of others."

But Edwin Stanton had far more troublesome characteristics than these. During the Buchanan administration he so flattered the president that Buchanan considered him one of his greatest allies. Yet Stanton was simultaneously contacting arch-Republican William Seward and beginning the unprecedented effort of providing the Republicans daily reports on the most secret and important happenings within the administration. Amazingly, when Buchanan retired and Lincoln took office, Stanton began communicating information not only to Buchanan about Lincoln, but to Seward and the Radicals, who opposed Lincoln from the other end of the political spectrum.

electioneering material. The Negroes don't want to vote. They want to work and enjoy property, and they are no friends of the Negro who seek to complicate him with new prejudices.

And he exploded publicly against Stanton. Through friends, Sherman's brother John (a powerful Ohio senator), and even Sherman's wife Ellen, attempted to reconcile the two; the break peaked the day the massed Grand Army of the Republic paraded triumphantly into Washington. There, mere feet from President Johnson, General Grant, and ranks of the nation's most powerful men William Sherman humiliated Edwin Stanton by ignoring his proffered hand, staring past him, and then walking on. All of this, however, but presaged the bitter strife that lay ahead over the soul of the United States, North and South.

Black Plight

The destruction of the South meant suffering and deprivation not only for whites, but for blacks. Hundreds of

Tenacious

Still, in terms of winning the War, selecting Stanton proved one of the most profoundly wise decisions Lincoln ever made. No one in the United States was more tenacious than Edwin Stanton once he locked onto a mission. When other politicians, government officials, and soldiers quailed as battlefield defeats multiplied, Stanton grew only more determined to win.

When Lincoln died, Andrew Johnson inherited his cabinet—including his Secretary of War. So, Stanton began to feed information to Johnson's Radical enemies. By now the political climate was such that Stanton's spying multiplied in value to the Radicals. And he himself grew less patient with the whole process. His opposition to Johnson, at first surreptitious, grew increasingly visible, even brazen.

Finally, in October, 1867, Johnson fired him. But Stanton and the Radicals actually welcomed this, because it broke Congress's newly-passed Tenure-of-Office Act. This measure, whose constitutionality Johnson disputed, prohibited a President from dismissing members of his own cabinet if Senate approval had been required for their appointment.

Johnson, however, had the Constitution on his side—among other reasons because the Senate approved Stanton for Lincoln's cabinet, not Johnson's. Nonetheless, Stanton showed his customary perseverance, going so far as to barricade himself in his office and call for the protection of Federal soldiers. A historic solution emerged for this dilemma—the impeachment and near-removal from office of Johnson. When the President survived that ordeal, Stanton finally capitulated. Within a year, Johnson was out of office and Stanton, duplicitous and perfidious to the end, was dead.

Stanton showed his customary perseverance, going so far as to barricade himself in his office and call for the protection of Federal soldiers.

thousands of emancipated black men found themselves without work, money, or land, and often without work skills or even food and sustenance for themselves and their families and kin. After all, the farms, businesses, and plantations that had sustained them were bankrupt, destroyed, or otherwise unable often to provide even for their white owners.

Tens of thousands of other former slaves had joined or been forced to join the Federal armies during the War. They returned to the same devastation. But worse yet awaited these men. Southern whites, and some blacks, looked on them as traitors to their country, and participants in its savage destruction. Confederate Southerners had seen what these men and the white Federals did to the South even with Southern armies in the field. Now the South lay prostrate, its armies surrendered and disbanded, and an ominous stream of Radical Republican cant cascaded from Washington and elsewhere about how Southern civilization would either acquiesce to a fundamental restructuring of itself or suffer complete and final extermination.

Fear and anger washed over the South. And the mass of blacks, especially those who had gone with the United States, experienced a resentment, in places a violent resentment, they had never before known. Yet few of them could go North, because that section for the most part wanted nothing to do with them. It was vigorously maintaining its own laws barring blacks from entering, and even crafting new ones to strengthen the previous ones.

As the War wound down, and for some months after, groups of blacks appeared around the South, heading

The Year of Jubilee

Nobel Prize-winning author William Faulkner presented a classic portrait of emancipated blacks massed and heading down Southern roads—to where they knew not—in his classic novel of 1860s Mississippi, *The Unvanquished*:

> *Granny was already sitting up in the wagon, I could see her head against the branches and the stars; all of a sudden all three of us were sitting up in the wagon, listening. They were coming up the road. It sounded like about fifty of them; we could hear the feet hurrying, and a kind of panting murmur. It was not singing exactly, it was not that loud; it was just a sound, a breathing, a kind of gasping murmuring chant and the feet whispering fast in the deep dust. I could hear women too and then all of a sudden I began to smell them. "[Negroes]," I whispered.*
>
> *"Shhhhhh," I whispered. We couldn't see them and they did not see us; maybe they didn't even look, just walking fast in the dark with that panting hurrying murmuring, going on. . . . That night we waked up three times and sat up in the wagon in the dark and heard [blacks] pass in the road. . . . And then the sun rose and It was a big crowd of them this time and they sounded like they were running, like they had to run to keep ahead of daylight. Then they were gone. Ringo and I had taken up the harness again when Granny said, "Wait. Hush." It was just one; we could hear her panting and sobbing, and then we heard another sound. Granny began to get down from the wagon. "She fell," she said. "You all hitch up and come on."*
>
> *When we turned into the road the woman was kind of crouched beside it, holding something in her arms and Granny standing beside her. It was a baby, a few months old; she held it like she thought maybe Granny was going to take it away from her. "I been sick and I couldn't keep up," she said. "They went off and left me."*
>
> *"Is your husband with them?" Granny said.*
>
> *"Yessum," the woman said. "They's all there."*
>
> *"If I give you something to eat, will you turn around and go back home?" Granny said . . . . You see you can't keep up with them and that they ain't going to wait for you," Granny said. "Do you want to die her in the road for buzzards to eat?" But she didn't even look at Granny, she just squatted there.*
>
> *"Hit's Jordan we coming to," she said. "Jesus gonter see me that far."*

The Jubilee Singers, students who had all been slaves, were the first to take black spirituals around the world. They raised funds to build Jubilee Hall at Fisk University in Nashville.

down roads, lanes, and highways on foot. Purpose and determination marked many of their faces. It took observers awhile to realize most of these trekkers had no idea where they were headed. After a few days, a few weeks, or a few months, most such folks returned to their former homes, or at least to the environs around their former homes.

32 Extremes

Henry L. Stephens's watercolor of an elderly black man reading a newspaper in the 1860s.

If a white man kills a colored man in any of the counties of this State, you cannot convict him.

—Post-war Florida sheriff

At the outset of his presidency, some Northern Republicans had significant cause for optimism that Tennessee Democrat Andrew Johnson would aid their comprehensive overhaul of Southern society. He detested the Southern planter class; he had demonstrated a powerful enmity to the Confederacy by backing the North when war began (at great cost to himself), and, especially following Lincoln's assassination, he promised a hard peace and retribution against his native section.

The South's estimation of Johnson certainly gave the Republicans no cause for discouragement. Jefferson Davis called him "the embodiment of malignity toward the Southern people, perhaps the more so because he had betrayed and deserted them in the hour of their need." President Johnson, however, left the issue of franchising black voters to the states themselves. He did set three requirements each seceded state must meet before readmission to the Union. The only exceptions were Virginia, Louisiana, Arkansas, and Tennessee, which already had puppet Union governments in place. The others must ratify the Thirteenth Amendment, which constitutionally outlawed the practice of slavery; officially disavow the ordinance of secession; and repudiate, or give up all claims, to the Confederate war debt.

The Southern states' lack of enthusiastic cooperation surely disturbed Johnson. Numerous factors contributed to it. For one, the states had guaranteed during the War they would pay their debts to the many they owed. They also had good cause to suspect the Radically-dominated Congress would accelerate a provision of the Thirteenth Amendment that could immediately make eligible to vote all adult black males in the South—but not those in the North.

Black Codes

Southern leaders had no illusions about what the Radical Republicans intended for them. Johnson's lack of concern over black voting rights, as well as other emerging differences he had with the Radical Congressional majority, further hardened their position. The ex-Confederates determined to maintain control of their own state governments—which was what Lincoln had intended—before someone else got hold of them.

They also determined to protect themselves and their families from an ominous threat they saw looming with the blacks. Thousands of the latter, especially the still-blue-coated war veterans, remained armed, while huge numbers of white Confederates had

The Thirteenth Amendment

Section 1. Neither slavery nor involuntary servitude, except as a punishment for crime whereof the party shall have been duly convicted, shall exist within the United States, or any place subject to their jurisdiction.

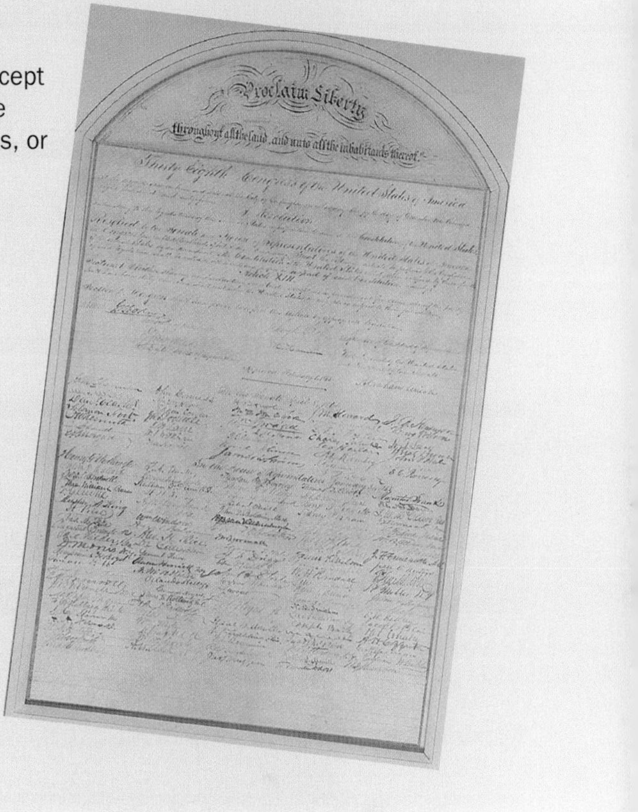

lost their weapons. Too, there was not enough food to go around, and they feared losing what they had to blacks. Desperate people commit desperate acts, and no few of these in the post-war South involved blacks stealing from whites. This further incensed and worried whites because they had rarely before witnessed blacks commit such acts. And increasing numbers of blacks were being promised by an array of Northern officials that they would receive free land and provisions in the "New South," and white Southerners knew this.

Between July and November of 1865, six Southern states established a set of "Black Codes." The objective was to define the new place of blacks in these states. With them, the white Southern majority found every way they could to deny the newly-freed slaves full citizenship rights. Though less harsh than the later Jim Crow laws, these Black Codes still short-circuited what many in the North, especially the Radicals, intended.

The Black Codes did include some improvements over the previous plight of Southern blacks. For instance, they provided access to the courts for them, allowing them to file suit on their own behalf. They also established hiring standards that enabled many former slaves without means and unable to find work, to reconnect with society. And they allowed blacks to own property.

The codes, however, specifically denied blacks the right to vote. And they established vagrancy standards. These said that former slaves who did not receive property from their erstwhile masters or some other source, thus becoming landed, could be run out of town by the sheriff. They also forbade racial intermarriage, and they prohibited blacks from testifying against whites in criminal cases.

All God's Chillun' Got Wings!

Before, during, and after the War, the life of many black communities centered around the church. Elizabeth White captured the spirit of that reality in her painting, "All God's Chillun's Got Wings!" Courtesy of the Sumter Gallery of Art, Sumter, South Carolina.

The Black Codes actually met Constitutional guidelines. And they mirrored many of the laws Federal military occupation officers had imposed on Southern blacks. Too, their vagrancy laws were no harsher than those established by some Northern states.

Committee of Fifteen

Northern Radicals had already observed the Southern states' lethargic fulfillment of President Johnson's requirements for readmission. Once they realized the import of the Black Codes, they were outraged. *The Chicago Tribune* spoke for many: "The men of the North will convert . . . Mississippi into a frog pond before they will allow any such laws to disgrace one foot of soil."

When Congress reconvened in December, Speaker of the House Schuyler Colfax threw down the gauntlet with an opening salvo that made clear the Radicals who controlled both the house and the senate had no intention of deferring to Johnson in determining the future of the conquered territory. Then the Republican of both chambers met in caucus. Thaddeus Stevens, now the most powerful man in America, ramrodded through the formation of the Committee of Fifteen. It would formulate its own policy regarding the disposition of the South and other important national affairs. Then it would inform the remaining Republicans in both houses of the plans and programs they should support. They, in turn, would override Johnson's vetoes and overwhelm his plans for a conciliatory reunification of the United States.

The Committee of Fifteen wasted no time in unsheathing its collective sword. When the lawfully elected representatives of the Southern states—most of them stalwart Confederates—returned to Congress in November 1865, the Northern Republican majorities in both houses voted to reject the membership of those states back into the Union. They refused to seat the representatives and told them to go home. Soon Stevens and the Committee of Fifteen would be known as the Joint Committee on Reconstruction. And soon he and it would determine the post-war fate of the ravaged South, and indeed all of America.

Underground Resistance

If the Southern people had been defeated, they had not agreed to it. By the end of 1865, they had been strangled by the Federal blockade, crushed militarily, devastated on the home front, denied independence as a country, and, finally, deprived of all political voice in their own affairs. Fury, sorrow, starvation, bewilderment, and exhaustion combined to beset them. Soon, underground societies and organizations like the the Knights of the White Camellia, the Knights of the Golden Horseshoe, the White League, and most famously, the Ku Klux Klan, sprang up. Some, including the Klan, began as fraternal organizations designed for fun and socializing.

As the Federal military occupation grew harsher, however, and Southern whites realized the Radical Republican government and armies intended to replace them with former slaves as the dominant force in Southern politics and society, the secret groups embraced a new agenda. They formed an underground resistance to defend their civilization from the utter extinction the War had not accomplished but the

Thaddeus Stevens Speaks

But there was nothing cowardly or underhand about Thad Stevens. The old man, shut up in his house, was forging his thunderbolt, and on December 18, with (Congressional) galleries packed, with a sprinkling of negroes, the floor crowded, he rose to challenge the Administration. It was a historical moment. Here spoke a man who was determining the immediate destiny of a people, and he spoke with the decision and force of an absolute monarch laying the law down to a cringing parliament.

Who could reconstruct? he demanded. Not the President, he said, for Congress alone had power. "The future condition of the conquered power depends on the will of the conqueror," he continued. "They must come in as new States or come in as conquered provinces.' Thereafter he referred to them as provinces—"provinces that would not be prepared to participate in constitutional government for some years." Then what? "No arrangement so proper for them as territorial governments," where they "can learn the principles of freedom and eat the fruit of foul rebellion." And when consider their restoration? Only when the Constitution had been so amended "as to secure perpetual ascendancy to the party of the Union"—meaning the Republican Party.

—Claude G. Bowers, *The Tragic Era*

post-war occupation was beginning to look as though it might. Well has Ludwell Johnson catalogued the tactics employed by this resistance movement:

> *conventional political methods . . . economic retaliation against blacks, social ostracism against whites, fraud, intimidation, and many forms of violence, including cold-blooded murder.*

That many of these acts contrasted so greatly with the wartime practices of most Confederates was another sad dividend of a dirty war and a dirty peace. After all, many Southerners said, they were only emulating the actions being perpetrated against them by a harsh occupation government, for which they had not asked, and its supporters. Charles Adams relates in *When in the Course of Human Events* how organizations like the Sons of Liberty rose up in a similar way against British loyalists in the early American colonies. These "patriots" beat the loyalists,

Thaddeus Stevens (1792-1868)

This larger-than-life giant towers over the post-war and Reconstruction periods. None in that era's dominant Republican ranks excelled him for courage, tenacity, earnestness, single-mindedness, guilelessness, concern for the plight of the blacks as a race, and disregard for personal gain. Neither did they better him for bitterness, cruelty, cynical mistrust of his fellow man, disdain for the Constitution, or lack of feelings of others and particularly for the plight of millions of Southerners. None, too, excelled him as a hater.

Speaker of the House, Vice President, and political ally Schuyler Colfax said, "the intensity of his hatred was almost next to infernal." Claude G. Bowers said of Stevens in *The Tragic Era* that "His tremendous power as a party leader lay in the biting bitterness of his tongue and the dominating arrogance of his manner, before which weaker men shriveled." "Genius and audacity without wisdom," wrote one observer, "imagination but not sagacity, cunning but not principle."

Born into poverty in Vermont, he had scant remembrance of his father. He early developed a loathing for the upper socio-economic classes that never departed. Ironically, his entire career would find him supporting those who advanced a centralized, nationalistic agenda—and the leaders of that were nearly always of the highest aristocratic class.

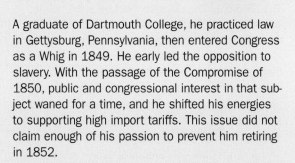

A graduate of Dartmouth College, he practiced law in Gettysburg, Pennsylvania, then entered Congress as a Whig in 1849. He early led the opposition to slavery. With the passage of the Compromise of 1850, public and congressional interest in that subject waned for a time, and he shifted his energies to supporting high import tariffs. This issue did not claim enough of his passion to prevent him retiring in 1852.

His energies revived with the emergence out of the ashes of the Northern Whig party in the mid-

tarred-and-feathered them, threatened them with death, destroyed their (and the British government's) property, and drove thousands of them out of the colonies. The Tory majority considered them terrorists, but American history calls them heroes.

Stevens' Plan

The government in Washington, meanwhile, was growing anything but more understanding with the South. They pressed forward with a constellation of political initiatives. At their head was Stevens, grim, lion-hearted, and seventy-four-years of age. He championed a program as controversial as it was comprehensive. Ludwell Johnson well summarized its key features in *North Against South:*

1) Outlawing of slavery
2) Elimination of laws discriminating by race or color

1850s of the Republican Party, a sectional party of the North founded on centralized government, ambitious internal improvements programs, industrial and big business subsidies, and high protective tariffs to fuel it all. He returned to Congress a Republican in 1858 and, by the time of the war, had acceded to the pivotal position of Chairman of the Ways and Means Committee.

Every Traitor

Like other Radicals inculcated with the Marxist spirit of the 1848 European Revolutions, Stevens saw in the War great opportunities. These included freeing the slaves; obliterating the leadership, social framework, and agrarian, Christo-centric philosophy of the South; and melding it into a sprawling transcontinental Union everywhere organized and governed by the principles and precepts of the Radical Republicans.

Stevens long dreamed of the remaking of American institutions "as to have freed them from every vestige of human oppression, of inequality of rights, of the recognized degradation of the poor, and the superior caste of the rich."

He expected, even hoped, that the South must "be laid waste, and made a desert, in order to save this Union from destruction," and he propagated the need to "slay every traitor—burn every mansion," without which he did not believe victory could come. He championed the most extreme brand of war against the South—certainly unlike any ever envisioned by the nation's Founding Fathers, for whom he held scant respect. He had no vision like Lincoln's of "binding up" the nation's wounds or helping the South to its feet and welcoming it back into the Union. His plans did not even really constitute "Reconstruction" of the defeated region. "Deconstruction" more accurately describes his vision.

The only sentiment he exhibited toward any organized religion was the Baptist Church of his mother, who was likely the one person he ever loved. Yet he displayed no outward religious profession nor practice, and his friend, the famed barrister Jeremiah S. Black, declaimed that "his mind was a howling wilderness, so far as his sense of his obligation to God was concerned." A newspaper in Lancaster, the Pennsylvania town of his home the last many years of his life, wrote that "he had been all his life a scoffer at religion and a reviler of sacred things."

Loved Blacks

Whether or not Stevens' methods for aiding Americans of African descent were wise may be debated. That he possessed keen concern for their welfare is indisputable. The year before he died, the Home for Friendless Children in Lancaster solicited him for a contribution. Fond of children, though he never had any of his own, he only donated after gaining assurance that black children would be as welcome at the institution as white.

The most intimate friend of his adult life was his housekeeper Lydia Smith, a fetching mulatto many years his junior. After her husband died, she moved into Stevens' home, and the two of them lived together, alone, for years, until he passed away. The community came to refer to her as "Mrs. Stevens," and he never disputed the many newspaper reports and editorials portraying him as living in open adultery with her.

He long dreamed of the remaking of American institutions "as to have freed them from every vestige of human oppression, of inequality of rights, of the recognized degradation of the poor, and the superior caste of the rich." No distinction would be tolerated in this purified Republic "but what arose from merit and conduct." Indeed, no distinction, no Bible, no Constitution, no international or common law would be tolerated that did not contribute to his agendas.

Perhaps no one has penned an epitaph for Thaddeus Stevens superior to that of Bowers:

> *And he could not compromise—that was at once his strength and weakness. It made him a leader while he lived, and a failure in the perspective of the years. He held no council, heeded no advice, hearkened to no warning, and with an iron will he pushed forward as his instinct bade, defying, if need be, the opinion of his time, and turning it by sheer force to his purpose.*

A striking figure on the canvas of history—stern, arrogant, intense, with a threatening light in his eye, and something between a sneer and a Voltairian smile upon his thin, hard lips. Such was the greatest party and congressional leader of his time.

3) Prohibiting payment of Confederate war debts
4) Support of heavy export tariffs—primarily to tax Southern cotton
5) Reduction of Southern states to territorial status
6) Granting blacks the right to vote
7) Confiscation of Southern plantations for redistribution to blacks

The first pillar of Stevens' program, the passage of the Thirteenth Amendment officially terminating slavery in areas of the North not addressed by the Emancipation Proclamation, was grafted into the Constitution that same December. The amendment's guarantee of emancipation for all slaves held additional import because some people said Lincoln did not have the authority to free the slaves in his Emancipation Proclamation. Thus, the Thirteenth Amendment settled the constitutional question. Ironically, though slavery had ceased to exist in the South, it survived in isolated instances in the North 1868, when the U.S. Supreme Court put down the final challenges to it.

Now the antebellum concerns of Robert E. Lee grew more pertinent than ever:

> The best men in the South have long desired to do away with the institution, and were quite willing to see it abolished. But with them in relation to this subject the question has been: What will you do with the freed people? That is a serious question today. Unless some humane course, based on wisdom and Christian principles, is adopted, you do them a great injustice in setting them free.

"Young Woman with a Basket" of cotton after the War in Georgia.

The Ku Klux Klan

Few names in the English language symbolize the specter of villainy and hatred more chillingly than the Klan. Since the 1920s, this organization has epitomized brutality, racism, religious bigotry, and atop it all, hypocrisy, as the names of Christ and God are invoked in its defense and banners emblazoned with Christian crosses are brandished alongside those of the American flag and the Confederate Battle Flag.

The Klan began after the War as a young men's fraternal organization. But the hard, often-brutal peace the North waged through the Radicals' Reconstruction agenda drove it in a different direction. Klansmen initially fought in the political arena against the Radicals' usurious cotton tax, and they fought in the fields and streets and homes to protect the cotton itself, cotton gins, and virtually every other type of Southern property, including people's homes. Klansmen saw themselves as defenders of Southern civilization against carpetbag and scalawag politicians and hundreds of thousands of armed, increasingly-militant Union Leaguers.

Warnings, threats—many of them delivered in a friendly manner—and intimidation against these adversaries constituted the vast majority of the Klan's aggressive acts. A common Klan trick involved asking blacks for water while "Night Riding" in white linen hood, cloak, and trousers, atop a horse similarly cloaked. The Klansman would pour

C. K. Berryman's portrayal of an original white-hooded and -cloaked, night-riding Ku Klux Klansman. The Klan of the 1860s and 1870s in the South was very different from the national organization that sprang up in the 20th century and was most numerous in the Midwest.

large amounts of water through his mouth opening and down a tube into a rubber sack hidden under his garb. Then he would announce that he had traveled a thousand miles in twenty-four hours and "that was the best water I have had since I was killed at the battle of Shiloh."

Another Night Riding ruse was to arrive at a black's hut, visit for a few moments while remaining mounted, then remove the garbed Klansman's "head"—in reality a pillow wrapped in linen sheets and positioned atop his actual head—hold it in his arms, and continue conversing. These and many other stunts did not fool all their intended victims, but they fooled many, enough so that the ex-Confederates noticed a general improvement in attitude from the blacks, an elevated work ethic, and a return to work by many of them. All this encouraged Klansmen to persist, and even increase their campaign.

Klansmen saw themselves as defenders of Southern civilization against carpetbag and scalawag politicians and hundreds of thousands of armed, increasingly-militant Union Leaguers.

Vicious Violence

Often, however, Klansmen committed deeds that were anything but good-natured or humorous. The South was devastated, its manhood slaughtered, its women widowed, and its children fatherless or orphaned. The Radicals had a vice-grip on power North and South; they were blaming Southerners for the War, and their intentions to utilize black freedmen as their agents for assuming permanent control of the South and its institutions grew ever more clear. Former Confederates not only saw their opportunity, power, and often their safety vanishing, they saw the Radicals wanted nothing less than to reverse the societal position of Southern whites and blacks.

A harvest of hate bloomed in the hearts of the white South. Many ex-Confederates retaliated against the outrages of freedmen and Union Leaguers. Many others did not wait to be wronged; coarse and hardened by years of fighting, they plunged into a new cycle of violence sometimes more vicious than anything seen in the War.

Charles Adams in *When in the Course of Human Events* recounted a horrifying specter. Broad sections of Confederate veterans considered former slaves who had joined the Federal army as part of the United States Colored Troops, then killed Southerners, helped burn their homes, plunder their goods, and starve many of them, as criminals and traitors to their own civilization. Unfortunately for many of these black U.S. veterans, they were not then allowed to emigrate North because of Northern Black Codes that prohibited them from entering many of those states. One group of Confederate veterans, executing vengeance on an ex-USCT soldier, Adams writes, "swore they meant to kill every black son-of-a— they could find that had ever fought against them."

In numerous Southern states, including Louisiana, South Carolina, Mississippi, and Tennessee, pitched battles broke out between members of the Klan or similar organizations, and Radical blacks and whites. The numbers of dead and wounded sometimes climbed into the hundreds.

What They Did

And, indeed, they did kill many. The log of accusations is virtually endless. Armed whites killed four blacks and wounded fifty-four at an October 1870 Republican campaign in Eutaw, Alabama. Blacks were lynched in many sections of the South.

Many blacks elected to office while the sweep of white Southerners were not allowed even to vote feared for their very lives. Black United States politician Emanuel Fortune fled Jackson County, Florida for fear of the Klan. He said: "The object of it is to kill out the leading men of the Republican Party . . . men who have taken a prominent stand."

At least one-tenth of the black members of the constitutional conventions spawned in the South by the Radicals' Reconstruction Acts suffered violence; seven were murdered. Historian Eric Foner recounts how Andrew Flowers was whipped by whites after he defeated a white for a Chattanooga justice of the peace position. "They said they had nothing particular against me, that they didn't dispute I was a very good fellow . . . but they did not intend any n— to hold office in the United States," Flowers said.

These and countless other atrocities were claimed. Many indeed occurred, but how many—and how many were accurately recounted? Over and over, Radical politicians waved "The Bloody Shirt" at election time, announcing white Southern outrages against black and white Radicals, in order to fire up Northern voters. The records of many of these accusers demonstrate dishonesty and deception in other areas of their lives. What portion of their "Bloody Shirt" rhetoric was true?

For instance, a significant number of crimes apparently committed by the Klan and similar clandestine groups were carried out by the hand of pro-Radical forces. A Radical-appointed Federal Marshal in North Carolina wrote, "I have also heard of combinations of negroes calling themselves Ku Klux and committing outrages [against other blacks]. . . . It has been charged that they have mobbed negroes for the [Democratic] ticket." Mississippi passed an anti-Klan law in 1870. It offered large rewards for the conviction of anyone committing a crime while dressed in a disguise. The first men charged were a group of blacks dressed as Klansmen who attacked a black man named Adam Kennard.

John B. Gordon

The Vision

For what purpose did the Klan's leaders say it was berthed? General John Gordon, one of the greatest Confederate generals of the latter half of the War, and a leader of the post-war South, headed the clandestine group in his home state of Georgia. He told the Congressional committee investigating the Klan:

> *The Union League and Carpetbaggers were organizing the negroes and we were afraid to have a public organization because we supposed it would be construed at once by the authorities of Washington as an organization antagonistic to the Government of the United States.*
>
> *It was therefore necessary in order to protect our families from outrage and preserve our own lives, to have something that we could regard as a brotherhood—a combination of the best men of the country to act purely in self defense, to repel the attack in case we should be attacked by these people; mainly confined to soldiers of the Confederate States Army, men who had shown themselves plucky and ready for any emergency, and who were accustomed to command.*
>
> *We never had any apprehension from the conduct of the negroes until unscrupulous men came among them and tried to stir up strife. But for such men we never would have had any trouble with the negro and would not have any now. We can get along forever with the negro, loving him and having him love us, if you will take away these Carpetbaggers.*
>
> *I am willing to swear until I am gray that the negroes and the white people can live together in Georgia peaceably and happily if they are not interfered with.*
>
> *The feeling of resentment against the reconstruction policy of Congress was intensified by the admission of the State of Georgia to the Union with the [new state] Constitution upon which the people refused to vote.*

"Worse Than Slavery," *Harper's Weekly's* (www.harpweek.com) stinging post-war caricature of the efforts of conservative Southern organizations such as the White League and Ku Klux Klan to keep blacks in a subordinate societal position. As is evidenced elsewhere in this volume, New York City-based *Harper's* consistently supported the Radicals' Reconstruction agenda, and with the pens of Thomas Nast and others, missed no opportunity to paint those who opposed it in the worst possible light. Rarely if ever addressed by the publication was the crucial role played by the Federals' wartime and post-war policies in provoking what violent reprisals by white Southerners that did occur.

Gordon was only one of thousands of respectable Southern men from the leadership ranks who joined the Klan. Women from the leadership ranks did their part too. "The history of the Civil War South belongs to the 'men and women,' the history of Reconstruction (and the Ku Klux Klan) belong to the 'women and men,'" historian William D. Polk wrote, "for in that dire period when the men had almost collapsed, and were bewildered on their way, the women encouraged them to still fight on, for 'Field and Fireside,' under the leadership of the Ku Klux Klan, between the years 1865 and 1877." Susan Lawrence Davis recounts in her book *The Authentic History of the Ku Klux Klan* how Southern women produced the Klan's regalia, cap-tained their households when the men were away, and guarded the organization's secrets. Their goals, said Davis, were "safety for the white race, safety for separation of Church and State, safety for Civilization in saving our Republican form of government."

Requiem

Nathan Bedford Forrest was the first "Grand Wizard" of the Klan. That name, shameful in its 20th- and 21st-century manifestations, stemmed from Forrest's famed sobriquet of the War, the "Wizard of the Saddle." In 1869, the Democrats regained control of political power in Tennessee, where Forrest lived. Simultaneously, he witnessed the escalation of lawless acts by men in hoods—some Klan, some not. The intersection of these developments prompted Forrest to issue a general order disbanding the entire organization, and he resigned from it himself. Its legitimate purposes, he said, were fulfilled.

The Klan intimidated and it defended. It bullied and it lifted up. It destroyed and it built and rebuilt.

But many Southern whites had no intention of retiring from Night Riding and other Klan or Klan-type pursuits. Some of these were less principled men who simply wanted black men dead or gone. But many belonged to Klan-like organizations in states where the Radicals still had their heel on the throat of white Southern civilization. The fight for survival might be over in Tennessee, they reasoned, but it was not in their states. The Red Shirts of South Carolina, the Knights of the White Camelia and the White League of Louisiana, and men in other states who still claimed Klan and similar membership generally carried on their resistance until Democrats wrested political control from the Radicals.

Indeed, the "Klan" has evolved into an umbrella term covering many people in many organizations or no organizations at all, and sometimes impostors and enemies of the Klan. Clandestine white resistance movements in the South ceased their organized efforts at various junctures between 1869 and the final curtain of Reconstruction in 1877.

And so the question lingers—how to assess the original Ku Klux Klan? Like much else during the half-century between 1828 and 1877, that answer depends largely on the viewpoint of the observer. The Klan intimidated and it defended. It bullied and it lifted up. It destroyed and it built and rebuilt. It brought fear and loathing and shame—and pride and honor and hope. It murdered, and it arguably saved Southern civilization.

Resistance groups in Scotland, Ireland, Russia, France, England, the Netherlands, India, the Balkans, China, Mexico, South America, the Middle East, and nearly every other corner of the globe—including the early American colonies—have fought tyranny and despotism, imperfectly and sometimes wrongly and in some respects wickedly. Were they—the original Klansmen—terrorists and criminals, or patriots and martyrs for their cause? Or both?

Nathan Bedford Forrest, during Reconstruction. He reportedly helped lead the original Ku Klux Klan as a Southern resistance organization against the vindictive Federal occupation, then ordered its disbanding when he felt the regaining of Southern political power had rendered it obsolete.

The New Klan

One of the enduring canards of American popular culture is that the Ku Klux Klan of the 1860s was the same organization with the same objectives as the KKK of the 20th and 21st centuries. The original Klan arose in response to what its members felt was an oppressive foreign empire drenched in the blood of Southern patriots. This Klan, whatever its admixture of good and evil, went out of existence in the 1870s.

Not until around 1920 did the "modern" KKK emerge. Its objectives and membership were vastly different from the original Klan. It sprang up in every corner of America; its most fervent activity centered in the Midwest, not the South. The new organization was nativist and anti-immigrant, except those from Protestant Northern Europe. It possessed a much longer list of enemies than the old. Its members considered blacks, Jews, Catholics, and people of every ethnic makeup besides full-blooded whites as mortal enemies—and mortal enemies of the Christian faith in which they have long blasphemously wreathed themselves. The new KKK has tarnished the names of Confederate heroes, brought infamy to the Confederate Battle Flag, and indeed made a byword and a mockery of the South itself with huge sections of the American population.

There never was a time before or since its organization when such an Order as the (1865–1877) Ku Klux Klan could have lived. May there never be again!

—Nathan Bedford Forrest's final words to the original Ku Klux Klan

Perhaps the most eloquent refutation of the aims and very existence of the latter-day Ku Klux Klan was uttered in 1875 by the original Klan's first Grand Wizard, Nathan Bedford Forrest, when he addressed a large barbecue gathering of Shelby County blacks at the fairgrounds east of Memphis:

> *Ladies and gentlemen—I accept the flowers as a memento of reconciliation between the white and colored races of the Southern states. . . . I came here with the jeers of some white people, who think that I am doing wrong. I believe I can exert some influence, and do much to assist the people in strengthening fraternal relations, and shall do all in my power to elevate every man—to depress none. I want to elevate you to take positions in law offices, in stores, on farms, and wherever you are capable of going. . . . I came to meet you as friends, and welcome you to the white people. I want you to come nearer to us. When I can serve you I will do so. We have but one flag, one country; let us stand together. We may be different in color, but not in sentiment. . . . I have been in the heat of battle when colored men asked me to protect them. I have placed myself between them and the bullets of my men, and told them they should be kept unharmed. Go to work, be industrious, live honestly and act truly, and when you are oppressed I'll come to your relief. I thank you, ladies and gentlemen, for this opportunity you have afforded me to be with you, and to assure you that I am with you in heart and in hand.*

33 Reconstruction

Matthew Brady's famous full-length portrait of Robert E. Lee, standing outside the back door of his rented home in Richmond following the War.

Is it not time that these [Southern] men be transplanted at least into the nineteenth century, and, if they cannot be suddenly Americanized, made to understand something of the country which was too good for them . . .

—Poet James Russell Lowell

All through 1866, the Radical-controlled Congress battled President Johnson over how to deal with the South. A tenacious battle it was, with results by no means certain at the outset. Johnson had siding with him both the Democrats and a significant minority of moderate Republicans. As mentioned earlier, this fight was only one front of the larger conflict to determine what would be the character of the United States of America.

I disagree with those who think these [Southern] States are but territories. We fought . . . upon the theory that a State cannot secede.

—Republican Senator John A. Logan

The Radicals pushed through their first big bill in early February. It continued, broadened, and strengthened the Freedmen's Bureau. Ostensibly designed with the laudable goal to aid blacks with food, supplies, land, and employment, the bill ignored existing American law in that pursuit.

The new Freedmen's Bureau bill declared up to three million acres of Southern land eligible to be given to freedmen, with no remuneration to anyone. The South was to be divided into hundreds of districts, which would be administered by thousands of new government bureaucrats. These bureaucrats had no oversight from Congress, because the Freedman's Bureau was an extra-governmental entity. Required to fend for itself financially, it found ingenious methods of doing so, including selling off Southern land to wealthy Northern merchants and politicos.

Bureau agents possessed the authority to arrest virtually anyone they wished. They required no indictment. Those they charged had no right to a jury trial. No law constrained members of a Freedmen's Bureau court-martial from exacting any penalty they decided, and no appeal of their sentence was allowed, no writ of error in any court of law. All this, and Southern states had no voice at all in any of it, because the Radicals considered them, variously, as "territories" (Sumner) or "conquered provinces" (Stevens).

Johnson thundered forth his opposition: "I cannot reconcile a system of military jurisdiction of this kind with the Constitution. Where in the Constitution is authority to expend public funds to aid indigent people? Where the right to take the white man's land and give it to others without 'due process of law'?" His veto at first stymied the bill. House and Senate alike passed a second Freedmen's Bureau Bill over his veto in June.

The Freedmen's Bureau

As Federal troops advanced in the final year of the War, increasing numbers of emancipated slaves came into their lines. Thousands of these were invited—or forced—to serve in the U.S. military forces. But Congress realized the need for a more comprehensive and long range plan to handle the huge numbers of erstwhile slaves.

The Freedmen's Bureau primary school for black children in Vicksburg, outside and inside, as rendered in *Harper's Weekly* (www.harpweek.com).

After a year of negotiation and political maneuvering and sparring, Congress passed a bill in March 1865 creating the Freedman's Bureau. It fell under the auspices of the War Department, but the Bureau had no budget and thus no official governmental jurisdiction. The Radical Republican Congress bequeathed it responsibility to gather its own budget—and authority to govern itself.

Among other directives, the Freedmen's Bureau was to provide food, shelter, and clothing for "destitute and suffering refugees and freemen and their families." And its Commissioner received authorization to give freedmen land stolen by the United States government from Southern citizens. According to Ludwell Johnson in *North Against South*, though the Bureau was "supposedly a relief and educational institution," it "materially assisted no more than 0.5 per cent of the four million ex-slaves'" or approximately 20,000 people. Though claiming to bring thousands of white Southerners back onto their farms and get those farms operating again, the agency's accomplishment in this area was at best negligible.

Southern blacks built and sustained many of their own schools without aid from the Freedman's Bureau.

Southern blacks built and sustained many of their own schools without aid from the Freedman's Bureau. Some Southern whites offered moral support for black schools and some did not. Some damaged or burned school houses and harassed or even attacked the teachers. Native whites, many of whom had lost all their possessions and their loved ones in the War, or themselves been maimed, directed particular resentment toward Northern teachers who criticized the Confederacy and championed the Yankee war effort as they taught Southern school children.

Accomplishments

One of the Freedmen's Bureau's most successful endeavors was its sending out waves of agents across the South to confiscate Southern property, which it then sold—to non-Southerners—to pay the agents hefty commissions and fund its own operations. A more noble accomplishment was the

Bureau's role in establishing black colleges, including Atlanta University, Fisk University, Hampton Institute, and Howard University, which was named in honor of Federal General Oliver O. Howard.

An August, 1867 report on the work of the Freedmen's Bureau that was signed by Howard and Supreme Court Chief Justice Salmon P. Chase helps place in perspective the challenges and objectives for the agency in the minds of those who supported and helped lead it:

> *The abolition of slavery and the establishment of freedom are not the one and the same thing. The emancipated negroes were not yet really freemen. Their chains had indeed been sundered by the sword, but the broken links still hung upon their limbs. The question, "What shall be done with the negro?" agitated the whole country. Some were in favour of an immediate recognition of their equal and political rights, and of conceding to them at once all the prerogatives of citizenship. But only a few advocated a policy so radical, and, at the same time, generally considered revolutionary, while many, even of those who really wished well to the negro, doubted his capacity for citizenship, his willingness to labour for his own support, and the possibility of his forming, as a freeman, an integral part of the Republic.*

Civil Rights Bill

In April, the Radicals rammed through a companion measure, the Civil Rights Bill. Once again, it was freighted with honorable objectives. For instance, it pronounced full citizenship benefits for blacks, with the right

> in every State and Territory . . . to make and enforce contracts, to sue, be parties, and give evidence, to inherit, purchase, lease, sell, hold, and convey real and personal property, and to full and equal benefit of all laws and proceedings for the security of person and property, as is enjoyed by white citizens, and shall be subject to like punishment, pains, and penalties, and to none other, any law statute, ordinance, regulation, or custom, to the contrary notwithstanding.

And as before, the methods the Radicals employed to advance the bill were extraordinary and unconstitutional. For one, it authorized (mostly Radical) Federal court-appointed "commissioners" to be paid incentive fees for every violation they booked. Again, Johnson boomed forth to the nation his opposition to the provisions:

> They interfere with the municipal regulations of the states, with the relations existing exclusively between a State and its citizens, or between inhabitants of the same State—an absorption and assumption of power by the General Government which, if acquiesced in, must sap and destroy our federative system of limited powers, and break down the barriers which preserve the rights of the States. It is another step, or rather stride, to centralization and the concentration of all legislative power in the National Government.

Johnson Opposes

Johnson cited numerous reasons for vetoing the Civil Rights Bill:

1) Eleven of the 36 states had no

Congressional representation and thus no voice in the matter, though it primarily concerned them, and they would have to live under its provisions.

2) The bill transferred long-held legislative rights from the state governments to the federal government—though, again, 11 of those states had say in the change.

3) It created "numerous . . . sort of police . . . agents irresponsible to the Government and to the people . . . in whose hands such authority might be made a terrible engine of wrong, oppression, and fraud," agents who could arrest at their pleasure.

4) The fees paid the commissioners for arrests and hearings "might convert any law, however beneficent, into an instrument of persecution and fraud."

5) He recognized that the agents responsible possessed a vested interest in fomenting discord between the two races, for "as the breach widens their employment will continue."

The Radicals, led by Stevens in the House and Sumner, Benjamin Wade, and others in the Senate, exerted party pressure against their fellow Republicans until they managed to override Johnson's veto. Indeed, party pressure began to tell in Washington, as key moderates like Oliver Morton, John Logan, and John W. Forney shifted their support from the President to the Radicals. And fiery James Lane, grim chieftain of the Kansas Jayhawkers, committed suicide. Lane's politics had trended away from the Radicals late in the War and toward the more moderate Reconstruction policies of Lincoln and Johnson. Withal, Johnson's contingent of support was thinning in both houses of Congress.

Fourteenth Amendment

This Stevens-spearheaded bill proved one of the most contentious in American history. It was a years'-long battle opened in May, 1866, when Stevens presented the version he had ramrodded through the pivotal Committee of Fifteen. Most positive about the amendment was its granting of full citizenship and legal rights to "All persons born or naturalized in the United States." The bill clearly had blacks in mind here. That race was prohibited from voting not only in the South, but in many Northern states as well.

You [Radicals] let the negroes vote in Ohio before you talk about negroes voting in Louisiana. Take the beam out of your own eye before you see the mote that is in your neighbor's. You are very much disturbed about New Orleans, but you won't let a negro go to the ballot box to vote in Ohio.

—President Andrew Johnson

It is important to remember that among the many enigmatic features of Radical Republican rule at this juncture of American history is the counting of former Confederate states in the three-fourths majority of states neces-

Robert E. Lee (Part 2) (1807-1870)

Ironically, Robert E. Lee's greatest legacy is perhaps as a peacemaker, rather than a warrior. Following the War, the South lay in rubble, its manhood decimated, a harsh Federal troop occupation further crushing it, and financial opportunists descending upon it from across the United States. Lee recognized the issue was no less than the survival of the Southern people and culture. Many Northerners desired the utter destruction of the South as a recognizable culture. Bitterness and hatred filled most Southerners.

But wisdom seasoned his thoughts and actions. He rebuked younger officers who advocated continuing the War with guerilla tactics; he refused to countenance or support large-scale emigration of Confederates to foreign lands; he urged Southerners to work lawfully and cheerfully within the existing laws of the United States to rebuild their fortunes and their land; and most of all, he beseeched them to forgive and forget wrongs committed against them by Federals past and present.

He counseled one of his many lovely, but bitter, young female admirers thus: "I want you to take a message to your friends. Tell them from me that it is unworthy of them as women, and especially as Christian women, to cherish feelings of resentment against the North. Tell them that it grieves me inexpressibly to know that such a state of things exists, and that I implore them to do their part to heal our country's wounds."

Over 20,000 people attended Robert E. Lee's funeral, even though it took place in the remote Shenandoah Valley town of Lexington, easy transportation there was not available, and terrific floods had cut off most of the normal routes to the town.

All the while, offers and opportunities cascaded in from around the South, across the United States, and even other nations. Railroads, insurance companies, corporations of every stripe offered Lee positions of leadership. One wealthy Englishman offered him a sprawling estate in the land of his forefathers, for life, at no cost. Leaders of the Democratic Party—most of them former Federal military officers—petitioned him to accept their party's nomination for President, and oppose Republican nominee U. S. Grant—and some of the North's most powerful newspapers cheered him on in print!

College President

But, as he often did, despite his simple dignity and guileless ways, he surprised nearly everyone when he took the helm of tiny, war-ransacked Washington College in the backwater Virginia mountain village of Lexington—where Stonewall Jackson spent the decade before the War. With no assistant, scant budget, and beset by the burgeoning health problems of his aging body, Lee set about rebuilding the school, placing special emphasis on what curricula would best prepare the young men of the South to rebuild their land.

Yet many times, in many ways, he voiced his primary concern. Rev. Dr. Thomas J. Kirkpatrick, professor of moral philosophy at Washington College, recalled Lee's words: "Oh, Doctor! if I could only know that all the young men in this college were good Christians, I should have nothing more to desire!"

Time and again he counseled forbearance and forgiveness on the part of his students, friends, family, and people across the South toward mercenary Northern carpetbaggers, Southern blacks, and Federal occupation forces. No one ever tabulated how many thousands of letters he received from Southerners seeking his counsel on what to do.

Lee was not without opposition even until he died. Many of the Radical Republican leaders wanted him hanged for treason. An austere Congressional committee grilled him more than once in Washington, seeking evidence with which to prosecute him. They failed at every turn, as the Constitutional course of Lee's actions became obvious even to those who despised both him and the Constitution.

Abolitionist leader and *Liberator* publisher William Lloyd Garrison decried Lee's place at the head of a college:

> *Who is . . . more obdurate than himself? He at the head of a patriotic institution, teaching loyalty to the Constitution, and the duty of maintaining that Union he so lately attempted to destroy! . . . Has Lucifer regained his position in Heaven? . . . If the South could reasonably hope to succeed in another rebellious uprising, and should make the attempt, who can show us any ground for believing that Gen. Lee would not again act as generalissimo of her forces?*

One of the many legacies left Robert E. Lee was Lee Chapel, on the campus of Washington College (now Washington and Lee University), where he served as president the last five years of his life. Lee designed the building himself and chose to keep his office in its basement. He and many of his family members now rest in crypts inside the structure.

Peacemaker

Still, as Lee's peaceable, forbearing example became manifest, as well as the fruits of his leadership at resurgent Washington College, his legion of admirers grew, even in the North. "My whole trust is in God, and I am ready for whatever He may ordain," Lee said. The last morning of his own life, Abraham Lincoln had been given by his soldier son Robert a photograph of Lee. "It is a good face; it is the face of a noble, noble, brave man," Lincoln said. "I am glad that the war is over." By the time of his death in 1870, most Southerners had followed his example, remained in their homeland, pursued peaceable ways, and put their hand to the plow of rebuilding their country.

*How Firm a Foundation** Author unknown

How firm a foundation, ye saints of the Lord,
is laid for your faith in His excellent Word!
What more can He say than to you he hath said,
To you who for refuge to Jesus have fled?

The soul that on Jesus hath leaned for repose
I will not, I will not desert to his foes;
That soul, though all hell should endeavor to shake,
I'll never, no, never, no never forsake!

*Robert E. Lee's favorite hymn

"I have never so truly felt the purity of his character as now, when I have nothing left me but its memory," the person who knew him better than anyone else, Mary, wrote a close friend. "God knows the best time for us to leave this world and we must never question either His love or wisdom. This is my comfort in my great sorrow, to know that had my husband lived a thousand years he could not have died more honoured and lamented even had he accomplished all we desired and hoped."

"He is an epistle, written of God," Edward Gordon, Lee's former assistant at Washington College, wrote, "and designed by God to teach the people of this country that earthly success is not the criterion of merit, nor the measure of true greatness."

My experience through life has convinced me that,
while moderation and temperance in all things are commendable
and beneficial, abstinence from spiritous liquor is the
best safeguard of morals and health.

—Robert E. Lee, near the end of his life

sary to amend the Constitution—though they had no Congressional representation and Congress did not consider them states. Among other things, the proposed Fourteenth Amendment outlawed anyone who supported the Confederacy from voting (much less holding office) in any election until July 4, 1870 and it entered into the Constitution the framework of the Civil Rights Act.

Viewed in its totality, Stevens' package wrested almost complete control over their lives and communities from Southerners and placed them into the hands of the Radical-controlled U.S. government. Even many Republicans shrunk back. Congressman and *New York Times* publisher Henry Raymond accused Stevens of designing the amendment so that Southern states could not adopt it. It would make the South another Ireland, Raymond

Riots and Lynchings

The North had crushed the South militarily. Now its Radical Republican majority determined to do the same politically. But these and other events were spawning a whirlwind that is still being reaped in America. Even those like Thaddeus Stevens and William Lloyd Garrison who genuinely sought the welfare of black Americans were in the process of undermining their own goals for political and social change.

In seeking to use—with the evident authority of bayonets—black freedmen as a lever of power against the white conservative majority in the South, the Radicals gave many blacks a false sense of security and hope and turned masses of Southern whites against them. Too, they engendered with their "Reconstruction" a bitter hatred from Southern whites far beyond what had existed at the end of the War.

The post-war era was a time of greed and arrogance in the North and poverty, hunger, and bitterness in the South. It was a mean low time of uncounted corrupt schemes and violent acts. Two particularly bloody episodes exploded into the national spotlight in 1866. The first occurred in May in Memphis. The combination of Federal disfranchisement of Southern whites and a wave of Irish immigration into the city elevated the Irish to prominence in local government and law enforcement. This, coupled with a tidal wave of former black slave emigration into the city from the surrounding countryside, generated a similarly uneasy social admixture as that which fueled the bloody New York City draft riots of 1863.

The post-war era was a time of greed and arrogance in the North and poverty, hunger, and bitterness in the South.

A garrison of 4,000 black Federal soldiers had stirred mounting controversy in the city for drunkenness, bullying of white citizens, and other misbehavior. When a group of these men, who were drunk, stoned some Irish policemen attempting to break up a fight and apparently shot one of them, the Irish police and a mob of laborers, also mostly non-Southern Irish, hurtled into the black soldiers, and a full-scale race riot ensued.

The Irish-dominated white mob gained the upper hand in the vicious fighting and proceeded upon an indiscriminate slaughter of blacks in the community. Robberies abounded, hundreds of buildings were sacked, damaged or destroyed, and nearly fifty people died, hundreds were injured, and five raped, the overwhelming majority of people in all these categories black.

New Orleans

In July, Northern Radicals sought a convention in New Orleans to reverse the lawful city and state government elections of the year before. These had replaced Unionists backed by the Federal occupation forces with native Louisianans elected by popular vote.

Numerous community leaders attempted to dissuade the organizers from the convention, which had no legal basis. However, Thaddeus Stevens and other Radical congressmen gave their assent. Even more importantly, Secretary of War Stanton ignored the request of the local Federal military commander for permission to prevent the convention. This, even though Stanton knew President Johnson had already sanctioned that course of action.

So the convention proceeded. One of its leaders, Dr. A. P. Dostie, shouted to a crowd of 2–3,000, mostly black: "I want no cowards to come. . . . We are 400,000 to 300,000 and can not only whip but exterminate the other party . . . . The streets of New Orleans will run with blood."

The next day, the convention itself met peaceably at Mechanics' Institute until a parade of blacks marched through city streets toward it, some shouldering rifles, the rest clubs and the like. Outside the institute, shouting and jostling occurred, then someone apparently shot at a policeman. Now the assembled police force and numerous deputized locals charged from police headquarters and waded into the black column as well as the conventioneers. Respectable whites in the community were conspicuously absent from the donnybrook that ensued.

No accurate accounting of casualties ever emerged from the maelstrom, though at least 40 police and deputies are thought to have died or been wounded. As in Memphis, black casualties appeared much higher, though no official total was ever produced. At least some of the blacks were murdered for their skin color.

The Radicals exploited these riots in the 1866 elections to paint the South as a savage land of lawless racist butchers. Philip Sheridan, however, in command of New Orleans though in Texas when the melee occurred, agreed that Dostie's speech helped provoke the slaughter, and that the convention organizers were "political agitators and bad men." By the close of Reconstruction in the late 1870s, thousands of conservative Southerners—black and white—had been intimidated, robbed, assaulted or murdered by Federal legions. And thousands of pro-Union blacks had suffered similar fates, at the hand of blacks and whites alike, many by lynching.

No Love Lost

The words of Radical Republican Congressman (and future House Speaker) Oliver P. Morton of Indiana provide a glimpse of the intensity of emotion generated by the political battles of the 1866 election season:

> *Every unregenerate rebel . . . calls himself a Democrat. Every bounty jumper, every deserter, every sneak who ran away from the draft calls himself a Democrat . . . Every man who murdered Union prisoners . . . who invented dangerous compounds to burn steamboats and Northern cities, who contrived hellish schemes to introduce into Northern cities . . . yellow fever, calls himself a Democrat. Every dishonest contractor . . . every dishonest paymaster . . . every officer in the army who was dismissed for cowardice calls himself a Democrat . . . . Every wolf in sheep's clothing who shoots down negroes in the streets . . . and murders women and children by the light of their own flaming dwellings, calls himself a Democrat. In short, the Democratic Party may be described as a common sewer and loathsome receptacle.*

Oliver P. Morton

declared, in reference to that then-unhappy subject of Britain. Another colleague asked Stevens if he could build a penitentiary large enough for eight million people. "Yes," Stevens thundered, "a penitentiary which is built at the point of the bayonet down below, and if they undertake to come here we will shoot them down."

The House passed the measure, and the Senate too, though the latter made revisions. Still, the act remained sufficiently devastating that voices howled in disbelief across the South, most of which still lay in ruins. All that now stood between the South and this watershed bill becoming law was that three-fourths of the states' legislatures' approval.

1866 Elections

Twenty-first century Americans, concerned that modern elections have deteriorated from honorable affairs of statesmanship to mud-slinging and character assassination, have not studied the remarkable 1866 election season. This marked the midpoint of Andrew Johnson's inherited term, so there was no presidential election. Congressional and gubernatorial races, however, abounded.

All this shaped up as a titanic struggle between Johnson and Stevens, though millions stood in support of both. The President, the Democrats, and the conservative wing of the Republican Party urged a conciliatory agenda that featured freedom for former slaves as well as readmittance to the Union with full rights for the Southern states. The Stevens-led Radical brigades, meanwhile, wanted expanded rights for freedmen, partly to accomplish their aim that the Southern states, if ever they hoped readmittance to the Union, must first be made over into mirror societal and cultural images of the New England states.

It was a fight over control of the destiny not only of the South, but of the entire nation. And a vicious fight it was. Johnson was called, among things, "vulgar," "despicable," "mobocrat," "besotted," "traitorous," "a dog," and "the great criminal of our age and country." Radical House leader Wendell Phillips of Massachusetts wanted him impeached. So did fellow Massachusetts Congressman Ben Butler, and arrested as well.

Abolitionist Wendell Phillips of Massachusetts, a leading Radical Republican before, during, and after the War.

There is danger from the growing corruption which festers when far-off States are put under the control of agents with unusual and undefined powers, meddling not only with public concerns, but with private business and family affairs. These agents, mostly adventurers and men unknown to the people, and beyond the reach of the eye of those who pay the cost of keeping them, are more tempted by love of power and lust for money to act corruptly. This form of government for the South, base and debasing, lives only by keeping up the passions and hates of the people of this country.

—New York Governor Horatio Seymour

The Democrats actually won a higher percentage of the national vote than they had in either 1860 or 1864, and they gained seven seats in the House. But the Republicans won every contested governor's race and kept control of both houses of Congress.

As the champagne glasses of Republican powers Henry Cooke, Schuyler Colfax, John Sherman, and others clinked in the Washington branch bank of Jay Cooke & Company, the *London Telegraph* penned a different reaction: The United States "may remain a republic in name, but some eight million of the people are subjects, not citizens." "We may read our destiny in the indications just at hand from the Northern elections," wrote one Southerner, "utter ruin and abject degradation are our portion." Bowers in *The Tragic Era* summed it up so: "It was in these elections that the old Republic of Jefferson went down and the agriculturists were definitely shunted aside to make way for the triumphant industrialists and capitalists."

Sowing the Wind

The Southern "former" states could not do much about it, but what they could they did. Every one of them, except now-Radical-ruled Tennessee, voted against the Fourteenth Amendment. So did Kentucky and Delaware, and thus the amendment failed for lack of the needed three-fourths majority.

Former North Carolina Governor Jonathan Worth declared his opposition to the legislation: "If we are to be degraded, we will retain some self-esteem by not making it self-abasement . . . If we were voluntarily to adopt this amendment I think we should be the meanest and most despicable people on earth." "It is one thing to be oppressed, wronged, and outraged by overwhelming force," *Mobile Register* editor John Forsyth agreed. "It is quite another to submit to voluntary abasement."

Radical fury erupted. Even as it did, then came the Supreme Court's long-awaited *Ex parte Milligan* decision. It

Henry Ward Beecher (1813-1887)

"Like a stump speaker who has mistaken his way and stumbled into church," this life powerfully demonstrates the perils of a Christian minister immersing himself in politics. Hailing from one of New England Puritanism's most respected families, his father was the famed Presbyterian cleric Lyman Beecher and his sister (Harriet Beecher Stowe) wrote *Uncle Tom's Cabin*. Before, during, and after the War, Beecher pastored the famed Plymouth Church in New York City, where attended many of America's most powerful families. An ardent abolitionist, he earned the highest salary of any pastor in the country.

Upon passage of the Compromise of 1850, which included the Fugitive Slave Law decried by Beecher and other abolitionist, he proclaimed: "Whenever the Union comes between a Christian people and their Christianity, it becomes a snare. . . . There are many evils greater than dissolution of our Union. . . . Religion and humanity are a price too dear to pay even for the Union." During the "Bleeding Kansas" troubles in the 1850s, Beecher advised that guns might be more useful than Bibles in some situations. Thereafter, the many rifles shipped from New England abolitionists to Free Soilers in boxes marked "Bibles" were roundly referred to as "Beecher Bibles."

Following John Brown's capture at Harper's Ferry for attempting to engineer a violent slave insurrection, Beecher said: "Let no man pray that Brown be spared. Let Virginia make him a martyr. His soul was noble, his work miserable. But a cord and gibbet will redeem all that and round up Brown's failure with a heroic success." After Browns' hanging, Beecher ridiculed what he considered the North's lethargy on the slavery issue: "What is average citizenship when a lunatic is a hero?" he asked.

After the War

Beecher, generally a supporter of Lincoln, initially backed Andrew Johnson and the Democrats' mild program for Reconstruction. When the Radical political and media establishment excoriated him, however, he recanted and plunged headlong in the other direction: "When in a matter of politics I am overruled, what shall I do? Shall I sulk and refuse to work?"

Theologically, Beecher symbolized the departure of the New England Puritans' progeny from their stalwart Biblical orthodoxy. Though Beecher held in form to many of those tenets, material success, social Darwinism, and the unworthiness of the poor were also among his frequent themes.

He did applaud Robert E. Lee's conciliatory postwar temper, and his application for pardon. He went so far, in fact, as to champion Lee and Washington College at a New York fundraiser for the school. Lee, Beecher said, was "pleading for mental bread for his students" and laboring to build their loyalty and love for all of the United States."

In the end, as it did many others of that generation, scandal overwhelmed this man of fame and fortune who had so sought the respect of other men. Friend, associate, and famous reform editor Theodore Tilton publicly accused Beecher of participating in an inappropriate relationship with Tilton's wife. "The greatest national spectacle" of the 1870s resulted in a hung jury regarding Beecher's guilt, but the evidence against him was overwhelming.

The Indians

The War left the Indian Territory, where the United States government had forcibly relocated Cherokees, Chickasaws, Choctaws, Creeks, and Seminoles, in ruins. These Indians, split in their allegiance to the Federals and Confederates, had seen not only those armies rampage through their lands, but the Indians themselves had turned and fought against one another among their own homes and communities.

The Southern Cherokees sent a delegation to Washington in 1866 to negotiate a new treaty with the United States. The delegates were, left to right: John Rollin Ridge, Saladin Watie (son of Stand Watie), Richard Fields, Elias C. Boudinot, and William Penn Adair. Delegates not in the picture were Stand Watie and Joseph A. Scales.

Violence came even to many Indians who attempted to retreat out of the line of fire. Many pro-Federal Indians seeking refuge in Kansas were ambushed en route by Confederate Indians. Once there, they faced attacks by William Quantrill and other Missouri "Bushwhackers," other pro-Confederate irregulars, and some aligned with neither side.

Pro-Southern Indians faced even worse odds. As U.S. Regular army control gradually spread throughout Indian Territory, Confederate Indians were forced to flee their homes en masse because of the depredations primarily of pro-Federal Indians. By war's end, many of the homes and communities of pro-North Indians were burned out and most of the pro-Southerners' were as well. Pro-North Principal Cherokee Chief John Ross's men burned long-time rival and pro-South Cherokee Chief Stand Watie's home to the ground. Later, Watie and his men burned down Ross's home.

Large numbers of pro-Confederate Indians refugeed down the Texas Trail to Confederate Texas, where they spent the remainder of the War, separated from their loved ones, fighting for the South. These Indians experienced particularly acute poverty. Even though these Indians had a non-voting representative, Watie's nephew Elias Cornelius Boudinot, in the Confederate Congress, he could secure little aid for them, because the Confederate States themselves were starving to death.

After the War

Intra-tribal contention continued after the War. Pro-Northern Indians attempted to persuade the U.S. that they had been forced to support the South. The Cherokees illustrate the problem. Separate delegations, pro-North and pro-South, traveled to Washington when the Federal government decided to "renegotiate" its treaties with the Cherokees, Creeks, and Seminoles. The Federals paid scant heed to these claims and determined to punish the tribes. They also decided to deal with the pro-Northern delegations, leaving the pro-Southern ones out of the process.

Among other adjustments to their treaty, the Cherokees had to give up 800,000 acres of their land in present-day Kansas, as well as additional land in Indian Territory for railroad right-of-ways. And they had to allow nearly a thousand Delawares and 700 Shawnees, themselves newly and forcibly removed by the United States, onto their land, and accept them as new members of their tribe.

These developments stunned the pro-Northern Indians; Cherokee Chief Ross died within days of the new treaty's signing. Meanwhile, the erstwhile Confederate Indians felt betrayed by the United States. Colonel William Penn Adair, Watie's second-in-command in the Cherokee Mounted Rifles and a pro-Southern post-war delegate to Washington, announced that the treaty "is not binding upon the Southern Cherokees, as we refused to sign it, and fought it to the last and are still fighting it."

Siding with the Confederates cost the Indians dearly. Siding with the Federals did them no good.

Siding with the Confederates cost the Indians dearly. Siding with the Federals did them no good. In the end, war devastated the five civilized tribes' homeland, and peace took away yet more of their land, liberty, and unity as they remained in bitterly divided factions.

Other Indians

To the south of Indian Territory, the Federal government would soon begin a "final solution" campaign against all Indians remaining in Texas, whether warlike or peaceful. By the time Ranald MacKenzie, Benjamin Grierson, and others finished their work in the 1870s, scarcely an Indian—man, woman or child—in all of Texas had not been killed or driven out of the state.

Farther North, through the Plains to Canada and across the Rocky Mountains into the Mojave Desert and Far West, post-war Presidential administrations unleashed a colossal effort against the Indians well summarized by the words "reservation or extermination." Of course, many were not given the opportunity for the reservation; many that were, found their reservations gradually reduced in size or moved.

The utter massacre of now-General George Armstrong Custer's 7th U.S. cavalry regiment near the Little Big Horn River in Montana by 6,000 warriors from a host of tribes, including Cheyenne and Sioux, showed what the American Indian was capable of accomplishing when united and organized. Never again would they be so, however, and an enraged American public sanctioned the Federal army's gradual grinding down of the remaining non-confined tribes until the 1890 massacre at Wounded Knee, South Dakota. There, Federal troops slaughtered three hundred Nez Perce. Most of the dead Indians were women and children.

Prior to his spectacular 1876 demise at the Battle of the Little Big Horn River, U.S. General George Armstrong Custer hunted Indians and wild game alike out West, including this grizzly bear. (National Archives and Records Administration)

"The only good Indian I ever saw was dead," Phil Sheridan told the surrendering Comanche Chief Tosawi at Fort Cobb, Indian Territory, in 1870. Sheridan himself ordered both the botched attack that became the Marias River, Montana massacre, in which 173 Piegan Indians died, one-third of them women and children, and the Cheyenne village massacre at the Battle of the Washita River in present-day Oklahoma.

No significant armed Indian opposition materialized after the Battle of the Little Big Horn. One modern-day Cherokee chief, himself the descendent of pro-Northern Cherokees, recalled recently how the Confederacy's wartime treaty with the Cherokees solved most of the latter's problems. "What if the South had won?" he wondered aloud. "It could have been a good deal for the Cherokees."

ruled unconstitutional the Federal military's capturing, imprisoning, trying, and convicting any American citizen—as happened with Northerner L. P. Milligan, whom the army sentenced to death—unless the case had direct involvement with military operations.

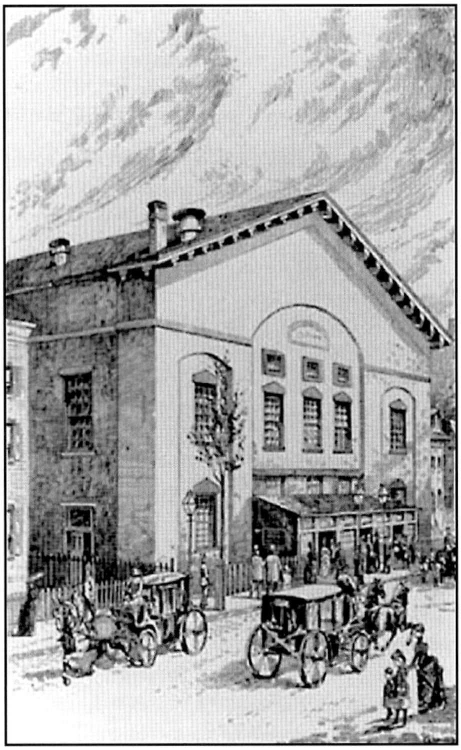

Plymouth Congregational Church in Brooklyn, New York, where Henry Ward Beecher drew weekly worship crowds of 2,500 people, and gained national renown as an orator.

(By implication, it also condemned the execution of former Andersonville Prison commandant Henry Wirz.)

Congress, declared Justice David Davis and the Court, had no right to suspend the constitutional right to a trial by jury of one's peers. Democratic Indiana Senator Thomas A. Hendricks, long a champion of the Constitution and of magnanimous reconciliation between North and South, cheered the decision as "among the landmarks of human liberty." Stevens took a rather different view, calling it "far more dangerous" than the Dred Scott decision and saying, "That decision has unsheathed the dagger of the assassin and places the knife of the rebel at the breast of every man who dares proclaim himself . . . a Union man."

Thaddeus Stevens and his brigades rolled up their sleeves. They had had their fill of the Supreme Court, the Constitution, Andrew Johnson, and the Southern state governments he sanctioned. The 1866 congressional elections gave the Radicals their mandate from the voters of the North. Reconstruction was about to begin.

34 Impeachment

Thaddeus Stevens closes the impeachment debate of President Andrew Johnson in the House of Representatives.

Yankees went to war animated by the highest ideals of the nineteenth-century middle classes, but they waged their war in the usual spirit of vengeance. . . . But what the Yankees achieved—for their generation at least—was a triumph not of middle-class ideals but of middle-class vices. The most striking products of their crusade were the shoddy aristocracy of the North and the ragged children of the South. Among the masses of Americans there were no victors, only the vanquished.

—Historian Kenneth Stampp
And the War Came: The North and the Secession Crisis, 1860–61

Now began that second, inestimably more hostile and contentious post-war phase. The 40th Congress—elected in November, 1866—possessed lopsided Republican majorities. This, partly because so many obstacles already existed to electing men in the Southern states who reflected the conservative beliefs of the majority of those people. Only two of twenty two senators from the former Confederate states were not Republicans, and only fourteen of fifty eight representatives.

Thaddeus Stevens spearheaded the passage, over presidential vetoes and the protests of the Democratic Congressional minority, of a series of historic Reconstruction Acts.

With party dominance in both houses, bold vision, and iron will, Thaddeus Stevens spearheaded the passage, over presidential vetoes and the protests of the Democratic Congressional minority, of a series of historic Reconstruction Acts. They proved the heart of the Radical Republican Reconstruction program. The spirit of these acts could be divined by examining Stevens' personal desires for Reconstruction. Among other wishes, he hoped for ten years of Federal military rule in the South; the Southern states' reduction to territories; and control of the education of black and white Southern school children alike, not locally, by state or regionally, but uniformly by the Federal government in Washington. The Reconstruction Acts, rather than working toward the confirmation of the ex-Confederate states' membership in the Union, or even their readmittance, virtually abolished them as political entities.

Reconstruction Acts

Dealing first with what he considered Supreme Court encroachment on the Radical agenda, Stevens hammered home the First Reconstruction Act, the Military Reconstruction Act. Passed on March 2, 1867, this law grouped ten of the former Confederate states into five military districts. This, nearly two years after the War had ended. Some of the states so ordered had existed longer than the American Union itself. Only Tennessee, ruled by corrupt Radical Governor W. G. "Parson" Brownloe, was excluded.

Each military district was appointed its own commanding general, whose

The Union League

Like other organizations and movements spawned during America's remarkable battle with itself, the famed Union League organization demonstrated greatness and pettiness, heroism and villainy, the best in the American character and the worst. By the end of the Reconstruction Era, no one on the continent had proved more vigorous in the pursuit of a Radical-dominated America, or more willing to use whatever means necessary to get there, than the Union Leagues.

Robert Newell's post-war photograph of Union League headquarters in Philadelphia. From the Brenner Collection.

Union League Clubs first sprang up in the wartime North as largely-white, middle-class patriotic clubs. The most successful chapters were those in Philadelphia and New York City. The latter accomplished a number of honorable deeds on behalf of the city's blacks, including improving their living conditions and integrating the streetcars.

By the end of the War, however, the future appeared uncertain for the Union League Clubs of the North. Many other civic and patriotic clubs and organizations existed, and the Leagues faced difficulty in fleshing out a *raison d'etre* capable of drawing a large enough following to insure their survival. Some Union League leaders suspected their best opportunities might lay in the South. In that section lived a significant number of white, pro-Federal hill and mountain Southerners; large numbers of Republicans were headed there; and huge masses of black freedmen now resided there, without organization or plans for their newly-free lives.

> *I believe, my friends and fellow citizens, we [blacks] are not prepared for this suffrage [voting]. But we can learn. Give a man tools and let him commence to use them, and in time he will learn a trade. So it is with voting.*
>
> —Beverly Nash, black delegate to 1868 South Carolina Republican Convention

The first Union Leagues in Southern states emerged during the War in South Carolina and Georgia. According to Eric Foner, they included local freedmen, black Federal soldiers, and Freedmen's Bureau agents, demanding the vote and an end of laws discriminatory to blacks. A St. Helena Island club declared, "By the Declaration of Independence, we believe these are rights which cannot justly be denied us."

Pro-Federal Southern whites dominated Union Leagues in the former Confederate states immediately after the War. Clubs in the South then transitioned into what Foner, in his book *Reconstruction: America's Unfinished Revolution*, called "the political voice for impoverished freedmen." Or at least many of them. But that did not happen without struggle, even within the Leagues themselves.

Many pro-Federal Southern whites proved no great friends to the blacks, and either left the clubs or formed their own, segregated, branches.

League Objectives

Union League Clubs held some uniform goals, and others varied from club to club. Two primary objectives were bringing black freedmen into the Radical fold and instructing them for whom to vote, and securing for them equal political and social status with whites. The latter was conspicuously specific to the South and not the North. Union League Clubs also selected black delegates for Republican political conventions in the Southern states, and entertained, hosted, and paid for expenses for delegates to Loyal Union Conventions in the North and South.

League representatives, helped by Freedmen's Bureau agents and Northern ministers, worked tirelessly to organize freedmen politically. These agents traveled the South day and night, recruiting blacks wherever they found them, whether in cotton fields, bar rooms, cabins, plantations, or at picnics. Many Union Leaguers hoped every township in the South would one day have its own club.

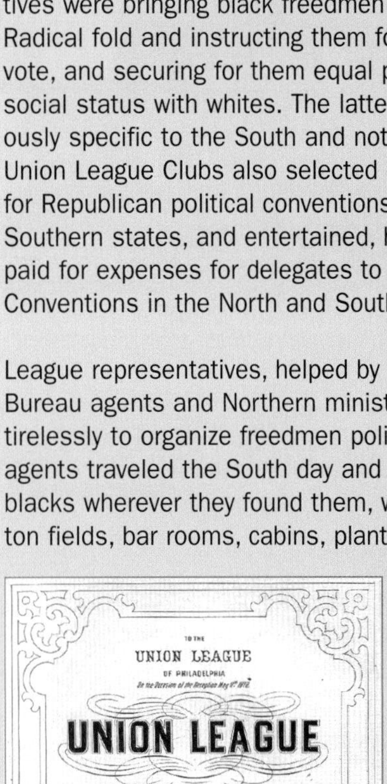

An 1870 Union League Philadelphia fund-raising reception poster. (Penn Library Department of Special Collections)

The first landmark event for these efforts were the 1867 elections, followed by the Presidential and other elections the following year. Union Leagues exercised their political influence in a myriad of legal and illegal ways, from courthouse to state house, and even White House, as that influence helped elect three straight Republican administrations.

Union League meetings addressed such issues as disfranchisement, government schooling, and debtor relief. As the Leagues grew, many of them attempted to build schools and churches, and some succeeded. They also raised money for charitable efforts such as providing for the sick. Like many other organizations of that generation, including white Southern resistance organizations, the Union Leagues featured emotionally-charged night meetings, elaborate ceremonies and rituals, secret passwords, solemn oaths, and dramatic initiation rites.

Ex-Confederates watched with mounting concern as Union League ranks multiplied under the guidance of their Radical sponsors. Membership grew to 80,000 in North Carolina alone, and was responsible for re-electing Radical-controlled Governor W. W. Holden. Many of the clubs converted into military companies and drilled day and night on the roads. A quarter of them carried muskets, pistols, or Bowie knives. In addition to free land, Union League speakers promised them all arms.

Violent Side

Pro-Democrat and pro-Confederate groups like the Ku Klux Klan, the White League, and the Knights of the White Camelia frequently resorted to violence to accomplish their ends, and so did the pro-Radical Union Leagues. League spokesmen continually portrayed white Southern Democrats as the freedman's arch enemy. In fact, as tempers and bloodshed mounted, some Union League Clubs began refusing admission to pro-Radical whites.

To attain unfettered influence with Southern blacks, the Radicals believed they needed to turn them against their white neighbors. One way they attempted this was by attempting to demonstrate that ex-Confederate-types no longer had power, especially power over the blacks. Radical newspapers in the South, bankrolled with the confiscatory tax payments of white Southern taxpayers, reinforced and broadcast this same message in print. So did the thousands of pro-Radical pamphlets, again courtesy of the taxpayer.

Non-Radical Southern blacks were no safer in locales where the Union Leagues were strong than were pro-Radical blacks in areas dominated by the Klan and similar organizations. The Union Leagues used a myriad of tactics to woo, intimidate, and threaten blacks they did not deem sufficiently compliant. They delivered incendiary speeches promising redistribution of white land in the South to blacks. They branded the accused as traitors to their race and party. They persuaded wives and girlfriends to turn against the offending men, and black women in general not even to associate with them and certainly not to marry them.

Death threats, destruction, and even whippings were commonplace. Sometimes murder was employed. In fact, much of the infamy attached to the Klan and the subsequent trouble suffered by it and similar resistance organizations stemmed from violent acts perpetrated by Union Leaguers posing as Klansmen. Typical was this notice pegged to one stubborn black man's door: "You mind me of the son of Esaw and who sold his birth Right for one mossel of meat, and so now you have sold your wife and children and yourself for a drink of Liquers and have come to be a Conservative bootlicker. Tom I would not give a d— for your back in a few days; you Conservative." A sign in one polling booth warned, "Death to Colored Democrats." A banner during the 1868 Presidential campaign in Georgia blared, "every [black] man that didn't vote the Radical ticket, this is the way we want to serve him: hang him by his neck."

A Union League Catechism

Q: With what party should the colored man vote?
A: The Union Republican Party.

Q: What is the difference between Radicals and Republicans?
A: There is none.

Q: Is Mr. Sumner a Republican?
A: He is, and a Radical; so are Thad Stevens, Senator Wilson, Judge Kelley, Gen. Butler, Speaker Colfax, Chief Justice Chase, and all other men who believe in giving colored men their rights.

Q: Why cannot colored men support the Democratic Party?
A: Because that Party would disfranchise them, and if possible return them to slavery and certainly keep them in inferior positions before the law.

Q: Would the Democrats take away all the negro's rights?
A: They would.

Q: The colored men then should vote with the Republican or Radical Party?
A: They should and shun the Democratic Party as they would the overseer's lash and the auction block.

Retrospect

Though the Union League fomented in hundreds of thousands of blacks the false hope that they would be given the land of other men as their own, the League's influence did help many thousands of blacks to demand post-war sharecropping arrangements with white landowners whose crops they worked, rather than less-attractive wage payments. Eventually, the Klan and other resistance groups blunted Union League power in the South. And the Republican Party itself, to the protests of black Radicals, strived to absorb the League clubs into the more disciplined, less violent, mainstream party structure.

Union League goals for black rights in the South towered above those held by almost any other group of that generation. The blacks themselves were often led to a knowledge and conviction of such ideals by the Union Leaguers. Sadly, corruption and backlash, generated from the hate spawned by unconstitutional actions on a still-unprecedented scale, rendered much of the blacks' gains only temporary.

Some major breakthroughs, however, such as the right to vote and other Constitutional rights, though delayed or diluted when white conservatives returned to power after Reconstruction, were at least committed to law. It was upon this basis that blacks would later claim and exercise various of their legal rights. According to historian Kenneth Stampp, if the abolition of slavery was worth four years of civil war, the Fourteenth Amendment was worth the morass of Reconstruction.

During the exceptional events surrounding the Union League Clubs in the Southern states, a Northern woman living near Orange Park, Florida, wrote to her brother of her support for President Johnson and her opposition to the Radicals: "Corrupt politicians are already beginning to speculate on [the blacks] as possible capital for their schemes, and to fill their poor heads with all sorts of vagaries." She also wrote to her friend the Duchess of Argyll: "My brother Henry . . . takes the ground that is unwise and impolitic to endeavor to force negro suffrage on the South at the point of the bayonet." So thought the writer. Her brother was Henry Ward Beecher, and she was Harriet Beecher Stowe, author of *Uncle Tom's Cabin*.

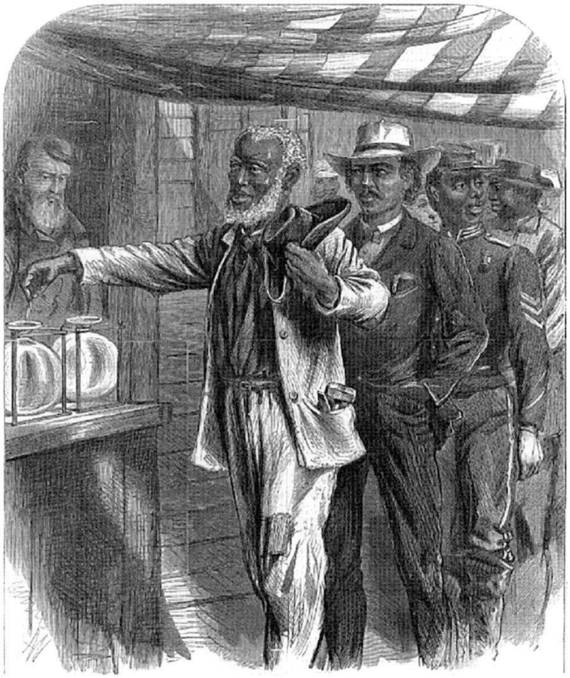

"The First Vote" of black freedmen in the South, as depicted by *Harper's Weekly* (www.harpweek.com). Though dramatically chronicling the historic event, the publication failed to mention that most Northern states were continuing to prevent blacks from voting *north* of the Mason-Dixon line.

range of authority included discretion to remove elected officials as he pleased and replace them with men of his choice, and replacement of peacetime juries and courts with military tribunals. "The power thus given to the commanding officer . . . is that of an absolute monarch," President Johnson told the nation. "His mere will is to take the place of law."

But the preamble to the first act declared that "no legal State governments or adequate protection for life or property now exists in the rebel state." Thus, the Radicals declared, it was "necessary that peace and good order should be enforced . . . until loyalty and republican State governments" be "legally established." This meant governments both "republican" and "Republican." Stevens calmed protesting moderate fellow-Republicans, who decried the extremity and questionable legality of the Military Reconstruction Act, by telling them the bill "would assure the ascendancy of the Union [Republican] party."

The act provided no date of termination for Federal military rule in the South. It also empowered the U.S. army to supervise conventions in each military district that would draw up new constitutions for the people of the South. The Federals, however, disfranchised tens of thousands of Southerners who had supported the Confederacy, and who were now allowed no voice in the constitutional conventions, or in subsequent elections. In other words, a significant portion of the people over whom all these new laws would rule, would have no say whatsoever in their composition.

W. G. "Parson" Brownlow, carpetbag governor in post-war Tennessee.

President Johnson's pardoning of thousands of ex-Confederates had incensed the Republicans, so the Reconstruction Acts now eliminated the President's right to pardon or return voting rights to ex-Confederates. With *Ex parte Milligan* in view, the acts also restricted the Supreme Court from hearing appeals by citizens invoking their right to habeas corpus. In other words, they had no appeal beyond United States military tribunals to civilian courts. This provision had particular application to those complaining of arrest and trial by the Federal military.

And the acts required approval of the new military district constitutions by Congress, passage of the lingering Fourteenth Amendment by the new Southern "governments," and cooperation by the Southern people in all these processes. Then, and only then, would military rule possibly end, and Congressional representation—by the same Republican-friendly group—resume. That the Southern states were forced and coerced into ratifying the Fourteenth and Fifteenth Amendments before being allowed back into the Union is perhaps the greatest irony of Reconstruction.

The Fifteenth Amendment not only paved the way for black men to vote, but many gained political office, some even in the United States Congress. This Currier & Ives painting shows the first black Congressmen, who served in either the 41st or 42nd Congresses or both after the War. Far left is Senator Hiram R. Revels, along with Representatives Benjamin S. Turner, Josiah T. Walls, Joseph H. Rainey, Robert Brown Elliot, Robert D. De Large, and Jefferson H. Long.

While I have considered the preservation of the constitutional power of the General Government to be the foundation of our peace and safety at home and abroad, I yet believe that the maintenance of the rights and authority reserved to the states and to the people, not only are essential to the adjustment and balance of the general system, but the safeguard to the continuance of a free government. I consider it as the chief source of stability to our political system, whereas the consolidation of the states into one vast republic, sure to be aggressive abroad and despotic at home, will be the certain precursor of that ruin which has overwhelmed all those that have preceded it.

—Robert E. Lee, in a December 15, 1866 letter to Lord Acton.

New Forces in the Reconstruction South

The Radical Republican Congress's Reconstruction Acts mandated bold new voter registration standards in the South. These produced a dramatic transformation of the political power structure in that region. Three significant new groups of people, all living in the South after the War, but none of them friendly to the old power structure, spearheaded the change.

Carpetbaggers—Northerners who came South looking for financial and political opportunity. Because of how the new Southern military districts were organized, people often rode a train or stagecoach from their home in the North to a destiny such as South Carolina. And three days later they might be a state representative. In one case, a man was "elected" governor of Florida before he had even moved from New Hampshire. When notified, he turned to his wife and said, "I didn't even know I was running!"

Slavery, in fact, remained legal even after the War for a couple of years in some Northern states, and some of the military district governors themselves owned slaves.

They were called carpetbaggers because they threw their belongings into large travel bags covered with material that looked like scraps of carpet, then made their way into the South. They comprised a new political phenomenon that supplanted the old power of the Southern elite.

Scalawags—Southern natives who saw an opportunity to improve their post-war fortunes by cooperating with the Federal military governors, and who exercised every opportunity to perpetuate that military rule—often to the ruination of their former neighbors. Scalawags did not hesitate to compromise their principles or their neighbors in the interest of their own personal gain. General James Longstreet is the most famous figure of this group, though it included wartime Georgia Governor Joe Brown and former North Carolina Governor W. W. Holden.

Ascendants—Former slaves given places of political "ascendancy" in the Reconstruction Southern governments because they could read and write, maybe had some level of higher education, and perhaps had made their way to the North. There, some even secured a college education, then returned South after the War.

Some ascendants received significant opportunities during this period, but not so incredible that they dominated Reconstruction Era politics in the South. Actually, very few ascendants made a permanent mark on the political landscape. Fifteen blacks won election to Congress, three as state lieutenant governors, and two as U.S. Senators. None were elected governor. And none won election to any such offices in the North until decades later.

Racial prejudice endured as strongly in the North—whose agents engineered ascendant political opportunities in the South—as in the former Confederacy. Slavery, in fact, remained legal even after the War for a couple of years in some Northern states, and some of the military district governors themselves owned slaves. American slavery did not end until the United States Supreme Court rejected the final appeals to the application of the Thirteenth Amendment. This did not occur until late 1867 in some states, and 1868 in Delaware. The Reconstruction South was ruled primarily by the military governors, the scalawags, and the carpetbaggers.

Thomas A. Hendricks (1819–1885)

Eclipsed by the famous chieftains of Radical Republican Reconstruction in the chronicles of American court historians is bold, dashing, conservative Democratic Indiana Senator and Governor Thomas Hendricks. "Purity," "courtesy," and "fidelity" were among the adjectives most frequently uttered in description of Thomas Hendricks. He consistently led the fight against those portions of bills such as the Freedman's Bureau and Civil Rights Bill that overthrew Constitutional principles and erected military and law enforcement structures unaccountable to it or their people. One leading statesman of the era called Hendricks, "The acknowledged champion of that great conservative sentiment . . . that brought about the return of the seceded States."

Born in Zanesville, Ohio, Hendricks moved with his family to Indiana the next year. He graduated from Hanover College and after passing the bar exam practiced law in Shelbyville, Indiana. Between 1848 and 1859, he served as a state legislator, Congressman, and Commissioner of the Indiana General Land Office. He failed in an 1860 run for governor, but won election to the U.S. Senate in 1863, where he served until 1869.

For the three years following the War, historian Claude Bowers writes, Hendricks was to speak the verdict of history in "debate. . . . [He] was the moral and intellectual equivalent of any man on the floor." Nineteenth-century U.S. Secretary of State William Maxwell Evarts recalled about Hendricks during the Reconstruction struggle that "among the eminent men who took part in debate no man appeared better in his composure of spirit, in his calmness of judgment, in the circumspect and careful deliberation with which,

Kate Chase Sprague (1840–1899)

Kate Chase Sprague was the daughter of Supreme Court Chief Justice Salmon P. Chase and wife of Rhode Island manufacturing magnate, "millionaire boy Governor," and Senator William Sprague. Favored by fortune as were few others, even as a tiny child, she and her famous, doting father would pray and read poetry and the Bible together.

Kate Sprague loomed as the most glamorous, charismatic, and perhaps most beautiful of a new generation of post-war Washingtonians. She was roundly acclaimed the most dashing and popular woman in official American society since Dolley Madison. "Not a gown, not a chain, not an ornament ever attracted attention except in so much as it shared her beauty," wrote a *Chicago News* correspondent. "She had more the air of a great lady than any woman I ever saw. She could make all the Astors look like fishwomen beside her." "No queen has ever reigned under the Stars and Stripes, but this remarkable woman came closer to being Queen than any American woman has," declared the *Cincinnati Enquirer*.

The Reconstruction Era saw the Federal capital where she "reigned" grow from a provincial avoiding extreme extravagances, he drew the line which should mark out fidelity to the Constitution as distinguished from addition to the supremacy of party interest and party passions."

No voice in the nation denounced the post-war frenzy of western land giveaways as loudly—or eloquently—as his. As the railroads and the financial titans who owned them gobbled up these lands, Hendricks was pronounced a "demagogue" for daring to challenge American progress and expansion.

Hendricks also fought against the Tenure-of-Office Act. When David Davis and the Supreme Court electrifyingly denied Congress the right to suspend the citizens' trial by jury (in lieu of Federal military tribunals), Hendricks lauded it as "among the landmarks of human liberty."

So highly regarded was Hendricks among Democrats that he became one of the leading contenders for the 1868 Presidential nomination. At one point during the convention balloting, he was only four votes behind the front runner. He narrowly lost, but the people of Indiana elected him governor in 1872.

He emerged anew as a front runner for the Presidential nomination in 1876. He finished second again, but had such strength that Samuel Tilden the nominee chose him as his Vice Presidential running mate. Corrupt scheming between Northern Republicans and Southern Democrats stole the election from them, but in 1884 Hendricks again held the vice presidential spot on the Democratic ticket. This time, with Grover Cleveland, Hendricks won election to the nation's second-highest post. But he held it less than nine months before he died.

Thomas A. Hendricks fought the lonely fight of a leader whose views are not popular in his generation. But he often influenced questionable policies toward the good, and he doggedly pressed accountability on powerful men who would likely have acted even more unconstitutionally than they did if not for Hendricks.

Southern town with pigs rooting amidst its muddy streets to a cosmopolitan center of international power and intrigue. Empires and destinies were made and lost at fashionable hotels like the Willard and Wormley and resplendent mansions like those along Lafayette Square.

Alas, all the gilded blessings the world could offer could not prevent her husband's alcoholism, her loneliness and infidelity with New York Senator Roscoe Conkling and possibly others, her husband's fury, her fleeing from him with her children, and their divorce. Even the stupendous mansion she had built on Sprague's farm on the Rhode Island coast burned to the ground a few years after her death, its ashes bearing mute testament to the transient nature of earthly favor.

THE SITUATION.

The dramatic showdown between President Andrew Johnson (far right) and Congress, utilizing its Tenure of Office Act, Secretary of War Edwin Stanton, and cooperative General-in-Chief of the Army U. S. Grant, as depicted in the March 7, 1868, *Harper's Weekly* (www.harpweek.com).

Impeached President

The same day the First Reconstruction Act was passed, Congress passed two other bills designed to reduce President Johnson's power. One, the Command of the Army Act, required Senatorial approval for the army's General-in-Chief to be removed or changed. But it was the other, the Tenure of Office Act, that struck Johnson like a trip hammer and set in motion a monumental series of events.

The Tenure of Office Act prevented the President from removing government officials whose original appointments were subject to Senate approval. This included his own cabinet members. Most conspicuous in this number was Secretary of War Edwin Stanton. That man had served three Presidents, from two parties, and he had wrought a sad record of duplicity, perfidy, and self-serving in every administration. Most recently, Stanton had undermined Johnson by serving the Radicals both as a forceful advocate for their policies within the administration and as a brazen in-house spy for them.

Frustrated and endangered once too often by Stanton's machinations, Johnson demanded his resignation on August 10 and asked U. S. Grant to take over the position. Stanton refused, then the Radical-controlled Senate sided with him. In February, 1868, Johnson fired him. Washington was thunderstruck. Stanton physically barricaded himself in his office; Grant turned against Johnson, stepped aside as Secretary of War, and made the army available for Stanton and the Radicals' purposes; and the Radicals (incorrectly) accused Johnson of marching a citizens' army from Maryland to deal with Stanton and Congress.

Most importantly, Congress pounced upon the dismissal, claiming their arch-foe Johnson broke the Tenure of Office Act. In an epic duel not matched until the disgrace of Bill Clinton over a century later, Stevens and the Radicals threw everything they had at Johnson. Stevens drew up eleven documents of impeachment for removing the President from office. The House voted for impeachment on all counts. Thus, was Andrew Johnson the first President in United States history to be impeached by Congress. A Senate trial was now all that stood between him and removal from office. With the mood of the Radicals, criminal prosecution might follow that. Such historic acts demonstrate that Stevens, Benjamin Wade, and the like were no small yet powerful Congressional cabal; rather, Radical philosophies indeed dominated the width and breadth of that body throughout the post-war years.

Impeachment, even removal from office, did not satisfy some of the more extreme Radicals. Missouri Senator B. F. Loan created a sensation when he insinuated in session that Andrew Johnson helped orchestrate President Lincoln's murder. Then his Senate colleagues James B. Ashley and Benjamin Butler spearheaded a plot to frame Johnson in the historic crime. They procured supposed witnesses, some of them already languishing in jail, to testify that Johnson had conspired with John Wilkes Booth.

Ashley had previous entanglement in bribery and influence peddling, and he would eventually be voted out of office, then later dismissed from his appointed position as governor of Montana. For now, when one of his key, incarcerated, conspirators refused to proceed without a pardon and pressure mounted against him, Ashley denied publicly accusing Johnson in Lincoln's death, and the scheme crumbled.

Senate Showdown

Then it was time for the Senate to decide whether Andrew Johnson remained in office. The Constitution called for Supreme Court Chief Justice Salmon Chase, sympathetic to the President, to preside. That Ohio Senator and President Pro Tempore

The Ladies' Gallery of the Senate During the Impeachment Trial of President Andrew Johnson, as it appeared in the April 18,1868 *Harper's Weekly* (www.harpweek.com).

Ben Wade, one of the harshest and most unrelenting of all Radicals, stood to accede to the Presidency, underscores how momentous were the stakes.

Standing again in the front ranks of battle for the Radicals was Ben Butler. His speech opened the proceedings, and press correspondents from America and beyond wrote of its unsurpassed rage and invective. He led the Radical charge in subsequent weeks to "persuade" fence-sitting Republican Senators to support removing Johnson from office: "Tell the d----- scoundrel," he said to one Senator of another, "that if he wants money there is a bushel of it to be had." After the proceedings concluded, Butler brought additional shame on himself and his party by attempting a smear campaign against Republicans who had sided with Johnson.

Even more popular than bribery that season was intimidation. The Radicals threatened and cajoled any Republican

When the Senate Voted on Andrew Johnson

Claude A. Bowers penned this dramatic account of the U.S. Senate's showdown vote on whether Andrew Johnson would remain President in the book *The Tragic Era*.

> *Cloudy and dull was the dawn, but through the morning the sun seemed trying to break through, and then the skies darkened again. The congested galleries amused themselves during the wait looking down on the celebrities. At the managers' table, Logan, Stevens, Sumner, the last two in earnest conversation. At times Stevens shook his head violently and his wig bobbed; at times he laughed sardonically.*
>
> *In his seat sat Howard, wrapped in a shawl, the stretcher that had borne him hence on the portico. Soon the desperately ill Grimes was carried in on the arms of four men to vote, his face pale and twisted with pain, and Fessenden sprang forward to grasp his hand and give him a "glorified smile" the sick man never was to forget.*
>
> *And now, the roll call. In the galleries, faces tense with anxiety; the faces of members pallid, some sick with fear. A deathlike stillness with the calling of each name, and then a heavy breathing. When a doubtful Senator's name was called the spectators seemed to hold their breath, and then, with the vote, came a simultaneous vent.*
>
> *Fessenden— "Not guilty."*
>
> *That was expected.*
>
> *Fowler—Grimes—Henderson—all know to be lost, and then—*
>
> *Ross—"Not guilty."*
>
> *Nearly all hope having fled, the last chance was with Van Winkle, and when he, too, voted to acquit, "a long breathing of disappointment and despair." The vote had been on Stevens's eleventh article, and, that failing, there was no hope for any other.*
>
> *Then, with adjournment, the excited throngs in the corridors looked upon an unforgettable spectacle—Thad Stevens, carried by his negro boys, far above the crowd, his face black with rage and disappointment, waving his arms at friends and saying, "The country is going to the devil."*

who offered the merest hint that he might support President Johnson. They rallied Senators' constituents to bully them. They conducted searches for a thread of blackmail material anywhere in their lives. Union League Clubs deluged wavering Senators with threatening telegrams from all over the country. One key swing vote who went for Johnson, Lyman Trumbull of Illinois, was warned by Republican Campaign Committee President Charles S. Spencer that Spencer would have him hanged from a lamp post if ever he came to Chicago.

When all the arguments ended and the great day came, in May, 1868, thirty-five Senators voted against Johnson, only nineteen for him. But that was just enough for the President to escape—by one vote—the two-thirds majority required for impeachment. Stevens and the Radicals were apoplectic with rage. Yet whatever Reconstruction program President Johnson had for the nation was sunk, and his influence was torpedoed for the remainder of his term.

Fourteenth——Again

Perhaps the greatest of all Reconstruction Era examples of breaking the law with the intent to improve it came with the resurrection of the Fourteenth Amendment in the summer of 1868. Defeated two years before by the opposition of non-Radical Southern state governments, the Radicals now felt sure they had enough puppet regimes installed in the South to assure passage.

Included in the amendment's four sections were:

1) Full citizenship and legal rights for all people born or naturalized in the United States.
2) Reduction of an individual state's representation in Congress if the Federal government determines that state's citizens have deprived their fellow citizens of their legal rights.
3) Proscription from holding elected state or Federal office of any former Confederate who had previously sworn an oath in any antebellum state or Federal military or civil capacity to uphold the Constitution.
4) Agreement that the full United States war debt should be paid.
5) Agreement that no part of the Confederate States war debt was to be paid.
6) Agreement that no former slaveowner was due any compensation for his slaves.
7) Congress's right to enforce all provisions of the amendment.

> *If he is a rebel, he is just such a rebel as I am and no more.*
>
> —John Quincy Adams II speaking of Wade Hampton

It was not only the South that the Radicals were dragging to the franchise trough for their black residents. Many Northern states and territories still disallowed black voting; Ohio, Kansas, and Minnesota had voted it down the year before, and the District of Columbia, home to the U.S. capital, voted down in 1867.

The Fate of President Davis

Confederate President Jefferson Davis did not fade from history after the War. If anything, his story grows even more singular. In disregard of international law, the Rules of Just War, and the American Bill of Rights, Davis was shackled in irons the first day of his imprisonment. Edwin Stanton authorized the action and decorated Federal war hero Brigadier General Nelson Miles, commanding general of Fort Monroe, ordered it.

Public pressure in the North caused the removal of Davis's shackles after five days, but that was only the beginning of his prison troubles. As Shelby Foote relates in his trilogy *The Civil War*, Miles ordered two sentries to remain in the room with Davis twenty-four hours a day, seven days a week, month in and month out, marching their booted feet back and forth without respite, even when he used the toilet. He also ordered a bright lamp kept perpetually burning near Davis, day and night.

More than two months passed before the frail, sickly fifty-seven-year-old man was allowed any exercise, more than three before he was allowed to read a letter from his wife, and nearly seven before he was allowed to see anyone but his doctor, his guards, and the twenty-six-year-old Miles—who sneered at him and called him "Jeff." Federal surgeon and Lieutenant Colonel John J. Craven's efforts led to the improvements in Davis' confinement.

Davis' first visitor was his wartime pastor, Charles Minnigerode, who served him communion—which the erstwhile President had not had, nor worship, those many months. Only after this was he again allowed to see his wife Varina.

After fifteen months, President Johnson himself ordered Miles's dismissal as commander of Fort Monroe. But the general had become a darling of the Radical leadership. His cruelty would continue in his later treatment of the Plains Indians as he worked his way all the way up to succeeding Grant, Sherman, and Sheridan as general-in-chief of the American army.

"Am I Your Equal?"

Davis biographer Hudson Strode chronicles the great loyalty the erstwhile Confederate President earned from friends, bishop and slave alike. One of the latter, Robert Brown, "simply ignored emancipation and stayed with the Davises as a friend and servant for the rest of their lives." So great was the esteem in which the Davises held Brown that shortly after the War's end, with Davis in prison and his wife ordered to remain in a Savannah, Georgia, rent by lawlessness, she sent her children north with Brown to Canada for safekeeping.

On the ship, Brown heard a white abolitionist insulting Davis within earshot of the Davis children. According to Strode, Brown approached the abolitionist and asked, "Do you believe I am your equal?" Certainly, replied the abolitionist. "Then take this from an equal," said Brown, cold-cocking the man with a single powerful blow.

Trial Sought

The Radicals were determined to see Davis tried in court before a worldwide audience, condemned of treason—and the ideal of secession with him—and hanged. As Speaker of the House Schuyler Colfax put it, they wanted him "hanging between heaven and earth as not fit for either."

But two infuriating obstacles appeared in their path. First, for years they had dispensed with *habeas corpus* when they did not want it, and they had used the military—and military courts—when they did want them. Slowly, however, it dawned on them that the American people, even in the North, would not stand for these practices in peacetime.

Coupled with the sobering realization that the government would have to try Jefferson Davis in a straight-up fight with his defenders in court, was the even more disturbing suspicion that shouting from the housetops that Davis was a traitor and murderer and all around fiend would not necessarily translate into a conviction in a straight-up fight. Why was that?

"If you bring these leaders to trial it will condemn the North," said Republican Supreme Court Chief Justice Salmon Chase, "for by the Constitution secession is not rebellion. . . . Lincoln wanted Jefferson Davis to escape, and he was right. His capture was a mistake. His trial will be a greater one. We cannot convict him of treason. Secession is settled. Let it stay settled." Chase would preside over any Davis trial, as the Virginia venue lay within jurisdiction. "Davis will not be found guilty and we shall stand there completely beaten," jurist Francis Lieber of "Lieber Code" fame told the government.

Indeed, the best lawyers in the North stumbled over each other to help defend, not prosecute, Davis. Most of them remained incensed at the Federal government's battering of the Constitution and Bill of Rights throughout the War. Now those that studied Jefferson Davis's case saw in it a sure winner, and one in which they could humble the government that had humbled them.

When President Johnson's attorney general saw the caliber of legal opposition lining up against the government, he recruited one of the greatest trial prosecutors in America, John J. Clifford, to lead their team. But Clifford stunned them by quitting the team and warning them if they pressed forward against Davis, the United States might up "end up having fought a successful war, only to have it declared unlawful by a Virginia jury."

Varina Davis, wife of Confederate President Jefferson Davis.

Varina Davis's courageous trip to the North during her husband's harsh prison ordeal brought her lasting renown. The man did not live that could intimidate her from soliciting his aid in seeking her President Davis's freedom. Indeed, it was not Southerners, but rather some of the richest and most powerful men in New York and New England who mustered the then-colossal $100,000 bail money for Davis's release.

And it was Varina who had called upon them, many of them in no way sympathetic toward her husband or the South, and petitioned them, for their honor and that of the nation before a watching world, not only to speak out on behalf of Davis, but to pay for his release. She earned a private audience with President Andrew Johnson himself, and helped to persuade him not only of the unjustness of the incarceration, but of the scant chance of winning the case in court for the Federal government.

Refuses Pardon

Another year passed as Davis languished in prison. Then the government appointed another special prosecutor; he too pulled out. When Johnson named a new attorney general, not even he would take the case.

Gradually, as legal, political, and moral pressure mounted on the Federals to let Davis go, his conditions of confinement improved. When President Johnson advised Davis's beautiful wife Varina of his support for her husband's cause and advised him to seek a pardon, Davis appreciated the former announcement and renounced the latter. The South rose in a crescendo of support for him. Then Johnson pardoned Davis himself, and the former President refused the offer, preferring to remain in prison and mount the case he believed would vindicate the constitutionality of Southern secession. The whole country was now calling it "The Trial of the Century."

After more than two years of imprisonment, wealthy Northerners like Horace Greeley and Cornelius Vanderbilt paid the [then] enormous $100,000 bond to release Davis from jail.

Finally, Chief Justice Chase conjured the idea not to prosecute Davis, while making no concession to the Constitutionality of Southern secession. Davis, Chase said, had already been punished by being denied the right under the Fourteenth Amendment to hold public office because of his insurrection against the U.S. The Bill of Rights' protection of a citizen against double jeopardy, or being tried and punished twice for the same crime, thus prevented any further legal action. The tortured nature of all these deliberations is evidenced by the fact that Davis had not been tried for, much less convicted of, anything.

And so did Jefferson Davis remain free. Many Southerners who castigated him during the War had come to love and respect him during his harsh and humiliating incarceration in a way they never otherwise would have. Henceforth until the end of his life the Southern people would continue to call him "The President."

" . . . for by the Constitution secession is not rebellion." Thus had the Federal Chief Justice himself said.

Dixie (Daniel Decatur Emmett)

I wish I was in the land of cotton,
Old times there are not forgotten;
Look away, look away, look away, Dixie Land!
In Dixie Land, where I was born in,
Early on one frosty mornin';
Look away, look away, look away, Dixie Land!

Chorus:
Then I wish I was in Dixie, hooray, hooray!
In Dixie Land I'll take my stand,
To live and die in Dixie;
Away, away, away down south in Dixie;
Away, away, away down south in Dixie.

This world was made in just six days,
And finished up in various ways;
Look away! Look away! Look away! Dixie Land!
They then made Dixie trim and nice,
But Adam called it "paradise,"
Look away! Look away! Look away! Dixie Land!

Chorus:
Then I wish I was in Dixie, hooray, hooray!
In Dixie Land I'll take my stand,
To live and die in Dixie;
Away, away, away down south in Dixie;
Away, away, away down south in Dixie.

Last Hurrah

A greater challenge yet for Stevens and the Radicals was the inconvenient detail that even with Federal military occupation, disfranchising of most of the Confederate South, and mass Radical coercion of freedmen, the House of Representatives could still only account for twenty seven of the thirty seven states having ratified the Fourteenth Amendment. The same three-fourths requirement, by which the amendment had gone down two years before, still necessitated at least twenty eight of them doing so. So, near the end of July, Congress simply passed a resolution declaring three-fourths of the states had ratified the amendment and that the Secretary of State should attest as such, and the amendment passed into law.

All this, and the Southern states knew they had to ratify the Fourteenth Amendment, like they had the Thirteenth, and like they must the Fifteenth, and see it made law, if they hoped to regain representation in the United States government. It would be one of Thaddeus Stevens' last hurrahs. He lived to see Ulysses S. Grant nominated by the Radicals as their Presidential candidate, though Grant had never in his life voted for a Republican for that office. But by mid-August, Stevens was dead, his live-in housekeeper Lydia Smith at his bedside, his only heir.

Claude Bowers wrote, "And so the tale of Thad Stevens was told, and his movement passed to men less able, less sincere, and far more selfish." In November, a lackluster Democratic campaign, disfranchisement of white Southerners, Radical coercion of the black vote, and rampant voter fraud brought Grant a narrow victory over conservative New York Governor Horatio Seymour. The latter favored a Reconstruction program perhaps even more moderate than that of Johnson,

"'Tis But a Change in Banners," Frank Ballew's November 16, 1868, *Harper's Weekly* cartoon evidencing the "wave the bloody shirt" strategy employed by the Republicans after the War to saddle the Democratic party with the onus of secession and the Confederacy. Couched within a scene of disloyalty and violence, the cartoonist depicts the Democrats' "Seymour and Blair" Presidential banner taking over for the Confederate flag and the Ku Klux Klan hat replacing a Confederate one.

whose impeachment had throttled his hopes for renomination.

Thus the Radicals no longer had Stevens, but they had his agenda well in motion, both houses of Congress, puppet regimes across the South, and now the White House, too. The most corrupt and larcenous era of government in American history was not coming to a close; it was about to begin.

1860s America witnessed violence on the battlefield and the newspaper editorial page alike. The pro-Radical *Harper's Weekly* (www.harpweek.com) announced Republican Ulysses S. Grant's presidential election victory over Democrat Horatio Seymour with this cover-page beheading. Grant's horse, meanwhile, rears its front legs over the fallen horse and body of supposedly-drunken Democratic Vice Presidential candidate Frank Blair, as whiskey flows from his bottle.

My sands are nearly run, and I can only see with the eyes of faith. I am fast descending the downhill of life, at the foot of which stands the open grave. But you, sir [Speaker Schuyler Colfax], are promised full length of days, and a brilliant career. If you and your compeers can fling away ambition and realize that every human being, however lowly or degraded by fortune, is your equal . . . truth and righteousness will spread over the land and you will look down from the top of the Rocky Mountains upon an empire of one hundred million of happy people.

—Thaddeus Stevens, speaking in Congress shortly before his death

35 Black and White

German native Thomas Nast's passionate Radical views animated his pen for decades and brought him world fame. He was not without fierce opposition, however. Perhaps his greatest foe was the equally-talented Matt Morgan, whose brilliant editorial artistry graced the pages of *Frank Leslie's Illustrated News* and many other publications. Morgan and Nast not only presented sharply contrasting social and political viewpoints, they frequently launched none-too-subtle broadsides and ripostes at one another's work through their own.

Here, Morgan's sprawling, double-page "Dark Horde" depicts an America besieged by a sea of supposedly corrupt, big-government Republican villains. On the sacred but threatened high ground, Lady Columbia, representing the heritage and spirit of the nation, clutches a tattered U.S. flag and calls forth George Washington, Abraham Lincoln, Benjamin Franklin, William Penn, and other past giants of American history. She cries out, "Shall these things be! Is not this state of things enough to cause the Fathers of the Republic to rise from their graves to protest against the iniquity and folly of the hour?"

You brethren at the North think that you have a great deal for which to forgive the South for the four years of war. I will not discuss that. But I tell you, brethren, we of the South have a great deal for which to forgive the North for the four years since the war.

—Dr. John A. Broadus
Co-founder, Southern Baptist Convention

On the surface, it seemed the Radicals had carried the field on so many fronts, they might never lose their grip, and that the doctrines espoused by Marx and Engels in their *Communist Manifesto* and fought for the last two decades by transplanted European Revolution "Forty-Eighters" and other Radicals might come to pass. But even as the Radicals consolidated their power in Washington and took firm control of Southern state governments like Louisiana and Mississippi, fissures began to emerge in the superstructure of their program.

It did not take long for Grant to evidence that his political inexperience, especially in high office, was exceeded only by his poor judgment and dangerous associations.

For one, cracks were widening within the Republican Party itself over economic issues. A growing minority agreed with conservative Democrats that tariffs—now near or above 50%—needed sharp reduction. This minority also backed the "sound money" system that provided for redemption of greenback paper money with gold, constraining the national debt while maintaining interest payments, and keeping down inflation. And it did not take long for Grant to evidence that his political inexperience, especially in high office, was exceeded only by his poor judgment and dangerous associations.

Black Friday

President Grant's absence of political, commercial, and financial experience—coupled with his lack of interest in learning—his association with men of questionable character, and his lack of guiding philosophical principles plunged him quickly into a parade of historic scandals. First to come to light, only eight months into his administration, was the infamous "Black Friday" stock market crash of September 24, 1869. This tragedy commands attention not only for its consequences, but because it exemplifies many of the Reconstruction Era's abiding pathologies.

Two of New York's preeminent financial speculators, Jay Gould (supposedly F. Scott Fitzgerald's inspiration for Jay Gatsby in his novel *The Great Gatsby*) and Jim Fisk, attempted to buy up enough gold to corner the entire American gold market. If accomplishing that, they would hoist high the price and reap a windfall of unfathomable proportions from merchants forced to purchase gold for the custom house.

The Radicals and Communism

During the closing years of the War, the early post-War years, and the Reconstruction Era, the Radical Republicans systematically implemented all or part of every plank of the Marx-Engels *Communist Manifesto*, which undergirded the many bloody revolutions of 1848 Europe. The Marxist aims follow, the Radicals' plans alongside them.

Communist Manifesto Doctrines	*Radical Reconstruction Goals*
Elimination of private property ownership.	Mandatory property taxes, determined by and payable to the government, else the taxpaying "owner's" property is confiscated.
Development of a graduated income tax.	The Internal Revenue Service.
Abolition of the inheritance of a deceased person's property by family members, churches, and others.	Heavy inheritance taxes.
Confiscation of the rights of certain peoples, these "rebels" and "aliens."	Revocation of citizenship, voting, and other among foremost Constitutional rights from thousands of ex-Confederates.
State-controlled banking.	The Federal Banking Act.
State-controlled transportation.	The Railroad Commission and the first (Federally funded and controlled) railroads themselves.
Control over mechanisms of the economy such as imports, exports, duties, and trading.	Federal price controls.
State-controlled currency.	The National Banking Act, passed in 1863, mandated uniformity in banking and bank note currency.
State-controlled labor.	Federal wage controls.
State-controlled agriculture.	The Southern Redistribution Act redistributed property into large combines or collectives, under the jurisdiction of carpetbaggers.
State-controlled education.	The Morrill Land Grant Act authorized Federal aid, including land grants, to established government-controlled (public) colleges. With the aid came increased government accountability and regulations.

The most frightful swindles are on foot and likely to go through, and the general wreck of the Republican Party through its espousal of these schemes is quite probable. . . . I have never seen such lobbying before as we have had in the last few weeks and such crookedness and complicity among members.

—Republican Indiana Representative George Julian

The plotters' expertise and resources enabled them to ensnare a number of high government officials in their scheme, including former Federal General Daniel Butterfield, whom Grant had appointed as sub-treasury agent for New York City. And unfortunately for almost everyone, they managed to enlist Abel Corbin—none other than the brother of the President's wife Julia—to discourage the President from releasing government gold for sale. This, to reduce the available supply Gould and Fisk needed to buy before the price rose. As if this were subsequently not enough of a blow to Grant's reputation, he himself, though never charged with wrongdoing, fraternized socially with Gould and Fisk.

Lasting Trouble

In the end, Grant approved Secretary of the Treasury George Boutwell's releasing of several million dollars worth of government gold, in the nick of time, to drive down the market price. This thwarted Gould and Fisk's audacious caper—but not before a nervous Gould proved anew the old adage about no honor among thieves by secretly selling much of his own gold even as Fisk, unawares, continued to buy.

The nimble pair, however, both rebounded from the adventure, even banking a modest profit from it. Many others caught up in the scheme did not. A correspondent witnessing panic sweep the New York financial district attested as such to Boutwell: "Nobody was in their offices, and the agony depicted on the faces of men who crowded the streets made one feel as if Gettysburg had been lost and the rebels were marching down Broadway." More than one sharper, speculator, and investor chose a bullet to the brain as his way out of the calamity.

Black Friday at first appears an appropriate inauguration of a decade of financial and economic turmoil in the United States. However, the many unsound post-war financial and political decisions executed by the increasingly centralized Federal government had already spawned a troubled national economy. Among many problems were Western farmers' suffering from usurious railroad prices and practices; conflict raging between management and laborers in Northern industrial and manufacturing plants; and the Federal military occupation, greedy commercial opportunists, and crushing taxes prostrating the poverty-racked South. The "Gilded Age" had arrived.

Southern Suffering

Most Southerners likely paid scant attention to the Black Friday debacle. By the end of what had proven the blackest decade in their history, most of those not killed in the War were sunk in poverty, uncertainty, and harsh military occupation and rule. Most of the best Southern land was in the process either of being taken over by Northerners or kept in Southern hands through the monetary credit—and thus, sufferance—of Yankee banks.

For instance, the War destroyed fully one-half of all the property in South Carolina. Yet, nearly a decade after Appomattox, that state's puppet legislature had quadrupled its property taxes from 1860, impoverishing thousands, bankrupting thousands more, and costing yet more thousands the land many had owned for generations. At one juncture, twenty percent of all the land in Mississippi was up for sale.

Tens of thousands of white former landowners lost their property, while masses of black freedmen never received the land promised them by Federal agents. These black and white Southerners alike could only work the land of others as sharecroppers or tenant farmers, wherein they shared the produce of the land with its owners or paid a fee to work it. Most of the money available for credit in Southern states went to carpetbag or scalawag office holders and their consorts. So did much of the money appropriated by the office holders in the various Radical-run Southern state legislatures.

Tax and Steal

Meanwhile, these puppet regimes ratcheted taxes ever-upward, even as most of the citizenry possessed less with each passing year. Time and again, carpetbag-dominated Southern legislatures voted enormous tax increases supposedly to fund new railroad tracks, roads, and canals—all of which could have benefitted the devastated South at this point. Few of these projects ever saw the light of day. Instead, the suffering people's money went to businessmen and opportunists who, instead of producing the declared service or product, pocketed most of

On a Sunday drive in Tennessee several years after the War.

the funds and shoveled a portion of them back to the puppet representatives who had voted it to them.

One singularly heinous example was the exorbitant "cotton tax," up to five cents per pound, which few cotton farmers could afford to pay. When they could not, they lost their cotton, the cotton gins on which they depended, and frequently the land on which they lived. And according to President Johnson's own Federal investigator, Sherrard Clemens, cotton tax revenues usually never made it past the personal bank accounts of the U.S. Treasury agents who collected them.

As this was happening, the state budgets approved by the Radical legislatures—comprised largely of white Northern carpetbaggers and black freedmen from both North and South—skyrocketed. Projects classified as "internal improvements" only comprised part of the story. "Mileage" expenses for individual legislators rose to astronomical levels across the South. Legislative sessions in Louisiana cost ten times what they had in 1860. So did the state's "printing" bill. The 1869 printing bill in Florida was larger than the budget to run the entire state government for the whole year in 1860, and more than the collective printing bill for the state from 1798–1868.

All this, and former white Confederates were told their sin precipitated the war that brought on their own just ruin. Their children were taught the same thing in the new government public schools springing up in communities across the South. Black former Confederates heard all this, and worse. They had their property stolen, their bodies whipped, and their lives taken on many occasions.

Few have summarized the malodorous situation better than E. Merlin Coulter in his famous book *The South During Reconstruction:*

> Saddled with an irresponsible officialdom, the South was now plunged into debauchery, corruption, and private plundering unbelievable—suggesting that government had been transformed into an engine of destruction. . . . Corruption permeated government from the statehouse to the courthouse and city hall. . . . The variety of means used to debauch government and plunder the public treasury bespeaks the vivid imaginations and practical ability of the perpetrators. Every seceded state came under the withering hand of Radical rule, but it was reserved to South Carolina, Louisiana, and Arkansas to suffer most. Legislatures piled up expenses against their impoverished states to fantastic heights.

State Railroads

If the transcontinental railroads provided a gateway to breathtaking wealth in the milieu of big government Radicalism, War profiteering, and Reconstruction, the "Military Districts" of the South proved lucrative in their own right. In Georgia, H. I. Kimball, an official in the administration of carpetbag Governor Rufus Bullock, used his influence to gain

The Railroads

One of the gargantuan feats of modern history, the crosshatching of America from one ocean to the other, symbolized many of the country's most singular traits—courage, vision, innovation, energy, greed, ruthlessness, and violence. Transcontinental railroads were a pillar of the internal improvements section of the Republican Party platform from the birth of the organization in the early 1850s. So was their fellow traveler, a homestead law, that would provide free land for the people which the railroads needed to settle the land along their routes and build communities and civic order.

Conservative Southern Democrats supported the free enterprise opportunities of railroad building, but not the forced participation of the citizenry through the confiscation of tax money for it. While the South remained in the Union, it stymied government-subsidized railroad construction at every turn. It did not take long after Southern secession, however, for the Northern Congress to pass the Pacific Railway Act of 1862. This chartered the Union Pacific Railway and officially launched the westward rail boom. Of equal import was the "purchase" of influence with individual Congressmen that generated colossal—and generous—monetary loans to the Union Pacific and other railroads; abolished Indian lands along rail right-of-ways; and required the use of iron manufactured by American companies.

Titans of industry made the railroads—and the railroads made them. J. P. Morgan, Cornelius Vanderbilt, Collis P. Huntington, James J. Hill, and that most cynical of robber barons, Jay Gould, as well as many other men of American industrial lore and legend recognized in railroads the preeminent vehicle of their generation by which to both multiply their financial kingdoms and garner political clout. So they poured in their money, energy, and vision. As they did, respected publications like *The Nation* warned that in terms of political and financial influence, the railroads had "the most formidable in any community" in the country; they lamented what they considered their poisoning of politics and domination of government.

The climax of a spectacular and historic race between the eastward-tracking Central Pacific and the westward-heading Union Pacific railroads, whose newly-laid tracks met at Promontory, Utah Territory, June 10, 1869. (National Archives and Records Administration)

John Carbutt's 1866 photograph of Union Pacific Railroad directors in western Nebraska Territory. They and their train, background, await a party of Eastern capitalists, journalists, and other prominent figures invited west by the railroad executives. (National Archives and Records Administration)

control of the construction and sale to the state of everything from hotels to opera houses. Authorized to employ state funds for the building of railroads, he became a partner in the Tennessee Car Company, purchased rail cars from himself with state money—then neglected the matter of delivering any cars.

Other Radical officials in Georgia secured enormous "compensations" from that state for their carpetbagging Brunswick and Albany Railroad. This scheme regarded iron the Southern government took from the company during the War—even though the Confederates paid for it and the Georgia state government had nothing to do with the action.

Former Federal General M. S. Littlefield, a mandarin power in the North Carolina state government in the late 1860s and beyond, operated an upstairs bar in the State House itself. There, he provided free whiskey and sometimes oysters in return for control of the state's railroads—from which many of the legislators themselves would receive hefty profits. Later, in 1875, Littlefield set up shop in Florida. There he used money, champagne, and beaver hats, among other things, to purchase legislators' votes for policies favorable to other railroads, the Georgia and the Tallahassee.

Their Legacy

One of the lasting enigmas of American history is the legacy of the railroads and the men who built them. Not blizzard, nor mountain, nor desert, nor Indian attack, nor political opposition, nor even malfeasance of funds on an unparalleled scale could stop them. They accomplished so much, and left so much to succeeding generations. Yet their cost in human capital perhaps exceeded that of the untold millions of dollars they cost the often-unsupportive taxpayer.

The financial looting and fraud surrounding the railroads was a direct and primary cause of the Panic of 1873. This in turn resulted in perhaps the worst depression in American history, which drove down wages in the major Eastern-based rail lines. These powerful corporations cut wages again in 1877, by ten percent. Now rail workers in Martinsburg, West Virginia, then from Maryland clear to San Francisco, walked off their jobs, demonstrated, and destroyed property. Violence and unrest beset hundreds of cities and towns. Over 100 people died, and millions of dollars in property was lost. Militiamen could not stanch the surging workers; U.S. Regular army soldiers finally did.

Relations between management and labor were never the same after the Great Railroad Strike. It played a pivotal role in the forming of America's labor union colossus. Labor chieftain Samuel Gompers later acknowledged this when he said, "The railroad strike of 1877 was the tocsin that sounded a ringing message of hope for us all." The final accounting for the moral ruin left by railroad plundering, theft, and character destruction will never be known.

Black Gains

Blacks who supported or migrated into the Radical camp gained numerous benefits from Federal Republican rule. A significant number of blacks won seats in Southern legislatures; a few won offices ranging from state lieutenant governor to governor and Congressman. Two became United States Senators. The Radicals facilitated no such ascendancy for blacks in the North during this period or for many years after.

Did we cease to throw shells into Vicksburg or Atlanta because women and children were there?

—Philip Sheridan defending his campaign of total war in the early 1870s on Plains Indians men, women, and children to William T. Sherman

Rampant corruption tainted the Radical-dominated constitutional conventions mandated by the Reconstruction Acts for the former Confederate states. The new constitu-

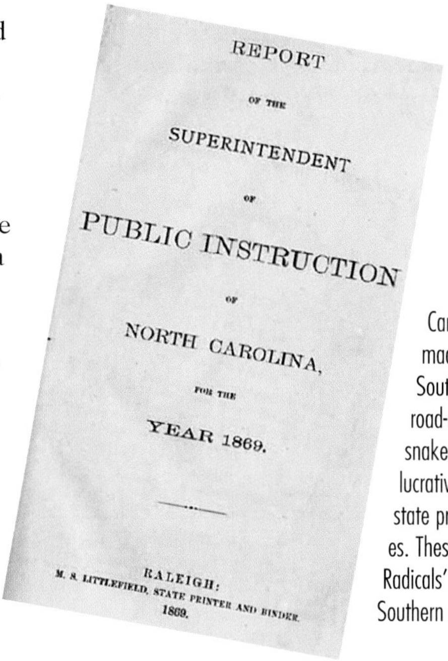
REPORT

OF THE

SUPERINTENDENT

OF

PUBLIC INSTRUCTION

OF

NORTH CAROLINA,

FOR THE

YEAR 1869.

RALEIGH:
M. S. LITTLEFIELD, STATE PRINTER AND BINDER.
1869.

Carpetbagger M. S. Littlefield made a fortune fleecing Southern state treasuries in railroad-related schemes, but he snaked his way into many other lucrative pies as well, including state printing and binding businesses. These mushroomed with the Radicals' expansion of the size of Southern state governments.

tions they produced, however, improved upon their predecessors in many ways. They provided that black men, as well as white, could vote. They also improved the legislative apportionment process for rural districts, made penal codes more humane, upgraded the legal status of women, and provided for insane asylums, homes for the poor, and other services.

And blacks served as delegates in every state that produced them. For awhile, men of African descent actually held the majority of seats in the South Carolina legislature.

On a different front, Northern schoolteachers and missionaries came South and taught thousands of black children reading and other educational skills.

Black Suffering

But black Southerners supportive of the Radicals suffered, too. Many Radical promises to them, such as free land, seldom came true, especially after Southern Democrats ousted the Republicans from power in the 1870s. Even many Northern blacks and more educated Southern freedmen opposed land giveaways to rural Southern blacks. One black Alabama Republican leader said, "We do not ask that the ignorant and degraded shall be put on a social equality with the refined and intelligent." Conversely, many Southern ex-slaves did not appreciate the prominence of Northern blacks, especially in Republican Party circles and political offices.

Masses of blacks found sudden emancipation in a land fraught with physical destruction, social turmoil, and economic despair, a difficult opportunity to master. And they found huge numbers of whites who were formerly their friends, or at least friendly to them, now hostile and even dangerous. The explosive growth of underground Southern resistance organizations multiplied the threat for blacks.

"End of the Track, Near Humboldt River Canyon, Nevada," by Alfred A. Hart. An 1868 Central Pacific Railroad train and campsite on the way to Promontory. (National Archives and Records Administration)

Granted, the blacks brought some of this backlash upon themselves when they acted foolishly and even violently against other blacks and white former Confederates. Most of it occurred, however, by virtue of the blacks getting caught in the crossfire—sometimes literally—between Radicals and Southern whites, as the former used them in an attempt to gain permanent national political hegemony over the latter. When Reconstruction ended and Federal bayonets departed, the majority of Southern blacks were left in the lurch by the departing Radicals, and cast into a long dark age that eventuated with Jim Crow laws and forcible segregation.

Race War

As Reconstruction ground on year after year; Radical forces grew richer and stronger while the bulk of the South suffered on; and violence begat violence, relations between the mass of Southern whites and blacks soured to where they have not yet fully recovered. Driven to desperation as they saw outside forces destroying their very civilization, Southern whites grew bolder in their resistance to tyranny. Intimidation of pro-Radical blacks increased, and against white carpetbaggers and scalawags too. And so did violence, including beatings, arson, and even murder.

Armed whites killed four blacks and wounded about fifty at an Alabama Republican gathering in 1870. Three white scalawags were murdered in Georgia. Eleven blacks were murdered in the area around York County, South Carolina during Reconstruction. An 1871 attack on a Union County, South Carolina jail by a masked mob hundreds strong left eight black prisoners lynched. Scores more such brutal examples can be cited.

But the Radical forces of the Union League, the Freedmen's Bureau, and others continued their own marauding, which additionally included the depredations of government power backed by legions of Federal bayonets. They too, bullied, beat, burned, and murdered their white—and black—Southern adversaries. Blacks attacked a Victoria, Texas jail, captured a white prisoner, dragged him out, and lynched him. A black lynch mob in South Carolina headed by black Federal soldiers kidnapped a jailed white man and murdered him. Pogroms by Federal military occupation forces—black and white—slaughtered white Southerners in Shreveport and Alexandria, Louisiana. One Northern journalist claimed the parade of "atrocities" and "daily outrages" committed by black soldiers against the white Southern citizenry seemed endless. Often, they too, donned disguises to commit crimes, many times against their own allies, so they could blame their acts on the Ku Klux Klan and other pro-Southern resistance movements.

> *All race antagonism [in the South] came from the carpetbaggers using the Negro votes to get their fingers into the Treasury.*
>
> —Federal General Donn Piatt

Klansmen Diverge

In 1869, Klan Grand Wizard Nathan Bedford Forrest evidently perceived the slow but determined political gains of the Southern majority, at

Hiram Revels (1822–1901)

The Reverend Hiram R. Revels rose up through racial prejudice, financial hardship, and a sea of corruption to leave a lasting legacy as a man who loved his God, his country, and his fellow man. Born to free black parents in North Carolina, from an early age he evidenced a zeal for learning and ministering to others. After he moved to Indiana in the early 1840s to pursue opportunities for higher education not available to blacks in the South, he became involved with the African Methodist Episcopal (AME) Church, a vigorous and gospel-preaching denomination in the black community.

In the mid to late 1840s, Revels pursued clerical training, received ordination as a minister in the AME Church, and became an elder. While preaching in the early 1850s, he married Phoeba A. Bass, with whom he sired and raised six children. He attended college in Illinois and in 1857, still preaching, became principal of a black high school in Baltimore.

The War brought new opportunities for service to the tall, handsome minister with the dignified manner and rich deep voice. He established a school for freedmen in St. Louis, aided the U.S. Provost Marshal in handling the affairs of ex-slaves, and moved to Vicksburg to preach and minister to the needs of freed slaves and help establish churches and schools for blacks.

Revels's talents, education, work experience, and character, as well as passage of the Fourteenth Amendment, led to his winning a City Council position in Natchez, Mississippi. While there, and while serving as presiding elder of the Methodist Episcopal church denomination for the southern part of Mississippi, he was asked by the Federally-imposed Radical state legislature to open their 1868 session with a prayer. According to John R. Lynch, a black political leader from Natchez, "That prayer was one of the more impressive and eloquent prayers that had ever been delivered in the Senate chamber. He made a profound impression upon all who heard him." So profound, in fact, that Lynch encouraged Revels to run for the state senate, which he did, victoriously.

Faithful to the End

Then in 1870, Revels gained the distinction of becoming the first black United States Senator in history when he won election to fill the final year of an unexpired term. He impressed a correspondent from the conservative, pro-Democratic *New York World* as a man "able to take care of himself . . . who will not suffer himself to be browbeaten even by (Charles) Sumner." During Revels's term, he persuaded the War Department to hire qualified black mechanics for its Washington Navy Yard, and he spoke against racial segregation in the schools of the U.S. capital city. He served on both the Committee on the District of Columbia and the Committee on Education, and introduced several bills and petitions.

None of the bills he presented to the Radical-dominated Senate passed, and he actually proved more conservative than some of the Radicals wished. Revels did support the Federal military occupation of the South, because he thought that necessary to protect the rights of Southern blacks. His Christian sense of justice, however, caused him to oppose the Radicals' depriving former Confederates of the right to vote. He did not believe that was any fairer than preventing black men from voting. A gradual but mounting dissatisfaction developed within him for Reconstruction and its flawed agenda.

After Revels left the senate, Alcorn College, a newly-formed college for blacks in Mississippi, named him its president. He served there until 1873, when he reentered the fulltime ministry as pastor of the Holly Springs Church, in the Methodist Episcopal denomination, in Mississippi. During this pastorate, his disapproval of Reconstruction grew. When some blacks began to vote for the Democrats and against the Republicans in the 1874 election campaigns, Revels wrote, "A great portion of them have learned that they were being used as mere tools, and determined, by casting their ballots against these unprincipled adventurers, to overthrow them."

In 1870, Hiram Revels gained the distinction of becoming the first black United States Senator in history.

The more he saw of the rampant corruption and lack of wisdom practiced by Carpetbag Governor Adelbert Ames and others, the less Revels liked it. Despite the opportunities Reconstruction policies had brought Revels and other blacks, unlike other men—black and white, in his own time and ours—he considered the means to an end as important as the end itself. His spiritual depth and that sense of justice filled him with disgust at the unfairness and lawbreaking he witnessed all around him. He electrified the whole nation in 1875 when he left the Republican party and declared that Reconstruction should end in the South.

Revels wrote a letter directly to President Grant, a letter that received wide publication and in which he accused the Republicans of using blacks to help them cling to political power. "If the state administration had adhered to Republican principles, advanced patriotic measures, appointed only honest and competent men to office, and sought to restore confidence between the races," he wrote, "bloodshed would have been unknown, peace would have prevailed, Federal interference been unthought of, harmony, friendship, and mutual confidence would have taken the place of the bayonet."

After several years in the ministry, Revels returned for a lengthy stint at the helm of Alcorn College. During his latter years, he preached and taught theology at Rust University in Holly Springs.

On January 16, 1901, while attending a church conference in Mississippi, Hiram R. Revels, faithful husband, father, minister, educator, and statesman, suffered a fatal stroke and passed from this world into the next. Surely he was received with the blessed words, "Well done, thou good and faithful servant."

least in Tennessee where he lived. He also recognized the multiplying violence, and the blaming of much of it on his friends that was done by his enemies. Someone—probably Forrest—issued a general order to disband the Ku Klux Klan.

At this point and soon after, many of the more respectable members of the Klan and similar organizations around the South indeed forswore their involvement. Klan activity in Tennessee petered out as the Democratic majority was able to

The Fifteenth Amendment

Section 1. The right of citizens of the United States to vote shall not be denied or abridged by the United States or by any State on account of race, color, or previous condition of servitude—

Section 2. The Congress shall have power to enforce this article by appropriate legislation.

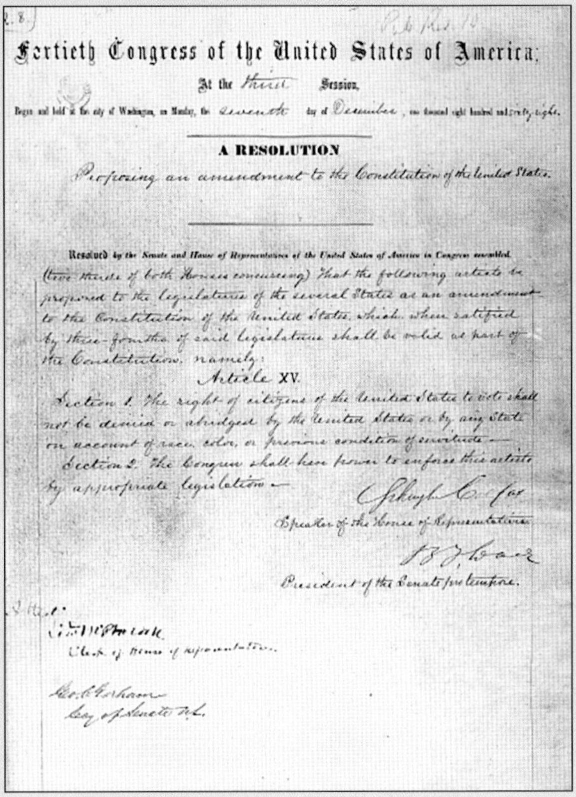
Fortieth Congress of the United States of America;

At the third Session,

Begun and held at the city of Washington, on Monday, the seventh day of December, one thousand eight hundred and sixty-eight.

A RESOLUTION

Proposing an amendment to the Constitution of the United States.

Resolved by the Senate and House of Representatives of the United States of America in Congress assembled, (two-thirds of both Houses concurring) That the following article be proposed to the legislatures of the several States as an amendment to the Constitution of the United States, which, when ratified by three-fourths of said legislatures shall be valid as part of the Constitution, namely:

Article XV.

Section 1. The right of citizens of the United States to vote shall not be denied or abridged by the United States or by any State on account of race, color, or previous condition of servitude—

Section 2. The Congress shall have power to enforce this article by appropriate legislation—

Schuyler Colfax
Speaker of the House of Representatives.

B. F. Wade
President of the Senate pro tempore.

Attest:
Edw. McPherson
Clerk of House of Representatives.

Geo. C. Gorham
Secy of Senate U.S.

The Joint Resolution of the United States Senate and House of Representatives proposing the Fifteenth Amendment to the Constitution. The signatures of House Speaker (and future Vice President Schuyler Colfax) and Senate President Pro Tempore Benjamin Wade are visible lower right.

reassert their electoral desires. Some men of less reputable nature, however, who likely committed the majority of the unsavory acts of the original Klan and similar groups, ignored Forrest's directive and continued on with their underground war, in Tennessee and elsewhere. In some states, too, such as Louisiana, Alabama, and Mississippi, the repressive conditions of Radical rule remained violent and corrupt enough that the vicious fight continued generally, with outrages large and small committed by both "sides."

In summary, the Klan and similar organizations faded out at different times in different places, usually depending on when the local white population again felt safe and somewhat empowered politically. This did not mean that rights for or friendliness toward blacks resumed, North or South. They did not. One of the great sad legacies of the War and Reconstruction is that Southerners of African descent lost much of what the Radicals promised them after the War and much of what Southern whites had provided them before the War.

Kirk's Rampage through North Carolina

Reconstruction conflict turned violent at times in South Carolina, Mississippi, Louisiana, and other states. Federal soldiers seemed always to play a central role at some point in these dramas, whether as policing agents, or precipitators of trouble, or both, or something else.

Nowhere was a Federal force more remarkably—or infamously—employed than in the "Kirk War" of 1870 North Carolina. The brainchild of arch Radical Senator John Pool, it called for a special army of Federal irregulars, designed ostensibly to corral Klansmen and other masked perpetrators of periodic violent deeds. Its covert design was to help the Republicans keep the reins of power in North Carolina. To do this, they needed an imposing force to cow those ready to issue indictments against the railroad-swindling juggernaut within the state government. "We are unable to administer the laws, and we feel that unless you can get our country under military rule we cannot protect our people," one of Pool's comrades wrote to vacillating Governor W. W. Holden.

When Holden flinched at hiring a rough man to ramrod the rough army of seven hundred—two thirds of them underage and illiterate, a third from out-of-state—Pool warned him, "Governor, you do not know how they are talking about you in Washington. The Republicans there say you are a failure, and Grant says you and Smith in Alabama were made Governors by the Republican Party under the Reconstruction Acts and you are sitting still and permitting these Ku-Klux to take them away from you, or cause them to slip away from you." Indeed, Grant promised Holden in Washington, "Let those men resist you, Governor, and I will move with all my power against them."

Colonel Kirk

And so, "Colonel" George W. Kirk, living in Tennessee, and notorious for his wartime brutality and desperate audacity as a Federal officer, took the reins of this special army. Some in North Carolina's Republican community applauded the selection of Kirk. Many did not. "For God's sake, don't send troops here. The town is quiet and all works well." "The Republicans do not want troops in this section, Governor. It will kill us in the next election." "Colonel Kirk is universally detested by the people as a military man. They fear and hate him." One recalled how "the very worst of troops, or men pretending to be such," commanded by Kirk, overran the county during the War. "We look upon Colonel Kirk as a man of bad character."

In the summer of 1870, Kirk led his motley column out of Morganton, headed east across the state. They cursed and insulted citizens as they passed, exposed themselves before women headed to church, and threatened, beat, and tortured "prisoners"—which were anyone they chose to arrest. The courts were ordered to accommodate them accordingly.

Josiah Turner, a brilliant *Raleigh Sentinel* newspaper reporter (and Klan member) excoriated Kirk and his mob. In return, Turner had his life threatened, his house stoned, and was finally captured, thrown into an iron cage swarming with rodents, and told he would be executed the next day. When his wife came to visit him, Kirk's men stoned her.

But Kirk's marauding only kindled the wrath of the state. In August, not even Radical control of the election machinery could turn back a Democratic landslide in the legislature, so overwhelming was the voter turnout. Then the Federal judiciary intervened, Grant failed to support the soon-to-be-impeached Holden, and Kirk was arrested—though a Radical sheriff allowed him to escape to Washington, where he served unmolested on the Capitol police force.

Meanwhile, Kirk's army disbanded quite near where its chaplain deserted his wife and children to elope with another woman. He was soon caught and arrested for bigamy.

Congress versus the Klan

Indeed, Southern resistance to Reconstruction rule grew rough enough that the still-Radical-controlled U.S. Congress, bolstered by Union League influence, established a committee to investigate the Ku Klux Klan. The Northern press and politicians depicted the Klan as a vast, coordinated, pan-Southern conspiracy. Extant evidence and eyewitness accounts point, rather, to a multitude of separate, usually unconnected small groups and individuals.

Americans have liked ice cream for a long time, as evidenced by this state-of-the-art Ice Cream Freezer advertised in the April 6, 1872 edition of *Harper's Weekly* (www.harpweek.com)

The twenty-man Congressional committee reflected the Radical majority of the larger House, and so did its report. It denounced and condemned the Klan, and recited a litany of offenses perpetrated against Republican whites and blacks in the South. Klan members did commit many of these offenses. Members of other resistance organizations committed some of them. So did anti-Radicals belonging to no such organizations. And some of them Union loyalists black and white did. But the majority of the committee was in no mood to brook such distinctions, and it condemned the Klan in the harshest possible terms. Its findings set the stage for legislation to exterminate as many Southerners as necessary to eradicate resistance activity.

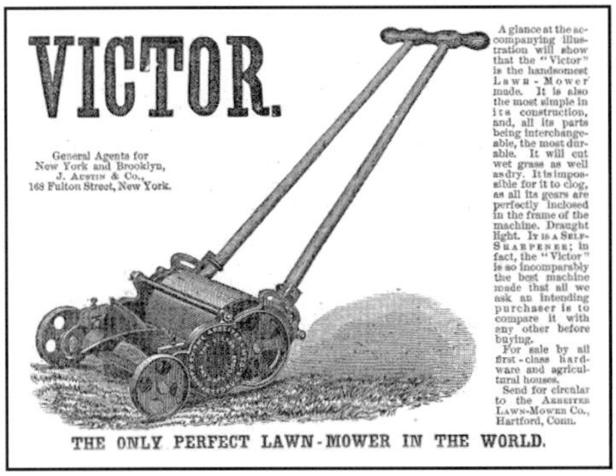

Victor declared itself "the only perfect lawn mower in the world" in the April 20, 1872 *Harper's Weekly* (www.harpweek.com).

Enforcement Acts

The Congressional committee report served as the catalyst for the three Enforcement Acts of 1870 and 1871, the third of which was the Ku Klux Klan Act. These measures were aimed to insure proper observance of the Fifteenth Amendment, ratified by the three-fourths of the states earlier in 1870, and designed to protect the voting rights of all citizens, specifically Southern blacks wishing to vote Republican.

These acts each featured a moral component that strived for the inclusion of the aforementioned blacks in the electoral process—even as they disfranchised non-Republican Southern whites from the same. And they featured a newfound sense of urgency. The Southern Democratic majorities were making inroads in several states, despite the broad and vigorous Federal Reconstruction policies. The Radicals needed their supporters—which included Northern carpetbaggers, Southern scalawags, and black freedmen—to vote Republican and do so without interference from white Democrats.

The Forgotten Minority Report on the Klan

Mostly lost to history is the minority report of the Congressional committee that investigated the Ku Klux Klan. While the entire committee condemned Klan violence, more than a third of it—none of them Southern Democrats—pointed the finger of blame for the bloodshed and other outrages straight at the Radicals' Reconstruction program, especially the actions of Union Leaguers.

> *Many of them took the law into their own hands and did deeds of violence which we neither justify or excuse. But all history shows that bad government will make bad citizens.*
>
> —Minority Report on the Klan

Charles Adams, in *When in the Course of Human Events*, catalogues the reasons cited in the minority report:

1. The Ku Klux Klan arose as an inescapable consequence of the Union League's brutality.
2. Many of the crimes against black people were committed by Union League men disguised as Klansmen.
3. Had there been no wanton oppression in the South, there would have been no rule of the tyrannical, corrupt carpetbagger or scalawag (white Southerners supporting Reconstruction for personal gain) rule, and there would have been no secret organizations.
4. From the oppression and corruption of the one sprang the vice and outrage of the other.

The minority report itself included this passage:

> *[The Union League] hatred of the white race was instilled into the minds of these ignorant people by every art and vile that bad men could devise. . . . Arson, rape, robbery and murder were things of daily occurrence; when the great mass of the most intelligent whites were disenfranchised and the ballot was put into the hands of the negro by the government in Washington. . . . In short, when the people saw that they had no rights which were respected, no protection from insult, no security even for their wives and children, and that what little they had saved from the ravages of war was being confiscated by taxation . . . many of them took the law into their own hands and did deeds of violence which we neither justify or excuse. But all history shows that bad government will make bad citizens.*

After the committee interviewed Nathan Bedford Forrest—believed to be the former leader, or Grand Wizard, of the Klan—in 1871–72 and amassed a mountain of other material regarding the Ku Klux Klan, they announced:

> *It is only necessary to turn to the official documents of Tennessee to show that all Forrest said about the alarm which prevailed during the administration of [Tennessee] Governor Brownlow was strictly true. No state was ever reduced to such humiliation and degradation as that unhappy commonwealth during the years Brownlow ruled over her.*

Forrest himself confused many and angered others in North and South alike when he proclaimed, "Abolish the [Union] Loyal League and the Ku Klux Klan; let us come together and stand together."

Steinway was a respected name in pianos even when this November 25, 1871 *Harper's Weekly* (www.harpweek.com) ad ran.

With the Ku Klux Klan Act, the government threw off all restraints. It discarded the legal jurisdiction guaranteed to states by the Constitution; deprived hundreds, perhaps thousands, of their Constitutional right to trial by a jury of their peers for crimes ranging from assault to murder; filled juries with Radical sympathizers and supporters; gave President Grant the unilateral right both to unleash martial law and suspend the writ of habeas corpus. No Southern citizen had any right to redress in any of these situations. Federal soldiers poured into one section of upcountry South Carolina in such numbers and arrested, prosecuted, imprisoned, and attacked with such vengeance that for a period of time in 1871 commercial activity in the area virtually ground to a halt.

New York Tribune publisher and 1872 Liberal Republican presidential candidate Horace Greeley

Sadly for everyone, in the most contentious areas, where the U.S. government appeared to have stymied Klan activity, the perpetrators—and angry men who subsequently joined their ranks—merely adjusted their tactics, went farther underground, and bided their time. The least of their intentions was to give up. Grim and hardened, they rested on one hope—they would be in South Carolina longer than would the Yankee troops.

Many would no doubt have concurred with the words of former Unionist and anti-secessionist Robert E. Lee. Near the end of his life, he told wartime Texas Governor Fletcher Stockdale, in private: "Governor, if I had foreseen the use those people designed to make of their victory, there would have been no surrender at Appomattox Courthouse; no, sir, not by me. Had I foreseen these results of subjugation, I would have preferred to die at Appomattox with my brave men, my sword in this right hand."

Elections of 1872

Aghast both at the tactics and results of Radical Reconstruction, a whole segment of the Republican Party splintered into a group known as "Liberal Republicans. Though not taking issue with the Radicals' support of high tariffs, they decried their party's "vindictive" Reconstruction policy and clamored for an end to the rampant corruption besetting government service. The Liberal Republicans included party stalwarts like Charles Sumner, Carl Schurz, and others. But they nominated Horace Greeley, who was not conservative enough to inspire Democrats and had too little to offer to Republicans to pull them away from their party's candidates and support.

Artist Matt Morgan's "The Cincinnati Snowball—It Grows As It Rolls," a May 4, 1872 *Leslie's Illustrated* editorial cartoon conveying the Liberal Republican movement's tide of momentum going into its Cincinnati convention prior to the 1872 Presidential contest. Artist Matt Morgan reveals the scene only thirty days before in the upper right corner, with President Grant and his lieutenants scoffing at the tiny snowball. Now its molders, Carl Schurz (with beard) and Charles Sumner, backed by a host of other disaffected Republicans, are rolling it over the Radical Republican establishment, including a fleeing Grant.

Grant, with the North solidly supporting him and most of the South still ruled by carpetbaggers, trounced Greeley, who carried only six states. Now Grant had the people's mandate to carry on the Radical brand of Reconstruction for four more years. And he had both houses of Congress to partner with him, as the Radicals retained control there, too. "The election of 1872 was a sweeping triumph for reaction," historian Claude Bowers summarized, "and the South found itself in more dire straits than ever, as the corruptionists and carpetbaggers, triumphant, mounted and rode."

The Race of the Time-Keepers.
ELGIN AHEAD.

Elgin leads the race of watches in a clever February 10, 1872, *Harper's Weekly* (www.harpweek.com) ad.

36 Corruption

"Colored Rule in a Reconstructed State," Thomas Nast's front-page March 14, 1874 *Harper's Weekly* (www.harpweek.com) depiction of the carryings-on of the Federals' Reconstruction-era South Carolina legislature. Lady Columbia, upper right, calls the members to account. The vivid work is particularly notable because Nast had long used his high-profile platform to exhort American society to improve its treatment of blacks. The many reports from government officials, journalists, and other citizens regarding the offensive behavior of the South Carolina state house prompted this dramatic broadside. *Harper's* did speak favorably in the same issue of the performance of South Carolina's Radical black Federal Congressmen.

Why, the war has corrupted everybody and everything. It is money that achieves success . . . nowadays. Thank God, my political career ended with the beginning of this corrupt political era.

—Republican Iowa Senator Ross Grimes

Immediately following the Radicals' sweeping 1872 election victories, a new sensation came crashing down, and never would the stain of scandal and disgrace depart the Grant administration until the end of his second term. It stemmed back to passage of the Pacific Railway Act of 1862 that chartered the Union Pacific Railroad. This and other wartime Congressional measures unleashed one of the great land-giveaways in history as that rail company and others hurtled toward completion of transcontinental lines. It also set in motion a frenzy of payoffs and bribes as railroads and other corporations purchased favor from government officials in the awarding of land grants and other valuable considerations.

James Garfield, Crédit Mobilier profiteer and future U.S. president.

Crédit Mobilier

And it produced companies like Crédit Mobilier. Formed as a construction company to build the Union Pacific's cross-country line, Crédit Mobilier possessed the same board of directors as the railroad company. These men mortgaged Union Pacific to the hilt and threw these proceeds, the company's enormous taxpayer-funded endowment, and every other Union Pacific resource they could manage toward Crédit Mobilier as payment for its construction work.

A Congressional investigation later determined that Crédit Mobilier charged Union Pacific $94 million for construction that cost $44 million or less. Those comprising the board that "served" both companies reaped the breathtaking harvest. Union Pacific shareholders, and the American taxpayer, were left holding the bag.

What raised Crédit Mobilier to a name of historic proportions was the men who profited by it and were implicated to varying degrees by the Congressional investigation. They included the Vice President, the Vice President-elect, the chairmen of the most crucial House committees, various Republican Party leaders, and even one Democrat, their House floor leader. Many of these leaders of the

American government received huge amounts of stock without paying for them; when dividends began cascading in, the purchase prices of the stock were declared paid, and the statesmen began receiving their windfalls.

Prominent Congressman and war veteran James A. Garfield provides one example. Despite abundant evidence to the contrary, he maintained he never owned such stock, nor received dividends. As historian Claude Bowers recalled, the Congressional committee found "that he had owned stock, did receive a dividend, and had perjured himself—and was therefore innocent." Garfield was elected President in 1880.

In the end, the Radical Congressmen dominating the investigation declared everyone innocent except the lone Democrat (who, unlike the others, abstained from voting on Union Pacific-related issues, except when voting against the railroad's wishes) and the Republican who had revealed the gigantic scheme. Still, *The Nation* announced that the scandal's "effect on congressional reputations may be briefly summed up in this way: total loss, one Senator; badly damaged and not serviceable for future political use, two Vice-Presidents and eight Congressmen." Indeed, Crédit Mobilier torpedoed the career of Schuyler Colfax, long a leader in the Radical juggernaut; he failed even to retain his position as vice president in Grant's second term.

Schuyler Colfax, Vice President in U. S. Grant's first term, whose political career the Crédit Mobilier scandal brought down.

National Unrest

Whatever the violence in the South during the dark days of Reconstruction,

Though political fraud and lawbreaking was rampant throughout the Republican Party—particularly its dominant Radical wing—during the post-war and Reconstruction Era, Democrat W. M. "Boss" Tweed headed the infamous New York-based "Tweed Ring." Headquartered in Albany, the state capital, the Tweed Ring offers one of the most notorious examples in American history of large-scale graft and influence-buying. So great were its offenses that bringing Tweed and his ring down in 1871 helped propel Samuel Tilden to the Democratic Presidential nomination in 1876.

and whoever was responsible for which part of it, contemporary newspaper accounts establish that the region was no more violent than the North. Gangs and mobs of jobless, sometimes homeless, men, marauded through the North, beating, robbing, and killing. "From all over the East came reports of thefts, incendiary fires, rapes and even murders committed by vagrants," one historian recounts. "Assassinations swept Northern coal fields. Harsh management practices by the railroads against their own employees led to burning, pillaging, and pitched battles between Federal soldiers and railroad workers."

Congress passed the Amnesty Act in 1872, which removed most restrictions placed on ex-Confederates in the Fourteenth Amendment.

Thousands of men, women, and children walked the streets of Northern cities in hopeless search of employment. A huge meeting at the Cooper Union assembly center in New York City featured placards that told the ugly story for that city:

> 10,000 homeless men and women in our streets. 7,500 lodged in the overcrowded "charnel" station houses per week. 20,250 idle men from 11 trade unions, while only 550 are employed. 182,000 skilled workmen belonging to trade organizations of the State idle. 110,000 idle of all classes in New York City.

As railroad and other industrial executives grew wealthy beyond imagining, some Northern states banned the often-underpaid workers from participating in either strikes or unions. And farmers from every section rose up against the cabal they now knew existed between the railroads, other corporate monopolies, and the Federal government. In some states, their demands for government control of railroads and staunching railroad landgrabs, followed by sweeping actions at the polls, constituted nothing short of revolution. In Illinois, for instance, voters replaced Radical establishmentarians with Democrat and Republican Reformers across the state.

Panic of 1873

Then fell like a crashing redwood tree the banking and financial empire of Jay and Henry Cooke, the largest dispenser of financial largesse in the nation to the Radical Republican government. The fall of Cooke set off a chain of toppling king-sized dominoes across the American financial community. Down went Henry Clews and Company, down went scores of Wall Street stalwarts, down went the nation's business in general. Thus came the Panic of 1873 and a crushing, six-year-long depression, worse than any in the nation's history, at least until that spawned by the Stock Market Crash of 1929.

The United States Treasury itself evidently needed a $200,000 securities injection to assure its safety—and they got it from Jay Cooke and Company. That remarkable transaction brought this comment from *The Nation*, one of the country's leading publications:

> Where Jay Cooke and Company got this money, no one seems to know, as the firm are insolvent and making terms with their creditors; and the creditors . . . who find the Government treated as having a preferred claim, are naturally alarmed. Altogether it is a very mysterious piece of business.

How could it have happened?

Claude Bowers offered his answer in *The Tragic Era:*

> Railroads, wastefully and sometimes criminally built, had been built greatly beyond the demand for their services. Overtrading, expansion of credits, rash investments, and unreasonable speculation on the part of those who thought it good to be rich, all enter into the explanation of the collapse.

Whiskey Ring

A new scandal lurched into the maelstrom of Reconstruction chicanery in the spring of 1875.

For years, a criminal ring based in Missouri had skimmed huge amounts of money from whiskey tax proceeds. The enterprise stemmed back to a Republican party feud in the late 1860s in Missouri between Radical party regulars and a reform group led by Senator Carl Schurz and others.

Grant had intervened by naming one of his close friends, Federal General John McDonald, as state party chairman and supervisor of the internal revenue office in St. Louis. The reformers warned that McDonald's dishonest reputation would mean trouble down the road, but Grant saw their protests as directed toward himself, not McDonald, and ignored them. Soon, a sordid conspiracy began encompassing McDonald, other internal revenue officers, Grant administration personnel and Treasury Department officials in Washington, and whiskey distillers. They stole huge amounts of whiskey tax revenue, funded Federal political campaigns, bankrolled anti-reform efforts in the party, and grew quite rich as individuals.

With complicity ranging through the highest levels of the national government, the Whiskey Ring plied its sordid, money-drenched trade for years. Year after year, the press screeched about corruption in the whiskey tax.

Grant's Disgraced Officials

1869	Abel Corbin, brother-in-law
1875	John McDonald, Internal Revenue Commissioner for St. Louis
1875	William W. Belknap, Secretary of War
1876	Robert Schenck, Ambassador to Britain
1876	Orville Babcock, Private Secretary

Ulysses S. Grant (Part 2) (1822–1885)

After the War, both major political parties courted Grant as a surefire Presidential election winner. At first, he seemed inclined toward the Democrats. He had only voted in two Presidential elections, both times for the Democratic candidate. And he served for awhile as Secretary of War to the first postwar president, who was Lincoln's second vice president and presidential successor, Democrat Andrew Johnson.

Withal, Grant had never really fit the mold of a Republican, certainly of a Radical Republican. He owned slaves, brought to his marriage by his Missouri wife Julia, long after his chief Southern adversary Lee did. It was not until passage (and eventual Supreme Court sanction of) the Thirteenth Amendment forced him to free them that he did—two years after the War ended. "If the war had been about slavery," Grant said, he "would have fought for the South." But Grant and Johnson ran afoul of one another, at least partly because powerful Republicans in Congress as well as Johnson's own administration were intriguing both to win Grant to their party and to destroy Johnson's Presidency.

U. S. Grant, dying of throat cancer, writes his memoirs.

So Grant won election in 1868 as a Republican against one of his former subordinates, William Rosecrans. But his Presidential career was as disappointing as his War record was brilliant. Personally honest and sincere, he committed errors of judgment, many of them big ones, from the beginning. He won reelection in 1872, but by the end of his second term in 1877, corruption and scandal abounded in his administration.

Scandal and Depression

Grant's brother-in-law Abel Corbin was found culpable in the historic "Black Friday" stock market crash of September 24, 1869, when stock manipulators Jay Gould and Jim Fisk tried to corner the gold market and instead sent the nation into a decade-long economic slump. His own brother was accused of wrongdoing by figures possessing national stature, his private secretary proven corrupt, and his bribe taking Secretary of War forced to resign. Black Friday, the Santa Domingo statehood scheme, the Crédit Mobilier scandal, the Whiskey Ring, the Emma Mine affair, and numerous other tawdry affairs chipped away at Grant's reputation and ability to lead, though he was not found guilty of personal wrongdoing in any of them.

Many with whom he directly dealt, however—diplomats, judges, Congressmen, the Vice President, and a future President—were. In short, Ulysses S. Grant was President during a time of unprecedented greed, high-level chicanery, and crooked dealings, and he possessed no ability to correct any of them, nor in most cases even recognize them. Grant's political incompetence and the corruption of many of his colleagues left a permanent stain on his own name and that of his administration. When he sought the Presidency for a third time in 1880, he could not even win his own party's nomination, losing to another former subordinate, James Garfield.

Former Confederate General Simon Bolivar Buckner and former Federal General U. S. Grant meet once last time, just thirteen days before Grant's death. The two had been good friends since their days at West Point, nearly half a century before. Buckner had loaned money to Grant when the latter was in dire straits before the War, and Grant was kind to him when Buckner surrendered to him at Fort Donelson. Buckner's wife Delia recalled that, "The sole object of General Buckner's visit was to assure him that the Southern people appreciated his magnanimity at Appomattox and give pleasure to a dying man."

By the end of his second term, the nation had descended into a years-long depression that was perhaps worse even than the one that began in 1929; tens of thousands of people declared bankruptcy, a shameful act in that generation. Grant did accomplish good during his eight years as President. Passage of the Amnesty Bill in 1872 restored civil rights to many Southerners, relieving some of the harsh conditions of Reconstruction. And, against considerable opposition, he took courageous steps to fight the growing threat of inflation.

Woeful money problems beset Grant during his last years. From the fall of 1884 until his death on July 23, 1885, he raced against the ravages of throat cancer to finish his memoirs so that his widow would not live out her days as a pauper. During his final days, he could only communicate, and work on his book, with short written notes. Grant won this final battle, and his well-received chronicle generated nearly half a million dollars in income for Julia, a colossal amount in that day.

Henry McNeil Turner (1834-1915)

Henry McNeil Turner provides a memorable illustration of the evolution of the spiritual-political leader as champion for the emerging American black community and its causes, and by extension, the causes of all Americans. Born a slave in South Carolina, President Lincoln appointed McNeil before he was thirty years of age as the U.S. Army's first black chaplain. At the end of the War, he became a Freedman's Bureau agent in Georgia. From 1868-1870, he served in Georgia's Reconstruction legislature.

Turner left the Freedman's Bureau, however, and according to the book *The Life and Times of Henry McNeil Turner*, redirected his focus toward spiritual ends and resumed his practice as an "active member of the Gospel and traveling over the state to organize the Freedman into churches." Indeed, Turner, ever a passionate advocate for what he believed right, endured many frustrations after the War. One that brought him much grief was the phenomenon of mixed-race elites, especially in larger Southern cities, greeting the mass and sudden entrance of black slaves into the ranks of the free with decided ambivalence. "The blacks were arrayed against the brown or mulattoes, and mulattoes in turn against the blacks,"' he witnessed with sorrow.

Another frustration involved his efforts to lobby Congress toward extending civil rights, including the right to vote, to blacks. "Several Congressmen tell me, 'the negro must vote,' but the issue must be avoided now so as 'to keep up a two thirds power in Congress,'" he reported to Georgia's statewide black convention in 1866. Even when blacks gained the right to vote in the South, they faced sometimes-violent opposition in some quarters, while numerous Northern states prohibited them voting for years to come.

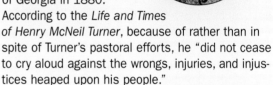

From 1870–1874, Turner pastored St. Philip's Methodist Episcopal Church in Atlanta, founded in 1865 as the "Mother Church of African Methodism" in Georgia. His denomination elected him Bishop of Georgia in 1880. According to the *Life and Times of Henry McNeil Turner*, because of rather than in spite of Turner's pastoral efforts, he "did not cease to cry aloud against the wrongs, injuries, and injustices heaped upon his people."

Not one to back away from controversy, Turner questioned the prevailing notion of his day that God was "white":

> *We have as much right biblically and otherwise to believe that God is a Negroe, as you white people have to believe that God is a fine looking, symmetrical and ornamented white man. For the bulk of you and all the fool Negroes of the country believe that God is white-skinned, blue eyed, straight-haired, projected nosed, compressed lipped and finely robed white gentleman, sitting upon a throne somewhere in the heavens. Every race of people since time began who have attempted to describe their God by words, or by paintings, or by carvings, or any other form or figure, have conveyed the idea that the God who made them and shaped their destinies was symbolized in themselves, and why should not the Negroe believe that he resembles God.*

Back to Africa

By the mid-late 1870s, Turner came to the conviction that white America would never allow blacks to "rise above a state of serfdom." He took a leading role in the "Back-to-Africa" movement in which thousands of blacks chose to return to their ancient homeland. Ironically, the American Colonization Society championed by Thomas Jefferson, Andrew Jackson, Abraham Lincoln, and many others had advocated just such a plan.

In 1878, Turner endorsed the chartering of a ship on which 200 South Carolina blacks emigrated back to Africa. In the 1890s, he led two such expeditions from Savannah, Georgia, himself. These African emigration efforts paid dividends in another way. Turner engaged in extensive missionary work to the unchurched people living on the continent of his heritage, particularly in west and south Africa.

Turner's passion did not leave him even in his later years. Ever-sympathetic to the underdog, he blasted America's brutal subjugation of the Philippines. President William McKinley claimed that blood-drenched conflict, which was part of the Spanish-American War and which took the lives of over 200,000 Filipino men, women, and children, was an effort to "Christianize and civilize" the (already largely-Catholic) Filipinos. President Theodore Roosevelt ferociously continued its prosecution when he came into office. But Henry McNeil Turner declared it "an unholy war of conquest."

But it was not until Benjamin A. Bristow's appointment as Secretary of the Treasury that honest men began to pursue the culprits. By the time the Whiskey Ring fell, government officials as high as Grant's personal secretary, Orville Babcock, had been indicted. Despite abundant evidence of Babcock's influence peddling and graft-taking, he was declared not guilty—though soon another scandal loomed that drove him from office.

The Grant administration, meanwhile, had executed its influence at every stage of the fight. It fired prosecutor John Henderson once he got hot on Babcock's trail. It prohibited witness immunity, which precluded informers from stepping forward. By the end, the nation's press mocked the White House as the headquarters of the Babcock defense. The ring's tactics against Republican Party reformers in Missouri spawned the "Liberal Republican" backlash that helped cost the party the House of Representatives in 1874, nearly the Presidency in 1876, and Reconstruction itself in 1877.

I have always contended that if there had been nobody left but the soldiers we would have had peace in a year. . . . The trouble is now made by men who did not go into the war at all, or who did not get mad till the war was over.

—Ulysses S. Grant,
shortly before his death in 1885

Jay Gould and the Robber Barons (1836-1892)

A frail and sickly child whose father locked him in the cellar when he misbehaved, Jason "Jay" Gould parlayed independence, intellect, audacity, and cool calculation into one of the greatest fortunes of the Nineteenth Century. He was, perhaps, the quintessential "robber baron," that class of industrial captains marked by aggressiveness, ruthlessness, and an inexorable greed for acquiring more power and wealth. Jay Gould exemplified both the bright dream and the dark reality of the American Dream, and no man incited more awe and hatred of himself.

While still in his late teens, Gould entered into a hide-tanning business partnership with an older man. Many of the characteristics that would mark his entire career appeared here in incipient form. He put his brilliant and creative business mind to work secretly, deceitfully, and profitably, stealing company money to play the New York City futures market he had learned. Learning of his young partner's perfidy, the older man merely allowed Gould to buy him out at a low price.

In 1868, Gould and his flamboyant fellow-speculator Jim Fisk locked horns with the richest man in America, Cornelius Vanderbilt, for control of the Erie Railroad.

Securing another partner, wealthy leather merchant Charles Leupp, Gould continued siphoning company profits—through a secret private bank he had founded—into the hides futures markets. Again exhibiting that "the boy is the father of the man," he effectively cornered that market and made his first million dollars, an enormous amount in that day, all before the age of twenty-one.

Then the economic panic of 1857 struck, the hide market crashed, and Gould and his unsuspecting partner both went bankrupt. Confronted with a calm, evidently unrepentant reaction from Gould, the shocked Leupp soon committed suicide. Gould proceeded on his way, and by the end of the War, while not yet thirty years of age, he owned one of the largest fortunes in the country. In 1868, he and his flamboyant fellow-speculator Jim Fisk locked horns with the richest man in America, Cornelius Vanderbilt, for control of the Erie Railroad.

Rough and dogged, Vanderbilt proceeded to buy up enormous amounts of Erie stock. Gould and Fisk brazenly issued more stock to dilute the value of Vanderbilt's purchases, then bribed New York legislators to sanction this illegal practice. When Vanderbilt issued warrants for their arrest, they ferried their headquarters across the river into New Jersey, beyond his reach. This epic battle of financial titans continued for years, until Vanderbilt conceded defeat to his tenacious opponents. He had learned, he said, "never to kick a skunk."

Familiar Patterns

Despite his victory over Vanderbilt, Gould's mannerly amorality birthed big problems for himself, as government investigators discovered his issuance of millions of dollars worth of fraudulent Erie Railroad stock. This forced Gould's resignation as Erie president in 1872, but he rebounded to take over the potentially more formidable Union Pacific Railroad. Here, Gould demonstrated a pattern that became familiar to observers. He manipulated his way to ownership of the troubled company through bribery, deception, and astute assessment of Union Pacific's weaknesses; performed cosmetic improvements to it, while raising large amounts of money; looted the proceeds to fund his own speculation and payments to business and political leaders; then sold the business for a price far above its actual worth.

By 1880 he controlled over 10,000 miles of rail line, approximately ten percent of the total amount laid in America at that time.

In the midst of the "Erie War" as it was known, Gould and Fisk nearly managed to corner the nation's gold market, which led to the "Black Friday" Stock Market Crash discussed earlier in this chapter. These Wall Street pirates exemplified how varied could be the external appearances of robber barons, while they shared similarly single-minded inner motivations. Gould was slight, soft-spoken, a loyal husband and loving father, and singularly free from the pursuit of alcoholic beverages, tobacco, and extramarital philandering, that beset many of his peers. Fisk, meanwhile, preened while adorned with expensive clothes and audacious bravado, as well as an insatiable lust for women. "In the pursuit of gain," writes Claude Bowers, however, "one was no more scrupulous than the other, and neither had any scruples at all."

Gould organized and schemed to expand his ownership of Union Pacific into a virtual railroad empire. By 1880 he controlled over 10,000 miles of rail line, approximately ten percent of the total amount laid in America at that time. He also gained majority ownership of the telegraph giant Western Union, New York City's elevated railways, and many other ventures.

Alas, as with other late-Nineteenth Century Gilded Age luminaries, no amount of wealth could provide Jay Gould security or peace of mind. One biographer of the era, W. T. Stead, remarked of Gould that "It is the keeping of the fortune, not the making of it, that takes it out of a man." Upon his death at age fifty-six, Gould's friend and physician remarked that "Jay Gould had no organic trouble, but his heart had all it could do to irrigate a brain always hungry for more sustaining food." A longtime close associate named Morosini said:

> *My opinion is that his system gave way under the great strain resulting from the consciousness of his great wealth. It was a tremendous care and he was always weighed down with the anxiety and excitement of protecting his properties.*

Gould's estate totaled over $70 million at his death, equal to several billion early-21st-century dollars. Yet son George Jay Gould lost the family's entire rail empire within twenty years of his father's death. Indeed, the elder Gould had bequeathed all $70 million to his family, leaving not one penny to charity or church. Though some Gould associates claimed he gave large anonymous donations to a variety of projects, no evidence attests to this. In fact, W. T. Stead offered a prophetic insight regarding Gould's apparent lack of benevolence in life and death. That stinginess, said Stead, would accelerate popular support for the government to confiscate increasing portions of the inheritance funds of millionaires, for the good of society, since some had shirked the opportunity to voluntarily do so.

Big Ben Hill's Reconstruction Oratory

Some of the greatest oratory in American history thundered forth during the Reconstruction Era from the lips of 6-foot, 6 1/2-inch Ben Hill of Georgia. No one took the Radical Republicans and their policies of suppression more sternly—or more eloquently—to task than did Hill, first in the Georgia legislature, then later in the United States Senate.

Tinkers may work, quacks may prescribe, and demagogues may deceive, but I declare to you that there is no remedy for us of the South . . . but in adhering to the Constitution.

A great many Southerners flippantly say the Constitution is dead. They say your rights and hopes for the future, and the hopes of your children are dead. . . . They say the Constitution does not apply to us? Then don't swear to support it. They say again that we are not in the Union—then why swear to support the Union of these states? What Union does that mean? When you took the oath, was it the Union of the Northern states alone that you swore to support?

Oh, I pity the colored people who have never been taught what an oath is, or what the Constitution means. They are drawn up by a selfish conclave of traitors to inflict a deathblow on the Republic by swearing them into a falsehood. They are to begin their political life with perjury to accomplish treason. . . . They are neither legally nor morally responsible—it is you, educated, designing white men—who thus devote yourselves to the unholy work, who are the guilty parties. You prate about your loyalty. I look you in the eye and denounce you morally- and legally-perjured traitors. . . . Ye hypocrites! Ye whited sepulchers! Ye mean in your hearts to deceive him, and buy up the Negro vote for your own benefit!

Benjamin H. Hill

Go on confiscating! Arrest without warrant or probable cause; destroy habeas corpus; deny trial by jury; abrogate state governments; defile your own race and flippantly say the Constitution is dead! On, on with your work of ruin, ye hell-born rioters in sacred things! But remember that for all these things the people will call you to judgment.

Ah! What an issue you have made for yourselves. Succeed and you destroy the Constitution! Fail, and you have covered the land with mourning. Succeed, and you bring ruin on yourselves and all the country! Fail, and you bring infamy upon yourselves and all your deluded followers. Succeed, and you are the perjured assassins of liberty! Fail, and you are defeated, despised traitors forever! Ye who aspire to be Radical governors and judges, I paint before you this day your destiny. You are but cowards and knaves, and the time will come when you will call upon the rocks and mountains to fall on you and the darkness to hide you from an outraged people.

Ah! What an issue you have made for yourselves. Succeed and you destroy the Constitution! Fail, and you have covered the land with mourning.

They tell you [blacks] they are your friends—it is false. They tell you they set you free—it is false. These vile creatures never went with the army except to steal spoons, jewelry, and gold watches. They are too low to be brave. They are dirty spawn, cast out from decent society, who go South seeking to use you to further their own base purposes. . . . Improve yourselves; learn to read and write; be industrious; lay up your means; acquire homes; live in peace with your neighbors; drive off as you would a serpent the miserable dirty adventurers who come among you . . . and seek to foment among you hatred of the decent portion of the white race.

. . . that traitors may hold the power they desecrate, and riot in the wreck of the prosperity they destroy.

[The Military Bill brought] the ultimate but complete change of all American government from the principle of consent to the rule of force (and) a war of races.

[Liberty is] abrogated and withdrawn from ten million people of all colors, sexes, and classes, who live in ten unheard and excluded states; and that, too, by men who do not live in these states . . . who never think of them but to hate . . . never enter them but to insult. . . . Better to brook the courts' delay for ten years than accept anarchy and slavery for a century. . . . Those who outlaw patriotism and intelligence would not scruple to rob. The same train brings the bread to feed, the officer to oppress, the emissary to breed strife and to rob.

There is not a single Southern man who advocates the acceptance of this reconstruction scheme who was not bought, and bought with a price by your enemies.

To secure these ten states to keep the Radical party in power in the next presidential election . . . to retain by force and fraud the power they are losing in the detection of their treason in the North . . . they annul the Constitution in the name of loyalty; exterminate the black race in the name of philanthropy; disfranchise the white race in the name of equality; pull down all the defenses of life and prosperity in the name of liberty; and with blasphemous hosannas to the Union, they are rushing all sections and all races into wild chaotic anarchy; and all, that traitors may hold the power they desecrate, and riot in the wreck of the prosperity they destroy.

Go on and pass your qualifying acts, trample upon the Constitution you have sworn to support; abnegate the pledges of your fathers; incite raids upon our people; and multiply your infidelities until they shall be like the stars of heaven and the sands of the seashore, without number; but know this: for all your iniquities the South will never again seek a remedy in the madness of another secession. We are here; we are in the house of our fathers; our brothers are our companions, and we are home to stay, thank God.

There is not a single Southern man who advocates the acceptance of this reconstruction scheme who was not bought, and bought with a price by your enemies. Never . . . suffer a single native renegade who voted for the vassalage of these states and the disgrace of your children to darken your doors or to speak to any member of your family.

Shifting Tide

In sum, the general economic and social climate of Reconstruction Era America was edgy, uncertain, often brutal, and, in the end, disastrous. Amidst all the corruption, all the scandal, all the destruction of moral goodness and decency, U. S. Grant's preeminent lieutenant, Radical Republican Speaker of the House Oliver Morton announced, "The standard of public morals today is higher in this country than it has ever been before."

In sum, the general economic and social climate of Reconstruction Era America was edgy, uncertain, often brutal, and, in the end, disastrous.

A huge crowd turned out to greet Andrew Johnson's triumphant return to the nation's capital as a newly-elected Senator from Tennessee. "What kind of government have we now?" he asked. The people of America, North and South, answered in the 1874 elections, when they unseated Radicals across the country and swept them from power in the House of Representatives for the first time since before the War. One by one, the Southern states shoved them out too, and reclaimed the reins of their own local and state political institutions. And the reputation of U. S. Grant and his administration sank lower and lower.

The Radical leadership that had dominated both houses of Congress for nearly a generation lay in tatters. Stevens and Stanton were dead and Sumner too, after being abandoned and ridiculed by his own party and divorced by his wife, Wade passed over, Julian defeated, Morton ill and nearing the end of his career. The Radicals summoned up one last desperate titanic effort to save themselves and their vision for America in the 1876 Presidential election. And the Democrats—North and now South too—rose as if in a holy crusade to meet them.

"The Panic of 1873," from the pen of Thomas Nast in *Harper's Weekly* (www.harpweek.com). Lady (American) Liberty barely survives amidst the rubble of the Wall Street corporate community.

The U.S. government's spectacular derailment of the Jay Gould-led Erie Railroad juggernaut, as memorably depicted by *Harper's Weekly* (www.harpweek.com).

O, I'm a Good Old Rebel (James Randolph)

O, I'm a good old Rebel,
Now that's just what I am,
For this "Fair Land of Freedom"
I do not care at all;

I'm glad I fit against it—
I only wish we'd won,
And I don't want no pardon
For anything I done.

I hates the Yankee nation
And everything they do,
I hates the Declaration
Of Independence too;

I hates the glorious Union—
'Tis dripping with our blood—
I hates their striped banner,
I fit it all I could.

Three hundred thousand Yankees
Is stiff in Southern dust;
We got three hundred thousand
Before they conquered us;

They died of Southern fever
And Southern steel and shot,
I wish they was three million
Instead of what we got.

I can't take up my musket
And fight 'em now no more,
But I ain't going to love 'em,
Now that is sarten sure;

And I don't want no pardon
For what I was and am,
I won't be reconstructed
And I don't care a d–.

37 Redemption

"A Jewel Among Swine," a *Harper's Weekly* (www.harpweek.com) editorial cartoon reflecting the raw moral corruption dominating the Federal "Reconstruction" of Louisiana. The scene concerns Louisiana's hotly-disputed electoral votes in the 1876 presidential election. Republican Election Return Board Chairman James Madison Wells apparently sent John T. Pickett to offer the state's electoral votes—upon which the presidency depended—to both the Democrats and Republicans, in return for an enormous sum of cash. This scene reveals that, according to Pickett, politico and former New York City gambling-house proprietor John Morrissey boasted that he himself could buy the members of Wells's election board like he could buy pigs.

The noblest soldier now is he that with axe and plough pitches his tent against the waste places of his fire-blasted home, and swears that from its ruins shall arise another like unto it.

—Democratic North Carolina Governor Zebulon B. Vance

By 1876, only three Southern states—South Carolina, Florida, and Louisiana—remained under direct Radical political subjugation. This was not due to lack of effort or desire on the part of the Radicals. But, in general, the American people had wearied of both the colossal corruption and the extreme policies of Reconstruction. They may have tolerated them in the years following the War, but more than a decade had passed since Appomattox and, more importantly, the schemes and practices accompanying Reconstruction had helped sink the nation into the deep and prolonged depression in which it now found itself.

Scores of men, most of them ex-Confederate soldiers, put on the blood-red shirts their wives or sweethearts sewed them, mounted, and rode to support Hampton and the Democrats.

Each of the three still-occupied states saw its own saga unfold in the months leading up to the centennial elections. None proved more dramatic than that in South Carolina, where the conservative majority called forth that rare man whom even legend could not surpass. Wade Hampton was a leader of his people before the War, during the War, and after. They remembered that he refused to surrender himself or the cavalry of the Army of Northern Virginia at Appomattox. He had led them out, the Federals catching not a glimpse of them. He was ready to carry on the fight against Sheridan in Texas until he gathered reluctantly—bitterly—that he would help his people more by laying down his sword.

And the people wanted him for their governor and Democrat Sam Tilden as their President, so they could clear the Radicals out of South Carolina. Across the state, scores of men, most of them ex-Confederate soldiers put on the blood-red shirts their wives or sweethearts sewed them, mounted, and rode to support Hampton and the Democrats.

Grant and his minions, seeing the writing on the wall, sent Federal troops, tried intimidating Hampton's supporters, even tried provoking them into firefights so that he could buckle down martial law on the whole state again and take control of the state elections. As the Radicals had often done, they used blacks for their dirty work. Various fights were picked with Hampton supporters, some, like in Edgefield County, resulting in murders of the latter. Others, as at Ellerton and Cainhoy, left dead on both sides.

But Hampton was commanding his supporters like he had commanded the Confederate cavalry. He and his lieutenants spread constant admonitions, even threats, for their people to restrain

Samuel Tilden Takes Jefferson's Mantel

Samuel Tilden was the conservative 1876 Democratic Presidential standard-bearer. He made the centerpiece of his campaign a ringing call for the rejection of the Radicals' big government excesses and a return to Constitutional, limited government and separation of powers, as championed by Thomas Jefferson.

> *What the country now needs is a revival of Jeffersonian democracy, with the principles of government and rules of administration, and . . . the high standards of official morality which were established by the political revolution of 1800. . . . The demoralizations of war—a spirit of gambling adventure, engendered by false systems of public finance; a grasping centralization absorbing all functions from the local authorities; and assuming to control the industries of individuals by largesses to favored classes from the public Treasury of money wrung from the body of the people by taxation—were then, as now, characteristic of the period. The party that swayed the Government, though embracing many elevated characters, was dominated as an organization by the ideas of its master spirit, Alexander Hamilton. Himself personally pure, he nevertheless believed that our people must be governed, if not by force, at least by appeals to the selfish interests of classes, in all forms of corrupt influence. . . . As a means to the reaction of 1800, Jefferson organized the Democratic Party. He set up anew the broken foundations of governmental power. He stayed the advancing centralization. He restored the rights of the States and of the localities. He repressed the meddling of Government in the concerns of private business. . . . He refused to appoint relatives to office. He declined all presents. He refrained while in the public service from all enterprises to increase his private fortune. . . . The reformatory work of Mr. Jefferson in 1800 must now be repeated.*

themselves and avoid gunfights and other violence. Never could the Radicals instigate a large enough outrage to elicit the help they wanted from Grant, and that he wanted to give. To South Carolina, Hampton had come to mean everything that George Washington had meant to the old American colonies.

Election of 1876

But the big race, and one of the biggest in American history, was for President. The Republicans lacked several advantages they had possessed in recent elections. Whereas carpetbag rule had presented them a host of automatic electoral votes in the South, most of those votes would now go to the Democrats (and would continue to go to them until the 1960s).

Also, the Radicals found that "waving the bloody shirt," or stirring up wartime passions against the South, and hence, the Democrats, was decreasingly effective. Too, the Northern public no longer backed Grant's frequent dispatching of Federal troops to Southern hot spots. This limited the Republicans' ability to intimidate voters and manipulate the election process in Southern states.

In fact, the biggest problem facing the Republicans and their candidate, Rutherford B. Hayes, was related to

Rutherford B. Hayes (1822-1893)

Rutherford Hayes was one of American history's most enigmatic figures, and the 19th President of the United States. An Ohio native, Hayes graduated Kenyon College and Harvard Law School en route to practicing law. A decorated war hero for the North, he was wounded four times and rose to the rank of major general.

After the War, Hayes won election to Congress, then twice to the governor's house of Ohio. He appeared the darkest of dark horses in a crowded field of 1876 Republican Presidential challengers. Not only were House Speaker Oliver Morton, Senate powerhouse Roscoe Conkling, and front-running Senator James Blaine more popular than Hayes, they were united in their opposition to him because he did not share their passion for continuation of the Radicals' vindictive Reconstruction agenda.

In one of the ironies of the nation's life, the very blandness of Hayes's political ideology and gentlemanliness of his character landed him the stunning, multi-ballot nomination. All the other candidates either proved too extreme or alienated too many factions within the party. The Republican majority decided that it could at least live with Hayes.

His uphill battle continued against Democratic nominee Samuel J. Tilden. Famed nemesis of the New York-based Tweed Ring, Tilden evidenced clear superiority to Hayes in a number of notable areas, including intellect, oratory, political accomplishment, and—if not Hayes' battlefield exploits—the courage

that last item. Millions of Americans had changed their opinion of that party as one of idealism, ideas, and ideology, to one of cynical greed and corruption. As if to confirm this, the leading candidate for the Republican nomination, James G. Blaine of Maine, had been torpedoed by a corruption scandal. And President Grant found his desires for a break with precedent that would allow him a third term ruined by a one-word epithet for corruption in high places heard around the country: "Grantism."

North Carolina had its own memorable race for governor in 1876. There, wartime Governor Zebulon B. Vance wanted his old job back. Vance had equipped the "Rough and Ready Guards," a company of Confederate soldiers; preserved habeas corpus throughout the War (no other Confederate state did); and gotten thrown in prison by the Federals at war's end. Now the great mass of the Old North State adored him as their captain and leader. But he faced the formidable political organization of the Radicals, who had no intention of losing the governor's house.

not only to engage but lead the way in dealing with contentious issues. One chronicler of the Reconstruction Era said of the former New York governor, "In intellect, character, capacity, Tilden suffered nothing in comparison with anyone who has ever held the Presidency."

Even many of the most respected Northern leaders in Hayes' own Republican Party, including Charles Francis Adams, George Julian, and publishing magnate Joseph Pulitzer, regarded Tilden so highly that they cast aside party affiliation and threw their support to the Democrat.

Pulitzer wrote:

> *Who, pray, is Mr. Hayes? What great public service has he ever rendered, what eminent ability has he ever shown, what reform ever accomplished, what independence of character displayed, what public or private virtues manifested, to merit the dazzling dignity of filling the place once ennobled by a Washington and a Jefferson. The answer came—Hayes has never stolen. Good God, has it come to this? . . . Four years of dull mediocrity in Congress, and five years of mediocre dullness in the gubernatorial chair stare us in the face, without a single act of reform, without a single thought or utterance of ability, without a single vote of independence to redeem the long record of obscurity—with nothing to justify it but pretended personal respectability. If [Republican Senator Carl] Schurz will show but a solitary vote which Mr. Hayes ever declined to give for his party, or a single word of protest against any of the many wrongs committed by the party, I shall consider him right and myself wrong.*

Devout Character

Even more importantly, the American public in general seemed to have had its fill of the hard hand and corruption of Radical Reconstruction. Though Pulitzer may have raised valid questions regarding Hayes's professional accomplishments, however, any criticism of the Ohioan's character fell on shakier ground. In addition to Hayes's kindly demeanor, he was a devout Christian, abstained from liquor and other questionable habits, and both his personal and professional integrity was stainless.

He finished close enough to Tilden that less reputable men could secure him the additional votes he needed for victory. No evidence has ever been produced that Hayes endorsed the machinations of Zachariah Chandler, James Garfield, and many others on his behalf, nor that he was even aware of them. Southern Democratic leaders agreed to support the Presidential vote count rulings of the Republican majority Federal Election Commission. In return, when Hayes took office he ordered Federal occupation troops out of South Carolina, Florida, and Louisiana. He also appointed the first ex-Confederate Southern Democrat since before the War to a Presidential cabinet.

Most importantly, Hayes exerted his Presidential influence to begin the long arduous process of moving the American political process away from the Marxist and pseudo-Marxist ideals that had dominated it for over a decade and back toward a more balanced approach to American politics. His public actions supported this. Hayes toured the South speaking toward Southern whites in a tone of reconciliation unprecedented since Lincoln's death and encouraging Southern blacks to look toward their white neighbors rather than the Federal government for support. Left to history is the question of why he never before raised an objection to the more extreme aspects of the Radical Reconstruction agenda.

Of course, none of these later actions endeared him to the still-potent Radical wing of the Republican Party. They saw to it that Rutherford Hayes was a one-term President. This, even though the Republicans kept the White House in 1880. But they did it with a different man—Garfield.

The Dark Epic of Louisiana

The infamy of Reconstruction, on all sides, reached its apex in Louisiana. The seeds for post-war conflict were sown during the Yankee invasions and occupation of the state in the early 1860s. Across the state, everything from women's earrings—while in their ears—to cemeteries to churches were ransacked and plundered by the invaders. Civilians were beaten, shot, and hanged. Whole sections of the state were destroyed. The surrendered town of Alexandria, with no Confederate soldiers anywhere near, was burned to the ground, leaving nearly the entire population of women, children, and old folks homeless.

An eyewitness reporter for the pro-Northern *St. Louis Republican* recounted the inferno that drove most of the townspeople down to the river:

> *Women gathering their helpless babes in their arms, rushing frantically through the streets with screams and cries that would have melted the hardest hearts to tears; little boys and girls running hither and thither crying for their mothers and fathers; old men leaning on a staff for support to their trembling limbs, hurrying away from the suffocating heat of their burning dwellings and homes.*

Carpetbag Rule

Even before the War ended, thousands of carpetbaggers began descending upon the Pelican State, in particular New Orleans, the South's largest city and greatest port. The mass of Louisianans were unreconstructed, and would remain that way, and they did not like the Federals, nor their post-war occupation.

Meanwhile, none other than Philip Sheridan, the renowned Yankee cavalry chieftain, took charge of the new military district which included Louisiana and Texas. Sheridan said if he had the choice between living in hell or Texas, he would live in hell and rent out Texas. (One Texan responded, "Every man to his own country.") He liked Louisiana and its people little better, if any.

Meanwhile, the Federals sent a twenty-five-year-old Illinois carpetbagger, Henry Clay Warmoth, south

The Federal Electoral Commission in session in the United States Supreme Court chambers, working to determine the winner of the disputed 1876 presidential contest between Samuel Tilden and Rutherford Hayes. From the February 17, 1877, *Harper's Weekly* (www.harpweek.com).

as governor in 1868. That same year, the Radical legislature voted in a new state constitution that did many things, some of them good and some of them not. It gave blacks the vote, but it disqualified most whites from voting. Warmoth, with an annual salary of $8,000, amassed a fortune of millions during his four years in office. In less than three years the radical legislature saddled the state with $33 million in new debt.

Meanwhile, so harsh was Sheridan's military rule in Louisiana and Texas that President Johnson removed him and sent him north to Missouri. But by then it had spawned new offspring— the Knights of the White Camelia, a Klan-like resistance organization dedicated to resisting the unconstitutional rule of the Radicals and their black surrogates and keeping the state government "in the hands of the white race.

By 1871, the Radical occupation force had turned against itself and split into two bitterly-opposed camps, fighting for control of the state. So vicious was the fratricidal rivalry that it erupted at times into shootouts between the Radical factions, including at least one pitched battle in the streets of New Orleans.

Warmoth, who had attempted to reconcile the state's white Democrat majority with the Republicans, was beaten in the 1872 Republican primary by the more extreme "Custom House" contingent's candidate, William Pitt Kellogg. Democrat John McEnery beat Kellogg in the general election, but the Returning Board, notorious as a corrupt instrument of the Radicals, "disqualified" enough votes to declare Kellogg the winner. Now bitterness multiplied across the state, and with it escalated violence. Throughout this era, the

"The Battle of Liberty Place," the greatest street battle in American history, where thousands of ex-Confederate soldiers and Federal police - commanded by former Confederate General James Longstreet - squared off in downtown New Orleans during Reconstruction and shot it out.

Radicals clung to control only because President Grant provided as many Federal soldiers as necessary to back them up.

White League

By 1873, economic conditions in most Southern states had improved from their post-war nadir. In Louisiana, however, they were worse than ever. While Radical officials across the state grew richer, St. Landry Parish alone lost 821 plantations to tax foreclosure in two years. Statewide, the Radical sheriff in New Orleans had made nearly 50,000 tax seizures.

By the early 1870s, as many native black Louisianans were voting Democratic as native whites were voting Republican.

Louisiana's descent had far to go, however. Many of the state's most respected people joined a new organization, the White League. Its objective: to rid Louisiana of Radical control and establish a government run by whites. Unlike the Knights of White Camelia and other forerunners, the White Leaguers had no intention of keeping their organization secret.

"Gathering the Dead and Wounded," *Harper's Weekly's* elegiac, May 10, 1873, depiction of the aftermath of the bloody "Colfax Massacre," where white Southerners overwhelmed an armed black force whom white Radicals had provoked to take over a small Louisiana town.

One of the White League's primary objectives was to stop the killing of blacks when the carpetbaggers provoked a race riot, which they had repeatedly done. White Leaguers trusted they would some day regain control of the state and they wanted as little bad blood as possible to carry over between the races. Plus, they knew the Radicals wanted black blood spilled to help convince Grant to send more Federal troops to the state. Indeed, by the early 1870s, as many native black Louisianans were voting Democratic as native whites were voting Republican.

Almost immediately, white Radicals incited blacks in Grant Parish to seize and barricade the town of Colfax in case Democrats—who believed they had been rooked out of an election they won fair and square—attempted to take possession of the county government. Bristling with arms and drilled by black war veterans and militia officers, the force controlled the town for three days. Then a force of battle-hardened white Confederate veterans arrived and the scene exploded into a pitched battle.

> *If there is one man . . . responsible for the misfortunes of Louisiana, that man is General Phil Sheridan.*
> —New Orleans' *Picayune* newspaper, 1875

The whites suffered a few killed and wounded, but they overwhelmed the defenders, killing over seventy of them. Tragically, the attackers shot down about half of these in combat-frenzied murder as they tried to surrender. Next to the Battle of Liberty Place in New Orleans the following year, it was the single bloodiest episode of the Reconstruction Era.

Liberty Place

On September 13, 1874, the White League decided it had had enough of carpetbag rule. When it demanded Kellogg abandon office, he fled his building as armed Louisianans, again mostly Confederate veterans, streamed forth into formation from all corners of New Orleans.

The next day, the Metropolitan Police, a Federally-controlled force exercising jurisdiction over three counties around New Orleans, confronted the protesters. Both forces were commanded by ex-Confederate generals, the White Leaguers by Frederick N. Ogden and the Metropolitans by no less than James Longstreet, who years before cast his lot with the Radicals.

Over 3,000 armed men stood on both sides, but the police had artillery and heavy arms and an additional force of United States Regulars formed behind them. When the protesters refused Longstreet's order to disperse, the Metropolitans raked them with cannon shells and Gatling gun fire. Rather than retreat, the White Leaguers unleashed a Rebel yell and hurtled headlong into the police.

In broad daylight in the center of the largest city in the South, the two forces shot each other down. But when the full force of the White Leaguer charge hit the Metropolitans, the latter gave way and fled pell mell down the Canal Street levee and clear out of the city. Over 100 men fell in the fifteen minute battle. As the White Leaguers stampeded past, thousands of the Federal Regulars unleashed a roaring cheer for them.

The "Battle of Liberty Place" was a pivotal event, rippling across the country's political and social landscape, leading to major Democratic gains at the polls in 1874, and signaling the beginning of the end of Reconstruction.
—Nicholas E. Hollis

Longstreet lowered his head and shook it. The former Confederates left him alone.

Louisiana built a monument to the men who fell that day, in their minds attempting to restore free government to the state. No monument has yet been built to Longstreet anywhere in the South.

"To that God who gave us the victory we commit with confidence and hope the spirits of our heroic dead," said Ogden, "and, strong in the consciousness of right, record anew our holy purpose that Louisiana shall be free." But Grant once again sent an overwhelming force of troops, and the White Leaguers relinquished control of the city. "The President's soldiers may reinstate there the officials of fraud, but the moment the troops retire Mr. Kellogg will be expelled or killed," declared the *Shreveport Times* newspaper.

More Trouble

And again that year, the Returning Board overruled elections, this time that would have won the Democrats a majority in the state legislature. Now, however, Federal soldiers had to invade the legislative chamber itself, remove elected Democrats, and install Radicals in their place—all at the point of bayonets and loaded rifles. "This is the darkest day for the Republican Party and its hopes I have seen since the war," Federal General and Radical Congressional leader James Garfield wrote. "To march a file of soldiers into the Representative Hall of a State . . . will not be tolerated by the American people."

A large gathering composed of some of New England's most respected citizens gathered at Boston's Faneuil Hall. This historic hotbed of abolitionism now witnessed a chorus of demands for the removal of Sheridan and a likening of the White League to America's Founding Fathers as patriots, freedom fighters, and defenders of liberty.

Several of Grant's highest cabinet officers urged him to end Federal involvement in Louisiana. He rebuffed them all, and for the next two years, Louisiana descended into a state akin to that in the early American colonies during their struggle against Britain. Beatings, terrorism, and murders abounded, even of Radical officials.

In fact, as if the situation were not volatile enough, now Grant returned Sheridan to Louisiana as military occupation commander. He promptly urged the President to declare "the white people"—meaning men, women, and children—of Louisiana as "banditti," or outlaws beyond the protection of the United States Constitution—meaning they could be imprisoned, deported, or short on sight. "If there is one man . . . responsible for the

Former Confederate Chieftain James Longstreet, in the 1870s.

misfortunes of Louisiana, that man is General Phil Sheridan," cried New Orleans' *Picayune* newspaper.

"Redemption"

The Democrats won yet another election in 1876, and the Radicals yet again tried to steal it. This time, however, a "deal" was in the works between Rutherford Hayes's Republican Presidential campaign and Southern political leaders in Louisiana and elsewhere. Hayes would remove Federal occupation troops from Louisiana and meanwhile, Grant would not again send soldiers to enforce Radical claims. And so, in April, 1877, Francis Tillou Nicholls, a gray-bearded, one-legged and one-armed old general who fought under Stonewall Jackson, moved into the State House. Reconstruction in Louisiana was over.

Much had been lost through the hateful years of Reconstruction. The mass of blacks would suffer a hard segregation for nearly a century. Somewhere along the way, the state lost much of its civic virtue. The first post-Reconstruction Democratic State Treasurer would flee the country with embezzled funds, and for more than a hundred years, Louisiana would be a by-word for crooked politics. Hate between black and white had blossomed, and hatred for the North, too, by white Louisianans. The War, in the Pelican State at least, had lasted a long time beyond 1865.

Benjamin Morgan Palmer (1818–1902)

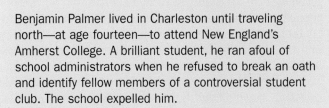

A golden chord amidst the lamentations of late-19th century Louisiana was pastor and theologian Benjamin Morgan Palmer. This spellbinding orator and tenderhearted shepherd of souls stood alongside Robert L. Dabney and James Henley Thornwell as pillars of the golden age of Southern clergymen. He began life in Columbia, South Carolina, and was the son and nephew of Presbyterian pastors. When his father Edward died in his nineties in 1882, he was the oldest living minister in the Southern Presbyterian Church.

Benjamin Palmer lived in Charleston until traveling north—at age fourteen—to attend New England's Amherst College. A brilliant student, he ran afoul of school administrators when he refused to break an oath and identify fellow members of a controversial student club. The school expelled him.

Palmer's return home to his family under such circumstances did not help his already somewhat distant relationship with his father. The latter's greatest concern for his son at this point, however, was whether the boy was yet a Christian. The younger Palmer taught for a few years, then continued his college education at the University of Georgia which, unlike the University of South Carolina, had a reputation as a good influence on Christian character.

Palmer's spiritual vitality bloomed and flourished during his years of teaching and his time at Georgia, and he attended Columbia Theological Seminary in South Carolina from 1839–1841. After ordination, he pastored the First Presbyterian Churches of Savannah and Columbia, respectively, from 1841–1855. All the while, churches from around the country sought to lure him away to their own congregations. Just as much in demand for his theological scholarship, Palmer taught at Columbia Theological Seminary from 1853–1856.

Modern-day Presbyterian Pastor and Palmer historian Mickey Schneider recalls that Palmer wore out a section of the carpet in his Columbia church manse, or home, so often did he pace back and forth practicing his sermons. Indeed, his dual duties as pastor and seminary professor drove him to the brink of exhaustion, which is why he resigned his pulpit in 1856 to concentrate on teaching. Palmer was at heart a shepherd of souls, however, and later in 1856 he accepted a call to the First Presbyterian Church of New Orleans.

Friends and family alike urged him not to go. Why? New Orleans was not a "Presbyterian city" as were Columbia and many other Southern cities. The South's largest Catholic population resided there, as well as a much more eclectic, foreign, and unchurched populace than elsewhere in the South, due in part to New Orleans's vigor as an international port city.

Palmer considered New Orleans nothing less than the greatest spiritual mission field in the entire country.

In addition, even by 1856, sorrows beset the South's largest city. Its heat, humidity, and enormous oceanic traffic rendered it vulnerable to epidemics such as yellow fever. In 1853 alone, that affliction killed 8,000 of the city's 154,000 residents. The following two years, 2,500 more died. Other pastors were actually leaving the city because of the plagues. These were all reasons, however, that convinced Palmer he must go to New Orleans. He considered it nothing less than the greatest spiritual mission field in the entire country.

New Orleans

It was also one of the nation's greatest cities. New Orleans was the fourth-largest city in the United States, the fourth-largest port in the world, and the fastest-growing city in America. (All that would crash to an end after the War.) Then in 1858, 5,000 more people perished by the plague. Palmer's arrival could not have been more difficultly-, and Providentially, timed. As other ministers continued to leave the sorrowing city, people in the afflicted homes placed signs on their front doors that said, "Plague here."

Rather than cowering before this, Palmer began daily walks through the city, neighborhood by neighborhood, street by street, house by house. Any time he saw a "Plague here" sign, he knocked on that door, went in, prayed with the people, and read them the Scriptures. Despite this audacious defiance of mortal danger, every member of Palmer's own family contracted the fever before he did. Miraculously, all the Palmers survived. "It was then that Palmer got the heart as well as the ear of New Orleans," one prominent Jewish rabbi observed.

Though Palmer's support of slavery when humanely practiced as a good for the slave, may offend modern sensibilities, he nonetheless possessed a powerful concern for the black residents of New Orleans. He sought and received the Mayor's permission to use First Presbyterian facilities to minister to them. From these efforts came a thriving, independent black congregation. Meanwhile, Palmer visited an average of 340 families in their homes every year for twenty-five years. This did not count the numberless people who came to his church office.

When war approached, Palmer delivered a stirring speech in favor of the Constitutional right of secession. It likely influenced Louisiana's decision to join the Confederacy. So powerful was an oration he delivered to the fledgling Southern Presbyterian Church General Assembly, that its members immediately voted him their first moderator, the denomination's highest office.

Once fighting began, he enlisted in the Southern army as a chaplain, serving among other places in Albert Sidney Johnston's army at Shiloh. When New Orleans fell to the Federals in May, 1862, however, Palmer was a marked man. Knowing the Federals would imprison him if they could catch him, he fled in exile to Mississippi, then to Columbia, where he rejoined the seminary faculty. The Southern Presbyterians appointed Palmer their commissioner to the Army of Tennessee in 1863. Unfortunately, the fire that wiped out most of Columbia when the Federals occupied it in 1865, burned down the home where the Palmer family was staying, and destroyed most of Palmer's splendid library.

When war approached, Palmer delivered a stirring speech in favor of the Constitutional right of secession. It likely influenced Louisiana's decision to join the Confederacy.

Following the War, Palmer at long last returned to New Orleans, where he would live until his death in 1902. He set about the business of rebuilding his church, which he pastored for nearly half a century, and the city. His oratorical renown continued to gain him speaking invitations all over the South. He also wrote a series of notable books, including *Life and Letters of J. H. (James Henley) Thornwell, Theology of Prayer; the Broken Home, or Lessons in Sorrow; Formation of Character,* and *The Family In Its Civil and Churchly Aspects.*

The Family has gained a new and wide audience through its recent reprinting by Sprinkle Publications. Well over a century after its writing, it is considered by many pastors and other churchmen as the greatest book ever written on the subject of the Christian family. Following is one of its many memorable passages:

> *The father's will is robust and unyielding—the granite rock against which the child must rub and be subdued. The mother's will brings in the element of gentleness; and, blending with its co-factor, tones down its severity, whereby the joint rule is rendered alike strong and loving.*

Lessons in Sorrow

Often overlooked in studies of Benjamin Palmer's eventful life is the series of profound losses he suffered during the decade between 1863 and 1873. During that time, four of his daughters, ranging in age from 17 to 25, died. These heartrending events inspired one of his most powerful books, *Broken Homes, or Lessons in Sorrow.*

One of the most dramatic accounts is that of Palmer's first-born daughter Sarah Frances, who had contracted a fever while in the New Orleans public schools. When her father left his family in Columbia, South Carolina, to take his wartime chaplain's post with the Confederate Army of Tennessee, she said, "Father, you are going so far, and I am so ill."

According to Palmer biographer Mickey Schneider, these words rang in his ears amidst

Final Years

One of Palmer's great speeches occurred when he was well into his 70s. The Federals' Reconstruction government had instituted a gambling lottery in Louisiana following the War, hoping for it to be a panacea for the crippled state's social, political, and economic crises. A New York City syndicate spearheaded the effort, and by 1891, when Palmer stood up in the Grand Opera House to inveigh against it, the people of Louisiana had had a bellyful of the scheme's corruption and broken promises. Men, women, and children alike stood on their chairs and cheered Palmer after he concluded.

When the people of Louisiana threw out the lottery in the subsequent vote, Rev. Schneider recalls that a distraught lottery supporter approached a Jewish rabbi on the street. "It looks like all is lost and the lottery has been defeated," the man said, "but I think we can get it back." "You will never get it back," replied the rabbi. "Why not?" asked the man. The rabbi looked at him and said, "Dr. Palmer has spoken."

Today, Benjamin Morgan Palmer is a forgotten name in New Orleans. When he is recalled, it is as likely as not to be as a slaveholding reactionary from another era. Such was not always the case. After being accidentally run down by a streetcar in 1902 and dying a few weeks later, his funeral drew the largest crowd in the city since that of Jefferson Davis. Perhaps the epitaph offered by *The Interior* was as good as any:

> *The decease of Dr. Palmer of New Orleans is like a change in the landscape of the South. As far as it is possible for one man in the space of a lifetime to be a part of the fixed order of things, Dr. Palmer has become identified like some old-time landmark with his denomination, his city and his section of the nation. . . . Dr. Palmer served God and his generation as a symbol of the immutability of the great essentials of our religion. His faithful witness to Jesus Christ in the word of his preaching and the example of his ministry gave him such power in New Orleans as few of the Lord's ambassadors have ever wielded in any age of the church. By all consent he was acknowledged for years to be the most influential man in that city, and he was so brave and outspoken that he made for righteousness not only in the private lives of men but in the civic life of the community.*

---

the drums and cannon of the camp. When the Confederates retreated from Shelbyville, he rushed back to Columbia, knowing his daughter was near death and hoping to look upon her pale face once more. He arrived early one morning and found her sleeping, but yet alive. He waited for her to awake. When she opened her eyes, she cried, "I knew he would come! I knew he would come!"

He rushed back to Columbia, knowing his daughter was near death and hoping to look upon her pale face once more.

They were among Sarah Frances's final earthly words. "It was an exclamation so full of love, so full of trust," Palmer recalled, " that I bowed my head and wept like a woman." In *The Broken Home*, he writes regarding Sarah Frances that he knows "there is a tendency to place a halo on the head of one who dies. I am not doing that, but since she was twelve years of age, I could find nothing in her to amend."

The Election that Ended Reconstruction

The extent of the Radicals' desperation during the 1876 Presidential campaign was displayed in a slough of "bloody shirt" harangues like those of renowned orator Robert Ingersoll. One of his incendiary but powerful speeches evidences anew that brutal politics is no recent innovation in America:

> *Every State that seceded from the Union was a Democratic State. Every ordinance of secession that was drawn was drawn by a Democrat. Every man that endeavored to tear the old flag from the heaven it enriches was a Democrat. Every man that tried to destroy the Nation was a Democrat. . . . Every man that shot down Union soldiers was a Democrat. . . . The man that assassinated Abraham Lincoln was a Democrat. . . . Every man that raised bloodhounds to pursue human beings was a Democrat. Every man that clutched from shrinking, shuddering, crouching mothers' babes from their breasts and sold them into slavery was a Democrat. . . . Every man that tried to spread smallpox and yellow fever in the North . . . was a Democrat. Soldiers, every scar you have on your heroic bodies was given you by a Democrat. Every scar, every arm that is missing, every limb that is gone is the souvenir of a Democrat. . . . Shall the solid South, a unified South, unified by assassination and murder, a South solidified by the shotgun—shall the solid South with the aid of a divided North control this great and splendid country?*

Conservative Democratic Indiana Senator Daniel Vorhees, a chief opponent of the Radical Republicans' Reconstruction agenda.

"I understand the tactics of the enemy in this fight perfectly," said Democratic stalwart and Congressman Daniel Vorhees of Indiana. "They will denounce the people of the South—this is cheap. They are helpless, then abuse them; they are powerless, then malign them. They are not here to answer, then manufacture lies about them, misleading the people."

Even the mild-mannered Hayes supported hoisting the bloody shirt. "Our strong ground," he wrote James Blaine, "is the dread of a solid South, rebel rule, etc., etc. I hope you will make these topics prominent in your speeches. It leads people away from 'hard times' which is our deadliest foe."

Tilden Elected?

Democratic candidate Samuel J. Tilden of New York built a popular vote lead of 250,000 and an electoral vote advantage of 184–166 (or 184–165 if not counting the Democrats' disputed electoral vote of Oregon.) But the Republicans challenged the vote totals in three states—the same three states where Federal occupation troops remained and where they had significant latitude to control election investigations.

In South Carolina, the vote was indeed close; though Wade Hampton swept to the governorship, Tilden had not supported him, and many of Hampton's supporters had not backed Tilden. Still, whether Hayes truly won the state, as declared by the fifteen-man Federal Committee, will never be known for certain.

Tilden, however, had clear majorities in both Florida and South Carolina. But in Florida, Federal troops under the command of Radical chieftains gave the Radical-controlled Election Board a shield to canvass the state's votes however it wished. When the "canvass" still showed Tilden ahead, the Board disfranchised large numbers of Tilden votes and fabricated scores of affidavits—228 of them were signed in the same person's handwriting.

Louisiana Shenanigans

In Louisiana, meanwhile, Tilden held a seemingly-insurmountable post-election lead of between six and eight thousand votes. But Garfield and a small army of other Federal officials had descended on New Orleans from Washington and around the U.S. And they were socializing regularly, and quite illegally, with the notorious Louisiana Election Returning Board.

Vote Counting Up Close in Florida

(Report of a Republican-controlled Florida State Board of Election Canvassers meeting as excerpted from the December 16, 1876, *Frank Leslie's Illustrated Newspaper*. The Board eventually ruled against Pasco and Democratic presidential candidate Samuel Tilden, and the state's electoral votes—and thus the presidency—went to Republican Rutherford Hayes. Courtesy Florida State Archives.)

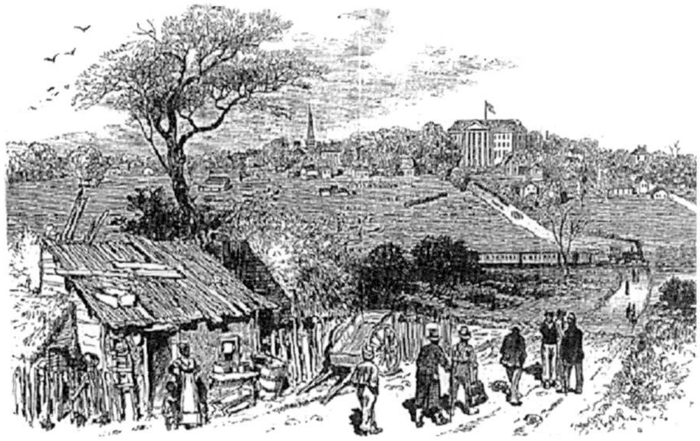

"Canvassing the Presidential Votes at Tallahassee, Florida," a sketch from the December 16, 1876, *Frank Leslie's Illustrated Newspaper.* The 2000 presidential election was not the first in which Florida provided bitter controversy and national significance. This scene depicts the U.S. Army's occupation of the Florida state capital as presidential votes were tabulated. The encampment appears between the rail line (center) and the state capital (upper). (Courtesy of Florida State Archives.)

As soon as the evening session opened Mr. Pasco arose and inquired of the Secretary of State, the Chairman of the Board, if he had not received another return from Baker County besides the one he had read. The chairman objected to the question, and would not reply. Mr. Pasco then charged openly and positively that such a return had been sent to the Board. He described the return... a certified copy of which he had in his hand... as being older in date than the one read by the Secretary; as having been legally attested, and as having been signed by the Clerk and Justice of the Peace, as the law requires. He then demanded to know why it had been suppressed, and insisted on it being produced at once. The chairman, though much confused, still refused to say whether he had received any such return or not.

Mr. Pasco then charged that, in utter violation of these plain rules, the Secretary of State, having received two returns from one county, had decided the question between them himself by suppressing one and presenting the other. He renewed his demand for the presentation of the suppressed return. The chairman then confessed that he had received another return, and, going to his desk, produced it. It was a return dated three days before the other, signed, as described by Mr. Pasco, and gave the Democrats 95 majority.

If this return is admitted Mr. Tilden's majority is over 100 (votes). With both returns before the Board under contest, Mr. Tilden has three electors and Mr. Hayes one.

The Federal Election Commission's declaration of Rutherford B. Hayes as winner of the 1876 presidential election, as rendered in the March 17, 1877 *Harper's Weekly* (www.harpweek.com).

Republicans comprised the entirety of the supposedly bipartisan Returning Board. They were uniformly considered by honest men of both major parties as corrupt and dishonest. Even General Philip Sheridan, Military Governor of Louisiana in the late 1860s and no friend of Democrats, had called Board Chairman James Madison Wells "a political trickster and a dishonest man" whose conduct was "as sinuous as the mark left in the dust by the movement of a snake."

Vote tabulations were conducted, in private, by a staff of Republican clerks. Five of these had criminal records and were under indictment at the time for crimes, some for murder. No Democrat was allowed in the room.

Again, Federal officials produced large numbers of affidavits, claiming all manner of wrongdoing by Democrats, such as intimidation of Republican voters. Many were no doubt legitimate. Rough characters there were in the white South who had no desire for pro-Republican blacks to vote, and had no intention of making it easy for them to do so. On the other hand, pro-Democrat blacks continued to experience similar treatment from Union League blacks and others.

But many other affidavits resembled that of a woman named Amy Mitchell. She later declared to Congressional investigators that Garfield personally grilled her with questions—after first prepping her—and that every answer she gave was a lie. Why? Because she was told to do so. Thomas A. Hendricks, Tilden's vice presidential running mate, later denounced Garfield's role in the affair as "one doubtful in character and worse than that of any other man now living."

A full three days before the Returning Board announced the Louisiana winner, the New Orleans Federal Marshal, a Radical, telegraphed Washington that he had "seen [Board Chairman] Wells, who says, 'Board will return Hayes sure. Have no fear.'" The next day, December 6, the Board disqualified 13,250 Tilden votes, which gave the state and its electoral votes to Hayes.

Plot Thickens

Historian John A. Rhodes, a Republican, summarized the majority opinion on these audacious and illegal conspiracies orchestrated by men in the highest echelons of power in the American nation: "Had these been Northern States the dispute would have ceased forthwith. These two States would have been conceded to Tilden, and his election secured; but under the carpetbag-negro regime, the canvassing boards of Florida and Louisiana had the power to throw out votes on the ground of intimidation or fraud, and these boards were under the control of the Republicans."

Emotions continued to mount, though a strange equation gradually took shape. Democratic voters across the country supported action as vigorous as necessary to assure the Republicans did not "steal" the election. But Democratic Party leaders in the North, including Tilden, exhibited a strange lethargy in prosecuting their case. Republican Party leaders, meanwhile, took a much more aggressive approach, partly because they had the army and most of the reins of government at their disposal. They pressed their case to the uttermost.

But it was Southern Democrats whose actions proved the most intriguing. Some of them, like Hampton and the South Carolinians, did not care one way or another for Tilden. All of them wanted the Yankee army and the carpetbag politicians out of the South. Yet they gradually concluded that, like it or not, the Republicans still possessed the political and military muscle to wrench the election away from Tilden.

And so, men of honorable heritage long treated with dishonor resorted to the methods of the new world in which they found themselves. They, too, feinted and finagled and jockeyed, in secret, in search of an "accommodation" with Hayes and the Republicans.

Deal and Decision

Meanwhile, Congressional moderates from both parties appointed a fifteen-member electoral commission to decide the issue once and for all. The commission included five men from the Supreme Court, five from the Senate, and five from the House. Seven were Democrats and eight Republicans; one of the latter, however, was David Davis, a "Liberal Republican," friend of Lincoln, thoroughgoing moderate, and the key swing vote. Then Davis won election to the U.S. Senate and the Republicans gained an eighth partisan. And partisan the decisions were, every step of the way, as the commission voted 8-7, along straight party lines, in favor of the Republicans' vote counts in all three Southern states. They also gave one disputed vote from Oregon to Hayes. These twenty votes nudged Hayes past Tilden for a 185–184 victory—the closest electoral "victory" in American history.

But that was not the whole story. Those Southern Democrats and Hayes's Republican minions indeed cobbled together a complex agreement. Electrifying then and now was the Southerners' agreement to support the electoral commission verdict for Hayes. In return, he made a host of commitments, including:

1) Removal of the remaining Federal occupation troops from the South (South Carolina, Florida, and Louisiana).
2) Naming of an ex-Confederate leader to a key position in his cabinet (Postmaster general, as it turned out).
3) Influencing the distribution of Federal funds toward internal improvements programs in the South such as the Texas & Pacific Railroad, as the North had received all along.

Hayes additionally hoped these and other concessions he made to the Southerners would help establish a legitimate and lasting base for the

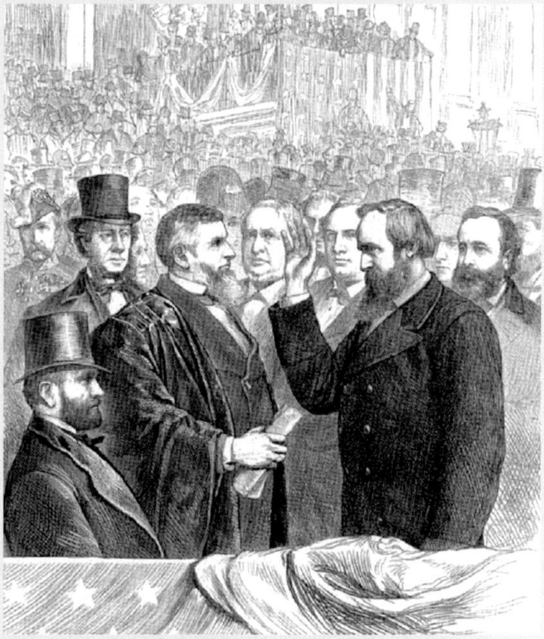

Supreme Court Chief Justice Waite swears in the nineteenth president of the United States, Rutherford B. Hayes, as depicted in the March 24, 1877 edition of *Harper's Weekly* (www.harpweek.com). Outgoing President U. S. Grant, seated lower left, watches.

Republican Party in the South. They did not do that, but they did deliver him the Presidency he did not win at the ballot box. And the Southerners got rid of their Yankee occupation force and their carpetbag governments, but the haunting question lingers—at what price to the virtue they had so long esteemed?

"Another such victory, and I am undone," the Republican Elephant, originally the creation of Thomas Nast, confesses to the vanquished Democratic Tiger (later Donkey), in the March 24, 1877 *Harper's Weekly* (www.harpweek.com). Though wearing the laurel wreath of victory after the Republican-majority Electoral Commission awarded Rutherford Hayes the presidency, the Elephant is battered and beaten, and has lost his tail. The quote originated with the ancient King Pyrrhus, who had won a costly victory that ultimately did lead to his ruin. Indeed, the Republican Party would win only one more presidential election in the 19th century.

Reconstruction Ends

The 1876 election season was another big one for the Democrats. Hampton won the governor's office in South Carolina, and so did scores of the party's candidates for other offices around the country. The Democrats even won the Presidency, by both electoral vote and a quarter of a million vote popular count—apparently. Then came Republican challenges to vote counts in three states won by Tilden—the three remaining occupied Southern states of South Carolina, Florida, and Louisiana—and one won by Hayes, Oregon.

The national temper, already at fever pitch on election day, now threatened to boil over. The nation had no winner and a tempestuous war of words between the two parties. But it had even more, as some Northern Democrats called for another "civil war" and Grant and the Republicans made clear they would fight before giving up the White House.

As before, nothing less than the direction of the whole country hung in the balance. The Republicans won all four challenges, at least two of them, Florida and Louisiana, with tactics that even many Republicans decried for their crookedness. And Hayes won the election by one electoral vote, 185–184.

To the everlasting shock and dismay of the Radicals, however, within months of his taking office on March 5, 1877, the mild-mannered Ohioan removed Federal occupation troops from South Carolina, Florida, and Louisiana. Without them, the carpetbag political organizations collapsed. This freed those states to resume the tending of their own affairs. It was all part of a complex, and quite illegal, deal with conservative Southern Democrats that precluded their objecting to Hayes' election. Reconstruction, at least in its most virulent form, was over.

"Our Uncle Going to Take a Rest," *Harper's Weekly's* (www.harpweek.com) April 7, 1877, sketch of America's Uncle Sam, headed for a much-deserved rest after the tumultuous 1876 Presidential campaign, the inauguration of President Hayes, and the swearing in and adjournment of Congress. The system has at length worked, *Harper's* suggests, and the Republic remains safe. Others then and since would disagree.

38 Epilogue

Religion in the South made its most useful contribution to Southern culture only after the war ended, when it emerged as a convincing symbol of the value of spiritual victory in midst of the earthly defeat.

—Gardiner A. Shattuck
A Shield and Hiding Place

That bravery, sacrifice, Christian fortitude and suffering, and spiritual revival revealed themselves through numberless lives and situations during the War Between the States, should give every American a sense of pride and admiration for those who came before us and sought, the best they knew how, to build a good and decent life for themselves and those who followed. But what cautionary lessons can we glean from America's uncivil and most tragic war?

Let us first look at the South and its Confederacy, which then and since have often demonstrated the dangers manifest in pugnacity and a ready willingness to settle disputes with arms. Also, the dangerous—and unchristian—practice of returning evil for evil, whether through vitriolic oratory, economic self-centeredness, bigoted attitudes toward others, or, again, a readiness to resort to the violent resolution of disputes.

Plus, be careful if you get three ardent Southern patriots in a room together, because it will not likely be long before one or more of them have seceded from agreement with the other(s). And to those who would even today yearn for Southern independence: whatever the merits of that objective, I wonder whether the temperament, patience, and wisdom necessary to succeed in such an undertaking has been demonstrated.

Here is a hard question for defenders of the Confederacy. The example of William Wilberforce and remembrance that a third of the slave states fought with the North notwithstanding, how and when *would* the South have ended slavery had war not come? How well did the South prepare the slaves for freedom when it came? Not very well. How well would it have prepared them if left to work out its own timetable on the matter? And would it have done so based only on the timing and criteria of its own economic interests?

The Christian foundations laid for American civilization by our Puritan and Pilgrim forefathers have lingered and aided America, despite our many flaws, to retain a stronger Christian influence than perhaps any other nation on earth. The great religious revival in the Southern armies during the War of 1861–1865, among other factors, has caused biblical Christianity to remain more pervasive in the South than anywhere else in the country. Still, the South, even if more slowly, seems increasingly supportive of a central national government ever-more-controlling of its own citizens' lives, even as it is ever more involved in the lives of people in other countries. Will Americans prove to be the exception to the rule of republics who become empires that collapse both from the weight of their own internal immorality and the fury of their ever-mounting legions of external enemies?

To those admiring of the North in the War, of its motivations, I would suggest that the latter is not geographic, but a particular mentaility, a state of mind. It incorporates the desire to "do good," to help others, to right the wrongs of the world—according to the judgment and perspective of those doing the righting. Such a mentality is the lingering echo of the Puritans' worthy desire to create a city on a hill to help illumine the way for all the nations to a better world. Yet it usually lacks the gospel that animated both the lives and the objectives of that earlier, amazing generation.

In its contemporary rendering, this do-goodism smacks of arrogance, imperialism, blindness, hubris, and—does this sound familiar—violence. It tends to right wrongs in such a way as to spawn battalions of other wrongs within itself and within others whom it has offended and/or wronged. The North's "Civil War" in many regards devastated the Republic and Constitution the Founders devoted their blood, their treasure, and their sacred honor to create. Never have either the Republic or the Constitution recovered from the savaging dealt them, however well-intentioned, by Lincoln, Stanton, Stevens, Wade, and others. Even the slaves were freed through violent and illegal means, and in a manner that doomed most of them, and their descendants, to generations of hardship and unfair treatment by white Americans.

Anyone in the United States who complains of high taxation, ballooning federal budgets, and ever-increasing national government power and involvement in the ordinary citizen's life, should hearken back to the watershed political policies of the Republican Party in the 1860s and 1870s.

One of the worst consequences of the War was the perpetuation of the treasured American fallacy that "might makes right," and that possessing the strongest military force provides the best remedy for curing the ills of the world, real or imagined.

Studying a lot of history can, indeed, be dangerous. A person eventually learns more than he wishes he knew. Perhaps you, dear reader, have that feeling now, if you have stayed with us through the entirety of this book. Many cherished myths and ideals must fall by the wayside for the honest Christian student who seeks to find the truth, whatever it might be.

In view of that, I grow more admiring with each passing year of America's Founding Fathers. I count among those fathers the Puritans and Pilgrims, and the Washingtons and Jeffersons alike. They increasingly appear, despite their failings and flaws, as a brief shining epoch in not only American, but world history, where the mistakes of the past were noted and abided, and liberty, freedom, responsible limited government, and moral virtue and trust in God clung to. Too seldom have great American leaders exhibited such virtues in the past two centuries, and the instances of their doing so seem to grow rarer and last more briefly.

The currents, consequences, and legacies of nations and peoples take long periods of time to gather, and long ones to unfold. The War of 1861–1865 was the hinge of American history in which, despite the "saving" of the union and the freeing of the slaves, many of those Founding Fathers' wise and hard-won principles were forfeited, and replaced by other, less beneficial ones, ones that are conspiring to form a dangerous future for our children and grandchildren. Treating others not as you would have them treat you, obeying the law only when it serves your immediate purposes, and resorting to violence to resolve differences are unwise practices for individuals and nations alike.

I teach my students that the saga of America is the story of a bold people striding through history conquering, winning, and loving the land before them, be it physical land or some other challenge. That unique story is made the more so in that every step of the way, we have, in effect, carried a Bible in one hand and a rifle in the other. There is much good in that, but much to reject and repent of. We spread the gospel to the utter ends of the earth like no other nation in history, and we destroy whole sections of other countries.

I tell the young men and women, too, of the words from long, long ago of Alfred the Great, son of Ethelbert, and king of the Saxons of the West. "The past is given to those in the present, to keep and guard those in the future," that humble, suffering, great and good Christian man declared.

May we American Christians learn from the past, and remember how good and faithful are the teachings of God. May we love our children and protect them best by following in the future in the way of the Lord Jesus, who only described Himself in the Holy Scriptures as "gentle and humble of heart."

—John J. Dwyer
28 December 2004
Denton, Texas

The War Prayer (Mark Twain)

It was a time of great and exalting excitement.

The country was up in arms, the war was on, in every breast burned the holy fire of patriotism; the drums were beating, the bands playing, the toy pistols popping, the bunched firecrackers hissing and sputtering;

On every hand and far down the receding and fading spreads of roofs and balconies a fluttering wilderness of flags flashed in the sun; daily the young volunteers marched down the wide avenue gay and fine in their new uniforms, the proud fathers and mothers and sisters and sweethearts cheering them with voices choked with happy emotion as they swung by;

Nightly the packed mass meetings listened, panting, to patriot oratory which stirred the deepest deeps of their hearts and which they interrupted at briefest intervals with cyclones of applause, the tears running down their cheeks the while; in the churches the pastors preached devotion to flag and country and invoked the God of Battles, beseeching His aid in our good cause in outpouring of fervid eloquence which moved every listener.

It was indeed a glad and gracious time, and the half dozen rash spirits that ventured to disapprove of the war and cast a doubt upon its righteousness straightway got such a stern and angry warning that for their personal safety's sake they quickly shrank out of sight and offended no more in that way.

Sunday morning came—next day the battalions would leave for the front;

The church was filled; the volunteers were there, their faces alight with material dreams—visions of a stern advance, the gathering momentum, the rushing charge, the flashing sabers, the flight of the foe, the tumult, the enveloping smoke, the fierce pursuit, the surrender!—then home from the war, bronzed heroes, welcomed, adored, submerged in golden seas of glory! With the volunteers sat their dear ones, proud, happy, and envied by the neighbors and friends who had no sons and brothers to send forth to the field of honor, there to win for the flag or, failing, die the noblest of noble deaths.

The service proceeded; a war chapter from the Old Testament was read; the first prayer was said; it was followed by an organ burst that shook the building, and with one impulse the house rose, with glowing eyes and beating hearts, and poured out that tremendous invocation:

God the all-terrible!
Thou who ordainest,
Thunder thy clarion
and lightning thy sword!

Then came the "long" prayer. None could remember the like of it for passionate pleading and moving and beautiful language. The burden of its supplication was that an ever–merciful and benignant Father of us all would watch over our noble young soldiers and aid, comfort, and encourage them in their patriotic work; bless them, shield them in His mighty hand, make them strong and confident, invincible in the bloody onset; help them to crush the foe, grant to them and to their flag and country imperishable honor and glory.

An aged stranger entered and moved with slow and noiseless step up the main aisle, his eyes fixed upon the minister, his long body clothed in a robe that reached to his feet, his head bare, his white hair descending in a frothy cataract to his shoulders, his seamy face unnaturally pale, pale even to ghastliness. With all eyes following him and wondering, he made his silent way; without pausing, he ascended to the preacher's side and stood there, waiting.

With shut lids the preacher, unconscious of his presence, continued his moving prayer, and at last finished it with the words, uttered in fervent appeal,"Bless our arms, grant us the victory, O Lord our God, Father and Protector of our land and flag!"

The stranger touched his arm, motioned him to step aside—which the startled minister did—and took his place. During some moments he surveyed the spellbound audience with solemn eyes in which burned an uncanny light; then in a deep voice he said

"I come from the Throne—bearing a message from Almighty God!"

The words smote the house with a shock; if the stranger perceived it he gave no attention.

"He has heard the prayer of His servant your shepherd and shall grant it if such shall be your desire after I, His messenger, shall have explained to you its import—that is to say, its full import. For it is like unto many of the prayers of men, in that it asks for more than he who utters it is aware of—except he pause and think.

"God's servant and yours has prayed his prayer. Has he paused and taken thought? Is it one prayer? No, it is two—one uttered, the other not. Both have reached the ear of Him Who heareth all supplications, the spoken and the unspoken. Ponder this—keep it in mind. If you beseech a blessing upon yourself, beware! lest without intent you invoke a curse upon a neighbor at the same time. If you pray for the blessing of rain upon your crop which needs it, by that act you are possibly praying for a curse upon some neighbor's crop which may not need rain and can be injured by it.

"You have heard your servant's prayer—the uttered part of it. I am commissioned by God to put into words the other part of it—that part which the pastor, and also you in your hearts, fervently prayed silently. And ignorantly and unthinkingly? God grant that it was so! You heard these words: 'Grant us the victory, O Lord our God!'"

That is sufficient. The whole of the uttered prayer is compact into those pregnant words. Elaborations were not necessary. When you have prayed for victory you have prayed for many unmentioned results which follow victory—must follow it, cannot help but follow it. Upon the listening spirit of God the Father fell also the unspoken part of the prayer. He commandeth me to put it into words. Listen!

> "O Lord our Father, our young patriots, idols of our hearts, go forth to battle—be Thou near them! With them, in spirit, we also go forth from the sweet peace of our beloved firesides to smite the foe.
>
> "O Lord our God, help us to tear their soldiers to bloody shreds with our shells;
>
> "Help us to cover their smiling fields with the pale forms of their patriot dead;
>
> "Help us to drown the thunder of the guns with the shrieks of their wounded, writhing in pain;
>
> "Help us to lay waste their humble homes with a hurricane of fire;
>
> "Help us to wring the hearts of their unoffending widows with unavailing grief;
>
> "Help us to turn them out roofless with their little children to wander unfriended the wastes of their desolated land in rags and hunger and thirst, sports of the sun flames of summer and the icy winds of winter, broken in spirit, worn with travail, imploring Thee for the refuge of the grave and denied it—
>
> "For our sakes who adore Thee, Lord, blast their hopes, blight their lives, protract their bitter pilgrimage, make heavy their steps, water their way with their tears, stain the white snow with the blood of their wounded feet!
>
> "We ask it, in the spirit of love, of Him Who is the Source of Love, and Who is ever-faithful refuge and friend of all that are sore beset and seek His aid with humble and contrite hearts. Amen."

(After a pause)

"Ye have prayed it; if ye still desire it, speak! The messenger of the Most High waits."

It was believed afterward that the man was a lunatic, because there was no sense in what he said.

Index of Names, Places, and Events

C

D

E

H

M

N

O

P

Q

R

S

T

U

V

W

Y